SEMANTIC AND LEXICAL UNIVERSALS

STUDIES IN LANGUAGE COMPANION SERIES (SLCS)

The SLCS series has been established as a companion series to
STUDIES IN LANGUAGE, International Journal, sponsored by
the Foundation "Foundations of Language".

Series Editors:

Werner Abraham　　　　　　Michael Noonan
University of Groningen　　University of Wisconsin-Milwaukee
The Netherlands　　　　　　USA

Editorial Board:

Joan Bybee (University of New Mexico)
Ulrike Claudi (University of Cologne)
Bernard Comrie (University of Southern California)
William Croft (University of Manchester)
Östen Dahl (University of Stockholm)
Gerrit Dimmendaal (University of Leiden)
Martin Haspelmath (Free University of Berlin)
Ekkehard König (Free University of Berlin)
Christian Lehmann (University of Bielefeld)
Robert Longacre (University of Texas, Arlington)
Brian MacWhinney (Carnegie-Mellon University)
Marianne Mithun (University of California, Santa Barbara)
Edith Moravcsik (University of Wisconsin, Milwaukee)
Masayoshi Shibatani (Kobe University)
Russell Tomlin (University of Oregon)
John Verhaar (The Hague)

Volume 25

Cliff Goddard and Anna Wierzbicka (eds)

Semantic and Lexical Universals

SEMANTIC AND LEXICAL UNIVERSALS

THEORY AND EMPIRICAL FINDINGS

Edited by

CLIFF GODDARD
University of New England

ANNA WIERZBICKA
Australian National University

JOHN BENJAMINS PUBLISHING COMPANY
AMSTERDAM/PHILADELPHIA

The paper used in this publication meets the minimum requirements of American National Standard for Information Sciences — Permanence of Paper for Printed Library Materials, ANSI Z39.48-1984.

Library of Congress Cataloging in Publication Data

Semantic and lexical universals : theory and empirical findings / edited by Cliff Goddard, Anna Wierzbicka.
 p.   cm. -- (Studies in language companion series (SLCS), ISSN 0165-7763; v. 25)
Includes bibliographical references and index.
1. Semantics. 2. Universals (Linguistics) I. Goddard, Cliff. II. Wierzbicka, Anna. III. Series: Studies in language companion series ; v. 25.
P325.5.U54S46   1994
401'.43--dc20   94-4253
ISBN 90 272 3028 5 (Eur.)/1-55619-377-7 (US) (alk. paper)   CIP

© Copyright 1994 - John Benjamins B.V.
No part of this book may be reproduced in any form, by print, photoprint, microfilm, or any other means, without written permission from the publisher.

John Benjamins Publishing Co. · P.O. Box 75577 · 1070 AN Amsterdam · The Netherlands
John Benjamins North America · 821 Bethlehem Pike · Philadelphia, PA 19118 · USA

Contents

Acknowledgements — vii

Opening Statement — 1
Anna Wierzbicka

Part 1: General

1. Semantic Theory and Semantic Universals — 7
   Cliff Goddard

2. Introducing Lexical Primitives — 31
   Cliff Goddard and Anna Wierzbicka

Part 2: Individual Language Studies

3. Ewe — 57
   Felix Ameka

4. The Exponents of Semantic Primitives in Mangap-Mbula — 87
   Robert D. Bugenhagen

5. Mandarin Semantic Primitives — 109
   Hilary Chappell

6. Thai — 149
   Anthony Diller

7. Acehnese — 171
   Mark Durie, Bukhari Daud and Mawardi Hasan

8	Kayardild *Nicholas Evans*	203
9	Lexical Primitives in Yankunytjatjara *Cliff Goddard*	229
10	Preliminary Observations on Lexical and Semantic Primitives in the Misumalpan Languages of Nicaragua *Ken Hale*	263
11	Mparntwe Arrernte and the Search for Lexical Universals *Jean Harkins and David P. Wilkins*	285
12	Longgu *Deborah Hill*	311
13	Samoan *Ulrike Mosel*	331
14	Semantic Primitives in Japanese *Masayuki Onishi*	361
15	Kalam Exponents of Lexical and Semantic Primitives *Andrew Pawley*	387
16	Semantic and Lexical Universals in French *Bert Peeters*	423

Part 3: Review

17	Semantic Primitives Across Languages: A Critical Review *Anna Wierzbicka*	445
	Notes on Contributors	501
	Index	505

Acknowledgements

Our thanks to the contributors who prepared the individual language studies which make up the bulk of this book. To explore and report on the translatability of three dozen postulated primitives within the relatively brief space available was an arduous task, but one which they discharged with insight, care and tenacity.

We would like to thank Igor Mel'čuk, Nicholas Evans, Jean Harkins and Andrzej Bogusławski, for detailed comments on the opening or concluding chapters.

Above all, we are indebted to Timothy Jowan Curnow, who worked tirelessly to prepare the final version of the book for publication. Aside from ourselves, he was the only person who had a comprehensive overview of the entire project. The volume as a whole has benefitted greatly from his many keen observations and insightful criticisms.

Cliff Goddard, University of New England
Anna Wierzbicka, Australian National University

Opening Statement

Anna Wierzbicka
Australian National University, Canberra

This set of papers represents a unique collection: it is the first attempt ever to empirically test a hypothetical set of semantic and lexical universals across a number of genetically and typologically diverse languages. In fact the word 'collection' is not fully appropriate in this case, since the papers report research undertaken specifically for the present volume, and shaped by the same guidelines; and because they constitute parallel and strictly comparable answers to the same set of questions.

Those questions all boil down to the following: Do all the peoples of the world have a shared set of concepts, forming the common conceptual foundation of all cultures? This question has a long history; but this is the first time an answer has been sought to it on a broad empirical basis.

In the seventeenth century, Leibniz advanced the idea of a universal 'alphabet of human thoughts' (1903 [MS]:435); and similar ideas were widespread among other seventeenth- and eighteenth-century philosophers. For example, in the entry on 'Dictionary' of the great French *Encyclopédie* (1754:959), d'Alembert put forward the idea of a 'philosophical dictionary' based on the philosophical roots of language, that is, on universal semantic primitives ("mots originaux et primitifs").

In the nineteenth century, however, this idea faded from philosophical discourse. Although it was never totally abandoned, by the early twentieth century the opposite view had become increasingly popular, culminating in the writings of the influential French sociologist Lucien Lévy-Bruhl, author of *Les fonctions mentales dans les sociétés inférieures* (1928) and *La mentalité primitive* (1925). As the titles of these books suggest, Lévy-Bruhl placed a strong emphasis on the (allegedly) fundamental differences between 'logical' (Western) thought and 'primitive' (non-Western) thought. Naturally, there was no place in this world-view for any notion of a shared conceptual foundation for all cultures.

At roughly the same time, however, the universalist position asserted itself again, notably in the writings of Franz Boas and his associates, and in the doctrine of the 'psychic unity of mankind' (Boas 1938). For a long time this doctrine overshadowed the theories of 'primitive thought', encouraging belief in universals, while recognising the tremendous differences between languages and cultures.

With time, the doctrine of the psychic unity of humanity gained wide acceptance, and as LePan notes (with regret), "the most influential anthropologists of the past fifty years have all been in agreement that the peoples of the world all think in the same ways" (1989:3).

But the doctrine of the psychic unity of humanity, too, has recently come to be seen increasingly as not much more than a pious slogan — and not only by latter-day adherents of the doctrine of primitive thought (cf. Hallpike 1979; LePan 1989; Bain 1992). Thus R. A. Shweder, a leading anthropologist and one of the founders of the new discipline of 'cultural psychology', is the author of a very critical review of Hallpike's *Foundations of primitive thought*, and can by no means be considered an adherent of the doctrine of primitive thought; yet he and a co-author make the point that

> although many anthropologists continue to be quite pious about the 'principle of psychic unity' (a principle that they often mistakenly believe to be an essential debating point in the battle against racism, thereby overlooking the fact that homogeneity is too great a price to pay for equality), it has today become thinkable that the processes of consciousness may not be uniform across the cultural regions of the world. After all, the idea of psychic pluralism is not really radical.
>
> (Shweder & Sullivan 1990:400)

But we do not have to choose between the ideas of psychic pluralism and psychic unity, since the two are fully compatible. In fact, the phrasing of Shweder and Sullivan's comments makes it clear that if they distance themselves from the tenet of psychic unity it is because of its apparent status as an assumption never to be questioned, rather than as a hypothesis supported by empirical data: "The current lack of a rich corpus of relevant data on the topic suggests that the 'principle of psychic unity' has been assumed more than it has been scrutinized" (Shweder & Sullivan 1990:401).

This volume attempts to vindicate the doctrine of the psychic unity of humanity by radically changing its status — from a faith (for some), and a politically correct slogan (for others), to a verifiable hypothesis, tested in and supported by empirical research. It presents a "corpus of relevant data on the topic" of the kind that Shweder and Sullivan are calling for. It also presents a theoretical framework within which such a corpus can be sought. No claim is made that only within this framework can a corpus of relevant data be sought. But without **some** suitable theoretical framework no relevant data can be looked for, and no hypotheses tested.

The process of testing launched in this volume needs to be carried much further. It has to be extended to a larger number of languages, and supplemented by a more thorough investigation of the 'universal grammar of thought' — a subject which could not be systematically investigated in the present volume, with its emphasis on the 'universal lexicon' of human concepts. But despite the need for further research, the overwhelming conclusion to which this book leads is that there is indeed a universal 'alphabet of human thoughts', which can be identified via a systematic and methodological study of different languages.

References

Bain, Margaret. 1992. *The Aboriginal–White Encounter in Australia: Towards better communication* (SIL-AAB Occasional Papers 2). Darwin: Summer Institute of Linguistics, Australian Aborigines Branch.

Boas, Franz. 1938. *The Mind of Primitive Man*. Rev. ed. New York: Macmillan.

d'Alembert, Jean le Rond. 1754. "Dictionnaire". *Encyclopédie* (Paris–'Neuchâtel' folio edition, 1751-1772) vol 4, 958-969. Paris: Le Breton.

Hallpike, Christopher R. 1979. *The Foundations of Primitive Thought*. Oxford: Clarendon Press.

LePan, Don. 1989. *The Cognitive Revolution in Western Culture*, vol 1: *The birth of expectation*. London: Macmillan.

Leibniz, Gottfried Wilhelm. 1903 [MS]. "Sur la caractéristique" (*Philosophie*, VII, C, 160-161). *Opuscules et fragments inédits de Leibniz* ed. by Louis Couterat, 435. Paris: Presses Universitaires de France. (Reprinted 1961, Hildesheim: Georg Olms.)

Lévy-Bruhl, Lucien. 1925. *La mentalité primitive*. 4th ed. Paris: Félix Alcan.

Lévy-Bruhl, Lucien. 1928. *Les fonctions mentales dans les sociétés inférieures*. 9th ed. Paris: Félix Alcan.

Shweder, Richard A. & Maria A. Sullivan. 1990. "The Semiotic Subject of Cultural Psychology". *Handbook of Personality* ed. by L. Pervin, 399-416. New York: Guilford.

Part 1: General

Semantic Theory and Semantic Universals

Cliff Goddard
University of New England, Armidale

This chapter lays out the semantic theory underlying the present work, reviews the literature on semantic and lexical universals, and explains the guidelines followed by contributors.

1.1   Semantic Theory: Main Principles

The most basic assumption underpinning the approach adopted in the present volume is what can be called the Semiotic Principle, as set out in (I). It was championed by C. S. Peirce (1932:2.230–231), among others, and is sometimes summarised in slogan form as 'the irreducibility of the sign'.

(I)   *Semiotic Principle.* A sign cannot be reduced to or analysed into any combination of things which are not themselves signs; consequently, it is impossible to reduce meanings to any combination of things which are not themselves meanings.

Principle (I) commits us to what philosophers know as a fully intensional conception of meaning. It is incompatible with reference-based or denotation-based approaches to meaning, such as classical truth-conditional semantics and more recent developments in 'formal semantics'. It also precludes attempts to reduce meaning to neurophysiological facts (in the way Kay and McDaniel (1978) went about 'defining' the meaning of colour terms), to statements about speakers' usage (in the way Labov (1973) went about defining the meaning of concrete objects), or to embodied action-schemata (in the style of Johnson (1987) and Lakoff (1987)).

Although Principle (I) is taken for granted in much semiotic work (cf. Eco 1984) and in many of the writings of the European structural semanticists (e.g. Greimas 1966, 1987),[1] it is only rarely endorsed in the mainstream Anglo-American linguistic literature. Two exceptions are to be found in the work of Yorick Wilks and Jerrold

Katz. Katz (1987) includes a spirited attack on the mainstream of twentieth-century philosophical semantics which, he says, can be viewed as "one attempt after another to treat meaning as something else". Such approaches are 'reductionistic':

> They seek to reduce the ordinary notions of sense and meaning away, replacing them with something else regarded from the metaphysical perspective of the reductionist as philosophically more respectable or scientifically more tractable ... [such as] behaviour-controlling stimuli, [to] images, methods of verification, stereotypes, truth conditions, extensions in possible worlds, use, illocutionary act potential, perlocutionary potential of various sorts, and even physical inscriptions.
>
> (Katz 1987:157–158)

Wilks has labelled the assumptions underpinning such attempts as the 'escape fallacy', the idea that "one can in language, or mental representations, or programs escape from the world of symbols to some formal but non-symbolic realm that confers significance" (Wilks 1988:235–236).

The next principle is set out in (II). It commits us to exhaustive decomposition into discrete terms.

(II) *Principle of Discrete and Exhaustive Analysis.* Meanings can be analysed in a fully determinate way; that is, any complex meaning can be decomposed into a combination of discrete other meanings, without circularity and without residue.

The pursuit of exhaustive analysis distinguishes the present approach from the tradition of componential analysis which attempts to capture only that portion of a word's meaning which enters into systematic opposition with other word-meanings, as in the work of Hjelmslev, Pottier, Coseriu, Nida, Katz, Lehrer and Jackendoff. Commitment to semantic representation in discrete terms distinguishes the present approach from that of Lakoff (1987), Coleman and Kay (1981) and others who propose scalar notations for semantics, such as 'fuzzy set theory'.

It follows from (I) and (II) that there must exist a set of meanings which cannot themselves be decomposed, but which comprise the terminal elements of the analytical process.[2]

(III) *Semantic Primitives Principle.* There exists a finite set of undecomposable meanings — semantic primitives. Semantic primitives have an elementary syntax whereby they combine to form 'simple propositions'.

The compelling logic that leads to (III) has been recognised by many semantic theorists of otherwise very different persuasions. In the seventeenth century, the existence of semantic primitives was upheld by Pascal, Descartes, Arnauld and

Leibniz. Representative of their general view was Arnauld, who writes:

> It is impossible to define all words. In defining we employ a definition to express the idea which we want to join to the defined word; if we then wanted to define 'the definition', still other words would be needed — and so on to infinity. Hence, it is necessary to stop at some primitive words which are not defined.
>
> (Arnauld 1964 [1662]:86–87)

Leibniz even began a program of lexical investigation with a view to discovering the primitive notions and rules of composition from which all complex notions were composed (Ishiguro 1972:36–48) — his *ars combinatoria* or 'universal characteristic', which is a direct ancestor of the present work (see section 1.3).

Peirce (1932:2.230), a great respecter of Leibniz, saw[3] that a fully articulated semantic interpretation (an 'interpretant', in his terms) would be "a Sign of itself, containing its own explanation, and those of all its significant parts". Similar reasoning led to the advocacy of semantic primitives (or their equivalents) by Sørensen (1958), Greimas (1966), Bogusławski (1965, 1970) and Bendix (1966, 1971), among others.

> The procedure in semantic analysis consists in reducing V [vocabulary of language L] to the smallest set of signs from which all the signs of V can be derived. A sign belonging to the smallest set of signs from which all the signs of V can be derived is a semantically primitive sign ... To set up the smallest group of signs which 'contain' the entire vocabulary of an 'ordinary' language L is the ultimate goal of the semanticist.
>
> (Sørensen 1958:42–43)

The revival of semantics in America in the early 1970s brought proclamations from all sides about the necessary existence of semantic primitives. Chomsky (1965) writes:

> It is important to determine the universal, language-independent constraints on semantic features — in traditional terms, the system of possible concepts. The very notion of 'lexical entry' presupposes some sort of fixed, universal vocabulary in terms of which these objects are characterised ...
>
> (Chomsky 1965:160)

From their different standpoints, Katz and Fodor (1963), Postal (1966; cited in Bierwisch 1967:3), Fillmore (1971), McCawley (1968, 1970) and Lakoff (1970, 1972) all subscribed to the existence of semantic primitives, also called elementary meaning components or atomic concepts.

> The meaning of a lexical item is not an undifferentiated whole. Rather, it is analysable into atomic conceptual elements related to each other in certain ways. Semantic markers and distinguishers are intended as the symbolic devices which represent the atomic

concepts out of which the sense of a lexical item is synthesised.
(Katz & Postal 1964:14)

Others interested in modelling the nature of language comprehension, such as psychologists Miller and Johnson-Laird (1976) and artificial intelligence researchers Wilks (1976, 1977) and Schank (1972), also upheld the concept of semantic primitives (even going beyond most linguists in proposing a concrete set).

Since the 1970s, general enthusiasm for semantic primitives has subsided, for reasons we will consider in section 1.2. To this day, however, their most persistent advocate has been Anna Wierzbicka.

The hallmark of Wierzbicka's approach is embodied in Principle (IV). The proper metalanguage of semantic representation is taken to be a minimal subset of ordinary natural language (hence the designation 'Natural Semantic Metalanguage (NSM) approach').

(IV)   *Natural Language Principle*. Semantic primitives and their elementary syntax exist as a minimal subset of ordinary natural language.

Principle (IV) is violated both in lexicography and in logic-inspired 'formal semantics', although in different ways. Lexicographers use ordinary language, but largely ignore the principle that the defining metalanguage should be as small as possible; logicians are generally more favourably disposed to the notion of a minimal metalanguage, but tend to see it as existing independently of natural language. Uriel Weinreich once wrote:

> Conventional lexicography apparently believes that the defining metalanguage should contain at least the entire object language. This belief may be unwarranted. Ideally we might wish for an 'absolute' metalanguage which is entirely independent of the object language, or of any natural language. But since this ideal in semantics is illusory (in contrast to phonetics), we should seek ways to make the metalanguage less rich ...
> (Weinreich 1980 [1962]:308)

And he went on to consider ways of "progressively reducing the defining metalanguage", such as "agreeing to use as few different words in definitions as possible, but to use each as often as possible". Though Weinreich himself did not progress far in this direction, it is, in essence, the approach which has been pursued by Wierzbicka over the past thirty years.

Most semantic theorists, however, have fallen prey, in one way or another, to the 'illusory ideal' of a defining metalanguage which is independent of natural language. For expository purposes, three sorts of position can be identified in the literature. Furthest from the spirit of Principle (IV) are proposals which employ obscure technical terms to represent posited primitives. Like many others since, McCawley (1968) used technical symbols borrowed from symbolic logic, such as $\exists$ and $\forall$. Schank

(1972) designated three of his fundamental conceptual categories as PACT, CACT and TACT. Since the meaning of such terms is obscure, they stand in need of explanation in ordinary English. This may be explicitly given, as is perforce the case with novel terminologies such as those of Schank (who explains the terms just mentioned as 'physical act', 'communication act' and 'transfer act'); or, if the technical notation is well-established within the academic community, as with logical symbols, it may simply be assumed that readers can supply the necessary interpretation for themselves. In any case, a technical term is a poor candidate as a semantic primitive, since the very fact that an explanation can be given for it establishes that it is semantically decomposable (unless it is completely synonymous with a single ordinary language word, in which case why use the technical term in the first place?).

In the heyday of generative semantics, writers like McCawley, Lakoff and Ross put forward analyses couched for the most part in English words — such as CAUSE, NOT, BECOME and ALIVE — but maintained quite explicitly that the intended meanings were not (exactly) those of the English words, but were more 'abstract'. McCawley (1972) even went so far as to propose that there were two atomic predicates $CAUSE_1$ and $CAUSE_2$, neither of which was identical with the English word *cause*, though the difference between them corresponded roughly to the slippery distinction between direct and indirect causation. Such manoeuvres have been rightly criticised (e.g. Kempson 1977:92–96; Wierzbicka 1980; cf. Lyons 1977:329–330) for rendering the 'abstract' semantic analyses unverifiable.

Thirdly and most commonly, there are proposals which use English words, usually of a learned and semi-technical nature, without any declaration about how the intended meanings might or might not correspond to those of ordinary English words. For instance, Katz (1987:186–187) uses labels like these to identify the 'conceptual components' of the English word *chase*: Activity, Physical, Movement, Fast, Direction, Toward location of, Purpose, Catching. As argued by Allan (1986:265–270), such semi-technical notations are nothing more or less than a "degenerate form of a natural language". To understand such 'markerese' we mentally undo the unstated deformation conditions and convert it back to a paraphrase in ordinary English (for instance, 'a physical activity of fast movement in a direction toward something, with the purpose of catching that something').

In other words, whether or not the analyst recognises it, it is an inescapable fact that "any formalism is parasitic upon the ordinary everyday use of language, in that it must be understood intuitively on the basis of ordinary language" (Lyons 1977:12). From this point of view, relying directly on ordinary natural language simply makes a virtue of necessity.

There is a further important contrast to be drawn between the NSM approach and that adopted by advocates of technical semantic jargons. It is this: because the elements of 'markerese' are not identified as English words, there is no natural syntax attaching to them. It is therefore up to the analyst to devise such a syntax.

In early versions of componentialism, the syntax of semantic representation was envisaged as merely the conjunction of features into a 'bundle', but it soon became obvious that something more elaborate was needed. Some scholars use a version of the predicate–argument syntax of predicate calculus; others use variants of phrase-structure tree diagrams or labelled bracketing; and various forms of labelled dependency diagrams are also in use. But never is the syntax of the notation viewed as a natural consequence of the fact that the items representing primitive meanings are lexemes or morphemes drawn from an ordinary language: it is rather an artificial, extra-linguistic syntax devised and imposed by the analyst.

In contrast, on the NSM approach the semantic metalanguage has what may be viewed as a natural, language-like syntax. The primitives drawn from a given natural language combine according to a subset of the morphosyntactic conventions of that language. Consequently, the metalanguage of semantic representation may be viewed as the smallest 'mini-language' with the same expressive power as the full natural language. The semantic primitives of any given language L, together with their rules of combination, comprise the Natural Semantic Metalanguage (NSM) derived from L.

This way of viewing semantic representation leads naturally to Principle (V).

(V)   *Expressive Equivalence of NSMs.* The NSMs derived from various languages will be semantically equivalent, that is, have the same expressive power. Any simple proposition expressible in an NSM based on L_1 will be expressible in an NSM based on L_2, L_3 and so on.

Principle (V) embodies the conviction that natural languages are equivalent in their expressive power. This entails complete inter-translatability between NSMs. There could never be an untranslatable residue of meaning present in the L_1 version of a particular simple proposition which was not carried over into the L_2 version of the same proposition. It should perhaps be noted that although a version of this principle is generally accepted within linguistics (e.g. Jakobson 1959; Katz 1981:226;[4] for a contrary view, Grace 1987), it has sometimes been rejected by anthropologists and other commentators on 'primitive thought' (e.g. Lévy-Bruhl 1925; Hallpike 1979); for discussion, see Wierzbicka (in press).

A far stronger form of semantic universalism is contained in the next principle, which is another of the distinctive hallmarks of the NSM program.

(VI) *Isomorphism of NSMs.* The simple propositions which can be expressed through the NSMs based on different languages will be fundamentally isomorphic.

The purport of Principle (VI) is that the linguistic exponents of semantically primitive meanings in different languages can be placed into one-to-one correspondence on a non-arbitrary basis. That is, that there is a unique set of universal semantic primitives, notwithstanding certain formal differences in their realisation in different languages (for instance, in allolexy and part-of-speech membership; see section 2.1 and chapter

17). Equally, Principle (VI) entails that the exponents of semantic primitives in different languages share a common set of combinatorial properties.[5]

It should be stressed that Principles (V) and (VI) are not advanced as dogma, but as hypotheses — the semantic equivalents of the universality hypothesis animating work in other fields of linguistics. It may not be logically necessary that the semantic cores of all human languages should coincide, but it is the strongest — and in our opinion the most interesting — hypothesis.

Clearly, the preceding principles imply the existence in all the world's languages of a set of lexical or morphemic items whose primary meanings are identical.[6] This conclusion is so fundamental to the present volume that it may be as well to spell it out in another form; Principle (VII) may be viewed as a corollary of the hypothesised isomorphism of NSMs.

(VII) *Strong Lexicalisation Hypothesis.* Every semantically primitive meaning can be expressed through a distinct word, morpheme or fixed phrase in every language.

This does not entail that there should be a single unique form for each primitive. Some languages have several forms (allolexes or allomorphs of the same item) functioning as contextual variants expressing the same primitive meaning. Conversely, it sometimes happens that the same form serves as an exponent of different primitives, although their distinct syntactic frames make it appropriate to recognise polysemy.[7] Also, an exponent of a semantically primitive meaning may be formally complex, including elements which function elsewhere as full morphemes. (These points are dealt with more fully in section 2.1.)

What we are postulating in Principle (VII) is that a semantically primitive meaning will always be expounded by means of specifically lexical material — be it a bound morpheme, a lexeme or a fixed phrase (or phraseme); to put it another way, that the linguistic exponents of primitive meanings will always be 'segmental signs'.

Though this is, in our opinion, the strongest and most plausible starting position, alternatives are conceivable. It is conceivable that a primitive meaning might be expounded by non-segmental means, such as reduplication or ablaut. It is conceivable that a primitive meaning might be expressed in some languages solely through a grammatical construction. Goddard (1989) floated the idea that the imperative construction could be taken as the true universal exponent of the notion of 'wanting', if it turned out that lexical equivalents for WANT were lacking in some languages. Evans (this volume) and Chappell (this volume) consider the possibility that the PART OF notion is not lexicalised in Kayardild and Mandarin, but might be expressible through an inalienable possession–type grammatical construction.

It is conceivable that a primitive meaning of a 'modifying' kind (such as LIKE or VERY) might lack a distinct lexical identity if a language possessed a set of portmanteau morphemes, one for each combination allowed by the elementary syntax. Such a proposal is made by Evans (this volume). It is conceivable that a primitive meaning may have no exponent at all, neither lexical nor grammatical. Hale (this volume) makes a concrete suggestion to this effect in relation to one of the Misumalpan languages.

It seems to us that such possibilities would create conceptual and methodological difficulties for cross-linguistic semantics. Although these would probably not be insuperable, at this early stage of investigation into lexical and semantic universals it seems methodologically sounder to provisionally adopt the Strong Lexicalisation Hypothesis.

In his discussion of universalism in semantics, Lyons (1977:331–332) applies a distinction familiar from syntax (Chomsky 1965). Formal universals concern the principles by which sense-components are combined to yield the meanings of lexemes; substantive universals concern the identity of semantic components. Lyons stated (and a similar observation was made by Zwicky (1973:474)) that, as far as he could see, no-one advocates the most extreme form of substantive universalism, that "there is a fixed set of semantic components, which are universal in that they are lexicalised in all languages". But that is precisely the thesis to be tested in the present work.

1.2   Semantic Universals in the Twentieth Century

The following review restricts itself to ideas about substantive semantic universals; it does not take in the work of Wierzbicka and associates, which is dealt with in section 1.3.

Linguistics, psychology and philosophy assumed their separate identities only this century, with the result that earlier theorising about semantic universals now seems (often awkwardly) to straddle these disciplines; but in classical, mediæval and Enlightenment times many thinkers addressed the relationship between language, thought and reality. The idealist–nominalist debate between Plato and Aristotle on categories and the empiricist–rationalist debate between Locke and Leibniz on simple ideas both presupposed the existence of semantic universals. Until Chomsky appropriated the term for his own a-semantic (or even anti-semantic) program, the long history of 'universal grammar' was semantic in orientation.

By the twentieth century, however, the old ideas about universal grammar, which had been conditioned by the relative uniformity of the grammatical categories of European languages and the pre-eminence of Latin, had begun to look decidedly shaky. The encounter with the exotic grammars of the New World led linguists increasingly to emphasise the differences, rather than the similarities, between languages. For instance, even in the nineteenth century, although conceding the existence in grammar and lexicon of a "midpoint around which all languages revolve", Humboldt was more concerned to emphasise the "far greater number" of conceptual and grammatical peculiarities of individual languages (Humboldt 1903–36, vol 4:21–23; cited in Wierzbicka 1992a:5).[8]

Similarly, in the influential *Handbook of American Indian languages*, Boas (1911) was at pains to dispel the preconception that there was anything natural or inevitable about the grammatical categories of the languages of Europe and western Asia, although he also held that grammatical forms did not say much about underlying thought processes, which he saw as common to humanity as a whole. Sapir laid great emphasis on the universality of language as part of "man's psychic or 'spiritual' constitution", and often said that the "fundamental groundwork" of language is everywhere the same. He even asked the question, "What, then, are the absolutely essential concepts in speech, the concepts that must be expressed if language is to be a satisfactory means of communication?" (Sapir 1921:93). But his answer (Sapir 1921:93–109) — in terms of a schema of "basic or radical concepts" on the one hand, and of "pure relational concepts" on the other — was formal rather than substantive; and the general emphasis of Sapir's *Language* is on the differences between languages, rather than on their similarities.

Even Jespersen (1924:46–57) went through a thorough rehearsal of the grammatical differences between languages before endorsing the existence of language-independent notional categories, hedging that they were "universal in so far as they are applicable to all languages, though rarely expressed in them in a clear and unmistakable way". In brief, one could say that although the great descriptive linguists of the early part of the century seemed confident that all human languages rested on a universal conceptual base, they did little to characterise that base in substantive terms.

The sole exception was the work of Sapir's student Swadesh (1955), which sought evidence for universal concepts in shared features of human life, such as the environment and the human body. Though Swadesh's search for 'basic vocabulary' has been of practical value for fieldworkers and comparativists, from a theoretical point of view its outcome rather weighed against the hypothesis that there were universals of vocabulary. For as well as recurrent overlaps in basic vocabulary, it was discovered that there were so many differences that the existence of absolute lexical universals seemed doubtful. Some languages (for example, Slavic languages) lack separate words for 'hand' and 'arm', some lack a general word for 'sun' or 'moon' (for example, the Australian language Nyawaygi (Dixon 1980:104)), and so on.

The second half of the century saw linguistics flourish, and brought the formation of distinct schools or approaches which we will now consider in a little detail, beginning with European structuralism and American generativism.

One might have expected that Saussurean structuralism, with its emphasis on the arbitrariness of the sign, would have sounded the death-knell for interest in substantive semantic univerals. Saussure had insisted that

> in a language there are differences, *and no positive terms* ... neither sounds nor ideas existing prior to the linguistic system, but only conceptual and phonetic differences arising out of that system.
>
> (Harris 1983:118; emphasis in original)

And what, after all, is a substantive semantic universal, if not a 'positive term'?

Nevertheless, as pointed out by Lyons (1977), both the major European schools of post-Saussurean structuralism, the Prague School and the Copenhagen School, arrived at the view that word-meanings, like phonemes, could be analysed into distinctive features, and that

> although the complexes of components ... and the paradigmatic and syntagmatic interrelationships of these complexes are unique to particular languages, the ultimate components of sound and meaning are language-neutral.
>
> (Lyons 1977:245)

Just as the Prague School (especially through the person of Roman Jakobson) had a formative influence on generativist ideas about phonology, so it was too with semantics. Shared human physiology was held to determine possible phonological and conceptual distinctions, subsets of which would be actualised by each different language.

These developments set the scene for generativist ideas about semantic primitives in the mid-1960s and the 1970s, mentioned in the previous section. Fillmore (1971:372) cited his eight examples of the "ultimate terms of semantic description" — identity, time, space, body, movement, territory, life and fear — with the comment that these were "presumably biologically given notions". Bierwisch (1967:3–4) believed that universal semantic markers corresponded to "certain deep seated, innate properties of the human organism and the perceptual apparatus", and spoke of a "biological determination" of the ultimate components of concepts. Katz maintained that the inventory of potential semantic markers is innate and universal because of their physiological basis (cf. Katz & Nagel 1974). Enthusiasm for a biological basis for semantic universals was also boosted by Berlin and Kay's (1969) discoveries about universals of colour terminology.

Now one unfortunate consequence of this 'biological turn' in thinking was the apparent assumption that semantic universals were not only language-independent (in the sense of language-universal), but extra-linguistic in nature. Perhaps this helps to account for the remarkable indifference of generative grammarians to the possibility that the identity of the non-arbitrary semantic universals could be established by linguistic analysis. For it is a very curious fact, looking back on it, that while so many espoused the necessity for substantive semantic univerals, so few made serious efforts to establish what they were (cf. Zwicky 1973). To the best of my knowledge, no-one from either the Interpretive Semantics or the Generative Semantics camps, or any of their intellectual heirs or successors, has proposed any substantial inventory of universal semantic elements. Where a few samples have been offered, such as those referred to above, it was on the basis of a handful of sketched analyses, with no detailed consideration of methodology. Not surprisingly, the whole notion of semantic primitives has been brought into disrepute.

It is now widely believed that it is imponderably difficult to decide whether something is or is not a semantic primitive; and the spectre is raised of it being impossible to decide between competing lists (cf. Burling 1964; Lyons 1977:330–335; Kempson 1977:96–101; Aitchison 1987:66–67). As argued by Wierzbicka (1987a), however, the criterion of non-decomposability — if taken seriously — is sufficient to disconfirm most posited primitives and to dispel doubts about arbitrariness. To give just a single example: Katz, Jackendoff and Fillmore all advocated 'Motion' as a semantic primitive, as well as 'Time' and 'Location', without addressing the possibility that motion can be defined as the changing of location over time (cf. Leibniz 1981 [1704]:297; Langacker 1987:167). As for being unable to decide between a proliferation of competing sets, this is hardly a worry, since scarcely anyone has proposed a complete set.

Aside from the scholars mentioned so far, the most important contemporary sources of proposals about substantive semantic universals (again excepting the work of Wierzbicka and associates) are to be found in the works of John Lyons, R. M. W. Dixon, and the linguists of the Moscow School.

Though associated with the term 'structural semantics', John Lyons is, on his own account, the inheritor of Jespersen's view that there are notional universals in language which spring from the nature of extra-linguistic reality. He has maintained consistently (Lyons 1966, 1989) that fundamental linguistic categories such as noun and verb are at least partly "determined by the language-independent structure of the world (i.e. ontologically)" (Lyons 1989:161). His ontological assumptions are unashamedly those of 'naive realism', such as that the external world contains a number of individual persons, more or less discrete physical objects, and places (or spaces). There is, however, no particular focus on lexical meanings in Lyons' work, and substantive universals that he discusses are relatively limited both in number and in nature.[9]

R. M. W. Dixon has long been an advocate of the priority of semantics over syntax, holding that "the syntactic properties of a lexical item can be largely predicted from its semantic description" (1982:8). But though Dixon has enjoyed a long and mutually stimulating association with Wierzbicka at the Australian National University, his ideas on semantics differ from hers on a number of important points (while agreeing on others). Though Dixon's approach has certain affiliations with that of Lyons also, it would be fair to say that his position is more or less unique.

As suggested by the existence in certain Australian languages of auxiliary vocabulary systems which merge most of subtler semantic distinctions of the full language, Dixon sees the lexicon as consisting of two natural and non-arbitrary groups — nuclear words and non-nuclear words. This distinction allows him to approach semantic description using a combination of what he calls the 'componential' and 'definitional' approaches; for instance, he writes in relation to verbs:

> Componential descriptions of nuclear verbs are generated from systems of primitive semantic features; non-nuclear verbs are defined in terms of the nuclear verbs (or of already

defined non-nuclear verbs) utilising the full grammatical possibilities of the language in
the formulation of these definitions.

(Dixon 1971:440–441)

But though "only a fairly small number of rather general systems of semantic features are required", these have not been Dixon's first priority. His approach has been more of an inductive–empiricist one: first to establish the broad outlines of the semantic organisation, and then the general principles of semantic–syntactic correspondence in various languages, before eventually working down to the fine details of semantic primitives.

Dixon proposes the existence of universal semantic 'types', into at least one of which each lexical item of a language must fall:

> A non-disjunctive definition can be given for the overall semantic content of each type. These types are almost certainly linguistic universals. By this I mean that each language has the same array of types, with more-or-less the same overall semantic contents; however, the morphological/syntactic properties associated with particular types will vary from language to language, and must be learnt for each individual language.

(Dixon 1982:9)

Examples are prototypical verb types like MOTION, AFFECT, GIVING and SAYING, prototypical noun types like OBJECTS and KIN, and typical adjective types like DIMENSION, COLOUR and VALUE.

This conception of the lexicon implies the existence in all languages of at least one word of each of the proposed semantic types, but it does not necessarily imply any exact semantic matching between the senses of lexical items of the same semantic type. For example, though universal types SAYING and GIVING are recognised, no claim is made that all languages possess words with senses identical to those of English *say* and *give*. Dixon's universal semantic types are not purely semantic, but have a mixed semantic–syntactic nature: they constitute a hypothesis, not about the ultimate elements of semantic theory, but about the mechanism of semantic–syntactic correspondence (see Dixon (1991) for an application in relation to the grammar of English).

Although the ultimate semantic basis for the whole system is supposed to be the 'primitive semantic features', Dixon has so far said little concrete about these. The implication of his componential versus definitional distinction, however, is that the primitive features are not senses of lexical items and that the principles by which they combine (whatever these may be) are not the grammatical possibilities of an ordinary language.

Finally, there is the Moscow School (now in part relocated to North America) consisting of Russian scholars like Jurij Apresjan, Lidija Iordanskaja, Igor Mel'čuk and Aleksandr Žolkovskij. These linguists have had a long-standing interest in the construction of a non-arbitary semantic metalanguage, their earliest work (Žolkovskij,

Leont'era & Martem'janov 1961) pre-dating that of Wierzbicka.

Apresjan has extolled the theoretical importance of semantic primitives in many works (for example, Apresjan 1973, 1992 [1974]):

> When we talk about different ways of expressing the same content or about the semantic equivalence of outwardly different expressions we assume the existence of some *semantic language* or *conceptual language* which is inaccessible to direct observation. ... The production of sensible sentences can be regarded as a process of translating from the semantic language into a natural language, and understanding sentences can be regarded as a process of translating from natural language into the semantic language.
>
> (Apresjan 1973:276–277; emphasis in original)

The semantic language (or metalanguage) has a vocabulary of 'elementary senses', which may be combined in various ways, according to the grammar of the semantic language (which is also non-arbitrary), to form the meanings of diverse words in natural languages.

In the early period of the development of the Meaning-Text Model (MTM), the semantic language and its lexicon was the main object of interest (cf. Apresjan 1992 [1974]:10–11). Žolkovskij (1964; cited in Mel'čuk 1989) proposed an inventory of 23 semantic primitives, including 'I', 'person', 'want', 'think', 'thing', 'property', 'number', 'more', 'time', 'space', 'norm' and a number of logical notions such as 'no', 'set/group', 'all', 'and', 'or', 'if-then' and 'true'. Apresjan (1992 [1974]:53) listed 27 'basic meanings' including, as well as the above, 'act', 'have', 'be able, can', 'manner', and 'one'. It was not held, however, that primitive meanings necessarily correspond to meanings of ordinary words, as shown by the case of the concept 'norm', which is not represented by a single word in ordinary Russian, and for which Apresjan used the 'fictitious' Russian word *norma*.[10] (This did not prevent him from insisting that its sense is indefinable, since he believed it could be made perfectly clear through examples.)

The later work of the Moscow School linguists, however, has become increasingly less interested in the fine details of semantic metalanguage, concentrating instead on documenting the semantic, syntactic and collocational properties of large numbers of lexical units in different languages, using language-neutral notations which could furnish a potential basis for automatic translation (cf. Mel'čuk & Žolkovskij 1970; Mel'čuk 1989). The 'semantic networks' by which the meaning of a lexical item is stated in the MTM are not constructed within any postulated set of elementary senses, and their syntax is based on predicate calculus, rather than being drawn from the language being analysed.

The contemporary attitude of the Meaning-Text Model linguists to the issue of semantic primitives has been summed up by Mel'čuk (1989) in a recent article devoted to just this question. On the one hand, Mel'čuk is quite explicit that:

(1) Within the framework of a MTM (Meaning-Text Model) we can be sure that semantic primitives exist. (2) They are the simplest lexical meanings of L — lexical meanings of L that cannot be represented in terms of other lexical meanings of L. (3) And they must be found in the process of semantic decomposition to which the entire lexical stock of L is necessarily submitted.

(Mel'čuk 1989:83)

Nevertheless, immediately following this passage, Mel'čuk concedes that he is "unable to produce even one semantic primitive for any language, let alone a complete inventory". He maintains that fruitful discussion of semantic primitives must await a generation of systematic large-scale lexical investigation, inaugurated in the monumental Russian and French 'Explanatory–Combinatorial Dictionaries' (Mel'čuk & Žolkovskij 1984; Mel'čuk et al. 1984, 1988, 1992). In addition, according to Mel'čuk there is no reason to believe, on the assumptions of the Meaning-Text Model, that the elementary lexical meanings of different languages correspond, that is, there is no reason to believe that there are any substantive semantic universals at all.

In summary, it should be clear that Wierzbicka's work stands virtually alone in being based on an explicit hypothesis about a complete set of indefinable universal semantic elements, represented through words or morphemes in ordinary language.

1.3   The NSM Search for Universal Semantic Primitives

As Wierzbicka (1992b) relates, her own interest in the pursuit of non-arbitrary semantic primitives was triggered by a 1965 lecture on the subject by Andrzej Bogusławski, who in his turn had been inspired by Leibniz (see also Bogusławski 1970):

The 'golden dream' of the seventeenth-century thinkers, which couldn't be realized within the framework of philosophy and which was therefore generally abandoned as a utopia, could be realized, Bogusławski maintained, if it was approached from a linguistic rather than a purely philosophical point of view.

(Wierzbicka 1992b:217)

Systematic lexical analysis was to be the procedure for discovering the Leibnizian 'alphabet of human thoughts'. Instead of speculating about the identity of the 'simple ideas' in terms of which all other complex notions were understood, or assuming that they would be self-evident on account of their clarity (as Descartes and Pascal had done), Wierzbicka set about a program of trial-and-error investigation of many areas of the lexicon. The spirit of this approach, incidentally, was just as Leibnizian as its goals; the philosopher–polymath had himself written:

we will get a better idea [of what the real primitives are] as we proceed in our analysis; and it is better to proceed than to get stuck at the very beginning because of excessive pedantry.[11]

(Leibniz 1903 [1686]:361)

After several years, Wierzbicka had formed a hypothesis about a set of semantic primitives which would be, as Sørensen had foreshadowed, expressively powerful enough to capture all intuitively perceptible semantic relations. This list, first published in English in the book *Semantic primitives*, comprised a mere fourteen elements (Wierzbicka 1972:15–16): I, YOU, SOMEONE, SOMETHING, WORLD, THIS, WANT, DON'T WANT, FEEL, THINK OF, IMAGINE, SAY, BECOME, BE A PART OF. In Wierzbicka's (1980) book *Lingua mentalis* this list was slightly modified — KNOW and BE IN A PLACE were tentatively added, and FEEL discarded (though the latter has since made a comeback). Overall, however, the inventory remained roughly the same, small size.

In the decade which followed, Wierzbicka continued her efforts to test the completeness and expressive power of the proposed inventory through numerous studies of diverse areas of the lexicon, including speech act verbs, emotion terms, simple and complex artefacts, mass nouns, natural kinds, superordinate functional categories, and ideological and value terms, among others (see references at end of this chapter). Wierzbicka's empirical–descriptive output stands in stark contrast to that of other semantic theorists; but as Albert Einstein is said to have once remarked, "there is nothing as practical as a good theory".

Another significant development was the extension of the approach to a widening range of languages. Wierzbicka herself did work on English, Polish, Russian and Japanese. Graduate students and other scholars at the Australian National University's Department of Linguistics — which under Dixon's influence always had a strong ethos of fieldwork and practical linguistic description — sought to apply it to Australian Aboriginal languages such as Yankunytjatjara (Goddard) and Arrernte (Wilkins, Harkins), to Chinese (Chappell), and to Ewe (Ameka), among other languages. Several of these scholars are contributors to the present volume.

The joint effect of widening the range of semantic phenomena being studied and the range of languages involved was to bring about a thorough overhaul of the primitive inventory. A couple of the earlier primitives (WORLD, IMAGINE) were discarded on account of non-translatability; but most of the changes resulted from the realisation that earlier analyses for the domains of time, space, quantification and cognition needed improvement (cf. Goddard 1989; Wierzbicka 1989). A significant turning point, in historical terms, was the Semantic Primitives Workshop held in Adelaide in 1986, organised by Cliff Goddard and David Wilkins.

The new inventory, which numbers some thirty-seven elements, also has the attractive quality of generating explications with a simpler, more readable syntax than its predecessor.[12] It is set out below and will be discussed in some detail in chapter 2 (see Wierzbicka (1992b) for a point by point comparison with earlier versions):

Substantives:	I, YOU, SOMEONE, SOMETHING, PEOPLE
Mental predicates:	THINK, SAY, KNOW, FEEL, WANT
Determiners/quantifiers:	THIS, THE SAME, OTHER, ONE, TWO, MANY, ALL
Actions/events:	DO, HAPPEN
Meta-predicates:	NO, IF, CAN, LIKE, BECAUSE, VERY
Time/place:	WHEN, WHERE, AFTER, BEFORE, UNDER, ABOVE
Partonomy/taxonomy:	HAVE PARTS, KIND OF
Evaluators/descriptors:	GOOD, BAD, BIG, SMALL

Table 1: Proposed lexical and semantic primitives

Though some account has been taken of other languages in the formulation of this proposed inventory of lexical primitives, it has been derived in the main through 'deep' semantic investigations conducted in European languages. It is important to understand that there is nothing inherently suspicious or invalid about this, any more than it is suspicious or invalid for Chomsky and his followers to seek hypotheses about universal syntactic principles from the in-depth study of a single language (and for similar reasons: exploratory, in-depth analysis requires native-speaker intuitions). Once detailed first-generation universalist hypotheses have been arrived at, however, they must be tested in detail against a range of typologically unrelated languages.

1.4 Goals and Methods of the Present Project

The purpose of the present project is to submit the list of proposed primitives in Table 1 to its first thorough cross-linguistic test.

The linguists who were invited to participate have both a sufficient familiarity with the assumptions and methodology of the NSM approach, and expertise in a non-English language.

In addition, they were furnished with an explicit set of Basic Assumptions, set out below:

(a) We are looking for meanings which have lexical exponents in all languages. These meanings may be expressed by words, affixes or phrases, but they must be associated with some lexical material.

(b) We assume that meanings are discrete and determinate; that is, that every word has a definite number of senses (one, two, or whatever), and that every meaning (except for the 'primitive' ones) can be stated in the form of one definition (without multiple glosses). We do not recognise any 'submeanings', 'shades of meaning' and so on.

(c) Consequently, we are not interested in similarities ('family resemblances' and so on); we are interested in identities.

(d)   To claim that two words are similar but not identical in meaning, it must be possible to identify the supposed difference in meaning.

An important common assumption about the cross-linguistic matching of meanings was that two words (morphemes, etc.) can be identical in meaning despite belonging to different parts of speech or having different grammatical status; for example, WANT can be either a verb or an adjective, FEEL can be a word in one language but a suffix in another, and so on. Naturally, two semantically identical words may have different patterns of allomorphy or allolexy in different languages; for example, SOMEONE may have just one lexical exponent in language A, but three or four in language B. Finally, semantically identical words may have very different ranges of use for cultural reasons, or because of different patterns of polysemy. (For discussion of all these points, see section 2.1.)

The common methodological approach was consolidated by a Workshop on Semantic and Lexical Universals held at the Australian National University, Canberra, in February 1992, attended by most of the authors represented in the present volume.

Finally, contributors were supplied with a list of canonical contexts (see Appendix to chapter 2) giving a selection of syntactic (combinatorial) contexts in which the proposed semantically primitive meanings can be expected to be found. Though this list was informed by on-going research into the 'elementary syntax' of semantic primitives, it is not possible to expound on this aspect of the NSM program here, in a book dedicated primarily to the lexical aspects of semantic metalanguage (but see Wierzbicka 1991). We can and should, however, point out some of the purposes served by the list of canonical contexts, in the context of the present project.

To begin with, it facilitated a degree of common ground in the type of data considered by contributors. More importantly, it assisted in overcoming potential confusion about which sense of a polysemous English word is proposed as semantically primitive. For instance, although English *know* is polysemous, the sense proposed as primitive can be indicated very simply by citing some example sentences such as *I know which way he went* and *We know that this is bad.* But perhaps most significantly, the list of canonical contexts acted as a tool which assisted contributors to identify the most plausible candidates for exponents of semantic primitives in the non-English languages they were addressing. For instance, in a given language there might be various ways by which notions involving causality may be expressed; reference to the list of canonical contexts would direct a contributor's attention to the exponent which would be used in examples equivalent to *There was a lot of noise; because of that I couldn't sleep* and *He hit me; that's why I'm crying.*

It will be apparent that the present project differs markedly from previous broad cross-linguistic lexical surveys, such as those of Cecil Brown and Stanley Witkowski (cf. Brown 1989), which have simply extracted data from bilingual dictionaries. The studies in the present volume are all authored by experts in the languages in question, they adopt a methodologically uniform approach, and all are located within a comprehensive and principled semantic theory.

Further discussion of methodological issues and a preliminary review of the entire proposed primitive inventory is provided in chapter 2.

Notes

1   In the Introduction to Greimas (1987), the English translation of various of Greimas's works, translator Paul Perron (1987:xxv) says: "Greimas's point of departure is that the investigation of meaning is by definition a metalinguistic activity that paraphrases and translates words and utterances by other words and utterances. It therefore follows that the first step in describing signification resides in the transposition of one level of language into another level, of one language into another language ... the next step is to develop a new terminology and construct an adequate metalanguage."
2   It does not necessarily follow from the existence of semantic primitives that semantic analysis must be exhaustive and discrete; as witness the views of Katz and Jackendoff, who both believe that for many words an unanalysable residue of meaning remains even after non-arbitrary analysis into elementary senses has taken place.
3   Admittedly, at other times Peirce sounds as though he believes that the process of explication must go on *ad infinitum*, a position which has endeared him to post-structuralist semiotics.
4   Jerrold Katz has long advocated a similar 'principle of effability'; in his formulation, 'each proposition (thought) is expressible by some sentence in every natural language' (Katz 1981:226). He too notes (1981:238) that this entails the inter-translatability of natural languages.
5   This is not to say that the combinatorial properties of exponents of semantic primitives will be fully identical from language to language — only that there be a shared subset of such properties.
6   The assumption that semantic primitives are realised as lexical universals does not mean that all lexical universals must also be semantic primitives. For example, it appears that all languages have a word corresponding to 'mother' (with different patterns of polysemy, but with one distinct sense corresponding to the basic sense of the English word *mother*; see Wierzbicka 1987a), even though the concept 'mother' is not semantically elementary.
7   Where the same phonetic form functions as an exponent of two distinct semantically primitive meanings each with distinctive syntactic properties, it would perhaps be more accurate to designate the situation as one of homonymy; but as explained in chapter 2, for the purposes of this volume the term 'polysemy' is used to cover both this situation and that of related meanings expressed by the same phonetic form.
8   This is not to suggest that Humboldt was uninterested in establishing semantic universals, as witnessed by his unfinished, yet to this day impressive, typological project on the dual (cf. Plank 1989).
9   Despite Lyons' affiliation with naive realism, there is a certain parallel with the latter-day Katz (1981), who expounds Platonist idealism. Katz too believes in "a language-independent semantic reality" — though of an altogether different type — while saying little about its contents.

10 'Fictitious' in the sense that *norma* exists as a Russian word, but not in the intended sense.
11 '... haec omnia, ut saepe dixi, ex ipso progressu melius apparebunt. Et praestat progredi, quam nimia quadam morositate obhaerescere in ipsis initiis.'
12 Reliance on English-specific syntax in early NSM explications (e.g. in Wierzbicka 1980) was noted with disapproval by a number of critics, for instance McCawley (1983:655), who called for the primitive vocabulary items to be supplemented with "a list of semantically primitive syntactic constructions". Considerable progress has since been made toward this goal, as explained in Wierzbicka (1991) and in chapter 2 of the present book.

References

Aitchison, Jean. 1987. *Words in the Mind: An introduction to the mental lexicon*. Oxford: Basil Blackwell.
Allan, Keith. 1986. *Linguistic Meaning*. London: Routledge & Kegan Paul.
Apresjan, Jurij D. 1973. *Principles and Methods of Contemporary Structural Linguistics*. Trans. by Dina B. Crockett. The Hague: Mouton.
Apresjan, Jurij D. 1992 [1974]. *Lexical Semantics: User's guide to contemporary Russian vocabulary*. Ann Arbor: Karoma. (English translation of: Jurij D. Apresjan. 1974. *Leksičeskaja Semantika — Sinonimečeskie sredstva jazyka*. Moscow: Nauka.)
Arnauld, Antoine. 1964 [1662]. *The Art of Thinking*. Trans. by James Dickoff & Patricia James. Indianapolis: Bobs-Merrill.
Bendix, Edward H. 1966. *Componential Analysis of General Vocabulary* (Indiana University Research Center in Anthropology, Folklore and Linguistics Publication 41). Bloomington, Indiana: Indiana University Press.
Bendix, Edward H. 1971. "The Data of Semantic Description". *Semantics: An interdisciplinary reader in philosophy, linguistics, and psychology* ed. by D. D. Steinberg & L. A. Jakobovits, 393-409. Cambridge: Cambridge University Press.
Berlin, Brent & Paul Kay. 1969. *Basic Color Terms: Their universality and evolution*. Berkeley: University of California Press.
Bierwisch, Manfred. 1967. "Some Semantic Universals of German Adjectivals". *Foundations of Language* 3.1-36.
Boas, Franz. 1911. *Handbook of American Indian Languages*. Washington: Government Printing Office.
Bogusławski, Andrzej. 1965. *Semantyczne pojecie licebnika*. Wroclaw: Ossolineum.
Bogusławski, Andrzej. 1970. "On Semantic Primitives and Meaningfulness". *Sign, Language and Culture* ed. by A. J. Greimas, R. Jakobson & M. R. Mayenowa, 143-152. The Hague: Mouton.
Brown, Cecil H. 1989. "Lexical Universals and Semantic Primitives". *Quaderni di Semantica* 10.2.279-295.
Burling, Robbins. 1964. "Cognition and Componential Analysis: God's truth or hocus-pocus?" *American Anthropologist* 66.20-28.
Chomsky, Noam. 1965. *Aspects of the Theory of Syntax*. Cambridge, Mass.: MIT Press.

Coleman, Linda & Paul Kay. 1981. "Prototype Semantics: The English verb *lie*". *Language* 57.1.26-44.
Dixon, R. M. W. 1971. "A Method of Semantic Description". *Semantics: An interdisciplinary reader in philosophy, linguistics, and psychology* ed. by D. D. Steinberg & L. A. Jakobovits, 436-471. Cambridge: Cambridge University Press.
Dixon, R. M. W. 1980. *The Languages of Australia*. Cambridge: Cambridge University Press.
Dixon, R. M. W. 1982. *Where Have All the Adjectives Gone? And other essays in semantics and syntax*. Berlin: Mouton.
Dixon, R. M. W. 1991. *A New Approach to English Grammar, on Semantic Principles*. Oxford: Clarendon Press.
Eco, Umberto. 1984. *Semiotics and the Philosophy of Language*. London: Macmillan Press.
Fillmore, Charles. 1971. "Types of Lexical Information". In *Semantics: An interdisciplinary reader in philosophy, linguistics, and psychology* ed. by D. D. Steinberg & L. A. Jakobovits, 370-392. Cambridge: Cambridge University Press.
Goddard, Cliff. 1989. "Issues in Natural Semantic Metalanguage". *Quaderni di Semantica* 10.1.51-64.
Grace, George W. 1987. *The Linguistic Construction of Reality*. London: Croom Helm.
Greimas, Algirdas Julien. 1966. *Semantique structurale*. Paris: Larousse.
Greimas, Algirdas Julien. 1987. *On Meaning. Selected writings in semiotic theory*. Trans. by Paul J. Perron & Frank H. Collins. Minneapolis: University of Minnesota Press.
Hallpike, Christopher R. 1979. *The Foundations of Primitive Thought*. Oxford: Clarendon Press.
Harris, Roy. 1983. *F. de Saussure Course in General Linguistics*. Trans. by Roy Harris. London: Gerald Duckworth.
Humboldt, Carl Wilhelm von. 1903–36. *Wilhelm von Humboldts Werke* ed. by Albert Leitzman. 17 vols. Berlin: Behr.
Ishiguro, Hide. 1972. *Leibniz's Philosophy of Logic and Language*. London: Duckworth.
Jakobson, Roman. 1959. "On Linguistic Aspects of Translation". *On Translation* ed. by R. A. Brower, 232-239. London: Oxford University Press.
Jespersen, Otto. 1924. *The Philosophy of Grammar*. London: Allen & Unwin.
Johnson, Mark. 1987. *The Body in the Mind. The bodily basis of meaning, imagination, and reason*. Chicago: University of Chicago Press.
Katz, Jerrold J. 1981. *Language and Other Abstract Objects*. Oxford: Blackwell.
Katz, Jerrold J. 1987. "Common Sense in Semantics". *New Directions in Semantics* ed. by E. Lepore, 157-234. London: Academic Press.
Katz, Jerrold J. & Jerry A. Fodor. 1963. "Structure of a Semantic Theory". *Language* 39.170-210.
Katz, Jerrold J. & Richard Nagel. 1974. "Meaning Postulates and Semantic Theory". *Foundations of Language* 11.311-340.
Katz, Jerrold J. & Paul M. Postal. 1964. *An Integrated Theory of Linguistic Descriptions*. Cambridge, Mass.: MIT Press.
Kay, Paul & Chad K. McDaniel. 1978. "The Linguistic Significance of the Meaning of Basic Color Terms". *Language* 54.3.610-646.
Kempson, Ruth. 1977. *Semantic Theory*. Cambridge: Cambridge University Press.
Labov, William. 1973. "The Boundaries of Words and Their Meanings". *New Ways of Analyzing Variation in English* ed. by C. J. Bailey & R. Shuy, 340-373. Washington: Georgetown

University Press.
Lakoff, George. 1970. "Natural Logic and Lexical Decomposition". *Papers from the Sixth Regional Meeting, Chicago Linguistic Society* ed. by M. A. Campbell, 340-362. Chicago: Chicago Linguistics Society.
Lakoff, George. 1972. "Linguistics and Natural Logic". *Semantics of Natural Language* ed. by D. Davidson & G. Harman, 545-665. Dordrecht: Reidel.
Lakoff, George. 1987. *Women, Fire, and Dangerous Things*. Chicago: Chicago University Press.
Langacker, Ronald W. 1987. *Foundations of Cognitive Grammar*, vol 1. Stanford, Cal.: Stanford University Press.
Leibniz, Gottfried Wilhelm. 1903 [1686]. "Generales Inquisitiones de Analysi Notionum et Veritatum" (*Philosophie* VII, C, 20-31). *Opuscules et fragments inédits de Leibniz* ed. by Louis Couturat, 356-399. Paris: Presses Universitaires de France. (Reprinted 1961, Hildesheim: Georg Olms.)
Leibniz, Gottfried Wilhelm. 1981 [1704]. *New Essays on Human Understanding*. Trans. by Peter Remnant & Jonathan Bennet. Cambridge: Cambridge University Press.
Lévy-Bruhl, Lucien. 1925. *La mentalité primitive*. 4th ed. Paris: Félix Alcan.
Lyons, John. 1966. "Towards a 'Notional' Theory of the 'Parts of Speech'". *Journal of Linguistics* 2.209-236.
Lyons, John. 1977. *Semantics*. Cambridge: Cambridge University Press.
Lyons, John. 1989. "Semantic Ascent: A neglected aspect of syntactic typology". *Essays on Grammatical Theory and Universal Grammar* ed. by D. Arnold, M. Atkinson, J. Durand, C. Grover & L. Sadler, 153-186. Oxford: Clarendon.
McCawley, James D. 1968. "The Role of Semantics in a Grammar". *Universals in Linguistic Theory* ed. by E. Bach & R. T. Harms, 124-169. New York: Holt, Rinehart and Winston.
McCawley, James D. 1970. "Semantic Representation". *Cognition: A multiple view* ed. by P. M. Garvin, 227-247. New York: Spartan Books.
McCawley, James D. 1972. *Syntactic and Logical Arguments for Semantic Structures*. Bloomington: Indiana Linguistic Society Club.
McCawley, James D. 1983. "Review of: Anna Wierzbicka's *Lingua Mentalis*". *Language* 59.654-656.
Mel'čuk, Igor A. 1989. "Semantic Primitives from the Viewpoint of the Meaning-Text Linguistic Theory". *Quaderni di Semantica* 10.1.65-102.
Mel'čuk, Igor A. & Aleksandr K. Žolkovskij. 1970. "Toward a Functioning Meaning-Text Model of Language". *Linguistics* 57.10-47.
Mel'čuk, Igor A. & Aleksandr K. Žolkovskij. 1984. *Tolkovo-Kombinatornyj Slovar' Sovremennogo Russkogo Jazyka*. Vienna: Wiener Slawisticher Almanach.
Mel'čuk, Igor A. et al. 1984. *Dictionnaire explicatif et combinatoire du français contemporain I* (Recherches lexico-sémantiques, I). Montreal: Les Presses de l'Université de Montréal.
Mel'čuk, Igor A. et al. 1988. *Dictionnaire explicatif et combinatoire du français contemporain II* (Recherches lexico-sémantiques, II). Montreal: Les Presses de l'Université de Montréal.
Mel'čuk, Igor A. et al. 1992. *Dictionnaire explicatif et combinatoire du français contemporain III* (Recherches lexico-sémantiques, III). Montreal: Les Presses de l'Université de Montréal.
Miller, George A. & Philip N. Johnson-Laird. 1976. *Language and Perception*. Cambridge:

Cambridge University Press.
Peirce, Charles S. 1932. "Speculative Grammar". *Collected Papers of Charles Sanders Peirce*, vol 2: *Elements of logic* ed. by Charles Hartshorne & Paul Weiss, 129-269. Cambridge: Harvard University Press.
Perron, Paul. 1987. Introduction to A. J. Greimas' *On Meaning: Selected writings in semiotic theory*, xxiv-xlv. Minneapolis: University of Minnesota Press.
Plank, Frans. 1989. "On Humboldt on the Dual". *Linguistic Categorization* ed. by R. Corrigan, F. Eckman & M. Noonan, 293-333. Amsterdam: John Benjamins.
Postal, Paul. 1966. "Review of: André Martinet's *Elements of General Linguistics*". *Foundations of Language* 2.151-186.
Sapir, Edward. 1921. *Language*. New York: Harcourt, Brace & World.
Schank, Roger C. 1972. "Conceptual Dependency: A theory of natural language understanding". *Cognitive Psychology* 3.552-631.
Sørensen, Holger Steen. 1958. *Word-Classes in Modern English*. Copenhagen: Gad.
Swadesh, Morris. 1955. "Towards Greater Accuracy in Lexicostatistic Dating". *International Journal of American Linguistics* 21.121-137.
Weinreich, Uriel. 1980 [1962]. "Lexicographic Definition in Descriptive Semantics". *Uriel Weinreich on Semantics* ed. by W. Labov & B. S. Weinreich, 295-314. Pittsburg: University of Pennsylvania Press.
Wierzbicka, Anna. 1972. *Semantic Primitives*. Frankfurt: Athenäum.
Wierzbicka, Anna. 1980. *Lingua Mentalis: The semantics of natural language*. Sydney: Academic Press.
Wierzbicka, Anna. 1987a. "Kinship Semantics: Lexical universals as a key to psychological reality". *Anthropological Linguistics* 29.2.131-156.
Wierzbicka, Anna. 1987b. *English Speech Act Verbs: A semantic dictionary*. Sydney: Academic Press.
Wierzbicka, Anna. 1989. "Semantic Primitives: The expanding set". *Quaderni di Semantica* 10.2.309-332.
Wierzbicka, Anna. 1991. "Lexical Universals and Universals of Grammar". *Meaning and Grammar: Cross-linguistic perspectives* ed. by M. Kefer & J. van der Auwera, 383-415. Berlin: Mouton de Gruyter.
Wierzbicka, Anna. 1992a. *Semantics, Culture, and Cognition: Universal human concepts in culture-specific configurations*. New York: Oxford University Press.
Wierzbicka, Anna. 1992b. "The Search for Universal Semantic Primitives". *Thirty Years of Linguistic Evolution* ed. by M. Pütz, 215-242. Amsterdam: John Benjamins.
Wierzbicka, Anna. In press. "Semantic Universals and 'Primitive Thought': The question of the 'psychic unity of [hu]mankind'". *Journal of Linguistic Anthropology*.
Wilks, Yorick. 1976. "Parsing English II". *Computational Semantics* ed. by E. Charniak & Y. Wilks, 155-184. Amsterdam: North-Holland.
Wilks, Yorick. 1977. "Good and Bad Arguments About Semantic Primitives". *Communication & Cognition* 10.3/4.181-221.
Wilks, Yorick. 1988. "Reference and Its Role in Computational Models of Mental Representations". *Meaning and Mental Representations* ed. by U. Eco, M. Santambrogio & P. Violi, 221-237.

Bloomington: Indiana University Press.

Žolkovskij, Aleksandr. 1964. "Leksika Celesoobraznoj Dejatel'nosti". *Mašinnyj Perevod i Prikladnaja Lingvistika* 8:76-108. (Translation: 1974. "The Vocabulary of Purposeful Activity". *Machine Translation and Applied Linguistics* ed. by V. Ju. Rozencvejg, vol 1.197-234. Frankfurt: Athenaion.)

Žolkovskij, Aleksandr, N. N. Leont'eva & Ju. S. Martem'janov. 1961. "O Principialnom Ispol'zovanni Smysla pri Mašinnom Perevode". *Mašinnyj Perevod* 2.17-47. (Translation: 1974. "On the Basic Use of Meaning in Machine Translation". *Machine Translation and Applied Linguistics* ed. by V. Ju. Rozencvejg, vol 1.115-141. Frankfurt: Athenaion.)

Zwicky, Arnold. 1973. "Linguistics as Chemistry: The substance theory of semantic primes". *A Festschrift for Morris Halle* ed. by S. Anderson & P. Kiparsky, 467-485. New York: Holt, Rinehart and Winston.

Introducing Lexical Primitives

Cliff Goddard
University of New England, Armidale

Anna Wierzbicka
Australian National University, Canberra

The main part of this chapter surveys the proposed primitive inventory whose crosslinguistic validity is being put to the test in this book. Before embarking on this exercise, we address some methodological issues.

2.1   Methodological Issues

Testing whether a proposed set of semantically primitive meanings can find lexical expression in a range of languages may seem to be a purely empirical task: laborious, to be sure, but relatively straightforward. In fact, however, the presence or absence of a word for a given concept cannot be established by any simple, checklist method. The search is empirical, but it necessarily has an analytical dimension, and it must be methodologically informed.

2.1.1   The Problem of Polysemy

It goes without saying that polysemy must never be postulated lightly, and that it has always to be justified on language-internal grounds; but to reject polysemy in a dogmatic and a priori fashion is just as foolish as to postulate it without justification. Polysemy is a fact of life, and basic, everyday words are particularly likely to be polysemous (cf. Zipf 1949). We may therefore expect that exponents of semantically primitive meanings will frequently be polysemous.

In English for example, *know* is polysemous between the semantically primitive sense of 'knowing that' (*I know that this is not true*) and its 'acquaintanceship/

familarity' sense (*I know this man/place*), distinguished in French as *savoir* and *connaître*. English *feel* is polysemous between its semantically primitive sense (*I feel good/bad*), its action sense (*I felt her pulse*) and its cognitive sense (*I feel it's wrong*). Even *you* is polysemous between *you*$_{SG}$ and *you*$_{PL}$.

It should be stressed that these assertions about polysemy are not purely impressionistic, and (notwithstanding the French example just given) are not based on comparisons between range of use across languages. To prove that a word is polysemous, rather than simply vague or general in meaning, one has to demonstrate that its various uses are genuinely semantically different; that is, that they call for distinct (though usually overlapping) reductive paraphrase explications. For instance, it can be shown that the action and cognitive senses of *feel* contain the elements DO and THINK respectively, thereby establishing these senses as complex and distinct from the semantically primitive FEEL.[1]

If such a 'purely semantic' demonstration is not practical for any reason, lexicographers agree on at least one mechanical diagnostic of polysemy, namely the possession of mutually exclusive syntactic frames or combinatorial possibilities (cf. Weinreich 1966:177–183). Thus, the polysemy of *know* can be established by the observation that the semantically primitive sense takes a sentential *that*-complement, and that the 'acquaintance' meaning is excluded from this syntactic frame. Similarly, the polysemy of Modern English *you* can be justified on the basis of the distinction between the forms *yourself* and *yourselves*, the choice between these being determined by the choice between *you*$_{SG}$ and *you*$_{PL}$ (compare *You must defend yourself* with *You must defend yourselves*).

There is really nothing surprising in the fact that a single word, as in these examples from English, may have two related meanings, one indefinable and the other definable. It is more surprising to discover that in some languages a single word-form may expound two different indefinable meanings. For instance, in Yankunytjatjara the same form *kutjupa* may expound both SOMEONE and OTHER; and in Mangap-Mbula the same form *-so* expounds both WANT and SAY. However, in both languages the lexical material is associated in each case with distinct syntactic properties, making the recognition of polysemy straightforward, even without a native-speaker semantic competence.

It could be argued that the term 'homonymy' would be more appropriate than 'polysemy' for situations like those just mentioned, since the meanings in question are unrelated semantically. We seem to be dealing with two distinct words with the same form, rather than with two related senses of the same word. 'Homonymy', however, suggests an arbitrary and unmotivated coincidence of form. In fact, one of the most exciting findings to emerge from the present studies is that there are recurrent patterns across languages in this respect: the lexical forms for DO and SAY, and for SOMEONE and OTHER, are identical in not one, but in many languages. (The rationale for, and contraints on, this phenomenon are among the main themes of chapter 17.) We therefore employ the term polysemy in a broad sense throughout this volume.

2.1.2 Formal versus Semantic Complexity

As we have just seen, a single form may well serve to express several meanings. But equally, a single, unitary meaning may find expression through a complex, analysable form.

Again, examples are readily furnished from English. The words SOMEONE and SOMETHING are both formally analysable, but in neither case is the meaning of the whole word the sum of the parts; on the contrary, SOMEONE and SOMETHING are semantically undecomposable (see below). This phenomenon is not restricted to word-level morphology. For instance, the two-word English expression THE SAME is also indivisible from a semantic point of view, even though (in the full English language, if not in the restricted language of semantic explication) its two parts may be separated, as in the expression *the very same*. Similarly, in English the basic locational primitive may take the form BE SOMEWHERE, but it is not possible to separate the meaning expressed into two components, one corresponding to the verb *be* and the other to *somewhere*. Comparable examples are found in many of the studies in the present volume.

None of this means, of course, that forms like *some*, *the* and *be* are not meaning-bearing in their own right elsewhere in the language. But it does mean that the implicit belief of many linguists that 'once a morpheme, always a morpheme' must be abandoned (just as the comparable formula about phonemes has been abandoned). The truth is that the same formal element may be a true morpheme in some contexts (i.e. be correlated with a distinct meaning), but a mere formative in others (i.e. lacking any correlated meaning).

Further examples of formal complexity associated with semantic simplicity can be found in the following section.

2.1.3 Allomorphy and Allolexy

The semantically primitive meaning which in English is represented by a single form THIS has in Latin not one but three forms: *hic* (masculine), *haec* (feminine) and *hoc* (neuter). These forms can be regarded as lexical variants (allolexes) of the same semantic unit. In this case, the variation is lexically conditioned by the gender class of the Latin noun.

A somewhat different type of example is furnished by English *me*, which can be regarded as a variant of the semantic element I; in this case, the distribution of the variants is conditioned by position — I is found pre-verbally, and *me* elsewhere.

Yet another type of contextual variation may be determined by combination. For example, in English the combination of the meanings THIS and SOMEONE is more naturally expressed as *this person*, rather than as *this someone*; because it is not possible to specify any semantic difference between *this person* and THIS SOMEONE, the term *person* may be regarded in this context as an allolex of SOMEONE.

A slightly different type of example of combinatorial allolexy is provided by the Japanese forms *kono* and *kore* which are both equivalents of the semantically primitive meaning THIS; the former is found where the meaning in question is a nominal modifier, and the latter where it is used as a referring expression in its own right, to refer to an extra-linguistic situation (compare *Kono hito wa yoi* 'This person is good' with *Kore wa yoi* 'This is good').

The concept of allolexy holds the key to an apparent difficulty for NSM semantics which has puzzled some observers (e.g. Moravscik 1991), namely, how to reconcile the existence of language-specific morphosyntactic categories with the NSM claim that the semantic metalanguage is isomorphic across languages. Strictly speaking, this matter is tangential to the lexical focus of the present volume, but the gist of the argument may be conveyed by a consideration of obligatory tense marking in English. Clearly, in an English sentence like *I did something*, as in (a) below, the word *did* is semantically complex, conveying both DO and 'past tense'. We may suppose that the semantic content of 'past tense' is, basically, *at some time before now* (where *now* is elliptical for *when I say this*). What happens if we 'paraphrase out' the past tense content of *did*, as in (b) below? Here, we would argue, the form *did* no longer conveys independent semantic content, aside from the lexical content of DO. That is, once the past time-reference aspect of meaning is, so to speak, extracted and made redundant as part of the sentential context, the choice of the form *did* as opposed to *do* becomes automatic, and can be viewed as allolexic, since in this context it would be ungrammatical to exchange the forms.

(a)   *I did something.*
(b)   *At some time before now, I did/*do something.*

For a similar example, consider the Latin forms *volo* 'I want' and *velis* 'you want'. In ordinary Latin, these forms often occur without any explicit subject pronoun, and must in such uses be regarded as semantically complex, that is, equivalent to *ego volo* 'I want' and *tu velis* 'you want', respectively. However, in the natural semantic metalanguage based on Latin, *volo* would never occur without an explicit subject *ego* (nor *velis* without *tu*); thus in Latin NSM, *volo* and *velis* may be regarded as contextually conditioned variants of the same semantic element.

2.1.4   Differences in Range of Use

Semantic equivalents across languages may have widely differing ranges of use in different languages, without this in any way invalidating their claim to semantic equivalence. What establishes semantic non-equivalence is the presence of a specifiable — that is, paraphrasable — semantic difference, but there are many factors aside from the existence of such a specifiable difference that may give rise to differing range of use.

One obvious and, in a sense, trivial factor is polysemy. If in a particular language the exponent of WANT, for instance, can also mean 'love, like' and 'need', then obviously the word will be likely to be more frequent than its monosemic equivalent in another language.

A more subtle factor is how the lexical element figures within the overall expressive dynamics of the linguistic system in which it is embedded. For instance, the Yankunytjatjara exponent of the semantic element BECAUSE, namely a particular use of the ablative case-marker *-nguru*, is much rarer in ordinary discourse than the word *because* (or *'cos*) is in English. Part of the reason is that Yankunytjatjara possesses two extremely common purposive constructions, expressing meanings which are an amalgam of BECAUSE together with WANTING TO DO SOMETHING and WANTING SOMETHING TO HAPPEN. In other words, the existence of these compact purposive constructions preempts much of the need for deployment of the bare, lexical BECAUSE.

Another cause of range of use differences are social and cultural factors. For example, Thai *chán* 'I' has a range of use incomparably narrower than its English equivalent, because in Thai society references to oneself are generally expected to be accompanied by expressions of humility or inferiority. A bare I therefore becomes pragmatically marked, and must be interpreted in most situations as either very intimate or very rude (cf. Cooke 1968; Diller (this volume)).

Similarly, in Javanese society, which lacks the ethos of individualist self-expression so characteristic of most Western cultures, it would be considered absurdly unrefined to come forth with frequent expressions of one's innermost feelings: consequently, the distribution of the Javanese exponent of FEEL would be much more restricted than its English counterpart; and explications for many 'feeling-laden' English expressions into a Javanese NSM would seem peculiar to native speakers of that language without cultural familiarity with the West.

2.1.5 Resonance

Another non-semantic difference between the exponents of semantically primitive meanings in different languages may be termed 'resonance'. Under this heading, we include, firstly, any non-paraphrasable effects resulting from the association between an exponent and other, complex meanings also expressible by the same lexical form. For instance, English *feel* may expound FEEL, but the same word also expresses meanings to do with the sense of touch; whereas the Malay equivalent *rasa* is polysemous with the meaning 'taste', and the Yankunytjatjara equivalent *tjuni* with the meaning 'belly'.

Secondly, resonance effects may exist as a result of formal complexity. For instance, there is conceivably some non-palpable effect proceeding from the fact that English *someone* and *something* have a morphological overlap; or that the semantic exponent of WANT in Yankunytjatjara *mukuringanyi* contains a formative which elsewhere indicates an inchoative meaning.

Thirdly, there may be resonance effects resulting from the sound shape (or even the graphic shape) of lexical exponents, and their interrelationships with other words in the language.

Such elusive effects have been accorded great weight by phenomenologists of language, such as Merleau-Ponty (1962 [1945]), and they are apt to play heavily also upon the minds of language learners and formally oriented linguists. Here we acknowledge the possible existence of resonance effects primarily for the sake of completeness. By definition, they inhere in relationships between form and meaning which cannot be captured in paraphrases, and they are inherently language-specific. From the NSM point of view, once having acknowledged their existence there is little choice but to invoke Wittgenstein's celebrated dictum and not attempt to speak of what — in principle — cannot be spoken of.

2.1.6 Non-Compositional Relationships

It used to be believed that semantically primitive meanings should be mutually independent (see Ishiguro (1972:45–46) on Leibniz; see also Wierzbicka 1972). The reason for this assumption was that it would seem that if two concepts had something in common they could not both be semantically indivisible.

But on the other hand, it was always clear that some elements from even the very earliest (and smallest) inventories of NSM primitives were not entirely independent of one another. For instance, YOU and I are not independent of SOMEONE, despite the fact that neither can be defined via SOMEONE (see below). Similarly, one could say that THINK, KNOW, WANT and FEEL have something in common, as they all stand for some sort of mental processes or states, although it is equally clear that such elements cannot be defined — at least not in terms which would be intuitively clear and self-explanatory. Again, GOOD seems to be intuitively related in some way to WANT, as a long line of philosophers have suggested; and BECAUSE and CAN seem to be related to IF (cf. Austin 1961).

In recent years it has become clear that semantic indivisibility is one thing and intuitive independence another. Affiliations of the sort just referred to are now known as 'non-compositional relationships', and are the focus of intense research interest. To appreciate the character of non-compositional relationships, it can be helpful to consider an analogy: numbers like 3, 7 and 11 do not have any numerical factor in common (aside from 1), but they nonetheless share a certain property, namely, that of being prime numbers. Among semantic primitives, many non-compositional relationships appear to have their basis in shared syntactic possibilities (see chapter 17).

In any case, for present purposes the important point is that to challenge the putative primitiveness of an element it is not enough merely to point out that it has some intuitive connection with another element. As ever, the test of semantic divisibility is the test of paraphrase. If the meaning is complex, then it should be possible to decompose it in a paraphrase; and conversely, for a meaning to maintain its claim to simplicity, it must withstand all attempts at paraphrase.

2.2 The Proposed Primitive Inventory

We will now run through the entire proposed primitive inventory, in the groupings used by authors of the individual studies to follow. In some cases, we will discuss and refute putative decompositions which are circulating in the general linguistic literature, or indicate areas of semantic analysis where the elements in question have proved themselves particularly indispensable.

It is, however, impossible to review here the very substantial corpus of descriptive semantic analysis which has already been conducted within the NSM framework — see, for example, Wierzbicka (1972, 1980a, 1980b, 1985a, 1985b, 1986a, 1986b, 1987a, 1988, 1990a, 1992a), Goddard (1979, 1985, 1986, 1990, 1991, 1992), Chappell (1980, 1986a, 1986b), Wilkins (1986, 1992), Ameka (1987, 1988, 1990, 1992), Harkins (1986, 1990). Nor can we undertake here a systematic review of how the present proposed mini-lexicon arose historically from earlier, smaller versions, such as those proposed in Wierzbicka (1972, 1980a); but see Wierzbicka (1989a, 1989b, 1992b).

2.2.1 Substantives: I, YOU, SOMEONE, SOMETHING, PEOPLE

SOMEONE and SOMETHING are among the best established semantic primitives. They clearly cannot be decomposed (without circularity) into simpler concepts, for example, 'personal entity' and 'non-personal entity' (cf. Wierzbicka 1980a:14–16). Often, the basic exponents of these concepts are described in grammars as 'interrogative pronouns', but more detailed descriptions make it clear that the use of the relevant words is not restricted to questions.

It should also be pointed out that the difference between SOMEONE and SOMETHING cannot be interpreted as a difference between persons and things. The concept of 'thing' implies discreteness, but SOMETHING does not imply discreteness. It seems to be a universal fact about human languages that the word for 'what' or 'something' applies not only to (discrete) objects but also to situations, 'stuffs', states of affairs, and so on, which may be neither clearly delimitable nor countable.

The so-called personal pronouns I and YOU are also well-established semantic primitives. They cannot be satisfactorily decomposed,[2] and they are attested, as distinct lexical elements, in every known human language — for rebuttal of the position that languages like Thai and Japanese lack personal pronouns altogether, see Diller (this volume) and Onishi (this volume).

Decomposition of the element I along the lines of 'the person who says this' cannot be accepted as valid because (as pointed out by Sørensen (1963:96, 1958)) the proposed paraphrase is semantically inadequate. 'The person who says this must be a fool' doesn't mean the same as 'I must be a fool'. It is simply not possible to reduce a sign in the first person (or in the second person, for that matter) to one in the third person. Another argument comes from concepts such as *self-pity* or *self-admiration*, which involve the concept of 'I', rather than the concept of 'the speaker'. Thus a person who feels self-admiration thinks, roughly: "I am very good, other people are not like me" (and he or she feels something good because of this). It would be untenable to suggest that a person who feels self-admiration thinks something like "The speaker is very good".

A second defect of the proposed 'person who says this' paraphrase is that the relative pronoun *who* contains I in its meaning (cf. Wierzbicka 1976; see also Castañeda 1966, 1977).

Similar arguments apply, *mutatis mutandis*, to YOU: putative paraphrases are not semantically adequate, attempts at decomposition lead to circularity. Paraphrases of YOU in terms of 'person' or 'someone' are inadequate because they imply a totally different perspective, and a totally different attitude, from YOU. A sentence such as *I love the person to whom I say this* sounds like a deliberate charade, and a deliberate attempt to avoid face-to-face interaction. It does not mean the same as *I love you*.

It might be objected that French *tu/toi*, say, cannot be the semantic equivalent of English *you*, because *tu* is perceived as either very intimate or very rude, and it might be proposed that *tu* can be decomposed along the following lines: *tu* = 'you, I don't have to show respect to you'. But this hypothesis is quite implausible. For example, it is hardly plausible to suggest that every time one addresses a dog as *tu* one wants to convey to the dog the message 'I don't have to show respect to you'. By using the form *tu*, one indeed shows that one finds it unnecessary to show respect to the addressee, but the absence of a manifestation of respect is not part of the intended message. Furthermore, the putative paraphrase could not even be formulated in French at all, since it would have to contain the very word which it seeks to explicate (*toi* = 'toi, je n'ai pas besoin de montrer du respect pour toi').

Finally among the substantive class of semantically primitive meanings is PEOPLE, the most recent addition to the proposed inventory. This element is needed for the explication of moral and social concepts such as 'charity', 'conceit', 'solidarity', 'service', and emotional concepts such as 'shame' and 'pride', which require components such as 'people (would) think this is bad/good'. The element PEOPLE also figures heavily in explications of the 'cultural scripts' embodying shared understandings about interactive conventions within a given society (cf. Wierzbicka, in press, forthcoming; Goddard 1992).

One might think at first that PEOPLE could be decomposed as the plural of SOMEONE or 'person', but such an analysis is not tenable because PEOPLE is restricted to humans in a way that SOMEONE is not. Also, the notion of 'plural' itself is by no means semantically simple; the meaning of plural personal pronouns, for instance, can be shown to be dependent upon the notion of PEOPLE, rather than the other way around (cf. Goddard, in press).

2.2.2 Mental Predicates: THINK, SAY, KNOW, FEEL, WANT

The canonical syntax of all these elements allows for a personal subject — I, YOU, SOMEONE or PEOPLE. Except for FEEL, they are complement-taking.

At one time, it was believed that KNOW THAT could be decomposed as 'can say that'; but this paraphrase is unsatisfactory if only because, as pointed out by Bogusławski (1979, 1989), a dog can know things, though it is unable to say anything. KNOW is indispensable in the analysis of illocutionary forces and in the area of syntactic complementation (cf. Wierzbicka 1987a, 1988), as well as for the explication of perception words like *see*, *hear* and so on, and propositional attitude verbs like *doubt*, *expect*, *wonder* and many others. It is also clear from empirical studies that KNOW has a much better chance of being a genuine lexical universal than, for example, *true*, which many semanticists treat as a fundamental concept, and take for granted. The canonical context for KNOW involves a sentence-like complement, that is, 'know that ...'.

Some languages have been reported not to distinguish lexically between THINK and FEEL (Lutz 1985; Levy 1973; Howell 1981), but it appears that in some such cases at least, the true exponent of FEEL has been overlooked (or treated as metaphorical) on account of it being identical with a concrete meaning such as 'belly' or 'insides'.

Presumably, little need be said to establish the plausibility of SAY as a semantic primitive. Attempts to paraphrase it lead immediately to greater obscurity, or to circularity.

The concept of WANT is so basic that it cannot possibly be decomposed into any simpler units, and any attempts to define it (e.g. in terms of 'positive volition') lead to circularity and obscurity.[3] Polysemy between WANT and SAY, however, is not uncommon in some parts of the world, such as New Guinea (Foley 1986:156–158); the Austronesian language Mangap-Mbula (Bugenhaugen, this volume) is one such example.

As for FEEL, it was for a time dropped from the NSM inventory (see Wierzbicka 1980a), but subsequent research has found that it appears to be both universal and indispensable for the semantic analysis of words for emotions and sensations, as well as for interjections, speech act verbs, 'experiencer constructions', and so on (cf. e.g. Ameka 1990, 1992; Bugenhagen 1990; Harkins 1990; Wierzbicka 1987a, 1990b, 1991, 1992a; Wilkins 1986). The canonical contexts for FEEL are, however, very restricted indeed: 'feel (something) good/bad'.

2.2.3 Determiners and Quantifiers: THIS, THE SAME, OTHER, ONE, TWO, MANY, ALL

THIS is another element which seems to be an indubitable semantic primitive. Attempts to explain its meaning only obscure it, as when, for instance, the meaning of

THIS is 'explained' in terms of 'spatial deixis' (cf. e.g. Anderson & Keenan 1985:280–282). For one thing, 'deixis' is hardly a simpler and clearer concept than THIS. For another, THIS is not an inherently 'spatial' concept at all (one can talk of *this time*, *this song*, *this word*, and so on, just as well as of physical objects). There can be no justification for calling THIS a 'spatial' concept and then resorting to labelling its wide range of common uses as 'metaphorical'.

A remarkable attribute of the element THIS is its neutrality with respect to animacy, personhood and discreteness: though every language appears to distinguish 'who' from 'what', none appears to distinguish between 'this$_{who}$' and 'this$_{what}$' (although many languages do distinguish between portmanteaus involving THIS: compare *he* with *it* in English).[4] And yet — curiously — in structures such as *This is good* and *This is bad*, the *this* is not neutral: it cannot refer to a person. We propose to account for this by saying that THIS is not necessarily restricted to a 'modifying' role, but may be used on its own to refer directly to a situation, or to some aspect of a situation. In support of this proposition, we adduce the fact that, even in English, *this* can be used to point directly to an extra-linguistic situation, activity or event. For example, one can say *Listen to this!*, *Look at this!*, *It went like this: [demonstration]*, *She did it like this: [demonstration]*. It would be highly unnatural to interpret sentences of this kind as elliptical, with *this* standing for THIS SOMETHING (as suggested in earlier work, e.g. Wierzbicka (1989a)).

We suggest, therefore, that THIS is not inherently a 'nominal modifier' or 'nominal determiner', and that its (semantic) syntax is not restricted to combinations with SOMEONE and SOMETHING.[5] Words such as *here* and *now* suggest that the same semantic element can also be combined, in semantic structure, with (SOME)WHERE and WHEN, and words such as *thus* and *so* suggest that it can also be combined with the element LIKE.

It must be conceded that, in many languages, the equivalent of THIS has a special form when used to refer to extra-linguistic situations. For example, in French one says *Ce garçon/couteau est bon* 'This boy/knife is good', but *Cela est bon* 'This is good'. As mentioned earlier, a similar situation is found in Japanese, where *kono* corresponds to *ce* and *kore* to *cele*. If the analysis proposed here is correct, pairs of words such as *ce* and *cele*, and *kono* and *kore* should be interpreted as allolexes.

The postulation of the element ONE as an indefinable semantic universal presumably needs little justification; it has been part of the lists proposed by Leibniz, Bogusławski and Apresjan. As for TWO, it appears to be attested as a lexical unit in all languages, and while it is decomposable in some sense (cf. Bogusławski 1965), one can doubt whether it can be decomposed into independently justifiable semantic units. It is needed, for example, for explicating words designating dual body parts such as *eyes*, *ears*, *hands* and *legs*. The wide occurrence of dual pronouns (especially in languages which don't have highly developed systems of numerals) provides additional support for the idea that TWO is a basic, and simple, semantic element (cf. Humboldt 1830). Both ONE and TWO are presumably needed, along with other elements such as PART OF, to explicate the higher numerals.

ALL is needed in many areas of both lexicon and grammar, including conjunctions, particles, and plurality. It is another element whose universality has been widely assumed, at least in the logical literature. Though it might appear at first brush that ALL can be decomposed along the lines of (a) or (b) below, neither analysis is satisfactory.

All dogs are faithful =
(a)   no dog is unfaithful
(b)   one can't say thinking of a dog: "this (dog) is not faithful"

Explication (a) fails because the use of *no* in this way is simply a variant of ALL, and a highly English-specific one at that. Explication (b) (proposed in Wierzbicka 1980a) may seem more convincing from a purely logical point of view, but it is less convincing from the point of view of psychological plausibility. As well, there are uses of ALL in volitive or expressive utterances, such as *Regards to all!* or *To hell with it all!* where (b) seems completely unworkable. (It would hardly be plausible to paraphrase *Regards to all!* as 'one can't say thinking of someone: I don't (send) regards to this person'.)

The elements THE SAME and LIKE correspond loosely to two fundamental logical relations, identity and similarity, which both occupy a prominent place in the philosophical literature concerning thought and knowledge. Attempts to define these concepts undertaken in earlier NSM work (Wierzbicka 1972) cannot be regarded as successful. Both are needed in semantic analysis across a wide range of areas. For example, THE SAME is needed to account for the meaning of many conjunctions and particles, such as *also*, *too* and *and* (cf. Goddard 1986, Wierzbicka 1986b, 1991), as well as for that of grammatical devices such as switch-reference.

OTHER is needed for reciprocals, comparatives and non-singular pronouns, for the decomposition of numerous lexical items involving the notions of parts and kinds, and for some grammatical phenomena such as switch-reference.

It may appear that since we have negation (or something like negation) at our disposal, we need either THE SAME or OTHER but not both (cf. Wierzbicka 1989b); for instance, that *another book* = 'a book, not the same book'. But this kind of explication will not work in contexts where the expression OTHER PEOPLE is contrasted with I or YOU, such as *I/you and some other people*. It can be added that the apparent symmetry between THE SAME and OTHER is deceptive, since THE SAME may apply to predication (e.g. *do the same*, *say the same*) whereas OTHER has to do exclusively with reference (*another person, another thing*).

All the determiner-like and quantifier-like elements in this grouping can be expected to be combinable with the substantives SOMEONE, SOMETHING and PEOPLE, although it appears that in many languages there are allolexes for some of these combinations. This may be readily illustrated from English. As mentioned earlier, the expression *this someone* (though comprehensible) sounds rather unnatural, but exactly the same meaning seems to be expressed by *this person*, suggesting that in this context *person* functions as an allolex of SOMEONE. Admittedly, not all languages have a general word like *person*, which would freely combine with the deictic THIS, but most have portmanteau exponents for this combination of concepts in the form of the so-called third-person personal pronouns (like *he* and *she*).

We would expect that other 'complex substantives' would include expressions like 'the same person', 'two people', 'the same two people', 'these two people', and so on; though again, in many languages, complex meanings of this kind are normally realised as simple lexemes, that is, as varieties of 'third-person pronouns'.

Finally, it should be noted that in some languages the elements in this 'determiner/quantifier' grouping are in fact verbs, or adverbial modifiers.

2.2.4 Actions and Events: DO, HAPPEN (TO)

In earlier NSM work, DO was treated as a semantic 'molecule' rather than as an 'atom', on the assumption that it could be decomposed in terms of WANT and HAPPEN (cf. Wierzbicka 1980a:177). However, arguments put forward by Bogusławski (1989) have shown that the proposed paraphrases are inadequate, and that there is something irreducible about 'doing' which can only be accounted for by treating DO as a semantic primitive. There is also a good deal of evidence suggesting that DO can be regarded as a lexical universal, although it appears that polysemy is often involved, particularly with exponents of SAY and HAPPEN.

We hypothesise that in any language one can say, in one way or another, the equivalent of 'I/you/someone did something'. The whole concept of 'agency', which plays such an important role in the grammar of natural languages, relies on that. Furthermore, the fundamentals of morality, and of law, rely on the concept of 'someone doing something' and more particularly, on the concept of 'someone doing something bad'.

One interesting difference between DO, on the one hand, and THINK, KNOW and SAY, on the other, involves their relationship to time. One does something at a particular time, and 'doing' seems to make sense only with reference to time. By contrast, thinking (believing, etc.), knowing, and perhaps even saying, can be viewed as only loosely related to time. We cannot conceive of someone doing something other than in terms of them doing it 'at some time' (whether specified or unspecified). By contrast, we can conceive of people thinking or knowing something without any reference to time (cf. Wittgenstein 1967:17).

This inherent relationship with time links DO not with the other personal predicates, but with the impersonal HAPPEN.[6]

It seems reasonable to expect that one should be able to say in any language something corresponding to the English sentences *What happened?* and *Something happened (at that time)*. One would expect, therefore, to find in any language not only some counterpart of 'what' or 'something', but an exponent of HAPPEN (and to find that they are able to co-occur with one another).

But just as action (DO) is necessarily linked with an agent, events are necessarily linked with a substratum: things don't just 'happen', they happen in (or to) a place, a thing, or a person. One would expect, then, to be able to say, in any language, not only that 'something happened (at some time)', but also, that 'something happened to a person' or that 'something happened to a thing'. The element HAPPEN should in fact be regarded as not different from HAPPEN TO or HAPPEN WITH. One would therefore expect to be able to say, in any language, the equivalent of 'Something (or this) happened to me/you/this person/this thing'.

The point is important, because the positing of two separate indefinables DO and HAPPEN might otherwise seem unnecessary: isn't 'doing' a type of event? It must be stressed, therefore, that what is meant by HAPPEN in the present system is not some abstract 'event' in the sense philosophers often give to this word, but an event affecting someone or something. It is closer, therefore, to the linguistic notion of 'patient' than to the philosophical notion of 'event'.

Like DO, the concept of HAPPEN (TO) is intrinsically linked with the concept of time. Presumably, any sentence referring to 'something happening' is also, explicitly or implicitly, referring to time. For example, the sentence *This happened to me* has to be understood as an elliptical version of *This happened to me at some time*.

There are, then, two predicates which are intrinsically related to time, DO and HAPPEN (TO), and perhaps it is this semantic link (i.e. that both are predicates with a 'temporal slot') which accounts for the frequent lexical links between their exponents.

2.2.5 Meta-Predicates: NO, IF, CAN, LIKE, BECAUSE, VERY

This is a very loose grouping of terms whose syntax is such that they combine, with a modifying or operator-like effect, with a predicate or clause.

The ability to say "No!" is surely a basic feature of human nature. NO has an inherently first-person orientation, representing the speaker's rejection of something — an offer, a request, a statement, food, unwelcome sexual advances or whatever. This meaning is comparable to that of the expression '(I) don't want' (which was the form in which it originally occurred in early NSM work), but the 'rejection' expressed by a particle/interjection such as English *No!* cannot really be analysed into 'I', 'not' and 'want' — it is a single semantic unit. (This, incidentally, is why NO cannot be identified with the abstract and impersonal 'negation' of logic or formal syntax.)

It should be added perhaps that many languages have a word which can be glossed as 'Don't!', and which is described as a marker of 'negative imperatives' (for example, Latin *Noli me tangere* 'Don't touch me'). Such words can be seen as an amalgam of the basic concept of NO with the combination YOU DO.

From the early days of NSM research it was recognised that imagination is a basic and irreducible aspect of human life, manifested in children's play, in fantasy, dreams, pretending, works of fiction, and so on. Originally it was represented in the

NSM lexicon by the verb 'imagine', but it is now clear that what is needed is not so much a verb, attributable to any subject, but a modal device indicating the speaker's attitude, that is, an element such as IF.

The concept of CAN may seem to be dispensable from the list of universal atomic concepts because CAN seems to be related to IF (as J. L. Austin (1961:153) put it, 'cans are iffy'). Indeed, it is tempting to try to decompose the 'can of ability' along the following lines (cf. Wierzbicka 1972:154, and 1987b): *I can* ... = 'if I want I will ...'. However, an analysis along these lines cannot really get rid of CAN, because the explication does not analyse away the notion of 'possibility', and 'possibility' cannot be convincingly defined via wanting or imagination. There are things which we can imagine but which we know cannot happen. (Imaginable does not mean possible: it only means possible to imagine.)

Something akin to possibility is needed in many areas of semantic analysis, and it is this function which is served by CAN (and its English allolex *could*); for instance, to express meanings like: 'people can know this', or 'something bad could happen to me'. It must be conceded that CAN is often difficult to identify cross-linguistically, partly because it is often involved in complex patterns of polysemy, and partly because its exponents often appear to be bound morphemes rather than distinct words.

As for the syntax of CAN, it would seem that the following combinations should all be possible: 'you (I, someone) can know/think/say: S'. In other words, CAN is similar to NO and IF insofar as it has an entire clause in its scope (that is, it applies to the combination of a subject and a predicate), but it doesn't have the inherent first-person orientation of these other two 'sentential operators'. If the other two are, so to speak, psychological, CAN is, so to speak, logical.

LIKE functions as a semantically primitive 'hedge' within the NSM meta-language, and is crucial for the prototype-style analyses needed for emotions, speech acts, colours and kinship, among other areas. In terms of syntax, LIKE seems to have a special affinity for THIS, and many languages have special allolexes for the combination LIKE THIS, or even for more specialised combinations such as DO LIKE THIS, HAPPEN LIKE THIS or SAY LIKE THIS. Nonetheless, one would also expect combinations such as SOMEONE LIKE ME and SOMETHING LIKE THIS to be sayable in any language.

As for BECAUSE, it was once believed (Wierzbicka 1972:17) that this concept could be defined away, by means of an analysis similar to that used by logicians for the relationship of 'material implication':

X happened because Y happened =
if Y hadn't happened X wouldn't have happened

However, the paraphrase above is incorrect. For example, it may be true that *If Mary hadn't met John, she wouldn't have married him*, but it doesn't follow from this that *Mary married John because she had met him*. This shows that BECAUSE cannot be reduced to IF.

It appears, then, that BECAUSE is a semantic primitive, and we hypothesise that it has lexical exponents in all languages. Although many languages do not have a word reserved solely for expounding BECAUSE, these languages are not necessarily counterexamples to the hypothesis that BECAUSE is universally lexicalised. Careful analysis shows that many words which can mean either BECAUSE or, for example, 'from' (or 'after') can be legitimately regarded as polysemous (just as English *since* is polysemous, having both a temporal and a causal meaning).

VERY is a recent addition to the list of hypothetical semantic primitives, and it is not fully certain that it is really needed. But it does seem to be universally available. The area where it seems most relevant is that of expressive evaluations, such as *wonderful*, *marvellous*, *terrific*, *awful* or *horrible*. Expressions of this kind seem to rely crucially on the combinations of the elements GOOD and BAD with VERY (VERY GOOD, VERY BAD).

In earlier work (see Wierzbicka 1972:86) it was assumed that VERY can be reduced to 'more' (an assumption questioned at the time by Dwight Bolinger, personal communication), along the following lines: *This is very good* = 'this is more than good'. But this analysis depends on the definability of 'more'. Now, even supposing that certain uses of 'more' (in relation to physical stuffs, e.g. *more butter*) could be defined away in terms of PART OF, it is hard to see how one could plausibly reduce the notions 'very good' and 'very bad' to the notion of PART OF. It therefore seems necessary to regard VERY as an indefinable.

2.2.6 *Time and Place:* WHEN, WHERE, AFTER, BEFORE, UNDER, ABOVE

Another basic concept which one would expect to find universally involves the concept of place (WHERE). One would expect to be able to say in any language that someone, or something, is somewhere (in a particular place), and to be able to ask where someone or something is.

It is important to note that the idea of 'being somewhere' cannot be analysed into 'being' and 'somewhere': the fact that in English (and in many other languages) it is expressed by means of a locative expression and a copula verb has to do with the language-specific realm of form, not with the language-universal realm of meaning.

Another basic meaning one would expect to be able to express in any language involves the concept of 'time' (WHEN). One would expect to be able to say the equivalent of 'When did it happen?' and 'It happened at this time'. In fact, it seems that 'time' (WHEN) can co-occur with 'place' (in sentences referring to location).[7] A sentence such as *John is in the garden* can be regarded as equivalent to *At this time (now) John is in the garden*. A locational sentence with a past tense, such as *John was in the garden* can be regarded as equivalent to *At some time before now John was in the garden*.

As implied by the preceding discussion, in addition to the semantically simple temporal adjunct 'at some time', there must be in any language some complex ones: 'at this time', 'at the same time', 'at some time before this time' and so on. And similarly for places, we predict or expect that in any language one could express meanings such as 'in this place' and 'in the same place'.

The pairs of elements BEFORE and AFTER, and UNDER and ABOVE are necessary to accommodate relational concepts in the temporal and locational domains, respectively. At present, it appears that in each case it is necessary to regard both members of these pairs of converse opposites as indefinable. Despite the obvious affinities between BEFORE and AFTER, for instance, it is not possible to convincingly paraphrase BEFORE in terms of AFTER, or vice versa.

2.2.7 Taxonomy and Partonomy: KIND OF, HAVE PARTS

These two concepts have in common the fact that both are inherently 'relational', and also that although both appear to be fundamental to human conceptualisation, they nevertheless present some difficulties in terms of cross-linguistic lexical identification.

The concept of KIND OF is at the heart of the human categorisation of 'the contents of the world'. The lexicon of every language is full of taxonomic concepts, which rely crucially on the concept of KIND OF. For example, in English, a *rose* is 'a kind of flower', an *oak* is 'a kind of tree', a *swallow* is 'a kind of bird' and so on. It is an inherently relational concept: one can speak about a kind of thing, a kind of person, or a kind of place, but not about a KIND without OF.

It might seem that KIND OF is too closely related to LIKE to be a separate indefinable. It seems natural to think that things which are of the same kind are also like each other. Yet recent work in cognitive psychology as well as linguistics has led to the growing conviction that human categorisation cannot be reduced to notions such as likeness or similarity. In particular, LIKE seems to create an ad hoc link between two entities, situations, or whatever, whereas KIND OF seems to appeal to something more permanent, more objective, and possibly more hidden: for example, all dogs are thought of as the same KIND OF animal although they are not really very much LIKE one another (cf. Atran 1990; Carey 1985; Gelman & Coley 1991; Keil 1986; Medin & Ortony 1989; Rips 1989). The concept KIND OF is necessary for the analysis of both natural kinds (e.g. *dog*, *oak*, *daffodil*) and cultural kinds (e.g. *cup*, *bottle*, *chair*) (cf. e.g. Wierzbicka 1985a).

Parthood seems essential for the explication of numerous items of the concrete vocabulary of any language (e.g. *arm*, *root*, *roof*). Though the concept of 'parthood' has always been an element in the NSM inventory of fundamental concepts, there has been a change in expectations about the kind of exponent that can be expected to be found cross-linguistically. Rather than it taking a form analogous to English *part of*, recent research suggests an exponent with the converse orientation is more widely attested, that is, an element like HAVE PARTS.

In English, the expression HAVE PARTS has plural morphology; obviously, there is no reason to expect that this aspect of the formal representation of the primitive will be found in other languages. On the other hand, it is interesting to note that the very concept of 'parthood' does imply the existence of more than a single part. It should also be noted that in some languages there is no separate lexical item for 'part', but the word meaning 'thing' can be used in a construction which manifestly expresses the concept of HAV(ING) PARTS; for example, a construction which word-for-word can be glossed as "has two things", but which overall expresses the meaning 'has two parts'.

2.2.8 Evaluators and Descriptors: GOOD, BAD, BIG, SMALL

We hypothesise that every language has some words or morphemes corresponding to the fundamental ideas GOOD and BAD. The existence of such elements seems crucial to human culture and to human society, since they provide a basis on which morality, law and religion rest.

Earlier NSM work (Wierzbicka 1972) assumed that the concepts in question were not elementary — that GOOD, for instance, could be defined in terms of WANT and negation. For example, *This apple is good* = 'this apple is as we would want apples to be'. But such analyses no longer seem convincing, because of the conflict between the inherently subjective perspective of WANT, as opposed the inherently objective perspective of GOOD and BAD. People's 'wants' and desires are subjective, changeable, unpredictable, but 'goodness' and 'badness' are conceived of as objective properties of objects, events or acts. Consequently, any attempt to equate GOOD with 'desirable' seems ultimately unconvincing. (The contrast between WANT and GOOD can be compared, in this respect, to that between THINK and KNOW.)

Evidence available at this stage (cf. Hill 1987) seems to suggest that all languages have exponents of these concepts. In fact, difficulties involved in identifying these concepts cross-linguistically are due more to the superabundance of plausible candidates than to their absence. In English, *good* and *bad* are clearly the most basic words in the relevant area. But Russian, for example, has two different words corresponding to the English *good* — *xorošij* and *dobryj* — and three words corresponding to bad — *ploxoj*, *durnoj* and *zloj* (in addition to *nexorošij*, formally a compound of *xorošij* and negation). The relationship between such synonyms or quasi-synonyms requires detailed investigation. As well, the range of use of the basic words for GOOD and BAD appears to differ somewhat from language to language. Again, the nature of this variation in use requires investigation.

As predicate types which have no relation to time (and which do not take temporal adjuncts) GOOD and BAD can be regarded as analogous to adjectives. We surmise that GOOD and BAD can combine with both personal and non-personal substantives, so that it would be possible to say in any language the equivalents of, for example, 'This is good/bad', 'This person is good/bad', 'You are good/bad', 'I am good/bad'.

As for BIG and SMALL, these are among the latest candidates added to the list of primitives, and so far they have not been researched to great depth. The main argument in their favour is the failure of earlier analyses to decompose them, as well as their wide lexicalisation in languages of the world.

This concludes our preliminary survey of the proposed primitive inventory.[8] For a review of the overall results of the present set of studies, see chapter 17.

Notes

1. It may be worth noting that regardless of polysemy in any 'full' natural language L, the mini-language of semantic explication (the NSM) based on L will be free of complex polysemic meanings, because all the non-primitive meanings will have been 'explicated away'. Thus there will be both lexical and full syntactic isomorphism between NSMs.
2. For a recently expressed contrary view, see Bogusławski and Herman (1991).
3. In earlier work, Wierzbicka has entertained the notion that I WANT may be a single semantic unit, incapable of further analysis (see e.g. Wierzbicka 1972, 1980a, 1989b). Strong arguments against this notion, which has now been abandoned, were expressed in Bogusławski (1988).
4. The Australian Aboriginal language Yidiny (Dixon 1977:180–182) has contrasting deictic forms 'whose use depends on the human-ness/animacy of the referent', at least in the oblique cases; *yinydyu-* is the only root for 'this' in respect of a human, whereas *yinggu-* is the favoured root for 'this' in referring to any inanimate referent. However, the distinction is neutralised in the absolutive case, and also in the locative forms, which are the very forms needed for the purpose of constructing an NSM based on Yidiny.
5. Presumably, what applies to THIS applies also, *mutatis mutandis*, to THE SAME, to TWO, and to ALL. For example, the sentence *This happened to me twice* can be viewed as 'atomic' and non-elliptical, composed of nine simple semantic units (i.e. sometime before this time, this happened to me two times). Similarly, the sentence *You did the same* can be viewed as composed of seven simple semantic units (i. e. sometime before this time you did the same).
6. In place of HAPPEN TO, earlier NSM work (Wierzbicka 1980a) had the element 'become', but HAPPEN TO has turned out to be more versatile in semantic analysis than 'become', and furthermore 'become' can be easily explicated in terms of HAPPEN, whereas the reverse is not true:

    X became Y =
    (a) at some time, X was not Y
    (b) after that something happened to X
    (c) after that X was Y
    (d) I say this after that time

In the philosophical and linguistic literature touching on this problem it has often been suggested that 'becoming' could be explicated in terms of only two components: essentially (a) and (c) above. Such an analysis is not satisfactory, however, because 'becoming' is a dynamic notion, referring to an event or a process, not only to two different states of affairs. Happening

is a dynamic notion par excellence, and it accounts for the dynamic character of 'becoming'.
7   Admittedly, there are also sentences such as *Portugal is in Europe*; these do not have a temporal slot and cannot include temporal adjuncts: *?At this time (now) Portugal is in Europe*. But in fact, sentences of this kind are only pseudo-locational (and they are by no means universal). What they really mean is that one entity is a part of another entity. What they really involve, therefore, is the concept of PART OF, not the concept of WHERE.
8   The current inventory remains, of course, subject to modification in the light of new empirical and analytical considerations. In particular, we would like to reserve the possibility that several additional primitives may be needed. For instance, work in progress suggests that the current inventory may not be capable of handling counterfactual conditionals; it may prove necessary to reinstate IMAGINE (or an analogue) for this purpose.

References

Ameka, Felix. 1987. "A Comparative Analysis of Linguistic Routines in Two Languages — Ewe and English". *Journal of Pragmatics* 11.3.299-326.

Ameka, Felix. 1988. "The Grammatical Coding of the Terminal Viewpoint of Situations in Ewe". *Australian Journal of Linguistics* 8.2.185-217.

Ameka, Felix. 1990. "The Grammatical Packaging of Experiencers in Ewe: A study in the semantics of syntax". *Australian Journal of Linguistics* 10.2.139-181.

Ameka, Felix (ed). 1992. *Journal of Pragmatics* 18.2/3 (Special issue on interjections).

Anderson, Stephen & Edward Keenan. 1985. "Deixis". *Language Typology and Syntactic Description* ed. by Timothy Shopen, 259-308. Cambridge: Cambridge University Press.

Atran, Scott. 1990. *Cognitive Foundations of Natural History*. Cambridge: Cambridge University Press.

Austin, John L. 1961. "Ifs and Cans". *Philosophical Papers* ed. by J. L. Austin, 153-180. Oxford: Clarendon Press.

Bogusławski, Andrzej. 1965. *Semantyczne pojecie licebnika*. Wroclaw: Ossolineum.

Bogusławski, Andrzej. 1979. "Wissen, Wahrheit, Glauben: Zur semantischen Beschaffenheit des kognitiven Vocabulars". *Wissenschaftssprache* ed. by T. Bungarten, 54-84. München: Fink Verlag.

Bogusławski, Andrzej. 1988. "Glosa do księgi aktów mowy". *Pamiętnik Literacki* 79.4.103-123.

Bogusławski, Andrzej. 1989. "Knowledge is the Lack of Lack of Knowledge, but What is that Lack Lack of? On Ziff's 'coherence theory of knowledge'". *Quaderni di Semantica* 10.1.15-31.

Bogusławski, Andrzej & Ewa Herman. 1992. "Prawda o sobie". *Posługiwanie się znakami* ed. by M. Kopfinger & S. Żółkiewski, 49-66. Warsaw: Ossolineum.

Bugenhagen, Robert D. 1990. "Experiential Constructions in Mangap-Mbula". *Australian Journal of Linguistics* 10.2.183-216.

Carey, Susan. 1985. *Conceptual Change in Childhood*. Cambridge, Mass.: MIT Press.

Castañeda, Hector-Neri. 1966. "'He': On the logic of self-consciousness". *Ratio* 8.130-157.

Castañeda, Hector-Neri. 1977. "On the Philosophical Foundations of the Theory of Communication: I. Reference". *Midwest Philosophical Studies*, 165-186.

Chappell, Hilary. 1980. "Is The Get-Passive Adversative?" *Papers in Linguistics* 13.3.411-452.
Chappell, Hilary. 1986a. "Formal and Colloquial Adversity Passives in Standard Chinese". *Linguistics* 24.1025-1052.
Chappell, Hilary. 1986b. "The Passive of Bodily Effect in Standard Chinese". *Studies in Language* 10.2.271-296.
Cooke, Joseph R. 1968. *Pronominal Reference in Thai, Burmese, and Vietnamese*. Berkeley: University of California Press.
Dixon, R. M. W. 1977. *A Grammar of Yidiɲ*. Cambridge: Cambridge University Press.
Foley, William. 1986. *Papuan Languages*. Cambridge: Cambridge University Press.
Gelman, Susan A. & John D. Coley. 1991. "Language and Categorization: The acquisition of natural kind terms". *Perspectives on Language and Thought: Interrelations in development* ed. by Susan A. Gelman & James P. Byrnes, 146-196. Cambridge: Cambridge University Press.
Goddard, Cliff. 1979. "Particles and Illocutionary Semantics". *Papers in Linguistics* 12.1/2.185-229.
Goddard, Cliff. 1985. *Yankunytjatjara Grammar*. Alice Springs: Institute for Aboriginal Development.
Goddard, Cliff. 1986. "The Natural Semantics of TOO". *Journal of Pragmatics* 10.5.635-644.
Goddard, Cliff. 1990. "The Lexical Semantics of 'Good Feelings' in Yankunytjatjara". *Australian Journal of Linguistics* 10.2.257-292.
Goddard, Cliff. 1991. "Anger in the Western Desert — A case study in the cross-cultural semantics of emotion". *Man* 26.2.265-279.
Goddard, Cliff. 1992. "Traditional Yankunytjatjara Ways of Speaking — A semantic perspective". *Australian Journal of Linguistics* 12.1.93-122.
Goddard, Cliff. In press. "Who are 'We'? The natural semantics of pronouns". *Language Sciences*.
Harkins, Jean. 1986. "Semantics and the Language Learner: Warlpiri particles". *Journal of Pragmatics* 10.5.559-574.
Harkins, Jean. 1990. "Shame and Shyness in the Aboriginal Classroom: A case for 'practical semantics'". *Australian Journal of Linguistics* 10.2.293-306.
Hill, Deborah. 1987. *A Cross-Linguistic Study of Value-Judgement Terms*. MA Thesis, Department of Linguistics, Australian National University, Canberra.
Howell, Signe. 1981. "Rules Not Words". *Indigenous Psychologies* ed. by P. Heelas & A. Lock, 133-159. London: Academic Press.
Humboldt, Carl Wilhelm von. 1830. "Über den Dualis". *Abhandlungen der historisch-philologischen Klasse der Königlichen Akademie der Wissenschaften zu Berlin aus dem Jahre 1827*, 161-187. (Reprinted: 1907. *Wilhelm von Humboldts Gesammelte Scriften* ed. by Königlich Preussiche Academie der Wissenschaften, vol 6.4-30. Berlin: Behr.)
Ishiguro, Hide. 1972. *Leibniz's Philosophy of Logic and Language*. London: Duckworth.
Keil, Frank C. 1986. "The Acquisition of Natural Kinds and Artifact Terms". *Language Learnability and Concept Acquisition* ed. by William Demopoulos & Ausonio Marras, 133-153. Norwood, NJ: Ablex.
Levy, Robert. 1973. *Tahitians*. Chicago: Chicago University Press.
Lutz, Catherine. 1985. "Depression and the Translation of Emotional Worlds". *Culture and Depression* ed. by A. Kleinman & B. Good, 63-100. Berkeley: University of California Press.
Medin, Douglas & Andrew Ortony. 1989. "Psychological Essentialism". *Similarity and Analogical*

Reasoning ed. by S. Vosniadon & A. Ortony, 179-195. New York: Cambridge University Press.
Merleau-Ponty, M. 1962 [1945]. *Phenomenology of Perception*. Trans. by C. Smith. London: Routledge & Kegan Paul.
Moravcsik, Edith A. 1991. "Review of Anna Wierzbicka's *The Semantics of Grammar*". *Studies in Language* 15.1.129-148.
Rips, L. J. 1989. "Similarity, Typicality, and Categorization". *Similarity and Analogical Reasoning* ed. by S. Vosniadon & A. Ortony, 21-59. New York: Cambridge University Press.
Sørensen, Holger Steen. 1958. *Word-Classes in Modern English*. Copenhagen: Gad.
Sørensen, Holger Steen. 1963. *The Meaning of Proper Names*. Copenhagen: Gad.
Weinreich, Uriel. 1966. "On the Semantic Structure of Language". *Universals of Language* ed. by J. H. Greenberg, 142-216. Cambridge, Mass.: MIT Press.
Wierzbicka, Anna. 1972. *Semantic Primitives*. Frankfurt: Athenäum.
Wierzbicka, Anna. 1976. "In Defense of YOU and ME". *Theoretische Linguistik in Osteuropa* ed. by W. Girke & H. Jachnow, 1-21. Tübingen: Max Niemeyer.
Wierzbicka, Anna. 1980a. *Lingua Mentalis: The semantics of natural language*. Sydney: Academic Press.
Wierzbicka, Anna. 1980b. *The Case For Surface Case*. Ann Arbor: Karoma.
Wierzbicka, Anna. 1985a. *Lexicography and Conceptual Analysis*. Ann Arbor: Karoma.
Wierzbicka, Anna. 1985b. "A Semantic Metalanguage for a Crosscultural Comparison of Speech Acts and Speech Genres". *Language in Society* 14.491-514.
Wierzbicka, Anna. 1986a. "Human Emotions: Universal or culture-specific?" *American Anthropologist* 88.3.584-594.
Wierzbicka, Anna. 1986b. "Precision in Vagueness: The semantics of English approximatives". *Journal of Pragmatics* 10.5.597-613.
Wierzbicka, Anna. 1987a. *English Speech Act Verbs: A semantic dictionary*. Sydney: Academic Press.
Wierzbicka, Anna. 1987b. "The Semantics of Modality". *Folia Linguistica* 21.1.25-43.
Wierzbicka, Anna. 1988. *The Semantics of Grammar*. Amsterdam: John Benjamins.
Wierzbicka, Anna. 1989a. "Semantic Primitives and Lexical Universals". *Quaderni di Semantica* 10.1.103-121.
Wierzbicka, Anna. 1989b. "Semantic Primitives: The expanding set". *Quaderni di Semantica* 10.2.309-332.
Wierzbicka, Anna. 1990a. "Color and Cognition: The semantics of color terms". *Cognitive Linguistics* 1.1.99-150.
Wierzbicka, Anna. 1990b. "The Semantics of Emotions: *Fear* and its relatives in English". *Australian Journal of Linguistics* 10.2.359-375.
Wierzbicka, Anna. 1991. *Cross-Cultural Pragmatics: The semantics of social interaction*. Berlin: Mouton de Gruyter.
Wierzbicka, Anna. 1992a. *Semantics, Culture, and Cognition*. Oxford: Oxford University Press.
Wierzbicka, Anna. 1992b. "The Search for Universal Semantic Primitives". *Thirty Years of Linguistic Evolution* ed. by Martin Pütz, 215-242. Amsterdam: John Benjamins.
Wierzbicka, Anna. In press. "'Cultural Scripts': A new approach to the study of cross-cultural

communication". *Intercultural Communication: Proceedings of the International Symposium held in Duisburg, March 1992* ed. by Martin Pütz.

Wierzbicka, Anna. Forthcoming. "'Cultural Scripts': A semantic approach to cultural analysis and cross-cultural communication".

Wilkins, David. 1986. "Particles/Clitics for Criticism and Complaint in Mparntwe Arrernte (Aranda)". *Journal of Pragmatics* 10.5.575-596.

Wilkins, David. 1992. "Interjections as Deictics". *Journal of Pragmatics* 18.2/3.119-158.

Wittgenstein, Ludwig. 1967. *Zettel*. Oxford: Blackwell.

Zipf, G. K. 1949. *Human Behavior and the Principle of Least Effort*. Cambridge: Addison-Wesley.

Appendix: Canonical Contexts for Lexical Primitives

This list gives syntactic (combinatorial) contexts in which the proposed semantically primitive meanings could be expected to be found, in any language. Put another way, the following sentences, or sentence fragments, represent things which we would expect or predict could be said in any language. A version of this list was provided to all contributors to this volume.

1   Substantives: I, YOU, SOMEONE, SOMETHING, PEOPLE

I want to go with you.
I want to see my grandfather.
Who did it?
I saw someone (else).
What is it?
What happened?
I can see something over there.
If you do this, people will say bad things about you.
People say that God knows everything.

2   Mental Predicates: THINK, SAY, KNOW, FEEL, WANT

I thought it was a possum.
I think she has eaten it.
We know that this is bad.
I know that he went this way.
I want to go with you.
I want to see my grandfather.
He said the same.
I feel good/bad.
I feel like this.

INTRODUCING LEXICAL PRIMITIVES

3   Determiners and Quantifiers: THIS, THE SAME, OTHER, ONE, TWO, MANY, ALL

Look at this.
He did it (sang, danced, etc.) like this.
I want to do the same.
She said the same.
It happened at the same place/time, not at another place/time.
She thought it was another man.
I saw you and two other people.
He has two sons and one daughter.
They have all died.
He has given away all his daughters (in marriage).
She has many daughters.

4   Actions and Events: DO, HAPPEN TO/IN

What did you do?
I want to do the same.
You did something bad.
What happened?
Something bad happened (to her).
The same thing happened again.

5   Meta-Predicates: NO, IF, CAN/COULD, LIKE, BECAUSE, VERY

No! I didn't do it (see it, etc.).
If it rains, I won't come.
If you do it, people will say something bad about you.
He did it like this: ...
This is like lilac (any plant), but it is not lilac.
It could rain tomorrow.
It could break (perhaps it will break).
There was a lot of noise. Because of that, I couldn't sleep.
He hit me. That's why I am crying.
It is very good/bad.
It is very big/small.

6   Time and Place: WHEN, WHERE, AFTER, BEFORE, UNDER, ABOVE

When did you do it?
When we went to the zoo, we ...
It happened at the same time.
They live in X now. Before this, they lived in Y.
After this, she got very sick.
X was born before/after Y.
Where did you do it?
Where is he now?
It happened in the same place, not in a different place.
There were black clouds above us.

7   Taxonomy and Partonomy: KIND OF, HAVE PARTS

We saw many kinds of fish (bird, etc.).
These two trees (birds, etc.) are different kinds, not the same kind.
This is not the same fish (bird, etc.), but it is the same kind of fish (bird, etc.).
An axe has a handle.
That horse has a long tail.
The face has a nose, a mouth and two eyes.
This thing has two parts.

8   Evaluators and Descriptors: GOOD, BAD, BIG, SMALL

You did something good/bad.
Something good/bad happened to me.
He is a good/bad man (person).
I saw a big/small tree.
I saw a big/small dog (bird, etc.).

Part 2: Individual Language Studies

Ewe

Felix Ameka
Leiden University

Ewe belongs to the Kwa branch of the Niger-Congo family.[1] It is spoken by about two million people in the south-eastern part of the Volta Region of Ghana across to parts of southern Togo as far as and just across the Togo–Benin border in West Africa. In the indigenous orthography of the language, it is spelled 'Eʋe'. It is pronounced [əβə].

Phonologically, Ewe, like most African languages, is a register tone language with high and non-high tonemes. It does not have downstep. It has a seven vowel system. Each of these has both an oral and a nasalised counterpart. It also has double articulated labial velar stops. There is a contrast between bilabial fricatives and labio-dental fricatives in the language. There is also a voiced apical post-alveolar stop which contrasts with a voiced dental stop.

Morphologically, Ewe may be said to be an isolating language with agglutinative features. It makes use of compounding, reduplication, triplication and affixation processes in the formation of new words. However, there are no productive morphological processes for the formation of new verbs. As such, predicate meanings are expressed by monomorphemic verbs, or a verb root and its inherent nominal complement, for example, *fo ɖi* 'strike dirt, i.e., be dirty', a verb root and its satellite, as in *kpɔ́ ɖá* 'see in the distance, i.e., look at', or by two verbs that colexicalise a single predicate meaning, as in *xɔ se* 'get hear, i.e., believe'.

Ewe is a grammatical word order language with basic SVO syntax (and subject and object are morphologically unmarked). Alternative orders of OSV, OVS and SOV are systematically linked to this basic one, determined by semantic and pragmatic factors. In general, the possessor precedes the possessum. But first- and second-person singular pronominal possessors may follow the possessum. 'Alienable' possession is indicated by a possessive marker *fé* which is interposed between the possessor and possessum. Body parts have 'alienable' syntax (cf. Ameka 1994). Relative clauses and other modifiers generally follow the noun head in a nominal phrase. Pronouns have syntactically conditioned allomorphs. The language also has a logophoric pronoun *ye* with its plural *yewó*. It is used in reportive contexts to designate the individual(s) (except for the first person) whose speech, thoughts, feelings and so on are reported or reflected in the linguistic context. It only occurs in clauses introduced by the dependent clause introducer *bé/béná* 'that' (cf. Clements 1979).

Ewe is a verb serialising language. In a serial-verb construction, each verb in the series has the same subject, which is only expressed with the first verb. Each verb is marked independently for tense, mood and aspect, although they must be semantically compatible. In some of the serial-verb constructions, serialising connectives may be used to link the verbs: *hé* for simultaneous or sequential relations and *ɖá* for purpose relations.

To express relational meanings, the language has both prepositions, which evolved from verbs, and postpositions, most of which have evolved from body-part nominals. Some relational meanings are expressed by complex adpositions comprising a preposition and a postposition which, so to speak, circumscribe the object nominal. For example, the relational meaning 'about' as in 'talk about X' is expressed by a complex adposition made up of *tsó* 'from' and the postposition *ŋú* 'side', *tsó X ŋú*. Ewe also has a number of utterance particles which signal the illocutionary force or the attitude of the speaker. In addition, there are particles for indicating the status of the information units and for framing discourse such as a focus marker *yé* and a background information or topic marker *lá* (cf. Ameka 1992).

Ewe has a future/non-future tense system where the non-future can be thought of as a past. The former is marked by *(l)á* while the latter has no overt realisation. The interpretation of a non-future eventive verb is that the action occurred prior to the temporal reference point. For a stative predicate, however, the interpretation is that the change of state occurred prior to the temporal reference point and the state currently exists. For this reason the non-future form of stative verbs is translated by the present tense and that of the eventive verbs by the past in English, as in the following examples:[2]

(1) a. *É-   yi   Gě*
       3SG go   Accra
       '(S)he went to Accra.'

    b. *É-   nyá   Gě*
       3SG know Accra
       '(S)he knows Accra.'

Standard written Ewe was developed in the last century. It is a hybrid of the regional variants of the various sub-dialects of the language. With it has also emerged a standard colloquial variety (spoken usually with local accent) that is very widely used in cross-dialectal contact situations such as in schools, markets, churches and so on. Because of this there are, as we shall see below, several sets of synonyms in the language which are dialect variants for some of the exponents. (For further information on Ewe grammar and lexis, see Ameka 1990, 1990/1991, 1991; Ansre 1966;

Clements 1972; Duthie 1988, in press; Westermann 1930, 1973 [1928].)
In general, one can identify lexical items and expressions which embody the proposed semantic primitives. Problems arise with respect to the translatability of some of the canonical phrases in which the items occur as I will try to indicate below.

3.1 Substantives

I and YOU are realised in Ewe by the following sets of syntactically determined allomorphic variants:

	Independent	Subject	Object	Logophoric
I	*nye*	*me-*	*-m*	
YOU	*wò*	*(n)è-*	*wò*	*ye*

The independent pronouns are used in a number of contexts: (a) in emphatic contexts when marked by a focus or topic marker or modified by an intensifier; (b) in nominal coordination as in *nye kplé wò* 'I and you'; (c) in possessive phrases, for example *dadá-wò* 'your mother'; (d) in appositive nominal phrases as well as vocatives; and (e) the first-person form is used in negative sentences. The subject forms are cliticised onto the first element within the verb phrase, and the object forms are used as the object forms of verbs and prepositions as illustrated in the translation of the following canonical sentence:

(2) Me- dí bé má- yi kplí wò
    1SG want that 1SG:SBJV go with 2SG
    'I want to go with you.'

If the subject of the main clause in sentence (2) were the second person, then the logophoric form would be used in the dependent clause to refer back to the subject of the main clause, as illustrated in (3). Note also the use of the object form of the first-person singular pronoun.

(3) È- dí bé ye- á- yi kplí- m- à?
    2SG want that LOG SBJV go with 1SG Q
    'Do you want to go with me?'

SOMEONE and SOMETHING are expressed by *ame* 'person' and *nú* 'thing' respectively. These nouns can co-occur with modifiers such as the indefinite article *áɖé* 'a certain'. This yields the forms *ame áɖé* 'someone' and the variants *náné* and *náɖé* for 'something'. When *ame* and *nú* combine with the content question marker *ka*, we get the forms *ameka* 'who, which person?' and *núka* 'what, which thing?' respectively. Consider these sentences:

(4) Ame- ka- é wɔ- e?
    person CQ aFOC do 3SG
    'Who did it?'

(5) Me- kpɔ́ ame áɖé / náné le afí- má
    1SG see person INDEF thing:INDEF at place that
    'I saw someone/something over there.'

(6) Nú- ka- é dzɔ?
    thing CQ aFOC happen
    'What happened?'

There is one problem with the translation of SOMETHING in explications when it occurs as the object of a verb of saying. For instance a more natural rendition of *something* in the sentence *I say/said something because of this* makes use of *nya* 'word' instead of *nú* 'thing', as illustrated in (7):

(7) Me- gblɔ nya áɖé le ésia- ta
    1SG say word INDEF at this because
    'I said something (some word) because of this.'

However, this does not mean that *nya* can be taken to be one of the exponents of SOMETHING. I believe that sentence (7) can always be paraphrased in Ewe using *náné* even if it sounds a bit technical and unnatural to the native speaker's ear.

The variants *náné* and *náɖé* may also be used to indicate an indefinite quantity. In this case it functions as a modifier. Consider its use in the following sentence:

(8) Ame náné-/náɖé- wó vá tefé lá
    person thing:INDEF PL come place DEF
    'Several people (I can't say how many) came to the place.'

PERSON can also be translated into Ewe as *amegbetɔ́* which is made up of *ame* and *gbetɔ́* 'the alive one'. Each of the three forms *ame*, *gbetɔ́* and *amegbetɔ́* can be used to mean 'person'. All three are therefore plausible candidates for the primitive SOMEONE. However, *ame* is the best candidate because it, unlike the other terms, can be used in contexts which involve reference to sentient entities including gods and devils, which is the idea behind SOMEONE. Thus the question in (4) above using *ame* can be answered simply by *Máwú-é* 'God'. It appears that *gbetɔ́* is added to *ame* to make it clear that God is excluded from the possible referents.

The more general nature of *ame* is perhaps the motivation behind its extended use in the language as a unit counter, similar to a numeral classifier, that can be applied to both animate and inanimate entities as in the following phrases:

(9) a. ɖeví wó ame adé
       child 3PL COUNTER six
       'six (individual) children'

   b. atí wó ame ene
      tree 3PL COUNTER four
      'four (individual) trees'

I conclude from these pieces of evidence that the exponent of the primitive SOMEONE in Ewe is *ame*, which is polysemous between the person sense and the unit counter sense.

The question that remains to be answered in this section is this: What is the realisation of PEOPLE in Ewe? It can be translated by the plurals of the three forms that we saw above which mean 'person', namely, *amewó*, *gbetɔ́wó* and *amegbetɔ́wó*. None of these, in my view, can be taken as primitive because they are semantically decomposable. From this point of view, we may conclude that there is no exponent of the form PEOPLE in Ewe which is independent of the term 'person'. This conclusion would not be unique for Ewe because I believe similar views have been expressed with respect to other languages (see Onishi, this volume, on Japanese, Evans, this volume, on Kayardild, and Harkins and Wilkins, this volume, on Mparntwe Arrernte). But we can also explore further the possibility that the *gbetɔ́* forms which are exclusively used for humans might have some uses that could be related to the term PEOPLE. Indeed there is a saying in the language in which the use of *gbetɔ́* is translated into English as *people*, as illustrated in (10).

(10) ... gbetɔ́ la- fo nu le ŋú wò
         person FUT strike mouth at side 2SG
     '... people will talk of you.'

Furthermore, *gbetɔ́* and *amegbetɔ́* are used in contexts where an opposition between God and people is intended as in the following extract from a novel (Akotey 1988:31) where the speaker is proclaiming her innocence in a matter before God and people:

(11) ... le Máwú kplé amegbetɔ́-wó ŋkúme lá,
         at God and person-PL face TP
     nye- mé- nyá nánéké le nú-sia ŋú o.
     1SG NEG know anything at thing-this side NEG
     'Before God and people, I do not know anything about this.'

By analogy with the use of *(ame)gbetɔ́* for 'people' in these sentences one could translate the canonical sentence *If you do this, people will say bad things about you* as follows:

(12) Né è-   wɔ ésia lá, gbetɔ́ á-   gblɔ nú   baɖa- wó
      if 2SG do this TP person FUT say thing bad   PL
      le ŋú wò
      at side 2SG
      'If you do this, people will say bad things about you.'

But the form *gbetɔ́* cannot be used to translate the canonical sentence *People say that God knows everything*. There is thus no conclusive evidence that *gbetɔ́* or any other element is an uncontroversial exponent of PEOPLE in Ewe. I must confess that I am sceptical about the primitive and universal status of PEOPLE.

To conclude the section on substantives, the exponents for the primitives I, YOU, SOMEONE and SOMETHING in Ewe are *nye*, *wò*, *ame* and *nú* and their allolexes. There is no uncontroversial primitive element for PEOPLE.

3.2 Mental Predicates

THINK has two main translation equivalents: *súsú* and *bu*. Each of these has a wide range of uses. One of the interpretations of *súsú* relates to the sense in which THINK is to be understood, viz: 'to occur to one, to cross one's mind'. In this usage the verb takes a sentential complement introduced by *bé* 'that' and may also be translated as 'assume, suppose' (see examples (15) and (16)).

Súsú may also be interpreted as 'to think of someone/something/some place' in the sense of missing that entity. The target of the thought in this case is coded as the direct object of the verb as in the following example:

(13) Me- súsú- á   afé   ŋútɔ́
      1SG think   HAB   home   very much
      'I think of (= miss) home a lot.'

In another usage, it may be interpreted as 'to opine, to express intellectual feelings about something'. Here the target or topic of the thought may be coded as the object of the complex adposition *tsó ... ŋú* 'about' as in:

(14) Áléké nè-   súsú tsó   nya   sia   ŋú?
      how   2SG think from   matter this side
      'What do you think about this matter?'

Bu also has a number of contextual uses. It may be translated as 'think, meditate, consider, calculate, count'. One of the interpretations of *bu* in the sense of THINK is 'to occur to one, to cross one's mind'. In this usage it takes a sentential complement introduced by *bé* as is the case in a similar interpretation of *súsú* as indicated above. Indeed both items can be used to translate the canonical sentences, as shown below:

(15) Me- súsú / bu bé adogló yé
      1SG think   that lizard aFOC
      'I thought it was a lizard.'

(16) Me- súsú / bu bé é- ɖu nú xóxó
      1SG think   that 3SG eat thing already
      'I thought she had eaten already.'

There are a number of lexical and syntactic clues which trigger the other interpretations of *bu* in context. Thus when its inherent object complement is *ta-me*, literally 'head-in, i.e., in the head', it is interpreted as 'think-meditate/consider'. The topic of the thought may be expressed as the object of the postposition *ŋú(tí)*. Such a postpositional phrase may in turn function as the object of prepositions such as *le* 'at' and *tsó* 'from', as in the following example:

(17) Me- bu ta-me tsó nya sia ŋú ʋuu
      1SG think head-in from matter this side long.time
      'I thought about (= meditated on) this matter for a long time.'

For the sense of 'count, calculate' the verb *bu* takes a nominal phrase as its object. It is synonymous with *xlẽ* 'count, read' in this usage. Thus in the following example *xlẽ* can be substituted for *bu*:

(18) Kofí bu ga lá
      Kofi calculate money DEF
      'Kofi counted/calculated the money.'

Given the different ranges of use of the two possible candidates of THINK, it is legitimate to ask whether one can be defined in terms of the other. It is very tempting to suggest that one could explicate *bu* via *súsú*. Part of the reason for this is that *súsú* seems to be more directly related to mind and thought than *bu*. A piece of evidence in support of this contention is that there is a nominal derivative of *súsú* — *sùsú* — which translates as 'mind, thought, brain'. This is the form used in the following example where the speaker is blaming himself at the time when he is suffering the consequences of something he had done on the spur of the moment earlier on:

(19) Afí-ka gɔ́- é me- ɖe nyě sùsú da ɖo?
      place-CQ INT aFOC 1SG remove 1SG:poss mind throw at
      'Where at all did I leave my brain (before doing this)?' (Akotey 1988:88)

This is an interesting and attractive suggestion but it is far from being conclusive. At this stage one has to say that there are two candidates for THINK in Ewe.

The exponent of KNOW is *nyá*. It may take a nominal phrase as its object as in example (20). In that syntactic frame it may be paraphrased as 'know something/someone'. When it has a nominalised complement, it may be paraphrased as 'know how to do something'. When it takes a sentential complement introduced by *bé*, it may be paraphrased as 'know that'.

(20) Me- nyá mɔ́ si wò- tó
    1SG know way REL 3SG pass
    'I know which way (s)he passed.'

(21) Me- nyá tsi- fú- fú
    1SG know water swim swim
    'I know swimming.' (i.e. 'I know how to swim.')

(22) Kofí nyá bé ga mé- le así- nye o
    Kofi know that money NEG be hand 1SG NEG
    'Kofi knows that I don't have money.'

Nyá can also combine with the satellite *ɖá* 'in that direction'. In this configuration, it typically occurs in the imperative and may be paraphrased as 'look at, observe', as in:

(23) Nya así- wò ɖá
    know hand 2SG DIR
    'Look at your hands.'

On the basis of such examples, Dzobo (1981, 1992) argues that the primary sense of *nyá* is 'to look at, to observe'. He further suggests and concludes that the kind of knowing involved in *nyá* is therefore knowledge based on observation. While this is an interesting claim it is not founded on strong empirical evidence. The claim does not take into account the fact that the 'observe' sense is only available when the verb satellite is present. One can draw a parallel between the behaviour of *nyá* and *kpɔ́* 'see' which also gets a 'look at' interpretation when it is in construction with the satellite *ɖá*. Thus I do not think that the primary sense of *nyá* is 'to observe, look at'. Its primary sense is KNOW.

There are three possible candidates for the concept SAY in (standard) Ewe. They are *gblɔ*, *dó* and *bé*. By and large, *gblɔ* and *dó* are dialect variants which are mutually substitutable for each other in many contexts. Thus either of them could be used to translate SAY in the following meaning components:

(24) Me- dí bé má- gblɔ/dó nya áɖé ná wò
    1SG want that 1SG:SBJV say word INDEF to 2SG
    'I want to say something to you.'

(25) Me-   gblɔ/dó ésia   ná   wò
      1SG   say   this   to   2SG
      'I said this to you.'

There is one difference, however, between *gblɔ* and *dó*: *dó* is used to form the report or delocutive expressions from formulae. Thus the report form of the one-word formula *agoo* 'May I come in?' is *dó agoo* 'to say may I come in'. *Gblɔ* is not used for this purpose.

Bé is used as a verb meaning 'say' to introduce direct quotes. It is thus the best translation of the primitive SAY for propositional content components of the form *I say: I want you to do it*:

(26) Me-   bé: me-   dí   bé   na-   wɔ-   e
      1SG   say   1SG   want that   2SG:SBJV do   3SG
      'I say: I want you to do it.'

A homophonous complementiser has developed from *bé*. It is used to introduce complement clauses of various verbs whether they are presented as reports or as direct quotes as in the example above and described for the other mental predicates.

In an earlier attempt to discover the exponents of the primitives in Ewe, I suggested that the equivalent of SAY in Ewe should be *bé* (Ameka 1986:287). I claimed that the other verbs *dó* and *gblɔ* could be defined via this item. This was at a time when the ideal thing in NSM research was to find only one exponent for each primitive. Thus one could not talk of allolexes. I do not think any longer that *dó* and *gblɔ* can be defined and I now think that the three items are the embodiments of SAY in Ewe. One problem with *bé* as the exponent of SAY is that it is not used with respect to 'mental' and internal speech. *Gblɔ* and *dó*, however, can be used in such a context.

(27) É-   dó/gblɔ/*bé   le   ta   me ...
      3SG say   at   head   in
      '(S)he said in his/her head (mind) ...'

The various differences between the three verbs suggest that they complement each other in the expression of the concept SAY in Ewe.

The exponent of FEEL may be taken to be *se* in one of its numerous senses. Some of the senses are easy to distinguish: for example, it may mean 'to obey' or 'to understand' or 'to know a language'. In these cases the object of the verb can help in determining the sense at issue. However, for other senses it is rather difficult. These other senses are: 'perceive', 'hear', 'smell', 'taste' and 'feel'. Consider the following text example in which it is obvious that the sense of 'feel' is intended, but it cannot be easily distinguished from the sense of 'perceive':

(28) Me-   fo-   e,
    1SG   strike   3SG
    gaké   éya   ŋútó bé   ye-   mé-   se-   e   o
    but   3SG INT   say   LOG   NEG   'hear'   3SG   NEG
    'I struck him, but he himself said that he did not feel it.'

There are two contexts in which this verb can be unambiguously rendered as 'feel'. The first is when its object is an emotion/sensation nominal. For example:

(29) É-   se   vevé / avuvɔ   ŋútó
    3SG   'hear'   pain   cold   INT
    '(S)he felt pain/cold a lot.'

The second context is when the locus of perception is specified as inside the body, as in the following example:

(30) Me-   se   le   nye   lã-me   bé   me-   le   dɔ
    1SG   'hear'   at   1SG:poss   flesh-in   that   1SG   be   sick
    lé   gé
    catch   INGR
    'I feel (within my body) that I am going to be sick.'

The verb *se* and the prepositional phrase *le lãme* may be compounded to yield *seselelãme* 'feeling', as in the following folk definition of 'jealousy':

(31) ŋuvava   nyé   ɖokui-tɔ-dídí   tó   sese-le-lãme
    jealousy   be   self-own-RED:seek   through   feeling
    si   nyɔ-   a   vevé-sese ...   le   ame   fé   susú
    REL   arouse   HAB   pain-RED:'hear'   at   person   poss   mind
    kplé   dzi   me   le   ame-hávi   fé   dzɔgbe-nyui
    and   heart   in   at   person-colleague   poss   fate-good
    aló   núwɔna   áɖé   ta
    or   act   INDEF   because
    'Jealousy is selfishness through a feeling that arouses pain in the heart and mind of somebody because of the good fortune or an action of his/her fellow human being.' (Nyɔmi 1980:9)

This raises the question as to whether the exponent of FEEL should be taken to be just the verb *se* or if it is the verb plus the prepositional phrase, that is, *se le lãme*. In fact to render the primitive in the canonical context sentences *I feel good/bad* and *I feel like this* in Ewe, the prepositional phrase has to be added; without it the translation would not make sense. The Ewe versions of these sentences are as follows:

(32) Me- se   sese- le- lãme   nyui áḍé
      1SG feel feeling at body-in   good INDEF
      'I feel something good.'

(33) Me- se   náné   le- nyĕ   lã-me   álé
      1SG feel something at   1SG:poss body-in like.this
      'I feel something (in my body) like this.'

In fact, without the prepositional phrase in (33), the verb *se* translates as 'hear':

(34) Me- se   náné   álé
      1SG feel something like.this
      'I heard something like this.' (Not 'I feel something like this.')

From the sentences above, it should be obvious that it is not possible to translate the sentences *I feel good/bad* and *I feel like this* without having a nominal like 'something' in the translation.

The exponent of WANT in Ewe is the verb *dí*. It is, however, polysemous. The different senses can be distinguished by the syntactic patterns associated with them. For the relevant sense of the primitive WANT, it takes an animate NP subject and an object complement clause introduced by the complementiser *bé* 'that' whose verb is marked for the subjunctive, as in (2) and (3).

(35) Kofí dí   bé   ye- a-   kpɔ́ wò
      Kofi want COMP LOG IRR see 2SG
      'Kofi wants to see you.'

When its object is an NP, then it may be translated as 'want', 'like', 'seek' or 'look for'. These senses imply that the subject does something actively in order to obtain the desired object. It is rather hard to differentiate between these senses in some cases. A useful clue is provided by the interpretation of the non-future form of the verb in context. For the 'want' sense the verb behaves like a stative verb in the sense that its non-future form is interpreted as present. For the 'look for, seek' sense *dí* behaves like an eventive verb. Thus its non-future form is interpreted as past. Consider the following sentence which has ambiguous readings, but which may be disambiguated in terms of temporal interpretation. Thus in the 'want' sense the only interpretation possible is the present tense one. Similarly, for the 'look for' sense the only interpretation possible is the past tense one.

(36) Me- dí   ésia
      1SG want this
      (i) 'I want this.' (Not 'I wanted this.')
      (ii) 'I looked for this.' (Not 'I look for this.')

The third sense of the verb is easier to identify. The verb is used to express prospective aspect, that is 'to be about to V' when it occurs in a sentence with an inanimate NP subject and a *bé* complement clause in which the verb is marked for the subjunctive, as in examples (37) and (38):

(37) *Tsi dí bé ye- a dza*
      water want that LOG SBJV fall
      'Rain wants to fall.' (i.e. 'It is about to rain.')

(38) *Dɔ dí bé ye- a lé- m*
      sickness want that LOG SBJV catch 1SG
      'Sickness wants to catch me.' (i.e. 'I am about to become sick.')

This last sense lends indirect support to the claim that the verb *dí* in Ewe means WANT because it is quite common and natural for a verb meaning 'want' to be grammaticalised to express a 'future' kind of meaning (cf. Ultan 1978:113).

The conclusion here is that the verb *dí* is the exponent of the primitive WANT in Ewe. Even though this verb is polysemous its different senses can be distinguished on semantic and syntactic grounds.

3.3   Determiners and Quantifiers

The exponent of THIS is *sia*. Some of its dialect variants which may be thought of as its allolexes are *ke* and *yi*. These forms can function as modifiers of nouns, as in (39). They may also be pronominalised by prefixing an *é-* to them. In this prefixed form they can stand on their own as noun phrases.

(39) *Ame sia/yi/ke wɔ nú baɖa áɖé*
      person this   do thing bad INDEF
      'This person did something bad.'

(40) *Kpɔ́ é-sia/é-yi/é-ke ɖá*
      see   this   in that direction
      'Look at this.'

The translation of THE SAME in many contexts involves the post-nominal intensifier *ké*, which may also be translated as 'very (the very one)'. As an intensifier it has to co-occur with another element that it modifies. Typically, the item that it provides intensification for has other modifiers, namely, the distal demonstrative *má* 'that' and the prenominal intensifier *nenémí* 'such' or its pronominal form *nenémá* 'as such'. When THE SAME is used pronominally and not as a modifier it may be translated by *nenémá* alone. Thus in this context the *ké* intensifier may be omitted, as in the following example:

    (41)   *É-*   *wɔ*   *nenémá (ké)*
              3SG do   as.such
              'She did the same.'

It was such a usage which led me to claim in an earlier work (Ameka 1991:22) that the exponent of THE SAME in Ewe was *nenémá*. However, this cannot be right because when THE SAME functions as a modifier of another nominal then *ké* is always present. If the item that it modifies is a pronominal then there is no other modifier required, as in (42). But if the item it modifies is a noun then there may be the prenominal intensifier and by all means the demonstrative *má* among its modifiers.

    (42)   *Wò*   *ké*
              2SG INT
              'the very you' (i.e. 'the same you')

    (43)   *(Nenémĩ)* *ame*   *má*   *ké*
              such   person DEM INT
              'the same person'

    (44)   *Nyɔ́nu-a-* *ga-* *biá* *nya* *má* *ké* *srɔ̃-* *a*
              woman-DEF REP ask word DEM INT spouse DEF
              'The woman asked her husband the same thing again.' (Akotey 1988:5)

In the light of all this, it seems better to say that the translation of THE SAME is *nenémá ké*, which is used in different configurations depending on the context.

THE SAME can also be expressed by the verb *sɔ* 'be equal, identical' or its adverbial derivative *sɔsɔe* 'equally'. These forms, however, involve the idea of similarity in a feature rather than precise identity in every respect, which is the notion embedded in the *nenémá ké* construction and in the primitive THE SAME.

    (45)   *Kofí* *kplé* *Áma* *wó-* *sɔ* *le* *kɔkɔ́-* *me*
              Kofi and Ama 3PL equal at height in
              'Kofi and Ama are the same in height/have the same height.'

    (46)   *Wó-* *vá* *ɖó* *sɔsɔe*
              3PL come arrive equally
              'They came/arrived at the same time.'

ONE is *ɖeká*, as used in (50). There is a distinct lexical item for the ordinal form, viz: *gbã*. Apart from its use as a numeral quantifier, it may be used in certain contexts

to translate THE SAME, as in example (79).
OTHER is embodied in the quantifier *búbŭ*, as in these examples:

(47) Me- kpɔ́ wò kplé ame eve búbŭ
 1SG see 2SG and person two other
 'I saw you and two other people.'

(48) É- súsú bé ŋútsu búbŭ yé
 3SG think that man other aFOC
 '(S)he thought it was another man.'

MANY may be translated with the quantifier *geɖe* 'many, several' or the predicate *sɔ gbɔ* 'be many, numerous', which is made up of a verbal and a nominal complement. An adjective may be formed from this predicate by compounding its verbal and nominal components yielding the form *sɔgbɔ* 'many, plenty'.

(49) a. Vi- nyɔ́nu- ví geɖe- wó le é- sí
  child- woman- DIM many PL be.at 3SG hand
  '(S)he has many daughters.'

 b. Vi- nyɔ́nu- ví- wó sɔ gbɔ le é- sí
  child- woman- DIM PL be.many be.at 3SG hand
  '(S)he has many daughters.'

TWO is expressed by the numeral quantifier *eve*. Like many other numerals (except *ɖeká* 'one') it forms its ordinal by the suffixation of *-liá*, yielding *eveliá* 'second(ly)'. Consider this example:

(50) Vi- nyɔ́nu- ví- ɖeká kplé vi- ŋútsu- ví eve le
 child- woman- DIM one and child- man- DIM two be.at
 é- sí
 3SG hand
 '(S)he has one daughter and two sons.'

ALL is embodied in the quantifying intensifiers *kátā* and *pétée*, which may be considered as allolexes because they are dialect variants:

(51) Wó kátā/pétée wó- kú
 3PL all 3PL die
 'They have all died.'

Both forms can be used as nominal modifiers, as in the above example, but it is only *pétée* which may be used as an adverbial to express the idea of 'completely':

(52) Wó- kú vɔ pétée / ?? kátã
      3PL die PFV all
      'They have died completely.'

3.4 Actions and Events

DO corresponds to *wɔ*, although it has a number of other uses and translations. In a simple transitive clause such as sentence (4) it is used to express the idea of 'do, make (in the sense of create)'. When it takes a sentential complement which may or may not be introduced by the complementiser *bé* it translates as 'do, act, make, cause', as in the following:

(53) Tsidzadza lá wɔ- e bé me- tsí megbé
      rain DEF do 3SG that 1SG remain back
      'The rain made it that I was late.'

Wɔ is also used to predicate a quality of an entity/person. In this usage the object of the verb denotes a property concept which is a nominal or an adverbial.

(54) É- wɔ ké / ba / nogoo / sue
      3SG do sand mud round small
      'It is sandy/muddy/round/small.'

The exponent of HAPPEN is *dzɔ*, as used in example (6). Apart from the sense of 'happen', it also means 'come into being, be born, originate'. The basic distinction between the two senses is in the animacy of the subject NP: if the subject is animate then it has the sense of 'come into being', as in example (55), and if it is inanimate then it has the 'happen' sense.

(55) Kofí dzɔ háfí Áma dzɔ
      Kofi happen before Ama happen
      'Kofi was born/came into being before Ama was born/came into being.'

HAPPEN TO/IN may be expressed in one of two ways. First, one can use the verb *dzɔ* with the experiencer of the happening coded as the modifier of the postposition *dzí* 'top' together with which it functions as the object of the allative preposition *ɖé*, as in example (56). Second, one can use the verb *wɔ* 'do' where the experiencer is its direct object (see Harkins and Wilkins, this volume, on a similar phenomenon in Mparntwe Arrernte). Compare the following examples:

(56) Náné   dzɔ   ɖé é-   dzí
     something happen to 3SG top
     'Something happened to him/her.'

(57) Náné   wɔ-   e
     something happen 3SG
     'Something happened to him/her.'

It should be noted that in this case we have a situation where exponents of two separate primitives (DO and HAPPEN) can be used to translate one of them (HAPPEN) in one of its canonical combinatorial frames. This kind of criss-crossing is, in my view, undesirable and calls for further investigation.

3.5   Meta-Predicates

NO is expressed by the interjection *ao!*. This form is used to convey the idea of rejection either as an answer to a propositional question or as a prohibition to prevent someone from doing something or in declining an offer. The notion of rejection is also expressed by the clausal negator *mé ... o* 'not' which is a discontinuous morpheme. *Ao* can occur as a co-utterance of a clause in which the clause negator is present, as in the following example:

(58) Ao,   nye- mé-   wɔ-   e   o
     No   1SG   NEG   do   3SG   NEG
     'No, I didn't do it.'

The concept of DON'T WANT is embodied in the verb *gbé* which has a number of translation equivalents such as 'refuse, reject, divorce, forbid'. However, this verb can be explicated via NOT and WANT along the following lines: *X gbé Y* = 'X does not want Y (any more)'.

IF corresponds straightforwardly to the conditional clause introducer *né*, as in

(59) Né   tsi   dza   lá, nye- ma-   vá   o
     if   water fall TP   1SG   NEG:IRR   come   NEG
     'If it rains, I won't come.'

Né also has a temporal interpretation. It may thus translate as 'when' with respect to the future time realisation of events (see section 3.6), as in this example:

(60) Né   mié- ɖó   tefé- á   lá, ma-   yɔ́   wò
     if   1PL   reach place DEF   TP   1SG:IRR   call 2SG
     'When we reach the place, I will call you.'

COULD is expressed by the irrealis marker *a* and the predicate *té ŋú* 'can', which consists of a verb and its inherent nominal complement. This predicate takes a VP complement and it is a moot point whether together they constitute a serial-verb construction or not. *Té ŋú* by itself can express both possibility and ability (cf. *ŋútété* 'ability' — the nominalised form of the verbal expression), but in combination with the irrealis marker it has the possibility meaning which is the notion underlying the primitive COULD.

(61)   *Tsi   a-   té ŋú   á-   dza   etsɔ*
       water IRR can IRR fall tomorrow
       'It could rain tomorrow.'

LIKE is embodied in the semblative construction *abé X (ené)*, where X is the standard of comparison syntactically coded as a phrase, as in (63), or a clause. If X is a clause it is typically introduced by *álési* 'how', as in (62).

(62)   *É-   zɔ-   na   abé   álési   fofó-   á   zɔ-   na   ené*
       3SG walk HAB like how father DEF walk HAB like
       '(S)he walks like the father does.'

(63)   *É-   fo-   a   nu   abé   ako*
       3SG strike HAB mouth like parrot
       '(S)he talks like a parrot.'

Álési is made up of the word *álé* 'thus, like this', the form that is used when demonstrating how something is or is to be done, and the relative marker *si*. *Álé* is thus the more appropriate form for translating 'like this' in the canonical sentences, as shown in (64). It also combines with a variant of the content question marker to form the manner question word *áléké* 'how'.

(64)   *É-   wɔ-   e   álé ...*
       3SG do 3SG like.this
       'S/he did it like this ...'

The form *abé ... (ené)* has two other uses which are linked to its semblative function and meaning. First, it is used to introduce the complements of verbs indicating the notions of 'appear', 'seem', 'look like' and so on (see (65)). Second, it is used in expressing approximations, as illustrated in (66).

(65)   *É-   wɔ   abé   tsi   le   dza-dza   gé   ené*
       3SG do like water be:PRES RED:fall INGR like
       'It looks like it is about to rain.'

(66) Mía-   vá   ɖó   abé   ga   etɔ̃   ené
    1PL:FUT come reach like hour three like
    'We will arrive around three o'clock.'

The conceptual links between likeness, similarity, appearance and approximation are quite transparent. Thus one can claim that *abé ... (ené)* is the exponent of LIKE although it has some other contextual meanings which are linked to its core meaning.

BECAUSE is expressed in two main ways: first, by the variant connecting particles *ta* and *ŋútí*, which have evolved from the body-part terms for head and skin respectively, and second, by the causal coordinating conjunction *élabéná*. *Ta* and *ŋútí* are more versatile syntactically than *élabéná*. They can have scope over phrases as well as clauses. Thus they combine with proforms such as *ésia* 'this', *éya* '3SG' and *núka* 'what' to form the molecules *ésiata/ésiaŋútí* 'because of this', *éyata/éyaŋútí* 'because of it, therefore' and *núkata/núkaŋútí* 'because of what, why?'. By contrast, *élabéná* is a sentence-level rather than clause- or phrasal-level operator. In addition, a 'reason' clause which is conjoined to another clause by *élabéná* always occurs after that clause. 'Reason' clauses involving *ta* and *ŋútí* can occur either before or after the main clause. Thus the *ta* and *ŋútí* forms are better candidates for translating the canonical sentences. For instance:

(67) É-   fo-   m.   Éya-ta   me-   le   avi   fa-   ḿ
    3SG hit 1SG 3SG-because 1SG be:PRES tear cry PROG
    'He hit me. Because of it, I am crying.'

Notice that if *élabéná* were substituted for *éyata* in the above sentence the meaning would be different. It would mean that the reason for his hitting me is that I was crying (and I may be crying for no reason).

Furthermore, sentences involving *élabéná* can be readily paraphrased using *ta* and *ŋútí* but not necessarily vice versa. One can conclude on the basis of the differences between the two sets of forms that the exponents of BECAUSE in Ewe are the allolexes *ta* and *ŋútí*.

The concept VERY is embodied in the intensifier *ŋútɔ́*, which can occur as a modifier of nominals (example (69)) or as an adverbial (example (68)).

(68) É-   nyó / túkúí   ŋútɔ́
    3SG good   small   very
    'It is very good/small.'

To translate sentences in which the intensified item cannot occur as a verb, such as *gã* 'big', one needs a full noun phrase in which the item and *ŋútɔ́* function as modifiers. This nominal phrase may be used as an utterance on its own, in which case it is marked by the focus particle, or otherwise the NP occurs in a clefted construction as illustrated below:

(69) Agbalẽ nyuí / gã áɖé ŋútɔ́- é (wò- nyé)
      book   good big INDEF very aFOC 3SG be
      'It is a very good/big book.'

As a nominal intensifier, *ŋútɔ́* has other interpretations. It may be used to express emphasis, in which case it may be translated as an emphatic reflexive 'self', or to indicate that the item in its scope is real:

(70) a. *Nye ŋútɔ́ me- wɔ- e*
         1SG   very   1SG do   3SG
         'I myself (I) did it.'

      b. *Siká ŋútɔ́- é*
         gold   very   aFOC
         'It is real gold.'

3.6 Time and Place

The concept of time can be expressed by two types of items: a set of words based on the word *ɣe* 'sun, time', and the clause introducers *ési* 'when' and *né* 'if, when'. The relevant words based on *ɣe* are *ɣe-ka-ɣi* 'time-CQ-time, when' (interrogative), *ɣe-yí-yi* 'time' (noun), *ɣe-siâ-ɣi* 'time-every-time, every time, always', *ɣe-si-ɣi* 'time-REL-time, time when' (relative) and *ɣe-má-ɣi* 'time-that-time, at that time'. The interesting thing about these and similar words based on generic temporal nouns such as *gbe* 'day' is that when they combine with determiners to form lexical units, the noun is recapitulated after the determiner, as is obvious from the words cited above.

To translate interrogative WHEN and TIME in the canonical sentences one can use *ɣekaɣi* and *ɣeyiɣi* respectively. It should be noted however that any generic time word in construction with *ka* 'CQ' can translate the interrogative 'when'. Thus the word *gbe-ka-gbe* 'day-CQ-day, what day' can also be translated as 'when'. But such words are more complex than *ɣekaɣi* because they contain additional components that relate to their specific semantics such as 'day'.

(71) ɣekaɣi nè- wɔ- e?
      when   2SG do   3SG
      'When did you do it?'

(72) É-   dzɔ   le ɣeyiɣi má   ké   me
      3SG happen at time   that same in
      'It happened at the same time.'

Non-interrogative WHEN corresponds to the clause introducers *ési* 'when' and *né* 'if, when' (see section 3.5). As indicated earlier, *né* expresses 'time when' with respect to irrealis events. *Ési*, on the other hand, expresses 'time when' with respect to realis or past events. Compare the following example with (60):

(73)   Ési   mié-   ɖó   tefé-   á   lá,   me-   yɔ́   wò
       when 1PL   reach place DEF TP   1SG call 2SG
       'When we reached the place, I called you.'

The difference between *ési* and *né* corresponds to a distinction that is widely attested cross-linguistically between a conditional marker that has temporal interpretations and a temporal clause introducer (cf. the difference between *toen* 'when' and *als* 'if' in Dutch).

Ési can be used in situations involving the simultaneity of events. In this usage the clause introduced by *ési* indicates the time that both events happened or the time during which the second event occurred. In the latter case it may be translated as 'while'.

(74)   Ési   dzi   nɔ   gbe   ɖe-   ḿ   lá
       when sky   be:NPRES   voice issue PROG   TP
       ɖeví- á-   wó   nɔ   ɣlí   dó-   ḿ
       child DEF   PL   be:NPRES   shout   make   PROG
       'While it was thundering, the children were shouting.'

Of course there are other grammatical means of expressing simultaneity of events such as through the use of verb-serialisation structures, but these relate only covertly to time.

Here as elsewhere we are confronted with two different sets of items as possible candidates for a semantic primitive. But it seems clear that the range of uses of one set, the clause introducers, are included in those of the other set. I am therefore inclined to say that the ɣe-based words *ɣekaɣi* and *ɣeyiɣi* are the best exponents of the primitive concept of TIME.

PLACE is also expressed by a number of forms in Ewe: two derivational formatives, *-gbé* 'place, region, area' and *-fé* 'place', and two nouns, *afí* 'place, here' and *tefé* 'place'. Of all these forms, *-gbé* is the least attractive as an exponent of the primitive for two reasons. First, it is restricted in its applicability and productivity. It only occurs on noun stems, as in *asigbé* '(place) for marketing' or *dɔgbé* 'for errand'. Second, *-gbé* seems to be complex because it always encodes a purposive sense. The best gloss for *N-gbé* structures as in the examples above seems to be 'place for (doing) N'. The purposive sense of this form is evident from the fact that one of its functions in some dialects is to express intention/purpose, especially when there is motion involved in the situation:

(75) É-   yi tsi- le-   gbé
      3SG go water bath INGR
      '(S)he has gone to have a bath.'

The other derivational formative -fé, which may have developed from the nominal root in the word a-fé 'home, hometown, house, dwelling, etc.', is highly productive and has a wide range of applicability. It can occur on a stem made up of a verb — as in dzɔfé 'birth place' — or a noun and verb compound — as in ɣedzefé 'sun-appear-place, east' — or a clause — as in nɔ-ma-nyá-fé 'mother-not-know-place, a place unknown to mother'. It can be paraphrased as 'place where event represented by the stem happens'.

There is an overlap in function between -fé and -gbé with respect to the intentional/purposive. Thus a sentence identical to (75) except for the morpheme -fé also has an intentional interpretation. In such contexts, however, -fé is vague. It has two interpretations, one for place and the other for purpose, as indicated in the example below:

(76) É-   yi tsi- le-   fé
      3SG go water bath INGR/place
      (i) '(S)he has gone to have a bath.'
      (ii) '(S)he has gone to the bathing place.'

Thus -fé also seems tainted with a purposive sense, if only as an inference in certain contexts, and is perhaps not a good candidate for the primitive.

Furthermore, all the uses of -fé (and for that matter of -gbé) involving 'place' can be paraphrased using the noun tefé. Morphologically and historically, tefé comes from te, probably a verb meaning 'push, drag', and the locative derivative -fé, described above. But this historical derivation and morphological complexity does not seem to have an impact on its semantic structure: it simply means 'place'. Consider the following intralingual paraphrase of a -fé word in terms of tefé:

(77) ɣedzefé = tefé   si   ye dze-   na   le
      east   place REL sun appear HAB at
      'east = place where the sun rises'

A close synonym of tefé is afí. They can be substituted for one another in several contexts (see examples below). Afí corresponds in behaviour with the ye-based words for TIME: there are general proform words for 'place' based on it such as afí-ka 'place-CQ, where?', afí-si 'place-REL, where', afí-sia 'this place' and afíí 'here'.

(78) Afí-ka/Tefé ka nè-   wɔ e   le?
      place CQ   2SG   do 3SG at
      'Where did you do it?'

(79) É-   dzɔ   le   afí/tefé   ɖeká má
      3SG   happen   at   place   one that
      mé-   nyé   afí/tefé   búbu o
      3SG:NEG   be   place   other NEG
      'It happened in the same place, not in a different place.'

However, there are two arguments against *afí* as the exponent of PLACE. First, it seems to always have a deictic implicature of a specific place as opposed to an indefinite place. *Tefé* does not carry such an implicature. Second, and more importantly, *afí* cannot be quantified whereas *tefé* can be. Compare the following:

(80) *afí / tefé   vovovo-   wó
       place   different PL
      'different places'

On the basis of these pieces of evidence, it could be concluded that *tefé* is the less complex word for PLACE in Ewe. But this is only part of the story, because all the words discussed so far for PLACE refer to places as entities. The sense intended for the primitive PLACE is that of "being somewhere" (Wierzbicka 1992:402). For this sense, the best exponent of (BE AT A) PLACE is the predicate *le* which can function as a preposition, as in (78) and (79), or as a verb, as in (83) and (84). *Le* has a number of uses: locative, existential, temporal and possessive (see example (89)). For each of these uses the predicate requires a specific object/complement. In the case of the locative, the usage which is of concern to us, it is required that the complement of *le* should designate a place or be construed as a place. Thus in examples (78) and (79), place words are the complements of the *le* form which expresses the locative relation.

It must be concluded from all this that the exponent of the primitive PLACE is *le* in Ewe. It should be pointed out, however, that there is an ambiguity inherent in the English term *place* which could refer to an entity or a relation. This could lead one to nominate the nominals discussed earlier as the representatives of the term PLACE in Ewe. But this is wrong since there is a clear exponent for the primitive BE AT A PLACE. It should also be noted that *le* in itself is not locative: its locative sense is completed by the semantic and pragmatic restriction on its complement to be a location.

AFTER is embodied in the word *megbé*, which also means 'back or back part of an entity, behind'. Historically and morphologically, *megbé* is derived from *mě* 'the back of a person' and the formative *gbé* 'region, area', discussed above. This derived form has become a distinct lexical item in the language (see Heine, Claudi and Hünnemayer (1991:65) and Ameka and Wilkins (in press) for some views on the different senses and developments of the word).

There is a syntactic distinction that corresponds to the meaning of *megbé* as 'back of a person or entity' on the one hand and its meaning as 'back, behind, after'. Whenever *megbé* is linked to another noun by the possessive connective *fé* then it has the meaning of a part term and not that of a spatio-temporal relational term. For the spatio-temporal relation sense the word is merely juxtaposed to the other constituents. This means that there is no overt syntactic means of distinguishing between a temporal after sense and a spatial after (i.e. behind) sense. Nevertheless it is a perfect match for AFTER in all its configurations in canonical contexts. For instance:

(81) Le ésia megbé lá, é- dze dɔ
      at this after TP 3SG land disease
      'After this, (s)he became sick.'

It is also possible to get an 'after' interpretation from the iconic ordering of clauses, and also in complex sentences where the first clause is introduced by *ési* 'when' and contains a perfective marker *vɔ*. For example:

(82) Ési   wó- ɖu nú   vɔ lá, wó ɖó dze
      when 3PL eat thing PFV TP 3PL converse
      'After eating, they conversed.'

It is worth noting that this construction involves a temporal 'when' word. In spite of this possibility, *megbé* is undoubtedly the best candidate for AFTER.

BEFORE can be expressed by a complex construction involving the word *ŋgɔ* 'front' as in the expression *dó ŋgɔ ná ésia* 'put front to/for this, i.e., before this'. BEFORE may also be expressed by the clause introducer *háfí* 'before'. This is, however, limited only to sentences of the form 'before doing X, (s)he did Y' or 'X happened before Y happened' (see (55)). It cannot co-occur with nominals on its own in expressions of the form 'before this ...'.

UNDER is expressed by three synonymous and dialect variant terms: *té, gɔme* and *ɖome*. Each of these items can be translated as 'under, bottom, beneath, base'. However they have different extended uses. For instance, *té* can be used to express the metaphor of 'being under someone', meaning 'to be subject of or subordinate to someone', and *gɔme* is used to talk about the meaning or content of something, as in *é-gɔme ɖé?* '3SG-under Q, i.e., what does it mean'. However, *ɖome* does not have any such extended usages. *Gɔme* and *ɖome* are related respectively to the body-part terms *gɔ(me)* 'buttocks' and *ɖo* 'female genital organ'.

Be that as it may, the three items are substitutable for each other in all contexts involving the spatial relational concept of UNDER:

(83) Míe- le lilíkpo- wó té/gɔme/ɖome
      1PL be cloud   PL under
      'We are under the clouds.'

ABOVE does not have any good straightforward translation equivalents in Ewe. The best approximations are the locative nominals *dzí* 'top of' and *tame* 'peak, top of, summit, upper part', which is related to the body-part term *ta* 'head'. Even though in some contexts, such as the canonical context sentence in (84), 'above' can be translated using these words, it is only a contextualisation of the more general meanings that the terms have.

(84)　*Lilíkpo yibɔ áɖé-   wó le miá- fé   tame*
　　　 cloud　 black　INDEF　PL　be　1PL　poss　top
　　　 'There are black clouds above us.'

Thus ABOVE and, as pointed out earlier, BEFORE do not seem to have good candidates in Ewe. But this is not a problem since there are good exponents in the language for the converses of the same relations, expressed by the words for UNDER and AFTER. It could be argued that the relations encoded by a converse member of the pairs of ABOVE/UNDER and BEFORE/AFTER are universal and they get an expression in different languages through one of the converse terms.

3.7　Taxonomy and Partonomy

KIND OF corresponds to the word *fomeví*, as is evident from its use in the following example:

(85)　*Me- kpɔ́ lã   fomeví vovovo-   wó*
　　　 1SG　see　animal　kind　 different　PL
　　　 'I saw different kinds of animals.'

In this example, *fomeví* functions as an adjective. It can also function as an intensifier. In its intensifier function it is synonymous and interchangeable with the dialect variants *tɔgbe/tɔgbi* and *kúme*, all of which translate as 'type of, sort of, kind of'.

(86)　*É-   nyé ame   áɖé   tɔgbi/kúme/fomeví*
　　　 3SG　be　 person　INDEF　kind
　　　 '(S)he is a certain kind of person.'

The lexical exponent of PART OF is the nominal *akpá*, which translates as 'part, side, division'. It is used to express the notion of 'part' when it is itself the head of a possessive construction, as is the case in the following line from a poem about the oil palm tree, whose parts are all said to be individually useful:

(87)　*É-   fé   akpá sia   'kpá nyó- ná*
　　　 3SG　poss　part　every　part　good　HAB
　　　 'Every part of it is good (for something).'

Similarly, this word is used in talking about parts of places, things and animals, as in (88):

(88)   *Gɛ̃ / kokló fé akpá ka nè- l5-- na wú?*
       Accra chicken poss part CQ 2SG like HAB surpass
       'Which part of Accra/chicken do you like best?'

However, this word is not normally used in expressing relations between parts and wholes embodied in constructions of the form 'X (whole) has Y (part)'. There are several syntactic constructions dedicated to the expression of such meanings in the language. These grammatical resources include syntactic compounding, juxtaposition, the use of a possessive marker, and a number of predicative constructions involving the locative/existential verb *le* 'be at' (see Ameka 1991, ch. 7, and 1994). A sentence such as 'That horse has a long tail' can be translated in the following ways:

(89)   a. *Asíkétí didi ádé   le-   e   ná só   má*
          tail   long INDEF be.at 3SG to horse that

       b. *Asíkétí didi ádé   le   só   má   sí*
          tail   long INDEF be.at horse that HAND

       c. *Só   má   fé   asíkétí didi*
          horse that poss tail   be.long

Thus while there is a lexical exponent for PART OF, it does not feature in the translation of the canonical context sentences (see Hill, this volume, for a similar situation in Longgu).

3.8 Evaluators and Descriptors

GOOD corresponds to the verb *nyó* 'be good' and its morphological derivatives: an adjective *nyuí/nyoé* 'good', a nominal based on the adjective *nyuĭ/nyoĕ*, and an adverbial *nyuié/nyoédé* 'well'. It is possible to explicate the meaning of the adverbial via the other forms. Thus the verbal, nominal and adjectival forms may be considered to be allolexes of GOOD whose distribution is syntactically determined, as illustrated in the following sentences:

(90)   a. *Ésia nyó*
          this be.good
          'This is good.'

b. Ésia-   é   nyé   nyui   a
   this   aFOC   be   good   DEF
   'This is (the) good (one).'

(91) È-   wɔ   nú   nyuí   áɖé
      2SG   do   thing   good   INDEF
      'You did something good.'

(92) È-   wɔ-   e   nyuié
      2SG   do   3SG   well
      'You did it well.'

BAD has several equivalents in Ewe. First there is a basic adjective *vɔ̃* and its nominal derivative *vɔ̃*, which carries the connotation of wrong or evil. Thus when it is compounded with *nú* 'thing' the resulting word *núvɔ̃* is translated as 'sin'. Second, there is the related word *vɔ̃ɖi*, which is probably derived historically from a predicate made up of *ɖi* 'look like' and *vɔ̃* 'evil'. This word can function both as an adjective and a verb in the same form. Similarly, a third word *vló* can also function as an adjective and a verb without any overt change in form. It is mainly used to talk about the character or behaviour of people. A fourth word, *baɖa*, can be used in the same form as an adjective, a verb and an adverb. It is applicable to a wide range of things. Finally, there is a verb *gblẽ* 'be bad, spoilt'. In the sense of 'bad' it is used in relation to moral character. An adjectival form of this verb, *gbégblẽ*, also translates as 'bad'.

By and large these words can be used interchangeably in the appropriate morphosyntactic form to express the idea of 'bad' in the canonical contexts, as illustrated in the following sentences:

(93) È-   wɔ   nú   vɔ̃/vɔ̃ɖi/vló/baɖa/gbégblẽ   áɖé
      2SG   do   thing   bad   INDEF
      'You did something bad.'

(94) É-   vɔ̃ɖi/vló/baɖa/gblẽ
      3SG   bad
      '(S)he is bad.'

At this stage it is not clear to me whether one of these terms could be used in defining the others. It would appear, though, that *vɔ̃ɖi* could be explicated via *vɔ̃*. It might also be suggested that since *gblẽ* is rather restricted in the sense of 'bad' it may not be a very good candidate. Even leaving these forms aside one is still left with at least three terms — *vɔ̃*, *vló* and *baɖa* — as the candidates for BAD in Ewe.

BIG corresponds to the adjective *gã*, which has a nominalised form *gã* and an adverbial form *gãɖé*. SMALL is expressed by a number of words. *Ví* is an adjective, and has morphological derivatives *vĭ* 'a little' (noun), *vié* 'a little' (adverbial) and a diminutive suffix -ví (see Heine, Claudi and Hünnemayer (1991:79–91) for a discussion of the uses of this suffix). *Sue* functions as an adjective, a verb or an adverbial without a change in morphological form. Similarly, *túkúí* can function as an adjective or a verb without a change in form. Its adverbial form is derived by adding a suffix to get *túkúíɖé*. *Túkúí* has connotations of 'tiny' and 'thin'. The three forms can be substituted for one another in the canonical context sentence, as in (95). Thus I consider them allolexes of the exponent of SMALL in Ewe.

(95) Me- kpɔ́ atí gã / ví/sue/túkúí áɖé
      1SG see tree big   small   INDEF
      'I saw a big/small tree.'

3.9 Conclusion

In general, Ewe seems to have lexical exponents for the proposed primitives. In several cases the items correspond straightforwardly with the primitive and its combinatorial frame. This is true for the exponents for I, YOU, UNDER and AFTER, for example. In other cases, it is easy to identify a lexical exponent for a primitive but the item is restricted in its range of use such that it is not easy to utilise it in all of the proposed canonical context sentences. This is evident, for instance, from the discussion of FEEL and THE SAME. These difficulties could be overcome by identifying language-specific combinatorial properties for the primitives.

In spite of the general success in identifying the semantic primitives and lexical universals for Ewe, the present exercise has brought to the fore certain methodological issues that need to be addressed. The first issue concerns allolexy. In the discussion of the Ewe equivalents, one finds many instances of 'allolexy'. Some of these can be explained as pertaining to dialect variation, as is the case for *ta* and *ŋútí* as exponents of BECAUSE. Other cases of allolexy can be attributed to morphological or syntactic variation on the same form. This obtains with respect to the exponents for GOOD, I and YOU, for example. One may well want to ask whether these two instances of allolexy are the same and whether they should be treated in the same way. In particular, if we assume that grammatical categories in themselves are meaningful — a perspective on grammar which I believe is shared by many contributors to this volume — then is it legitimate to consider the different morphological derivatives of a form as its allolexes, as I have done with respect to GOOD? My dilemma is that the canonical context usages require different derivational forms.

The notion of allolexy has also been appealed to in instances where there was not enough evidence to show that a particular equivalent is semantically prior to other exponents. The exponents for BAD, SMALL and THINK are cases in point. A similar argument has been used for the exponents of SAY. In this case it is worth noting that there are two different shades of allolexy at play. First, *dó* and *gblɔ* are dialect variants which overlap in function. Secondly, *bé*, *dó* and *gblɔ* can all be used to express SAY. But *bé* as a verb has a restricted range of uses, and these uses seem to be included in those of *dó* and *gblɔ*. One may question, as David Wilkins (personal communication) has done, whether the second instance of the relations is really a relation of allolexy. I am not sure, but the only way I can account for the contexts of use of the primitive SAY is to accept that all three elements share part of the primitive status. The moral of all this is that there is a need for a clarification of this notion of allolexy and the situations in which it is legitimate to invoke it.

A second methodological issue relates to the translational approach in identifying the primitives across languages. In particular it concerns the fact that in some instances we get one primitive notion being represented by candidates for other primitive notions, as is the case with DO and HAPPEN.

A third and final problem concerns the conceptual status of semantic primitives. As indicated in the discussion, some of the Ewe elements in which the primitives are embodied have developed from other more basic terms such as body parts. This is the case with the exponents for AFTER, BECAUSE and UNDER, for example. From a localist viewpoint, the body parts from which the locative terms have developed are more basic and more concrete than the the primitive notions they have developed into. Thus the locative terms are more complex and less prior conceptually. One can defend the primitive status of these terms by saying that although there is a semantic and conceptual link between their historical sources and the primitive notions, one cannot define these primitive terms through the body-part terms, so from a decompositional point of view these terms are primitive. It can further be argued that there is no semantic compositional relation between the terms and their sources.

All the issues raised here deserve further investigation. It is my hope that the data provided here on Ewe can help to throw some light on some of these issues.

Notes

1   I would like to express my gratitude to Debbie Hill and David Wilkins, who have been especially helpful to me in the writing of this paper, not only for their comments on an earlier fragment of the paper but also and above all for their concern, inspiration and encouragement. I am also grateful to James Esegbey, Cliff Goddard and Anna Wierzbicka for their suggestions and comments on a pre-final version of the paper. Thanks also to Tim Curnow for his editorial assistance and patience.

2   The following abbreviations are used in glosses: COMPlementiser, CQ content question marker, DEFinite article, DEMonstrative, DIMinutive, DIRectional verb satellite, aFOC argument focus marker, FUTure, HABitual, INGRessive, INDEFinite, INTensifier, IRRealis, LOGophoric pronoun, NP nominal phrase, NEGative, NPRES non-present, PFV perfective, PLural marker, poss possessive linker, PRESent, PROGressive, Question marker, REDuplicative formative, RELativiser, REPetitive, SBJV subjunctive, SG singular, TP terminal particle, 1 first person, 2 second person, 3 third person.

In the traditional orthography of Ewe only few tones are marked. In this paper, all high tones are marked throughout with an acute accent ´. Low tones, marked with a grave accent `, are only indicated when demanded by the orthography or to make explicit the tone of the item being discussed. Rising and falling tones are marked by ˇ and ˆ respectively where necessary.

References

Ameka, Felix K. 1986. *The Use and Meaning of Selected Particles in Ewe*. MA Thesis, Department of Linguistics, Australian National University, Canberra.

Ameka, Felix K. 1990. "The Grammatical Packaging of Experiencers in Ewe: A study in the semantics of syntax". *Australian Journal of Linguistics* 10.2.139-181.

Ameka, Felix K. 1990/1991. "How Discourse Particles Mean: The case of the Ewe 'terminal' particles". *Journal of African Languages and Linguistics* 12.2.143-170.

Ameka, Felix K. 1991. *Ewe: Its grammatical constructions and illocutionary devices*. PhD Thesis, Department of Linguistics, Australian National University, Canberra.

Ameka, Felix K. 1992. "Focus Constructions in Ewe and Akan: A comparative perspective". *Proceedings of the Kwa Comparative Syntax Workshop MIT 1992* ed. by Chris Collins & Victor Manfredi, 1-25. Cambridge, Mass.: MIT Dept of Linguistics and Philosophy.

Ameka Felix K. 1994. "Body Parts in Ewe Grammar". *The Grammar of Inalienability* ed. by Hilary Chappell & William McGregor. Berlin: Mouton.

Ameka, Felix K. & David P. Wilkins. In press. "Where Semantic Theory and the Comparative Method Meet: Grammaticalisation" (Review article of Heine, Claudi & Hünnemayer 1991). *Journal of African Languages and Linguistics*.

Ansre, Gilbert. 1966. *The Grammatical Units of Ewe*. PhD Thesis, University of London.

Clements, George N. 1972. *The Verbal Syntax of Ewe*. PhD Thesis, University of London.

Clements, George N. 1979. "The Logophoric Pronoun in Ewe: Its role in discourse". *Journal of West African Languages* 10.2.141-177.

Duthie, Alan S. 1988. "Ewe". *The Languages of Ghana* ed. by M. E. Kropp Dakubu, 91-101. London: Kegan Paul.

Duthie, Alan S. In press. *Introducing Ewe Linguistics*. Accra: Ghana Universities Press.

Dzobo, Noah K. 1981. "The Indigenous African Theory of Knowledge and Truth: Example of the Ewe and Akan of Ghana." *Conch* 13.2.85-102.

Dzobo, Noah K. 1992. "Knowledge and Truth: Ewe and Akan conceptions". *Person and Community: Ghanaian philosophical studies 1* ed. by Kwasi Wiredu & Kwami Gyekye, 73-84. Washington: Council for Research in Values and Philosophy.

Heine, Bernd, Ulrike Claudi & Friederike Hünnemeyer. 1991. *Grammaticalization: A conceptual framework*. Chicago: University of Chicago Press.

Ultan, Russell. 1978. "The Nature of Future Tenses". *Universals of Language* ed. by Joseph H. Greenberg, vol 4.83-123. Stanford: Stanford University Press.

Westermann, Diedrich. 1930. *A Study of the Ewe Language*. Trans. by A. L. Bickford-Smith. London: Oxford University Press.

Westermann, Diedrich. 1973 [1928]. *Ewefiala: Ewe–English Dictionary*. Berlin: Reimer.

Wierzbicka, Anna. 1992. "Lexical Universals and Universals of Grammar". *Meaning and Grammar:*

Cross-linguistic perspectives ed. by Michel Kefer & Johan van der Auwera, 383-415. Berlin: Mouton de Gruyter.

Ewe Texts

Akotey, Klu. 1988. *Ku ɖi fo na wo* [Death satisfied them]. 2nd ed. Accra: Bureau of Ghana Languages.

Nyɔmi, C. Kofi. 1980. *ŋuvava* [Jealousy]. Accra: Bureau of Ghana Languages.

The Exponents of Semantic Primitives in Mangap-Mbula

Robert D. Bugenhagen
The Summer Institute of Linguistics

This paper examines the applicability of the proposed set of lexical and semantic universals to Mangap-Mbula, an Austronesian language spoken in the Morobe Province of Papua New Guinea.[1] Before proceeding on to the universal elements themselves, however, a brief sketch of the morphosyntax of the language will be given.

Overall, the word order in Mangap-Mbula is summarised by the linear precedence rule that heads of phrases precede their phrasal complements. Thus, the language exhibits the following characteristics:

(a) verb–object order
(b) prepositions rather than postpositions
(c) complementiser–complement clause ordering
(d) post-nominal occurrence of most noun phrase modifiers

Three exceptions to this rule are: (a) the occurrence of subjects before the predicate phrase; (b) the occurrence of some genitives before the head noun; and (c) the occurrence of a number of modal adverbs either sentence-initially or between the subject and the predicate. Word order in the language is quite rigid, with the exception of the occurrence of various constituents sentence-initially for thematic purposes. Mangap-Mbula is, therefore, an SVOX language.

(1) *Nio   aŋ-kam=i   pa   mbeŋ   ma*
    1SG:NOM 1SG-do/get=3SG:ACC REF[2] night   and
    a-mar.
    1PL:EXC-come
    'I brought him along at night.'

Morphologically, the language is nominative–accusative. The person and number of subjects are indicated by co-indexing subject prefixes on the verb.[3] A number of the nouns are obligatorily inflected with suffixes indicating the person and number of a genitive. No distinction is made in the pronouns for gender.

As is the case in many Oceanic languages,[4] there are several genitive constructions in Mangap-Mbula. One type, the alienable genitive, is encoded by prepositional phrases headed by the form *ki/k-/t-*.[5] It is primarily used to encode ownership, but may also express location (e.g. 'the villages of this island'), production (e.g. 'my talk, what I said') and 'about' (e.g. 'a story about dogs').

The inalienable genitive construction consists of a noun obligatorily inflected with a set of genitive suffixes indexing the person and number of a genitive entity. The identity of this entity may be further specified by a free noun phrase which occurs before the head noun. This construction is relevant for this paper because it is a primary means of expressing part–whole notions.

(2) *Silas   kumbu-unu   / tama-ana*
     Silas   leg-3SG:GEN   father-3SG:GEN
     'Silas' leg/father'

A variant of the inalienable genitive relies on the mediating inalienable forms *ka-* and *le-*,[6] which are in turn followed by one or more nouns which indicate more precisely the entity bearing the relationship. The form *ka-* is used to encode ownership or reception of items intended for consumption, some unfortunate interpersonal relationships, as well as less inherent part–whole relationships. The form *le-* is used to express some beneficial personal relationships and to encode ownership or reception of items not intended for consumption.

This now concludes the brief summary of Mangap-Mbula morphosyntax. We shall now proceed on to an examination of the exponents of the proposed lexical and semantic universals.

4.1 Substantives: I, YOU, SOMEONE, SOMETHING, PEOPLE

The proposed substantives I, YOU, and SOMEONE/PERSON have obvious equivalents: the pronouns *nio/yo* 'I' and *nu/u* 'you', and the noun *tomtom* 'person, people'. I and YOU exhibit syntactically conditioned allomorphic variation, in which the shorter, accusative versions occur as objects and the longer, nominative versions occur as subjects. Recall from the introductory section that I and YOU are also distinguished by affixation on the verb and by affixation on those nouns having inalienable genitives. The primitive SOMEONE is expressed by a combination of the noun *tomtom* plus the determiner *ta* 'one, a'. Without the determiner *tomtom*, as a singular form, would always be interpreted as having definite reference.

(3) *Nio   aŋ-re   tomtom   ta.*
    1SG:NOM 1SG-see person   one
    'I saw someone.'

The category PERSON is also allolexically[7] represented by the interrogative pronouns of the language, *asiŋ* 'who?' and *ziŋoi* 'who plural?'. The form *asiŋ* is more neutral with respect to number than *ziŋoi*. It can be used either to refer to a single individual or more generically when no assumptions are being made about the number of people involved. *Ziŋoi* is used when the speaker explicitly assumes that there was more than one person involved.

If the noun *tomtom* occurs preceded by the overt pluraliser *zin* or is the subject of a verb or the genitive of a noun having third-person plural inflection, then it is interpreted as 'people'. Otherwise, its meaning is 'a/the person', depending upon whether or not it co-occurs with the determiner *ta*. Compare the following example with example (3):

(4) *(Zin)   tomtom   ti-kam   ŋgar   ŋoobo.*
    PL   person   3PL-do   thinking   incorrectly
    'People think incorrectly.'

A final note about the form *tomtom* is that the phrase *tomtom biibi* 'big person' is often used to refer to God.

Another form, *wal*, is used to mean 'a specific group of people'. It always occurs in conjunction with (a) numerals; (b) quantifiers like *boozo* 'many' or *pakan* 'some, a few'; and (c) the pluraliser *zin*; and, in contrast with the form *tomtom*, it never seems to be used generically.

The exponent of the primitive THING is somewhat problematic, because ideally a form is needed that subsumes both (a) activities/events ('you did something'/'something happened') and (b) entities ('you did something to **something**'/'something is good to eat'). Mangap-Mbula, however, seems to distinguish these two notions. There are two interrogative pronouns: *sokorei* 'what (thing(s))?' (probably derived from *so* 'what?' and *koroŋ* 'thing'), used to question only things; and *so*, used only to question events:

(5) *Zin   ti-kam   sokorei?*   *Zin   ti-kam   so?*
    3PL   3PL-do/get   what   3PL   3PL-do/get   what.event
    'What did they get?'   'What did they do?'

Although the noun *koroŋ* 'thing' can be used to refer to both events and entities, THINGS which are events are more typically expressed in Mangap-Mbula using a different noun, *mbulu* 'event, behaviour':[8]

(6) *Iti irao ta-kam mbulu ti pepe.*
1PL:INC should 1PL:INC-do event this PROHIB
'We shouldn't do this.'

(7) *To aŋ-re mbulu toro i-pet.*
then 1SG-see event other 3SG-happen
'Then I saw something else happen.'

Because the predicates used to express DO and HAPPEN are polysemous (*-kam* 'make/do, receive, give' and *-pet* 'appear, happen, come in a seawards direction'), if one wants to **unambiguously** express the meanings 'something happened' or 'someone did something', it is necessary to use the noun *mbulu* rather than *koroŋ*:

(8) *Nu kam koroŋ ambai-ŋa-na.*
2SG:NOM 2SG:do/get/give thing good-NMS-3SG:GEN
'You did/received/gave something good.'

Nu kam mbulu ambai-ŋa-na.
2SG:NOM 2SG:do event good-NMS-3SG:GEN
'You did something good.'

(9) *Koroŋ toro i-pet.*
thing other 3SG-happen/appear/come.seaward
'Something else happened/appeared/came in a seaward direction.'

Mbulu toro i-pet.
event other 3SG-happen
'Something else happened.'

(10) *Asiŋ i-kam koroŋ ta-na?*
who? 3SG-do/get thing SPEC-GIV
'Who did/got that?'

Asiŋ i-kam mbulu ta-na?
who? 3SG-do/get event SPEC-GIV
'Who did that?'

4.2 Mental Predicates: KNOW, FEEL, THINK, SAY, WANT

The exponent of the primitive KNOW is clearly the verb *-ute* 'know'. This form can be used to mean both 'know that …' and 'know someone (as a person)'.

(11) *Nio   aŋ-ute   ni   i-kam   mbulu*
      1SG:NOM 1SG-know   3SG:NOM 3SG-do   behaviour
      sanan-ŋa-na   kat.
      bad-NMS-3SG:GEN   very
      'I know he did something very bad.'

The exponent of the primitive FEEL is more problematic. One possibility is the verb *-yamaana* 'feel, sense'. In its experiential sense, it always occurs in the frame: *-yamaana + Reflexive-Emphatic Pronoun + kembei + Sentential Complement*.

(12) *Nio   aŋ-yamaana   itu-ŋ*
      1SG:NOM   1SG-feel   REFL-1SG:GEN
      kembei   mete   i-kam   yo.
      like   illness   3SG-do/get 1SG:ACC
      'I feel that I am sick.'

(13) *Nio   aŋ-yamaana   itu-ŋ*
      1SG:NOM   1SG-feel   REFL-1SG:GEN
      kembei   lele-ŋ   ambai   som.
      like   insides-1SG:GEN good   NEG
      'I feel that I am not happy.'

There are two problems, however, with designating *-yamaana* as the exponent of FEEL. First, because it always takes a sentential complement, it cannot occur in a canonical context like 'I feel good'. And secondly, although it **can** be used to express both physical sensations and emotions, these notions are far more commonly expressed using inalienable body part nouns like *kete-* 'liver', *ni-* 'body', and *lele-* 'insides'. *Kete-* tends to be used to express strong emotions which are not easily controlled, for example *kete- malmal* 'liver fight' (= 'angry') and *kete- ise* 'liver ascend' (= 'be excited to the point where one can no longer say "No" to oneself'). The form *ni-* is only used to express **physical** sensations like health, sickness, fever, and exhaustion. *Lele-* 'insides', on the other hand, is the most productive form of all for expressing emotions but cannot be used to express physical sensations.[9]

(14) *Ni-n   (i-)saana.*
      body-3PL:GEN   (3SG-)deteriorate
      'They feel exhausted.'

(15) *Ni   lele-ene   i-saana   p-io.*
      3SG:NOM insides-3SG:GEN 3SG-deteriorate REF-1SG
      'He feels bad on my account.' (Note that the bad feelings could be anger because of something I had done, or sorrow because of something bad which had happened to me.)

(16)   *Nio   lele-ŋ   ambai.*
       1SG:NOM insides-1SG:GEN   good
       'I feel happy/contented.' (Note that this sentence cannot mean 'I feel well'. To express this, the following example would be used.)

(17)   *Nio   ni-ŋ   ambai.*
       1SG:NOM body-1SG:GEN   good
       'I feel well/healthy.'

The problem, therefore, is that the most common expressions for FEEL in Mangap-Mbula, the ones which occur in canonical contexts like 'X feels good', require one to discriminate between physical sensations and emotions. In explications of various emotions using Natural Semantic Metalanguage, the component 'X feels something good/bad because of that' would often most naturally be rendered in Mangap-Mbula using *lele-*.

The active sense of THINK is unambiguously expounded by the verbal noun *ŋgar*, which occurs in periphrastic constructions like:

(18)   *Nio   aŋ-kam   ŋgar   pi-ni   ta   kembei:*
       1SG:NOM 1SG-do   thinking   REF-3SG SPEC   like
       Ni   i-kam   mbulu   ambai   som.
       3SG:NOM 3SG-do   behaviour well   NEG
       'I think concerning him like this: He did not behave well.'

Stative thinking, on the other hand, is expressed by the verb *-so₁* 'to think' (homophonous with *-so* 'say'), usually in conjunction with the modal adverb *ko*, which expresses uncertainty:

(19)   *Mazwaana   ta-na   nio   aŋ-so   (ko)*
       time   SPEC-GIV   1SG:NOM 1SG-think   UC
       ni   i-meete   kek.
       3SG:NOM 3SG-die   PERF
       'At that time, I thought he had died.'

This brings us to the primitive SAY, which is manifested by the verb *-so₂* occurring in the frame: *-so₂* + (*ta kembei.*) + (*-so₂*)+ *Sentential Complement/NP*.

(20)   *Ni   i-so   (ta   kembei.)*
       3SG:NOM 3SG-say SPEC   like
       (I-so)   "Nio   ko   aŋ-mar."
       3SG-say   1SG:NOM UC   1SG-come
       'He said (like this.) (He said), "I will come."'

(21) Zin   ti-so   sua   raraate.
      3PL:NOM   3PL-say   talk   the.same
      'They said the same.'

The two most frequent means of encoding WANT are: (a) the inalienable noun *lele-* 'insides' immediately followed by the non-factual complementiser *be* or the referent preposition *pa*; and (b) the verb *-so₃* 'want' plus (optionally) the complementiser *be*:

(22) Nio   lele-ŋ   be
      1SG:NOM   insides-1SG:GEN   NF
      aŋ-la   aŋ-re   Atai   kar   ki-ni.
      1SG-go   1SG-see Atai   village GEN-3SG
      'I want/would like to go see Atai's village.' (Literally, 'My insides (are) that I go see Atai's village.')

(23) Nio   aŋ-so(=(m)be)   aŋ-la   aŋ-re
      1SG:NOM   1SG-want(=NF)   1SG-go   1SG-see
      Atai   kar   ki-ni.
      Atai   village   GEN-3SG
      'I want/intend to go see Atai's village.'

Note that when *lele-* encodes WANT and takes a sentential complement, it is **obligatorily** followed by the non-factual complementiser *be*. When *-so* encodes WANT, it may or may not be followed by *be*, with no apparent difference in meaning.[10] If one wants to express that one wants some **thing**, where the thing desired is an entity and not a state of affairs, then only *lele-* can be used:

(24) Nio   lele-ŋ   pa   koroŋ   ta-na.
      1SG:NOM   insides-1SG:GEN   REF   thing   SPEC-GIV
      'I want/would like that (thing).'

The sequence *lele- be/pa* seems to be a better candidate for WANT because: (a) it is unambiguous; and (b) it can be used to express the wanting of both states of affairs and entities.

4.3 Determiners and Quantifiers: THIS, THE SAME, OTHER, TWO, ALL

The equivalents of the determiners THIS, THE SAME, OTHER, TWO, and ALL are as follows: *ti* 'this, here' (a demonstrative-cum-locative adverb), the adverb *raraate* 'same', the determiner *toro* 'other', the quantifier *ru* 'two', and the quantifier *taboozomen* 'all'. The form *taboozomen* is formally complex, consisting of *men* 'still, only', *boozo* 'many', and *ta*, a form whose contextual invariant appears to be 'the specific one'.[11]

With regard to the demonstrative *ti* 'this, here', it should be noted that the same form can function either as a modifier within the noun phrase or independently as a locative adverb:

(25) Re   koroŋ   ti.
      2SG:look   thing   this
      'Look at this.'

(26) Zin   ti-mbot   ti.
      3PL   3PL-stay   here
      'They stayed here.'

Although *ti* may have either anaphoric or cataphoric reference in texts, it is more frequently cataphoric. It contrasts in this regard with the demonstrative *tana* 'that, there', which only has anaphoric reference. *Ti* is used to refer to the place where the speaker is at; for example, *lele ti* 'this place'. It can also be used to refer to various parts of the speaker's body — for example, *kumbuŋ ti* 'this leg of mine' — and to entities located near the speaker — for example, *buza ti* 'this knife (near me)' versus *buza tana* 'that knife (near you)'.

Parallel to the demonstratives *ti* 'this', *tana* 'that' and *taŋga* 'that over there' are a set of three demonstrative pronouns: *iŋgi* 'this (one)', *ina* 'that (one)' and *iŋga* 'that (one) over there'. In the Mangap-Mbula equivalents of kernel sentences like 'This is good' or 'That is good', either these demonstrative pronouns or a phrase like 'this thing' can occur in the subject position. Similarly, it will be noted from example (25) that in the kernel sentence 'Look at this', the phrase *koroŋ ti* 'this thing' occurs in the object position. This is because the demonstratives do not normally occur in isolation as encodings of clausal arguments.

In the Mangap-Mbula encoding of a sentence like 'He sang like this', the realisation of THIS is slightly different, being *ta*. This form elsewhere functions as the numeral 'one', the indefinite article, a relative clause complementiser, and a component of a number of demonstratives and causal conjunctions.

(27) Ni   i-mbo   mboe   toro   ta   kembei.
      3SG:NOM   3SG-sing   song   other   SPEC   like
      'He sang another song like this.'

The notion THE SAME is expressed by the adverbial form *raraate* 'in the same way'. This form can also be used predicatively.

(28) *Tomtom taboozomen ti-kam mbulu raraate.*
person all 3PL-do behaviour in.the.same.way
'All the people did the same thing.'

(29) *Ke ru ta-na raraate kat.*
tree two SPEC-GIV the.same very
'Those two trees are exactly the same.'

4.4 Actions and Events: DO, HAPPEN

The predicate DO is expounded by the verb *-kam*, and the predicate HAPPEN is expounded by the verb *-pet*. *-Kam* also has a second sense of 'get, receive', but it most frequently occurs in causative constructions such as:

(30) *Ni i-kam ma lele-ŋ ambai som.*
3SG:NOM 3SG-do and insides-1SG:GEN good NEG
'He upset me.'

(31) *Kam buk i-la ki Aibike.*
2SG:do book 3SG-go LOC Aibike
'Take the book to Aibike.'

Recalling the discussion of THING, to unambiguously express that someone 'did' something or that something 'happened', *-kam* and *-pet* must occur in combination with the noun *mbulu* 'event, behaviour':

(32) *Ni i-kam mbulu*
3SG:NOM 3SG-do event
(toro / tamen / sanan-ŋa-na).
(other one-only deteriorate-NMS-3SG:GEN
'He did (something else/the same thing/something bad).'

(33) *Mbulu ta-na i-pet p-io na aŋ-murur.*
behaviour SPEC-GIV 3SG-happen REF-1SG GIV 1SG-shiver
'When that happened to me, I was surprised (literally, 'shivered').'

Like *-kam*, the verb *-pet* is polysemous. In addition to the sense HAPPEN, it can mean either 'to appear, come into view/being'[12] or 'to come in a seaward direction'. There is an important subcategorisation difference between *-pet*₁ HAPPEN and the other senses of *-pet*: the form *-pet*₁ takes only **referent** prepositional complements[13] whereas the other senses of *-pet* take both **locative** and **referent** prepositional complements.[14] Contrast example (33), where *-pet*₁ HAPPEN is used, with the following locative one, in which the post-verbal complement is encoded as a locative prepositional phrase rather than a referent one:

(34)   Ni   i-pet   t-io   neeri.
       3SG:NOM   3PL-appear   LOC-1SG   yesterday
       'He came to me yesterday.'

4.5   Meta-Predicates: DON'T WANT, IF, COULD, LIKE, BECAUSE, VERY

The notions NOT (NO) and DON'T WANT have distinct exponents in Mangap-Mbula. The former is expounded by the sentence final adverb *som* 'not'. This same form also functions as the interjection 'No!'.

(35)   Nio   aŋ-ute   koroŋ   ta-na   som.
       1SG:NOM   1SG-know   thing   SPEC-GIV   NEG
       'I didn't know that.'

(36)   Som,   zin   ko   ti-mar.
       no   3PL   UC   3PL-come
       'No, they will come.'

DON'T WANT is expounded by the sentence final adverb *pepe*:

(37)   Kan   koroŋ   ta-na   pepe.
       2SG:eat   thing   SPEC-GIV   PROHIB
       'Don't eat that.'

Pepe can also occur in isolation as an interjection meaning 'Don't do that!'.

There are three possible candidates for the exponent of IF. The first is a verb homophonous with the verb -so_2 'say' which takes a sentential complement,[15] as in (38), while the second is a phonologically identical modal adverb[16] *so(=(m)be)*, as in (39). The third possible exponent would be the modal adverb/complementiser *be*.

(38)   Yaŋ   i-so(=(m)be)   i-su,   (i)na-ko   aŋ-mar   som.
       rain   3SG-say(=NF)   3SG-descend   GIV-UC   1SG-come   NEG
       'If it rains, I won't come.'

(39)   Yaŋ   so(=(m)be)   i-su,   (i)na-ko   aŋ-mar   som.
       rain   if(=NF)   3SG-descend   GIV-UC   1SG-come   NEG
       'If it rains, I won't come.'

In these examples the phonologically bound clitic =be/=mbe 'non-factual' is optional, freely fluctuating with its absence.[17] A free form *be* functions as a complementiser introducing the sentential complements of predicates like *-miu* 'dream (that)', *-maŋga* 'start to do something', *-ŋgalsek* 'prohibit someone from doing something', *-ur sua* 'order someone to do something', *lele- be/pa* 'want', and so on. This same form also introduces purpose clauses.

In counterfactual conditionals, a modal adverb *be* fluctuates with *so* in the protasis, and *so* obligatorily replaces *inako* in the apodosis:

(40) *Nu   so / be   kam   mbulu   ambai-ŋa-na*
       2SG:NOM   if   NF   2SG:do   behaviour good-NMS-3SG:GEN
       pi-zin,   so   te-ndeeŋe   pata-ŋa-na
       REF-3PL   if   1PL:INC-find   heavy/trouble-NMS-3SG:GEN
       ti   som.
       this NEG
       'If you had behaved correctly towards them, we wouldn't be in this trouble.'

Regarding the choice between *so((m)be)* and *be* as the exponent of IF, *so* is probably a better choice, because it is the **essential** element in all hypothetical conditionals and a possible element in counterfactual ones. Despite its phonological similarity to the exponents of the primitives SAY and THINK, there would never be true constructional ambiguity between SAY and IF because of various syntactic differences. (These differences are outlined in section 4.9.)

If *be* were to be chosen as the exponent of IF, its function as a complementiser of a verb like *-miu* 'dream' would be easily explained. Also, it would have the advantage of being a distinct lexical item from those manifesting other primitives. It is a frequent element in both counterfactual and hypothetical conditionals. Against *be* is the fact that it is perfectly possible to omit it from a hypothetical conditional construction with no change in meaning.

The primitive COULD is expounded by the modal adverb *irao* 'able, can, could, should, permitted'. This form is phonologically identical to the third-singular form of the verb *-rao* 'adequate, sufficient', which is also used to express abilitative modality. The modal adverb *irao* is ambiguous/vague between abilitative, permissive, possible, and obligative readings. Only context gives it a more precise flavour. The 'could of possibility' is illustrated below:

(41) *Nu   kilaala   lele   be   padei?*
       2SG:NOM   2SG:recognise   place   NF   how
       Irao   yaŋ   i-su?
       could   rain   3SG-descend
       'What do you think about the weather? Could it rain?'

The primitive LIKE is expressed by the phrases *ke(mbe)i ta/ta ke(mbe)i*:

(42) *Puulu   i-tooro   ma   i-we   kei ta   siŋ.*
     moon   3SG-change   and 3SG-become   like SPEC blood
     'The moon (its colour) changed becoming like blood.'

(43) *Mburu   ki-zin   matakiŋa, kei ta   ki-zin.*
     clothing GEN-3PL   manifold   like SPEC GEN-3PL
     misis
     white.woman
     'They had many kinds of clothing, like that of the white women.'

(44) *Zoŋ   kembei   ta   puulu   mi   mata-ana*
     sun   like   SPEC   moon   and   eye/colour-3SG:GEN
     i-siŋsiŋ   kei   ta   you.
     3SG-red   like   SPEC   fire
     'The sun (was big) like the moon and its colour was red like fire.'

Regarding the exponent of CAUSE, one is faced with the opposite problem of Evans (1986), who notes the unimportance of causal notions for the Aboriginal language Kayardild. In Mangap-Mbula there is an embarrassment of riches when it comes to syntactic devices encoding causation. Given this abundant variety of causal devices, the notion of CAUSE is well established as a semantic category relevant to the language. *Pa*, a form homophonous with the referent preposition *pa* that governs most oblique arguments in the clause, is the best choice as the exponent of CAUSE, because it can govern both nominal and sentential complements:

(45) *Nio   kete-ŋ   malmal   pa*
     1SG:NOM   liver-1SG:GEN   fight   because
     zooro-ŋa-na   ki-ni.
     rebel-NMS-3SG:GEN   GEN-3SG
     'I am angry because of his rebellion.'

(46) *Niom   ka-mar   som   pa-so?*
     2PL:NOM   2PL-come   NEG   because-what?
     'Why did you not come?'

     Niam   a-mar   som   pa   a-moto.
     1PL:EXC:NOM   1PL:EXC-come   NEG   because   1PL:EXC-fear
     'We did not come because we were afraid.'

Despite their superficial resemblance to prepositional phrases headed by *pa* which encode other oblique clausal arguments, causal adjuncts headed by *pa* are distinguished syntactically because of their positioning at the rightmost periphery of the sentence, following even 'sentence-final' adverbs like *pepe* 'prohibitive', *som* 'negative' and *kek* 'perfective'. This is illustrated in the second line of example (46).

Another extremely frequent type of device used to express causal notions are intersentential connectives like *tana*, *ta*, *tanata* and *tabe*, which are based on the formatives *ta* 'specific' and *na* 'given information'. Recall from section 4.3 that the form *tana* also functions as a demonstrative indicating things which are near to the hearer and in anaphoric reference. All of these causal connectives occur in constructions of the form *X Conjunction Y*, where X is the cause of Y.

(47)   *Mooto   i-pakaam   yo   tana   aŋ-kam*
         snake   3SG-trick   1SG:ACC   therefore   1SG-get
         ke   ŋono-ono   mi   aŋ-kan.
         tree   fruit-3SG:GEN   and   1SG-eat
         'The snake tricked me, and therefore I took the fruit of the tree and ate it.'

Sentential causes are more typically encoded using forms based on *ta* rather than the form *pa*. Nominal causes are obligatorily encoded using *pa*. The interrogative *paso* 'why?' is based on a combination of *pa* and *so*[18] 'what'. The form *paso* can also function as a sentence-initial causal connective, freely alternating with *pa*. Note that when *pa* and *paso* are used as sentential causal connectives, the ordering is *X pa/paso Y*, where Y is the cause of X. This is the opposite of the ordering found with the connectives based on *ta* (compare examples (46) and (47)).

Some other syntactic devices encoding causation are:

(a)   morphological causatives (formed by adding the prefix *p(a)-*), e.g. *po-mbol* 'strengthen' (from *-mbol* 'be strong'), *pa-ute* 'teach' (from *-ute* 'know');

(b)   analytic causatives (formed by conjoining the verb *-kam* 'do' in a cosubordinate predicate combination), e.g. *-kam X ma imar* 'bring X' (literally, 'do X and it come'), *-kam ma X isaana* 'ruin X' (literally, 'do and X deteriorate');

(c)   purpose clauses, which are introduced by the non-factual complementiser *be*:

        (48)   *Nio   aŋ-la   Lae   be   aŋ-re*
                 1SG:NOM   1SG-go   Lae   NF   1SG-see
                 tizi-ŋ.
                 younger.sibling-1SG:GEN
                 'I went to Lae to see my younger brother.'

(d)   the form *uunu* 'reason, basis', related to *u-* 'source, base, clan'.

Pa and *uunu* are frequently combined, particularly in expressions like *pa uunu toro* 'for another reason', *pa uunu ti* 'for this reason', *pa uunu tana* 'for that reason' and *pa so uunu i* 'for what reason?'.

The primitive VERY is expounded by the adverb *kat* 'very, really, exactly':

(49) *Ni   i-kam   mbulu   ambai-ŋa-na*
       3SG:NOM 3SG-do   behaviour good-NMS-3SG:GEN
       kat   p-iti.
       very REF-1PL:INC
       'He does very good things for us.'

(50) *Koroŋ   ti   i-saana.   Mi   nu   k-u*
       thing   this 3SG-bad and 2SG:NOM GEN-2SG
       ta-na   na   i-saana   kat.
       SPEC-GIV GIV 3SG-bad very
       'This one is bad, but that one of yours there is very bad.' or 'That one of yours there is worse than this one here.'

Note from example (50) that comparative notions are typically expressed using *kat*. In negated utterances, *kat* is frequently (but not necessarily) replaced by *pe*. *Pe* only occurs in negated utterances:

(51) *Uraata i-loondo pe / kat som.*
       work   3SG-run   very   NEG
       'The work is not running very well.'

4.6 Time and Place: WHEN, WHERE, AFTER, BEFORE, UNDER, ABOVE

The primitive TIME is expounded by the interrogative word *ŋiizi* 'when?' and the form *mazwaana*, a third-singular form of the inalienable noun *mazwa-* 'space between'. Illustrations of both the spatial and temporal senses of *mazwaana* are:

(52) *Ruumu   ki-ni   i-mbot   la   Aikeŋ   ruumu   ki-ni*
       house   GEN-3SG   3SG-stay go   Aikeŋ   house   GEN-3SG
       mi   Alisa   ruumu   ki-ni   mazwa-n.
       and   Alisa   house   GEN-3SG   between-3PL:GEN
       'His house is in the space between Aikeng's and Alisa's houses.'

(53) *Mazwaana   ta-na,   tubudu   ti-mar*
       time   SPEC-GIV   ancestor.spirit/European 3PL-come
       zen.
       NEG:PERF
       'At that time, the Europeans had not yet come.'

It will be noted that when the noun *mazwa-* has the sense 'space between', it is always inflected with **plural** genitive morphology, since the concept 'between' implies at least two spatial loci with respect to which some third entity is located. When *mazwa-* has the sense 'time', however, it is invariably inflected with **singular** genitive morphology.

The concept PLACE is expressed by the noun *lele* 'place'. There is also a distinct interrogative form *swoi* 'where?' which refers to place.

(54) *Nu   ndeeŋe   koroŋ   ta-na   swoi?*
       2SG:NOM   2SG:find   thing   SPEC-GIV   where?
       'Where did you find that thing?'

(55) *Ni   i-kam   uraata su   lele   toro.*
       3SG:NOM   3SG-do   work   descend   place   other
       'He worked in another place.'

The concepts BEFORE and AFTER are expressed by the two temporal adverbs *muŋgu* 'before, first' and *kaimer* 'later, afterwards'. Resembling these both phonologically and semantically are the two verbs *-muuŋgu* 'precede' and *-kemer* 'come after'.

(56) *Koozi   ti-mbot   Lae. Mi   muŋgu na,   ti-mbot   kar.*
       today   3PL-stay   Lae   and/but before GIV   3PL-stay   village
       'Today they live in Lae. But before, they lived in the village.'

The spatial orientation UNDER is indicated by the inalienable noun *mbarma-* 'place underneath something', and the orientation ABOVE is indicated by the locative adverb *kor* 'high, above'.

(57) *Zin   moori   ti-mbot   ruumu   mbarma-ana.*
       3PL   woman   3PL-stay   house   under-3SG:GEN
       'The women are under the house.'

4.7 Partonomy and Taxonomy: PART OF, KIND OF

The exponent of the classifier KIND OF is the form *mataana*, a form homophonous with the third-person singular form of the noun *mata-* 'eye'. This same form also means 'colour'.

(58) Mbia   mataana   tel: soŋgol,   mbiagap,   mi   muŋesŋes.
     bat   kind   three soŋgol   mbiagap   and muŋesŋes
     'There are three kinds of bats: *soŋgol*, *mbiagap* and *muŋesŋes*.'

An interrogative form *parei-ŋa-na* (literally, 'how?-NMS-3SG:GEN') 'what kind of?' is used to question kinds. Another form, *matakiŋa*, is used to indicate a plurality of different kinds:

(59) Am-kan   kini   matakiŋa.
     1PL:EXC-eat   food   many.different.kinds
     'We ate many different kinds of food.'

The primitive PART is expressed in at least three different ways. First, there are a number of inalienable nouns which express specific, part–whole notions when the part is an **inherent** part of the whole:

> ute-   'top part of, head'
> lwo-   'middle part of, torso, trunk'
> u-   'base/bottom of'
> zilŋa-   'edge of'
> ndeme-   'back part of'

These inalienable nouns are textually the most frequent means of encoding part–whole notions and occur in constructions like the following:

(60) tomtom   ute-ene
     person   top-3SG:GEN
     'the person's head'

(61) Ke   ta-na   lwo-ono   biibi.
     tree   SPEC-GIV   middle-3SG:GEN   big
     'That tree's trunk is big.'

These two examples can serve to illustrate the fact that in Mangap-Mbula there is no predicate meaning 'have a part'. Part–whole notions are always expressed **within** the noun phrase as 'X's part'. To deny that something has a part, a nominalisation like the following is used:

(62) Iti   tomtom wi-som-ŋa-nda.
     1PL:INC person tail-NEG-NMS-1PL:INC:GEN
     'We people do not have tails.' (More literally, 'We people are no-tail ones.')

Non-inherent parts which are easily separated from their wholes are more typically encoded using the inalienable noun *ka-*:

(63) Ruumu   ka   kataama   i-saana   kek.
     house   PASSIVE:3SG:GEN   door   3SG-deteriorate   PERF
     'The house's door has deteriorated.'

(64) wooŋgo ka   saama
     canoe   PASSIVE:3SG:GEN   outrigger
     'the canoe's outrigger'

The most generic exponent of the notion PART is the textually infrequent form *koroŋŋana*, a nominalisation of the noun *koroŋ* 'thing' which co-occurs with *ka-* when the parts are non-inherent, as in (65), and without it when the parts are inherent elements of the whole, as in (66):

(65) Masin   ta-na   ka
     machine   SPEC-GIV   PASSIVE:3SG:GEN
     koroŋ-ŋa-na   boozo.
     thing-NMS-3SG:GEN   many
     'That machine's parts are many.'

(66) Iti   koroŋ-ŋa-nda   boozo: kumbu-ndu,
     1PL:INC thing-NMS-1PL:INC:GEN   many   leg-1PL:INC:GEN
     nama-nda,   ma   koroŋ   ta   kei.
     arm-1PL:INC:GEN   and   thing   SPEC   like
     'Our parts are many: legs, arms, and such things.'

4.8 Descriptors and Evaluators: GOOD, BAD

The exponents of the primitives BE GOOD and BE BAD are straightforward. BE GOOD is manifested by *ambai*, a non-inflecting verb,[19] whereas BE BAD is manifested by *-saana* 'be bad, deteriorate', an inflecting verb:

(67) Iŋgi   ambai.
     this.one good
     'This is good.'

(68) Buza ti   i-saana.
      knife this 3SG-bad
      'This knife is bad.'

The nominalised forms of both verbs are textually nearly as frequent as the verbs themselves:

(69) Iŋgi   kini ambai-ŋa-na.
      this.one food good-NMS-3SG:GEN
      'This is good food.'

(70) Zin   ti-kam   mbulu   sanan-ŋa-na.
      3PL   3PL-do   behaviour bad-NMS-3SG:GEN
      'They did something bad.'

Semantically, *ambai* and *-saana* can be used to refer to either amoral (as in (69)), or moral (as in (70)) goodness and badness.

4.9   Evaluation and Problem Areas

Overall, most of the proposed primitives are readily translatable into Mangap-Mbula. The only areas of difficulty involve: (a) SAY, THINK, WANT and IF; (b) THING; and (c) FEEL.

It is a striking fact in Mangap-Mbula that four of the proposed primitive notions — THINK, SAY, WANT and IF — can be expressed using the same phonological form, *-so*. It is only when their complementation possibilities are considered that these notions are formally distinguished. These possibilities are listed below:

THINK: *-so (ko) S*

SAY: *-so (pa NP) (ta kembei.) (-so) S*

WANT: *-so(=(m)be) XCOMP*   (if the matrix and embedded
                                clauses have the same subject)

        -so(=(m)be) S   (if the matrix and embedded
                                clauses have different subjects)

IF: *-so(=(m)be).XCOMP*

From this listing, it can be seen that only WANT with a same-subject sequence and IF are constructionally identical. However, if intonation is also considered, then these two are distinguished. The high rising intonation on the protases of conditionals, along with the morphemes *na, inako* or *so,* which introduce the apodoses of conditionals, will always distinguish the *-so* meaning IF from the one meaning WANT.

In the case of WANT, it should be reiterated that another, unambiguous exponent of this primitive is available: *lele- be/pa*. In the protases of conditionals, it is this exponent which always occurs:

(71) Ni   i-so-mbe   lele-ene   be   i-la,
      3SG:NOM   3SG-say-NF   insides-3SG:GEN   NF   3SG-go
      na   zem=i   ma   i-la.
      GIV   2SG:let=3SG:ACC   and   3SG-go
      'If he wants to go, then let him go.'

Although there are complementation differences between the various senses of the verb *-so,* this does not vitiate the fact that a single phonological form *-so* can be (and frequently is) used to express four distinct primitives: THINK, SAY, IF, WANT. The multifunctionality of the verb 'to say' has also been noted for the Papuan language Gahuku by Deibler (1971).

The primitive THING is problematic because the language appears to distinguish between entities (*koroŋ, sokorei*) and events (*mbulu, so*). And the primitive FEEL is problematic because no term subsumes both physical and emotional sensations except for the verb *-yamaana*. But *-yamaana* is relatively rare, takes sentential complements, and is not used in canonical expressions like 'X feels good'. The notion FEEL is more normally expressed using various inalienable body-part nouns like *lele-* 'insides' and *ni-* 'body'. These body-part nouns distinguish, however, between emotional and physical feelings.

Notes

1   The author and his wife have lived among the Mangap-Mbula since 1982. The data in this paper reflect the dialect spoken in Yangla Village. Special thanks are due to Mr Giemsa Apei and Mr Moses Gial of Yangla Village who helped me by providing some important contrastive examples. I would also like to express my appreciation to Anna Wierzbicka and Cliff Goddard for their comments on earlier versions of this paper, and to my wife Salme for proofreading it. Special abbreviations used in this paper are: ACCusative case, COMPlementiser, DEMonstrative, DETerminer, EXClusive, GENitive, GIVen from the linguistic or extra-linguistic context, INClusive, LOCative, NEGative, NF non-factual, NMS nominalising suffix, NOMinative case, NP noun phrase, PASSIVE, PERFective, PLural, PROHIBitive, QUANTifier, REFerent case, REFLexive, SG singular, SPEC points to something specific, UC uncertain.
2   REF here stands for referent. The referent preposition *pa/p-* is used in the encoding of almost every conceivable peripheral argument: source, instrument, benefactive, addressee, time, inani-

mate or relatively immobile animate goals and locations, *inter alia*. The only other preposition, *ki*, is used to encode alienable genitives, highly mobile animate goals and locations, and body parts of perception (e.g. 'see with one's eyes').

3   A subset of verbs is morphologically defective, however, and lacks such prefixing.
4   See Lynch (1982) and Lichtenberk (1985) for further discussion of Oceanic genitive constructions. Bugenhagen (1986, 1991) describes the Mangap-Mbula genitives in more detail.
5   The alternation of forms is morphophonemically conditioned, with the monophonemic forms occuring in pronouns.
6   Lichtenberk (1983, 1985) prefers the term 'possessive classifiers' for such forms.
7   Wierzbicka (1992:236, note 6) refers to this notion of allolexy, stating:

> One important theoretical point which became clearer concerns the 'allomorphy' (or 'allolexy') of semantic primitives. For example, if different case forms of the Russian word *kto-o* 'someone' (*kogo-to, komu-to, kom-to*) can count as exponents of the same primitive, so can English words such as *someone, who, person, one* (e.g. in *no-one* or *everyone*), and so on.

8   *Mbulu* can also refer to an individual's characteristic behaviour. For example, to say that someone is a good person, one would normally say *Mbulu kini ambai* 'His behaviour is good'. When it has its 'event' sense, it can refer to acts done by people as well as non-agentive happenings like earthquakes, unusual phenomena in the sky, and so on.
9   Note that there is also an alienable noun *lele* 'place' that is homophonous with *lele-* 'insides'. The form *lele-*, in conjunction with the complementiser *be* or the preposition *pa,* also functions to encode WANT. Two other inalienable nouns which commonly express emotions are *mata-* 'eye' (e.g. *mata- koikoi* 'shy', which is literally 'eye enemy-enemy') and *kopo-* 'stomach' (e.g. *kopo- ruru* 'anxious', which is literally 'stomach seek-seek'). The noun *kuli-* 'skin' is sometimes used in expressing physical sensations as in *kuli- ibayou* 'have a fever', which is literally 'skin be.hot'.
10 When *be* follows *-so*, it is phonologically bound to *-so* and has two alternating forms, *be/mbe*.
11 *Ta* functions as: (a) the numeral 'one'; (b) an indefinite article; (c) a relative clause complementiser; (d) a formative in demonstratives like *tana* 'that one', *taiŋgi* 'this one here, near you and me', *taŋga* 'that one over there away from both you and me'; and (e) a formative in causal conjunctions like *tana* 'therefore' and *tabe* 'and so ...'.
12 Note that the same two senses of 'happen' and 'appear, come into view/being' are also exhibited by the Tok Pisin form *kamap*.
13 Complements of $-pet_1$ which are governed by *pa* may encode either the person **to whom** something happens or the place **where** it happens.
14 The choice between locative and referent prepositional complements for the other senses of *-pet* is determined by animacy. Highly mobile animate locations and goals are expressed using locative prepositional phrases, whereas inanimate or relatively immobile animate locations and goals are encoded by referent phrases.
15 Actually, since the subject NP of the sentential complement is obligatorily omitted and obligatorily coreferential with the subject of the matrix clause, it would be more precise to term it an

XCOMP, following the terminology of Lexical-Functional Grammar (Sells 1985:165).
16 The modal adverbs are distinguished as a form class by their lack of verbal morphology and their ability to occur either before the subject or between the subject and the predicate, with no change in meaning. For example:

Sombe yaŋ i-su ina-ko aŋ-mar som.
if rain 3SG-descend GIV-UC 1SG-come NEG
'If it rains then I won't come.'

Yaŋ sombe i-su ina-ko aŋ-mar som.
rain if 3SG-descend GIV-UC 1SG-come NEG
'If it rains then I won't come.'

17 This same clitic occurs on the verb *-so₂* 'say'.
18 This *so* should not be identified with the verb *-so* 'say'. The *so* meaning 'what?' is a non-inflecting form that derives from Proto-Oceanic *sapa*.
19 *Ambai* is assigned to the verb part of speech despite its lack of verbal inflection because it can only be used predicatively. For it to occur internal to a noun phrase, it must be nominalised; for example, *koroŋ ambaiŋana* 'something good' (literally, 'thing good:one'). **Koroŋ ambai* is ungrammatical. The same phonological form *ambai* can also occur following the object as an adverb meaning 'well'. Thus, it resembles the colloquial American English *good*, which can function either adnominally or adverbially — *You did that real good*.

References

Bugenhagen, Robert D. 1986. "Possession in Mangap-Mbula: Its syntax and semantics". *Oceanic Linguistics* 25.1/2.124-166.
Bugenhagen, Robert D. 1991. *A Grammar of Mangap-Mbula: An Austronesian language of Papua New Guinea*. PhD Thesis, Department of Linguistics, Australian National University, Canberra.
Deibler, Ellis. 1971. "Uses of the Verb 'To Say' in Gahuku". *Kivung* 4.2.101-110.
Evans, Nicholas. 1986. "The Unimportance of CAUSE in Kayardild". *Language in Aboriginal Australia* 2.9-17.
Lichtenberk, Frantisek. 1983. "Relational Classifiers". *Lingua* 60.147-176.
Lichtenberk, Frantisek. 1985. "Possessive Constructions in Oceanic Languages and Proto-Oceanic". *Austronesian Linguistics at the 15th Pacific Sciences Congress* (= Pacific Linguistics C-88) ed. by A. Pawley & L. Carrington, 93-140. Canberra: Australian National University.
Lynch, John. 1982. "Towards a Theory of the Origin of the Oceanic Possessive Constructions". *Papers from the Third International Conference on Austronesian Linguistics*, vol I: *Currents in Oceanic* (= Pacific Linguistics C-74) ed. by A. Halim, L. Carrington & S. A. Wurm, 243-268. Canberra: Australian National University.
Sells, Peter. 1985. *Lectures on Contemporary Syntactic Theories. An introduction to Government-*

Binding Theory, Generalized Phrase Structure Grammar, and Lexical Functional Grammar. (CSLI lecture notes number 3.) Stanford: The Center for the Study of Language and Information.

Wierzbicka, Anna. 1992. "The Search for Universal Semantic Primitives". *Thirty Years of Linguistic Evolution* ed. by Martin Pütz, 215-242. Amsterdam: John Benjamins.

Mandarin Semantic Primitives

Hilary Chappell
La Trobe University, Melbourne

The belief in the existence of a universal language or 'alphabet of the human mind' shares part of its history with the study of the Chinese language by European scholars.[1] This gained momentum in the early seventeenth century, influencing philosophers such as Gottfried Leibniz in his search for this *universelle Begriffssprache* 'universal conceptual language' (q.v. Harbsmeier 1979:9–16; Mungello 1977:53–68). This view was reinforced by descriptions of the striking absence of grammatical categories such as case, person, number, gender, voice, mood and tense in Chinese in contrast with the noun declensions and verb conjugations of the classical Indo-European languages such as Greek, Latin and Sanskrit. Linguistic elements were seen to be used in their 'absolute' form without any designation of word class.

This set of features is, in fact, commonly associated with languages of the analytic or isolating type such as the Sinitic branch of the Sino-Tibetan language family, to which Mandarin belongs. Mandarin can thus be more appropriately described as a 'semantics prior' discourse-oriented language in terms of the primary level at which grammatical and syntactic strategies are determined (see also Li & Thompson 1978:226; Tsao 1978:189, 1979; Chen 1986; La Polla 1990). Discourse considerations can be used to explain why several word orders are possible for simple clauses in Mandarin: SVO, SOV, OSV and topic–comment including the double-subject construction SSV as a subtype.

In general, the structural principle of Mandarin grammar is for the modifier to precede the modified. Hence, attributive and relative clauses precede their head noun while not only adverbs but also locative, benefactive and instrumental phrases precede the main verb.[2] Specification of the category of number is linked to the semantic categorisation of nominals since the use of an appropriate classifier is obligatory upon enumeration in Mandarin. Most of the few affixes and grammatical morphemes in Mandarin are atonal suffixes used to modify verbs aspectually or to nominalise nouns, form their diminutives and derive new nouns. These atonal morphemes also include a large set of polysemous utterance-final modal particles which are used to express the speaker's attitude (see, for example, Chappell 1991b).

The approach taken in this analysis of Mandarin is that only a small subset of lexemes and expressions of a natural spoken language serves as a potential 'key' or metalanguage in directly representing basic conceptual building blocks, a framework of semantic analysis advocated and developed by Anna Wierzbicka (1972, 1980, 1985, 1989a, 1989b, 1991) and Cliff Goddard (1989, 1991). In the main section of the paper, the eight classes of primitives proposed by Goddard and Wierzbicka (see chapter 2) are discussed in turn for Mandarin: (1) substantives and pronouns; (2) mental predicates; (3) determiners and quantifiers; (4) actions and events; (5) meta-predicates; (6) time and place; (7) meronymy and taxonomy; and (8) evaluators and descriptors. Most of the data are elicited for the purpose of creating the set of test sentences with the primitives in their canonical contexts in order to provide a comparative corpus for this volume. Where possible, I have supplemented this with data from transcriptions of recorded conversations and narratives to add utterances from natural contexts. The data are transcribed using the *pīnyīn* system officially adopted in China in 1958 which is used as an ancillary writing system to the character script.

5.1 Substantives: I, You, Someone, Something, People

5.1.1 Wǒ *I* and Nǐ *YOU (SG); Pronouns*

(1) *Wǒ   xiǎng qù   kàn   wǒ   nǎinai*
    I   want go see I   grandma
    'I want to go and see my grandma.'

(2) *Wǒ   yào   hé   nǐ   yìqǐ   qù*
    I   want with you together go
    'I want to go with **you**.'

The deictic words referring to speaker and addressee in Mandarin are *wǒ* I and *nǐ* YOU (SG) respectively. Although Asian languages are well-known for their complicated politeness phenomena, Mandarin has no grammatically coded speech levels, possessing polite forms only for the second-person pronouns, *nín* 'you (singular, polite)' and *nínmen* 'you (plural, polite)'. The plural form is however rare in the spoken register. In agreement with Wierzbicka (1989a, 1989b, 1991), I do not consider these to be the basic forms. The singular neutral forms *wǒ* I and *nǐ* YOU (SG) are thus proposed as the two basic pronouns representing the indispensable discourse participants in face-to-face interaction — the speaker and the addressee.

5.1.2 Shéi *SOMEONE*: Indefinite Pronoun

It has been observed cross-linguistically that interrogative pronouns frequently double as indefinite pronouns (for example, see Wierzbicka 1991). I argue in this section that the pronoun *shéi* 'who, someone' is the best candidate to code SOMEONE in Mandarin, considering briefly the possibility of the expression *yǒu rén* 'there is a person/people'.

The Mandarin interrogative pronoun *shéi* 'who', exemplified in (3), can also function as an indefinite pronoun 'someone', 'anyone' or 'everyone', depending on the construction type.

(3)   *Shéi gàn de?*
       who   do   NOM
       '**Who** did it?'

The first function of *shéi* as an indefinite pronoun, meaning 'someone' or 'anyone', is not restricted to any syntactic position or semantic role. In (4), it is found post-verbally in a question utterance as semantic patient of the main verb, while in (5), it is in clause-initial position of a complement clause as semantic agent:

(4)   *Nǐ zhèlǐ rènshi shéi ma?*
       2SG here know who Q
       'Do you know **anyone** here?'

(5)   *Wǒ xīwàng shéi néng shèngrèn zhèige gōngzuò*
       1SG hope who can be:competent this:CL work
       'I hope **someone** will be competent to do this work.'

The second function of *shéi* as an indefinite pronoun, meaning 'everyone', is restricted to pre-verbal position, where in conjunction with the adverbials *dōu* 'all' or *yě* 'also', it codes 'everyone' or, correspondingly, 'no-one (not), anyone' in negated sentences, as in (6); that is, either all members of a class or none, depending on the polarity of the utterance:

(6)   *Shéi dōu (bù) yuànyì zuò*
       who all (NEG) willing do
       '**Everyone** (no-one) is willing to do this.'

Apart from the construction type in (6), *shéi* only occurs in utterance-initial position when used as either the interrogative pronoun 'who' (see (3) above) or in a third construction type, where it codes a representative member of a class, corresponding to English 'whoever':

(7)   *Shéi lái-wán le, shéi jiù méi yǒu diǎnxīn chī*
        who come-late CRS who then NEG provide snack eat
        '**Whoever** comes late, won't get any snacks.'

In contradistinction to these uses of *shéi* who, someone', the VO expression *yǒu rén* (literally, 'there:be person/people') can be interpreted as either 'there is a person', 'there are people' or simply 'someone'. It is subject, however, to a greater number of discourse, semantic and grammatical restrictions than *shéi*. This expression is used, for example, clause-initially as a discourse strategy for introducing nouns which are 'new' or non-referential in information status, since the discourse preference of Mandarin is for clause-initial nouns to be given (see also Chao 1968; Li & Thompson 1981).

(8)   *Yǒu rén huì bāngzhù nǐ*
        there:be person will help 2SG
        '**Someone** will help you.'

A grammatical restriction on *yǒu rén* 'someone' is that it cannot occur utterance-finally, as (9) shows. It may turn up as a pivot noun, however, where it acts as both post-verbal object of a matrix verb and agent of the following embedded verb in complex structures such as (10):

(9)   * *Wǒ kànjiàn yǒu rén*
        1SG see there:be person

(10)   *Wǒ kànjiàn yǒu rén zài qiāo tā de mén*
        1SG see there:be person PROG knock 3SG DE door
        'I saw **someone** knocking on her door.'

Semantically, *yǒu rén* 'someone' is restricted to humans, and cannot normally refer to supernatural beings such as spirits and gods, unlike *shéi*. Given these three kinds of restrictions on *yǒu rén*, I choose *shéi* 'who, someone' as the exponent of SOMEONE in Mandarin.

5.1.3   Shénme SOMETHING; *Indefinite Pronoun*

The two main candidates for this primitive in Mandarin are a noun, *dōngxi* 'thing', and the indefinite pronoun *shénme* 'something, anything', which also functions as an interrogative pronoun 'what, which', analogous to the situation described in section 5.1.2 for SOMEONE. The close relationship between the interrogative and indefinite uses of *shénme* in Mandarin is shown by example (11) for questions and (12) for the indefinite pronoun:

(11) *Zhè shì shénme?*
this be what
'**What** is this?'

(12) *Nǐ mǎi shénme le ma?*
2SG buy something CRS Q
'Have you bought **anything**?'

I argue that the indefinite pronoun *shénme* 'what, which' should be chosen in preference to *dōngxi* 'thing' as the equivalent to SOMETHING due to the fact that it is more general and vague in reference than *dōngxi* 'thing'. Consider the following pair of examples:

(13) *Zuótiān wǒ jìn-mén de shíhou, kànjiàn*
yesterday 1SG enter-door DE time see
*zhuōzi-shang yǒu yībāo **shénme***
table-on there:be one:CL something
'Yesterday, as I came in, I noticed there was a parcel of **something** on the table.'

(14) *Zuótiān wǒ jìn-mén de shíhou, kànjiàn*
yesterday 1SG enter-door DE time see
*zhuōzi-shang yǒu yībāo **dōngxi***
table-on there:be one:CL thing
'Yesterday, as I came in, I noticed there was a parcel of **things** on the table.'

When the term *shénme* 'what/something/anything' in (13) is changed to *dōngxi* 'thing' in (14), it implies that there is some concrete object which the speaker has seen but does not want to identify, whereas with *shénme* 'something', uncertainty as to the nature of the object is uppermost: it cannot be identified. Hence, the noun *dōngxi* 'thing(s)' refers to referentially vague objects in its prototypical use, not to indefinites, whereas *shénme* 'something' clearly retains its 'ignorative' sense when used in this way. Moreover, it is not restricted to tangible phenomena as is the case for *dōngxi* 'thing(s)' but may refer to concepts and events.

A third possibility, *mǒu shì*, literally 'certain matter', is virtually restricted to written rather than spoken Chinese and is excluded from consideration on these grounds.

5.1.4 Rénmen *and* Rén *PEOPLE; Nouns*

There are three lexemes in Mandarin coding notions related to the semantic field of

PEOPLE. These are: *rén* 'person, people', which lacks any inherent number distinction, typical of unmodified monosyllabic nouns in Mandarin; *rénmen* 'people', which morphologically appears to be the explicit plural of *rén* formed by adding the suffix *-men*, but is not semantically; and the political concept *rénmín* 'the people'. I argue that the noun *rénmen* 'people' should be chosen as the exponent of this primitive, with *rén* 'person, people' serving as its allolex when used in a complex noun phrase and compound noun function.

The term *rénmín* is a compound of two morphemes both separately meaning 'people' and is used in many expressions belonging to the domain of government and politics such as in the political slogan *Wèi rénmín fúwù!* (literally, 'for people serve') 'Serve the **people**!' or in the official name for China — *Zhōnghuá Rénmín Gònghéguó* — 'the **People**'s Republic of China'. Such examples indicate that *rénmín* is not a highly colloquial term used to express 'people'. Hence, we can exclude it from further discussion.

Although the term *rénmen* 'people' is morphologically composed of *rén* 'person' and the plural suffix *-men*, its semantic structure is not a simple addition of these meanings to form the plural, since it further conveys the popularist rather than political concept of 'people', in the sense of a community or society one belongs to, sharing certain values, beliefs and customs. This is uppermost in the following example:

(15) *Rúguǒ nǐ   zhèyàng zuò, **rénmen** huì shuō*
      if   2SG this:way do   people   will say
      nǐ   de huàihuà
      2SG DE bad:words
      'If you do this, **people** will say malicious things about you.'

The possession of human qualities is the significant conceptualisation behind the unmodified use of *rén* 'person, people' as a free morpheme, and not the idea of people as social beings. Hence *rén* contains an implicit contrast to animals and inanimate beings as its primary meaning:

(16) ***Rén** shì gāojí   dòngwù*
      people   be   high:class animal
      '**Humans** are higher order animals.'

(17) *Tā   bù   shì **rén***
      3SG NEG be   person
      'He is not **human**.'

It is thus not normally possible for semantic reasons to substitute either *rénmen* 'people (viewed as social beings)', a concept similar in meaning and register to the American English usage 'the folks', or *rénmín* 'the people (viewed as a political entity)' into this context, even though (18) is grammatically well-formed:

(18) ? ***Rénmen*** (/ ***rénmín***)   shì   gāojí   dòngwù
       people   (people)   be   high:class animal
     ? 'The folks (/the people) are higher order animals.'

In terms of syntagmatic relations, *rénmen* and *rén* are diametrically opposed: *rénmen* has to remain morphologically indefinite, that is, it cannot take any modifiers directly preceding it, iconically reflecting its inherently non-referential nature.[3] In (19), there is modification by a quantifier *xŭduō* 'many', while in (20) there is modification by a demonstrative pronoun and a plural classifier, *xiē*, yet neither is possible with *rénmen*. Similarly, in (21), it is only *rén* which can form a compound noun (see also (87) below):

(19)   * *xŭduō rénmen*   *xŭduō rén*
         many people   many person
                                  'many people'

(20)   * *zhèxiē rénmen*   *zhèxiē rén*
         this:CL people   this:CL person
                                  'these people'

(21)   * *Zhōngguó rénmen*   *Zhōngguórén*
         China   people   China:person
                                  'Chinese person/people'

The use of *rén* in complex noun phrases and in compounds can be viewed as an allolex of *rénmen* for 'people', given the complementary nature of restrictions on attributive modification for these two words. In this second function, it identically codes the generic sense of PEOPLE as members of a social group, but unlike *rénmen* permits referential specification and individuation.

These data show that *rénmen* codes the generic concept 'people' since it aptly codes the popularist, societal meaning as opposed to both the political concept of people coded by *rénmín* 'the people' and the unmodified use of *rén* 'person, people' focusing on human qualities. Hence, *rénmen* is the best candidate in Mandarin for the primitive PEOPLE.

5.2   Mental Predicates: THINK, KNOW, SAY, FEEL, WANT

5.2.1   Xiăng THINK; Cognitive Verbs

There is a large number of verbs which belong to the cognitive domain in Mandarin. In this section, I propose that the verb *xiăng* 'think' is the best candidate, since it is most appropriate if the sense is the Cartesian one of thinking as a uniquely human ability. This verb can take either a noun or a complement clause as its object:

(22)   Wǒ   **xiǎng**   shì   tā   gěi   chī   le
       1SG think   be   3SG GEI   eat   CRS
       '**I think** it's been eaten by him.'

Another posibility is *rènwéi* 'consider, think' which, however, is more typical of formal and written registers. It could be used, for example, during a discussion at an important political meeting to express one's thoughts on a matter, as in (23). This accounts for its more serious and forceful tone in comparison with both *xiǎng* 'think' and a third verb, *kàn*, that is highly colloquial in register and means 'be of the view' or 'according to'. This is related to its primary sense of 'look'. Its meaning does not necessarily include reference, however, to the process of thinking by which the subject arrives at the resulting point of view:

(23)   Wǒ   **rènwéi / kàn / xiǎng**   zánmen   zuì-hǎo   bié   qù
       1SG consider   view   think   1PL:INC   better   NEG   go
       '**I consider/I am of the view/I think** it would be better for us not to go.'

In addition to these three verbs, there is also the complementiser verb *juéde* which means 'to feel', not just with respect to physical sensation (see discussion of FEEL coded into Mandarin simplex clauses in section 5.2.4), but rather to one's conviction based on intuition and experience:

(24)   Wǒ   **juéde**   zhè   shìr   bù   duìjìnr
       1SG feel   this   matter   NEG   normal
       '**I feel** there's something fishy about this.'

It would be semantically and thus stylistically odd to substitute *rènwéi* 'consider' for *juéde* 'feel, think' in (24) since the use of *bù duìjìnr* 'fishy, irregular' makes the utterance highly colloquial. In addition, two semantically specialised verbs are excluded from consideration on the grounds of their restricted semantics. These are *kǎolǜ* 'to think over' (cf. German *sich überlegen*), which implies a time lapse before some decision is reached, and *yǐwéi*, which itself has two basic uses: (a) 'to mistakenly think' and (b) 'to think, consider'. The second use is largely restricted to academic writing and hence its primary meaning of 'mistakenly think' is the relevant one for (25):

(25)   Wǒ   **yǐwéi** *(rènwéi / kàn / xiǎng)*   shì   zhī   shùxióng
       1SG think   (consider   view   think) be   CL   koala
       '**I thought** it was a koala (but it turned out to be a cat).'

If *rènwéi* 'consider' were substituted for *yǐwéi* in (25), an appropriate context would be one of scientific determination of the species ('I consider (or judge) it to be a koala'), while *kàn* 'be of the view' would belong to a much less serious context and consequently serve as a less imposing claim as to which species of animal it was ('In my view, it's a koala (and not a cat)'), and *xiǎng* 'think' would be the semantically unembellished statement 'I think it's a koala', based on one's knowledge and implying the requisite amount of intellectual activity to arrive at this conclusion. The verb *juéde* 'to feel, have an opinion' cannot be used appropriately in the context of intellectual discrimination — in this example, of an animal species — since its meaning is based on the notion of feeling.

The basic verb of thinking is thus *xiǎng*, which is proposed here as the Mandarin primitive. In contrast to the other verbs described above, *xiǎng* 'think' has this concept as its primary meaning while not being restricted to either colloquial or written registers.

5.2.2 Zhīdao KNOW; Verb

The verb *zhīdao* 'know' contrasts with *rènshi* 'know, be familiar' in the same way that *savoir* contrasts with *connaître* in French, or *wissen* with *kennen* in German: it refers to factual and acquired knowledge, as opposed to the 'recognition' kind of knowledge gained through experience and familiarity coded by *rènshi*. The use of *zhīdao* in (26) refers to knowing the sequence of streets that will lead to one's destination, including contexts where the subject has never been to the place before but has carefully studied a map. If *rènshi* were used instead, it would refer to ability of the subject to recognise and identify the streets and roads through prior experience.

(26)   Wǒ   zhīdao   (rènshi)   zhètiáo lù
       1SG   know   (be:familiar)   this:CL   road
       'I **know** this way.'

Zhīdao may also be used with complement clauses whereas *rènshi* cannot:

(27)   Wǒ   zhīdao   (*rènshi)   tā   bù   néng lái
       1SG   know   (*be:familiar)   3SG   NEG   can   come
       'I know that she can't come.'

There are several other cognitive verbs in Mandarin — *tǐhuì* 'know, realise through experience', *dǒngde* 'know, grasp' and *liǎojiě* 'understand' — which have specialised meanings that result in certain semantic co-occurrence restrictions on their nominal and clausal object complements. As a result of this, none could be substituted for *zhīdao* in (27), and need not be further considered.

5.2.3 Shuō SAY; Verb

The verb *shuō* 'to say, speak, talk' is the most semantically general of the speech act verbs, contrasting, for example, with *tán* 'talk, chat', *liǎo-tiān* 'chat', *jiǎng* 'say, tell, explain' and *tǎolùn* 'discuss'.

Shuō codes not only a specific instance of a speech act, translated by 'say' in (28), but also the activity of talking, as in (29):

(28)   Tā   yě   shì   zhèyàng **shuō** de
      3SG   also be   this:way **say**   NOM
      'She **said** the same.'

(29)   Wǒ   **shuō**-le   bàntiān   tā   hái   shì   bù   tīng
      1SG   say-PFV   half:day 3SG   still be   NEG   listen
      'I've **talked** to him for ages, but he still won't listen to me.'

The verbs *shuō* and *jiǎng* are the only ones in this group which may be used as quotative verbs for direct speech. *Shuō* can be used in all kinds of situations, its quotative use exemplified by (30):

(30)   Tāmen **shuō** "Gǔpiào yào   zhǎng   jià"
      3PL   say   share   want   inflate value
      'They **said**, "The price of shares is about to go up".'

Jiǎng has a more specialised meaning of to talk with a didactic purpose as in a formal speech: *Máo Zhǔxí/Sūn Zhōngshān jiǎng-guo:...* 'Chairman Mao/Sun Yatsen once said:...'. This is also apparent in VO compound verbs such as *jiǎng-yán* 'give a lecture' and *jiǎng-kè* 'give a class'. As a result of these considerations, the more general and less formal verb, *shuō*, is chosen as the best candidate for this concept in Mandarin.

5.2.4 Expressions for FEEL: Gǎnjué and Gǎndào; Verbs

In informal spoken registers of Mandarin, feelings are typically directly expressed by the appropriate stative verb of emotion,[4] psychological event or physical perception (heat, cold, etc.) without it being necessary to use any of the verbs meaning 'to feel':

(31)   Wǒ   hěn   shēngqì / gāoxìng / shīwàng   / lěng
      1SG   very   angry   happy   disappointed   cold
      'I'm very angry/happy/disappointed/cold.'

It is possible, of course, to add in either of two verbs meaning 'to feel', namely *găndào* 'feel, perceive', as in (32), or *juéde* 'feel', as in (33), which can be used in combination with the specific verb of psychological or physical state. Note, however, that *juéde* 'feel' is much more restricted in its distribution than *găndào* 'feel, perceive' such that when it co-occurs with *lěng* 'cold' in (34), it is not understood as body temperature, unlike the case with *găndào* 'to feel' in (32), but rather as part of an elliptical complement clause referring to the weather or external temperature. Correspondingly, the syntactic structure with *juéde* 'feel' in (34) is interpreted as a complex clause containing the complementiser verb 'to feel that, find that':

(32) *Wǒ găndào hěn cánkuì / hàipà / lěng*
      1SG feel   very ashamed   afraid   cold
      'I **feel** very ashamed/afraid/cold.'

(33) *Wǒ juéde hěn cánkuì / nánguò*
      1SG feel   very ashamed   sad
      'I **feel** very ashamed/sad.'

(34) *Wǒ juéde hěn lěng*
      1SG feel   very cold
      'I **feel** (find) that it is very cold.' (Not 'I feel very cold.')

Another possible candidate is *gănjué* which functions both as a verb 'to feel, sense' and a noun meaning 'feeling'. Unlike *găndào* 'feel, perceive' and *juéde* 'feel, find that', in its verbal use *gănjué* cannot co-occur with specific verbs of psychological state, as (35) shows, but only with those denoting one's general state of well-being. This is exemplified by (36), a typical adjacency pair in a medical consultation or conversation with a concerned friend:

(35) * *Wǒ gănjué hěn nánguò / cánkuì / gāoxìng*
      1SG feel   very sad   ashamed   happy

(36) *Nǐ gănjué zěnmeyàng?*
      2SG feel   how
      'How are you feeling?'

      Wǒ gănjué hěn hǎo / bù hǎo
      1SG feel   very good   NEG good
      'I'm **feeling** very well/unwell.'

The syntactic distribution of these two types of verbs meaning 'to feel' is complementary, since neither *găndào* 'feel, perceive' nor *juéde* 'feel, find that' can make general reference to a person's well-being in simple clauses, as is shown by (37) and (38):

(37)   ? *Nǐ **gǎndào** zěnmeyàng?*
       2SG feel   how

   * *Wǒ **gǎndào** hěn hǎo   /   bù   hǎo*
       1SG feel   very good   NEG good

(38)   *Nǐ   **juéde** (zhè:běn xiǎoshuō) zěnmeyàng?*
       2SG feel   (this:CL   novel)   how
       'What do you think (of this novel)?'

       *Wǒ   **juéde** hěn hǎo   /   bù   hǎo*
       1SG feel   very good   NEG good
       'I **feel** it is very good/not very good.' (Not 'I feel very good/bad.')

The use of *gǎndào* in (37) is semantically awkward in a question about general state of health since it normally codes a judgement as to the specific feeling or emotion. (It could thus be used in a different context to question a person's particular state of well-being.) Furthermore, the answer in (37) is not acceptable with the stative verb *hǎo* 'be good, well' since it is not adequately specific, nor can it be interpreted as part of an elliptical complex clause. This contrasts to the use of *juéde* in both (34) and (38). The elliptical form of a complex clause in (38) asks for one's opinion about something (here, about a novel) and not about the addressee's inner state of well-being. (See also example (24) above with *juéde*.)

For the reasons discussed above, *gǎnjué* is chosen as the basic term for FEEL in terms of a person's well-being, while *gǎndào* 'to feel, perceive, realise' acts as its allolex in contexts specifying the precise psychological or physical state. The possibility of *juéde* is excluded since it focuses on the judgement of a psychological state and is restricted in the number of stative verbs for emotions with which it can co-occur.

5.2.5 Yào WANT; Verb

It is a simple matter to identify this primitive in Mandarin as the verb *yào* 'want', as in (39) below and (2) above:

(39)   *Gèng   zhòngyào   shì wǒmen **yào**   tígāo   xuésheng*
       more   important be   PL   want   raise   student
       xuéxí   Yīngyǔ   de   nénglì
       study   English DE   ability
       'It is more important that we **want** to improve the ability of students to study English.' (Kubler & Ho 1984:21)

Other potential candidates such as *yuànyì* 'to be willing' and *xǐhuan* 'to like, desire' can be excluded due to their more specialised meanings. The verb *yào* can also be used to express the related meanings of 'order, ask for', as in (40), or in another modal function to express the immediate future 'going to, about to' (see example (30)):

(40) Xiànzài nǐ   de dōngxi ne, nǐ **yào** wǒmen
      now   2SG DE thing RP 2SG ask 1PL
      bāng nǐ, shì bāng nǐ   zhǎo qiánbāo?
      help 2SG be help 2SG find wallet
      'Now how about your things, do you **want** us (*or* are you **asking** us) to help you, help you find your wallet?' (*Hong Kong Police* 1990:14)

5.3 Determiners and Quantifiers: THIS, THE SAME, OTHER, ONE, TWO, ALL, MANY

5.3.1 Zhè(ge) *THIS; Demonstrative Pronoun*

The equivalent of THIS in Mandarin syntactically requires a classifier when used to modify a noun, in the same way as a numeral does, in the spoken register. The general and default classifier in Mandarin, *ge*, is thus chosen here to represent this obligatory grammatical feature of the noun phrase. Example (41), from a recorded conversation, shows three instances of *zhè* 'this' with different classifiers including individuating *ge* and the plural classifier *xiē* to indicate referents that are given or specific in their information status. Example (42) shows its basic demonstrative (or deictic) use in post-verbal object position:

(41) Jiù   shì **zhè:ge** Xiānggǎng rén ... **zhè:xiē**
      then be this:CL Hong Kong person this:CL
      jǐngchá a   **zhè:xiē** rén
      police RP this:CL   person
      'So it's **the** Hong Kong people, **these** police, **these** people.'
      (*Hong Kong Police* 1990:3)

(42) Kàn-kàn **zhè:ge**
      Look-look this
      'Look at **this**.'

The Mandarin equivalent of the adverbial expression of manner 'like this' also uses *zhè* to modify another classifier, *yàng* 'sort, way' (see also section 5.5.4 on LIKE):

(43)   Tā   shì **zhèyàng** zuò / chàng / tiào de
      3SG be   this:way   do   sing   dance NOM
      'She did it/sang/danced like **this**.' (Literally, 'She did it this way.')

A third deictic use of *zhè* is where it occurs utterance-initially and does not require a classifier, as in (11): **Zhè shì shénme?** 'What is this?'. In this example, it deictically 'point outs' either an object or a situation. The common element in all cases can be identified as the morpheme *zhè* THIS.

5.3.2   Tóng *THE SAME*

The word *same* in English (as opposed to the primitive THE SAME) is ambiguous: depending on the context, it can mean either 'identical' ('one and the same') or 'similar' ('the same kind'). In many other languages, such as German and Mandarin, the two meanings are given separate morphological treatment. In German, there are two different lexemes: *der-, die-, dasselbe* (nominative case) for 'same (identical)', as opposed to *gleich* 'same (similar)'; while in Mandarin there are two analytical expressions based on the morpheme *tóng* THE SAME: *tóng yī* (+ CL) 'same (identical)' (literally, 'same one'), formed with the primitive for ONE — *yī(ge)* — as opposed to *tóngyàng* 'same (similar)' (literally, 'same:sort'). Mandarin clearly makes the type–token distinction explicit in this area of its lexicon. Hence for events or actions affecting one and the same individual, Mandarin uses *tóng yīge rén* 'the same person' for the 'identical token' meaning, as in examples (44) and (45), or *tóng yīge dìfāng* 'same place', as in (90), while for the identical course of action (used on a different occasion), *tóngyàng* 'same way' is used, as exemplified in (46):[5]

(44)   Zhè shì   fāshēng zài **tóng yī:ge**   rén   shēn-shang
       this matter happen   at   same one:CL person   body-on
       'This happened to **the same** person.'

(45)   Tā   yǐwéi shì **tóng yī:ge**   rén
       3SG think be   same one:CL person
       'He (mistakenly) thought it was **the same** person.'

(46)   Wǒ   xiǎng yòng **tóngyàng** de fāngshì qù zuò
       1SG intend use   same:way   DE method   go do
       'I want to do **the same**.'

Although *yīyàng* 'same' (literally, 'one:sort/way') appears, at first, to be another possibility, its meaning is restricted to that of 'similarity', that is, the same type or 'same sort'. It does not code the concept of identity of two objects or referents nor can it be substituted into the examples above in the relevant noun phrases in the form of *yīyàng de rén* ('same DE person') in (44) or (45) or *yīyàng de fāngshì* ('same DE method') in (46). The morpheme *tóng* THE SAME is thus chosen to represent this primitive in Mandarin.

5.3.3 Lìng(wài) OTHER

The term 'other' in English has two main interpretations: 'additional/extra' (cf. *another*) and 'different'. The first meaning is expressed in Mandarin by *lìng* or, more colloquially, by use of the compound *lìngwài*, and the second meaning by *bié(de)* 'other'. Consider the following example:

(47) Tā   yǐwéi shì   **lìngwài** yī:ge   rén   / **bié** rén
      3SG   think be   another   one:CL   person   other   person
      'She (mistakenly) thought it was **another** person.'

In example (47), the attributive *lìngwài* means 'other' when referring to additional objects, typically belonging to the same category (specifically, one's social group in this example), while *bié* is used in the sense of both different and separate (that is, belonging to a different social group from the speaker's). Thus, the choice hinges on whether the speaker's presupposition or the context involves additional tokens of the same type as the given referent (where no contrast is implicit) or a token of a different type which sets up an implicit contrast with the first one. The two following examples reinforce this explanation:

(48) Zhèjiàn   shì   wǒmen   jiù   tán-dào   zhèlǐ,
      this:CL   matter   1PL   then   talk-to   here
      ràng   wǒmen   tán   **bié**   de   shì   ba
      let   1PL   talk   other   DE   matter   RP
      'That's enough discussion of this. How about we talk about something **else**?'

(49) Zhèjiàn   shì   wǒmen   jiù   tán-dào   zhèlǐ,
      this:CL   matter   1PL   then   talk-to   here
      ràng   wǒmen   tán   **lìngwài**   yījiàn   shì   ba
      let   1PL   talk   other   one:CL   matter   RP
      'That's enough discussion of this. How about we talk about **another** item?'

In (48), the use of *bié* 'other' implies a completely different item, contrasted with the matter that has just been discussed. This contrast implies a greater scope for the set of possible items to be discussed than for *lìngwài*, exemplified in (49), which refers to an additional, possibly related matter on the agenda. The same applies to (90) with *lìng yīge dìfāng* 'another place' as referring to an additional token of the same type (not a contrasting location).

Although *lìngwài* '(an)other' frequently implies just 'one other' or 'another' in its scope, note that this can be more than 'one' other entity:

(50)   Wǒ   kànjiàn   nǐ-le,   hái   yǒu   **lìngwài**   liǎngge rén
       1SG   see   2SG-CRS   also   have other   two:CL person
       'I saw you and two **others** as well.'

The best choice for OTHER in Mandarin is therefore *lìng(wài)* 'another'. The concept of 'different type or kind' can be handled by the negation of *tóng yī:ge zhǒnglèi* 'same kind', discussed below in section 5.7.2. A third possibility is *qítā* 'other' which can be immediately excluded on the grounds that the term is typical of the written register and Classical Chinese.

5.3.4   Yī(ge) ONE and Liǎng(ge) TWO; Numerals

The concepts ONE and TWO are the basis of any counting system, where theoretically this process should involve adding on tokens of the same kind, one by one. There is a linguistic reflection of this in Mandarin in that objects can only be counted whose nouns can take the same classifier, whether it be the general classifier *ge* or a more specific one. In other words, the concepts of ONE (oneness or identity) and TWO ('twoness' or two of the same kind) are needed, since by means of a cumulative process, these can be used to arrive at any quantity. Support for this comes in the form of the primitive concepts SAME and OTHER, which both presume a minimum of two objects or concepts to compare. More than these two objects can be expressed either in a general manner by use of the primitive for MANY (see section 5.3.6) or by means of a specific numeral, noting, however, that numeral systems will differ greatly, being culture-specific — for example, being based on binary, quinary, septimal or decimal systems. Beyond TWO, it is a matter of the individual language as to which quantities and how many will be lexified.

The numeral for TWO in Mandarin is *liǎng(ge)* 'two(CL)' while that for ONE is *yī(ge)* 'one(CL)', discussed above in section 5.3.2 with respect to SAME (see examples (44) and (45)):

(51)   Nà   **liǎng**:ge   jǐngchá   yě   méi   fàn   chī   zuò
       that two:CL   police   also   NEG   food   eat   sit
       zài   nàr   xiě
       at   there   write
       'Those **two** police hadn't had anything to eat but were still sitting there writing.' (*Hong Kong Police* 1990:20)

When reference is being made to a particular category of objects (*zhǒng* KIND), the grammar obligatorily requires the use of the appropriate classifier for stating the quantity. The combination **liǎng jǐngchá* is therefore not grammatically acceptable in (51) for modern spoken Chinese without any classifier. The following qualification needs to be made, however, with respect to the use of *liǎng* TWO: in terms of abstract counting, where no set of objects is being enumerated, Mandarin makes use of the morpheme *èr* TWO for cardinal numbers. This also applies to ordinals based on TWO such as *dì' èr(ge)* 'the second', as **dìliǎngge* is not acceptable with the prefix *dì* which forms ordinals in Mandarin. In a classifier construction of the form *Numeral + Classifier + Noun*, *liǎng* must, however, be used with measure units less than ten for most individual classifiers, as shown in both (50) and (51), while for compound numbers, *èr* is used to form most measure units greater than ten, for example *èrshíèr(ge)* 'twenty-two'. The 'exception' to the rule is found in written and classical Chinese where one may find expressions such *xiōngdì èr rén* (literally, 'brothers two people') 'the two brothers'. Notably, the classifier is often absent in these styles of writing (see also Chao (1968:567–578) for further variation). Consequently, I propose that the concept for TWO represents a case of allolexy in Mandarin with both *liǎng* and *èr* being needed, while for the primitive ONE, *yī(ge)* is chosen.

5.3.5 Dōu *ALL; Adverb*

The concept ALL is expressed adverbially in Mandarin by *dōu*, which has the unusual feature of having the immediately preceding noun in its scope rather than the following predicate, unlike most other adverbs in Mandarin:

(52) *Ta   bǎ   nü'er   dōu   jià-chūqu   le*
      3SG BA daughter   all   marry-away CRS
      'He has given away **all** his daughters in marriage.'

Dōu 'all' is the unmarked semantically neutral choice for this primitive. Other lexemes in this general domain such as *suǒyǒu(de)* 'all, every (tokens of one kind)', *quán* 'entire(ly), complete(ly)', *quánbù* 'the whole lot', *yīqiè* 'everything (all different kinds)' and *zhěng(ge)* 'whole' show subtle differences in meaning. *Zhěng(ge)* 'whole' may only have a single entity in its scope, and thus can be dismissed from further consideration on these grounds. Similarly, the terms *quán* 'entire(ly)' and *quánbù* 'the whole lot' treat a group of objects as a collective or unity, defocusing any constituent parts, as opposed to the concept of ALL through which a totality is viewed as an accumulation of entities (see Sapir 1930). *Yīqiè* 'every, everything' can function as a noun or attributive but is more typical of formal registers. Furthermore, its scope includes a grouping of 'all different kinds', thus excluding it as a possibility. Of the remaining two words, the closest competition to *dōu* for expressing ALL would be *suǒyǒu* 'all', referring to a totality of entities of the same kind. However, it cannot be used in sentence constructions without *dōu* 'all' to accompany it, as (53) shows. Furthermore, it can only function as an attributive. The presence of two morphemes with the meaning 'all' in (53) creates a more serious and emphatic context:

(53)   Tā   bǎ   suǒyǒu:de   nǚ'er   *(dōu)   jià-chūqù   le
        3SG   BA   all:DE   daughter   all   marry-away   CRS
        'He has given away **all** his daughters in marriage (and not a single one is left).'

The use of the adverb *dōu* alone is neutral in this respect. A final example with *dōu* shows that there are subtle differences in meaning when it is replaced by either of the two terms, *quán* 'entirely' and *quánbù* 'the whole lot' in this adverbial function, since these adverbs focus on the collection of individual entities as a group, viewing it as a unified whole. Note that both *quán* and *quánbù* can co-occur with *dōu* 'all' but are not grammatically required to do so.

(54)   Tāmen   quán   /   quánbù   /   **dōu**   qùshǐ-le
        3PL   entirely   whole:lot   all   die-CRS
        'All of them have passed away./The whole lot of them has passed away./They have **all** passed away.'

For these reasons, *dōu* is the best candidate for ALL.

5.3.6   Xǔduō *MANY; Adjective*

There are two allolexes for MANY in Mandarin. These are *duō*, which can serve the function of a stative verb 'to be many' or an adverb 'more', and *xǔduō* 'many', which is an attributive quantifier. Mandarin does not morphologically distinguish between count and mass nouns, hence *duō* and *xǔduō* cover the semantic space of both 'many' and 'much' in English. It is important to note that only the lexeme *xǔduō* 'many' can be used attributively as the linguistic equivalent of MANY, since its allolex *duō* cannot be used unmodified in this structural slot. It syntactically requires the intensifier morpheme *hěn* 'very':

(55)   Tā   yǒu   **xǔduō**   nǚ'er   /   *(**hěn**)   duō   nǚ'er
        3SG   have   many   daughter   very   many   daughter
        'She has **many/very many** daughters.'

In (56), *duō* acts as the main verb and can thus be modified aspectually:

(56) Tā   dě dōngxi **duō** -zhe   ne
      3SG DE thing many   PROG RP
      'He has too **many** things!' (Literally, 'His things are too many!')

Although *xǔduō* cannot be used as a main verb, it is chosen for the primitive MANY since it is not subject to any restrictions when used in its basic function as an attributive quantifier, unlike its allolex *duō*.

5.4 Actions and Events: DO, HAPPEN TO (IN)

5.4.1 Zuò DO; Verb

The basic meaning of the verb *zuò* is the agentive one of 'to do'. It may be used in both formal and informal registers and for this reason is to be preferred over its colloquial allolex *gàn* 'to do' which is not found in all regional varieties of Mandarin (for examples with *gàn*, see (3) (58) and (68)). Although *zuò* may be replaced unproblematically by *gàn* in many examples, depending on the predicate type, there may be a slight shift in meaning. A possible reason for the colloquial preference for *gàn* is related to its use as an atelic activity verb meaning 'to do' without any purpose in mind or intended result, which explains why *zuò* is more appropriate than *gàn* in (57). The verb *zuò* not only means DO but also 'to make' and is used with accomplishment verbs and verbs of creation where some resultant state or object is produced, as in *zuò fàn* 'make a meal', *zuò zuòyè* 'do homework'.

(57) Wǒ   yě   xiǎng   zhèyàng **zuò** / ?gàn
      1SG also intend this:way do
      'I want to **do** the same.' or 'I want to do it like this.'

(58) Nǐ   gàn / zuò -le   huài shì
      2SG   do   PFV   bad   matter
      'You **did** something bad.'

Hence, *zuò* is chosen as the Mandarin primitive, given its less restricted semantic distribution (it covers both Vendlerian activities and accomplishments) and its occurrence in both formal and colloquial styles of language.

5.4.2 HAPPEN Semantics in Mandarin: Adversity and Fāshēng

The dichotomisation of verbs of happening in Mandarin into adversative and fortunate interpretations seems to cause problems at first in identifying the counterpart of the English verb *to happen*. It can be shown, however, that the verb *fāshēng* 'to happen' proves to be the best candidate, since it is semantically neutral in the construction type with locative NPs (as opposed, however, to that with human NPs, discussed below). This neutral construction is exemplified by (59):

(59)   Zhèlǐ **fāshēng** -guo yī:jiàn shì
        here happen -EXP one:CL event
        'Something **happened** here.'

The majority of verbs of happening in Mandarin tend to express misfortune. In other words, explicit verbs of bad luck and misfortune are more numerous than verbs of good luck (see Chappell (1986) for a similar phenomenon for passive markers). A striking semantic asymmetry thus becomes evident when we consider the following data. The main explicit verbs of misfortune are *dǎoméi* 'to have bad luck', exemplified in (60); as well as the separable verbs *chuǎng-huò* 'get into trouble, cause a mishap', *chī-kuī* 'be on the losing end, to have bad luck' and *zāo-nàn* 'suffer, meet with misfortune', the latter exemplified in (61). There appears to be just one general verb of good fortune, *zǒu-yùn* 'to have good luck' (or variations such as *yǒu yùnqì* 'to have good luck'), exemplified in (62):

(60)   Rúguǒ nǐ zhèyàng zuò, huì **dǎoméi** de
        if 2SG this:way do can have:bad:luck DE
        'If you do this, something **bad** can **happen**.'

(61)   Yóuyú zhè:ge yuányīn wǒ **zāo** -le **nàn**
        through this:CL reason 1SG meet PFV misfortune
        'Because of this, something **bad happened** to me.'

(62)   Wǒ **zǒu-yùn** le
        1SG go-luck CRS
        'I've had good luck.' ('Something **good happened** to me.')

Chū-shì 'to happen' and *fāshēng* + *Noun*_{Human} 'to happen' are formed of semantically neutral components, yet they, too, generally code misfortune. The separable VO compound verb *chū-shì* in (63), which is formed by the semantically neutral components *chū* 'to appear, come out' and *shì* 'thing, event, matter', can only be used for unfortunate events. In fact, (63) is a commonly used colloquial expression in Mandarin for a mishap or an accident (the same applies to example (92), with *chū-shì* in a backgrounded clause):

(63)   **Chū** -le shénme shì?
        appear PFV what thing
        'What's **happened**/what's wrong?'

Misfortune is a typical pragmatic inference of utterances of the construction type formed by *fāshēng* 'happen' with an overt human participant, as in (64), as opposed to the construction type with *fāshēng* 'happen' and a locative NP as the subject, exemplified in both (59) and (65):

(64) *Zhèyàng de shì   jīngcháng **fāshēng** zài tā   shēnshang*
     this:kind DE matter frequent   happen   at 3SG   body:on
     'This kind of thing often **happens** to her.'

(65) *Zhèlǐ **fāshēng** -le   jùdà de biànhuà*
     here   happen   -PFV huge DE change
     'Huge changes **have taken place**.'

Given this problem of the inherent adversity of 'happen' verbs in Mandarin, the solution is to choose the neutral construction type with *fāshēng* 'to happen' where it co-occurs with a locative NP, as in (65). This can be regarded as the general construction where *fāshēng* occurs as a pure event verb without reference to any human participants and thus appropriately captures the primitive meaning of HAPPEN. Note that human participants co-occur with *fāshēng* only in adjunct phrases, as in (64) — which is similar to their syntactic treatment in English: *happen to NP$_{Human}$* — and not as core participants, unlike the semantic subject of *zāo-nàn* in (61), which is a human participant. Typically only locative and event NPs may act as the intransitive subject of *fāshēng*.

5.5 Meta-Predicates: NOT WANT, IF, COULD, LIKE, BECAUSE, VERY

5.5.1 Bù NOT WANT (NO); Negative Adverb

Sinitic languages provide strong evidence for postulating a negative modal NO (NOT) or NOT WANT as the primitive for negation. The major dialect groups within Sinitic, including Mandarin, Yue, Min, Xiang, Hakka and Wu, all possess a monomorphemic general or 'volitional' negative marker coding both 'not' and 'not want' which is structurally opposed to a marker of existential negation (see Chappell 1992). In Mandarin, the primitive *bù* functions as this general negation marker. With most action verbs, it additionally expresses unwillingness on the part of an agentive subject to carry out the action, as opposed to the existential negative marker *méi* which negates the presupposition of a perfectivised event, that is, that the given event has taken place. Thus, there are both modal and aspectual differences between the two markers. Compare (66) and (67), which exemplify the Mandarin volitional and the existential negative respectively in a minimal pair of utterances:

(66) Wǒ   bù   qù
    1SG NEG go
    'I'm **not** going/I **won't** go/I **don't want** to go.'

(67) Wǒ   méi   qù
    1SG NEG   go
    'I **didn't** go/I **haven't** gone.'

Further evidence in favour of postulating *bù* as the primitive for pure negation is that in Mandarin it is also used in responses to polar yes/no questions to express the negative form:

(68) *B ù ,   b ù*   shì   wǒ   gàn   de
    NEG NEG be   1SG   do   NOM
    '**No!**, I **didn't** do it!'

Given the modal component of *bù*, it is not surprising to find that it is also used in irrealis contexts, including both expression of the future and conditionals:

(69) Rúguǒ xià yǔ,   wǒ   jiù   bù   lái   le
    if   fall rain 1SG   then NEG   come   CRS
    'If it rains, I **won't** come.'

Finally, note that this negative marker is not only used to negate agentive action verbs but also many stative verbs, including the copula *shì* 'to be', as in (68), as well as certain verbs of emotions and mental activities.

The problem with the presence of a minimum of two negative markers in each Sinitic language is how to analyse negation of events. Are we forced to conclude that there are two primitives for NOT/DON'T WANT in Mandarin and other Chinese languages? Presumably, the existential negative *méi* would have to be either defined in terms of the volitional negative *bù* or considered to be its allolex in past perfective contexts, to which it is aspectually restricted, apart from negating many achievement verbs and the possessive verb *yǒu* 'to have'. For Mandarin, I propose *bù* as the best candidate for NOT WANT (NO).

5.5.2 *Conditional Hypotaxis: IF in Mandarin*

There are several strategies in Mandarin for expressing conditional propositions. All involve complex clauses and may have explicit markers for either or both the condition and the consequence clause. There is strict sequencing in Mandarin for hypotactic complex clauses expressing condition or supposition: the condition or *if*-clause obligatorily precedes the consequence clause, as in (70) below and (69) above. There is no flexibility as in English where both orders are possible. The term *rúguǒ* 'if' can occur both sentence-initially and in the second position after the subject noun.

(70) ***Rúguǒ*** *nǐ   zhèyàng zuò,   huì   dǎoméi   de*
      if   2SG this:way do   could have:bad:luck DE
      '**If** you do it like this, something bad could happen to you.'

The term *rúguǒ* 'if' is a word which is found in formal contexts such as logic, mathematics and philosophy but can nonetheless also be used informally. In the colloquial conversation genre, the *if*-marker, *rúguǒ*, is however often omitted from verbalisation, as it could be, for example, in (70). Complex clauses without any overt markers at all may code the hypothetical, provided some kind of marker of the irrealis occurs in the consequence clause such as a negative or appropriate adverb to enable the first clause to be understood as a condition. This is shown in (71), where the use of *bù* in the second clause transposes the utterance into the realm of the irrealis:

(71) *Tā   bù   qù, wǒ   yě   **bù**   qù*
      3SG NEG go   1SG also NEG go
      '**If** she doesn't go, then I'm not going either.'

Note that the first clause — *Tā bù qù* — when used alone as an independent utterance means 'She's not going'. Hence, the hypothetical meaning arises from the juxtaposition of the two clauses in these cases (see also Li & Thompson 1981:633).

A second *if*-marker is the colloquial discontinuous expression *yàoshi ... de huà* which codes an *if*-hypothesis in the sense of 'supposing X to be the case', and hence is more semantically specialised. In informal colloquial speech, this backgrounding clause marker can be abbreviated to either *yàoshi* or *yào*, or else to the clause enclitic *de huà*, as in (72):

(72) *Zhè:ge ... nǐ   dào   Běijīng qù   **de huà**   (m),   yě*
      this:CL   2SG to   Beijing go   DE   speech   (hmm) also
      bù   yīdìng   tīngdedǒng   shì bu   shì ...
      NEG certainly listen:DE:understand be   NEG be
      'The ... **if** you go to Beijing, you won't necessarily understand either, will you? ...' (Liang, DeFrancis & Han 1982:13:61)

A third common way of expressing 'if' in colloquial Mandarin is to use *wànyī* (literally, 'one ten-thousandth') which means 'if by any chance, if it should'. In addition to these markers, there are also many formal markers which are typical of written genres such as scientific writing. These are *jiǎshǐ*, *jiǎrú* and *jiǎdìng* which are used to introduce the hypothesis or condition in the same structural slot as *yàoshi* or *rúguǒ*. All these *if*-markers are either more semantically specific or more restricted in distribution than *rúguǒ*, and for this reason I consider *rúguǒ* 'if' to be the best candidate for primitive status in Mandarin.

5.5.3   Mandarin Irrealis: Kěnéng COULD (POSSIBLY); Adverb

There are two main epistemic modal expressions of possibility in Mandarin: *huì* 'be likely; probable', typically used to translate the modal verb and future marker *will* in English; and the modal adverb *kěnéng* 'possibly, it is possible that, could'. Compare (73) with (74) for the difference in degree of the speaker's certainty as to the occurrence of the projected event:

(73)   Míngtiān **huì**   xià yǔ
       tomorrow be:probable fall rain
       'It **will** rain tomorrow.' or 'It's **likely to** rain to tomorrow.'

(74)   Míngtiān **kěnéng** xià yǔ
       tomorrow possibly fall rain
       'It **could** rain tomorrow.'

To reduce the degree of certainty expressed in (73), the adverb *kěnéng* 'possibly, perhaps' can also combine with *huì* 'can, will' to render the meaning of 'might':

(75)   Míngtiān **kěnéng**   **huì** xià yǔ
       tomorrow be:possible can   fall rain
       'It **might** rain tomorrow.'

Hence *kěnéng*, also exemplified in (76), is chosen as the Mandarin primitive for the concept of a projected chance happening, COULD (POSSIBLY), since the degree of certainty is less than that for *huì* 'be likely' but more than for the collocation *kěnéng huì* 'might':

(76)   Nàtiáo   shéngzi **kěnéng**   duàn   le
       that:CL rope   be:possible break CRS
       'That rope **could** be broken.'

5.5.4   LIKE: A Case of Allosyntax

For this primitive, allosyntax needs to be posited for Mandarin, since a distinction is made between similarity or likeness of two objects and similarity of two actions or events. In the first case, the verb *xiàng* 'to be like, resemble' is used:

(77) *Zhè:ge* **xiàng** *dīngxiāng dàn bù shì dīngxiāng*
       this:CL resemble lilac but NEG be lilac
       'This is **like** lilac, but it's not lilac.'

(78) *Xiǎo Méi hěn* **xiàng** *tā bàba*
       Xiao Mei very resemble 3SG father
       'Xiao Mei's very much **like** her father.'

In the second case, where two actions or events are likened to one another, *zhèyàng (zuò)* '(to do something) like this' (that is, a combination of the primitive *zhè* 'this' with *yàng* 'way') is used with the appropriate verb:

(79) *Tā shì* **zhèyàng** *zuò de*
       3SG be this:way do NOM
       'He did it **like** this.'

When two situations are likened to one another, an event, action or state of affairs is thus characterised as being performed in a certain manner. Consider also:

(80) *Wǒ bù yuànyì nǐ* **zhèyàng** *zuò*
       1SG NEG willing 2SG this:way do
       'I don't want you to do it **like** this.' (Literally, 'I am not willing for you to do it this way.')

Hence, similarity in appearance of two objects and similar action are treated in syntactically different ways in Mandarin. This can be accounted for in terms of allosyntax. First, the verb *xiàng* 'be like, resemble' is chosen in the case of likening two objects, as in (77) and (78). It has the basic syntactic form: *X xiàng Y*. Second, the meaning of like action or event is expressed by the combination of the primitive for THIS, *zhè* (see section 5.3.1), with the morpheme *yàng* 'way', as in (79) and (80). It has the basic syntactic form: *X zhèyàng Verb*.

5.5.5   *Causation:* Yīnwei BECAUSE; *Conjunction*

Causation can be expressed lexically in Mandarin by means of resultative verb compounds, syntactically by means of periphrastic constructions with pivot verbs such *ràng* 'let, have' and *jiào* 'make' (see Chappell, 1991a and forthcoming), and also by means of complex clauses with the unmarked order of *Cause + Result* (see also section 5.5.2 on IF hypotaxis). Causal hypotaxis in Mandarin uses the explicit markers *yīnwei* 'because' ... *suǒyǐ* 'therefore'..., with the first marker being able to occur either utterance-initially or after the subject/topic for same-subject clauses. The second marker *suǒyǐ* 'therefore' is often omitted in the conversational genre.

(81) *Yīnwei hěn duō rén shīyè le, suǒyǐ Gōngdǎng*
because very many people lose:job PFV so Labor:Party
zài dàxuǎn-zhong kǒngpà bù huì huóshèng
at election-in afraid NEG likely win
'**Because** there are so many unemployed, it's not likely that the Labor Party will win the elections.'

A more formal and literary marker of causation is *yóuyú* 'through, due to':

(82) *Yóuyú Wéizhōu de shīyèlǜ hěn gāo, Gōngdǎng*
through Victoria DE lose:job:rate very high Labor:Party
de wēiwàng dà-dà bù rú yǐqián
DE prestige big-RED NEG like before
'**Due to** Victoria's level of unemployment being very high, the prestige of the Labor Party is not the same as before.'

Since *yīnwei* is not subject to any such distributional restrictions, it is chosen as the best candidate for the primitive BECAUSE in Mandarin.

5.5.6 *Intensifier:* Hěn VERY; *Adverb of Degree*

The adverb *hěn* 'very' is the most common of the large set of intensifiers in Mandarin. It can be used to modify attributives and adverbs and also stative verbs, including a subset of emotion verbs and verbs of mental events. It is not restricted to any register. The examples of *hěn* 'very' in (83) show its use in modifying stative verbs coding size, *dà* 'to be big' and *xiǎo* 'to be small':

(83) *Zhè:ge dōngxi hěn dà / hěn xiǎo*
this:CL thing very big very small
'This thing is **very** big/**very** small.'

There are also compound adverbs of degree used as intensifiers such as *shífēn* (literally, 'ten parts') 'very, completely', typical of the written medium, not to mention *fēicháng* (literally, 'not common') 'extremely' and postverbal intensifiers such as *Stative Verb + de hěn* (literally, 'DE very') 'very (much)' and *Stative Verb + jí-le* (literally, 'extreme-CRS') 'extremely, awfully', which all express a greater degree of intensity than (preverbal) *hěn*. Reduplication of stative verbs coding properties is another strategy for expressing the degree of intensity of the given property, such as *hóng-hong* (literally, 'red-red') 'very red'. However, this strategy cannot be applied to all stative verbs, since many of the disyllabic ones in particular are excluded. In addition, other Chinese languages and the regional dialects of

Mandarin are reputed to be the source of further highly colloquial forms used as intensifiers such as *tǐng* (SV 'straight') 'very, quite', *mǎn* (SV 'full') 'completely' and *hǎo* (SV 'good') 'very', which may all be excluded from consideration due to either their semantics or their restricted distribution.

5.6 Time and Place: WHEN, WHERE, AFTER, BEFORE, ABOVE, BELOW

5.6.1 Shíhou TIME (WHEN); Noun

The noun *shíhou* 'time' is chosen in preference to the interrogative pronoun corresponding to English *when* as the best candidate for TIME since the term 'when' in Mandarin is a composite expression including the morpheme for TIME: *shénme shíhou* WHEN (literally, 'what time?'). In fact, it is composed with a second primitive *shénme* SOMETHING or 'what' (see section 5.1.3):

(84)   *Nǐ   shì shénme shíhou zuò de?*
      2SG be what   time   do NOM
      '**When** did you do it?'

In the case of clause combining, the term *shíhou* forms the backgrounded clause marker in conjunction with the marker *de*, functioning as a relativiser which allows complex attributives to precede the head noun. Following the general rule for hypotaxis in Mandarin, the 'when' clause must precede the main or foregrounded clause. A second noun *shíjiān* 'time' cannot be used in this way:

(85)   *Wǒmen qù dòngwùyuán de   shíhou / *shíjiān,*
      1PL   go zoo   DE   time   *time
      kàndào -le   yī:tiáo èyú
      see   -PFV one:CL crocodile
      '**When** we went to the zoo, we saw a crocodile.'

In colloquial and informal styles of Mandarin, the marker for backgrounded *when*-clauses is reduced to *shí* time' (*shíhou* is a disyllabic compound word and *shí* can be seen as its truncated form). The literary Chinese form of interrogative WHEN is *hé shí*, with the analogous structure to *shénme shíhou* of 'what time'. This can be excluded on the grounds of formality.

There is one other nominal for 'time', *shíjiān*. It is a compound word, which like *shíhou* has *shí* 'time' as the initial syllable and morpheme, and *jiān* 'interval, between' as its second. It is used to refer to both the concept of time and to 'time' when a specific period is intended. This word cannot be used to form the interrogative pronoun WHEN (**shénme shíjiān* 'what time') nor as the marker of a backgrounded *when*-clause (see (85)), but rather is used in questioning length of time — *duōcháng shíjiān* 'for how long?' — implying a specific and limited period of time as the answer. In contrast to this, *shíhou* 'time' is appropriately vague for this feature. For these reasons, *shíhou* is chosen as the best candidate for TIME (WHEN) (used in sequencing events as a marker of backgrounded clauses). The interrogative form *shénme shíhou* 'when' can thus be decomposed in Mandarin into two primitives: the indefinite pronoun SOMETHING (see section 5.1.3) and TIME.

5.6.2   Dìfāng PLACE (WHERE); Noun

The usual colloquial expression for interrogative 'where' in Mandarin is the interrogative *nǎr/nǎli* 'where', composed of *nǎ* 'which' with atonal suffix *-r* or *-li* 'in':[6]

(86)   *Zhè:jiàn shì   zài nǎr   fāshēng   de?*
        this:CL matter at   where happen   NOM
        '**Where** did it happen?'

Nǎli or *nǎr* may also be used to question place in an attributive function, as in (87). Neither can, however, be used as a free nominal.

(87)   *Nǐ   shì   nǎli (nǎr de) rén?*   *Wǒ shì Shànghǎirén*
        2SG be   where   person   1SG be   Shanghai:person
        '**Where** do you come from?'   'I'm from Shanghai.'

There is also the composite expression *shénme dìfāng* for 'where' (literally, 'what place'), which can be used as an alternative to *nǎli/nǎr*. This is analogous in structure to the composite expression *shénme shíhou* for 'when' (literally 'what time') discussed in section 5.6.1.

(88)   *Tā   xiànzài zhù   zài   shénme dìfāng / nǎr?*
        3SG   now   live at   what   place   where
        '**Where** does she live now?'

Choice of this term is closer to Wierzbicka's earlier proposals (1989a) regarding the primitive for the basic locative concept as being WHERE. The interrogative expression *shénme dìfāng* 'where' is slightly more formal than either *nǎr* or *nǎli*. Note however that when the tonal value of *nǎr/nǎli* changes from 3rd tone (low falling-rising) to 4th tone (falling), these interrogatives function as the spatial deictics 'there' and hence also combine an indefinite notion with that of place:

(89) Zánmen wǎnshang qù **nàr**, hǎo ma?
 1PL:INC evening go there good Q
 'Let's go **there** tonight, OK?'

The two forms, *nǎr* and *nǎli*, could be seen as colloquial allolexes of *shénme dìfāng* in some of its functions, given that it has the less restricted distribution in terms of register. The crucial factor is, however, that *dìfāng* can be used as a free nominal for 'place' whereas neither *nǎr* nor *nǎli* can be used in this way:

(90) Zhè:jiàn shì fāshēng zài tóng yī:ge **dìfāng** / *nǎr
 this:CL event happen at same one:CL place *where
 bù shì lìng yī:ge **dìfāng**.
 NEG be different one:CL place
 'It happened in the same **place**, not in another **place**.'

The term *dìfāng* 'place' is therefore chosen as the spatial primitive in Mandarin, combining with *shénme* WHAT to form the interrogative expression 'where'.

5.6.3 Yǐhòu AFTER and Yǐqián BEFORE; Clause-Final Subordination Markers

The spatial locative *hòu* 'behind' can also be used temporally to mean AFTER when it combines with grammatical function morphemes *yǐ* 'with, taking' (or *zhī* 'possessive' in literary Chinese):

(91) Nà **yǐhòu**, tā dà bìng -le yī:chǎng
 that after 3SG great ill -PFV one:CL
 '**After** that, he got very ill.'

In more colloquial registers, *hòu* can however be used alone as an enclitic to the backgrounded clause:

(92) Chū-shì **hòu**, yǒu rén shuō-le xiē shénme
 happen after there:be people say-PFV CL something
 '**After** this happened, someone said something.'

The analogous situation obtains with *qián* 'front', which has a temporal meaning BEFORE in combination with the aforementioned grammatical morphemes:

(93) Tāmen xiànzài zhù zài Quánzhōu. Zài zhè yǐqián,
     3PL   now   live at Quanzhou   at this before
     tāmen zhù zài Xiàmén
     3PL   live at Xiamen
     'They live in Chüanchow now. **Before** this, they lived in Amoy.'

As a final point, I note that it is very common cross-linguistically to find semantic change moving in the direction from spatial to temporal meanings (cf. Bybee 1985; Traugott 1975).

5.6.4 Shàng ABOVE and Xià BELOW; Postpositions

The terms for ABOVE and BELOW are the two bound atonal morphemes *shàng* and *xià* respectively. Structurally, both are postpositions to the noun they mark, and they can form discontinuous locative nominal phrases in conjunction with *zài* 'at', as in (94). *Shàng* can also be used to express the concepts 'on top of' or simply 'on' as a postposition, while *xià* can similarly express 'underneath' and 'under'.

(94) Yī:jià   zhí/shēngfēijī zài wǒmen tóu-shang   fēi-lái
      one:CL   helicopter   at 1PL   head-above fly-come
      fēi-qù bǎ wǒmen xià-huài   le
      fly-go BA 1PL   frighten-bad CRS
      'A helicopter flying around **above** our heads frightened us badly.'

(95) Wǒmen lóu-xia   zhù de   shì yī:jià Cháoxiānrén
      1PL   building-below live NOM be one:CL Korean
      'A Korean family lives **below** us.'

I choose *shàng* 'up, above' as the primitive since it has a much wider network of meanings than does *xià* 'below, under' and can be considered the unmarked member of the pair, a position argued for in Scott (1989). Chao (1968:622) also claims that *shàng* has more 'versatility' than *xià*.

5.7 Meronymy and Taxonomy: A PART OF, A KIND OF

5.7.1 Possession and Meronymy: A Case of Allosyntax

In this section we show that the concept of being a part of a whole is typically expressed syntactically rather than lexically in Mandarin and, further, that a case of allosyntax must be proposed.

There are two lexical expressions of meronymy in Mandarin in the form of the verb *shǔyú* 'be a part of, belong' and the classifier construction *yī-bùfēn* 'a part of, piece' (literally, 'one-part'). In the following discussion, I show that both expressions should be excluded from consideration, since neither can be used to refer to a possession relationship involving humans.

First of all, the verb *shǔyú* expresses a property or ownership relationship:

(96) Zhè:suǒ fángzi **shǔyú** tā
      this:CL house belong 3SG
      'This house **belongs** to her.'

Normally, this cannot be used to refer to a person belonging to a family, club or political party:

(97) *? Wǒ mèimei **shǔyú** dǎng de
      1SG sister belong party NOM
      'My younger sister **belongs** to the party.'

Secondly, the term *yī-bùfēn* 'a part' can be linguistically related to its whole in an equative construction, as in example (98). In fact, the genitive marker *de* is used to establish this relationship of association (see Chappell & Thompson 1992). However the Mandarin expression *yī-bùfēn* is not appropriately used with human subjects, as (99) shows:

(98) Shùzhī shì shù de **yī-bùfēn**
      branch be tree DE one-part
      'Branches are **parts** of trees.'

(99) Tā shì Chén jiā de yī-yuán / *yī-bùfēn
      this be Chen family DE one-member *one-part
      'She is a member of the Chen family.' (Not 'be part of')

Furthermore, neither *shǔyú* 'be a part of, belong' nor *yī-bùfēn* 'a part of' are typical colloquial means of expression for the 'part of' relation; rather an expression using the possessive verb *yǒu* 'have' in a construction of the form $Noun_{Subject, Whole}$ + *yǒu* + $Noun_{Part}$.[7] This construction codes simple possession and may be also used for generic expressions:

(100) Fǔzi yǒu bǎr
      axe have handle
      'An axe has a handle.' or 'Axes have handles.'

(101) *Liǎnshang yǒu yī:ge bízi, yī:zhāng zuǐ*
       face-on have one:CL nose one:CL mouth
       hé liǎng:zhī yǎnjing
       and two:CL eye
       'The face has a nose, a mouth and two eyes.'

In fact, the possessive verb *yǒu* will be used not only to describe regular features of an object in generic expressions such as (100) and (101), but also for the purpose of describing a special feature of an individual member of some category in non-generic statements:

(102) *Nèipǐ mǎ yǒu yītiáo cháng wěiba*
       that:CL horse have one:CL long tail
       'That horse has a long tail.'

In contrast to the *yǒu* construction, Mandarin also has a construction expressing inalienable possession that includes characteristics and personality traits (see Tsunoda (1994) on the same phenomenon in Japanese). This could be viewed as a feature that is either conspicuous, unusual or in some way contrastive with other members of the particular category and hence can be used to characterise it. For this purpose, the 'double subject' or 'double nominative' construction is the preferred coding strategy and not the possessive *yǒu* construction. The double subject construction takes the form $Noun_{Whole} + Noun_{Part} + Verb_{Intransitive}$ and expresses an inalienable relation between the whole and the part noun (see Teng 1974; Chappell 1994). For example, in the context of horse breeders looking for a particular kind of horse with a long tail, the double subject construction would be appropriate if the speaker views this as a conspicuous feature:

(103) *Nèipǐ mǎ wěiba cháng*
       that:CL horse tail long
       'That horse is a long-tailed one.' or 'That horse, its tail is long.'

Similarly, looking at a set of pictures of clown faces:

(104) *Zhè:zhāng liǎn hěn nánkàn, bízi wāi*
       this:CL face very ugly nose crooked
       zuǐ xié, yáchǐ huáng
       mouth slanted teeth yellow
       'This face is very ugly: the nose is crooked, the mouth is slanted and the teeth are yellow.'

The double subject construction cannot be used to make generic statements about the 'normal' possession of parts and attributes, but can be used only where these are further characterised. Example (105) is ungrammatical even though the verb *yǒu* 'have' is semantically stative, while equally stative (106), which characterises a particular axe as long-handled, is grammatical:

(105)   * *Fǔzi bǎr yǒu*[8]
        axe handle have

(106)   *Nà:bǎ fǔzi bǎr cháng*
        that:CL axe handle long
        'That axe is long-handled.'

This does not mean to say that the double subject construction cannot be used to make generic statements. On the contrary, as long as some special feature of the part noun is used to characterise the whole, this will be possible. Recall the well-known 'elephant' example used in Teng (1974) and Li and Thompson (1976):

(107)   *Xiàng bízi cháng*
        elephant nose long
        'As for elephants, their trunks are long.'

Do we thus have a case of allosyntax for meronymy? Indeed, this appears to be so, given the complementary semantic space of the *yǒu* construction and the double subject construction. This can be summarised as follows:

(a)   The *yǒu* construction is chosen in the case of simple possession for statements relating whole to part without any characterisation of that part: 'Xs have Ys'. The possessive relation is not restricted in either case to an inherent part–whole one but extends to ownership of artefacts and other concrete objects.

(b)   The double subject construction is chosen wherever the whole noun itself is characterised by some special feature of the part with a contrastive purpose. This can only be used for inalienable part–whole relationships. Hence, the choice will often depend on discourse considerations as to whether the speaker wants to say something new about the part (with the *yǒu* construction) or something new about the whole by means of a part (with the double subject construction).

5.7.2   Zhŏng *A KIND OF; Classifier*

Zhŏng is a classifier used to categorise nouns as a phenomenon in their own right, that is as a 'kind'. This morpheme has the further meanings of 'seed, species'. If the technical sense of 'species' is intended, then the compound noun *zhǒnglèi* 'kind, species' will be used. This compound is formed by *zhǒng* and the noun *lèi* 'type, category', a more erudite term that could itself be defined in terms of *zhǒng*.

(108) Wǒmen   qù dòngwùyuán   de shíhou,   kàndào
      1PL   go zoo   DE time   see:reach
      le   xǔduō gèzhǒng gèyàng   de dòngwù
      PFV   many each:kind each:sort DE animal
      'When we went to the zoo, we saw many different **kinds** of animals.'

(109) Zhèxiē shù   dōu   shì tóng yīge   zhǒnglèi
      this:CL tree all   be same one:CL kind
      bù   shì liǎng zhǒng   bù   tóng de
      NEG   be two CL:kind   NEG   same NOM
      'These trees are the same **kind**, not two different **kinds**.'

The use of *zhǒng* is to classify objects together as belonging to the same kind. Consequently, if *zhǒng* is reduplicated to form the plural 'kinds', the meaning 'different kinds' is expressed. This can be seen in example (110) from one of the written speeches of a former leader of China, Mao Zedong:

(110) Tāmen yǐ   **zhǒng-zhǒng**   lǐyóu fǎnduì
      3PL take   kind-kind   reason oppose
      'They used **all kinds** of reasons to oppose (it).'

The reduplication of *zhǒng* to mean 'all kinds' or 'different kinds' is, however, largely restricted to such written contexts.

Zhǒng KIND is the best candidate for this primitive, since, as I have shown, it is used to categorise objects as being the same (in kind).

5.8   Evaluators and Descriptors: GOOD, BAD, BIG, SMALL

5.8.1   Hǎo GOOD and Huài BAD; *Stative Verbs*

GOOD and BAD are semantically asymmetrical in Mandarin, *huài* 'bad' being semantically narrower in its range of application. In this case, the use of simple negation of the morpheme *hǎo* GOOD which gives *bù hǎo* might, in fact, be preferable since *huài* is more semantically specialised at its end of the scale to mean 'immoral', 'nasty' or 'evil' than *hǎo* is on the 'saintly' end of the scale. For example, consider the compounds *huàifènzi* 'evildoer', *huàidàn* 'bastard', *huàirén* 'scoundrel', *huàishì* 'evil deed' and *huàihuà* 'malicious remarks', versus the blander *hǎohuà* 'fine words', *hǎoshì* 'good deed', *hǎogǎn* 'good opinion', *hǎohàn* 'brave man, hero' and *hǎotiānr* 'lovely weather'. Examples (111) and (112) show the attributive use of *hǎo* and *huài* — note the asymmetry shown by the alternative English translations:

(111) Nǐ zuò -le yī:jiàn **hǎo** shì / **huài** shì
2SG do -PFV one:CL good matter bad matter
'You did something **good/bad** (*or* an evil deed).'

(112) Tā shì **hǎo** rén / **huài** rén
3SG be good person bad person
'She is a **good** person/**bad** person (*or* evildoer).'

The reader is referred to section 5.4.2 for discussion of the expressions 'Something good/bad happened to me' since the events of good luck and misfortune are expressed predicatively in Mandarin, not as postnominal attributives as in English, nor for that matter in any symmetrical relation.

5.8.2 Dà BIG and Xiǎo SMALL; Stative Verbs

Assuming that we accept these two concepts as primitives, BIG and SMALL are uncontroversial in Mandarin, being lexified as the stative verbs *dà* and *xiǎo* in (83) and (113) respectively:

(113) Wǒ kànjiàn-le yī:kè **dà** / **xiǎo** shù
1SG see-PFV one:CL big small tree
'I saw a **big/small** tree.'

5.9 Conclusion

In general, identifying the putative semantic primitives in Mandarin has not been problematic. In most cases, it has been argued that lexemes expressing the basic meaning and having the widest distribution linguistically should be chosen. The primitives thus typically fall into a class of lexemes which are neither semantically specialised nor have any syntagmatic co-occurrence constraints or register/style distinctions. Four cases of allolexy were identified and accounted for in terms of complementary semantic and syntactic restrictions. These were for the primitives PEOPLE (*rénmen* and *rén*), FEEL (*gǎnjué* and *gǎndào*), TWO (*liǎng(ge)* and *èr*), and MANY (*xǔduō* and *duō*).

Secondly, there were two cases of allosyntax where it was shown that some primitives may be syntacticised in Mandarin rather than lexified. This was the situation for meronymy, for example, where inherent part–whole relations and simple possession are expressed by means of two different syntactic constructions rather than at word level. No lexemes for 'part' or 'belong' could be identified that were able to express the same unrestricted range of meaning. Similarly, the primitive LIKE can be expressed in two different syntactic constructions in Mandarin, depending on whether the perceived resemblance involves two objects or two actions.

For the spatial and temporal primitives, an earlier proposal by Wierzbicka (1989a) that PLACE and TIME are the basic terms and not the interrogatives 'where' or 'when' was upheld. In fact, in Mandarin the interrogative markers are complex terms formed by the primitive for SOMETHING used interrogatively — *shénme* 'what' combined with the primitives *dìfang* and *shíhou* for PLACE and TIME respectively.

At the lexical level, it was pointed out that the primitive for the negative marker NOT WANT (NO) is monomorphemic in form in all Sinitic languages, not just in Mandarin. Diachronically and synchronically, these negative adverbs must be considered as modals meaning 'to not want', that is, as a kind of volitional negative, providing excellent evidence for the postulation of this concept as a primitive.

Notes

1   I wish to thank Liu Mingchen (La Trobe University/University of Otago), Wu Yunji (University of Melbourne) and Hongyin Tao (University of California at Santa Barbara) for their assistance in elicitation work and discussion of the Mandarin data. Needless to say, I am responsible for the interpretation of these data. This research was supported by an Australian Research Council Large Grant entitled "A typological grammar of Sinitic languages".

   Apart from contextualised elicited examples provided by the three native speakers acknowledged above, some data were taken from a transcription made by Hongyin Tao, *Hong Kong Police*, and from the published transcriptions by Liang, DeFrancis and Han (1982) and Kubler and Ho (1984). I have added the glosses and translations for these.

   The abbreviations used in the glossing of the Mandarin data are as follows: BA marker of preposed 'object' noun (or pretransitive marker), CLassifier, CRS 'currently relevant state' aspect marker (perfect aspect), DE marker of subordination for attributives in complex noun phrases or for nouns in a genitive (associative) relation and marker of subordination for relative clauses, EXPeriential aspect marker, GEI verb passivising prefix, GENitive marker, INClusive, NEGative marker, NOMinaliser, NP noun phrase, PFV perfective aspect marker, PLural, PROGressive aspect marker, Question particle, REDuplication, RELativiser, RP rhetorical particle, SG singular, SV stative verb, VO verb object sequence. For the 3SG pronoun, *ta*, the glossing of examples alternately uses 'she' or 'he' to avoid the clumsy disjunction 's/he' in English. The symbol (*x) indicates that the utterance becomes ungrammatical if element x is included while the notation *(x) indicates that the utterance becomes ungrammatical if element x is deleted. The interrogative marker (?) preceding a linguistic example indicates that although the utterance may be syntactically well-formed, the combination of elements is semantically odd .

   Tone values for Mandarin use the standard pīnyīn diacritics: High level tone V^{55} = v̄; High rising tone V^{35} = v́; Low falling-rising tone V^{214} = v̌; High falling tone V^{51} = v̀. Tone sandhi

2   has not been indicated. Syllables unmarked for tone are in the neutral tone (Chao 1968).
2   Exceptions to this rule are locative markers which take the form of postpositions (see section 5.6.4 for discussion) as well as some markers of backgrounded clauses which take clause-final position such as *shíhou* 'when' discussed in section 5.6.1; also *yǐqián* 'before' and *yǐhòu* discussed in section 5.6.3.
3   Note that preceding 'relative clauses' modifying *rénmen* are not excluded by this claim, for example *zhùzài zhè:ge cūnlǐ de rénmen* (literally 'live:at this:CL village REL people') 'people who live in this village'.
4   There is no adjective class in Mandarin. Stative verbs expressing properties and qualities may also function as attributives.
5   Note that colloquially the following Mandarin expressions would be preferred to (46) and (44) respectively, both using a combination of *yě* 'also' with the primitive deictic *zhè* THIS:

   Wǒ   yě   xiǎng zhè:yàng zuò
   1SG   also   want   this:way   do
   'I want to do **the same**.' (Literally, 'I also intend to do (it) this way.')

   Zhè shì   yě   fāshēng zài zhè:ge rén   shēn-shang
   this matter also happen at   this:CL person body-on
   'This happened to the **same** person.'

6   The difference between *nǎr* and *nǎli* appears to be mainly one of register: *nǎr* is more colloquial and *nǎli* slightly more formal.
7   The separate existential use of *yǒu* is discussed above in connection with *yǒu rén* 'someone' (literally, 'there:be people') in section 5.1.2.
8   The same sequence (but a different utterance) is possible in the form of a left-dislocation with an intonation break between 'axe' and 'have': Q: *Yǒu fǔzi bǎr ma?* 'Do you have any axe handles?' A: *Fǔzi bǎr, // yǒu.* 'As for axehandles, (we) have (them).' In this case, however, *fǔzi* 'axe' and *bǎr* 'handle' form a conceptual unit, unlike (105) above, where the intonation break occurs between *fǔzi* and *bǎr*: **Fǔzi, // bǎr yǒu.*

References

Bybee, Joan. 1985. *Morphology*. Amsterdam: John Benjamins.
Chao Yuen Ren. 1968. *A Grammar of Spoken Chinese*. Berkeley: University of California Press.
Chappell, Hilary. 1986. "Formal and Colloquial Adversity Passives in Standard Chinese". *Linguistics* 24.1025-1052.
Chappell, Hilary. 1991a. "Causativity and the *Ba* Construction in Chinese". *Partizipation: Das sprachliche Erfassen von Sachverhalten* ed. by Hansjakob Seiler & Walfried Premper, 563-584. Tübingen: Gunter Narr.
Chappell, Hilary. 1991b. "Strategies for the Assertion of Obviousness and Disagreement in Mandarin: A semantic study of the particle *me*". *Australian Journal of Linguistics* 11.39-65.

Chappell, Hilary. 1992. "Typology and Semantics of Negation in Sinitic Languages". Paper presented at the 25th International Conference on Sino-Tibetan Languages and Linguistics, University of California at Berkeley, October 14–18, 1992.

Chappell, Hilary. 1994. "Inalienability and the Personal Domain in Mandarin Chinese Discourse". *The Grammar of Inalienability. A typological perspective on body parts and the part–whole relation* ed. by Hilary Chappell & William McGregor. Berlin: Mouton de Gruyter.

Chappell, Hilary. Forthcoming. *Analytic Syntax in Mandarin Chinese. A semantic analysis of passive, causative, dative and benefactive constructions.*

Chappell, Hilary & Sandra A. Thompson. 1992. "The Semantics and Pragmatics of Associative *De* in Mandarin Discourse". *Cahiers de Linguistique Asie Orientale* 21.2.199-229.

Chen, Ping. 1986. *Referent Tracking in Chinese*. Doctoral Dissertation, Linguistics Department, University of California at Los Angeles.

Goddard, Cliff. 1989. "Issues in Natural Semantic Metalanguage". *Quaderni di Semantica* 10.1.51-64.

Goddard, Cliff. 1991. "Testing the Translatability of Semantic Primitives into an Australian Aboriginal Language". *Anthropological Linguistics* 33.1.31-56.

Harbsmeier, Christoph. 1979. *Zur philosophischen Grammatik des Altchinesischen im Anschluß an Humboldts Brief an Abel-Rémusat*. Stuttgart-Bad Cannstatt: Friedrich Frommann.

Kubler, Cornelius C. & George T. C. Ho. 1984. *Varieties of Spoken Standard Chinese*, vol II: *A speaker from Taipei*. Dordrecht: Foris.

La Polla, Randy. 1990. *Grammatical Relations in Chinese. Synchronic and diachronic considerations*. Doctoral Dissertation, Linguistics Department, University of California at Berkeley.

Li, Charles N. & Sandra A. Thompson. 1976. "Subject and Topic. A new typology of language". *Subject and Topic* ed. by Charles N. Li, 457-489. New York: Academic Press.

Li, Charles N. & Sandra A. Thompson. 1978. "An Exploration of Mandarin Chinese". *Syntactic Typology: Studies in the phenomenology of language* ed. by W. P. Lehmann, 223-266. Austin: University of Texas Press.

Li, Charles N. & Sandra A. Thompson. 1981. *Mandarin Chinese. A functional reference grammar*. Berkeley: University of California Press.

Liang, James C. P., John DeFrancis & Y. H. Han. 1982. *Varieties of Spoken Standard Chinese*, vol I: *A speaker from Tianjin*. Dordrecht: Foris.

Mungello, David E. 1977. *Leibniz and Confucius. The search for accord*. Honolulu: The University Press of Hawaii.

Sapir, Edward. 1930. "Totality". *Linguistic Society of America, Language Monograph* 6.

Scott, Amanda. 1989. *An Examination of the Syntactic and Semantic Characteristics of* Shàng *and* Xià *in Mandarin*. MA Thesis, Department of Linguistics, Australian National University, Canberra.

Teng, Shou-hsin. 1974. "Double Nominatives in Chinese". *Language* 50.3.455-473.

Traugott, Elisabeth. 1975. "Spatial and Temporal Expressions of Tense and Temporal Sequencing: A contribution to the study of semantic fields". *Semiotica* 15.207-230.

Tsao Feng-fu. 1978. "Subject and Topic in Chinese". *Proceedings of Symposium on Chinese Linguistics* ed. by Robert L. Cheng, Ying-che Li & Ting-chi Tang, 165-196. Taipei: Student Book Co.

Tsao Feng-fu. 1979. *A Functional Study of Topic in Chinese. A first step towards discourse analysis*. Taipei: Student Book Co.
Tsunoda, Tasaku. 1994. "The Possession Cline in Japanese and Other Languages". *The Grammar of Inalienability. A typological perspective on body parts and the part-whole relation* ed. by Hilary Chappell & William McGregor. Berlin: Mouton de Gruyter.
Wierzbicka, Anna. 1972. *Semantic Primitives*. Frankfurt: Athenäum.
Wierzbicka, Anna. 1980. *Lingua Mentalis*. New York: Academic Press.
Wierzbicka, Anna. 1985. *Lexicography and Conceptual Analysis*. Ann Arbor: Karoma Press.
Wierzbicka, Anna. 1989a. "Semantic Primitives and Lexical Universals". *Quaderni di Semantica* 10.1.103-121.
Wierzbicka, Anna. 1989b. "Semantic Primitives — The Expanding Set". *Quaderni di Semantica* 10.2.133-157.
Wierzbicka, Anna. 1991. "Lexical Universals and Universals of Grammar". *Meaning and Grammar: Cross-linguistic perspectives* ed. by Michel Kefer & Johan van der Auwera, 383-414. Berlin: Mouton de Gruyter.

Thai

Anthony Diller
Australian National University, Canberra

Thai is a tonal language with fairly typical isolating typological features, at least in its informal conversational registers.[1] There is no inflectional morphology at all, and basic 'low' vocabulary tends to be monosyllabic and monomorphemic. Zero nominal anaphora is widespread, grammatical relations and predicate arguments often must be interpreted from context and resulting bare-verb or serial-verb constructions account for much practical communication. On the other hand, formal 'higher' Thai tends to make grammatical relations clear, to state nominals overtly and to mark subordination types explicitly. 'Higher' Thai also uses less basic vocabulary, for example that referring to abstract concepts or polite alternate forms appropriate for non-intimate and formal contexts. This vocabulary, although tonally assimilated, is normally of Pali-Sanskrit or Mon-Khmer provenance and is typically polysyllabic and complex — often very complex — in terms of borrowed derivational morphology. (Neologisms can be compounded together from a stock of Indic roots, reminding one of how new Greek-derived scientific terms can be created in English.) But 'higher' Thai uses monosyllabic forms too and the intermeshing of these contrasting sorts of lexical structure gives the normative standard language a distinctive character. The speech-level issue also has interesting consequences for the project of determining how semantic and lexical universals would be represented in Thai, as we will see below.

As a first approximation, the language is of the SVO type, however, especially in 'low' Thai, other pragmatically sensitive orders occur and the semantic/syntactic status of 'subject' and 'object' in any case would require theoretical attention beyond our scope here. Nouns precede modifiers, including possessives and relative clauses, auxiliaries precede main verbs and adpositions precede their objects (that is, Thai has prepositions, although determining them as a set is complicated by certain verbs and nouns with decidedly preposition-like features).

Since there is no obligatory affixal indication of number, gender, case, tense, aspect, voice or the like, associated semantic notions are optionally conveyed in Thai by other means — for example, by individual words or construction types — or are simply understood from context. Important roles are played by so-called speech-act particles, serial-verb constructions and auxiliary verbs. An extensive system of nominal classifiers is an important feature of the language and classifiers are syntactically obligatory in some, but not all, contexts. The basis of co-occurrence is mixed, with agreement principles holding between classifiers and head nominals being (a) partly syntactic and arbitrary, (b) partly semantic and (c) partly pragmatic and sociolinguistic in nature (Juntanamalaga 1988). In noun phrases the most frequent (maximal) pattern is: *Head Noun + Qualifier + Number + Classifier + Specifier.*

In assessing how specific Natural Semantic Metalanguage (NSM) candidates could best be represented in Thai and how formulations could be constructed using these items, it is useful to keep a few general features of the language in mind. In fact, just what 'the language' might mean for Thai is perhaps the most critical feature. Different speech registers or what Sapir (1933) refers to as 'subforms of language' are especially salient in the Thai communicative context. Sociolinguistic, literary–stylistic and other factors would need to be analysed to clarify how Thai subforms are constituted and how these genres directly organise speakers' judgements of acceptability and even grammaticality. A simplistic assumption that Thai utterances could be classified merely as well-formed or not — made perhaps on the basis of how English speakers might feel about the status of their sentences — would be unworkable. As argued elsewhere (Khanittanan 1987; Diller 1988, 1993), native-speaker feelings about well-formedness in Thai depend on an evolving texture of socially situated linguistic registers or subforms.

NSM formulations in Thai would be a subform. If these formulations are to be represented in Thai they will need to find their place in the Thai landscape of other linguistic subforms and this will require a number of practical decisions, for example, the determination of lexical speech-level. Especially among less educated or refined speakers (and in private among more refined ones), colloquial conversation is typically characterised by 'low' lexical forms (e.g. *rú:* 'know'; *yà:k* 'want') differing from 'high' forms more characteristic of polite or formal situations (e.g. *sâ:p* 'know'; *tô'ngka:n* 'want, would like'), although intermediate forms may be in use too and only rarely, if ever, would speech-level alternates be entirely synonymous (for discussion of KNOW, see section 6.2).

Discussion in sections 6.1–6.8 **assumes** that the Thai version of a semantic metalanguage is best constructed as an intimate, informal linguistic subform, as though we were overhearing, say, a mother talking to her daughter. In section 6.9 we return to this issue.

6.1 Substantives

Considerations relating to how NSM primitives I and YOU should be represented in Thai are postponed to section 6.9. Tentatively, the I/YOU pair *chăn/thoe:*, shown in (1), will be satisfactory for purposes at hand:

(1)   chăn   yà:k   pay   kàp   thoe:
       1SG   want   go   with   2
       'I want to go with you.'

In sentences like (2), first-person possessive indication is omitted in Thai, although to avoid ambiguity the first-person pronominal (here *chăn*) could be repeated in the predicate as a postnominal modifier, as in (3). Sentence (4) shows that the 'default interpretation' of zero-anaphora actor/subject is frequently the speaker, but if a third-person referent were salient in prior discourse, that would be apt to attract anaphoric interpretation instead. In such a case, to force first-person reference an overt form would be needed, as in (1). Examples (10), (12), (13) and others provide further examples of typical zero-anaphora interpretations.

(2)   chăn   yà:k   pay   hă: pù:
       1SG   want   go   seek father's-father
       'I want to see my grandfather.'

(3)   chăn   yà:k   pay   hă: pù: chăn
       1SG   want   go   seek father's-father 1SG
       'I want to see my grandfather.'

(4)   yà:k   pay   kàp   thoe:
       want   go   with   2
       '(I) want to go with you.'

In Thai there is a convergence of main indefinite and *wh*-question forms (or rather '-*ay*–question' forms, in the Thai case). Thus *khray* in preverbal position normally translates as an English 'who?' question, as in (5), and elsewhere as 'whoever' or 'someone', as in (6), but even here a question interpretation may be appropriate in certain contexts. Similarly *aray* sometimes translates as 'what?', sometimes as 'whatever' or 'something', as in (7)–(9) and (38). A question interpretation can be facilitated by particles, as in (7). Indefinite interpretation can be secured in various ways, for example by inserting assertion marker *kô'* after the *wh*-form or by reduplication (e.g. *aray-aray* 'something, anything'), but here there is a nuance of plurality. Preceding negative and existential forms tend to induce the indefinite interpretation, but not irrevocably; see (8). NSM candidates SOMEONE and SOMETHING could be directly handled by indefinite interpretations of *khray* and *aray*, but, as above, in some discourse contexts where English might require overt indefinite forms, in informal Thai discourse zero anaphora would be the normal selection; see (64). In literary styles of the language other indefinite forms are available, but they tend to be used for universal indefinites: *phû:-day* 'anyone'; *sìng-day* 'anything'. For plural reference, *ba:ng* + *Classifier* is used: *ba:ng khon* 'some people'.

(5) khray   tham
     who(ever) do
     'Who did it?'

(6) kháw hěn   khray   ma:
     3   see   who(ever) come
     (i) '(She) sees someone coming.'
     (ii) 'Who does (she) see coming?'

(7) aray   ná
     what(ever) PCL
     'What is it?'

(8) kòe:t   aray   khû'n nìa
     occur   what(ever) arise PCL
     (i) 'Something happened.'
     (ii) 'What happened?'

(9) chǎn hěn   aray   yù: thî:-nô:n
     1SG   see   what(ever) stay over-there
     'I see something over there.'

For NSM candidate PEOPLE the clear choice is Thai *khon*, a word functioning syntactically both as a common noun and as a classifier for normal humans. Since Thai has no obligatory number marking, this form translates both as 'person' and as 'people', depending on context. In common NSM expressions such as 'people think' or 'people say', Thai equivalents in *khon* would receive the desired interpretation unproblematically, as in (10) and (11). A redundant third-person pronoun *kháw* illustrated in (11) assists in establishing a non-specific plural interpretation that evokes social norms or majority views, but *kháw* is not strictly necessary to establish the desired NSM interpretation.

(10) thâ: tham yà:ng   ní: khon   ca   wâ:
     if   do   like/CLF this person IRLS say(-bad)
     'If you do like this, people will say bad things about you.'

(11) khon   kháw wâ: ta:m   bun   ta:m   kam
     person 3   say   follow merit follow karma
     'People say that events take their own course.'

6.2 Mental Predicates

NSM candidate WANT is clearly *yà:k* if an equi-subject complement clause is the construction type required, as in (1)–(4). Either a different construction type or a different lexical verb would be needed if a switch-reference postverbal nominal object were to be indicated, followed by a clause. 'I want you to know this', for example, would require a complement clause introduced by switch-reference–indicating form *hây*, elsewhere a verb meaning 'give, allow'. Only rarely does *yà:k* function as a simple transitive verb with nominal object, mainly in set expressions such as *yà:k ná:m* 'want water', that is, 'to be thirsty'. Otherwise, fully transitive verbs such as *tô'ng-ka:n* (closer to 'would like') or *aw* (more literally 'take') would be appropriate ways to translate English transitive 'want (something)'.

NSM candidate FEEL is represented in straightforward manner by Thai *rú:sù'k*, as in (12) and (13). Although etymologically this is a compound (see KNOW below) it now clearly functions as a single lexical item. Culturally, although Thais are taught that emotional detachment is a Buddhist goal of existence, in practice they relish conversation about feelings and *rú:sù'k* would be heard in a wider range of Thai contexts than 'feel' would be in corresponding English ones.

(12) *rú:-sù'k saba:y*
      feel   healthy/comfortable
      'I feel good.'

(13) *rú:sù'k yà:ng ní:*
      feel   like/CLF this
      'I feel like this.'

Thai *rú:sù'k* sometimes corresponds to English 'think' with a complement clause in the 'suppose' sense, but colloquial English can use 'feel' in this way too (e.g. 'I feel this is not a good idea'). For NSM purposes, THINK is probably better represented by *khít*, although the verb has potential connotations of reckoning or figuring out: *khít lê:k*, literally to 'think number(s)', means 'to calculate' and a pocket calculator, which presumably would not THINK in the NSM sense, is a *khrû' ang-khít-lê:k* 'machine-think-number'.

(14) *khít wâ: kin   láe:w*
      think COMP eat   already
      'I think she has eaten it.'

A complication is the verb *nú'k* which also translates into English sometimes as 'think', but sometimes also as 'feel' or colloquially as 'guess', as in (15). This verb is particularly appropriate for situations of musing, wondering, attempting to recall or emphasising that one is not entirely sure of something. If a fact is 'on the tip of one's tongue' but one cannot think of it, an expression in *nú'k* is appropriate. In past time contexts, as in (16), a contrary-to-fact interpretation is often natural; compare with (35) and (36).

(15) nú'k   wâ: pen   ôn   chanít   nu'ng
      think COMP   be   bamboo:rat kind:of   one
      'I guess it's a kind of bamboo rat.'

(16) to':n   nán   nú'k   wâ: pen   ôn
      period that think COMP   be   bamboo:rat
      'At that time I thought it was a bamboo rat (but it wasn't).'

NSM expressions in THINK typically have an interpretation that one holds a particular opinion or, perhaps as the result of cognitive processes, one has come to a certain conclusion. For this type of thinking *khít* is more appropriate than *nú'k*.

For KNOW the most direct Thai selection is *rú:*, particularly if a general principle is adopted for Thai NSM selections to be at the lower, more intimate level of speech. *Sâ:p* is the usual high-level counterpart of *rú:* but it is also more restricted. *Sâ:p* is most frequent in contexts where one indicates whether or not one has learned of a specific piece of currently relevant information. For a deeper, more permanent kind of knowing, either through study or by intuition, *rú:* is more appropriate. Thus the prefixal nominalisation *khwa:m-rú:* directly translates 'knowledge', but a corresponding nominalisation with *sâ:p* seems awkward or unacceptable. 'Know' in the sense of 'be acquainted with' is *rú:càk*; this form takes a postverbal nominal object rather than a complement clause.

(17) rú: wâ: pay   tha:ng   nǎy
      know   COMP   go   way   which(ever)
      'I know which way he went.'

Given the way in which SAY (THAT) is used in NSM formulations, Thai *phû:t (wâ:)* is probably the best choice, as in (18), but *phû:t* without a complement clause usually translates as 'to speak'. Other possibilities are *bò':k (wâ:)* and *lâw (wâ:)*, both of which fall closer to English 'tell' or 'relate'.

(18) kháw   phû:t   wâ: ca   pay
      3   say   COMP   IRLS   go
      'He said he would go.'

The form *wâ:*, glossed in examples (14)–(18) and elsewhere as COMP (complement marker), represents a full or partial grammaticalisation of the verb *wâ:* 'say' in serial-verb–derived constructions of expression, cognition, feeling and certain other subordinate relationships, as in (39). For a main-verb use of *wâ:*, see

(10) and (42), where, used alone, the verb takes on a connotation of saying something **contrary** — of criticising or opposing. With an adverbial adjunct or quotative complement, the effect is more neutral, as in (11) and (19). However, for NSM candidate SAY, the likelihood of disparaging nuances when *wâ:* is used alone as a main verb makes this a poor choice:

(19)   kháw   wâ: yà:ng   nán   dûay
        3   say   like/CLF   that   too
        'He said the same.'

Apart from the possibility of representing SAY, the form *wâ:* would certainly have a role to play in NSM formulations, as it is obligatorily present for embedded clauses in constructions shown in (14)–(18), (35), (36) and so on. There is considerable disagreement among Thai authorities as to whether *wâ:* in such clauses still retains properties of a verb 'say', and if so, which specific properties. Namtip Pingkarawat (1989:133–151) summarises the debate and, on (possibly circuitous?) syntactic grounds, sides with a full-verb analysis, with *wâ:* meaning 'say' retaining its essential verbhood. On the other hand, at least from a logical or truth-value point of view, some form of the complement analysis is indicated by disjunct co-ordinate statements like (20). These show that one can think something, with the 'something' introduced by a *wâ:* clause, without actually expressing anything about the thought. Whatever *wâ:* may mean in the first clause of (20), it does not mean that the person thinking actually said anything. Therefore in NSM formulations, *wâ:* can occur in complement clauses predictably and be safely taken as a semantically transparent grammaticalised form as may be required by syntax.

(20)   khít   wâ: di: tàe: mây   dây   phû:t   yà:ng   nán
        think   ?   good   but   not   ACMP   say   like/CLF   that
        'I think it is good but I did not say so.'

6.3 Determiners and Quantifiers

THIS in Thai is fairly straightforward as to basic lexical selection. The form *nî:* occurs as an independent pronominal in most contexts, as in (21), but the function is especially demonstrative-emphatic and *nî:* is often accompanied by facial pointing. The physical context of the speech situation is usually evoked, so the best translation in English is sometimes 'here!'. The 'milder' tone-shifted variant *ní:* is used anaphorically as a modifier to another nominal form in a noun phrase. When the referent is thought of as individuated, *ní:* normally occurs in specifier position in the basic noun phrase pattern, preceded by a classifier, as in (22). The form *ní:* is also used after a few prepositions and in some adverbial constructions, as in (23) (see also Diller & Juntanamalaga 1989).

(21) du: ní: sî
      look   this   PCL
      'Look at this!'

(22) du: mǎ: tua   ní: sî
      look   dog   CLF   this PCL
      'Look at this dog.'

(23) kháw   tham   yà:ng   ní:
      3   do   like/CLF   this
      'He did it like this.'

In (22) the classifier *tua* is used preceding *ní:* if an individual, specific dog is being referred to, and this classifier is also required for counting dogs and in certain other quantifying expressions. Also, the classifier and deictic alone, without the head noun, is a common anaphoric device — *tua ní:* 'this one' (that is, the dog previously mentioned or obvious from context). Now a common function for THIS in NSM formulations is to refer anaphorically back to a prior segment of the formulation ('I say this because ...'). To use *ní:* alone for THIS in such cases would be perhaps intelligible but improperly emphatic; conservative language authorities might object to it and brand it incorrect. A headless anaphoric classifier construction — such as *rû'ang ní:* 'this matter', *khô': ní:* 'this item', *sìng ní:* 'this thing' or *yà:ng ní:* 'this sort (of thing)' — would sound more natural, but would raise the question of the semantic basis of classifier selection.

TWO could only be *sǒ':ng* in Thai, but classifiers are obligatory when counting most discrete items, as in (24). Note that for sentences like (25) the head noun, but not the classifier, is regularly omitted if recoverable from context, for example if the sentence is answering a question in 'how many?'.

(24) kháw   mi: lû:k-cha:y   sǒ':ng   khon
      3   have   son   two   person/CLF
      'He has two sons.'

(25) mi: sǒ':ng   khon
      have   two   person/CLF
      'He has two.'

THE SAME in the sense of 'the same one' or 'the same thing' would usually be in Thai a classifier construction of the above type, as in (26), using the form *Classifier + diaw-kan*, a lexicalised compound consisting of *diaw* 'single' and *kan* 'together', a reciprocal and gathered-plural marker. In (55) the form is shown with locative and temporal items patterning as though classifiers. When English 'the same thing' has an adverbial function such as '(act) in the the same manner', as in (27), a further compounding is indicated for Thai — *yà:ng-diaw-kan* 'in the same way', with a higher speech-level alternate *chên-diaw-kan*. In extended discourse, deictic expressions such as *yà:ng nán* 'like that' are used more frequently for indicating sameness when anaphoric linkage is clear, as in (19). To use *yà:ng-diaw-kan* in contexts like these seems rather emphatic: '(to say) exactly the same thing'.

The simple adjectival verb *mŭ'an* 'to be of the same type or quality' is another good NSM candidate. It also forms an adverbial in *-kan*, sometimes translating into English as 'the same', as illustrated in (28). Thai speakers report that *mŭ'an-kan* sentences like (28) can have paraphrases of the (27) type in *yà:ng-diaw-kan* (or *chên-diaw-kan*). But in addition *mŭ'an-kan* has a number of extra possible interpretations, depending on context, such as 'also', 'rather' and sometimes a disjunctive or concessive nuance of 'even so'. This range would seem to complicate its use for NSM purposes.[2] This would leave *diaw-kan* and *yà:ng-diaw-kan* as the leading contenders to represent NSM candidate THE SAME, with syntax to decide the exact form.

(26)   *nî: mă: tua diaw-kan*
       this dog CLF same
       'This is the same dog.' (As the one we saw here yesterday, for example.)

(27)   *chăn yà:k tham yà:ng-diaw-kan*
       1SG want do same
       'I want to do the same.'

(28)   *chăn yà:k tham mŭ'an-kan*
       1SG want do same
       (i) 'I want to do the same.'
       (ii) 'I want to do it too (but ....).'

Possibilities for NSM candidates MANY (MUCH) and ALL (EVERY) are shown in (29). As a first approximation, it appears that Thai regularly makes a mass/count distinction for quantified nominal entities. For mass entities, *mâ:k* 'much' and *mòt* 'all' would seem appropriate as NSM representatives. On the other hand, if a speaker has sets of discrete individual items in mind, different lexical items are used to quantify, and syntactic construction type differs as well. Forms *lă:y* 'many' and *thúk* 'all, every' require classifiers in final position, as in (30). Also, these forms are regularly reduplicated to intensify the quantification.

(29)   'many'   Noun + *lă:y (-lă:y)* + Classifier
       'much'   Noun + *mâ:k*   (Rare: + Classifier)
       'every' Noun + *thúk (-thúk)* + Classifier
       'all'   Noun + *mòt*   (Rare: + Classifier)

(30) kháw mi: lû:k-să:w lă:y khon
    3   have daughter many person/CLF
    'She has many daughters.'

The quantifier *mòt* 'all' is particularly appropriate when something is thought of as exhausted, entirely used up or all gone, as in (31). This meaning is salient if the form is used with individuated items which could also take the construction *thúk* + *Classifier*. The meaning of the latter construction is perhaps logically equivalent to *mòt* in truth-value terms, but a different nuance is present stressing a distributive plurality (each and every one) rather than a notion of anything being all gone. However these meanings are not contradictory and the two sorts of quantifiers can be merged together, as in (32).

(31) kháw yo':m hây lû:k-să:w tàeng-nga:n mòt
    3   allow give daughter marry all
    'He has let all of his daughters marry.'

(32) kháw ta:y mòt thúk khon
    3   die all every person/CLF
    'They have all died.'

Example (33) shows that OTHER/ANOTHER is represented by forms *ì:k* and *ù':n* occurring in several construction types. As above, referents thought of as countable or in some sense individuated take classifier constructions, whereas those thought of as mass entities do not (with the normal English translation being 'more'). The exception to this is that classifiers may be proper measures and applied to masses ('another kilogram of rice'). If NSM candidate ANOTHER has the sense of an additional discrete item of a given type, this would be coded by *ì:k* in a classifier construction with *nu'ng*, a form of 'one' suggesting indefiniteness, as shown in (33). For higher numbers (e.g. 'another two' of something) — also for 'one' with some focus on the act of counting itself — the reverse order is used, as shown in (34).

(33) 'another'   Noun + ì:k   + CLF   + nu'ng
    'another', 'more'   Noun + ì:k   + Number + CLF
    'more'   Noun + ì:k
    'other'   Noun + ù':n (-ù':n)
    'other'   Noun + CLF   + ù':n (-ù':n)

(34) chăn hĕn thoe: kàp khon ì:k sŏ':ng khon
    1SG see 2   with person additional two person/CLF
    'I saw you and two other people.'

Ù':n, also reduplicated for plurality as *ù':n-ù':n*, represents NSM candidate

ANOTHER/OTHER if it is to have a general dominant sense of 'different' rather than 'additional'; see (55). Contrast in usage between *ù':n* and *ì:k* is subtle and subject to some speaker variation. In (35), *ù':n* clearly signals difference, but for some speakers a minimally different sentence with *ì:k*, as in (36), has two interpretations: one equivalent to (35) — indicating difference — and one focusing instead on addition, as noted in the translation of (36). For these speakers then *ì:k* would have about the same range as 'another' has in English. (Compare also the adverbial usage in (38).) Yet another possibility for 'different', emphasising comparative variability (for example, that two colours do not match), are the the forms *tà:ng* and *tà:ng-kan*, reduplicated for distributive plurality as *tà:ng-tàng* 'different, various'; see (59). Probably these forms are too specialised for NSM considerations.

(35) nù'k wâ: pen   khon   ù':n
      think that be   person/CLF   other
      'She thought it was another person (i.e. a different one, not the one expected).'

(36) nù'k wâ: pen   ì:k   khon   nu'ng
      think that be   additional   person/CLF   one
      'She thought it was another person (i.e. an extra person not counted on previously).'

6.4   Actions and Events

DO is directly represented by *tham*, as in (37); for further examples, see (5), (10), (23), (27), (28), (40) and (42).

(37) thoe: tham mây   dì:
      2   do   not   good
      'You did something bad.'

HAPPEN is somewhat problematic but is well represented by a very common serial-verb expression *kòe:t ... khû'n*, composed of components *kòe:t* 'be born, become, occur' and *khû'n* 'arise'. In higher speech levels a single etymologically related word *bangkòe:t* is available, but this is so unusual and stylistically marked as to devalue it as a NSM representative.

The form *kòe:t* is used either as a main verb with meanings 'to be born' and 'to occur' (taking a nominal subject) or as a quasi-auxiliary verb (followed by a clause). In the 'occur' meaning and in the quasi-auxiliary function it imparts a note of unpredictability and usually, but not irrevocably, a further nuance of undesirability, 'bad luck' or deterioration. For example, it is common in reports of fires, floods or other disasters. (Compare 'it befell' in archaic English.) These nuances suggest that *kòe:t* alone is unsuitable to represent NSM candidate HAPPEN, which should lack these negative associations. Also, the item is somewhat exceptional syntactically in that *kòe:t*, along with other existential verbs, shows an argument patterning sensitive both to pragmatic or discourse factors as well as to the (more semantic) attributes of co-occurring arguments.³

On the other hand, the serial verb construction *kòe:t ... khû'n* is more promising. Difficulties remain: (a) the construction is potentially discontinuous as in (38); (b) Thai speakers would certainly think that two separate words were involved, not a single compound; (c) some of the negative nuances reported above for *kòe:t* alone may remain. Nevertheless *kòe:t ... khû'n* seems to be accurate as a NSM representative for HAPPEN or HAPPEN TO, and NSM formulations in Thai using *kòe:t ... khû'n* have a well-formed effect — lacking, say, if *kòe:t* 'be born' were used alone to represent HAPPEN. For example, sentences (53) and (55) both contain *kòe:t ... khû'n* — if *kòe:t* were used alone in these sentences, it would be given default interpretation not as 'happen' but rather as 'be born'.

(38)   lò':n   kòe:t   aray   khû'n   ma: ì:k   láe:w
       3F   occur   what(ever)   arise   come   additional   already
       'Something (bad) happened to her again.'

(39)   rû'ang   ní: kòe:t   khû'n   phró'   wâ: khon   mây   rú:
       matter   this   occur   arise   because   COMP   person   not   know
       'This happened because people didn't know about it.'

6.5   Meta-Predicates

Negating in Thai is mainly done with preverbal *mây*. The best way to say 'no' in Thai is to negate the verb *chây* 'to be so', as in (40) (see also (43)).

(40)   mây   chây.   mây   dây   tham.
       not   so   not   ACMP   do
       'No. I didn't do it.'

Conditional IF is represented by *thâ:*, as in (41). The apodosis of the condition optionally includes the linking assertive marker *kô'*, as in (42). Alternatively, the protasis may be unmarked — in that case, the occurrence of *kô'* in effect marks the apodosis.

(41)   thâ: fŏn   tòk   chăn   ca   mây   ma:
       if   rain   fall   1SG   IRLS   not   come
       'If it rains, I won't come.'

(42) thâ: tham   khon   kô'   ca   wâ:
      if   do   person LINK   IRLS   say(-bad)
      'If you do it, people will say something bad about you.'

Being LIKE or SIMILAR TO in Thai is well represented by *khlá:y*, which optionally takes preposition *kàp* to introduce the nominal which something is similar to, as in (43):

(43) nî: khlá:y (kàp) kulà:p tàe: mây chây kulà:p
      this   like   with   rose   but   not so   rose
      'This is like a rose but it is not a rose.'

For so-called epistemic modals, indicating degree of speaker's certainty, one has a choice of several preverbal auxiliary elements in Thai. Expressing uncertainty, especially if concerning the future, most naturally involves irrealis particle *ca* following the auxiliary as well. The best choice for COULD is probably *à:t*, or better expanded as *à:t + ca*, as in (44) and (45). Note that the so-called root modal sense of English 'could' that involves having a potential or the ability to do something can be achieved in different ways in Thai, for example as in (46), although in some contexts *à:t* may have this reading as well.

(44) phrûng-ní: fǒn   à:t   ca   tòk
      tomorrow   rain   might IRLS   fall
      'It could rain tomorrow.'

(45) à:t   ca   tàe:k
      might   IRLS   break
      'It could break.'

BECAUSE in Thai is fairly well represented by *phró'*, which can take a directly following nominal or similar phrase, as in (46) and (47). Note that NSM sequences like 'because of this' and 'because of that' have corresponding Thai compound phrases in which a deictic is incorporated into a compound expression. Also possible is a complement clause introduced by *wâ:*, as in (39). A connective morpheme *loe:y* frequently occurs between subject and predicate of the following (result) clause, as in (47), and perhaps should be used in NSM formulations. In fact, in a two-clause sequence in 'lower' Thai *loe:y* alone in the second clause is a normal way of indicating that an unmarked preceding clause is to be interpreted as a reason or causal factor. (Compare 'so then' or 'so therefore' in English.) If NSM research were to favour SO or THEREFORE rather than BECAUSE (OF) to deal with causality, then Thai would have *loe:y* available as the obvious NSM candidate.[4] Otherwise, as in (47), it could be added as a predictable element.

(46) mi: sĭang   dang.   phró'-chan-nân   no':n   mây làp
      have sound   loud   because-of-that   recline not sleep
      'There was a lot of noise. Because of that, I couldn't sleep.'

(47) kháw tǐ: chăn.   phró'-chan-nán   chăn loe:y   ró':ng-hây
      3   hit   1SG   because-of-that 1SG   so   cry
      'He hit me. That's why I'm crying.'

VERY in Thai is best represented by *mâ:k* used with an adjectival verb. The same form with a mass noun means 'much' (see section 6.3). Intensification is a complex issue in Thai (Haas 1946) and for a number of idiomatic phrases, such as being 'very sick', other intensifiers are more common than *mâ:k*; see (54).

(48) di: mâ:k
      good very
      'It's very good.'

(49) yày   mâ:k
      big   very
      'It's very big.'

6.6 Time and Place

WHEN functioning to ask a question, direct or indirect, is best represented in Thai by *mû'a-ràу*, and as as a general temporal conjunction by *mû'a*, with *kô'* again optionally in the second clause, as in (51). The conjunction *mû'a* is most common in sequential clauses. A number of additional *when*-like words are used in the language to emphasise other temporal relations, such as *to':n* for simultaneity, *pho':* 'as soon as', and so on. Spans of time may also be indicated with expressions in *to':n*, as in (52), or in 'higher' Thai by *we:la:*, as in (53). *We:la:* elsewhere functions as an abstract noun translating English 'time' quite closely.

(50) tham mû'a-rày
      do   when
      'When did you do it?'

(51) mû'a   thŭ'ng sŭan-sàt raw   kô'   hĕn co'rakhê:
      when   reach   zoo   1PL   LINK see crocodile
      'When we reached the zoo we saw the crocodiles.'

(52) to':n ní: yù: krung-thê:p. kò':n   ní: yù: chiang-mày
      span this   stay Bangkok   before this stay Chiangmai
      'They live in Bangkok now. Before this, they lived in Chiangmai.'

(53) kòe:t   khû'n   we:la: diaw-kan
      occur   arise   time   same
      'It happened at the same time.'

For AFTER Thai makes etymological use of the body-part term *lăng* 'back' in a sense that seems virtually opposite to how English extends 'back' for temporal purposes. Unlike English, Thai temporal *lăng* or *lăng-cà:k* (where it is coupled with a preposition meaning 'from') seems to suggest that one has 'turned one's back' on something and passed on from it:

(54) lăng-cà:k-ní: kô'   rôe:m   pùay   nàk
      back-from-this   LINK   begin   sick   heavy
      'After this, she got very sick.'

Many locative notions in Thai are formed with *thî:*, which can function as a noun meaning 'place, space', as in (55). Locative questions are regularly formed with *thî:-năy*, as in (56) and (57), which would be the best representative for WHERE as a question.

(55) kòe:t   khû'n   thî: diaw-kan   mây   chây   thî: ù':n
      occur   arise   place   same   not   so   place   other
      'It happened in the same place, not in a different place.'

(56) tham   thî:-năy
      do   where
      'Where did you do it?'

(57) to':n-ní: yù: thî:-năy
      span-this   stay   where
      'Where is he now?'

If notions like UNDER or ABOVE were to be accorded NSM status, then in Thai they could be represented by the prepositional/adverbial forms *tây* and *nŭ'a*:

(58) mi: mê:k   mû':t-mû':t   yù: nŭ'a   phu:-khăw
      have   cloud   dark-dark   stay   above   mountain
      'There were black clouds above the mountains.'

6.7 Partonomy and Taxonomy

KIND can be represented in Thai directly as *chanít*, which can function syntactically either as a common noun or as a classifier. Another good possibility for KIND is *yà:ng*, already introduced in considering THE SAME in section 6.3. Whereas *chanít* is limited to classifying, *yà:ng* has a wider scope of usage; see (10) and (23). In (59) *yà:ng* could easily be substituted for *chanít*, but in (60) *chanít* seems especially appropriate since the purpose of the statement is obviously to discuss classification *per se*. (There are other candidates: a more scientific classificatory form *praphê:t* is a possibility but its speech-level seems too high for NSM; *bàe:p* 'style, type' might be considered, but it evokes strong associations of models, prototypes and copies — often of human-made items.)

(59) raw dây   du: sàt   tà:ng-tà:ng   lǎ:y   chanít
     1PL accomplish watch animal different   many   kind
     'We saw many different kinds of animals.'

(60) tôn-máy phûak ní: khu': tôn   chanít   diaw-kan
     tree   group this be   CLF   kind/CLF same
     mây chây sǒ':ng chanít
     not so   two   kind/CLF
     'These trees are the same kind, not two different kinds.'

The notion of PART, HAVING PARTS or of BEING A PART OF has at least two possibilities in Thai as it does in English. A noun/classifier *sùan* is available which answers well to the English noun *part*. In addition, the verb *mi:* translates into English either as an existential 'there is/are' or as a quite general verb 'to have'.[5] Thus Thai, like English, can represent part–whole relationships either through a specific nominal meaning 'part' or through a verb of 'having' (i.e. as a part, understood), as in (61)– (63). As a lexical item *mi:* is far more frequent than *sùan* and NSM formulations with Thai versions in *mi:* tend to seem accurate and natural, whereas those in *sùan* may feel awkward or unduly technical, especially in otherwise 'low' speech. It is likely that NSM decisions concerning English *part of* versus *to have* would have parallel consequences for Thai.

(61) khwǎ:n yô':m   mi: dâ:m
     axe   normally have   handle
     'An axe has a handle.' (Intended as a generalisation.)

(62) má: tua nán mi: hǎ:ng ya:w
     horse CLF that have tail   long
     'That horse has a long tail.'

(63) nâ: mi: camù:k   pà:k   kàp   ta: sŏ':ng   duang
      face have nose   mouth   and   eye two   CLF
      'The face has a nose, a mouth and two eyes.'

6.8 Evaluators and Descriptors

GOOD in Thai would best be represented by *di:*, as in (20), (48) and (64), but there are a few complications: 'feeling good', that is physically well and/or in a good mood, is usually indicated in other ways, as in sentence (12), for example. BAD is most frequently *mây di:* 'not good', as in (37). Other ways of translating English *bad* are more specific and include *le:w* 'inferior (quality)', *rá:y* 'wicked, cruel', *chûa* 'morally evil', *nâw* (and other forms) 'rotten', *phìt* 'wrong, incongruous', *yâe:* 'be very unpleasant', and so on. Note also 'bad' nuances of many main verbs, for example: *wâ:*, as in (10) and (42), discussed in section 6.2; and *kòe:t*, as in (38), discussed in section 6.4.

(64) thoe: tham di:
      2   do   good
      'You did something good.'

(65) kháw pen khon   di:
      3   be   person good
      'He is a good person.'

BIG, if intended in a general sense, would be *yày* in Thai, as in (49) and (66), but if one has in mind something which has **grown** big, such as a person or animal, a different word *to:* could be selected to put emphasis on the change of state, 'to (now) be big'. SMALL would be directly represented by *lék*. If a qualifier like BIG or SMALL is used in a simple attributive sense, it follows its head noun directly, as in (66), but if used in a specifying sense, it occurs in the specifier position after a classifier in the general noun phrase pattern, as in (67).

(66) chăn hěn tôn-má:y yày
      1   see tree   big
      'I saw a big tree.'

(67) chăn hěn mă: tua lék
      1   see dog CLF small
      'I saw the/a small dog.' (That is, not the big one.)

6.9 Conclusion

The preceding sections have claimed that, given the right presuppositions, NSM candidates under current consideration can all be represented in Thai, but with varying degrees of directness or plausibility. In particular THIS, TWO, KNOW, WANT, FEEL, DO, GOOD, BIG, SMALL, IF, BECAUSE, NOT, AFTER/BEFORE, UNDER/ABOVE, KIND OF and LIKE can be represented in Thai by individual words which, although in some cases polysemous, do at least in one reading directly represent the core NSM meanings. Thai speakers could thus rather naturally come to delimit the usage of these items in a way capturing the intended NSM semantic values — just as users of English NSM formulations would need to delimit, for example, the polysemy of English *know* to the required NSM sense. Optimistically, this could be done "on the basis of an example", as suggested by Wierzbicka (1992:236, note 5).

For other NSM candidates, the selection of Thai representatives depends how several 'NSM ground-rules' are interpreted. The question of 'distinct lexical item' is one area needing attention for Thai. In Wierzbicka's (1992:221) formulation, "conceptual primitives will present themselves in all languages in the form of distinct lexical items (whether morphologically simple or complex ...)". It would seem then a trivial and language-specific fact about English that, by convincing tests, certain distinct lexical NSM items like SOMEONE would be morphologically complex and other items would sometimes require articles or prepositions in their intended NSM interpretations, as in **THE** SAME or PART OF. Perhaps the potentially discontinuous Thai sequence *kòe:t ... khû'n*, which semantically appears to represent HAPPEN quite accurately, is on a par with these English forms, since *khû'n* arguably functions as a predictable grammaticalised element in this lexicalised expression.

There remains however some tension between the **recognition** of individual NSM representatives in Thai and the realistic **construction** of a full Thai version of semantic metalanguage — an effectively functioning linguistic subform — complete with syntax and taking into account the semantic nuances conveyed by particular Thai syntactic construction types. The extent to which sociolinguistic or so-called pragmatic variables could be 'bracketed out' of this enterprise or rendered innocuous extras remains to be seen.

For example, what to do about classifiers, overt pronouns and zero anaphora? Syntactically, we have seen that few full nominals are needed in 'low' Thai, although classifiers are frequently required, sometimes adding their own semantic nuances. Section 6.3 shows that good Thai NSM candidates for THIS, THE SAME, TWO, MANY, ANOTHER and so on usually require classifier constuctions. In many cases, as when these items refer to normal humans, classifier selection is straightforward and can be considered syntactically predictable, as in (25). On the other hand, when anaphoric linkage is back to entire statements made in prior discourse or to referred-to events, states and so forth, then classifier selection intrudes more into the NSM enterprise. For formulations like 'I say this because ...' or 'This happened because ...' Thai would not normally use *ní:* THIS alone; rather, an appropriate classifier would be selected in pre-position, as in (39). Recall that a lone deictic in Thai is emphatic, as, for example, in (21). Although the constrained nature of current versions of NSM would not require many classifiers in Thai, it is unlikely that they could be excluded completely.

As noted already, a constituting feature of subforms of colloquial Thai is zero anaphora — the absence of overt nominals — and the resulting high frequency of serial-verb constructions. Substantive reference is apt to be construed on the basis of speaker–listener assumptions, from prior discourse, from the physical setting of speech or from other shared background information. Similarly, classifiers are often used in anaphoric situations (where pronouns might be used in English) providing 'just enough information', as it were, to allow identification of nominal referents. The assumption that such nominal information will be automatically supplied establishes or reinforces a kind of solidarity among interlocutors which is integral to the 'low' register. It is as though the speaker were operating on the principle: "I know that you will think that I am saying something about **this**, because you and I think the same thing about this, you are like me."

On the other hand, formal or literary Thai typically 'fills in' much nominal material of this sort overtly, as well as opting for 'high' lexical alternates. A good way for a Thai speaker to underscore formality and social distance is to supply nominal information that the listener(s) would know already. Such discourse tends to be scripted, ceremonial, non-interactive and probably not the appropriate speech-level choice for NSM-based formulations.

Related critical concerns are raised by overt substantives when they **do** occur in 'low' registers of Thai. In this context, it is worth returning to NSM candidates I and YOU (section 6.1). Thai distinguishes a number of first-person/second-person pairs, as in (68). Pairings shown are based merely on normative tradition and probably reflect frequency; other combinations are possible. All of these forms should be considered preliminary possibilities to represent I and YOU in Thai.

(68)   *ku:/mu'ng*   non-deferential, speaker either sex, considered rude or insulting in educated urban speech; common in rural speech;

khâ:/e:ng   non-deferential, speaker either sex, considered rustic or coarse in urban speech; common in rural speech;

chăn/thoe: non-deferential, speaker either sex;

kan/kae: non-deferential, intimate, mainly male interlocutors;

dichăn/khun   non-intimate, non-deferential, female speaker;

phŏm/khun   deferential, male speaker;

kraphŏm/thân   very deferential, male speaker;

khâphacâw/thân   impersonal, formal, speaker either sex;

úa/lú':   non-deferential (Chinese associations).

For NSM purposes, why select *chăn/thoe:* instead of some other pair? To answer this, some selectional issues are first illustrated through an imaginary 'case study'. Suppose a girl wanted to go out shopping with her mother; she could easily express this desire through (69):

(69) yà:k   pay   dûay
      want   go   along
      '(I) want to go too.'

(70) nŭ   yà:k   pay   kàp   khun   mâe: khâ
      rat   want   go   with   'virtuous' mother PCL
      'I'd like to go along with you, please, mother.'

In situations where pronominal meanings are directly retrievable from context of discourse, if overt pronominal or other personal reference forms are **not** omitted then they are typically present because speakers are wanting to achieve communicative goals relating to sociolinguistic dynamics. If, instead of (69), the child said (70), her chances of being taken along could well be improved, since *nŭ:*, literally 'rat' or 'mouse', when used as a first-person pronominal substitute by girls to elders brings a respectful deference into the communicative act, as does the final polite female particle *khâ*. When *nŭ:* is used along with *mâe:* 'mother' functioning in effect as a second-person form, the tone of the sentence is at once respectful and intimate, evoking the mother–daughter relationship. To precede *mâe:* with *khun*, a polite form etymologically meaning 'virtuous', is all the more deferential. The underlying message conveyed by the overt marking of (70) might be something like: "a nice mother like you would naturally take her polite and respectful little daughter along with her shopping."

In the same situation, an almost unimaginable effect would be achieved by using the true pronominal forms selected as NSM representatives, *chăn* 'I' and *thoe:* 'you':

(71) chăn   yà:k   pay   kàp   thoe:
      1SG   want   go   with   2
      'I want to go with you.'

A Thai speaker could hardly conceive of a daughter saying this seriously to her own mother, even in anger. (Sarcasm or a pouting jest might be barely possible.) These pronominal forms signal quite strongly a lack of respect and deference that would be truly shocking coming from a child, or even from an adult woman to her mother. On the other hand, given a reversal of interlocutor roles, the sentence becomes a normal possibility: a mother could easily say (71) to her daughter with no feeling of inappropriateness at all.

In constructing the novel Thai linguistic subform of NSM-based formulations, *chăn* and *thoe:* are selected for I and YOU. This is **not** because they are technically 'neutral' with respect to other forms in (68). In fact no form in (68) is sociolinguistically neutral and even zero anaphora used to avoid other selections is not an entirely transparent discourse move. Rather, a decision has been made to allow Thai NSM-users to imagine a particular sort of interlocutor dyad. The articulation of NSM formulations is to be as though a mother were speaking to her child. In the natural course of events in virtually every speech community, this is a prior type of communication in ontogenetic terms. If mother-to-child speech can be taken universally as the first and foremost type of human discourse, then it would not seem inappropriate for the NSM subform to reflect this articulation when specific decisions need to be made, as in the *chăn* and *thoe:* case.

In fact, all of the Thai items suggested for NSM representation above have been selected with this particular interlocutor dyad in mind. Perhaps this specific decision is arbitrary and will need to be reviewed, but a general principle remains. As NSM research progresses, formulations may well approach the status of a universal semantic consensus, but to express such agreement as understandable discourse, local sociolinguistic constraints, such as those imposed by Thai personal pronouns, will inevitably evoke culturally situated modes of articulation. Further cross-cultural research is needed to work out how the articulation issue may affect the NSM enterprise generally. In such work perhaps technical labels like 'formal/informal' or 'high' and 'low' speech levels need to be supplemented by considering typical or prototypical interlocutor dyads like the one suggested above.

Notes

1   I am indebted to several authorities, especially to Preecha Juntanamalaga and Orawan Poo-israkit, for useful comments on a draft of this paper. Transcription follows the tone-marking system of Mary R. Haas (1964) with some straightforward adaptations, including long vowels indicated by a colon. Segmentals follow the romanisation system of the Thai Royal Institute. High vowels: i, u', u; mid vowels: e, oe, o; low vowels: ae, a, o'. Special abbreviations: ACMP accomplishment marker, COMPlement marker, IRLS irrealis, CLF classifier, LINKing assertive marker, NP noun phrase, PCL sentence final particle, PLural, SG singular.
2   A more throrough examination of how sameness, similarity and difference are expressed in Thai clearly warrants further research.
3   For a modest class of existential verbs in Thai, including *mi:* '(for) there to be', *khà:t* 'to be lacking', and so on, the normal SV(O) characterisation for Thai basic word order is somewhat disrupted: topical (especially old-information or deictically specified) subjects do precede these verbs, but new-information subject-like arguments and indefinite ones regularly follow. In the latter case, the preverbal NP position may be occupied by an extra dative experiencer or genitive possessor argument which — depending on theoretical inclinations — might or might not be identified as 'subject'. (Note that English 'lack' is a so-called middle-verb with reminiscent characteristics.) It is further interesting that verbs of this type tend in Thai to have two rather distinct readings (or at least two separate translations into English), one following general SV(O) organisation and an (existential) one following the pragmatic principles sketched above:

mi: 'to have' (normal SVO) or 'to be' (existential); *khà:t* 'to be torn' (normal SV) or 'to lack' (existential). Now *kòe:t* is clearly a verb of this general type, with alternate readings 'be born' (SV) and 'to occur, happen (unexpectedly)' (existential) — the latter pragmatically sensitive in the way sketched above. Derived from the latter main-verb use is the semantically similar auxiliary function mentioned in the text. The serial construction *kòe:t ... khû'n* inherits the main syntactic *kòe:t* (existential) characteristics, which explains why in example (38) the experiencer of NSM candidate HAPPEN precedes *kòe:t*, whereas the new-information indefinite argument — the thing that happens — follows it. On the other hand, example (39) demonstrates that if the thing that happened is topical old information, for example if its noun phrase includes a deictic form such as *ní:* 'this', then such a noun phrase regularly precedes *kòe:t* with no experiencer mentioned. Note also (8), which follows the same principles.

4   The form *loe:y* is characterised by a high degree of 'Thai-style grammaticalisation' — semantic derivation and syntactic reorganisation of verbs and nouns into preposition-like, adverb-like or auxiliary-like elements (see also preceding note). The lexical form *loe:y* can still function in a (diachronically prior) main-verb sense of 'to pass beyond', but it has acquired at least three frequent adverb-like functions, each with distinct syntactic properties: (a) 'so, consequently'; (b) 'exceedingly'; (c) 'at all' (negative intensifier). If *loe:y* were used alone in NSM formulations to achieve the effect of BECAUSE in a preceding clause, care would need taken that other functions and meanings did not intrude.

5   See Note 3.

References

Diller, Anthony. 1988. "Thai Syntax and 'National Grammar'". *Language Sciences* 10.2.273-312.

Diller, Anthony. 1993. "Diglossic Grammaticality in Thai". *The Role of Theory in Language Description* ed. by William A. Foley, 393-420. Berlin: Walter de Gruyter.

Diller, Anthony & Preecha Juntanamalaga. 1989. "Deictic Derivation in Thai". *Prosodic Analysis and Asian Linguistics: To honour R. K. Sprigg* (= Pacific Linguistics C-104) ed. by D. Bradley et al., 169-196. Canberra: Australian National University.

Haas, Mary R. 1946. "Techniques of Intensifying in Thai". *Word* 2.127-130.

Haas, Mary R. 1964. *Thai-English Student's Dictionary*. Palo Alto: Stanford University Press.

Juntanamalaga, Preecha. 1988. "Social Issues in Thai Classifier Usage". *Language Sciences* 10.2.313-330.

Khanittanan, Wilaiwan. 1987. "Some Aspects of Language Change in the Linguistic Usage of Kings Rama IV, Rama V and Rama VI". *Proceedings of the International Conference on Thai Studies, Australian National University, Canberra, 3-6 July 1987*, vol 3.1.53-70.

Pingkarawat, Namtip. 1989. *Empty Noun Phrases and the Theory of Control, with Special Reference to Thai*. PhD Thesis, University of Illinois at Urbana-Champaign.

Sapir, Edward. 1933. "Language". *Encyclopedia of Social Sciences*, vol 9.155-169. New York: Macmillan.

Wierzbicka, Anna. 1992. "The Search for Universal Semantic Primitives". *Thirty Years of Linguistic Evolution* ed. by Martin Pütz, 215-242. Amsterdam: John Benjamins.

Acehnese

Mark Durie
University of Melbourne

Bukhari Daud and Mawardi Hasan
Universitas Syiah Kuala, Banda Aceh

Acehnese is an Austronesian language, spoken by approximately two million people in the Special Region of Aceh in Indonesia.[1] There are also some speakers in Malaysia and in Medan, North Sumatra. Dialect diversity is quite considerable. Within Austronesian, Acehnese is now believed to be most closely related to the Chamic languages, spoken in Vietnam, Cambodia (with some refugee communities in Malaysia) and Hainan. Acehnese itself exhibits many typological features characteristic of Indonesian languages, but more notably the marked influence of languages from the Southeast Asian mainland, particularly of Mon-Khmer languages.

Like other languages in the region, Acehnese has no inflectional morphology, and virtually no grammatical categories such as voice, tense, gender, case, number and so on. Quite a good case can be made that number is not even a category within the pronominal system, however it does make a distinction between ego, first-person inclusive, and first-person exclusive pronouns, which can be understood as involving a contrast in personhood, rather than in number. In general, Acehnese linear precedence within constituents is organised according to the head-first/right-branching principle. Thus it has prepositions, and most modifiers of nominals, for example relative clauses, follow their heads. At the clause level there is an overall preference for (A)V(O) order for transitive sentences, with either (S)V or V(S) order for intransitives. Aspectual particles and polarity marking tends to immediately precede the verb. In addition to verbal predicates, Acehnese makes heavy use of NP and PP predicates, with a preferred (S)NP/PP$_{(PRED)}$ order in discourse.

Acehnese displays an 'active' grammatical structure: some intransitive verbs take an argument, S_A, which has properties of the transitive A, and others take an argument, S_O, with the properties of the transitive O. For this paper it is important that this difference reflects a quite consistent semantic contrast between volitional and non-volitional predicates. In morphosyntactic terms the difference is reflected most clearly in the cross-referencing system: the actor (A and S_A) is cross-referenced on the verb by a proclitic, the undergoer (O and S_O) by an enclitic. In this paper these clitic pronominals are glossed using English pronouns, except that the third-person clitics are glossed as '3'.

Like other languages of the region, Acehnese uses classifiers to support enumeration of nominals, thus *si-droe ureueng* (literally, 'one-CLASS person') 'a person'.

Acehnese is traditionally written with a script derived from the Arabic-based Malay Jawi script. Many recent publications use a Latin-derived script. The system used here is that of Durie and Daud (in press), and differs in some small details from the standard system that was established by a team of Acehnese scholars at Universitas Syiah Kuala in 1980 (see Hasan et al. 1980).

7.1 Substantives

I is *kèe*. This has some affixal allomorphs: *ku-* and *-kuh*. Other first-person forms are for use in more formal context, and to those with higher status. They are: *lôn*, *lông*, *ulôn*, *lôntuan*, *ulôntuan*.

YOU is *kah*. Allomorphs are *ka-* and *-keuh*. More formal second-person forms are *gata* and *droeneuh*. For decontextualised examples of the kind presented here, the forms *lôn* 'I' and *droeneuh* 'you', which are rather more formal, are appropriate, and these would be the forms offered by an Acehnese native speaker if you asked him/her to translate simple English sentences out of context. The use of *kah* and *kèe* is considered impolite in a formal conversation, especially in talking with an older person. However, there seems little doubt that the lower status forms are the proper lexical instantiations of the first- and second-person pronominals. Evidence for this is that these forms are used: (a) among those for whom social status is not relevant, for example between children; (b) when talking to oneself; (c) when talking with God (*kèe* only), implying that this first-person pronoun has no inherent derogatory implications towards to the addressee, even though in other contexts, such as in an argument, its use may imply derogation; and (d) when addressing non-people, where social context is also irrelevant. *Kèe* and *kah* are also the forms which are phonologically simpler and internally unanalysable (more formal pronominal terms are longer and often complex). A rather nice example illustrating some of these principles is the following proverb (suitable for a young unmarried man), in which the speaker is *ku-* (*kèe*) I and the rain is *ka-* (*kah*) YOU:

(1) *Hai ujeuen, bèk   ka-tôh   ilèe; bijèh   kayèe gohlom*
     Hey rain   DONT! you-excrete yet seedling tree not:yet
     ku-pula. Hai tuboh bèh,   bèk   maté ilèe; bungong
     I-plant. Hey body come:on! DONT! die yet   flower
     mangat bèe gohlom ku-rasa.
     sweet smell not:yet I-feel
     'Hey rain, don't rain yet: I haven't yet planted my tree. Hey body, don't die yet: I haven't yet experienced (smelled) that fragrant flower.'

SOMEONE/WHO is quite unambiguously *soe*. This is an 'epistemological classifier' (Durie 1985a): it can be used for 'who' in questions, and for indefinite expressions of various kinds expressing meanings like 'someone' or 'anyone'. Thus:

(2) *Soe pubuet nyan?*
     who do   that
     'Who did that?'

(3) *Ku-ngieng soe laén nyang duek ateueh panteue.*
     I-see   who other REL   sit top   platform
     'I see someone else sitting on the platform.'

Soe is applicable to non-humans, such as God or spirits, in addition to people:

(4) *Soe tuhan gata?*
     who god   your
     'Who is your god?'

Another form to mention in the context of discussing WHO/SOMEONE is *droe* 'person', which is the classifier for counting 'someones', including, for example, God:

(5) *Tuhan si-droe.*
     God   one-CLASS
     'God is one.'

Droe is also the base for forming reflexives and a set of personal pronouns (all for persons). Note that in Acehnese all pronouns are 'someones': there is no equivalent of English *it*. The classifier *droe* is perhaps interpretable as an allolex of *soe*.

SOMETHING/WHAT is clearly *peue* (dialect *pue*). Like *soe*, this is an epistemological classifier: it can be used alone as 'what' in questions, and also as 'something', and in formally complex constructions meaning, for example, 'anything, nothing, whatever, everything'.

(6) *Peue nyan.*
what that
'What's that?'

(7) *Na peue lôn-tanyöng.*
BE something I-ask
'There is something I want to ask.'

Sometimes there may be ambiguity in the use of *peue*:

(8) *Nyoe peue?*
this/here what
'What is this?' or 'Here is something.'

Acehnese has no very good candidate for a noun 'thing'.

For PEOPLE the word is *ureueng* 'person/people'. Acehnese has no number category hence the vagueness of 'person/people'. This term is restricted to human beings: it cannot be used for God, spirits or, say, fairy-tale talking animals, in the way that *soe* can be:

(9) *Ka ureueng-peugah lagèe nyan.*
already people-say way that
'People said that.'

Note that translation of sentences using the English expression *people say* will not necessarily elicit this expression, for Acehnese has a word *gop* 'other person/people' which is used where in English we would often say *people say*. Certainly this would be used when one is describing opinions of others that one does not wish to own for oneself, as for example in 'People will say bad things about you'.

7.2 Mental Predicates

THINK is *piké* (from Arabic *fikr*). This can be used intransitively, 'I am thinking', and also in the frame *piké S* 'think that S', where S is a clausal complement. A non-sentential object of thought can be expressed with a preposition *keu* — *piké keu X* means 'think about, consider X', as in 'consider the lilies of the field' — but this is clearly a different meaning from 'think that S'. The meaning of English *think of* in *think of mother* is expressed by a completely different verb, *ingat keu*, which may be translated as 'think of, call to mind, remember'. Note that *keu* is the preposition used generally with all objects of mental attention and emotion; it contributes no other specific meaning of its own:

(10) Ku-piké nyan rimueng.
      I-think that tiger
      'I think that was a tiger.'

Acehnese has a considerable number of other verbs of similar meaning, for example *sangka* 'guess, suspect', but clearly *piké* is the primitive member of the group.

KNOW presents some complexities in Acehnese. Acehnese has a number of 'know' verbs, composed of the form *tu-* 'know' in combination with an epistemological classifier (for a full list, see e.g. Asyik (1972:104, 1987:96)). Thus *tu-peue* (dialect *teupue*) 'know (that)' or 'know what', *tusoe* 'know who', *tudum* 'know how much', *turi* 'be acquainted with' (German *kennen*) and so on.[2]

(11) ... hana   soe   toepeue   rasia nyan.
          NOTBE who   know:what   secret that
      '... no-one would have known that secret.'

(12) Lôn-tupeue   angèn malam bahaya.
      I-know:whether   wind   night dangerous
      'I know a night wind is dangerous.'

(13) Na ta-tujan   kapay bungka?
      BE you-know:when   ship   leave
      'Do you know when the ship leaves?'

(14) Lôn-tusoe   ureueng nyan.
      I-know:who   person   that
      'I know who that person is.'

(15) Lôn-tu-ho   geu-jak.
      I-know-whither   3-go
      'I know which way he/she went.'

One possibility might be to take *tu-* itself as the exponent of KNOW. Since *tu-* cannot be used independently, one then needs to account for the semantic contribution of the compulsory epistemological classifier used in conjunction with *tu-*. If this always makes a substantial semantic contribution, then in Acehnese it is impossible to talk about knowing without simultaneously classifying the type of knowledge involved, using one of the epistemological classifiers. (This was the interpretation adopted in Durie (1985a).) Such apparent exuberance would present a potential difficulty for NSM theory in that Acehnese would aways require one to say more than just KNOW. If NSM representations developed with other languages do not require such epistemological classification of KNOW, then we would have a classic type of non-translatability, but at the most primitive level in the metalanguage.

There seem to be two possible ways around this. It may be that Acehnese is making explicit something that is true for all language: that knowledge must be universally classified into types, roughly equivalent to *wh*-categories. So when we say *I know Mary* what we really mean is that we know X concerning Mary, where X is some kind of knowledge category. Similarly when we say *I know the answer* what we really mean is that we know **what** the answer is. Let us now consider the status of our presumed primitve KNOW. This is intended to be applicable to 'know that'-type contexts, as in *I know (that) Mary is sick*. If Acehnese really represents the universal situation, what then is the categorisation of knowledge for this kind of sentence? The Acehnese verb form used for this kind of knowledge is *tupeue* (from 'know+whether'), which suggests that the appropriate knowledge category is perhaps a non-ignorative[3] equivalent of 'whether'. This is the interpretation of this function of *tupeue* assumed in Durie (1985a). So following this line of reasoning, the obvious Acehnese exponent of KNOW is the prefix *tu-*.

On the other hand, it may be the case that Acehnese *tupeue* as used in 'know that' contexts is not semantically decomposable at all, and the apparently connected meaning of *peue* 'whether' is just a red herring. In this case, the morphological complexity of *tupeue* does not correlate with semantic complexity, and this word is in fact an Acehnese exponent of KNOW. This seems a more conservative approach, given previous assumptions about KNOW in NSM research. It still leaves us with a certain amount of complexity in the Acehnese system of verbs of knowledge, however. For in the case of verbs like *tusoe* 'know who', *tuho* 'know whither' and *tupat* 'know where', we must take it that semantic complexity **does** correlate directly with the morphological complexity, and that here *tu-* is also an exponent of KNOW. In fact, since *tupeue* itself is polysemous, having a 'know what' reading in addition to 'know that', we must assume that the 'know what' reading of *tupeue* is decomposable into *tu* 'know' + *peue* 'what', whilst for the 'know that' reading, *tupeue* simply means KNOW. So, following this line of reasoning, Acehnese has two exponents of KNOW, the bound form *tu-* and the free form *tupeue*.

SAY is *peugah*. We are sure that this is right candidate for the lexical primitive, but it is formally complex. *Peu-* is the causative morpheme, forming a transitive verb from the predicate *gah* 'known, famous'. Taken literally this verb should thus mean 'make known'. But this is etymology, not semantic analysis, and *peugah* does not mean this. It means simply SAY: we believe that one could *peugah* something to oneself, for example.

FEEL is probably best identified with *rasa* (from Sanskrit; it is also found in Malay), which has various presumably distinct meanings: 'feel by touch', 'taste', 'hold an opinion', 'experience states and emotions':

(16) *Lôn-rasa   seunang.*
      I-feel   happy
      'I feel happy.'

Another candidate is *nyeum* 'feel, taste, have an opinion'. Between *rasa* and *nyeum*, the distinction seems to be a matter of objectivity. *Rasa* implies objective experience, and *nyeum* implies something like experiencing a feeling. If one were to say 'feel cold', the sense with *rasa* would be 'feel the cold', and with *nyeum* would be simply 'feel as if I was feeling the cold'. Thus *nyeum* seems to be the more complex of the two. *Nyeum* has at least one marginal feature of an epistemological classifier: it can form a 'know' compound with *tu-*: *tunyeum* 'know what feeling'. *Nyeum* can be used as a conjuction meaning 'it is as if'. Note that *rasa* is also a noun, meaning 'taste, impression'.

WANT is a rather difficult mental predicate to locate as a verb in Acehnese, and deserves some careful discussion. The difficulty is that clear lexical distinctions are made according to the different kinds of causal links between wanting and the actual realisation of the thing wanted (as always in Acehnese, the semantic status of volition is crucial). At the same time there is no uncontroversial lexical candidate in Acehnese for WANT itself. One can distinguish the following different kinds of 'wanting' verbs:

(a) 'X wants X to do something', where X is both the wanter and the intended agent (e.g. *tém* 'want'). The sense of this is thus close to 'be willing to';
(b) 'X wants Y (= addressee) to do something', where Y is an addressee (e.g. *lakèe* 'ask for'). The sense of this is thus 'ask or tell someone to do something';
(c) 'X wants Y to happen or be the case' (e.g. *galak* 'happy, want', *meuh'eut* 'desire'). The sense of these types of verbs are thus either 'hope or wish for Y', or 'be happy if Y happened'.

When Acehnese people are asked to translate English expressions with *want*, typically verbs of any of the above three kinds will appear, according to the context.

The verb *tém* is applicable with a clausal complement that describes a volitional action of the one wanting.[4]

(17) *Lôn-tém woe.*
      I-want   return
      'I want to return.'

It is a strict requirement that the complement verb in this construction be volitional, taking either an A or an S_A (what is described as 'agent' in Durie (1985a) and (1985b), and 'actor' in Durie (1987)). For a discussion of complementation in Acehnese and this particular constraint, see Asyik (1987:365–367). Note that *tém* itself also takes an actor (Durie 1987), which is coreferential with the actor of the complement verb.

Rather less frequently there is no complement, as in example (18) where the following clause is a conditional adverbial clause, and not a complement of *tém*. Here the use of *tém* still implies that the actor (who happens to be a dog) would agree and be actively willing to be involved or take part if he were to be married off by the master of the house:

(18) Ta-tém   teuma   ro   adak geu-peukawén?
      you-want thus   PARTICLE   if   3-marry
      'So you (would) want (to go along with it) if he married you off.'
      (Sulaiman 1978:59)

The use of *tém* in contexts where active agreement or disagreement is at issue is quite characteristic.

The necessary causal link between the wanter and the fulfilment of the desire is perhaps reflected in a related but polysemous use of *tém* with non-volitional complements, meaning 'have the ability or potential to'.

Any English expression containing 'I want you ...' would often be most easily rendered in Acehnese, if imprecisely, with the verb *lakèe* 'ask', which takes an actor.

(19) Lôn-lakèe droeneuh beu-neu-woe.
      I-ask   you   DO!-you-return
      'I want you to return.'

Things wanted, but not yet come to pass, and not under the control of the speaker or addressee are often introduced with *galak* 'happy, like'. On its own *galak* can mean 'happy':

(20) Ka   galak-neuh.
      already happy-you
      'You are happy now.'

However the verb is at least two-ways polysemous: it can take an 'object' of happiness, and the meaning is 'like':

(21) Jih   hana   galak-jih keu droeneuh.
      She   NOTBE   like-3   to   you
      'She doesn't like you.'

Interestingly *galak* 'like' is one of the 'fluid-S' verbs of Acehnese. It can occur with either an actor or an undergoer (the latter is more usual), with the predictable semantic difference: use of an actor implies volitional control over the 'liking', and it is, for example, consistent with use of the imperative:

(22) *Bék ka-galak keu ureueng inöng nyan.*
    DONT! you-like to person woman that
    'Don't hanker after that woman.'

Galak can be used with a clausal complement, and here the 'happy' and 'like' meanings seem able to be distinguished. It is this clausal complement 'happy' reading of *galak* that provides a rendering of what Acehnese people would often say instead of, for example, 'I want you/him/her to do this'.

(23) *Lôn galak droeneuh neu-pubuet lagèe nyoe.*
    I happy you you-do way this
    'I am happy if you do this/for you to do this.' (Inexact translation of 'I want you to do this.')

(24) *Di lôn galak lôn-pajôh bu ngön eungkôt laôt.*
    FOCUS I like I-eat rice with fish sea
    'I like eating rice with sea fish.' (Djajadiningrat 1934, vol 2:435)

So frequent is the use of *galak* 'happy' with a sentential complement, that it is easy to misinterpret this meaning of *galak* as 'want', and indeed in Bakar et al. (1985) one of its senses is given as Indonesian *mau* 'want', and in Djajadingrat (1934) its first sense is given as Dutch *gaarne willende* 'gladly wanting'. But these translations are both too exuberant, and *galak* simply means 'happy that' or 'be pleased that', and such a meaning falls short of WANT.

Another putative verbal candidate for WANT is *meuh'eut* (from the noun *h'eut* 'desire, inclination', which is attested as an independent form in only some dialects). This verb can be used to describe anything from an inclination to a lustful desire. It takes an undergoer, and there is no implication of control over the thing wanted, nor of active readiness to do something, in contrast to *tém*. On the contrary, with *meuh'eut* there is a suggestion that there is some obstacle and the desire may not or ought not be fulfilled.

(25) *Di jih meuh'eut-jih that keu maté.*
    FOCUS (s)he want-3 very to death
    'She wants to die (but cannot).'

(26) *Lôn meuh'eut lôn-jak u Makah.*
    I want I-go to Mekka
    'I want to go to Mekka.' (Djajadiningrat 1934, under *h'eut*)

(27)   *Di   gopnyan meuh'eut-geuh that   aneuk-geuh ji-jak*
       FOCUS (s)he   want-3   very   child-3   3-go
       sikula.
       school
       'They very much want/wanted their children to go to school (but it wasn't possible or seems impossible).'

Both *h'eut* and *meuh'eut* can be used for wanting something or someone, as well as a clausal complement:

(28)   *Lôn meuh'eut that keu inöng nyan.*
       I   want   very to woman that
       'I really want that woman.'

Before leaving WANT, we should mention the particle *beu-* 'I want, may it be/happen that' (glossed DO!), and its negative counterpart *bèk* 'I don't want/may it not be/happen that' (glossed DONT!). These can be used with great productivity, in many contexts.

(29)   *Beu-neu-tupeue   ubat   nyoe peunténg.*
       DO!-you-know:that medicine this important
       'I want you to know that this medicine is important.'

(30)   *Beu-geu-riwang lom Teungku Jôhan u Acèh.*
       DO!-3-return   again title   Johan to Aceh
       'I want Johan to come back to Aceh again.'

(31)   *Bèk   neu-pubuet buet nyan.*
       DONT!   you-do   deed that
       'Don't do that.'

(32)   *Nyoe bèk   sagai jadèh.*
       this DONT! at:all happen
       'I don't want this to happen at all.'

(33)   *Bèk   p'iep rukok.*
       DONT! smoke tobacco
       'Don't smoke!'

These two particles are often used in imperative and negative imperative constructions, but the imperative sense is by no means obligatory. Both are also used in forming subordinate purposive clauses. Of course they can only be used for wanting by the speaker, thus 'I want', but not 'she wants'. However, within the limitation of this restriction, *beu* seems to provide the closest Acehnese exponent of WANT.

7.3 Determiners and Quantifiers

THIS is *nyoe*. It forms one of a set of three with *nyan* 'that' and *jéh* 'that, further away'. These demonstratives can be used as modifiers, or pronominally:

(34)   *Ka-beuet (kitap) nyoe.*
       you-read (book) this
       'Read this (book).'

A bound suffixal allomorph is *-noe*:

(35)   *Geu-meunari meu-noe.*
       3-dance   way-this
       'Dance like this.'

THE SAME should be clearly matched with Acehnese *sa* 'the same'. *Sa* is homonymous with but distinct from the word for 'one': the latter has allomorphy between *sa/si*, but *sa* 'the same' has no such allomorphy, and unlike *sa* 'one' it is used on its own as a predicate (e.g. 'These are the same') and also in productive combinations with epistemological classifiers: for example, *sa-jan* 'the same time/when',[5] *sa-ho* 'the same direction/whither', *sa-kri* 'the same manner/how', *sa-pat* 'the same place/where', *sa-ban* 'the same manner'.

(36)   *Kamoe   sa.*
       we:inclusive the:same
       'We are the same.'

(37)   *Jih ngön lôn sa-ban.*
       she with I   the:same-manner
       'She and I are the same (in some way).'

(38)   *Kamoe   sa-jan   lahé.*
       we:exclusive   the:same-when   born
       'We were born at the same time.'

But not **sa-soe*: to express 'the same person': *si-droe* 'one-person' can be used but only in some contexts ('John and Mark are *si-droe* = one and the same person').

OTHER is *laén*, which is polysemous, also having the meaning 'different':

(39) *Geu-piké ureueng laén.*
    3-think person other
    'He/she thinks (it was) another person.'

(40) *Geu-peugöt rumoh laén.*
    3-make house another
    'She/he made another house.'

Pronominal 'another' is *nyang laén* 'REL other', literally, 'what is other'.
TWO is *dua*. This is straightforward:

(41) *Gopnyan dua droe aneuk agam, si-droe aneuk inöng.*
    he/she two CLASS child male, one-CLASS child female
    'He/she has two sons and one daughter.'

ALL is *dum*. This can be used in combination with epistemological classifiers, for example, *dum-soe* 'everyone', *dum-peue* 'everything'. *Dum* is itself also an epistemological classifier with the meaning 'how much, what quantity'. When used alone, it often is compounded with *man*, a phonological variant of *ban* 'the whole lot':

(42) *Ka maté man-dum.*
    already die/dead whole-all
    '(They) have all died.'

Note that *dum* cannot have the sense MANY, although as an epistemological classifier it means 'how many'. The usual Acehnese term for MANY is *lè*.

7.4 Actions and Events

The best verbal candidate for DO is *pubuet*.[6] This is in fact a causative derivative, from the noun *buet* 'work, deed'. *Pubuet* is thus literally constructed as 'do a deed'. It is transitive, taking a nominal object which refers to the deed. Here there is a potential difficulty, since it needs to be established whether the formally derived form is actually semantically more basic: perhaps the noun *buet* is the more basic. This is conceivable, but the prima facie assumption based on the morphology would tend to go the other way. In English *deed* is clearly more complex and more restricted in reference than *do*: one might be doing something without it being describable as a 'deed', for example sitting on a bench. And 'I have no deed to do' is not the same as 'I have nothing to do'. However in Acehnese this is not true of *buet* compared to *pubuet*. Thus 'having nothing to do' is quite normally expressed with *buet*; the question 'What are you doing?' can also be expressed in this way:

(43) *Hana   buet laén.*
      NOTBE deed other
      'There is nothing else to do.'

(44) *Peue buet droeneuh?*
      what deed you
      'What are you doing?'

(We should also note that *buet* is polysemous — another, derivative meaning is 'job, work', so the previous examples have alternative readings: 'There is no other work', and 'What is your job?'.)

If the noun *buet* is indeed basic, and the Acehnese exponent of DO, then 'You did something bad' would be rendered as the quite acceptable:

(45) *Buet droeneuh brôk.*
      deed you   bad
      'You did something bad.' (Literally, 'Your deed (is) bad.')

And this is how one of the co-authors preferred to translate this English expression.

Significantly, another co-author suggested a formulation with *pubuet*, but also including *buet*:

(46) *Droeneuh ka   neu-pubuet buet brôk.*
      you   already you-do   deed bad
      'You did something bad.'

The complement *buet* is not required: it is used in order to give the adjectival predicate *brôk* a nominal head. A headless relative clause *nyang brôk* could have been used instead, and a question may be asked without *buet*:

(47) *Peue neu-pubuet?*
      what you-do
      'What are you doing?'

The meaning 'I want to do the same' can also be rendered with either *buet* or *pubuet*:

(48) *Beu-sa-ban   buet lôn.*
      DO!-same-manner deed I
      'I want to do the same.' (Literally, 'May my deed be the same.')

(49) Beu-lôn-pubuet sa-ban   buet.
      DO!-I-do   same-manner deed
      'I want to do the same.' (Literally, 'May I do the same deed.')

Without more evidence, the most straightforward hypothesis for Acehnese would seem to be that *buet* is the exponent of DO.

A difficulty related to the status of DO is one that affects several of the predicates discussed here. Durie has argued elsewhere that Acehnese divides predicates into two groups: those that take grammatical actors, incorporating within their semantic structure something like the meaning of 'something happens because the actor wants it' (Durie 1985a), and predicates that do not take actors, and have no such component. Causatives formed with *peu-*, including *pubuet*, always take actors. (For our purposes here, we define actor purely grammatically, as an argument which controls proclitic cross-referencing on the verb.) This analysis would imply that every predicate taking an actor argument is inherently complex, decomposable, and not primitive. The above-listed candidates for THINK, KNOW, SAY, FEEL, WANT and DO all take actors, and thus these would be treated as semantically complex. The semantic component of 'want to' is particularly strongly evident in clauses that are simply positive or negative, with no preceding aspectual or modal particle such as *ka* 'already':[7]

(50) H'an ku-pubuet nyan.
      not I-do   that
      'I won't (don't want to) do that.'

To suppress the semantic element of volition something must be **added**, for example *na*, generally 'be, exist', and here understood as 'be the case that', as in:

(51) Hana (< h'an+na) ku-pubuet nyan.
      NOTBE   I-do   that
      'I don't/didn't do that.'

Many verbs have derived counterparts of which the distinctive semantic feature is the absence of volition: thus *teupiké* means 'to occur to, to happen to think of', and *teupeugah* means 'say by accident, happen to mention'. So a contrast exists between verbs with and without this semantic component of volition. Only a few verbs have no such counterparts, for example *tém* 'want to'. If Durie's analysis is correct, then it seems to be problematic that the best Acehnese translational equivalents of some primitive predicates would include this distinct component of meaning.

This difficulty may be overcome by adopting a more complex interpretation of Acehnese verbal semantics, whereby not all predicates which take actors would necessarily include within their semantic representation a specific component involving WANT, but rather volition is an unmarked inference for particular classes of verbs.

This could resolve any difficulty that the Acehnese data present for the NSM hypothesis. We would not wish to rule such an analysis out, but it is too difficult, given the constraints on space, to explore this option here, which would involve a complex interaction of pragmatics and semantics. Whatever model is adopted, it must be able to account for the unavailability of, for example, *piké* 'think' for referring to non-volitional (e.g. daydreaming[8]) mental activity.

The predicate HAPPEN is also not without its difficulties: it seems to require a particularly wide range of alternative translation strategies when being rendered in Acehnese. The most likely candidate would seem to be *rôh*, which has two senses, 'come to be in a place' and 'happen'. These two senses appear in distinct argument frames. The first takes an undergoer NP argument and a locative expression. In this frame *rôh* can be used, for example, to speak of fish coming into a net, a hand getting caught in a cleft, or something happening to be in the sun's rays. The second frame provides the candidate for our primitive HAPPEN, and it involves a sentential complement, or possibly an NP complement that describes a state of affairs, such as *raseuki* 'good fortune'. The sense is thus not 'Y happens to X', but 'S happens'. 'What happened?' would thus be *Peue rôh?*, and 'Something bad happened' could be:

(52) Ka   rôh   brôk.
      already happen   bad
      'Something bad happened.'[9]

There is no Acehnese predicate that takes two arguments with the meaning 'X happens to Y'. We would go further, and state that it is impossible for Acehnese to have a single predicate 'happen (to)', such that one could say both:

(53)   a. 'X happened.'
       b. 'X happened to Y.'

where X and Y are NPs. The difficulty is a matter of permissable argument structures. In (53a), X would have to take the undergoer grammatical role — note that we are using the term 'undergoer' strictly to refer to a grammatical relation — since for semantic reasons it could not be an actor. In (53b), X would still be the undergoer, because in Acehnese monovalent and divalent constructions involving the same verb form, grammatical role assignments do not change (it is impossible in Acehnese to have the analogue of 'The bread is cooking' and 'John is cooking the bread', where the same semantic role is realised as different grammatical relations, but the verb form is the same). How then to code Y? Semantically it is, as Wierzbicka points out, the patient, and must be the preferred candidate for undergoer, a slot which is already taken. Y is therefore uncodable. There is simply no way in Acehnese to code the Y argument of expressions like 'do X to Y', or 'X happens to Y' except as undergoer. The problem is then the impossibility of simultaneously coding both X and Y of (53b) as grammatical undergoers of the same predicate.

How then would one render an expression like 'X happened to Y' in Acehnese, even if perhaps inexactly? One way is with the structure 'X happened', where X is a clausal expression, and Y is understood as an actant in that clause. The sense is thus 'X happened', where Y happens to be part of or involved in X. For example:

(54) Na rôh   ji-kap lôn lé uleue.
      BE happen 3-bite I   by snake
      'It happened that a snake bit me.'

One can further topicalise a participant from the complement clause:

(55) Lôn na rôh   ji-kap lé uleue.
      I   BE happen 3-bite by snake
      'I happened to be bitten by a snake.'

Finally, there is a productive grammatical structure that should be mentioned here. Acehnese has a number of verbs which can be used with the sense of 'happen' or 'be located', including *keunöng* 'to strike, coincide, meet the target', *trôk* and *teuka* 'arrive', *rhèt* 'fall', *na* 'be, be a fact that, come to pass' and also *rôh* 'happen'. These are monovalent verbs, taking something that happens or is located in time or space as their primary undergoer argument — in the following example the undergoer is 'something bad':

(56) Nyang brôk ka   rhèt ateueh lôn.
      REL   bad already fall on   I
      'Something bad happened to me.'

With such verbs a productive grammatical structure of Acehnese allows a NP, understood as the 'location'[10] (although sometimes only metaphorically so) of the event, to be topicalised before the verb, with the undergoer NP — the thing located — immediately following (actually incorporated) after the verb. Thus:

(57) Lôn ka   keunöng geulanteue.
      I   already strike lightning
      'I got struck by lightning.'

(58) Jaroe lôn ka   keunöng èk   leumo.
      hand I   already strike dung cow
      'My hand got cow dung on it.'

This contruction is quite unlike true transitive constructions with an actor and undergoer. Firstly, there is no actor, as shown by the lack of proclitics. Secondly, the incorporated undergoer (the thing that happens or is located) is syntactically inert: it cannot be relocated, relativised, and so on.

The point is that this structure can provide a way of rendering English expressions of the kind *X happens to Y*:

(59) *Lôn ka keunöng raseuki.*
I already strike good:fortune
'Good fortune happened to me.'

7.5 Meta-Predicates

There are three main negative particles in Acehnese. *Bèk* 'don't, I don't want' has already been mentioned under WANT, and is fairly straightforward. *H'an* 'not' is used to negate verbal predicates. *Kön* has two functions: (a) to negate non-verbal (i.e. NP and PP) predicates; and (b), with verbal predicates, to express the meaning 'on the contrary'. The following examples illustrate these four types of negation:

(60) *Bèk neu-woe.*
DONT! you-return
'Don't come back.' or 'I hope you don't come back.'

(61) *H'an lôn-woe.*
not I-return
'I won't return.'

(62) *Lôn kön guru.*
I not teacher
'I am not a teacher.'

(63) *Kön lôn-woe.*
not I-return
'It is not that I returned.' (on the contrary)

A complication is provided by the special distinction between *h'an* 'not' and *hana* 'not' (from *h'an* 'not' + *na* 'be'),[11] parallelling a distinction between the absence and presence of *na* used as a pre-verbal 'auxiliary'.[12] It has already been mentioned that in Acehnese, verbs which take an actor would appear to include a volitional semantic component. Without any preverbal auxiliary, such verbs can be read in an irrealis sense, with a meaning 'want to':

(64) *Lôn-jak.*
I-go
'I am going.' (I intend to and will go.)

(65)   *H'an lôn-jak.*
       not   I-go
       'I'm not going.' (I don't want to and I won't.)

The use of *na* 'be' (and also some other auxiliaries such as *ka* 'already') produces a realis reading:

(66)   *Na lôn-jak.*
       BE I-go
       'I did go.' or 'It is the case that I will go.'

(67)   *Hana lôn-jak.*
       NOTBE I-go
       'I didn't go.' or 'It is the case that I will not go.'

For non-volitional verbs, taking an undergoer, a similar realis–irrealis effect is observed, with a contrast is between potentiality (without *na*) versus actuality (with *na*):

(68)   *Awak nyan mandum h'an maté.*
       person that all   not die
       'All of them will not die.' (None will die.)

(69)   *Awak nyan mandum hana maté.*
       person that all   NOTBE die
       'They are all not dead.'[13] (or 'They all didn't die.')

Thus 'I didn't do it' would have to be translated with *hana*, indicating negation plus realis, rather than just with the more primitive *h'an*.

The meta-predicate IF is very straightforwardly found in Acehnese *meu(ng)-*. This is a clitic, which is often formed into *meunyö* 'if' ('if'+'yes') and *meungkön* 'if not' ('if'+'no/not'). There is no subjunctive:

(70)   *Meung-na ujeuen, h'an lôn-jak.* (or *Meunyö na ujeuen, ...*)
       if-BE   rain   not I-go
       'If it rains I won't go.'

For MAYBE a potential candidate is *(s)alèh*:

(71)   *Alèh ji-tôh ujeuen singöh.*
       maybe 3-excrete rain tomorrow
       'Maybe it will rain tomorrow.'

However in such expressions there is a strong epistemic sense, an expectation that the thing actually will happen or be the case: 'I suppose that it will rain, but I don't know whether it will.' Simple non-epistemic possibility is expressed with *jeuet* 'can, be possible', which takes a clausal complement:

(72) *Nyan jeuet beukah.*
      that can break
      'That can/could break.'

With *jeuet* any suggestion that it might break is pure inference: all that is said is that the possibility is there. *(S)alèh* implies, however, that the event may well come to pass.

The meta-predicate LIKE is *meu-/ban*. These appear to be variant forms of the same lexeme, which might normally be translated as a noun meaning 'manner'. *Meu-* is a clitic form, and *ban* can be either a free noun, or an epistemological classifier which may occur bound, as in *tu-ban* 'to know what manner'.[14] Acehnese allows a nominal predication of the type *X this manner* meaning 'X has this manner', or 'X is like this'. Likewise a very productive grammatical construction allows a manner NP to function adverbially: for example, *John runs this manner* meaning 'John runs like this'.

(73) *Ta-pubuet meu-noe.*
      you-do   manner-this
      'Do it like this.'

(74) *Ta-pubuet ban   nyang lôn-peugah.*
      you-do   manner REL   I-say
      'Do as I say.'

It is unclear what difference in meaning there is between *ban/meu-* and another noun *lagèe* 'manner', which is used in a similar way:

(75) *Nyan ban / lagèe rimueng, tapi kön rimueng.*
      that manner   tiger   but not tiger
      'It is like a tiger, but is not a tiger.'

BECAUSE is the noun *keureuna* (or *kareuna*) (from Sanskrit) a term which makes no distinction between prior cause and purpose. *Keureuna* is often used, conjunction-like, to head a nominal dependent phrase or clause:

(76) *Ji-moe kareuna nyan.*
      3-cry cause   that
      'She is crying because of that.' (Literally, 'She cries that cause.')

(77)   *Bak si-uroe, keureuna hana buet nyang laén,*
       at   one-day   because NOTBE deed REL other,
       ji-jak-jak lam beuluka.
       3-go-go   in   brush
       'One day, because he didn't have anything else to do, he was
       walking through the bush ...' (Sulaiman 1978:7)

It is not clear how *kareuna* differs from *sabap* (from Arabic) which is also a noun and has an apparently identical function.

The productive causative morpheme *peu-* is clearly complex, involving both the concept of cause and either 'want' or 'do' (or both), and is not a candidate for this primitive.

VERY is quite simply found in the word *that*:

(78)   *Nyan göt that.*
       that   good very
       'That is very good/beautiful.'

7.6 Time and Place

WHEN is *jan*. This is both a noun 'time' and an epistemological classifier 'when', whence the interrogative *pajan* 'when', in which *pa-* is a prefix used in Acehnese to derive ignoratives (Wierzbicka 1980) from a number of epistemological classifiers.

(79)   *Pajan neu-pubuet nyan.*
       when you-do   that
       'When did you do that?'

(80)   *Lôn ngön gopnyan sa-jan   na kamoe.*
       I   with he   same-time BE we:exclusive
       'He and me, we were born at the same time.'

For 'time' Acehnese has *watèe*. This is used to head temporal relative clauses, for which *when* might be used in English:

(81)   *Watèe neu-woe ...*
       time you-return
       'When you return ...' (Perhaps more literally, 'At the time you return ...')

(82) Bèk   riyôh   watèe ureueng beuet.
      DONT! be:noisy time person   recite
      'Don't be noisy when someone is reciting.'

(83) Pajan na watèe ta-pajôh   kuwah pliek?
      when   BE time   1:inclusive-eat kind:of:dish[15]
      'When will we have a time to eat *kuwah pliek*?'

WHERE is *pat*, an epistemological classifier. The noun for 'place', *teumpat*, is clearly the historical source for *pat*. These two terms might be regarded as allolexes.

(84) Pat   gopnyan jinoe (< jan + nyoe)?
      where she   when   this
      'Where is she now?'

(85) Beu-ta-duek   sa-pat.
      DO!-we:inclusive-dwell   same-place
      'Let's live at the same place.'

Some potential difficulties exist with possible exponents for the temporal expressions AFTER and BEFORE. There are two basic alternative pairs of words that could provide exponents of these putative primitives. One of the possible approaches of rendering 'X before Y' or 'X after Y' is transparently analysable in such terms as 'X (when) not yet Y' and 'X (when) Y has happened/has finished'. That is, putative exponents for AFTER and BEFORE are formally derived from non-relational verbal aspectual modifiers together with implicit (pragmatically inferred) temporal coincidence. A full account of the issues demands more space than is available here: it would require a detailed analysis of Acehnese verbal aspect, using putative Acehnese lexical primitives in Acehnese grammatical structures.

AFTER may be rendered as *lheueh*, *'oh lheueh*, *ka* or *'oh ka*, where *'oh* is originally an epistemological classifier meaning 'how far, as far as' but here just means 'when', and is an optional component. *Lheueh* means 'finished, completed',[16] and the alternative *ka* means something like 'already', implying: (a) for a state, that it has begun and now applies; and (b), for an event, that it has been completed (if having a duration) or past (if punctual):[17]

(86) 'Oh   lheueh   sakét,   geu-beudöh.
      when finished sick/hurt   3-arise
      'After his sickness (or pain) was over, he got up.'

(87) 'Oh   ka   sakét,   h'an geu-beudöh lé.
      when already   sick/hurt not 3-arise   anymore
      'After he got sick (or the pain started), he couldn't get up anymore.'

Clearly *lheueh* and *ka* are hardly good candidates for the primitive AFTER. The situation for BEFORE is much the same. An obvious candidate is *goh lom*,[18] an aspectual marker coding an incomplete process, or an as yet unattained state:

(88)   Goh lom   geu-jak   lôn   ka   lon-woe.
            not:yet   3-go   I   already   I-return
            'Before they went I had returned.'

Thus in Acehnese, coding of temporal sequencing can be based upon the **simultaneity** of temporal reference points, but distinctive aspectual categorisation. 'X comes after Y' is thus rendered as, for example, 'At a particular time, Y is finished or complete but X is not'. In such constructions the temporal sequencing is strictly speaking an inference, and because of this, as far as temporal sequence is concerned, the meanings AFTER and BEFORE find no lexical realisation in Acehnese in such constructions. If such aspectual notions as 'complete' and 'incomplete' are to be decomposed in terms of AFTER and BEFORE, and if Acehnese had no other candidates for BEFORE and AFTER then we would have a serious problem for NSM methodology within Acehnese.

The way out of this tangle seems to be provided by *awai* 'early/earlier, former' (from Arabic) and *dudoe* 'late/later'. These are verbs, but are usually used adverbially (as is quite normal in Acehnese) to characterise an event as early or late in time:

(89)   Cuba muplueng-plueng keu-déh, soe awai tôk
            try   race   to-there   who   earlier   arrive
            meuteumèe pèng.
            get   money
            'Let's race over to there: whoever gets there first gets the money.'
            (Djajadiningrat 1934, under *awai*)

(90)   Awai that tôk   droeneuh.
            early very arrive you
            'You've come very early.' (Djajadiningrat 1934, under *awai*)

They can also be used attributively, thus, for example, *peurumoh awai* 'former wife'. The following example shows both attributive and independent adverbial use:

(91)   Jôh awai ji-kheun "tan",   dudoe ka   na.
            time earlier 3-say   NOTBE   later   already   BE
            'First (s)he said there wasn't (any), but later there was (some) after all.' (Djajadiningrat 1934, under *awai*)

The NSM requirement is for a divalent relational predicate here, yet the examples of *awai* and *dudoe* we have considered so far are monovalent. It is important to note that Acehnese gradable predicates (they are in fact all verbs) make no distinction between comparative and non-comparative readings. Thus *soe tuha* (literally, 'who old') can mean 'Who is old?' or 'Who is older/oldest?'. However in Acehnese comparison is formally distinguished by the use of the preposition *nibak* to mark the pivot of comparison, and in this way a divalent reading of *awai* and *dudoe* is possible:

(92) Lôn lahé duwa thôn away nibak droeneuh.
 I born two year early than you
 'I was born two years earlier than you.'

(93) Ji-beudöh dudoe nibak nyan.
 3-get:up later than that (= then)
 'She got up after that.'

The primitives UNDER and ABOVE are quite straightforwardly realised respectively as *(mi)yup* and *ateueh*.

(94) Awan nyan di ateueh kamoe.
 cloud that at place:above we:exclusive
 'That cloud is above us.'

7.7 Partonomy and Taxonomy

For the proposed primitive PART OF it seems quite certain that no reasonable equivalent can be found in Acehnese. In the light of Wierzbicka's proposal to locate PART OF for Warlbiri in a morpheme that would normally be treated as a grammatical marker of an adnominal 'possessive' construction, we will first consider the possibility that PART OF can be found in grammatical constructions.

There are only two grammatical constructions that are relevant, one adnominal and one clausal. In neither case is there any lexical material that is available for a possible intereperation as having the meaning 'part of' or 'has a':

(95) Gö sikin.
 handle knife
 'the knife's handle'

(96) Sikin nyan na gö.
 knife that BE handle
 'The knife has a handle.'

This latter expression involves a kind of clause-internal syntactic extraction: the verb *na* is intransitive, taking a single argument *gö sikin nyan* 'that knife's handle', and on the basis of this the possessor *sikin nyan* 'that knife' appears in the topical fronted position. This is a quite general possibility for undergoer arguments in Acehnese (see discussions in Durie (1985a:183–185, 1987:375)), and as a grammatical phenomenon it conforms to the general construction type known as 'possessor ascension' (for definition of this Relational Grammar term, and illustration of the construction type, see papers in Perlmutter and Rosen (1984)). The construction is further illustrated by the following examples:

(97) a. *Ka   gadöh gènsè lôn.*
         already lost   pencil I

      b. *Lôn ka   gadôh gènsè.*
         I   already lost   pencil

      'My pencil is lost.' (or 'I have lost a pencil.')

(98) a. *Ka   ji-tèt rumoh lôn.*
         already 3-burn house my

      b. *Lôn ka   ji-tèt rumoh.*
         I   already 3-burn house

      '(Someone) has burned down my house.' (or 'My house has been burnt down.')

Using this construction one can certainly can say the equivalent of 'Y has an X', as in (96), but there is no way of saying 'X is a part of Y', so the construction is of little use in forming the requisite NSM representations.

Quite apart from this difficulty, it seems unacceptable that something as fundamentally syntactic as the adnominal construction, or the possessor ascension construction which is based directly upon it, could be treated as a polysemous construction with a range of decomposable meanings. A range of such adnominal meanings exist, and they themselves can presumably be defined through semantic decomposition, but it is not so certain that the construction itself (*NP* + *NP*) is polysemous. A parallel exists with the status of the subject–verb relationship. Clearly one can specify a range of meaning-types that a subject holds in respect of its verb (e.g. agent, experiencer, etc.),[19] but it does not obviously hold that the subject–verb construction itself is polysemous. Rather the variations in meaning reside in the verb meanings. Similarly any PART OF meaning that can be found in an expression like 'John's leg' is presumably to be located in the meaning of *leg*, rather than in the adnominal construction itself. To see this even more clearly, in Acehnese 'The knife has a sheath' and 'The knife has a blade' are expressed in exactly the same way:

(99)   *Sikin nyan na sarông.*
       knife that BE sheath
       'That knife has a sheath.'

(100) *Sikin nyan na mata.*
       knife that BE blade
       'That knife has a blade.'

If the second expression is asserting that a blade is part of a knife, why isn't the first asserting that a sheath is part of a knife? This construction cannot be used to say 'A sheath is not a part of a knife': *Sikin nyan hana sarông* means only that the knife has no sheath, and likewise *Sikin nyan hana mata* only means that the knife has no blade. Since the adnominal construction cannot be used either to affirm or deny that, for example, 'A sheath is a part of a knife', it is of no use to propose that the construction itself is an exponent of this putative primitive.

We have not exhausted our discussion of PART OF, which can only be complete when we have described how an Acehnese person deals with the task of trying to translate 'X is a part of Y', 'X has many parts' or 'What is this a part of?'. For such expressions, one is forced in Acehnese either to use a formulation which makes no distinction between actual parts and other non-part attachments or appendages (e.g. to talk of 'things' or 'objects'), or to use a more specific word for a particular kind of part (e.g. a 'blade', a 'handle', a 'side'), and the relational concept is that of belonging to, or coming from something. Below we present some examples of the many sentences with the English source sentences which were produced as Acehnese people attempted to translate such expressions. Where appropriate we have given the comments of the translator (rendered into English from Acehnese in some cases).

(101) *Bak geuritan angèn na lè peue.*
       at vehicle wind BE many what
       { bicycle }
       'A bicycle has many things.' (From 'A bicycle has many parts.')
       Comment: 'It is precisely this which is exceeding difficult to translate.' Another comment: *'Cannot be translated unless the parts have names',* with no translation offered at all.

(102) *Lè that peue macam bak geuritan angèn nyan.*
       many very what kind at vehicle wind that
       { bicycle }
       'There are many kinds (of things) on a bicycle.' (From 'A bicycle has many parts.')
       Comment: 'We would say this very rarely, because it seems impossible to work out a context for this sentence.'

(103) *Gunténg na dua blah mata, ban dua blah saban.*
scissors BE two side blade, both two side same:manner
'Scissors have two blades; both sides are the same.' (From 'Scissors have two identical parts.')
Comment: 'Your original sentence cannot be translated.'

(104) *'Oh ta-kalön gunténg nyan, yup ateueh ban dua*
when we-see scissors that below above both two
mata-jih sa-ban.
blade-3 same-way
'When you look at a pair of scissors, both its blades are the same from below and above.' (From 'Scissors have two identical parts.')

(105) *Nyoe gö galang.*
this handle axe
'This is an axe handle.' (From 'This is a part of an axe.')
Comment: 'In Acehnese you don't say "that is a bagian *(Indonesian for 'part') of an axe", but directly "axe handle", "axe blade", etc. We don't have "part of" in Acehnese because we say the name of something straight out.'*

(106) *Sang nyoe atra bak moto.*
apparently this object from car
'It seems this comes from/belongs to a car.' (From 'I think that this is a part of a car.')
Comment: 'Your original sentence cannot be translated.'

(107) a. *Peue atra nyoe?*
   What object this
   'What is this object?'

   b. *Pat ji-duek barang nyoe?*
   where 3-sit object this
   'Where does this thing go?'

   c. *Atra nyoe pat geu-ngui?*
   object this where 3-use
   'Where do you use this?'
   (a, b and c from 'What is this a part of?')

(108)   *Si-blah   ka   gadöh.*
        one-side   already lost
        'One side (or one of two juxtaposed parts) is lost.' (From 'One part is lost.')
        Comment: 'But not all parts can be translated as siblah.'

We note that the editors have suggested that Acehnese *peue* 'thing' actually has PART as one of its meanings. We disagree. In the first example above, the bicycle's 'things' are not just parts: they could be parts and non-parts. Also if *peue* were polysemous in the way suggested, then the difficulty experienced in translating this example is inexplicable. Polysemies do not provide such difficulties for translation as this example presents. For example the polysemy of Acehnese *sa*, meaning both ONE and THE SAME, is quite obvious to an unsophisticated native speaker, and presents no difficulties in translation.

KIND OF presents very particular difficulties in Acehnese. Four rather different construction types can be distinguished: predicative 'X is a kind of Y', referential '(I saw) a kind of Y', interrogative 'What kind of Y?', and the enumerative '*n* kinds of Y'. Let us consider the first expression. Both Acehnese co-authors initially offered the following as the translation of 'This is a kind of bird':

(109)   *Nyoe lagèe   cicém.*
        this   manner bird
        'This is like a bird.'

Here it seems a matter of inference that the speaker means something that actually **is** a bird. An alternative to the noun *lagèe* 'manner' is *macam* 'manner, kind'. This was also offered by informants to translate English expressions with *kind of*. It seems a likely exponent of KIND OF:

(110)   *Na   lhèe   macam   musang.*
        BE   three kind   civet:cat
        'There are three kinds of civet cat.'

(111)   *Na   lhèe   macom   bak   mamplam   lam   lampôh   nyoe.*
        BE   three kind   tree   mango   in   garden   this
        'There are three kinds of mangoes in this garden.'

(112)   *Nyoe   peue   macam?*
        this   what   kind/manner
        'What kind/manner (of thing) is this?'

Again, a problem with *macam* is that, like *lagèe*, it can often have the (English) reading 'manner, like', and it hard to see how to distinguish 'X is a kind of bird' from 'X is like a bird' using *macam*. It is not clear to us whether *macam* is polysemous or vague: in the latter case, the one meaning of *macam* (and also of *lagèe*) would be equally applicable in Acehnese to talking about taxonomies of things, and to manners and likenesses.[20]

Note that in Acehnese there is a clear structural difference between an enumerative expression of the type '*n* kinds of Y' and the predicative 'X is a kind of Y', although both can be expressed with *macam* and *lagèe*. In the first construction the Acehnese equivalent of '*n* kinds' forms an attributive measure phrase modifying the head Y, whereas in the 'a kind of Y' construction, *macam* is the head of the NP. Thus in the enumerated expression, the whole NP is headed by Y, and it must refer to something that is a Y, and in this context any putative distinction between a 'manner of Y', and a 'kind of Y' is redundant. However in predicative expressions of the type 'X is a kind (*macam*) of Y' the issue is important, because the whole nominal phrase *macam Y* is headed not by Y but *macam*, and it refers not to a Y, but to a manner or kind of Y.

Of course if one wanted to say that something was indeed a bird, this is simplicity itself, and one wonders whether such a formulation wouldn't be adequate in NSM formulations, at least for Acehnese:

(113)   *Nyoe cicém.*
         this   bird
         'This is a bird.'

Other putative candidates for KIND OF are *biek* 'kind, type' (*biek* is polysemous, also having the meaning 'lineage', this perhaps being the older meaning), and *bangsa* 'race, kind, type'. But all these seem to mean something more like 'type', thus *biek ureueng* means 'a person: human kind', rather than 'a kind of human'.

Interestingly the epistemological classifier *peue* (normally 'what') would be rendered into English as *what kind* when it is followed by a nominal expression: *peue eungkôt* 'what kind of fish'; compare also *sa-peue* 'same kind', and *lè peue* 'many kinds':

(114)   *Na   lhèe peue musang.*
         BE   three what civet:cat
         'There are three kinds of civet cat.'

So *peue* may be considered a candidate for this primitive. We note that *peue* can only be used with the reading 'what kind of' in the expressions 'What kind of Y' and '*n* kinds of Y', not to express 'X is a kind of Y' (for this one can say 'X is a Y', as we noted above). However an alternative interpretation is that *peue* here simply means 'what', and the sense of 'what kind' dervies from the adnominal construction which the 'what kind' reading of *peue* partakes of. The parallel is with expressions like *eungkôt yèe* 'shark fish', where the noun *yèe* 'shark' specifies the kind of *eungkôt* 'fish'. Thus *lè peue* 'many kinds' may in fact mean 'many somethings', where 'something' is understood to have an adnominal modifying function. If this is a valid interpretation, then *peue* is not the exponent of KIND OF in these constructions. Rather, the construction *peue X* only means 'what kind of X' to the extent that adnominal modification can encompass this kind of semantic relation.

7.8 Evaluators and Descriptors

Acehnese *göt* is GOOD (dialect variant is *gèt*). Unlike English *good*, the Acehnese term is also used for 'beautiful, scenic, handsome'; however it is not clear whether this usage is polysemous. BAD is *brôk*, which, corresponding to *göt*, can also be used for 'ugly'. Likewise, while *göt* means 'fixed, working, usable', *brôk* can mean 'rotten, broken down, ruined'. *Göt akai* ('good character/mind') means 'good-natured' and *brôk akai* means 'evil-natured'. *Göt rupa* ('good appearance') means 'handsome/beautiful', whilst *brôk rupa* means 'ugly'. Causative *peugöt* means 'to fix' and *peubrôk* means 'to wreck'.

Notes

1. Mark Durie gratefully acknowledges the financial support of the Australian Research Council through the projects "Studies in Grammaticization and Lexicalization" and "Grammatical Structures of Mon-Khmer and Austronesian Languages in Mainland Southeast Asia and Sumatra". The following symbols are used in the glosses: BE the verb *na*, CLASS a classifier (used for enumeration), DO! the enclitic *beu-*, DONT! the particle *bèk*, FOCUS a focus marker, NOTBE the compound *hana* (from *h'an + na*) or its synonym *tan*, REL complementiser, introducing a relative clause.

2. Note that *tu-* itself only appears as a bound form in this kind of construction. Historically it derives from an independent verb **tahu* 'know', which has survived in Acehnese as *thèe*. However Acehnese *thèe* now has a more restricted sense of 'know by personal experience'. Thus the following example is appropriate when I have experienced the earthquake and thus know about it, but not when the earthquake has happened somewhere else, and I have only heard about it:

    Ka   ku-thèe na   geumpa.
    already I-know BE   earthquake
    'I know there was an earthquake.'

    Because of this, we would not propose *thèe* as the exponent of KNOW.

3. For discussion of the 'ignorative', see Wierzbicka (1980).

4. The editors have suggested to us that *tém* in fact means 'intend'. We reject this, since 'intend' does not imply wanting or willingness in the same way that *tém* does. (The best Acehnese

candidates for 'intend' are *keumeung* and *keuneuk*. We have not discussed these here because they do not seem relevant to the discussion of WANT.)

5   *Sajan* is polysemous: it also means 'together'.
6   We note also the existence of the predicate *saja* 'to do intentionally, purposefully', which is clearly not primitive.
7   In response to a query from the editors, we note that the 'don't want to' component is also evident for verbs such as 'feel' or 'know'. For example *H'an geu-turi lôn* 'not 3-know I' means something more like 'He refused to recognise me' than 'He didn't know me'. Likewise *H'an kurasa nyan* means something more like 'I refuse to feel/taste that' rather than 'I don't feel that'. We also note that such verbs have 'non-volitional' derivatives, thus *teurasa* from *rasa* 'feel': of these two, *rasa* could be used in an imperative, but *teurasa* could not. Compare also the discussion of volitional versus non-volitional 'see' in Durie (1985b). As we note in the main text, this aspect of Acehnese verbal semantics needs further exploration.
8   To describe someone daydreaming one would use the word *tahè*, which takes an undergoer, not an actor.
9   The expression *something* in the English expression seems vacuous.
10 Clearly the term 'location' cannot always be interpreted literally, as the preceding example shows. However we would suggest that its metaphorical use is consistent in general with other metaphorical extensions of locative senses in Acehnese.
11 A good description is provided in Djajadiningrat (1934) under the appropriate lexical entries.
12 The analysis of auxiliaries as main verbs is well known in contemporary approaches to English syntax: in Durie (1985a) the use of *na* as an 'auxiliary' is also treated as a case of a superordinate main verb.
13 It is quite systematic in Acehnese that no lexical distinction is made between the process of reaching a state and the resulting state itself: thus *maté* can be interpreted as 'die' or 'dead', *na* as 'exist' and 'come into existence' (or 'be born' also), *rhèt* as 'fall' and 'fallen'.
14 Traditional scholarship has tended (wrongly) to analyse the clitic *meu-* as a derivational prefix. See e.g. Djajadiningrat (1934, vol 2:51–52), under sections 1b, 2c and 5b of the lexical entry for the derivational prefix *meu-*. And, quite consistently, Djajadiningrat omits any mention of *meu-* under *ban*.
15 *Kuwah pliek* is a spicy Acehnese culinary speciality in which the distinctive ingredient is the flesh of coconuts that has been allowed to ferment, and from which the oil has been expressed. This *pliek* is then cooked with various vegetables and spices to form the *kuwah pliek*, which is eaten with rice.
16 As an independent verb *lheueh* means 'loose, released'.
17 The editors have pointed out that they see as untenable the application of this analysis to punctual events. We disagree: for punctual events the relevant reading is simply that of a past event.
18 Or *golom*. The derivative *sigohlom* 'before' is a loan translation based on Malay *sebelum*: its analysis does not lead us in any other direction than that of *gohlom*.
19 We do not wish to imply that such notions as 'agent' are components of semantic representations. Rather they are types of structural configurations within the semantic representations. See e.g. Wierzbicka (1980:176), Mel'čuk (1988:88–89, note 6; 1992:97, note 8), Jackendoff (1990).

20 The editors have suggested a direct comparison with English *kind of* as in *her eyes were kind of blue*, versus *a kind of blue*, in support of the polysemy interpretation. We don't agree that English *kind of* is strictly speaking polysemous. In English there is a formal distinction between *a kind of* and *kind of*, they have quite different syntactics (in the sense of Mel'čuk): one is enumerable and takes an article, whilst the other is not enumerable and takes no article. Nevertheless it is not implausible that Acehnese *macam* could be polysemous in this way: we just wish to reserve judgement on this matter.

References

Asyik, Abdul Gani. 1972. *Atjehnese Morphology: Pase dialect*. MA Thesis, Institute Keguruan dan Ilmu Pendidikan (IKIP) Malang.

Asyik, Abdul Gani. 1987. *A Contextual Grammar of Acehnese Sentences*. PhD Dissertation, University of Michigan, Ann Arbor.

Bakar, Aboe, Budiman Sulaiman, M. Adnan Hanafiah, Zainal Abidin Ibrahim & Syarifah H. 1985. *Kamus Aceh Indonesia*. 2 vols. Departemen Pendidikan dan Kebudayaan, Jakarta: Pusat Pembinaan dan Pengembangan Bahasa.

Djajadiningrat, Hoesein. 1934. *Atjèhsch-Nederlandsch Woordenboek*. 2 vols. Batavia: Landsdrukkerij.

Durie, Mark. 1985a. *A Grammar of Acehnese*. Dordrecht: Foris.

Durie, Mark. 1985b. "Control and Decontrol in Acehnese". *Australian Journal of Linguistics* 5.43-53.

Durie, Mark. 1987. "Grammatical Relations in Acehnese". *Studies in Language* 11.365-399.

Daud, Bukhari & Mark Durie. In press. *Acehnese Lexicon and Thesaurus*. Canberra: Pacific Linguistics.

Hasan, Ibrahim, Abidin Hasyim, Abdullah Ali, A. Gani Hanafiah, Darwis A. Soelaiman, Budiman Sulaiman, Zaini Ali & Adnan Hanafiah. 1980. *Hasil Perumusan Seminar Pembinaan dan Pengembangan Bahasa Aceh, Darussalam, Banda Aceh, August 25-26, 1980*. Universitas Syiah Kuala, Banda Aceh.

Jackendoff, Ray. 1990. *Semantic Structures*. Cambridge: MIT Press.

Mel'čuk, Igor. 1988. *Dependency Syntax: Theory and practice*. Albany: State University of New York Press.

Mel'čuk, Igor. 1992. "Toward a Logical Analysis of the Notion 'Ergative Construction'". *Studies in Language* 16.91-138.

Perlmutter, David M. & Carol G. Rosen (eds). 1984. *Studies in Relational Grammar 2*. Chicago: University of Chicago Press.

Sulaiman, Budiman (ed.) 1978. *Haba Peulandôk*. Edited from a manuscript by Teungku Yahya Baden. Pustaka Mahmudiyah, Bireuen, Aceh, Indonesia.

Wierzbicka, Anna. 1980. *Lingua Mentalis: The semantics of natural language*. Sydney: Academic Press.

Kayardild

Nicholas Evans
University of Melbourne

Kayardild (phonetically [kajaɟilt]) is an Australian language spoken in the South Wellesley Islands in the Gulf of Carpentaria by a population traditionally numbering around 120 people. The work on which this paper is based has been carried out since 1982,[1] with a total of some fourteen months in the field; a special fieldtrip to Bentinck Island to check questions arising from an earlier version of this paper[2] was made over Easter 1992, and some further questions were checked over Christmas 1992.

Though genetically non–Pama-Nyungan (Tangkic subgroup), Kayardild is typologically more like a Pama-Nyungan language: morphologically, words are entirely suffixing; there is a rich set of case suffixes but no verb agreement; and word-order is free. The three most unusual features of Kayardild grammar are discussed briefly below; all involve unusual extensions of case-like phenomena.

Modal Case. Most NPs in a sentence — objects, instruments, places and so on, but not the subject — take what is etymologically a case suffix, that shows tense and mood in agreement with the verb; I term such suffixes 'modal case'.[3] Compare[4]

(1)   *dangka-a   raa-ja   bijarrba-ya   ngakan-ki*
        man-NOM   spear-ACT   dugong-ACT   sandbank-ACT
        wumburu-nguni.
        spear-INST
        'The man spears a dugong on the sandbank with a spear.'

with its equivalent in three other tense/moods, examples (2)–(4). As can be seen, objects and locations simply take the modal case suffix; other NPs such as instruments first take a normal (or 'relational') case suffix, then a modal case suffix outside it. The four commonest modal case values are illustrated here — actual (found with the verbal 'actual' and others), future (found with the verbal 'potential' and others), prior (found with the verbal 'past' and others) and emotive (found with the verbal 'apprehensive', 'desiderative' and 'hortative'):

(2) *dangka-a   raa-ju   bijarrba-wu   ngakan-ku*
    man-NOM spear-POT   dugong-FUT   sandbank-FUT
    wumburu-ngun-u.
    spear-INST-FUT
    'The man will spear a dugong on the sandbank with a spear.'

(3) *dangka-a   raa-jarra   bijarrba-na   ngakan-kina*
    man-NOM spear-PST   dugong-PRIOR sandbank-PRIOR
    wumburu-nguni-na.
    spear-INST-PRIOR
    'The man speared a dugong on the sandbank with a spear.'

(4) *dangka-a   raa-nyarra   bijarrba-ntha   ngakan-inja*
    man-NOM spear-APPR dugong-EMOT   sandbank-EMOT
    wumburu-nguni-nj.
    spear-INST-EMOT
    'The man might spear a dugong on the sandbank with a spear.'

Verbal Case. In addition to a set of twelve or so 'normal' case suffixes such as the instrumental in (4) (which behave like regular case inflections in other languages except that they can be followed by further 'modal case' inflections), Kayardild has a set of 'verbal case' inflections. These express case-like meanings (e.g. beneficiary, source of motion, goal), can be subcategorised for by main verbs, and appear on all words of the relevant NP; however they convert the words they attach to into morphological verbs which take the full set of regular verbal inflections. Sentence (5) illustrates the use of the 'verbal dative' to mark the indirect object of 'give'; note that it takes the verbal tense/mood inflection (the potential) rather than the modal case (the future) found on the object 'money'. Example (6) illustrates another verbal case, the 'verbal allative'; note that the NP bearing it shows negative polarity, unlike the temporal adjunct 'tomorrow', whose 'modal case' suffix does not show polarity. (The semantic value of the verbal category 'potential' and the modal case category 'future' will be discussed in more detail in section 8.2.2.)

(5) *ngada   wuu-ju   wirrin-ku*
    1SG:NOM give-POT   money-FUT
    ngijin-maru-thu   thabuju-maru-thu.
    my-VD-POT   elder.brother-VD-POT
    'I will give the money to my elder brother.'

(6) ngada   warra-nangku   dathin-kiiwa-nangku
     1SG:NOM   go-NEG:POT   that-VALL-NEG:POT
     ngilirr-iiwa-nangku   balmbi-wu.
     cave-VALL-NEG:POT   morrow-FUT
     'I will not go to that cave tomorrow.'

Complementising Case. The oblique case suffix[5] may also appear on all words of a subordinate clause (after their other inflections) under certain conditions, such as when it is a complement of a main clause predicate; such a use of this case will be glossed COBL:

(7) ngada   mungurru,
     1SG:NOM   know
     [maku-ntha   yalawu-jarra-ntha   yakuri-naa-ntha.]
       woman-COBL   catch-PST-COBL   fish-PRIOR-COBL
     'I know that the woman caught a fish.'

Such complementised clauses may often be 'insubordinated' — used independently without a main clause, something like an independent subjunctive in German or Romance — as in (8). These clauses have a wide range of pragmatically informed interpretations, basically conforming to the semantic range of possible main clause predicates (essentially perception or knowledge verbs, though some volitional verbs are also included). The gloss in (8) is that appropriate to the context in which this utterance was recorded, but in other contexts glosses like 'I hear' or 'I know' could be appropriate.[6]

(8) [Dan-kurrka   riin-kurrka
       here-LOC:COBL   from:east-LOC:COBL
       thardawankawuru-ntha   burri-jurrk!]
       aeroplane-COBL   appear-IMMED:COBL
     '(I can hear) the aeroplane coming in just now, here from the east!'

These brief grammatical remarks should enable the reader to understand the examples discussed below — for fuller details of Kayardild grammar see Evans (forthcoming), and of the Kayardild lexicon see Evans (1992). We now pass to a consideration of the various Kayardild candidates for the proposed primitives.

8.1   Substantives: I, YOU, SOMEONE, SOMETHING, PEOPLE

All of these have straightforward translations in Kayardild.

8.1.1 I and YOU

I is expressed by *ngada* and the various case-inflected forms built on the stem *ngijin-*; see (11) for a sentence example.

YOU (SG) is expressed by *nyingka* and the various case-inflected forms built on the stem *ngumban-*; a sentence example is (10).

8.1.2 SOMEONE (WHO) and SOMETHING (WHAT)

SOMEONE may be expressed by *ngaaka dangkaa*; SOMETHING by *ngaaka thungalda*. These are phrasal expressions; each component word inflects. The element *ngaaka* only rarely appears alone (though see (13) for an example), so I treat the phrase as a single lexical item. Sometimes additional members of the series are used, such as *ngaaka nida* 'what name' and *ngaaka wuranda* 'something; what creature'. This latter may in some circumstances be opposed to *ngaaka thungalda* 'something; what (inanimate) thing', although *ngaaka thungalda* is regularly used with the semantic range of English *something*, to include animals.

As in many Australian languages there is a set of ignorative words (Karcevski 1969) exhibiting systematic polysemy between interrogative and indeterminate-pronoun meanings. When used with interrogative intonation (represented here by a question mark) these words will be translated as 'who', as in (9), or 'what', as in (10), respectively; when used with declarative intonation they will usually be translated as 'someone ... who is it?' and 'something ... what is it?', as in (11) and (12).

(9) *Ngaaka   dangka-a   dathin-a   riin-da*
    what:NOM person-NOM there-NOM from.east-NOM
    {   who-NOM   }
    jawi-j?
    run-ACT
    'Who is running there from the east?'

(10) *Ngaaka   thungal-da   nyingka   jani-j?*
    what:NOM thing-NOM you:NOM look.for-ACT
    {   what-NOM   }
    'What are you looking for?'

(11) *Ngada   ngaaka-na   dangka-na   kurri-jarra*
    1SG:NOM what-PRIOR person-PRIOR see-PST
    thaldi-n-kina.
    stand-N-PRIOR
    'I saw someone there, who's that person there?'[7]

(12) *Ngaaka thungal-da dan-da riin-id.*
what:NOM thing-NOM here-NOM from.east-STILL
'I saw something coming from the east here, what is it?'

Although the pragmatics of making an assertion like 'I saw someone ...' typically implicates the question 'who is it?', this is not an invariant part of the semantics: as (13) illustrates, it is possible to use *ngaaka* to translate 'someone' in circumstances where there is no implicated 'who' question:

(13) *Ngada ngaaka-na kurri-jarra dan-kina*
1SG:NOM who-PRIOR see-PST here-PRIOR
bath-ina, ngada kinaa-nangku ngumban-ju.
west-PRIOR 1SG:NOM tell-NEG:POT 2SG-FUT
'I saw someone here in the west, (but) I won't tell you (who).'

8.1.3 PEOPLE

PEOPLE can be expressed by *dangkawalada*, the plural of *dangkaa* 'person', but this is rather marked, since only about twenty nouns can be pluralised in this way, and it would be used only if the number is to be emphasised. More often the singular form is used, especially in generic statements like 'People used to ...', so that a more natural exponent of PEOPLE is simply *dangkaa*. B's question in (14) exemplifies the generic use of *dangkaa*.

Aside from the question of number, *dangkaa* is polysemous between 'person, human' and 'man, adult male'; moreover it is often used like English *one* as a dummy head to an NP, in which case the referent need not be human at all. The equivalents in many other Australian languages I know (e.g. Mayali *bininj*) have a further sense, 'Aboriginal person', but this is not the case in Kayardild[8] — 'Aboriginal person' is *ngumuwa dangkaa* (literally, 'dark person') and 'European' is *balarra dangkaa* (literally, 'white person'). An example illustrating both the 'people' and the dummy head (here glossed 'feller') uses is:

(14) (The speaker is reminiscing about a time when Sweers Island, having been abandoned by its temporary white occupants, still carried a few horse and sheep which the Kayardild hunted and ate.)

A: *dan-da yarraman-d, dan-da rajurri-j,*
this-NOM horse-NOM here-NOM walk.around-ACT
dikakulinjuru, warngiid-a yarraman-d ngalda diya-j.
horse:NOM one-NOM horse-NOM we:NOM ate-NOM
'This horse, it was walking around here, a horse, we ate one horse.'

B: *dangka-a yulaa-j?*
   people-NOM afraid-ACT
   'Were people afraid (of white retribution)?'

A: *na, I can't, nothing dangka-warri, waydbala-warri,*
   no   person-PRIV whitefeller-PRIV
   no waydbala, dana-thirrin-da warngiid-a dangka-a,
   no whitefeller leave-RES-NOM one-NOM feller-NOM
   warngiid-a dangka-a diya-a-j, kantharrk.
   one-NOM feller-NOM eat-M-ACT alone:NOM
   'No, there were no people, no white people, no white people, but one feller (i.e. one horse) was left behind, one feller got eaten, it was all by itself.'

8.2 Mental Predicates: KNOW, WANT, THINK, FEEL, SAY

WANT and THINK raise a number of problems; the other mental predicates have straightforward equivalents.

8.2.1 KNOW

KNOW is translated by the nominal predicate *mungurru* 'know, knowledgeable'. This is freely combinable with nominal objects, as in (15), as well as clausal complements, as in (16) and (17), with the senses 'know, be familiar with' and 'know how to' distinguished by syntactic frame and the nature of the object:

(15) *nyingka mungurru ngijin-ji.*
     you:NOM know me-ACT
     'You know me.'

(16) *nyingka mungurru-wa*
     you:NOM know-NOM
     [ngumban-inja kajakaja-ntha buka-nth?]
        your-COBL daddy-COBL dead-COBL
     'Do you know that your father's dead?'

(17) *niya mungurru wirrka-j.*
     (s)he knowlegeable dance-ACT
     '(S)he knows how to dance.' (Literally, '(S)he dances knowledgeably.')

8.2.2 WANT

We shall see shortly that there are some problems translating WANT with scope over a clause; but first let us consider certain uses of 'want' that are quite straightforward. Sentences like 'I want a fish' or 'I want money' will be translated using the purposive or translative case suffixes on the desired noun, but these mean more than simply WANT, respectively conveying purposeful activity to obtain the desired object, or inactive waiting for it: *ngada yakurijaniij* 'I want a fish, and am seeking one' (*-janiij* is the purposive), *ngada manimariij* 'I want money, and am waiting for it (e.g. in a queue outside the post office)' (*-mariij* is the translative). Occasionally the translative is used with nominalised verbs, for example *nyingka warraja dayiinmariij* 'You're going out, wanting to get laid', but this still has the added sense of passive expectation: 'in the hope of getting laid'. The etymologies of these cases are revealing: the translative is from 'putting oneself', and the purposive from 'seeking, searching for'. 'Want' in the sense of sexual desire will usually be translated with a sense of the verb 'see, look at': *niya kurrija dathinki makuy* 'He wants that woman', but more accurately 'He is looking at that woman with desire'.

Sentences like 'I want: X' confront problems. Certainly, two verbal inflections — the potential and the desiderative — have a semantics that includes WANT, but does not allow it to be freely combined with all subjects, or expressed as an isolated predicate. The potential inflection (in concert with the future modal case) has a number of senses: one, usually translated as 'should', expresses the speaker's wish that the action occur (one sense of (18)); another, usually translated with 'want', expresses the subject's wish to undertake the action (another sense of (18), and the only sense of (19) allowed by the text in which it appears).

(18) *kunyawunya kunawalad-a rarumban-ju kang-ku*
little:NOM children-NOM southern-FUT language-FUT
kamburi-ju.
speak-POT
(i) 'The little children should speak Kayardild.'
(ii) 'The little children want to speak Kayardild.'

(19) *waydbala kurri-ju. raba-tha dathin-ki dulk-i.*
white.man:NOM see-POT defile-ACT that-ACT place-ACT
'Some white men wanted to see (that place). They defiled that place.'

There is no morphosyntactic distinction between the 'should' and '(subject) want' constructions, although context often makes the intended sense clear. I have been unable to find a way of disambiguating between these constructions (other than context and background knowledge), and as far as I have been able to determine it is impossible to directly translate, for example, 'X wanted to come, but I didn't want X to come'. Instead, one would say 'X come-POT, (but) I said to X: don't come!'.

A third sense of the potential inflection is 'can, able to'; this is morphosyntactically distinct from the other two in that it can combine with the actual modal case if the ability (or lack of ability in the case of a negative) is located in the past:

(20)   barruntha-ya   ngada   kurri-nangku   mala-y.
       yesterday-ACT   I   see-NEG:POT   sea-ACT
       'Yesterday I couldn't see the sea.'

The desiderative inflection expresses a more circumspect desire — 'it's good that X', 'it would be good if X', 'one would want that X':

(21)   dathin-a   dangka-a   dali-d.
       that-NOM   man-NOM   come-DES
       'That man should come; it would be good if that man comes.'

It is clear, then, that WANT can be expressed in various contexts. But because it is an element in the meaning of an inflectional category, rather than a free lexeme, there remain situations where it is impossible to translate. An example is a sentence of the type 'A wants B to V', since the use of the potential inflection on V can only mean 'B wants to V', or 'Speaker wants B to V'. In attempting to translate 'Mum wants me to stay', I was given such sentences as *Ngamathu kamburijarr, nyingka ngakath!*, literally 'mother said: you stay!', but this is only available if the mother actually says something. Pushing this further, and asking how one would express the idea if the mother wanted the outcome, but didn't actually say anything, the only possible sentence was said to be *Ngada kurrijarra ngijinjina ngamathuna kirrkina, ngada warranangku, ngarrkuna miburina kurrijarr*, literally, 'I looked at my mother's face; I would not go, since she looked at me angrily'. The unavailability of translations for such sentences shows that even though the potential verb inflection has a meaning that contains WANT, there is no translation that just means WANT, and that would allow all combinations involving it to be expressed.

Note that the ex-primitive DISWANT is unproblematic: the verb *warnaja*, whose semantic range includes 'avoid', is often used for 'dislike' and 'diswant'.

8.2.3 THINK

Bardakamarutha (literally, 'stomach-put') and *marralmarutha* (literally, 'ear-put') can both be used in the sense of 'think of (an absent person or thing)'. The first always has an additional component either of 'wanting to be in the place as him/her/them' (e.g. *ngada bardakamarutha dathinki makuy* 'I'm thinking about that woman, wishing she's here, or wishing myself to be there') or of sympathy — of feeling what he/she/they think. *Marralmarutha* and *nalmarutha* (literally, 'head-put') are both used in contexts of deliberate, purposive intellectual activity with a specified goal and are best translated 'think of, recall, come up with something through thinking', for example, *kakuju nalmarutha nithi* 'Uncle will think of the name, will recall the name', *dathinki yakuriya ngada marralmarunmarri* 'I can't manage to think of (the name of) that fish'.

There are three further means of translating *think* in certain contexts, though none of these contains a lexical or constructional unit directly corresponding to THINK.

Firstly, in contexts of mistaken thought the counterfactual[9] particle *maraka* 'as if; should have been; one would have thought; (some unspecified agent) wrongly thought' may be used: *kurrija manharriy, maraka dangkakarranji, birra niwanji* '(they) saw a torch, and wrongly thought it was the man's, but it too was his (the monster's)'; although the explication of this clearly **contains** THINK it always includes a notion of 'wrongly, incorrectly' as well.

Secondly, in cases like 'I thought it was a fish (on seeing/hearing/smelling it)' where an inference results directly from a particular sensory modality, the appropriate perception verb may be used along with a secondary predicate on the object: *ngada kurrija/marrija/barndija niwanji yakuriy* 'I saw/heard/smelled it (as) a fish'. Although it was suggested at the Workshop on Semantic and Lexical Universals that this may represent polysemy in which perceptual verbs have a second sense, I reject this argument for two reasons. Firstly, this would not explain why all the perceptual verbs can be used in this way (rather than simply extending one, such as 'see', on the lines of the extension of English *see* to 'know'). Secondly, Kayardild speakers whom I asked about this said the relevant verb could only be used if a specific perception had taken place: if one had not actually seen, heard or smelled it one should use the negative of a perceptual verb and then an interrogative: *ngada kurrinmarri, ngaaka yakuriy?* 'I didn't see it, what (is it,) a fish?'.

Thirdly, various grammatical means may be used to translate THINK plus some information about certainty or source of information. The potential verbal inflection can translate THINK in cases where the speaker is fairly certain: *niya balmbiwu daliju* '(I think) he will come tomorrow'. And statements based on inference from contextually present evidence (e.g. 'I think sister has eaten the fish', when confronted with its remains) may be translated using an insubordinated clause in the past, as in (22) (Evans 1993). However a more faithful translation is 'Sister must have eaten the fish' or even more faithfully to the elliptical nature of the construction, '(There's nothing) because sister has eaten the fish'.

(22) *kularrin-inja   diya-jarra-ntha   yakuri-naa-nth.*
      sister-COBL   eat-PST-COBL   fish-PRIOR-COBL
      '(There's nothing left,) because sister has eaten the fish.'

There are thus a large number of strategies that one can employ to translate various canonical sentences involving THINK. The question arises whether any of them can be taken as the exponent of exactly, and only, THINK. Clearly the extensions of perception verbs are too specific, and the counterfactual particle has an additional component, 'mistakenly'. The verbs *bardakamarutha, marralmarutha* and *nalmarutha* are better candidates, but they also have additional components: 'wanting X to be here' for the first, and 'purposefully' for the other two. However, on my most recent field-trip I did record a couple of instances in which *marralmarutha* was used as a simple translation of THINK, without the added purposeful component:

(23)   ngada   marralmaru-th,   dali-nangku   bil-d.
       1SG:NOM think-ACT   come-NEG:POT 3PL-NOM
       'I think that they won't come.'

I conclude that this verb has the second sense THINK in addition to its primary sense 'think of, think about', and that second sense, though rarely used, is a reasonable translation of this primitive.

8.2.4   FEEL

Bardaka is a polysemous noun with the primary meaning 'stomach', and a secondary meaning 'feeling'. It can occur with this second meaning in a wide variety of collocations, such as *mirraa bardaka* 'feel good' (literally, 'good stomach/feeling'), *mildalatha bardaka* 'feel grief stricken' (literally, 'cut through one's stomach'), *bardaka warriliija* 'feel uneasy, feel that someone is saying something bad about one' (literally, 'stomach causes itself to go away'), *birdiya bardaka* 'feel bad' (literally, 'bad stomach'), *danda bardaka* 'feel like this' (literally, 'this stomach').

8.2.5   SAY

SAY is unproblematic: it is one sense of *kamburija*, though this can also mean 'speak, speak to':

(24)   *Kalthuriya   kamburi-j:*   "*nguku.   nguku-wuru*
       Kalthuriya   say-ACT   water   water-PROP
       dangka-a   ngambura-th!"
       person-NOM dig.well-IMP
       'Kalthuriya said: "Water. (You) people dig wells for water!"'

8.3   Determiners and Quantifiers: THIS, THE SAME, OTHER, ONE, TWO, MUCH/MANY, ALL

None of these present problems.

8.3.1 THIS

Danda represents THIS, for example *danda thungalda* 'this thing'. The roots *dan-* and *dathin-* 'that' are polysemous, also possessing the spatial-adverb meanings 'here' and 'there', although the complex agreement rules of Kayardild can assign different cases to spatial adverbs than to demonstratives.

8.3.2 THE SAME

Two words may translate THE SAME. *Niida*, probably a lengthened form of *nida* 'name',[10] is used attributively (for example *niida kala kirrwand* 'You two are the same colour'), and an extended sense of *warngiida*, whose primary sense is ONE, can be used either attributively or predicatively. An attributive example illustrating the semantic neutralisation between 'one' and 'same' is *birra warngiijina bardakana* 'they two are from the one womb, from the same womb'.

However, this extension of *warngiida* is limited to cases where one is talking about a single object, whereas *niida* lacks this restriction: *niida kiyarrngka maku* '(the) same two women' versus **warngiida kiyarrngka maku*. I therefore take *niida* as the more general exponent of THE SAME.

8.3.3 OTHER

Kayardild distinguishes *jathaa* 'another of the same type, another in a series, another about which I shall say a similar thing'[11] from *jangkaa* 'another about which I shall say a different thing, a different one'. For example, in (25) the 'other corner' (*jathaa wurduwa*) is added to an enumerated list of corners built by the same protagonist onto a giant fishtrap, whereas in (26) the 'other (Kaiadilt)' (*jangkaa*) suffer a different fate. Although there is a tendency for the choice to correlate with whether the 'other' is a different token of the same type (*jathaa*) or a different type (*jangkaa*), I think this is a secondary effect following from the different discourse choices — there is a natural correlation between making a different predication of two objects and contrasting them in other ways.

> (25) *wurdu-maru-th,   bad-a   jirrma-ja   wurdu,*
> corner-put-ACT   west-NOM   build.up-ACT   corner:NOM
> *jatha-a   wurdu-w*
> other-NOM   corner-NOM
> 'Put a corner on, and in the west built up a corner, and another corner.'

(26) jangka-a   yuuma-th,   jangka-a   thungkuwa-y,
     some-NOM   drown-ACT   some-NOM   mangrove-LOC
     jangka-a   jingka-ri.
     some-NOM   swamp-ALL
     'Some (Kaiadilt) drowned, some (hid) in the mangroves, some (were) scattered about in the swamp.'

Of the two, *jathaa* is more general and I take it as the exponent of OTHER. For example, to translate 'I do this, but other people don't' one would say:

(27) ngada   dandanangand,   jatha-a   dangka-a   warirr.
     I   like.this   other-NOM   person-NOM   nothing
     'I do this, but other people don't.'

8.3.4 ONE, TWO and MUCH/MANY

Warngiida means ONE, for example *warngiida maku* 'one woman'.[12] *Kiyarrngka* means TWO, as in *kiyarrngka kunawuna* 'two children'. *Muthaa* means MUCH or MANY, there being no syntactic distinction between mass and count nouns.[13] Examples are *muthaa dulka* 'many places', *muthaa nguku* 'much water, lots of water'.

8.3.5 ALL

There are several means of expressing ALL in Kayardild.

The invariant particle *maarra* can qualify a noun in its scope (for example, *maarra yaluluwuru kurriju* '(You) will see all the lights'), or can stand alone like English 'everyone, everything':

(28) maarra   waydbala-karran-ji   marri-ja   kang-ki.
     all   whitefeller-GEN-ACT   understand-ACT   language-ACT
     'All understand the white people's language.'

(29) maarra   diyaankuru.
     all   edible
     'All are edible.' (after discussing a number of different yams)

A second sense, or perhaps the same sense in a second construction, is 'only':

(30)   miida   maarra   maku-karran-d.
       louse   all/only   woman-GEN-NOM
       'Lice are only women's (food).', that is 'All lice are women's (food).'

Another semantic extension is to 'just, only do', as in *maarra kurrija ngijinji, kamburijarri* 'He just looked at me (literally, 'all (he did) was look at me'), and said nothing'. *Maarra* thus has a richly polysemous semantic structure, but its basic ALL sense, at least as used in examples (28) and (29), is an unproblematic translation of ALL. However, when it is required to quantify over a nominal not in the nominative there are problems, as it is incapable of bearing case but it is normal for Kayardild NPs to manifest full agreement. In these contexts two other constructions, both using the root *bakii-*, are used.

In its underived form, *bakiija* is a coverb[14] meaning 'all (intransitive subject) do, do to all (object)'; there is an additional semantic component of 'doing to completion'. This use can be exemplified by:

(31)   bala-tha   ngada   bakii-ja=da   munda   kurri-j.
       kill-ACT   I   all-ACT=SAME   arse   see-ACT
       'I killed them all, killed them until there were none left.' ('Saw their arse' is an idiom used for emphasis in this example.)

The nominalised form of this coverb, *bakiinda*, is also used freely to translate ALL, especially when the NP in its scope bears some case other than the nominative. It lacks the extra 'do to completion' sense found with the coverb.

(32)   ngada   kurri-ja   bilwan-ji   bakii-n-ki   kalajala-n-ki.
       I   see-ACT   them-ACT   all-N-ACT   wander.round-N-ACT
       'I saw them all wandering around.'

I thus regard *maarra* and *bakiinda* as allolexic exponents of ALL, with the first being preferred where the NP in scope is nominative, and the second preferred elsewhere.

8.4   Actions and Events: DO, HAPPEN (TO/IN)

8.4.1   DO

There is an interrogative verb, *ngaakawatha* 'do what',[15] as in *nyingka ngaakawath?* 'What are you doing?'. There are also demonstrative adverbs *dandananganda* 'this way, like this, happen like this, do like this' and *dathinananganda* 'that way, like that, happen like that, do like that'. But all these are over-specific. It is interesting that a large proportion of NSM definitions with DO occur in collocations like 'do this', 'do the same' and so on.

Expressions like 'do something bad' will be translated by specific verb lexemes in Kayardild. Many have the verb formative *-yalatha* which I gloss 'do' in my grammar (Evans, forthcoming); for example, *birdiyalatha* (literally, 'bad-do') 'do evil things, act immorally', *mirrayalatha* 'do well'.[16]

The existence of these various exponents means DO can usually be translated, but not in a consistent way. It would make the manipulation of DO in Kayardild definitions extremely difficult — for example one cannot use any direct translation equivalent of DO, but must retranslate in sentences like 'I'll do the same' (which would be translated as 'I will copy/imitate') and 'I'll do what you say' (which would be translated as 'I will follow your words').

8.4.2 HAPPEN

The interrogative *ngaakawuru*, one of the senses of which is 'why, for what purpose', is also used with the meaning 'what happened?'; and we saw in section 8.4.1 that the demonstrative adverbs can be used to mean 'happen like this', 'happen like that'.

However, the best translation of HAPPEN in non-interrogative contexts is using the nominal *birrjilka* whose primary senses are 'time, occasion', 'way, manner, pace', 'law, custom' and 'morals, way of living', but which has a further sense, discovered only after specific questioning on my last field-trip, of 'event, happening'. Consider (33), which juxtaposes the interrogative *ngaakawuru* 'what happen' with the nominal *birrjilka* 'event; happening'; and (34), 'A bad thing happened', which illustrates how the verbal morphology is actually associated with what in English would be the adjective, while HAPPEN is translated by the nominal *birrjilka*.

(33) *ngaakawuru?*   *niid-a*   *birrjilk.*
      what.happen   same-NOM   event:NOM
      'What happened?   The same thing happened.'

(34) *birdiwa-tharra*   *birrjilk.*
      be.bad-PST   event:NOM
      'A bad thing happened.' (Literally, '(There) was a bad event.')

HAPPEN TO X is expressed by X (subject) *burutha birrjilki*, literally 'X get/receive event', as in *mirrana birrjilkina niya burutharr* 'Something good happened to him/her' (literally, '(S)he received a good event').

The use of *birrjilka* to translate HAPPEN is thus a further example of the possibility, discussed by Goddard in section 1.4, of a particular primitive having a felicitous translation provided one does not require the part of speech to be held constant.

8.5 Meta-Predicates: NO, IF, COULD, LIKE, BECAUSE, VERY

8.5.1 NO

NO is expressed by a number of allolexes. The interjection *warirra* can mean either 'No!' or 'nothing, there is none'. The privative (adnominal) case suffix *-warri/-marri* means 'having no, without', for example, *ngada thaatha wirrinmarri* 'I came back with no money, without money'. Negative predications with verbs use a special set of portmanteau inflections that show negative and tense/mood, for example, *-nangku* 'negative potential' in *ngada kurrinangku* 'I won't, can't see/look', *-tharri/-jarri* 'negative actual' in *ngada kurrijarri* 'I didn't/don't see/look'.

8.5.2 IF

There are a number of *if-then*-constructions in Kayardild that provide for the grammatical expression of IF: various tense/mood sequences, such as past–potential (as in (35)) and precondition–actual (as in (36)), are used, and even actual–actual, which repeats the unmarked tense/mood choice, can be given a conditional reading with the right intonation. Some tense/mood sequences (notably the past–future) only allow the conditional interpretation, others (e.g. precondition–actual) also allow a 'when' interpretation.

(35) ngada   kurri-jarra   bukaji-na   dii-n-kina,
     1SG:NOM   see-PST   seahawk-PRIOR   sit-N-PRIOR
     ngada   raa-ju.
     I   spear-POT
     'If I had seen a sea-hawk landing, I'd have speared it.'

(36) jatha-a   dangka-a   ngakan-kinaba   wungi-jarrb,
     other-NOM   man-NOM   sandbank-PRIOR   steal-PRECON
     dul-marra   dangka-a   jul-iya   barrki-j.
     country-UTIL man-NOM   bone-ACT   chop-ACT
     'If/when another man stole (one's) sandbank, the boss of that country would chop some bones (in a spell of vengeance).'

8.5.3 COULD/CAN

One sense of the potential verb inflection in Kayardild is deontic 'can'; this inflection also covers future tense and prescription ('must'), but the existence of different rules for assigning modal case makes this is a clear case of polysemy: past predicates with the potential assign the actual modal case (see (19) for an example), which cannot happen with the future and prescriptive senses of this verbal category. The negative potential verb inflection expresses 'cannot'. Affirmative and negative examples are:

(37)   *kiija-tha*   *bathin-d,*   *kiija-tha*
        approach-IMP   west.from-NOM   approach-IMP
        bathin-d,   *marrwa-a*   *ngijuwa*   *kurri-juu-nth.*
        west.from-NOM   near-NOM   I:COBL   see-POT-COBL
        'Come near from the west, come near from the west, so that I can see you close up.'[17]

(38)   *dali-j!*   *ngada*   *kantharrkuru*   *ngudi-nangku*
        come-IMP   I   alone:NOM   throw-NEG:POT
        banga-walath-u.
        turtle-many-FUT
        'Come! I can't turn all these turtles over on my own.'

The epistemic qualification expressed by *maybe* or *can* in English is translated in traditional Kayardild by one or another combination of verbal inflection with modal case. Such qualification of past events will be expressed by the past verbal inflection in concert with the prior modal case, as in (39).[18] Future events so qualified will, if undesirable, be expressed with the apprehensive verb inflection plus the emotive modal case, as in (40). Future events neutral or positive with respect to desirability may be expressed with the desiderative verbal inflection and the emotive modal case (not exemplified here).

(39)   *dangka-karran-jina*   *thungal-ina*   *wungi-jarr.*
        people-POSS-PRIOR   thing-PRIOR   steal-PST
        'Maybe (he)'s been stealing people's things.'

(40)   *warkurr-inja*   *daman-da*   *dara-a-nyarr.*
        dugong.hide-EMOT   tooth-NOM   break-M-APPR
        '(You) might break your tooth on the dugong hide.'

The restriction of CAN to one sense of a grammatical category is not problematic due to the natural combinatorics, or should we say 'primitive syntax', of CAN: definitions always combine CAN with verbs anyway. However, the fact that epistemic possibility is but one sense of a rather rich set in the case of the potential and desiderative inflections makes the exact and decontextualised expression of COULD rather problematic in traditional Kayardild, so it is not surprising that the English-derived particle *marrbi* (from *might be*) is the most current means of expressing this category. Sentence (41), a paraphrase of (39) using this particle (and note the substitution of the unmarked verbal and modal case inflections), is a far more natural sentence in ordinary Kayardild today:

(41) marrbi   dangka-karran-ji   thungal-i   wungi-j.
      maybe   people-POSS-ACT   thing-ACT   steal-ACT
      'Maybe (he)'s been stealing people's things.'

8.5.4 LIKE

'Like an X' can be translated in two ways. The prefix *minyi*-[19] is used in some contexts — for example, *niya minyi-thabuju* 'He is like (his) brother' — and several lexical items based on explicit simile employ this prefix: *ngarnala* 'white cockatoo', *minyi-ngarnala* '(a) witchetty grub; (b) termite' (both are white like a white cockatoo). Although *minyi* is probably a good equivalent to LIKE, it is rather limited in use — it mainly occurs in abusive comparisons with particular debauched relatives.

More freely combinable is the polysemous particle *maraka*, which is frequently used, with clausal scope, as a counterfactual (see Evans (forthcoming)):

(42) maraka   yuuma-thu   barruntha-y.
      counterfactual   drown-POT   yesterday-ACT
      '(He) could have drowned yesterday (but didn't).'

But *maraka* is also used frequently to express LIKE; for example: *kirrmaku, maraka maku* 'He is effeminate, like/as if he were a woman'; *danda kunawuna jungarr, maraka niwanda kanthathu mankarr* 'This child is big, he is sturdy like his father'. *Maraka* may also mean 'like' where the comparison takes a whole clause as its argument:

(43) jatha-wuru   maku-wuru,   maraka   nyingka   ngumal-d
      other-PROP   woman-PROP   like   you:NOM   single-NOM
      '(You) have got another woman, (you're carrying on) like you're single!'

I therefore take this sense of *maraka* as the exponent of LIKE.[20]

8.5.5 BECAUSE

I have argued elsewhere (Evans 1986) that the expression of BECAUSE is not straightforward in Kayardild, often being formally conflated with pure temporal sequence. Such apparent conflation occurs in three sets of exponents: the locative case *-ki(ya)/-i(ya)/-ya*, encoding 'ambient cause' and also 'ambience' more generally (this case may also go on verbs); the consequential case *-ngarrba*, encoding 'prior cause' (contingent succession) and also 'temporal priority' (non-contingent succession); and the factitive suffix, which derives verbs meaning either 'cause to be X' or 'do until X' — from *kabin-da* 'low tide', for example, the factitive verb *kabilutha* can be derived, meaning either 'cause the tide to become low' or 'do until the tide is low'.

There are two possible interpretations of these facts: either the relevant forms are polysemous between causal and non-causal readings, or they encode more abstract relations which will be interpreted as having causal readings in certain contexts, possibly supplemented by pragmatics. Since the appearance of my article both Goddard (1991) and Wierzbicka (1991) have argued for a polysemy interpretation of this data. One argument, given by Wierzbicka, is that the interrogative *ngaakangarrba* (formally the interrogative base plus the consequential case), which I gloss as 'why, because of what', is a clear exponent of unalloyed causality. However, this word can also have the purely temporal meaning 'after what, after when': on asking someone *ngaakangarrba nyingka kalkath* (literally, '*ngaakangarrba* you got.sick') one could receive an answer either in terms of cause (e.g. 'because of a stonefish') or in terms of temporal consequence (e.g. 'after I was on Sweers Island'). So it would be possible to maintain the 'abstract' position by arguing that this interrogative simply means 'after what', with 'why' a context-specific sense.

A second line of argument in favour of polysemy, given by Goddard (1991) for Yankunytjatjara data that resembles Kayardild in many ways, involves decisive situations in which the cause is concurrent with the effect (e.g. not being able to sleep because one is thinking about one's grandfather), but in which the ablative (normally used for temporal succession) is used; in this way the independence of temporal and causal expression is demonstrated. Following Goddard's idea, I tried to elicit similar sentences in Kayardild and found that it is in fact possible to use the consequential in situations where the cause is concurrent with the effect; an example is (44), which exemplifies both the use of the locative for 'ambient cause' in B's sentence, and the use of the consequential for concurrent cause in A's second statement:

(44) A: *ngada wulji-ya yiiwi-n-marri.*
 1SG:NOM last.night-LOC sleep-N-PRIV
 'I couldn't get to sleep last night.'

 B: *yeah, kungul-muth, ngada yiiwi-jarri*
 yeah mosquito-many 1SG:NOM sleep-NEG:ACT
 mutha-ya kungul-i.
 many-LOC mosquito-LOC
 'Yeah, (there were) lots of mosquitoes, I couldn't sleep for all the mosquitoes.'

 A: *kungul-warri, ngada marralmaru-tha mungkiji-Ø*
 mosquito-PRIV 1SG:NOM think.about-ACT own-ACT
 kanthathu-y, dathin-ngarrba ngada yiiwi-jarri.
 father-ACT that-CONS 1SG:NOM sleep-ACT
 'No, it wasn't the mosquitoes, I was thinking about my own father, it was because of that that I couldn't sleep.'

I conclude that the consequential suffix is polysemous between 'temporal consequence' and 'causal consequence' meanings, and in the latter meaning is an appropriate translation of BECAUSE.

8.5.6 VERY

The exact answer here depends on the scope of VERY. Modern English *very* is restricted to adjectives, but in Chaucer's time could qualify nouns (*a verray partait gentil knyght*); the Russian equivalent *očen'* can also qualify verbs, as in *Ja očen' ustal* 'I am really tired' or *Ona očen' ljublju menja* 'She really loves me'. Assuming this enlarged notion of VERY, Kayardild has a number of allolexes. Adjectives take suffixed *-mirra*, a reduced form of *mirraa* 'good', as in *kunyamirra* 'very small', *birdimirra* 'very bad'. Nouns combine with the particle *kalala* 'real, dinkum', as in *kalala ngunguka* 'a real, proper story'. There are a large number of idiomatic extensions of other words that can mean 'very' — such as *ngulmu* (literally, 'deadly'), as in *wardunda bandija ngulmu* 'Cats smell very well, cats can really smell', and *kurulutha* (literally, 'kill'), as in *ngada balatha niwanji wangalkuru kuruluth* 'I really hit him with the boomerang' — but often their combinatorial possibilities are limited.

8.6 Time and Place: WHEN, WHERE, AFTER, BEFORE, UNDER, ABOVE

8.6.1 WHEN and WHERE

WHEN is translated by *jinawarrku* (literally, 'where sun') if a time of day is being sought (e.g. *jinawarrkuru thaathu?* 'When (what time of day) will you come back?'), and by *jinaa darri* (literally, 'where time')[21] in a more general sense (e.g. *jinana darrina dathina dangkaa dalijarr?* 'When did that man come?', *jinadarru kantharrkuru diyaju malawu?* 'When will I ever be able to drink my beer on my own?').

Jina-a WHERE is quite unproblematic. An example is:

(45)   *jina-a*   *mirra-a*   *wara-a*   *dangka-a?*
       where-NOM   good-NOM   mouth-NOM   person-NOM
       'Where is the healer?'

8.6.2 AFTER and BEFORE

The polysemous consequential case *-ngarrba*, discussed in section 8.5.5 in connection with BECAUSE, is used with NPs to mean 'after NP': for example, *wunngarrba ngada thaathu* 'I will return after the rains'. The adverbial *buda*, basically 'behind', can mean simple 'after', so that 'Jill came tumbling after' would be *Jill buda barjija dalij*. 'Happen after' can be rendered by *buthiiwath*, the inchoative of the locative of *buda*: *wirrkanda buthiiwath* means 'the dance happened after, the dance was last'.

There is no simple way of exactly expressing the converse, 'before X'. One way would be to use the translative case and say 'while waiting for X'. But the verb *yuulutha*, literally 'go ahead', is sometimes used with the meaning 'first, happening first', as in *X yuulutha bukawath* 'X died first, before'.

The verb *ngariija* means 'go in front, happen first', and *danaaja*, a lexically specialised passive of *danatha* 'leave', means 'go behind, happen last'; each can be nominalised, giving *ngariinda* 'first one', *danaanda* 'last one'. In discussions of sequence, *ngariija* and *jinkaja* 'follow' are often used in successive clauses:

(46)   *bil-da*   *wirrka-ja*   *ngarii-j,*
        they-NOM   dance-ACT   first-ACT
        ngakul-da   *jinka-ja*   *wirrka-j.*
        we-NOM   follow-ACT dance-ACT
        'They danced first, and we danced last.'

In context, where attention is focused on the relative chronology of two events, there is no requirement that they be strictly first or last in a larger sequence, so that translation as 'before' and 'after' rather than 'first' and 'last' is possible.

I therefore take AFTER as having two allolexic exponents: the suffix *-ngarrba* when AFTER governs an argument ('after the rain'), and the adverbial use of the verb *jinkaja* 'follow; after'. BEFORE can only be expressed by the adverbial use of *ngariija*.

8.6.3   UNDER and ABOVE

Yarka has a range of senses that includes 'down, underneath, oriented downwards'; its locative, *yarki*, means more specifically 'underneath, below'. *Walmu* means 'above; above NP (in locative case)'; *walmathi* means 'on top of, above'. Both of these are good translations of ABOVE. An illustrative sentence with the former is *ngumuwa wunda walmu (ngakuluwanji dulki)* 'Dark clouds are above (our-LOC place-LOC)'; with the latter, *ngamathu wijiri yarka, kunawuna wijiri walmathi* 'The mother firestick is underneath, the baby firestick is on top'.

8.7   Partonomy and Taxonomy: PART OF, KIND OF

8.7.1   PART (OF)/HAVING AS A PART

There is no noun meaning 'part'; two nouns sometimes translated as 'piece' refer specifically to pieces of meat and would therefore be more accurately rendered as 'morsel'.

The 'part–whole' construction, in which the nouns denoting part and whole are syntactically apposed, agreeing in case, is certainly sensitive to the part–whole relationship, but is not suitable for definitions. For example, one can use it to say 'I burned the tree on its bark' but not 'The bark is part of the tree', since the apposition is only possible when a lexical verb is present.

Recently Wierzbicka (1989) has argued that in Warlpiri 'part of' is one sense of the polysemous genitive case, which includes both 'part of' and 'belonging to'. The Kayardild genitive can be treated similarly, except that it partially overlaps with the ablative (see Evans (forthcoming, ch. 4) for details of the semantic distinctions). Among older speakers the genitive suffix *-karra* is used only for possession in attributive position (e.g. *dangka-karra wangalk* 'the man's boomerang') and for severed body parts (*bijarrbakarra marld* 'a dugong's (severed) flipper'), though younger speakers can also use it for the part–whole relation: *dangka-karra marld* 'the man's hand'. In predicative position it can be used for the part–whole relation by all speakers: *dathina marlda dangkakarrand* 'That hand is a man's, is part of a man'. Two example sentences given by Kayardild speakers as translations of 'part (of)' are:

(47) *dathin-a   thungal-da   ngaa-karra   / ngaaka-na?*
      that-NOM   thing-NOM   what-GEN   what-ABL
      'What's that thing a part of?'

(48) *dan-kina   diwal-ina   /   wumburung-kina.*
      this-ABL   tree-ABL   spear-ABL
      'It's a part of this tree/of this spear.'

8.7.2 KIND (OF)

After writing in the first draft of this paper that there was no straightforward translation of KIND OF, I discovered that there was in fact a special use of the word *minyi*, usually translated 'colour', for KIND. Since this use is far from common, I would like first to discuss some other ways of translating KIND, even though none of them are general enough to qualify as a good transcontextual equivalent.

In discussing taxonomies that would call up *kind of* in English, one simply uses a nominal predicate: instead of 'the great trevally is a kind of fish' one says simply *wakabinya — yakuri* '(the) great trevally (is a) fish'. 'Both X and Y are kinds of Z' will be expressed by 'X, Y one Z': *bijarrb, bangaa, kunbulka warngiid. yakarr, warngiid kunbulk* 'Dugong, turtle, they are sea-game alike. Porpoises, they are one (with them) as sea-game'. Kinship terms are also frequently used in discussing taxonomies: for example, to say 'The porpoise and the whale are both kinds of cetacean' one says *yakarra duujind, kanithu thabuju* 'The porpoise is the younger brother, and the whale is the older brother'.

The word *wuranda* 'food' may also have the senses 'creature' and, sometimes, 'kind', as in *dathina jangkaa wurand, Dicky, ngulmuwa wurand* 'that Dicky is another kind/sort (of person), a fantastic kind/sort'; and the collocations *niida wurand* 'same kind' and *jangkaa wurand* 'another kind' are often used as predicates. Neither can be used as a two-place predicate like *kind of* in English. The meta-terms *jungarra nid* 'big name' and *kunyaa nid* 'small name' translate English 'superordinate' and 'hyponym' in discussions of taxonomy: *bilwanda warngiida jungarra nid, kunbulk. jathaa nida kunyaa, bijarrb, bangaa, yakarr, kanithu* 'They have the one big (superordinate) name, *kunbulk* ('big game', 'large marine animal'). The other names are small (hyponyms): dugong, turtle, porpoise, whale.'

Turning now to the term *minyi*, this is normally translated into English by Kayardild speakers as 'colour', as in *muthaa minyi: bana balarr, bana ngumu, bana karndukarndu* 'Many colours: light, and dark, and red'. However, the word *colour* in Mornington English, though including the English sense, is in fact much broader and can apply to all kinds of physical resemblance, though with the connotation that they are due to common ancestry. For example, in discussing a mother and daughter, one could say *birra warngiida minyi* 'They two (are of) one colour', and this could mean either that they have the same colour in the English senses (either of race — that is, they are both full-blood Aborigines — or of complexion or hair colour, e.g. they both have golden hair) or that they resemble each other in some other way, for example in their face or build. In discussing the pair of elephants in Noah's Ark, the following sentence was offered:

(49)   *dathin-a   kiyarrng-k ... warngiid-a   minyi*
       that-NOM   two-NOM   one-NOM   kind:NOM
       dali-jarrma-th.
       come-CAUS-ACT
       'Those two ... he brought one kind (of them on board).'

The expression 'kinds of' is translated by reduplicating the proprietive form of this word: *minyiwuru minyiwuru*, literally 'kind-having kind-having'.

Minyi is thus a good translation equivalent of KIND in many contexts. However, it cannot be used transitively to express 'X is a kind of Y' (where Y is superordinate) — in this case a simple equational sentence will be used, as discussed above.

8.8   Evaluative and Descriptive: GOOD, BAD, BIG, SMALL

All are straightforwardly expressed by adjectives: *mirraa* 'good', *birdi* 'bad', *jungarra* 'big', *kunyaa* 'small'.

8.9 Conclusion

Most of the proposed primitive set find unproblematic translations into Kayardild. The problems that arise can be divided into the following groups:

Problems of Combinability. This is most obvious with those primitive candidates expressible only as one sense of an inflectional grameme: WANT (potential verb inflection), COULD (potential, apprehensive, past or desiderative verb inflections depending on tense and other mood factors), IF (particular tense sequences, or sometimes just intonation) and PART OF (the genitive or ablative cases).

With WANT, for example, one can translate 'I want X' or 'I want to V' into Kayardild but not 'X wants Y to V'. Further, the polysemous nature of most of the gramemes involved (e.g. WANT and COULD are two senses of the potential) and the impossibility of giving contrastive stress to inflectional suffixes means that it is impossible to translate statements such as 'He could swim, but doesn't want to swim', since this would come out as the conjunction of the potential and the negative potential, giving an apparent contradiction. The only way around this would be to use another way of expressing 'could swim' in the first clause, such as *biyankuru*, the proprietive-suffixed nominalised form of the verb that translates ability, 'one able to swim'; a sentence like *niya biyankuru, biyanangku* would then be understood as 'He is able to swim, but doesn't want to swim/won't swim' through implicature selecting the WANT sense of the negative potential on the second verb.

Problems of Exuberance. These arise in cases where there is no 'pure' lexical exponent, even though there may be words whose explication contains the relevant primitive: this is the case with DO (which appears in the definition of *ngaakawatha* 'do what?' and *mirrayalatha* 'do properly', among others). In such cases it will be perfectly possible to translate certain combinations into Kayardild, since these combinations are lexicalised (e.g. 'do something bad' *birdiyalatha*, 'do like this' *dandananganda*) but others (e.g. 'do what I want', 'do as you please') are impossible; here we again find limitations on combinability.

Viewed from another angle, these two types of problem underscore the distinction between **semantic** and **lexical** universals: the Kayardild evidence suggests that all the primitives considered in this volume are **semantic universals**, but that some fail to be **lexical universals**. In a case like THINK or DO there exist many Kayardild words that contain the relevant semantic component, supporting the claim that they are semantically universal, but they have not been lexicalised in a pure form. The case of putative universals expressible only as senses of gramemes is directly comparable: WANT and COULD are required in the explication of certain gramemes, but are not available in a pure form as lexemes. Yet only when a meaning is lexicalised does it become fully available for translation, which requires the ability to combine freely. Conversely, it may not be until one attempts translation that a particular lexical gap is even noticed, since all the commonest configurations involving a particular semantic primitive may be lexicalised — Kayardild, for example, has 'do this', 'do that', 'do well', 'do badly', 'do what', 'do like someone else' and so forth. By lexicalising all the regularly used combinations, a language can in some cases get by perfectly well without lexical exponents of the primitives themselves.

Notes

1 I would like to thank the many Kayardild speakers who have taught me their language over the years, especially Darwin Moodoonuthi, Roma Kelly, Pluto Bentinck and Arthur Paul. Roland and Anne Moodoonuthi, Alison Dundaman, Paula Paul and Netta Loogatha were particularly helpful in checking the various questions discussed in this paper. My research on Kayardild has been supported by the Australian Institute of Aboriginal and Torres Strait Islander Studies, the Australian National University, the University of Melbourne, the Australian Research Council (grant "Non–Pama-Nyungan Languages of Northern Australia"), the Kaiadilt Association and the Mornington Shire Council, all of which bodies I thank for their assistance.

2 My warm thanks to Anna Wierzbicka and Cliff Goddard for organising the Workshop on Semantic and Lexical Universals at which an earlier version of this paper was discussed, as well as providing very detailed critical comments on an earlier draft of this paper, and to all the participants of that workshop for their helpful comments. Without this seminar I would not have had the sobering but enlightening experience of discovering that after so many years working on the language, and even preparing a reasonable dictionary, I still did not understand how to express such simple concepts as 'happen', 'kind' and 'want', concepts which a subsequent field-trip showed to be straightforwardly translatable.

3 In fact modal case can to some extent be varied independently of the verb; this is irrelevant to the present paper.

4 The following glosses are used: ABLative, ACTual, ALLative, APPRehensive, COBL complementising, CAUSative, CONSequential, CTRFCT counterfactual, DESiderative, EMOTive, FUTure, GENitive, IMMEDiate, IMPerative, INCHoative, INSTrumental, LOCative, Middle, NEGative, Nominaliser, NOMinative, NP noun phrase, OBLique, PLural, POSSessive, POTential, PRECONdition, PRIOR, PRIVative, PROPrietive, PST past, RESultative, SAME, SG singular, STILL, UTILitive, VALL verbal allative, VD verbal dative, VPURP verbal purposive, VTRANSL verbal translative.

5 The locative may also be used, but for simplicity of exposition is not illustrated here. See Evans (1988) for details.

6 The issue of how grammatical and pragmatic constraints interact here is discussed in Evans (1993).

7 The translations of (11) and (12) are verbatim translations given by Kayardild speakers; in (11) and (12) the speaker, Roland Moodoonuthi was careful to stress the double nature of the ignorative as indeterminate pronoun implying a question.

8 Perhaps because the Kayardild first became aware of white people and other Aboriginal people at the same time.

9   This particle is labelled 'counterfactual' after its most frequent sense, but some of its uses (e.g. to translate 'like' — see section 8.5.4) are not directly counterfactual.
10 This semantic extension appears to have been bridged by the special religious context of talking about sacred sites and the people or things associated with them, and of whom the sites are to be considered another manifestation, or in other words 'the same'. *Niida dulk* (literally, 'same place') has been variously translated for me as 'name place', 'same place for him' and so on, and *niida dangkaa* (literally, 'same person') as 'same person, boss for that place', and so on, but probably a more revealing translation would be 'person who is in some ways the same as that place'.
11 Note that in the closely related language Yukulta, *jathara* means 'one', and even in Kayardild counting proceeds by saying *Jathaa, jathaa, jathaa* ... where English would say *One, another/two, another/three* ...; this implies that *jathaa* is more accurately characterised as meaning 'one in a series' rather than 'another in a series'.
12 Note that *warngiida* (like the other numerals) is not used as one counts objects: one says *jathaa, jathaa, jathaa* ... 'one, another, another ...'. But in answer to *jinamulu* 'How many?', *warngiida* ONE is an appropriate answer.
13 Though a subset of count nouns are distinguished by being able to take the suffix *-walada/-walath-* 'many', as with *bangawalathu* 'many turtles' in (38). No mass nouns can take this suffix.
14 Coverbs are morphologically verbal words that share a clause with a main verb, with which they agree in tense, mood and polarity.
15 Anna Wierzbicka (personal correspondence) has pointed out that if this verb patterned like the other ignoratives it should allow the meaning 'do something'. However I have never heard it used this way.
16 Goddard (Yankunytjatjara, this volume) argues that the Yankunytjatjara equivalent is polysemous between 'make' or 'fix' and 'do'; I have no evidence for *mirrayalatha* including simple 'do' in its semantic range, although it does include 'make' and 'repair, fix up' in addition to 'do properly, do well'.
17 The complementising oblique case here marks the last three words as belonging to a subordinate clause whose subject is not the same as the main clause; it does not affect the interpretation of the potential verb inflection.
18 Although the grammatical coding here is far from unambiguous, since (39) is also compatible with a past declarative interpretation. The exact interpretation would depend on the choice between 'assertive' and 'suggestive' intonation.
19 This is the only prefix in Kayardild and is etymologically related to the free noun *minyi* 'kind', discussed in section 8.7.2.
20 Counterfactual/like polysemy is also found in several other Australian languages (see Breen 1984) and one might try and postulate a single invariant meaning, defining 'X is like Y' as 'one would think X a Y' (and a rather similar analysis was at one point proposed by Wierzbicka (1971), who suggested paraphrasing 'like X' by 'you'd say that it could be X'). Although this is not a bad first definition of 'like', especially with nouns, it does not work so well with verbs — 'X danced like this' does not mean 'X danced, one would think this was him doing it' — and Wierzbicka has recently rejected the validity of this paraphrase.

21 Like other time NPs this inflects for modal case; it behaves as a compound in some modal cases, such as the future (*jinadarru*) and as a two-word idiom in others, such as the prior (*jinana darrina*).

References

Breen, Gavan. 1984. "Similarity and Mistake in Two Australian Languages". *Language in Central Australia* 1.2.1-9.

Evans, Nicholas. 1986. "The Unimportance of CAUSE in Kayardild". *Language in Aboriginal Australia* 2.9-17.

Evans, Nicholas. 1988. "Odd Topic Marking in Kayardild". *Complex Sentence Constructions in Australian Languages* (= Typological Studies in Language 15) ed. by Peter Austin, 219-266. Amsterdam: John Benjamins.

Evans, Nicholas. 1992. *Kayardild Dictionary and Thesaurus*. Melbourne: Department of Linguistics & Language Studies, University of Melbourne.

Evans, Nicholas. 1993. "Code, Inference, Placedness and Ellipsis". *The Role of Theory in Linguistic Description* ed. by William A. Foley, 243-280. Berlin: Mouton de Gruyter.

Evans, Nicholas. Forthcoming. *A Grammar of Kayardild*. Berlin: Mouton de Gruyter.

Goddard, Cliff. 1991. "Testing the Translatability of Semantic Primitives into an Australian Aboriginal Language". *Anthropological Linguistics* 33.1.31-56.

Karcevski, Serge. 1969. "Introduction a l'étude de l'interjection". *A Geneva School Reader* ed. by Robert Godel, 196-212. Bloomington, Indiana: Indiana University Press.

Wierzbicka, Anna. 1971. "Porównanie — Gradacja — Metafora". *Pamiętnik Literacki* 62.4.127-147.

Wierzbicka, Anna. 1989. "Semantic Primitives and Lexical Universals". *Quaderni di Semantica* 10.103-121.

Wierzbicka, Anna. 1991. "Lexical Universals and Universals of Grammar". *Meaning and Grammar: Cross-linguistic perspectives* ed. by Michel Kefer & Johan van der Auwera, 383-415. Berlin: Mouton de Gruyter.

Lexical Primitives in Yankunytjatjara

Cliff Goddard
University of New England, Armidale

Yankunytjatjara is a minority dialect of the Western Desert Language, spoken by several hundred people, primarily in the north-west of South Australia.[1] By Australianist standards, it is reasonably well-described. A grammar (Goddard 1985) and dictionary (Goddard 1992) are both available, and there is a range of technical and pedagogical material published for the neighbouring dialect Pitjantjatjara (e.g. Eckert & Hudson 1988, Bowe 1990). In addition, there are a variety of texts published in both Pitjantjatjara and, to a lesser extent, Yankunytjatjara.[2]

The Western Desert Language is a typical Pama-Nyungan language in being agglutinative (chiefly suffixing), with a well-developed system of nominal and verbal derivation. Phrasal ordering is flexible, with a preference for core NPs to precede and other NPs to follow the verb. Constituent order is fixed within the NP, with the head preceding all modifiers. For most NP types, case marking applies only to the final word of the phrase. Ellipsis of 'understood' third-person arguments is very common.

The case system has three core cases — nominative, accusative and ergative — applying to NPs in S, O and A functions respectively, but a 'split' system of case marking: pronouns have identical (zero-marked) nominative and ergative case forms, whereas other nominals have identical (zero-marked) nominative and accusative forms. This is a classic example of what is commonly referred to as 'split ergativity'; see Goddard (1982) for discussion and defence of the three-case analysis assumed here. The existence of different grammatical cases for S and A raises the question, addressed in section 9.1.3, of whether nominals have different semantic content in the two roles.

Yankunytjatjara verbs strictly subcategorise their subjects for either ergative or nominative case. Verbs inflect for tense/aspect/mood, but not person. There are four conjugational classes, strongly correlated with the transitivity and with the mora-parity of the verbal stem. Although there is a solid base of monomorphemic verbal lexemes, the majority of verbs are derived from nouns, adjectives or adverbs. The most productive process for creating intransitive verbs involves the prolific *-ri/-ari* suffix, glossed as 'inchoative'. Transitive verb creation is done primarily by zero-derivation: the root is simply assigned to one of the transitive verb classes and inflected accordingly. These facts will be relevant when we come to consider semantically primitive verbal meanings such as DO and HAPPEN.

All the posited lexical primitives find good candidates in Yankunytjatjara, once polysemy and allolexy are taken into account. In general, the posited exponents are formally simple (monomorphemic) words or clitics; but sometimes they are affixes, and occasionally they are formally complex (i.e. apparently polymorphemic) expressions.

9.1 Substantives

9.1.1 *I and YOU*

I and YOU have free (subject) forms *ngayulu* and *nyuntu* respectively, as in (4) and (8a), and (3) and (8b). Also common are their clitic (or 'bound') equivalents -*na* and -*n* respectively, which attach to the first phrase in a sentence, as shown in examples (1), (2), (9) and (58), and (26), (42), (63) and (68). These must be regarded as allolexes of *ngayulu* and *nyuntu*.

9.1.2 *SOMEONE, SOMETHING and PEOPLE*

There is a degree of overlap in the formal means by which these three primitive meanings are expressed in Yankunytjatjara. The form *kutjupa* (which as a modifier means OTHER, see section 9.3.3) plays a role akin to that of *some-* in English, which figures in the morphology of the English exponents of SOMEONE and SOMETHING, but does not, in these expressions, carry an independent meaning. As well, the word *anangu*, which is the primary exponent of PEOPLE, features in some expressions as an allolex of SOMEONE (in some ways analogous to English *person*).

These complications can be confusing, so it may be well to emphasise at the outset that the distinction between SOMEONE and SOMETHING is very clear in the interrogative system, in the contrast between *ngananya* 'who' and *nyaa* 'what'. Like English *what*, *nyaa* may be used to make an inquiry about something thought about, as in (8b), or said, as in (26), as well as about physical things and 'stuffs'. Both words often occur as in (1) and (2), consistent with Yankunytjatjara discourse style, to signal that a new participant is to be introduced into the conversation. The 'who' word[3] may also be used as in (3), with a 'you-know-who' meaning, that is, to allude the identity of someone without mentioning the person's name.[4]

(1) *Munu-na   nyaa   nyangu   — malu.*
     and-I   what   see:PAST   kangaroo
     'Then I saw something (what) — a kangaroo.'

(2) Ka-*na* *ngananya nyangu — wati panya Witjikinya.*
 and-I who:ACC see:PAST man that.one Witjiki:NAME
 'I saw someone (who) — that fella Witjiki.'

(3) *Nyuntu ngana-ku wangkapai!*
 you who-PURP talk:CHAR
 'You've been talking (favourably) about you-know-who.' (e.g. an accusation by a jealous boyfriend)

The fact that neither *ngananya* 'who' nor *nyaa* 'what' is confined to interrogative uses suggests that they do not contain an ignorative component (Wierzbicka 1980b) *sensu stricto*, that is, a component including the specification 'I don't know'. On the other hand, it can be argued that both words contain a weaker form of ignorative component, acknowledging the speaker's failure to identify the person or thing concerned; roughly, 'I don't say now, thinking of something/someone: it was this something/someone'. Wierzbicka's original article on the ignorative contains a discussion (pp. 323–328) of such components, which she terms 'indifferentives'. To decide whether an indefinite expression in given language contains such a component in a "truly semantic" sense, as opposed to it being "merely a common inference" calls for careful case-by-case analysis (Wierzbicka 1980b:323). English *someone* and *something*, for instance, can be shown not to express any such component, partly on account of their being the only semantically neutral nominals available to frame the ignorative and indifferentive components themselves, which involve locutions like 'I'm thinking of someone/something'.

Applying this consideration to Yankunytjatjara suggests that despite the fact that *ngananya* and *nyaa* are more semantically versatile than English *who* and *what*, they are not the premier exponents of SOMEONE and SOMETHING. Rather, these both seem to be furnished by forms based on *kutjupa*. As mentioned, adnominal *kutjupa* means OTHER, but since it plays such an important role in the formation of Yankunytjatjara indefinite expressions, I have given it the interlinear gloss 'some' in these contexts.

Consider examples (4) and (5). Here *kutjupa* alone functions as an exponent of SOMEONE. Example (4), for instance, could not mean 'I saw something', and (5) could not mean 'Something threw it away' (even though the verb *waningu* 'threw away, cast aside' can be used with non-personal subjects, such as *walpa* 'wind').

(4) *Ngayulu kutjupa nyangu.*
 I 'some' see:PAST
 'I saw someone.'

(5) *Kutjupa-ngku waningu.*
 'some'-ERG throw.away:PAST
 'Someone threw it away.'

One possible interpretation would be that the word *aṉangu*, which may closely approximate 'person', is an implicit nominal head in such examples; that is, that *kutjupa* in (5) is short for *aṉangu kutjupa*, and *kutjupangku* in (5) is short for *aṉangu kutjupangku*. A suggestion along these lines is made by Harkins and Wilkins (this volume) for comparable data from Mparntwe Arrernte.

There is a problem with this however. *Aṉangu* is not usable in reference to non-human entities such as monsters and the personae of Dreaming stories, even when these have clear 'personal identities'. (I suggest below that *aṉangu* is better construed as an exponent of PEOPLE.) Consequently, the expression *aṉangu kutjupa* 'another person' has a narrower referential range than *kutjupa* alone. For instance, in traditional folktales, babies and children are often stolen away from their families by such creatures as *pangkalangu* 'ogre' and *kungkapaṉpa* 'bogey woman'. Looking at the tracks leading away from where the baby had been left, a protagonist could say the likes of (6); since there is no presumption that a human being is responsible, *aṉangu kutjupa(ngku)* is not substitutable here:

(6) *Kutjupa-ngku iṯi katingu!*
    'some'-ERG baby take:PAST
    'Someone's taken the baby!'

Many Yankunytjatjara people have adopted Christianity. Example (7) shows *kutjupa* being used to make an indefinite reference which turns out to relate to God; *aṉangu kutjupa* 'another person' could certainly not be substituted for *kutjupa* here:

(7) *Kutjupangku rawangku nyuntunya nyanganyi*
    'some'-ERG always you:ACC see:PRES
    munu kulini. Nganalu? Godalu.
    and think:PRES who:ERG God:ERG
    'Someone is always watching and thinking about you. Who? God.'

I conclude therefore that *kutjupa* alone may function as the head of an NP, and when it does it expounds the meaning SOMEONE.

Consider next the examples in (8), adduced by Eckert and Hudson (1988:40) to show a culturally natural way of bringing up a touchy topic in conversation. Example (8a) shows the reduplicated form *kutjupa-kutjupa* expounding SOMETHING:

(8) a. *Kutjupa-kutjupa ngayulu kulini.*
       'some-some' I think:PRES
       'I'm thinking of something.'

    b. *Nyaa nyuntu kulini?*
       what you think:PRES
       'What are you thinking (about)?'

Sentence (9) is another example of *kutjupa-kutjupa* referring to abstract things. It can also refer to an 'object of perception', as in (10), which could be a whole scene or a specific physical object.

(9) Munu-na   kutjupa-kutjupa   tjutaku   nintiringkupai.
     and-I   'some-some'   many:PURP   know:INCHO:CHAR
     'I would learn about many things.'

(10) Ngayulu   kutjupa-kutjupa   nyangu.
     I   'some-some'   see:PAST
     'I saw something.'

We will see in section 9.4.1 that the inchoative suffix *-ri/-ari* is the Yankunytjatjara exponent of HAPPEN (TO). It is very telling, therefore, that in the Yankunytjatjara expression for 'something happened', the form *kutjupa-kutjupa* corresponds to SOMETHING:

(11) Tjinguru   kutjupa-kutjupa-ri-ngu,   Nangatjunya.
     maybe   'some-some'-INCHO-PAST   Nangatju:NAME
     'Maybe something's happened to Nangatju.'

Thus, the situation is that *kutjupa* as the head of an NP means SOMEONE; and the reduplicated version *kutjupa-kutjupa* as the head of an NP means SOMETHING.

The expression normally volunteered by bilinguals as an equivalent for PEOPLE is *anangu tjuta*, where *tjuta* 'many' is the pluralising word (see section 9.3.2), but closer investigation suggests that *anangu tjuta* is more referentially specific than English *people* — that it is more like English *the people*. In generic uses, such as (12) and (13), *anangu* alone is the exponent for PEOPLE. Also, the expression equivalent to English *all people* is simply *anangu uwankara*, with no *tjuta* needed. Note also examples (15), (23) and (41).

(12) Anangu-ngku   kulilpai,   nyangatja   kura.
     people-ERG   think:CHAR this   bad
     'People think this is bad.'

(13) Nyangatja   anangu   wiya,   ngayulu   kutju.
     here   people   no   I   only
     'Here (there are) no people, only me.'

One problem remains — how are expressions like 'someone else' and 'something else' formed in Yankunytjatjara, given that the primary words for SOMEONE, SOMETHING and OTHER all involve the same form? In broad terms, the answer appears to be that under certain conditions *anangu* functions as an allolex of

SOMEONE, thus partially parallelling the association between *people* and *person* in English. However, these conditions are more complex than one might expect, and I do not yet fully understand them. For instance, in (14a) *anangu kutjupa* may mean only 'another person'; it cannot mean 'other people', which would have to be expressed as in (14b), using the modifier *tjuta* 'many':

(14) a. *Ngayulu   anangu   kutjupa   nyangu.*
         I   'people'   other   see:PAST
         'I saw another person.'

      b. *Ngayulu   anangu   kutjupa   tjuta   nyangu.*
         I   'people'   other   many   see:PAST
         'I saw other people.'

On the other hand, there are indications that one of the conditions forcing the readings given in (14) is the fact that the NPs are understood to be referentially specific, that is, that a particular person or group of people is meant. For instance, in a referentially non-specific context, such as (15), the expression *anangu kutjupa* appears to mean 'some people':

(15) *Ka   mai   wiyangka   anangu   kutjupa*
      and   food   no:LOC   people   some
      tjangara-ri-ngi   munu   anangu   pungangi.
      cannibal-INCHO-PAST/IMPRF   and   people   hit:PAST/IMPRF
      'Because there was no food some people turned cannibal and took to hunting people.'

The complexity of this matter prohibits any further exploration in this paper.

A similar allolexy operates for collocations of SOMETHING with deictic and determiner-like elements. Where what is being referred to is a material thing, the form *punu* — also 'tree, stick, wood' — is used, as in (16) and (17). Example (16), for instance, occurred as a speaker was trying to think of the name of a kind of bird:

(16) *Nyaa?   Punu   panya   nyaa?*
      what   'tree'   that   what
      'What (is it)? What is that thing?'

(17) *Ngayulu   punu   kutjupa   nyangu.*
      I   'tree' other   see:PAST
      'I saw something else.'

There is an additional complication, however. *Punu* cannot be used in relation to dicta, where instead we find *tjukurpa* (also 'word, message, story'):

(18)   *Ngayulu   tjukurpa   kutjupa   wangkangu.*
       I   'word'   other   say:PAST
       'I said something else.'

In this respect, Yankunytjatjara appears to differ from Mparntwe Arrernte, where the cognate form *arne* 'something, tree, stick, wood' is much more semantically versatile, and may indeed be taken as a good primary exponent of SOMETHING (Harkins & Wilkins, this volume).

Finally, it should be noted that in the Yankunytjatjara equivalents of expressions like 'do something good' and 'do something bad', no lexical item occurs corresponding to English *something*, as in examples (48) and (49).

In summary, lexical exponents for the substantives SOMEONE, SOMETHING and PEOPLE are readily identifiable when the meaning in question is unmodified: their primary Yankunytjatjara exponents are *kutjupa*, *kutjupa-kutjupa* and *anangu* respectively. When these meanings enter into phrasal collocation with modifiers, however, they are expressed by a set of allolexic variants which is not yet fully understood.

9.1.3   Case Allolexy

As mentioned in the opening remarks, Yankunytjatjara has distinct cases for NPs in S (nominative), A (ergative) and O (accusative) functions, though there is zero-marking for S and A pronouns, and for S and O nouns, making these case-forms homophonous. My convention of leaving zero-marked categories unglossed has obscured differences in case category in many of the examples so far, but the issue becomes very clear on comparing examples like (4) and (5), or (12) and (13), which show *kutjupa* SOMEONE and *anangu* PEOPLE both with and without the ergative marker *-ngku*.

Is this formal difference associated with any specifable semantic difference? That is, is the ergative versus nominative case contrast meaning-bearing? In my opinion, for Yankunytjatjara the conclusion must be that it is not meaning-bearing, at least in this context.[5] The argument depends on data presented in detail in sections 9.2, 9.4 and 9.7. The crucial fact is that some of the semantically primitive verbs of Yankunytjatjara — *kulini* THINK, *wangkanyi* SAY and *palyani* DO — require an ergative subject, whereas *mukuringanyi* WANT demands a nominative subject. Nominative case is also called for in the ascriptive-type constructions involving exponents of KNOW and HAVE PARTS (the adjective *ninti* and 'having' suffix *-tjara*, respectively).

Now if the case-category of the subject carried independent meaning, this would entail that the words for SOMEONE have different meanings in the Yankunytjatjara expressions corresponding to 'someone did ...' and 'someone wants ...'; and similarly that the word for I would have a different meaning in expressions like 'I think ...' and 'I want ...'. In my opinion, this amounts to a *reductio ad absurdum* of the original proposition. The case-marking contrasts cannot be viewed as originating in the compositional semantics of the verbs, since these verbs are primitive and have no compositional semantics.

A second and similar argument is that if ergative case in Yankunytjatjara were meaning-bearing there would be a meaning difference between a sentence composed in Yankunytjatjara semantic primitives with an ergative case subject and the corresponding sentence composed in English primitives. We must conclude that ergative case-forms are allolexic variants of their unmarked counterparts.

The question then arises: how is the distribution of the variants to be stated? Perhaps the first formulation that comes to mind would be that the conditioning is grammatical, based on whether the argument in question is functioning as an A or as an S. But this explanation is not available, since the notions of 'A' and 'S' are not applicable to the NSM mini-language. Conventional definitions of A (e.g. Dixon 1979; Andrews 1985:68–69) rely on making reference to a prototypical or primary transitive verb, such as *kill* or *kick*, which takes an 'agent' (a potentially deliberate doer or causer) and a 'patient' (something affected by what happens to it). Since 'agent' and 'patient' are clearly notions of some semantic complexity, it would be circular to use them (or grammatical notions dependent upon them) to state allolexic conditions within the NSM itself. Related to this, and just as important, is the fact that there simply are no prototypical or primary transitive verbs within the NSM lexicon. One might perhaps regard THINK, KNOW and even DO as complement-taking, but there are no NSM verbs which take prototypical patients (and WANT is also complement-taking). We must therefore regard the ergative allolexy as lexically conditioned — as determined by the identity of the verbal lexeme.

This is not to say that it is purely coincidental that the Yankunytjatjara exponents of THINK, DO and SAY select ergative case subjects, and those of WANT and HAPPEN TO do not. Presumably there is indeed some affinity between those in the first group, which is not shared by those in the second, but it is an affinity of a non-compositional nature (cf. chapters 2 and 17), such as the fact that thinking, doing and saying are subject to some voluntary control, whereas wanting and having things happen to one are not.

9.2 Mental Predicates

9.2.1 KNOW and THINK

KNOW is *ninti*, which — interestingly, in view of the fact that *know* is a stative verb in English — is an adjective-like element, not a verb.

(19) *Ngayulu ninti, nyara paluṟu alatjikutu yanu.*
     I   know that   DEF like.this:ALL go:PAST
     'I know he went that way.'

Ninti can also be used to convey the notion of 'knowing' a person, and knowing how to do something, as shown in (20) and (21), but these are additional polysemic meanings. Notice that they involve *ninti* taking a purposive case complement, thereby distinguishing them syntactically from the semantically basic KNOW shown above, which takes a paratactic clausal complement.

(20) Ngayulu tjana-mpa   ninti.
     I   they-PURP   know
     'I know them.'

(21) Ngayulu mutuka-ku   ninti.
     I   car-PURP   know
     'I know about cars.' (e.g. how to fix or to drive them)

THINK is *kulini*, though the word is polysemous, and can also mean 'hear, listen' and 'heed'. Bain (1979:126, cited approvingly in Harris 1990) states unequivocally that "there is no way to differentiate the concepts of thinking, listening and heeding in Pitjantjatjara. The same verb *kulini* does duty for all." But although the same word-form does indeed 'do duty for all', it is not difficult to differentiate the meanings on language-internal grounds, since each of the senses just mentioned has a distinctive syntactic frame, from which the others are excluded. Only the THINK sense can take a 'quasi-quotational' clausal complement (often introduced by *alatji* 'like this'), as in (22). Only the 'hear, listen' sense can take a non-finite circumstantial complement, as in (23). Only the 'heed' sense can take a locative case complement, as in (24).

(22) Ngayulu alatji   kulini,   "Tjinguru-la .."
     I   like.this   think:PRES   maybe-we
     'I think this about it, "Maybe we ...".'

(23) Ngayulu anangu-ngku   wangkanytjala   kulinu.
     I   people-ERG   talk:NOML:LOC   hear:PAST
     'I heard people talking.'

(24) Wati katjangku   mamangka   kulintja   wiya.
     man son:ERG   father:LOC   heed:NOML   no
     'The son won't heed his father.'

9.2.2 WANT

The semantically primitive sense of English *want* (as in 'I want to do such-and-such') is expressed by the formally complex word *mukuringanyi*, consisting of root *muku-* (which does not occur independently) and the inchoative formative *-ri*; but in canonical contexts with a clausal complement, there is no trace of any inchoative ('become/happen') meaning. Sentence (25a) shows the normal, hypotactic complement, formed with the intentive complementiser *-kitja*; (25b) shows a semantically equivalent sentence employing a more language-neutral hypotactic complementation strategy:

(25) a. *Ngayulu yankunytjikitja mukuringanyi.*
     I   go:INTENT   want:PRES
     'I want to go.'

   b. *Ngayulu alatji mukuringanyi: Ngayulu yananyi.*
     I   like.this want:PRES   I   go:PRES
     'I want to go.'

It should perhaps be noted that *mukuringanyi* also has nominal complement constructions (with the purposive case), in which it has meanings similar to English *like*, *love* and *need*. This gives Yankunytjatjara *mukuringanyi* a far broader range of use than English *want*; but these semantically complex, language-specific constructions do not form part of the NSM based on Yankunytjatjara. For more detailed argumentation on *mukuringanyi*, see Goddard (1990, 1991).

9.2.3 SAY

The verb *wangkanyi*, illustrated in (26)–(28), is the Yankunytjatjara exponent of SAY. There is an alternative candidate in the verb *watjani*, but this is closer in meaning to English 'tell'.

(26) *Nyaa-n wangkangu?*
     what-you say:PAST
     'What did you say?'

(27) *Ngayulu wangkangu, "Ngayulu yananyi,*
     I   say:PAST   I   go:PRES
     ngura nyara Mimilalakutu".
     place that Mimili:ALL
     'I said, "I'm going off to Mimili."'

(28) *Munu kutangku palupurunypatu wangkangu.*
     and older.brother:ERG same   say:PAST
     'And my brother said the same.'

As shown by (28), *wangkanyi* as SAY selects an ergative case subject. The verb also occurs with a nominative case subject, expressing a range of more complex polysemic meanings. These include 'talk, speak', as in (29), where the subject denotes a person or people, and 'blow', as in (30), where the subject is *walpa* 'wind'; if the nominative subject denotes a type of bird or insect, as in (31), the meaning conveyed[6] is something like 'sing', 'chirp' or 'call':

(29) *Kungka kutjara nyaratja wangkanyi.*
 woman two here talk:PRES
 'Two women are talking over there.'

(30) *Walpa alinytjaranguru ngalya-wangkanyi.*
 wind north:ABL this.way-blow:PRES
 'The wind's blowing this way from the north.'

(31) *Punpun wangkanyi.*
 fly buzz:PRES
 'A fly is buzzing.'

9.2.4 FEEL

The exponent of FEEL in canonical contexts like 'I feel good/bad' is one of the more interesting of the Yankunytjatjara set of primitives. This meaning is expressed by the ascriptive-type construction in (32) utilising the word *tjuni*, which can also mean 'belly' or 'guts':

(32) *Ngayulu tjuni palya/kura.*
 I 'belly' good/bad
 'I feel good/bad.'

The locution appears to provide the precise semantic equivalent of English *feel good* and *feel bad*; for instance, in both languages the expressions are vague as to whether the feeling in question is bodily or mental.

In relation to the present time, no verb is required, but in relation to a non-present time, the existential verb *ngaranyi* 'be (in a state)' is used to support the appropriate tense inflection, as in (33). The present tense form of *ngaranyi* is possible with (32) also, suggesting that the basic construction ought to be regarded as including *ngaranyi*, which is subject to elision in the present tense.

(33) *Ngayulu tjuni palya/kura ngarangu,*
 I 'belly' good/bad be:PAST
 nyara palula ara-ngka.
 that DEF time-LOC
 'I felt good/bad, at that time.'

Combined with the inchoative verbalising morpheme, identified in section 9.4.1 as the exponent of HAPPEN, *tjuni kura* gives rise to the common expression illustrated in (34), which means roughly 'something happened, because of which I felt bad':

(34) *Ngayulu   tjuni   kura-ri-ngu,*
      I   'belly' bad-INCHO-PAST
      kutjupangku   wangkanyangka.
      someone:ERG   say:NOML:LOC
      'I came to feel bad, because of what someone had said.'

In addition to this straightforward collocation, there is a range of more or less idiomatic emotional expressions which involve *tjuni*, such as *tjuni pupanyi* (literally, 'belly crouching') 'having a grudge' and *tjuni tjulypily* 'upset'.

Identifying *tjuni* (in the appropriate construction) as the exact semantic equivalent of FEEL challenges preconceptions about the dividing line between literal and figurative language. The widespread use of body-part words (such as 'heart' and 'liver', as well as 'belly') in expressions for feelings is almost always assumed in the anthropological and linguistic literature to be metaphorical or figurative, but as far as I know, such a judgment has never been taken in the light of a rigorous semantic methodology. From the NSM standpoint, it is a judgment which now seems mistaken, at least in relation to Yankunytjatjara. Paradoxical as it may seem from an English-speaker's viewpoint, the FEEL sense of *tjuni* is semantically prior, simply because this sense is semantically primitive. It is the more concrete 'belly' sense which is the semantically complex, extended meaning. (The link may have to do with the fact that a full or empty stomach makes one FEEL GOOD or FEEL BAD, presumably a very salient consideration in a hunting and gathering society.)

Note that uses of English *feel* in relation to specified sensations are rendered in Yankunytjatjara not by *tjuni* but by *kulini*, advanced above as the exponent of the primitive THINK. For instance:

(35) *Ngayulu pika   kulini*
      I   pain   'think':PRES
      'I feel pain.'

I must admit that there are some posited canonical uses of FEEL which I am not certain how to express in Yankunytjatjara. I am not sure if it is possible to say merely 'I feel something', without making any evaluation of the quality of the feeling. Another potential difficulty is with the expression 'feel the same'. A possibility here is the expression *tjuni kutju* (formally identical with 'one belly'), as shown in (36a). This identifies one of the ideals of Yankunytjatjara social life — a state akin to social harmony — and it seems possible (to me) that it means, essentially, 'feeling the same'; in contrast, the expression *tjuni tjuta* (literally, 'many belly') indicates discord, as in (36b):

(36) a. *Wati, wanyu-la wirura nyinama, tjuni kutju.*
man just-1PL well live:POT 'belly' one
'Men, can't we just live properly, (all) feeling the same.'

b. *Wati nyaaringu-lanku nyangatja munu-la*
man what:INCHO:PAST-1PL:REFL here and-we
tjuni tjuta-ri-ngu.
'belly' many-INCHO-PAST
'Men, what's happened to us here, that we're feeling so many (different) ways.'

9.3 Determiners and Quantifiers

9.3.1 ONE, TWO and ALL

These are straightforward: *kutju* is ONE, *kutjara* is TWO, *uwankara* ALL. See examples (93) and (97); (29), (85), (86), (92) and (99); and (50), (95) and (97).

9.3.2 MANY

This notion is expressed by the 'plural' word *tjuta*, seen in (9), (14b), (59), (73c) and (93). In fact, however, plural is something of a misnomer. An expression like *wati tjuta* or *malu tjuta* (*wati* 'man', *malu* 'kangaroo') would not be appropriate for two, or even three, men or kangaroos. The older generation of ethnographers captured its quality better when they described the system of number-reckoning as consisting basically[7] of: *kutju* 'one', *kutjara* 'two', *mankur* 'three, a few', and *tjuta* 'many'.

9.3.3 OTHER

The form *kutjupa* has featured earlier (section 9.1.2): as a nominal head, it expounds SOMEONE, and, reduplicated, it is an exponent of SOMETHING. As a modifier however, *kutjupa* is the Yankunytjatjara exponent of OTHER, as illustrated below (see also examples (14), (17), (18), (69) and (98)):

(37) *Palu ngayulu munu kungka kutjupa. Panya*
but I and woman other that.one
nganaku? Yaritjiku nyanga ngunytju.
who:GEN Yaritji:GEN this mother
'But (there was) me and another girl. Now whose (relation) was it? Yaritji here's mother.'

The background to (38) is that the narrator's father has just brought in two kangaroos which he has killed; the tail is the portion normally taken by children:

(38) Kangku*r*u   pu*l*kangku   wirtjapaka*r*a   wipu
      older.sister   big:ERG   run:SERIAL   tail
      mantjinu   ka   wipu   kutjupa   ngayuku   ngaringi.
      get:PAST   and   tail   other   1SG:GEN   lie:PAST/IMPRF
      'My oldest sister ran and got a tail and the other tail was lying (there) for me.'

9.3.4 THIS

The morphologically related words *nyanga* and *nyangatja* both mean THIS. The difference between them is syntactic. *Nyanga* is used adnominally and participates in the system of case inflection. *Nyangatja* is invariable in form, and is mainly used in equational and ascriptive sentences and to give ostensive identifications of persons, places and things.[8]

Nyanga and *nyangatja* must be regarded as allolexes, for although one would prefer to see the morphologically simpler word *nyanga* appear as the primary exponent of THIS, it cannot be used in one of the canonical contexts:

(39) Nyangatja / *nyanga   kura.
      this   *this   bad
      'This is bad.'

On the other hand, *nyangatja* cannot be used in equally canonical adnominal contexts:

(40) A*n*angu   nyanga-ngku / *nyangatja   katingu.
      person   this-ERG   *this   take:PAST
      'This person took it.'

It should also be noted that the form *alatji* functions as a portmanteau expressing the meaning LIKE THIS; that is, *alatji* is semantically equivalent to *nyanga-pu*r*uny(pa)*.

9.3.5 THE SAME

Here we seek an exponent which may be used adverbially, in expressions like 'do the same', 'be the same' and 'say the same'. Adverbial THE SAME is expressed by the formally complex form *palupu*r*unypa*t*u*: *palu-* is the root which acts as the base for what I call the definite nominal (see below), *-pu*r*unypa* is identical with the suffix expounding LIKE, and *-*t*u* is an emphatic suffix. Nevertheless, in canonical contexts the combination *palupurunypatu* does not mean 'just like this' or 'likewise', as one might suspect, but THE SAME, as illustrated in (28) and (41):

(41) Munu ngula ... anangu nyara palumpa tjitji
 and in.future people that DEF:GEN child
 tjutangku pakara nyakunytjaku, munu
 many:ERG get.up:SERIAL see:NOML:PURP and
 palupurunypatu palyantjaku.
 same do:NOML:PURP
 'So that in future those people's children can grow up and see, and be able to do the same.'

The definite nominal (nominative/ergative form *paluru*) is a feature of Yankunytjatjara grammar which straddles the division between pronouns and other nominals. It may occur alone, in which case it functions much like a third-person singular pronoun (see examples (19) and (81)); its case-marking pattern is also that of a pronoun, that is, it has identical nominative and ergative forms, an accusative marked by suffix -*nya*, and it takes the pronominal allomorphs of the purposive and locative case-markers, namely -*mpa* and -*la* respectively. On the other hand, it may — and very frequently does — occur as the final modifier of an NP, specifying that the intended referent is the same as that previously mentioned or otherwise established in the discourse (hence the designation 'definite nominal').

9.4 Actions and Events

9.4.1 HAPPEN (TO)

The Yankunytjatjara equivalent of HAPPEN (TO) is the inchoative verbalising suffix -*ri*/-*ari*, which may be exemplified in the word *nyaaringu?* 'what happened?', where the affix is applied to the stem *nyaa* 'what' — see (36b) and (42). It is also possible to say *alatjiringu* 'happened like this', where the inchoative affix is applied to *alatji* 'like this'.

(42) Tjitji, nyaa-ri-ngu-n?
 child what-INCHO-PAST-you
 'Child, what's happened to you?'

(43) Ka mulapatu alatji-ri-ngu, Godalu
 and true:EMPH like.this-INCHO-PAST God:ERG
 wangkanyangka.
 say:NOML:LOC
 'And indeed it happened like this, just as God said.' (Genesis 1:9)[9]

As mentioned earlier, 'something happened' is rendered by a -*ri*/-*ari* verb based on *kutjupa-kutjupa* SOMETHING, as in (11). Though the verb in such cases tends to be interpreted as indicating something bad, I take this to be a pragmatic implication.

9.4.2 DO

The primitive sense of DO is intransitive, or rather, non-transitive: a person may do something (e.g. laugh, leave) without doing anything **to** anything else. Prototypically, transitivity seems to be strongly associated with causativity, but it appears that languages which maintain a strict distinction between transitive and intransitive verbs tend to use the formally transitive verb in the semantically unmarked case, for instance to ask 'What did you do?'. This is certainly the case in Yankunytjatjara. The candidates for DO are all quasi-transitive, in that their subjects require the ergative case.

The best candidate, and the word usually volunteered by bilinguals, is *palyani*, formed by zero-derivation from the root *palya* GOOD. *Palyani* is a polysemous verb. In its most frequent uses it generally means 'make' or 'fix'. But it also occurs as below, with *alatji* 'like this' (or a related form) apparently functioning as a kind of complement, meaning simply DO:

(44)   *Munu pula punungka   unnguwanu   ankula*
      and   3DU tree:LOC   under:PERL go:SERIAL
      katanankupai,   kuranyitja,   tjitji   punungka
      break:CHAR   ahead:ASSOC   child   tree:LOC
      pirintjaku tawara.   Alatji   palyalpai.
      scratch   AVERSIVE like.this do:CHAR
      'They used to go through the scrub breaking it off, ahead (of us),
      so the kids wouldn't get scratched. This (is what they) used to do.'

(45)   *Munu waru   panya   kulingku   tjina*
      and   heat   that.one summer:ERG   foot
      kampanyangka,   alatji-alatji-tu   palyalpai.
      burn:NOML:LOC   like.this-like.this-EMPH   do:CHAR
      'And when the summer heat was burning (the kids') feet, (they)
      used to do the same kind of thing.'

(46)   *Nganana putu   iritilpi   alatji   palyaningi.*
      1PL   vainly long.ago   like.this   do:PAST/IMPRF
      'We've already been doing that for ages.'

Palyani was volunteered by a bilingual informant to help translate the following sentences, for use in explications for emotion terms. Notice that in the first example there is no object present; and in the second the expression *X-ku wiru* '(something) nice for X' seems to function as a kind of complement:

(47) *Ngayulu palyantjikitja mukuringanyi.*
I do:INTENT want:PRES
'I want to do (something).'

(48) *Ngayulu X-ku wiṟu palyantjikitja mukuringanyi.*
I X-PURP nice do:INTENT want:PRES
'I want to do (something) nice for X.'

Palyaṉi is also used in the Bible translation to form an expression for 'to do something bad' or 'to sin'. Here the word *kura* BAD appears as the complement, apparently at odds with the formal make-up of the verb (which is based on *palya* GOOD):

(49) *Ka wati tjiḻpingku tjinguṟu kura palyanyangka ...*
and man old:ERG if bad do:NOML:LOC
'For if an old man does something bad ...' (1 Timothy 5:1)

(50) *Ka nyuntu wiṟungku kulinma uwankara palyantjikitja.*
and you nice:ERG listen:POT all do:INTENT
'And you must listen well, so you do all (these things I have told you).' (1 Timothy 5:21)

Notice that though *palyaṉi* continues to select an ergative case subject in all the examples above, we are very far from a prototypical transitive situation with a discrete and fully affected 'patient'. This again testifies to the lack of any necessary correlation between ergativity and full 'semantic' transitivity.

A weaker candidate for DO is *nyaaṉi*, formed by zero-derivation from the root *nyaa* 'what'. This may be used as an interrogative, as in (51), or with an indefinite sense, as in (52). As indicated by the English *whatever* in the gloss for (52), I suspect that such indefinite uses carry an additional semantic component of the 'indiffertive' type mentioned in section 9.1.2:

(51) *Nyuntu nyaaṉu?*
you what:PAST
'What did you do?'

(52) *Walangku nyaala, ka-li ara!*
quick:ERG what:IMP and-1DU go:IMP
'Quickly do whatever it is and we'll be on our way.'

Two further indefinite verbs of doing are a pair of morphological causatives, both meaning 'do like this' — *nyanga alatjinga*ṉ*i* (based on *alatji*, the portmanteau form for LIKE THIS) and *nyanga puṟunymananyi* (*nyanga* THIS, *puṟuny* LIKE). The examples below are from the Bible, or Bible-related materials. The first is a comment on an account of the Jewish custom of bathing the feet of a visitor. The second follows a series of instructions on good conduct, as part of Paul's first letter to Timothy (4:16).

(53) Tjuu   tjuṯangku   tjakangku   nyanga   alatjingalpai.
     jew   many:ERG   usual:ERG   this   like.this:CAUS:CHAR
     'The Jews used to do this as a matter of custom.'

(54) Panya   nyanga   puṟunymankunytjatjanungku,
     that.one   this   like:CAUS:NOML:SEQ:ERG
     nyuntu-nku   wankaṟunkuku.
     you-REFL   save:FUT
     'For by doing like this, you will save yourself.'

9.5 Meta-Predicates

9.5.1 NO

NO is *wiya*, which functions as an exclamation, and also as a negative particle (following a nominalised verb form):

(55) Wiya.   Ngayulu   nyakunytja   wiya.
     No.   I   see:NOML   no
     'No. I didn't see it.'

Wiya may also function as a nominal, meaning 'nothing', and as a suffix in a contrastive paradigmatic relationship with the 'having' suffix *-tjara*, in which function it means 'not having, without'.

It is interesting to note the existence of another negative word, the pre-verbal particle *puṯu*, 'try but fail, do in vain': compare (55) with (56). It is clear, however, that the meaning of *puṯu* is semantically complex, and it can presumably be decomposed into *wiya* and a combination of other elements.

(56) Ngayulu   puṯu   nyangu.
     I   vainly   see:PAST
     'I looked but didn't see it (i.e. I couldn't find it).'

9.5.2 BECAUSE

A good exponent of BECAUSE is furnished by the ablative case marker *-nguru*:[10]

(57) *Nyaa-nguru nyuntu ulanyi?*
what-ABL you cry:PRES
'Why are you crying?'

(58) *Kutangkuni pungu.*
older.brother:ERG:1SG:ACC hit:PAST
Pala palulanguru-na ulanyi.
that DEF-ABL-I cry:PRES
'Big brother hit me. (It's) because of that I'm crying.'

(59) *Tjinguru tjanpi panya nyaa tjuta raitiyatangka*
maybe grass that.one what many radiator:LOC
tjarpangi ka palula-nguru kapi pailiringi.
enter:PAST/IMPRF and DEF-ABL water boil:PAST/IMPRF
'Maybe spinifex grass (or) some other things were getting into the radiator, and because of that the water boiled.'

As the designation 'ablative' suggests, the *-nguru* marker is polysemous, and with the appropriate types of verb can be used to indicate a point of origin of motion, as well as the material from which something is made, and an elapsed time. See Goddard (1991) for more discussion of these uses, and arguments establishing that they represent distinct, and complex, meanings.

9.5.3 LIKE

There is a clitic *-puruny(pa)* LIKE, usually written as a separate word, as in (60) and (61). The same element is used to express combinations like 'do like this', as in (54).

(60) *papa purunypa*
dog like
'like a dog'

(61) *Ngayulu mutuka nyanga purunypa kanyinma.*
I car this like have:POT
'Would I had a car like this.'

9.5.4 CAN

The CAN we seek is the 'can of possibility', which is expressed by the so-called future (better called the potential) verbal inflection -*ku*. This inflection is frequently found in sentences also containing *tjinguṟu*, in the sense of 'maybe' (see section 9.5.5), but even by itself -*ku* clearly indicates possibility, rather than certain futurity. It is frequently used in making polite requests, suggestions and warnings:

(62) *Ma-pitja-ku-ṉa?*
away-come-FUT-I
'Can I come in?'

(63) *Punkal-ku-n.*
fall-FUT-you
'You could fall.'

9.5.5 IF

It has sometimes been said (Bain & Sayers 1990; cf. McConvell 1991) that the Western Desert Language lacks any lexical exponent for IF, and even that the culture itself has no concept of the hypothetical. Following a suggestion made by Amee Glass (personal communication) however, I would nominate one sense of the word *tjinguṟu* as equivalent to IF. *Tjinguṟu* is, admittedly, more commonly found as a free particle or exclamation meaning 'maybe, perhaps'. But the word may also introduce a clause or phrase which functions as the protasis for a following one, as in the examples below, which seem impossible to gloss with 'maybe' or 'perhaps' alone. (The verb of the following clause usually bears an imperative, or other irrealis, inflection.)

In this first example, the speaker was explaining that she had not made a very large amount of spinifex gum because the weather was too hot to do this easily:

(64) *Tjinguṟu ngayulu waringka, puḷka palyanma.*
if   I   cold:LOC big   make:POT
'If I was in cold (weather), I'd make a bigger (amount).'

In (65) the speaker concludes the story of a near disastrous trip deep into the Gibson Desert. The vehicles had broken down, and their water had run out. Luckily, they had a two-way radio, and so were saved. Example (66) comes from the preface to a book of New Testament stories, which points out that the Old Testament is available in a separate publication. (See also (49).)

(65) *Tjinguṟu-la wiyampa iluma.*
       if-we   no:INTEREST die:POT
       'If we'd been without (a radio) we would've died.'

(66) *Ka nyuntu tjinguṟu tjukurpa irititjatjara*
       and you   if   story   long.ago:ASSOC:HAVING
       nyakula   kulintjikitja   mukuringkula, nyiri
       see:SERIAL think:INTENT   want:SERIAL   paper
       pala palunya nyawa.
       that DEF:ACC see:IMP
       'So if you want to read Old Testament stories, look at that book.'

9.5.6 VERY

The Yankunytjatjara exponent for VERY is the adverb *kutu*, found in expressions like *palya/kura kutu* 'very good/bad', *puḻka/tjukutjuku kutu* 'very big/small' and so on. (*Kutu* can also be used adnominally with a meaning something like 'simply' or 'pure and simple', but this presumably a separate, though related, meaning.)

A possible rival candidate would be *mulapa* (also 'true'). This can be used in expressions close in meaning to those just mentioned, but with an additional 'superlative' flavour. *Puḻka mulapa*, for instance, is more like 'big as can be' or 'really, really big' than a mere 'very big'.

9.6 Time and Place

9.6.1 WHERE and WHEN

Interrogatives *yaaltji* WHERE and *yaalaṟa* WHEN are the clearest exponents of the posited locational and temporal primitives. Both words are formally complex, with the initial formative *yaal-* serving a function much like that of the *wh-*segment in the English interrogative paradigm. Both are also polysemous.

The WHERE meaning of *yaaltji* is shown below. Though it can be used uninflected, as in (67), it is frequently suffixed with the locative, as in (68), or with the allative or ablative case-markers:

(67) *Ngura nyuntumpa yaaltji?*
       place you:GEN   where
       'Where is your place(camp)?'

(68) *Yaaltji-ngka-n   tjunu?*
      where-LOC-you   put:PAST
      'Where did you put it?'

The closest nominal corresponding to *yaaltji* is *ngura* 'camp, country, place', and it is this word which would be used to render canonical contexts such as that in (69). However, there would seem to be some link between *ngura* and the concept of PEOPLE (perhaps that *ngura* is 'somewhere people could be'). In any case, the range of use of *ngura* is narrower than English *place*: it could not be used as in English sentences like 'The elbow is the place on the arm where the arm can bend'.

(69) *Ngura   nyangatja   alatji-ri-ngu,   ngura*
      place   here   like.this-INCHO-PAST   place
      kutjupa-ngka   wiya.
      other-LOC   no
      'It happened in this place, not in (any) other place.'

Yaaltji has other meanings aside from WHERE. In association with verbs of cognition and speech, it can be used to express meanings which would be rendered in English with *how*, as in (70), or with *what*, as in (71):[11]

(70) *Yaaltji   wangkanyi   Yankunytjatjarangku?*
      'where'   say:PRES   Yankunytjatjara:ERG
      'How do (you) say it in Yankunytjatjara?'

(71) *Nyuntu   yaaltji   kulini?*
      you   'where'   think:PRES
      'What is your thinking (on this)?'

Though it seems clear enough that the 'how, in which way?' meaning in examples (70) and (71) is semantically distinct from the WHERE sense, one may well ask how the same form came to have these two meanings, especially since this is a phenomenon with parallels in other languages. Historically, it appears that *yaaltji* derives from *yaal+alatji*, where *alatji* 'like this' is the deictic used in conjunction with acts of demonstration. In the Western Desert, the link between location and demonstration is perhaps provided by the practice of indicating location by pointing with the lips or chin, a gesture which can be, and often is, accompanied by the word *alatji*.

The Yankunytjatjara equivalent for English interrogative *when* is *yaalara*, a compound of *yaal-* and the nominal word *ara*, which may be variously glossed as 'time', 'occasion', 'episode' or 'scene':

(72)   *Yaalara-na   piruku   pitjaku?*
       when-I   again   come:FUT
       'When can I come again?'

Nominal *ara* enters into many collocations whose natural English translation equivalents involve *time*:

(73)   a. *palula-ara*
          DEF-time
          'at that time, then'

       b. *yaaltjitu   ara*
          how.many   time
          'how many times, how often?'

       c. *tjuta-ara*
          many-time
          'many times, often'

       d. *kutjupa-ara*
          'other'-time
          'sometimes'

In view of examples like these, there can be little doubt that *ara* is a serviceable exponent of WHEN (TIME). On the other hand, the word is polysemous (as is English *time* and French *temps*). One common expression involving *ara* seems at first blush to have much the same meaning as 'in the same place', namely *arangka*, composed of *ara* and the locative case, as in (74). I would suggest this is a complex meaning combining temporal and spatial notions — something like 'where it was at that time'.

(74)   *Ara-ngka   tjura!*
       'time'-LOC   put:IMP
       'Put it (back) where it was.'

Among the other meanings of *ara* are the following: 'stories, yarns', in collocations with the verbs *wangkanyi* 'say' and *watjani* 'tell', as in (75); 'situation, matter', in collocation with verbs of speech or of thinking, as in (76); 'custom, role', when preceded by a genitive noun denoting a type of person, as in (77):

(75)   *Nganana   yankula   ara   watjaningi.*
       we   go:SERIAL   'time'   tell:PAST/IMPRF
       'We were telling yarns as we went.'

(76) Ngyaulu *ara* nyangatja nyanga alatji kulilpai.
I 'time' here this like.this think:CHAR
'I think this about the present situation.'

(77) Watiku *ara* panyatja.
man:GEN 'time' that.one
'That's a man's way after all.'

9.6.2 AFTER

The primary exponent of AFTER is *malangka*:

(78) (*Ara*) palula malangka, palu*ru* pikatjararingu.
time DEF after DEF sick:INCHO:PAST
'After that (time), she got sick.'

(79) Nyanga palula malangka pi*ru*ku wax
this DEF after again wax
tjunanyi, arinytji nga*ra*nytjaku.
put:PRES orange be:NOML:PURP
'After (doing) this, one applies more wax, so the orange will stay.'
(from a description of the stages of batik fabric dyeing)

Formally, *malangka* consists of root *mala* followed by the locative case suffix, but *mala* on its own means 'coming behind' in physical motion contexts like (80):

(80) Ka ngayulu mala pitjangi mamangka tjinangka.
and I behind came:PAST/IMPRF father:LOC feet:LOC
'I was coming along behind, in father's tracks.'

For this reason, we must recognise the formally complex *malangka* as the semantically primitive exponent of AFTER, perhaps viewing the locative morphology as akin to the use of English *at* in expressions like *at that time*. (Also, only the form *malangka* can be used in combination with 'this' or 'this time'.)

It perhaps should be noted that the ablative case-marker *-nguru* also has a role in expressing notions involving AFTER, as in (81), but it can be argued (Goddard 1991) that this is a complex meaning indicating immediate or close succession:

(81) ... *munu palula-nguṟu paluṟu kuliningi*
       and   DEF-ABL   DEF   think:PAST/IMPRF
      "Tjinguṟu-ṉa ..."
      maybe-I
      '... and after that he was thinking, "Maybe I ...".'

9.6.3 UNDER and ABOVE

The Yankunytjatjara exponent for ABOVE is clearly *katu*, as in *apungka katu* 'above the hill' or *Mimilila katu* 'above Mimili'. Notice that the reference point takes locative case. *Katu* may also be used without any reference point, in which case, perhaps unsurprisingly, it means 'high' or 'up'.

The best candidate as exponent of UNDER is *unngu*, which can usually be glossed as either 'under', as in (82) and (83), or as 'in, inside', as in (84) and (85):

(82) *Munu kuṟu pati mantangka unngu nyinapai.*
     and   eye   closed   ground:LOC   under   live:CHAR
     'And (the burrowing frog) lives under the ground.'

(83) *Ka tjananya katira puṉu altarta*
     and   3PL:ACC   take:SERIAL   tree   mallee.gum:LOC
     unngu tjarpatjuṟa kanyiningi.
     under   put.in:SERIAL   keep:PAST/IMPRF
     'And they took (the children) and put them in under the mallee gums and kept them there (out of sight of a circling aircraft).'

(84) *Maku puṉu unngu ngaripai atuṟungka.*
     grub   tree   inside   lie:CHAR   root:LOC
     'Witchetty grubs live in a tree/bush, in the roots.'

(85) *Ka wati kutjarangku tjaliṟa tjunu Toyota unngu.*
     and   man   two:ERG   carry:SERIAL   put:PAST   Toyota   inside
     'The two men carried (the sick woman) and put her inside the Toyota.'

In the limited fieldwork time I have spent on this question, I have not been able to establish conclusively that the UNDER meaning and the 'in, inside' meanings are indeed distinct, as opposed to contextual variants of a single more general meaning, although it is suggestive that only the UNDER reading is in a relationship of complementary antonymy with *katu*. One syntactic fact which may be relevant is the tendency for the reference point in the UNDER meaning to take locative case, as opposed to being unmarked in the 'in' reading.

9.7 Partonomy and Taxonomy

9.7.1 HAVE PARTS

In Yankunytjatjara, as apparently in many languages, there is no word which may be used in a way which is completely analogous to English *part of* (as in *The nose is part of the face*, or *A trigger is the part of a gun which* ...), yet it is difficult to imagine how paraphrase semantics could apply to a language unable to lexicalise the part–whole relationship, given its importance to the semantic structuring of numerous areas of concrete vocabulary. Growing awareness of this fact was responsible for the decision (first put into action at the Workshop on Semantic and Lexical Universals in Canberra, 1992) to seek lexical exponents for the 'part of' relationship from the converse orientation, as it were — that is, to seek exponents for HAVE PARTS.

This move was partly prompted by the fact that many Australian languages, though lacking a nominal corresponding to English *a part*, possess a 'having' suffix (Dixon 1980:324) and by indications that, though the semantic range of such suffixes is very broad (much like that of English *have*), in at least some sentence types the suffix seems to express precisely the notion 'have as a part' (cf. Wierzbicka (1989:109–110) in relation to Warlpiri).

These points can be illustrated from Yankunytjatjara, where the 'having' suffix is *-tjara*. It seems indisputable that in sentences like (86)–(88), where the arguments denote concrete things, the relationship being depicted is that of a whole possessing a designated part or parts:

(86)   *Yunpa   mulya-tjara,   tjaa-tjara,   kuru*
        face   nose-HAVING   mouth-HAVING   eye
        kutjara-tjara.
        two-HAVING
        'A face has a nose, mouth and two eyes (as parts).'

(87)   *Katji   mukul-tjara.*
        spear   hook-HAVING
        '(A) hunting-spear has a hook (as a part).'

(88)   *Nyantju   pala   wipu   wara-tjara.*
        horse   that   tail   long-HAVING
        'That horse has a long tail.'

The challenge facing the proposed identification of *-tjara* as the exponent of HAVE PARTS is to account for its broad range of use. Examples include *-tjara* used in relation to concrete bodily symptoms, as in (89), and to express a meaning something like 'equipped with, making use of', as in (90):

(89) Ngayulu putju/nyapi-tjara.
I rash/boil-HAVING
'I've got a rash/boil.'

(90) a. Wati tjilpi kukaku yanu, katji mankur-tjara.
man old meat:PURP go:PAST spear three-HAVING
'The old man went hunting, with three spears.'

b. Paluru tjana tuutji-tjara-ngku
DEF 3PL torches-HAVING-ERG
nguriningi.
search:PAST/IMPRF
'They were searching for it with torches.'

On the hypothesis advanced here, such uses in Yankunytjatjara represent distinct, polysemic meanings, presumably including HAVE PARTS in some cases at least, but containing other components also. It is not possible in the space available to establish this conclusively. However, I would suggest that the 'concrete bodily symptom' meaning in (89) is mediated through the complex notion of 'body', which involves both SOMEONE (PERSON) and SOMETHING: rashes and boils are things which people can sometimes have as parts of their bodies (as opposed to things like noses and eyes which people have as parts generically, so to speak).[12] As for the 'using' meaning in (90), this is possible only where the phrase containing -tjara is a syntactic adjunct to a verb depicting an action; the -tjara phrase will even carry an ergative inflection if this verb is transitive, as shown in (90b). Thus, this meaning is associated with a distinct syntactic frame from that of the (hypothesised) 'pure' HAVE PARTS meaning, which is an ascriptive-type construction with no verb. Another use of -tjara is to express the abstract 'having' relationship which a language or way of speaking has with one of its characteristic words, as in (91). I mention this to satisfy the curiosity of readers who have noticed that -tjara forms part of the dialect names Yankunytjatjara and Pitjantjatjara, but there can be little doubt that this too is a specialised, complex meaning.

(91) wangka yankunytja-tjara
speech 'go':NOML-HAVING
'speech variety using the word yankunytja (for 'go')'

A sceptic might still insist that the true meaning of -tjara is vague and generalised, having no direct counterpart in English, and that the apparent HAVE PARTS meaning in (86)–(88) is a consequence of the meaning of words like mulya 'nose', tjaa 'mouth', wipu 'tail' and mukul 'hook'. In fact, this position begs the question of how the lexical semantics of these words could be described at all if the notion of 'part' were not available. But let that pass. In my view we can refute the notion that the 'part' reading of -*tjara* is dependent on complex lexical semantics by falling back on examples which use semantically simple substantives.

Consider the question posed in (92), where *puṉu* is an allolexic exponent of SOMETHING (cf. section 9.1.2). In a word-for-word calque rendition this could be read as 'This things has two whats?'; but this is not ordinary English, nor does it express a clear, unambiguous meaning. In fact, the meaning of (92) is quite clear — the question is unambiguously about 'parts':

(92) *Puṉu nyangatja nyaa kutjara-tjara?*
thing this what two-HAVING
'What two parts does this thing have?'

This shows that the association between -*tjara* and the notion HAVE PARTS is not dependent upon the lexical semantics of either of the substantive words. (It would be no good replying that the HAVE PARTS meaning is just the 'default' meaning: that is essentially the proposition at issue.)

Similarly, in (93) we see *kutjupa-kutjupa tjuṯa-tjara* (literally, 'having many something') conveying the meaning 'having many parts'; recall from section 9.1.2 that *kutjupa-kutjupa* (literally, 'other-other') as the head of an NP is the Yankunytjatjara exponent of SOMETHING (my thanks to Paul Eckert for this example):

(93) *Puntu kutju, palu kutjupa-kutjupa tjuṯa-tjara.*
body one but something many-HAVING
'(It is) one body, but with many parts.' (from St Paul's Epistle to the Romans)

Further evidence of the association between suffix -*tjara* and HAVE PARTS is the existence of a nominal form *tjara*, with a closely related meaning, as illustrated in (94) and (95). For although Yankunytjatjara has no nominal word which can be used of a discrete detachable part, it does have a nominal meaning 'part of' a group of people, as in (94), of a mass object like meat or water, or area of land, as in (95) (see also (97)):

(94) *Ka-ya yanu, tjara. Ka tjara kutjupa nyinangi.*
and-3PL go:PAST part and part other stay:PAST/IMPRF
'So they went, some (of them). And the other part (of them) stayed.'

(95)   *Munu-la   manta   uwankara   mantjinu — tjara NT,*
       and-1PL   land   all   get:PAST   part NT
       tjara SA,   tjara WA
       part SA   part WA
       'And we got (back) all the land — the part in the Northern
       Territory, the part in South Australia, the part in Western Australia.'

There is also a corresponding transitive verb *tjarani*, formed by productive zero-derivation, meaning 'divide, split up'; it is used to speak, for instance, of dividing food into portions or separating people into groups.

9.7.2   KIND OF

Among the Yankunytjatjara, as no doubt in many cultures, explicit reference to taxonomic classification is rather rare; rather than saying something like 'A crow is a kind of bird' one normally says simply 'A crow is a bird'. Even so, the KIND OF concept is clearly present. Indeed, it is virtually inconceivable that any human society could lack this concept, given the ubiquity of typonymic classification (cf. Brown 1984). For Yankunytjatjara, additional linguistic evidence is furnished by the existence of the generic–specific (or noun classifier) construction — for example, *kuka malu* 'game kangaroo', *punu apara* 'tree river-gum' — which is widespread in Australian languages (Dixon 1980:102–103). Example (96) shows a categorial inquiry being made simply with the word *nyaa?* 'what?' (unassisted by any lexeme corresponding to KIND OF), and the answer (characteristically) in the form of a generic–specific construction:

(96)   a. *Mai   nyaa   nyangatja?*
          food   what   this
          'What (kind of) food is this?'

       b. *Mai   ili.*
          food wild-fig
          'Wild-fig food.'

Furthermore, there is a common Yankunytjatjara expression meaning 'different kinds of', namely *kutjupa-kutjupa tjuta* (literally, 'other-other many') used as a modifier, as in *punu kutjupa-kutjupa tjuta* 'different kinds of tree'. An expression like this was drawn upon by the Bible translators to deal with the story of Noah, who had to select some of each kind of animal to take aboard the Ark. God's instruction to Noah is rendered as:

(97) *Munu kuka panya palya kutjupa-kutjupa*
      and   animal that good 'other-other'
      uwankaranguru tjara kutju mantjira tjarpatjura...
      all:ABL   part one   get:SERIAL put.in:IMP
      'And from all the kinds of good (i.e. ritually clean) animal, put one group aboard ...' (Genesis 7:2)

It might seem at first that the existence of an expression for 'different kinds of' would be sufficient to capture taxonomic relationships within the vocabulary. For instance, suppose we explicate *tjulpu* (roughly 'bird') as 'something that flies and has feathers; there are many different kinds of this thing' — could we then not simply begin all explications for individual birds, such as *kaanka* 'crow' and *nyii-nyii* 'zebra-finch', with the words 'this is (a) *tjulpu*'? The answer is no, for this would lead to the incorrect result that there must be many different kinds of crow and zebra-finch. In other words, to articulate taxonomic relationships the ability to express meanings like 'this is a kind of bird (tree, etc.)' would seem to be indispensable.

Fortunately, at this level of metalinguistic classification, there is a natural way in Yankunytjatjara of expressing the requisite meaning. It employs the word *ini*, which can also mean 'name'. To say that '*kaanka* is a kind of bird' one says (to give a calque rendition) '*kaanka* is a bird name'; but this is surely a different sense of 'name' than that used in relation to a person or a place. I would suggest in fact that *ini* is a precise exponent of (A) KIND OF. Examples of *ini* in this use are shown in (98) and (99):[13]

(98) *Wiya, kuka   kutjupa palatja!*
      no   animal other   that
      Kuka   ini   kutjupa. Wai   wayuta!
      animal 'name' other   not.at.all possum
      'No, that's a different animal. An animal (of) another kind (name). No way is it a possum!'

(99) *Kuka   nyanga kutjara ini   kutjutu,*
      animal this   two   'name' one:EMPH
      kutjupa wiya.
      other   no
      'These two animals are of the one kind, not of different kinds.'

9.8 Evaluators and Descriptors

These are straightforward. *Palya* is GOOD and *kura* BAD: see (32) and (97), and (12), (32), (39) and (49), respectively. An alternative to *palya* might perhaps be *wiru* 'fine, nice', as in (48) and (50), but this seems to have a component involving wanting, as well as evaluation. *Puḻka* is BIG and *tjukutjuku* is SMALL, as in *tjitji puḻka/tjukutjuku* 'big/small child' and *apu puḻka/tjukutjuku* 'big/small rock' (see also (64)).

9.9 Concluding Remarks

When I embarked upon this investigation, I remember thinking that I would be sufficiently pleased if two-thirds of the proposed NSM inventory of lexical primitives were to be clearly locatable in Yankunytjatjara. At earlier stages of my work on the language, I had been convinced that there was no true exponent of WANT or of HAVE PARTS (cf. Goddard 1989), and I was unsure if it would be possible to identify lexical exponents for IF, DO and KIND OF. The outcome has shown these doubts to be unfounded. All the proposed primitives — it now seems to me — can find ready lexical expression in Yankunytjatjara.

This is not to say that all problems are solved. In particular, there are still some uncertainties about allolexic variants of some primitives, and about how to express certain collocations which the theory predicts to be possible. We are not yet in full possession of a Natural Semantic Metalanguage based on Yankunytjatjara. What has been done, however, is to establish its basic lexicon. There would seem to be no serious barrier to the construction of a full NSM based on Yankunytjatjara and mutually translatable with expressively equivalent NSMs (Thai, Japanese, Longgu, etc.), whose foundations have been laid in the other papers in this volume.

Notes

1   I would like to thank Lizzie Ellis, Lorna Wilson, Yami Lester and Paul Eckert for helpful discussions about different aspects of the present work. I am also grateful to Tamsin Donaldson, Jean Harkins and Anna Wierzbicka for helpful comments on earlier versions of this paper.

2   Most published Pitjantjatjara materials have been produced either for use in local bilingual schools or for religious purposes. From the first category, among the most reliable materials are McDonald (1986), Aṉangu Schools Resource Centre (1990), Lennon (1989), Pingkayi (1989), and issues 1–6 of the magazine *Kurparu*; and from the second category, the Old Testament sections of Bible Society of Australia (1987), Wycliffe Bible Translators (1982) and Gross (1986). Full details of current titles may be obtained from the Aṉangu Schools Resource Centre and the Pitjantjatjara Bible Translation Project, respectively, both at Ernabella, South Australia. Other useful texts are contained in HALT (1991) and Pitjantjatjara Council (1990, 1991). A collection of Yankunytjatjara texts may be found in Goddard and Kalotas (1988).

3   Interestingly, *ngananya* is also be used to ask about the name of a place, e.g. *ngura nganala?* (literally, 'place 'who'-LOC') 'at what (named) place?'. Goddard (1985:126) glossed it 'who, what name', leaving open whether the alternate glosses arose from polysemy or from semantic generality. I am now confident that *ngananya* must be regarded as polysemous, because: (a) used alone, i.e. without *ngura* 'place', it always means 'who', never 'what named place'; (b) when it

is used alone, inquiring about a person, a name is not required as an answer; and (c) it seems impossible to formulate a single general meaning which would cover both uses.

4. Yankunytjatjara material is presented in the practical orthography in use in Central Australia. An underlining indicates retroflexion; *tj, ny* and *ly* are lamino-dental stop, nasal and lateral respectively; the other symbols have their familiar values. Interlinear glossing symbols are as follows: ABLative, ACCusative, ALLative, ASSOCiative suffix, AVERSIVE marker, CAUSative, CHARacteristic mood, DEFinite nominal, DUal, EMPHatic, ERGative, FUTure, GENitive, HAVING suffix, IMPerative (perfective aspect), INCHOative derivational suffix, INTENTive marker, INTEREST clitic, LOCative, NAME proper noun marker, NEGative marker, NOML nominaliser, PAST tense (perfective aspect), PAST/IMPRF past tense imperfective aspect, PERLative, PLural, POTential mood, PRESent tense, PURPosive, REFLexive clitic, SEQuentive suffix, SERIAL verb, SG singular. In the interests of simplicity, I have not indicated morphosyntactic categories expressed by zero-marking, and have shown segmentation only where it is relevant. Polysemy can cause problems with interlinear glossing: to assign the glosses on a formal basis is deceptive, but glossing on a purely semantic basis obscures the fact that the form elsewhere expresses a different meaning, which may be more salient for speakers if the form is taken in isolation. For expository purposes, I sometimes use the convention of labelling the form according to its most salient meaning, but enclosing the interlinear word in 'scare-quotes'; the true meaning of the form in context is readily apparent from the free English gloss.

5. Wierzbicka (1980a:125–143), which considers the semantics of ergative case in relation to the instrumental case, may seem to imply the contrary, that is, that ergative case is meaning-bearing, but a careful reading shows that her observations about the links between ergative and instrumental (such as active, causal involvement on behalf of the case-marked entity) properly apply to the fully transitive ('ergative + accusative') construction as a whole.

6. This range is actually not as broad as that reported for similar verbs in some other Australian languages which can be glossed as 'to make the characteristic sound of a thing of this kind'; *wangkanyi* is not applicable to dogs or cattle, for instance.

7. There are also the higher number categories *kutjara-kutjara* 'four', *kutjara-mankur* 'five' and *mankur-mankur* 'six', but these are morphological and (presumably) conceptual compounds.

8. I have suggested elsewhere (Goddard 1985:57) that *nyangatja* contains the presupposition that the referent is evident or obvious to the addressee. But this obtains only in situations where there is a contrast, i.e. where either form could be used, as in *Papa nyanga anymatjara* 'This dog is hungry' versus *Papa nyangatja anymatjara* 'This here dog is hungry'.

9. Bible translations, and translations generally into Pitjantjatjara and Yankunytjatjara, have to be used with some care. The earlier works, dating back to the 1950s, are awkward and prone to errors of various kinds, but the more recent output of the Pitjantjatjara Bible Translation Project, based at Ernabella, is excellent.

10. Like the pronouns, the definite nominal occurs in its 'locative' form when suffixed with ablative *-nguru*, allative *-kutu* or perlative *-wanu*. This explains why it occurs as *palula-* in (58), (59) and (81), rather than as *palu-*. The locative form of the definite nominal is also called for in collocation with *malangka* 'after', as in (78) and (79).

11. Note that (71) does not mean 'What are you thinking about?', which would be expressed using

nyaa 'what': it is an open-ended question seeking to elicit the addressee's views on a topic which is already under consideration.

12 Note that *-tjara* is not used to express meanings like 'have a fever' or 'have a cough', cf. *Tjitji nyangatja waru* 'This child is hot (i.e. has a fever)'. Admittedly, the common word *pika-tjara* (literally, 'pain-HAVING') covers 'be sick/ill' generally, including fever, malaise, diarrhoea, etc., but I would surmise that this is a recent extension of meaning, and that prior to contact with the European medical system it was restricted to designating concrete painful symptoms.

13 It is even possible that *ini* 'name' might be implicit in constructions like *punu kutjupa-kutjupa* 'different kinds of tree'; i.e. that this is elliptical for *punu ini kutjupa-kutjupa* 'tree name other-other = trees of various kinds'.

References

Andrews, Avery. 1985. "The Major Functions of the Noun Phrase". *Language Typology and Syntactic Description* ed. by Timothy Shopen, 62-154. Cambridge: Cambridge University Press.
Anangu Schools Resource Centre. 1990. *Tjukurpa Mutu-Mutu*. Ernabella: Anangu Schools Resource Centre.
Bain, Margaret S. 1979. *At the Interface: The implications of opposing views of reality*. MA Thesis, Monash University, Melbourne.
Bain, Margaret S. & Barbara J. Sayers. 1990. "Degrees of Abstraction and Cross-Cultural Communication in Australia". Paper presented at the 6th International Conference on Hunting and Gathering Societies, University of Alaska, Fairbanks.
Bible Society of Australia. 1987. *Tjukurpa Palya. Irititja munu Kuwaritja*. Canberra: Bible Society of Australia.
Bowe, Heather. 1990. *Categories, Constituents and Constituent Order in Pitjantjatjara*. London: Routledge.
Brown, Cecil H. 1984. *Language and Living Things: Uniformities in folk classification and naming*. New Brunswick, NJ: Rutgers University Press.
Dixon, R. M. W. 1979. "Ergativity". *Language* 55.59-138.
Dixon, R. M. W. 1980. *The Languages of Australia*. Cambridge: Cambridge University Press.
Eckert, Paul & Joyce Hudson. 1988. *Wangka Wiru: A handbook for the Pitjantjatjara language learner*. Underdale: South Australian College of Advanced Education.
Goddard, Cliff. 1982. "Case Systems and Case Marking in Australian Languages: A new interpretation". *Australian Journal of Linguistics* 2.1.167-196.
Goddard, Cliff. 1985. *Yankunytjatjara Grammar*. 2nd ed. Alice Springs: Institute for Aboriginal Development.
Goddard, Cliff. 1989. "Issues in Natural Semantic Metalanguage". *Quaderni di Semantica* 10.1.51-64.
Goddard, Cliff. 1990. "The Lexical Semantics of 'Good Feelings' in Yankunytjatjara". *Australian Journal of Linguistics* 10.257-292.
Goddard, Cliff. 1991. "Testing the Translatability of Semantic Primitives into an Australian Aboriginal Language". *Anthropological Linguistics* 33.1.31-56.

Goddard, Cliff (ed). 1992. *Pitjantjatjara/Yankunytjatjara to English Dictionary.* 2nd ed. Alice Springs: Institute for Aboriginal Development.

Goddard, Cliff & Arpad Kalotas (eds). 1988. *Punu: Yankunytjatjara plant use.* North Ryde: Angus & Robertson.

Gross, Arthur W. 1986. *Tjukurpa Nyanganpa Bible-itja: Malatja Tjuta.* Trans. by Colin Brown. Kangaroo Ground, Vic.: Wycliffe Bible Translators.

HALT (Healthy Aboriginal Life Team). 1991. *Anangu Way.* Alice Springs: Nganampa Health Council.

Harris, Stephen. 1990. *Two-Way Aboriginal Schooling: Education and cultural survival.* Canberra: Aboriginal Studies Press.

Lennon, Manyiritjanu. 1989. *Walawurunya Munu Tjuuny-tjuunynga.* Ernabella: Anangu Schools Resource Centre.

McConvell, Patrick. 1991. "Cultural Domain Separation: Two-way street or blind alley? Stephen Harris and the neo-Whorfians on Aboriginal education". *Australian Aboriginal Studies* 1.13-24.

McDonald, Deborah. 1986. *Tjukurpa 4 Kuwaritja.* Ernabella: Anangu Schools Resource Centre.

Pingkayi. 1989. *Papa Natji-natjinya.* Ernabella: Anangu Schools Resource Centre.

Pitjantjatjara Council. 1990. *Minyma Tjuta Tjunguringkula Kunpuringanyi.* Alice Springs: Pitjantjatjara Council.

Pitjantjatjara Council. 1991. *Commemorating 10 Years of the Pitjantjatjara Land Rights Act.* Alice Springs: Pitjantjatjara Council.

Wierzbicka, Anna. 1980a. *The Case for Surface Case.* Ann Arbor: Karoma.

Wierzbicka, Anna. 1980b. *Lingua Mentalis: The semantics of natural language.* Sydney: Academic Press.

Wierzbicka, Anna. 1989. "Semantic Primitives and Lexical Universals". *Quaderni di Semantica* 10.1.103-121.

Wycliffe Bible Translators. 1982. *Anangu Tju: Tjutaku Tjukurpa.* Kangaroo Ground, Vic.: Wycliffe Bible Translators.

Preliminary Observations on Lexical and Semantic Primitives in the Misumalpan Languages of Nicaragua

Ken Hale
Massachusetts Institute of Technology

Misumalpan is the name given to the small family of languages comprising Miskitu, Sumu, and Matagalpa-Cacaopera. Of these, only Miskitu and two branches of the Sumu subfamily are still spoken today. Both are spoken in the Atlantic Coast region of Nicaragua and Honduras. The two branches of Sumu are the Northern and the Southern. Northern Sumu has two dialects, Twahka and Panamahka, while Southern Sumu has a single form, called Sumu Ulwa, or simply Ulwa, as it will be termed here. In this paper, Misumalpan will be represented by examples from Miskitu, from the Panamahka variant of Northern Sumu, and from Ulwa.

Northern Sumu is spoken in a number of towns in the mountainous area around Las Minas, to the west of Puerto Cabezas within the North Atlantic Autonomous Region (RAAN), Nicaragua, and in various locations in Honduras. It speakers number at least 6000 (Norwood 1987). Southern Sumu, or Ulwa, is spoken only at Karawala, a town of about 800 people, near the mouth of the Rio Grande de Matagalpa on the Atlantic Coast of Nicaragua — geographically in the RAAN, but administratively in the South Atlantic Autonomous Region (RAAS). Miskitu is the principal indigenous language of the Atlantic Coast, particularly in the north, and it enjoys the status of a lingua franca in the area. Consequently, there is much Miskitu-Sumu bilingualism. All of the Ulwa of Karawala, for example, speak Miskitu, and the two languages exemplify strongly the situation of 'grammatical merger'. And a similar situation exists in Northern Sumu communities.

The lexicons and bound morpheme inventories of Miskitu and Sumu are quite distinct, except for a few common Misumalpan retentions and, more importantly, the borrowings from Northern Sumu into Miskitu which date from the period of stressful contact between the two groups concomitant to early British commercial and piratical programs in the area. The merging of some Sumu communities into Miskitu society during this period left a recognisable body of Northern Sumu vocabulary items in Miskitu. And in more recent times, Northern Sumu has taken a large number of lexical items from Miskitu. Generally speaking, however, modern Ulwa keeps its vocabulary quite distinct from Miskitu, to the extent that speakers will consciously coin its own items for the Miskitu terms taken from English. And, in some cases, Ulwa speakers will avoid using an original Sumu term, where that happens to exist in Miskitu because of the earlier period of borrowing.

While it is possible for Ulwa speakers consciously to maintain lexical distinctions between Ulwa and Miskitu, the same is not true, or desired, in the case of grammar. It is only a slight exaggeration to say that the two languages have the same grammar. Translation between the two languages is entirely straightforward, involving simple substitution of lexical items and affixes, with minor exceptions, of course. From the point of view of syntax, the languages are typologically identical.

Some of the typological features of Misumalpan grammar are illustrated in the following sentence, the first line being Miskitu, the second Panamahka, and the third Ulwa:[1]

(1) Witin raks wal sula kum ik-an.
    Witing arakbus kau sana as iina.
    Alas arakbus karak sana as iit-ida.
    he gun with deer one kill-PAST3
    'He killed a deer with the gun.'

This sentence illustrates the prevailing SOV word order, and, in general, the language is head-final — thus, the instrumental expression is formed with a postposition. Functional category heads are also final, in general — thus the indefinite article *kum/as* 'a, one' follows the nominal head which it governs, as does the definite article *ba/kidi/ya*, as in (2) and (3), and inflection for tense and subject agreement, represented here by *-an/-na/-(i)da* 'past, third-person', follows the verb (as a suffix, in this case). Subject agreement is morphologically bound to the suffixal inflection. Object agreement, however, is prefixed to the verb (as illustrated in (2)).

In modification structures, the adjective follows the noun, observationally:

(2) Sula tara ba ai-kaik-an.
    Sana nuhni kidi yaa-tal-na.
    Sana sikka ya yaa-tal-da.
    deer big the me-see-PAST3
    'The big deer saw me.'

But this is not an exception to the head-final principle, since it has been shown (Green 1991) that these structures are relative clauses, in which the predicate (here a predicate adjective) is final, as expected. The Misumalpan relative clause is of the head-internal type:

(3) [[Yang sula kum kaik-ri]   ba]   plap-an.
     [[Yang sana as   tal-na-yang] kidi] iira-na.
     [[Yang sana as   tal-ikda]   ya]   iir-ida.
     I   deer one see-PAST1   the   run-PAST3
     'The deer which I saw ran (away).'

The relativised argument here — that is, *sula kum/sana as* 'a deer' — is internal to the relative clause. The modificational structure of (2) is simply a special case of this. It is a relative clause in which the subject is relativised. Thus the structure as a whole is head-final, since the predicate (the adjective) is the true structural head of the dependent clause.

In summary, the Misumalpan languages are head-final languages employing a head-internal relative clause. There is, incidentally, also a right-headed alternative to this, in which the relative argument appears (in the construct state, see below) external to the clause, between the latter and the article. The languages have a system of pronominal agreement for subject (by suffix) and object (by prefix). Nominals are inflected for possessor. This involves suffixal elements added to the 'construct state' of the noun, as in Miskitu *aras-k-i*, *aras-k-am*, *aras-k-a* 'my horse, your horse, his/her horse', in which *-k-* marks the construct, and the suffixes immediately following mark the person category. The person markers are sometimes infixed, as in *wa-i-tla*, *wa-m-tla*, *wa-Ø-tla* (cf. the absolute form *utla*). In Ulwa, the possessive forms are built on the construct, but the positioning is regulated by metrical considerations. The inflections are suffixed to the first full foot in the word, as in Ulwa *suu-ki-lu*, *suu-ma-lu*, *suu-ka-lu*, from *suulu* 'dog', and *mis-ki-tu*, *mis-ma-tu*, *mis-ka-tu*, from *mistu* 'cat', but *sana-ki*, *sana-ma*, *sana-ka*, from *sana* 'deer'. The Northern Sumu inflections are essentially the same as in Ulwa, except that the construct and third-person have *-ni* in place of *-ka*.

A final typological remark concerns the system of subject obviation, or switch-reference. Certain finite dependent verbal inflections indicate whether the subject of the dependent clause is bound or free in relation to the subject of the main clause. The following illustrates the 'proximate' or 'same-subject' inflection (glossed PROX):

(4) Waitna ba   plap-i   kauhw-an.
     Al   kidi k-iir-i   buk-na.
     Al   ya   iir-i   wauhd-ida.
     man   the   run-PROX   fall-PAST3
     'The man ran and fell.'

And in the following, the dependent verb is marked obviative (OBV), for different subject:

(5) Yang waitna ba   kaik-ri   kauhw-an.
     Yang al   kidi tal-ing   buk-na.
     Yang al   ya   tal-ing   wauhd-ida.
     I   man   the see-OBV1   fall-PAST3
     'I saw the man and he fell.'

The obviation system is involved in a wide range of constructions in Misumalpan, including the causative and a large collection of semi-idiomatic complex lexical entries of the type referred to as 'serial-verb constructions'. The device assumes an impressive share of the expressive burden in the language.

With these few typological remarks, I will turn now to a preliminary consideration of the manner in which the Misumalpan languages, as represented by Miskitu and Sumu, realise the lexical and semantic primitives. The term 'preliminary' must be taken seriously, since a full-scale study of this aspect of the Misumalpan lexicon has not been undertaken. The following remarks are based upon the information which exists as a result of on-going work on the lexicon as a whole, as part of the dictionary project being carried out in collaboration with the Ulwa Language Committee (Ulwah Yulka Tunak Muihka Balna or UYUTMUBAL) of Karawala. As the project continues, we hope to produce a more finished discussion of the lexical and semantic universals as realised in Misumalpan. In what follows, where interlinear glossing cannot express perfectly both the Miskitu and the Sumu — due to slight morphological differences, or differences in word divisions — it will follow the pattern represented by Ulwa (the third line).

10.1 Substantives: I, YOU, SOMEONE, SOMETHING, PEOPLE

The following sentences illustrate the use of the first- and second-person pronouns, which are identically *yang* and *man*, respectively, in Misumalpan languages (a fact which no doubt reflects early Sumu influence on Miskitu, mentioned above):

(6) Yang sula kum kaik-ri.
     Yang sana as   tal-na-yang.
     Yang sana as   tal-ikda.
     I   deer one see-PAST1
     'I saw a deer.'

(7) Man sula kum kaik-ram   ki?
     Man sana as   tal-na-man yah?
     Man sana as   tal-dam   pih?
     you deer one see-PAST2   INTER
     'Did you see a deer?'

In Miskitu the non-singulars of these pronouns are formed with the enclitic *nani* 'non-singular, more than one', normally written as a separate word — thus, *yang nani, man nani*. In Sumu, the pronouns have non-singular forms in the suffix *-na*, which may optionally combine with the general non-singular enclitic *balna* — thus, *yangna (balna), manna (balna)*. These first-person non-singular forms are generally used as exclusives. Inclusive non-singular pronouns also exist: Miskitu *yawan*, Panamahka *mayang*, and Ulwa *mining*.

The Misumalpan expressions corresponding to the indefinites SOMEONE and SOMETHING are built upon the nouns *upla/muih* 'person' and *dyara/dii* 'thing', respectively. These nouns are simply combined with the indefinite article, thereby forming the standard Misumalpan realisations of the suggested universal items:

(8) Upla   kum raks-ki   implik-an.
    Muih   as   arak-i-bus   mal-na
    Muih   as   arak-ki-bus nuut-ida.
    person one rifle-my   steal-PAST3
    'Someone stole my rifle.'

(9) Yang dyara kum atk-amna.
    Yang dii   as   bakan-ki.
    Yang dii   as   bakanta-ring.
    I   thing one buy-FUT1
    'I will buy something.'

The latter form is not limited to physical objects, but also applies to utterances or thoughts, as in Miskitu and Ulwa: *Witin dyara kum win/Alas dii as yultida* 'He said something'.

The interrogatives *ya/wai/wai* 'who' and *dia/ais/ai* 'what' are generally restricted to the interrogative use, as in the root question *Man dia atkram/Man ais bakannaman/Man ai bakantidam?* 'What did you buy?'. They also appear in embedded questions, as in the Miskitu *Yang nu apu witin dia atkan sapa* 'I don't know what he bought'. There is no direct relation between the interrogative words and the indefinites of (8) and (9).

The Misumalpan expression corresponding to PEOPLE is the non-singular of *upla/muih* 'person', as in the following (in which the nouns appear in their construct forms, as required following a pre-nominal demonstrative, possessor or relative clause; the gloss CNSTR will generally be suppressed hereafter):

(10) Naha   uplika   nani   Miskitu bila
     Aadika muihni   balna Wayah   yulni
     Aaka   muihka   balna Wayah   yulka
     this   person:CNSTR   NSG   Miskitu language:CNSTR

yulda-i.
yuyulw-i.
aisi-sa.
speak-PRES3
'These people speak Miskitu.'

Without the determiner *naha/aadika/aaka* here, and with the noun in the absolute (i.e., *upla/muih*), these sentences can receive a generic interpretation: 'People speak ...'. These nouns are also used in one standard definition of the Miskitu and Ulwa names *Dawan/Ah* 'God', namely *pura uplika/takat muihka* 'person up above'.

10.2 Mental Predicates: THINK, KNOW, SAY, FEEL, WANT

Misumalpan *lukaia/kulnin/pumnaka* THINK take nominal or clausal complements, as in:

(11) Dyara ailal   luk-aia   ba   yamni pali apia.
     Dii   manas   kul-nin   kidi yamni palni awas ki.
     Dii   isau   pum-naka   ya   yamka palka-sa.
     thing many   think-INF   the   good   very-NEG3
     'It is not very good to think (too) many things.'

(12) Yang   luk-isna   yauhka   li   auhw-bia.
     Yang   kult-ayang   yahan   was   lauwa-s(a)k-arang.
     Yang   pumt-ayang   yan   was   laut-arang.
     I   think-PRES1   tomorrow water rain-FUT3
     'I think it will rain tomorrow.'

Miskitu and Panamahka use the English-derived *nu*, often in combination with *takaia/kalahnin* 'become' or *kaia/atnin* 'be', in most situations where the putative universal KNOW is expressed. Ulwa uses the native Sumu form *kanglaawanaka* in those same situations:

(13) Yang   nu apia   witin   ani-ra   wa-n   sapa.
     Yang   nu awas-yang   witing   ang-kat   k-iu-na   pa.
     Yang   kanglaawa-sing   alas   aayau-h   yaw-ang   pan.
     I   know-NEG1   he   where-to   go-PAST3   Q
     'I don't know where he has gone.'

Misumalpan SAY is *wiaia/(kal)yulnin/yulnaka*. In this use, these verbs often take both a direct and an indirect object, as in:

(14) Yapti-ki   ra   bila   kum   wi-aisna.
      Naanang-ki yakat yul   as   kal-yul-ki sak-yang.
      Maamah-ki   kau   yul   as   yult-uting.
      mother-my   to   word   one   say-IMFUT1
      'I'm going to say a word to my mother.'

Panamahka and Ulwa use the reflexive expression *kal-dakanin/kal-dahnaka* (literally, 'hear/feel self') in expressing the putative universal FEEL. Miskitu uses a somewhat different expression (also based on 'hear'), *dahra walaia*, as in:

(15) Win-i tara   yamni   dahra wal-isna.
      Muih-ki nuhni   yamni   kal-daka-yang.
      muih-ki   yamka   kal-dah-yang.
      body-my   good   feel-PRES1
      'I feel good in my body.'

It is not necessary to mention the body, or a part of the body, here. Explicit reference to the body could be omitted from (15); in that case, however, the sentence would have a prominent reading according to which the feeling is emotional or psychological, rather than physical. In the following example, the expression under consideration refers again to a psychological, rather than to a physical, condition:

(16) Yang dahra wal-ri   pruw-aia   baku   kan.
      Yang kal-daka-na-yang   dau-ni   kapat dai.
      Yang kal-dak-ing   iwa-naka   yapa   dai.
      I   feel-RPST1   die-INF   like   PAST
      'I felt as if I was going to die.'

Ulwa *walnaka* corresponds both to WANT and 'seek'. Miskitu sometimes uses *plikaia* 'seek' for WANT, though the favoured form now, in both Miskitu and Panamahka, is the English borrowing *want*, categorially an adjective, typically augmented by the verb *kaia/atnin* 'be':

(17) Miskitu:
      (Andris ba dus ma kum pain,)
      upla   sut   dab-aia   plik-isa.
      Ulwa:
      (Aransa ya pan mak as yamka,)
      muih   luih   uk-naka   walda-i ka.
      people all   suck-INF   want-PRES3
      '(The orange is a good fruit,) all people want/seek to eat (literally, suck) it.'

(18) Yang   dusa   pihni   di-aia   want sna.
     Yang   panan   pihni   dii-nin   want-yang.
     Yang   panka   pihka   buih-naka   walt-ayang.
     I   stick   white   smoke-INF   want-PRES1
     'I want to smoke a cigarette.'

In general, the polysemous *walnaka* of Ulwa is used in circumstances in which universal WANT is expected, as is the English-derived *want* of Miskitu, as in *Bilwira waia want sna/Bilwi kau yawanaka waltayang* 'I want to go to Puerto Cabezas', or in *daukaia want sna/yamnaka waltayang* 'I want to do it'. But the Ulwa verb is also used where Miskitu would use *plikaia* 'to seek', as in *dyara kum tikri ba plikisna/dii as luktikda ya waltayang* 'I am looking for the thing I lost'. In Miskitu, the verb *plikaia* 'to seek' is more common in this latter use than in that corresponding to WANT. This verb also figures in the common Miskitu serial expression *pliki sakaia* 'to seek and find, to locate', corresponding precisely to its Ulwa counterpart *walti yaknaka*.

10.3 Determiners and Quantifiers: THIS, THE SAME, OTHER, ONE, TWO, ALL

The demonstratives of Misumalpan include the proximate corresponding to the suggested universal THIS: *naha/aadi(ka)/aaka*. These precede the head noun, and trigger the construct, as was exemplified in (10). There are also post-nominal uses of these demonstratives, the Miskitu variant being reduced to *na*, as in:

(19) Aras   na   isti   pali   plapi-sa.
     Aras   aadi   sirihni   palni   k-iir-i.
     Pamkih   aaka   sirihka   palka   iira-i.
     horse   this   fast   very   run-PRES3
     'This horse runs very fast.'

The post-nominal determiner does not itself induce the construct state. The proximate demonstrative is opposed to a non-proximate in both languages — *baha/kidi(ka)/yaka* 'that' — and these are opposed to a distal locative expression, sometimes appearing in demonstrative function — *bukra/kutkau/yakau* 'that (yonder)'.

Miskitu uses the English borrowing *sim* in most situations where *the same* would be appropriate in translation, as in *Naha sim sa* 'This is the same' or *Witin sim dukia daukan* 'He did the same thing', in which *sim* combines with the noun *dyara* (construct *dukia*) 'thing' (cf. (9)). In some such cases, Panamahka extends the Northern Sumu form *kapat* (LIKE) to this use, where Ulwa uses the form *suinka*, as in the following:

(20) Upla   yari   nani   kum kum ba   dus
     Muih   nanaini   as as   kidi pan
     Muihka   yuhka   balna   as as   ya   pan
     person   tall   NSG   some   the   tree
     yari   wal   sim   pawi-sa.
     naini karak kapat   baratw-i.
     yuhka karak suinka alawada-i.
     tall   as   same   grow-PRES3
     'Some tall people grow the same height as tall trees.'

More research is needed in order to determine the proper Misumalpan equivalents for this element. In Miskitu usage, the English-derived *sim*, or the expression *simsat* (from *same sort*), is the standard, and has eclipsed any Misumalpan equivalent, so far as we can tell. The same is probably true of unguarded Ulwa speech, though speakers of that language consciously avoid the use of borrowings. Ulwa *suinka* is not limited to the use illustrated in (20), being the term for 'unit' and applied primarily, if not exclusively, to the divisions of an hour, that is, to 'minutes', as in *Aakatka as ya 60 suinka watahka* 'An hour has 60 minutes'.

The Misumalpan elements corresponding to OTHER are *wak/uk/wala*, as in:

(21) Upla   wala   bal-an.
     Muih   uk   k-ai-na
     Muih   wak   waa-da.
     person other   come-PAST
     'Another person came.'

In Miskitu and Sumu, though more in the former than in the latter, these elements may be combined with the English derived *sat* 'sort', giving *satwala/satuk/satwak* 'different, strange, of a different kind'.

The cardinality expressions ONE and TWO are, respectively, *kum(i)/as(lah)* and *wal/bu*. The longer forms of ONE — *kumi/aslah* — are used in counting or in isolation, except in Panamahka, where the short form is used in counting. The shorter forms are used in noun phrases, as in sentence (3). The same element reduplicated renders SOME, as in (20). The dual *wal/bu* is used both in counting and in noun phrases; the latter use is illustrated in:

(22) Upla   wal   duri   ra   tauki   pyua ra
     Muih   bu   kuring yak   likmayang   kat
     Muih   bu   kuring kau   rihwadai   kau
     person two   dory   in   travel-PRES when

```
pain      sa.
yamni     ki.
yamka     ka.
good      be:PRES3
```
'It is good (more stable) when two people travel in a dory.'

The universal quantifier ALL is *sut/bitik/luih* in the Misumalpan languages:

(23) *Tangni ba   dyara wlihkaia pali   sa   upla*
      Dii pulu kidi dii as laik   palni ki   muih
      Pulu   ya   dii   suyu   palka ka   muih
      flower the   thing pleasant very   is   person
      sut   ra.
      bitik kau.
      luih   kau.
      all   to
      'The flower is a thing of great beauty to all people.'

10.4 Actions and Events: DO, HAPPEN

In Misumalpan, the verbs *daukaia/yamnin/yamnaka* 'make, do' correspond to DO, in most expressions of that concept, though the verbs also refer to the actual production or manufacture of concrete and abstract entities:

(24) *Dia   dauk-isma?*   *Yang wark tak-isna.*
      Ais   yamt-aman?   *Yang wark alahw-ayang.*
      Ai   yamt-ayam?   *Yang tukw-ayang.*
      what do-PRES2   I   work-PRES1.
      'What are you doing/making?' 'I am working.'

(25) *Utla   kwarika   kum   dauk-aia   luk-i*
      Uu   nuhni   as   yam-nin   kulti
      Uu   itukwana   as   yam-naka   pumt-i
      house   large   one   make-INF   think-PROX
      ais-isna.
      yulbaut-ayang.
      yult-ayang.
      say-PRES1
      'I'm considering building a large house.'

In the representatives of Misumalpan under consideration here, the verbs *takaia/kalahnin/bungnaka* corresponding to HAPPEN also correspond to 'exit' or 'go/come out', 'become' and 'appear/materialise':

(26)   Dia   tak-an?   Nu apia   dia
       Ais   kalah-na yah?   Nu awas-yang   ais
       Ai   bungp-ida?   Kanglaawa-sing ai
       what happen-PAST3   know-NEG1   what
       tak-an   sapa.
       kalah-na   pa
       bungp-ida?   pan.
       happen-PAST3   Q
       'What happened?' 'I don't know what happened.'

(27)   Naha   watla bila   wina   tak-aia
       Aadi   uuni   pas   kaupak   alahwi-nik
       Aaka   uuka   pas   aakaupak bung-naka
       this   house interior from   exit-INF
       want apia sna.
       want awas-yang.
       walta-sing.
       want-NEG1
       'I don't want to go out of this house.'

(28)   Luhp-i   tara   tak-an.
       Wala-ki-bis nuhni   kalah-na
       Baka-ki   tukwana   bungp-ida.
       child-my   big   become-PAST3
       'My child has become big.'

(29)   Raun   ba   dyara ailal   ra   tak-isa.
       Tuyulni kidi   dii   manas   kau   kalahw-i.
       Aran   ya   dii   isau   kau   bungpa-i.
       circle   the   thing many   in   appear-PRES3
       'The circle shape appears in many things.'

10.5   Meta-Predicates: IF, CAN, NO, BECAUSE, LIKE, VERY

The protasis of a conditional is marked by means of the complementisers *kaka/kat*, as in the following:

(30) Traus-ki   slihw-an   kaka, trit   wal   sip-s.
    Kalkan-ik   kur-na   kat,   trit   kau   biita-h.
    Kal-ki-sung kurud-ang   kat,   kaara karak biita-h.
    pants-my   unstitch-PAST if   thread with sew-IM
    'If my pants have come unstitched, sew them with thread.'

In this function, Ulwa also uses the particle *laih*, which also functions to set off a left-dislocated or introductory topic expression and may, therefore, not represent the universal IF perfectly. The latter use corresponds to Miskitu *lika*, which does not enter into the conditional in that language. The use of Ulwa *laih* in conditionals is illustrated in (31), where the Miskitu and Panamahka equivalents are given as *kaka/kat*:

(31) Aman   kaik-rasna   kaka, skiru   ba   ai klak-bia.
    Aman   tala-s-yang kat,   kuhbil kidi yaa-dakw-arang.
    Amang tal-sing   laih, kuhbil ya   yaa-dakt-arang.
    care   see-NEG1   if   knife   he   me-cut-FUT3
    'If I do not take care, the knife will cut me.'

The semantic connection between topic constructions and the conditional is sometimes quite evident, particularly where the topic is clausal. In fact, in the following, the conditional seems most natural in the Panamahka version, beside the topic construction in the other two languages:

(32) Silak   ba   apu   lika, sip utla pask-ras.
    Silak   kidi dis   kat,   sip uu   yamwa-s ki.
    Yasamah   ya   aisau   laih, it   uu   yamda-sa.
    nail   the   NEGEX   'if'   can house build-NEG3
    'Lacking nails, one can't build a house.'

The immediately preceding sentence serves to introduce the Misumalpan modal of possibility and capability, corresponding to the universal CAN. This element is grammatically unique in Misumalpan, as it enters into completely different grammatical constructions in the affirmative and negative. Sentence (32) illustrates the standard use of this element in the negative — it is not combined with a copula, and it is followed by the fully finite negative verb phrase. This pattern is essentially that of a serial-verb construction, in which the non-final verb appears in a dependent participial form (proximate or obviative, as the case may be) while the final (that is, main) verb is fully inflected as a finite verb. While *sip/sip/it* is not a verb, it behaves in the negative precisely like a participial in the serial construction. In the affirmative, by contrast, these elements inflect for person of the subject (via a copular element), and they take an infinitival complement, as in:

(33) *(Kiwa ba waitna ra hilp yabisa untara),*
      (Wah kidi al yakat ilp kal-aaw-i asang pas yak),
      (Wah ya al kau wal aatai damaska kau),
      sip sa   dyara   wilk-aia.
      sip ki   dii   sip-nin.
      it ka   dii   sit-naka.
      can-3   thing   tie-INF
      '(Vines can help a man in the bush), he can tie things (with them).'

The above examples illustrate the use of Misumalpan *sip/sip/it* in reference to ability on the part of the entity denoted by the subject. It is also used in reference to permission and possibility, as in Miskitu *Man sip sma naha briaia* 'You may have this' and *Sip sa yauhka li auhbia* 'It is possible that it will rain tomorrow'.

Sentence (32) contains one of the elements corrresponding to universal NOT, NO: *apu/dis/aisau*. These normally function as predicates and are primarily negative existentials, as in (32) and in:

(34) Wa-m-tla   ra   wa-ri   upla   kumi   sin
      Uu-ma   yak   yawana-yang   muih   as   bik
      Uu-ma   kau   yaw-ing   muih   as   bik
      house-your to   go-OBV1   person one   even
      apu   kan.
      dis   dai.
      aisau   dai.
      NEGEX   PAST3
      'I went to your house and no one was there.'

The Miskitu and Ulwa elements may be used as the negative response to an existential yes/no question; otherwise the proper negative response in Ulwa is *diahka*, and Miskitu has an additional negative *apia*, also used in negative responses and as the regular negative formative in sentences with non-verbal predicates (see (11)) and verbal predicates in certain tenses (e.g. the future). In the latter situations, Panamahka employs the negative auxiliary *awas*. Where the negative is not itself the predicate, as it is in (34), Ulwa uses a special inflected form for the negative, as in (11) and in:

(35) *(Kakaras ba daiwan lupia kum taski),*
      (Lapit kidi dii as taski ki),
      (Lapit ya dii baka as minisihka),
      upla   sut   alk-aia   want apia sa.
      muih   bitik   laih-nin   want awas ki.
      muih   luih   wat-naka   walda-sa.
      person   all   grab-INF   want-NEG3
      '(The cockroach is a dirty little animal), nobody wants to touch it.'

The English borrowing *want* is not a verb in Miskitu or Panamahka, hence the negative is formed with *apia/awas* here. Miskitu and Panamahka, like Ulwa, also possess a suffixal negative *-ras/-s* (see the main verb of (32)). This nominalises the verb and is often extended by means of an auxiliary or copular element.

The Misumalpan realisations of the universal causal linker BECAUSE are the postpositional complementisers *(ba) mihta/yulni kat/bahangh*, as in (53) and in:

(36)   Usus   ba   daiwan   pru-an   apu
        Kusma   kidi   dii   dau-na   dis
        Kusma   ya   dii   iiw-ang   aisau
        buzzard   the   animal   die-RPST   NEGEX
        mihta   sari   iw-isa.
        yulni kat   saari   du-w-i.
        bahangh   amatd-i   lau ka.
        because   sad   be PRES3
        'The buzzard, because there are no dead animals around, is depressed.'

The Misumalpan postpositional elements *baku/kaput/yapa* correspond to the comparative of similarity LIKE, as in:

(37)   Twaina   ba   inska   nani   wala   baku apia sa,
        Twaina   kidi   inska   uk   balna   kaput awas ki,
        Nangkirit   ya   bilam   balna   wak   yapa-sa,
        sawfish   the   fish   PL   other   like-NEG3,
        sa   kum   bri sa.
        saa   as   du-w-i.
        kirit   as   watah ka.
        saw   one   have PRES3
        'The sawfish is like no other fish, it has a saw.'

The languages also have predicates which express the similarity relation. These are *(ai) talya/ka(pa)pat/(kal)nakaabah*, as in:

(38)   Kruhbu ba   limi   wal   ai talya sa.
        Kuruh   kidi   nawah   karak   kapapat ki.
        Kuruh   ya   nawah   karak   kal-nakaabah ka.
        tigrillo   the   tiger   with   RECIP-similar-PRES3
        'The tigrillo and the tiger are mutually similar.'

Miskitu uses the Northern Sumu borrowing *pali* (from *palni*) VERY, while Ulwa uses the Southern Sumu equivalent *palka*. These elements follow the predicate (usually adjectival or adverbial) which they modify; they are exemplified in (11),

(19), (52), and in the following:

(39) Tininiska   ba   daiwan lupia (kum)   sirpi   pali sa.
    Rumhsik   kidi   dii   bin as   binibin palni ki.
    Surh   ya   dii   baka as   bisika   palka ka.
    sparrow   the   animal small one   little   very-PRES3
    'The sparrow is a very little "small animal" (i.e. bird).'

10.6 Time and Place: WHEN, AFTER, BEFORE, WHERE, UNDER, ABOVE

Interrogative WHEN is realised as Misumalpan *ahkia/mampat/mampa*, and the temporal relative involves a postpositional complementiser *bara/kat* (see also Sumu IF, section 10.5) or *taim/taim/kau* (*taim* is derived from English; cf. also the synonymous indigenous Miskitu *pyua ra*, 'at the time of' exemplified in (22)):

(40) Ahkia   bal-ram?
    Mampat   aiwa-na-man
    Mampa   waa-dam?
    when   come-PAST2
    'When did you come?'

(41) Utla   lama   ra   bui kap-ri   bara, yul
    Uu   yaihnit yak   lawa-na sak-yang   kat,   suul
    Uu   labaka yau   sak-yang   kat,   suulu
    house   near   at   stand-be:PAST1   when   dog
    ai sam-an.
    yaa-kas-na.
    yaa-kas-da.
    me-bite-PAST3
    'When I was standing near the house, the dog bit me.'

(42) Kasbrika ailal   iw-i   taim sip dyara
    Mukus   mahni   yak-lakw-a   taim sip dii
    Mukus   isau   lakwa-i   kau   it   dii
    cloud   much   descent-PRES   when can thing
    kaik-ras sma.
    tala-s-man.
    tal-sa-man.
    see-NEG-2
    'When there is a lot of fog, you can't see things.'

Miskitu speakers readily use the postposition *ningka ra* 'after, behind' (from *ninka ra*, literally, 'at the back/rear of') in expressing the temporal relation AFTER, and the Panamahka equivalent *us-t yak* is also used in this function. The Ulwa equivalent *dang-t kau*, primarily a spatial term, is used less often in this meaning — although this use is possible, as in the following passage from the history of Karawala:

(43) Baha sut ningka ra waitnika ba naku
    Kidi bitik usnit yat alni kidi aaput
    Yaka luih dangkat kau alka ya aapa
    that all after at man the thus
    wi-n kan.
    yulna dai.
    yult-ang dadang.
    speak-RPST be:RPST
    'After all that, the man said the following.'

More often, Ulwa uses clause sequencing (with obviation or switch-reference) or the general postpositional complementiser *kau* 'at, when', as in:

(44) Ulwa:
 a. Maa singka laaw-ak, watd-i
    day five pass-OBV3 travel-PROX
    yawa-na asang-kana kau.
    go-RPST3PL land-their to
    'Upon five days passing, they travelled back to their place.'

 b. Yaka balna luih laaw-ang kau,
    that PL all pass-RPST3 when,
    kuma kungka kau yawa-na.
    sea edge to go-RPST3PL
    'When all those things had passed, the went to the edge of the sea.'

These usages are also frequent in Miskitu and Panamaka, though the use of *ningkara/us-t yak* is probably equally common.

The Misumalpan postpositions *kan ra/taa-t yak/taa-t kau* 'in front of, before' are used primarily in expressing the spatial relation, as in (45):

(45) Yang   kain-am   ra   wa-mna.
      Yang   taa-ma-t   yak   yawa-ki,
      Yang   taa-ma-t   kau   yawa-ring.
      I   before-2   at   go-FUT1
      'I will go before you/ahead of you.'

A favoured usage in expressing the temporal relation between events involves the use of the pre-verbal particles *kau/baisa/katka* 'still, yet' in combination with the negative. This combination appears in the protasis (the BEFORE clause), which is followed by the postpositional complementisers *bara/kau* (see above):

(46) Kau   kabu   ra   tak-ras sma   bara,
      Baisa   kuma   yak   alahwa-s-man   kau,
      Katka   kuma   kau   bungpa-sa-man kau,
      still   sea   to   exit-NEG-2   when
      duar-kam   tara   ba   sip-s.
      kuring-ma   nuhni   kidi biita-h.
      kuring-ma   sikka   ya   biita-h.
      dory-your   big   the   caulk-IM
      'Before you go out to sea (i.e. while you have not yet gone), caulk your boat.'

This device may well predominate in Misumalpan for expressing the temporal precedence relation between punctual events, as in Miskitu *Witin pruan yang kau aisubi takras bara* 'He died before I was born' (literally, 'when I was not yet born').

Misumalpan interrogatives of location are *ani ra/angkat/aayau*, as in:

(47) Witin   ani ra   wark tak-isa?
      Witing   angkat   wark kalahw-i?
      Alas   aayau   tukwa-i?
      he   where:at   work-PRES3
      'Where does he work?'

The sub- and supralocative postpositions are *mu(nu)nhta ra/di-t yak/ana-t kau* 'under' and *ta-t kau/mi-t yak/pura-ra* 'on, above, on top of':

(48) Taira   ba   tasba   munhta
      Ukmik   kidi   sau   dinit
      Ukmik   ya   sau   anakat
      armadillo the   ground   under

> ra   watla   bri-sa.
> yak   uu-ni   duw-i.
> kau   uuka   watah-ka.
> at   house   have-PRES3
> 'The armadillo has its dwelling under the ground.'

(49)   Tuktan   kum   walpa   pura
       Muih bin   as   kiipala   minit
       Baka   as   kiimak   takat
       child   one   stone   top
       ra   iw-isa.
       yak   yalah-na sak ki.
       kau   lau-ka.
       at   sit-PRES3
       'A child is sitting on top of a stone.'

The simple locational relation according to which some entity 'is in a place' is generally expressed in Misumalpan by means of a nominal in a locative case functioning, in Miskitu, as the complement of the copula or, in Sumu, as the predicate itself, there being no overt copula. The copula is verbal in Miskitu, being based on the irregular verb *kaia* 'to be', as in *Witin ai watlara sa* 'She is in her house'. In Sumu, locative predicates combine directly with the system of subject agreement inflections otherwise associated with stative predicators, as in the Ulwa sentence *Alas uuka kau ka* 'She is in her house'.

10.7   Partonomy and Taxonomy: PART OF, KIND OF

Miskitu and Panamahka use the borrowed term *pis* (from English 'piece') in such sentences as (50), where Ulwa uses the Sumu noun *pah* 'place':

(50)   Yang   utla   pis-ka   kum   pask-aisna.
       Yang   uu   pis-ni   as   yam-ki ki.
       Yang   uu   pah-ka   as   yamt-uting.
       I   house   part-CNSTR   one   make-FUT1
       'I'm going to repair a part of the house.'

In discussions of the part–whole relation, however, it is more common to use the terms *dyara/dii* 'thing' (construct *dukia/diini/diika*), as in expressions like *wan wina tara dukia/maamuihki nuhni diini/muihni diika* 'a thing of our body', in reference to *auya/ising/asung* 'liver'. But this usage is not limited to the part–whole relation, strictly speaking, as it is also used for the spatial, or locational, relation exemplified in such expressions as *wan byara dukia/maabaaki diini/yasni diika* 'a thing of our stomach', in reference to the intestinal worm called *liwa/baabil*. In Miskitu, the English-derived *pis* is used in composing definitions for the new Miskitu dictionary currently being compiled, as in *Kabu wina tingni baku taki dimi wih pis kum kau tara taki ba* 'It (a lagoon) is an enlarged part of a river-like inlet from the sea' or *Upla tnata swapnika pura saitka piska ba nina* '(Waist is) a name of the part above a person's hips'.

The English borrowing *sat* 'kind, sort' is fully integrated into the Miskitu and Panamahka lexicons, and it is sometimes heard in Ulwa speech (as in the terms *satwala/satuk/satwak* cited in section 10.3). This term is also used with great frequency by those compiling the new Miskitu dictionary, as in *Lakatan ba siksa satka kum sa* 'The *lakatan* is a kind of *siksa* (banana)', and in the definition of *rumatis* 'rheumatism': *Siknis satka kum uplara alki ba* 'A kind of illness which attacks people'. But original Misumalpan terms such as *dyara/dii* 'thing', *upla/muih* 'person' and *daiwan/dii* 'animal' are often found in contexts where KIND OF is being expressed, as in *unta daiwra/asang diini/damaska diika* 'animal of the bush country', *li daiwra/was diini/was diika* 'animal of the water', *kabu uplika/kuma muihni/kuma muihka* 'people of the sea', and so on.

10.8 Evaluators: GOOD, BAD

The Miskitu equivalents of GOOD happen to be borrowings, *yamni* and *pain*, from Northern Sumu and English (*fine*), respectively. Ulwa uses the original Southern Sumu *yamka*, with the characteristic construct suffix *-ka*, corresponding to the characteristic Northern Sumu *-ni*. Sentences (51) and (52) illustrate, respectively, the attributive and predicative uses of these adjectives:

(51) Tasba nara upla kum kum ba lukanka
     Sau aa-kat muih as as kidi kul-nin-na
     Asang aa-kau muih as as ya pumnaka
     world this-in person one one the idea
     yamni bri-sa.
     yamni du-w-i.
     yamka watah-ka.
     good have-PRES3
     'In this world, some people have good ideas.'

(52) Bins ba pi-aia pain pali.
     Bins kidi kas-nin yamni palni ki.
     Sinak ya kas-naka yamka palka.
     beans the eat-INF good very
     'It is good to eat beans.'

The Misumalpan realisations of the universal BAD are *saura/dutni/dutka*:

(53) *Tairi   ba   dyara   kum   saura,   wan talya*
     Sasah   kidi   dii   as   dutni ki, maa-aa-ki
     Tasah   ya   dii   as   dutka,   aa-ni-was
     mosquito the   thing   one   bad   our blood
     dii   ba mihta.
     dii-w-a   yulni kat.
     dii-ya   bahangh.
     drink-PRES3   because
     'The mosquito is a bad thing, because it drinks our blood.'

10.9 A Remark on Lexical and Semantic Universals

The comment which I wish to make here is not based solely on the brief and very tentative survey just given of the possible Misumalpan realisations of the lexical and semantic universals. It is based partly on several decades' work in both practical and theoretical studies of the grammars and lexical resources of a number of Native American and Australian Aboriginal languages. My own experience, and the results of many years of study on the part of Anna Wierzbicka and her colleagues, as well as the work on lexical conceptual structure by people like Ray Jackendoff and others, lead me to accept virtually without reservation the notion that there are universal fundamental concepts, or 'conceptual primitives'.

I do have reservations about one aspect of the overall program which this short study of Misumalpan attempts to represent. Specifically, I doubt that all languages 'have words for' the conceptual primitives. This in no way challenges the idea of conceptual primitives, since concepts do not have to have names to be real. The 'reality' of the concepts can be determined in other ways. And I do not deny that 'shared words' exist, of course, nor do I deny the importance of determining what those shared words are or the importance of having a semantic metalanguage based on universal semantic primitives.

Nevertheless, it is well known that 'mismatches' abound in comparative lexical semantics. It is immediately apparent, from the existence of such polysemous terms as English *know*, embracing both the universal $KNOW_1$ and the derived '$know_2$', for example, that the words of a language are not isomorphic with the universal semantic primitives. Observations of this nature, to my way of thinking at least, cast doubt on the strongest requirement — that is, the isomorphism requirement — on the naming of conceptual universals in the world's languages.

It seems to me to be more interesting to yield in relation to the isomorphism requirement and to examine the evidence which remains in favour of the basic idea of conceptual universals. An interesting source of evidence, perhaps, is borrowing. In this connection, Miskitu, an enthusiastic borrower, is instructive. Consider, for example, the English-derived Miskitu and Panamahka word *pis* (English *piece*). In the absence of this term, there really is no perfect match for the concept PART. But the borrowing, so far as I can tell, corresponds well, if not precisely, to the proposed universal concept. This would be a miracle, if PART were not itself a universal, unnamed before the borrowing. The same is true, I think, of the English-derived Miskitu term *want*, which corresponds well, perhaps perfectly, to the universal idea. The indigenous ways of referring to 'wanting' were not exactly the universal WANT, so far as I can tell. One expression was more like 'seeking', now generally abandoned as a term for WANT in Miskitu; the other referred more to longing or deprivation. Interestingly, the Ulwa verb *walnaka*, originally 'seek', is now clearly polysemous, with one of its uses precisely parallelling the Miskitu *want*. This sort of extension also proves the basic point — an introduced usage is easily and accurately adopted, given the universality of the concept named.

Although I am not fully certain of this, I think the English-derived Miskitu and Panamahka *nu* corresponds to the universal $KNOW_1$, rather than to the polysemous English *know*. Original Miskitu items for 'knowing' were based on the verb *kaikaia* 'see', and the current derivative *kakaira* 'knowing' (literally, 'knower, seer') corresponds primarily to '$know_2$'. If Miskitu borrowed *nu*, applying it to $KNOW_1$, in the absence of a perfectly isomorphic indigenous term, then that is striking confirmation for the integrity of the universal $KNOW_1$ in the mental lexicon.

In summary, I think that a criterion of terminological isomorphy for universal concepts is too strong. While the proposed universality of fundamental concepts might be contradicted by empirical data at some point, it is not contradicted by the well-known fact that it is sometimes difficult or impossible to 'find a word for' some universal concept in a given language.

Note

1   The following abbreviations are used in glossing examples: 1/2/3 first/second/third-person, CNSTR construct state, FUTure tense, IMperative, IMFUT immediate future, INFinitive, INTERrogative complementiser (root clause), NEGative, NEGEX negative existential predicator, NSG non-singular, OBViative participial (different subject), PLural, PAST tense, PRESent tense, PROXimate participial (same subject), Question complementiser (subordinate clauses), RECIProcal, RPST remote past tense.

References

Green, Tom. 1991. "The Miskitu Noun Phrase: A minimalist approach". Manuscript, Massachusetts Institute of Technology.

Norwood, Susan. 1987. *Sumu Grammar*. Manuscript, Centro de Investigaciones y Documentación de la Costa Atlántica.

Mparntwe Arrernte
and the Search for Lexical Universals

Jean Harkins
Australian National University, Canberra

David P. Wilkins
State University of New York at Buffalo

Mparntwe Arrernte, previously known as Central Aranda or Alice Springs Aranda, is the traditional language spoken in and around Alice Springs in Central Australia. It is a member of the Arandic subfamily of Pama-Nyungan Australian languages, and apart from its relatively aberrant phonology, it is fairly typical of Pama-Nyungan languages. The language is still being acquired by children, and is one of the languages used in the Aboriginal-controlled bilingual-bicultural education program of the Yipirinya School in Alice Springs.

Morphologically, it is an agglutinative language which employs only suffixes, no prefixes. It has an extensive system of case marking involving fourteen cases marked on the final element of the noun phrase; marking is by peripheral attachment only. Unlike many Pama-Nyungan languages, Mparntwe Arrernte has a complex verb structure with seven distinct positions in the verb stem: the root, a slot for derivational suffixes, and then five positions for different types of inflectional suffix. It has the three 'core' (grammatical/syntactic) case system common in Australian languages: nominative, ergative and accusative (cf. Goddard 1982). This is realised through a split case-marking system in which marking for pronouns is nominative–accusative, while that for common nouns is ergative–nominative. Other aspects of the morphosyntax show a clear tendency towards a nominative–accusative grammar (a tendency to treat S and A arguments in parallel fashion as against the O argument). The verb may carry a non-obligatory inflection indicating the number, but not the person, of the subject (S or A). Unlike many Australian languages, Mparntwe Arrernte does not have bound pronominals, nor does it have distinct verb conjugations. An interesting feature of the verb morphology is a distinct slot for an elaborate category of inflections which Koch (1984) has named the 'category of associated motion' and which is used to indicate that the verb-stem action happens against the background of a motion event with a specific orientation in space (see Wilkins 1991).

Syntactically, noun phrases have a fixed constituent order. Phrase order in the clause is pragmatically governed, but there is a tendency for core arguments to precede the verb and peripheral elements to follow the verb. Dependent clauses can be of the embedded or the adjoined type. Relative clauses may be embedded or split from their head, and there are cases of internally headed relatives and headless relatives, as well as externally headed relatives. Reference tracking across clauses may be done by pronouns or zero anaphora, but there is also extensive use of switch-reference marking, indicating whether the subject (S or A) of the dependent clause is the same as or different from the main clause subject. A detailed grammar of the language can be found in Wilkins (1989), and studies of particular morphological, syntactic, semantic and pragmatic aspects in Wilkins (1984a, 1984b, 1986, 1988, 1991, 1992a, 1992b) and Van Valin and Wilkins (1993). The Arandic Dictionary Project in Alice Springs has done extensive work on the lexicon of Arandic languages, and a dictionary of Central and Eastern Arrernte is due out shortly.

11.1 Substantives

I and YOU are represented by a set of grammatically determined pronoun forms: *ayenge* '1SG:S/O', *the* '1SG:A', *unte* (with an allomorph *nge*) '2SG:S/A', *nge-nhe* '2SG-ACC'. These forms can readily be used in metalanguage sentences, for example:[1]

(1)   *Ayenge   nhenhe   re-nhe   unte   mpware-tyeke*
       1SG:S   this   3SG-ACC   2SG:A   make/do-PURP
      ahentye-kwenye.
       want-NOMNEG
      'I don't want you to do this.'

By virtue of their cases, both *ayenge* and *the* contain additional specifiable information besides just I (cf. Wierzbicka 1980, 1981; Goddard 1982), but these additional components are not morphologically separable from a lexical equivalent of I. On the assumption that these additional components will also be specified in any predicate which assigns case, we may say that the pronominal allolexes are to be understood only for the new information they provide, the components I and YOU, not for the redundant information they contain. Interestingly, in the context of devising a family tree, one speaker insisted that the Ego point in the tree should be labelled *ayenge*. If this may be considered a grammatically neutral environment (one that does not involve grammatical conditioning from a predicate), then perhaps *ayenge* is semantically the more basic of the two first-person forms.

Other Arandic languages show three allolexes for the primitive pronouns. Western Arrernte has *athe* '1SG:A', *yenge* '1SG:S' and *yenge-nhe* '1SG-ACC'. Alyawarre has S, A and O forms for both I and YOU. Arandic *(a)the* '1SG:A' is cognate with common A forms of the first-person pronouns in other parts of Australia (e.g. *ngatha, ngadyu*). These cognate forms are believed to have been morphologically complex: *nga-* '1SG' + *DHu* 'ergative (A)'. With the Arandic loss of the first syllable this complex form would be reduced to the part originally considered to be the ergative suffix, *the*. Thus, it does not seem unreasonable to suggest that what was originally a morphemically complex form is still a semantically complex form.

SOMETHING and SOMEONE, as primitives, identify entities that seem to be similarly identified by the interrogative forms *iwenhe* 'what' and *ngwenhe* 'who':

(2) *Ngwenhe-me   yalange?*
     who-Q   there(mid,uncert)
     'Who (if anyone) is out there?'

(3) *Iwenhe-ke?*
     what-DAT
     'What is it for?'/'What for?'

These forms are found only in interrogative uses, or in compounds like *iwenhe-peke* (literally, 'what-maybe') 'whatever', *ngwenhe-peke* (literally, 'who-maybe') 'whoever', *iwenhe-kweye* (literally, 'what-selfdoubt') 'whatchamacallit', *ngwenhe-kweye* (literally, 'who-selfdoubt') 'whosisname'; and so it seems that both in interrogative and in compound uses they include at least one other component along the lines of 'I don't know'. While the Arrernte forms seem more restricted to interrogative uses than the Yankunytjatjara forms discussed by Goddard (Yankunytjatjara, this volume), they cannot be entirely dismissed as possible equivalents of SOMETHING and SOMEONE.

In declarative sentences SOMETHING can be translated as *arne* 'thing'. *Arne* also means 'tree', 'wood' and 'stick (piece of wood)'; it can be used as a classifier for woody plants, and for artefacts of all materials. It can refer to non-material things as well (as in (5)) (unlike its probable cognate in Yankunytjatjara, *pu‍nu*; see Goddard, Yankunytjatjara, this volume).

(4) *Itne-rle   kenhe knge-tye-ke   arne   nhenhe map-aye.*
     3PL:A-TOP   but   take-HITH-PC   thing this   group-EMPH
     'But it was **them** (white people) who brought these things (infectious diseases).'

(5)   *Ayenge   ahentye-ane-me re   atyenge   arne*
       1SG:S   want-be-NPP   3SG:A   1SG:DAT   thing
       mpware-tyeke.
       make/do-PURP
       'I want him to do something for me.'

(6)   *Arne iwenhe-le   relhe   Mpetyane   re   ke-lhe-ke?*
       thing what-INST   woman   Mpetyane   3SG:S cut-REFL-PC
       'With what thing did that Mpetyane woman cut herself?'

Arne cannot translate 'something' in 'I feel something bad', but this may not be a problem (see example (13) and section 11.8).

SOMEONE is more problematic. In declarative sentences it is usually translated by *arrpenhe* OTHER:

(7)   *Arrpenhe   kwenhe   irrkwentye   ine-tyeke.*
       other   ASSERT   police   get-PURP
       'Someone should get the police.'

(8)   *Alakenhe-arle   irre-me-nge   arrpenhe-le-ante*
       thus-FOC   happen-NPP-ABL   other-ERG-only
       mpware-me-nge.
       make/do-NPP-ABL
       'Because this happened, someone did something.'

In these examples *arrpenhe* is fully interchangeable with *tyerrtye arrpenhe* 'other person':

(9)   *The   are-ke   (tyerrtye)   arrpenhe.*
       1SG:A   see-NPP   (person)   other
       'I saw someone.'

Arrpenhe can only be taken to mean SOMEONE when there is no specific antecedent. In the absence of an antecedent it is assumed that *arrpenhe* refers to some person *(tyerrtye)*, that is to SOMEONE **other** than the speaker and the interlocutor; and this makes *tyerrtye*, or *tyerrtye arrpenhe*, look like a better equivalent for SOMEONE than *arrpenhe*.

PEOPLE is also translated by *tyerrtye*, because Arrernte nominals normally have indeterminate number:

(10) *Ayenge ahentye ane-tyekenhe tyerrtye atyenge*
1SG:S want be-VBNEG people 1SG:DAT
akenge-ntye itirre-tyeke.
bad-VALADV think-PURP
'I don't want people to think something bad about me.'

Usually it is clear from the context whether singular or plural reference is intended, and when necessary a quantifier can be used: *tyerrtye nyente* 'one person', *tyerrtye mape* 'a group of people'. This seems to raise some doubt about whether separate primitives are needed for PEOPLE and SOMEONE, if we have 'person' and quantification. *Tyerrtye* can refer to any human person; it is sometimes used to mean 'Aboriginal person' as opposed to *alhentere* 'white person', but this is a secondary meaning. *Ngwenhe* 'who' and *arrpenhe* 'other' can more easily be used in reference to non-human 'someones' than can *tyerrtye* (or *tyerrtye arrpenhe*), but more experimentation using these terms in Arrernte explications would be needed before a firm distinction could be drawn between SOMEONE and PEOPLE. *Tyerrtye* also means 'body' (see example (50)); it appears to have been borrowed into Arandic languages, and probably originally meant 'skin' (Ngarri and Warlpiri have *jarrja* 'skin', Kukatja has *tyartinpa, tyartin* 'skin').

11.2 Mental Predicates

KNOW has two main translation equivalents, *kaltye* 'know (stative), be knowledgeable of; wise, learned' and *itelare-* 'know (actively); recall, remember':

(11) a. *Ayenge kaltye unte kurne mpware-ke.*
1SG:S know 2SG:A bad make/do-PC

b. *Ayenge itelare-me unte-rle kurne mpware-ke.*
1SG:S know-NPP 2SG:A-THAT bad make/do-PC

'I know you did something bad.' (i.e. (a) I am knowledgeable of the fact that you did something bad; (b) I am actively aware that you did something bad.)

Kaltye is a predicative nominal, and can take dative or purposive complements (in 'know about', 'know how to do' contexts, cf. example (22)) as well as sentential complements, as in (11a). The verb *kalty-irre-* 'learn' is derived from *kaltye* plus the inchoative suffix *-irre-* (see section 11.4). Either we should regard both *kaltye* and *itelare-* as equivalents of KNOW with the choice conditioned by the active/stative distinction; or we might be able to define *itelare-* in terms of *kaltye* KNOW plus *itirre-* 'think' (*itelareme* = ? *itirre-me kaltye-irre-ke-rle-ke* 'think-NPP know-INCH-PC-

REL-DAT', i.e. 'be thinking about that which has come to be known'), which could be compatible with the 'recall, remember' sense of *itelare-*. *Itelare-* probably comes from *ite-* (from 'throat') plus *are-* 'see' (John Henderson, personal communication), and in Mparntwe Arrernte particles can split *itel-* from *are-* (see Van Valin & Wilkins 1993).[2]

THINK, *itirre-*, can take sentential complements as in the example below, or dative or purposive complements in 'think of' contexts:

(12) *Ayenge   itirre-me   tyerrtye   yanhe-le   akurne   anthurre*
      1SG:S   think-NPP   person   that-ERG   bad   very
      mpware-ke.
      make/do-PC
      'I think (that) that person did something very bad.'

Itirre- is synchronically indivisible but probably comes from *ite-* (from 'throat') plus inchoative *-irre-*. *Itirre-* and the nominalised form *itirrentye* are also used to translate 'feel', 'feelings' in contexts like 'What are your feelings about this?', but only when the feelings involved are intellectual-emotional ones, like pride or worry, not physical and/or basic emotional ones like hunger or fear. This suggests that this use really corresponds to THINK rather than FEEL.

FEEL, *awelhe-*, is used for emotional or physical feelings such as anger, happiness and thirst:

(13) *Ayenge   akurne   awelhe-me.*
      1SG:S   bad   feel-NPP
      'I feel something bad.' (*'I feel badly'; see section 11.8.)

Although synchronically indivisible it probably comes from *awe-* 'hear' plus reflexive *-lhe-*. It applies to perceptions in which the source stimulus of the perception is thought to come from some part of the body itself (especially internally generated states and emotions, but also pain, hunger, etc.), as opposed to there being an external source for the perception as with *anperne-* 'touch, feel (an object)'.

SAY, *angke-*, is used in both direct and indirect quotes (see example (22)). It can also mean 'speak' (i.e. 'say something'):

(14) *Nhenhe   alakenhe-irre-ke-iperre,   tyerrtye   arrpenhe   angke-ke.*
      this   thus-happen-PC-after   person   other   say-PC
      'After this happened, someone said something.'

Angke- is not limited to human speech, but can refer to an animal or machine making its characteristic sound. Similarly, the nominalised form *angkentye* is usually 'language' but can also mean 'characteristic sound'. *Angke-* can also be used when something is 'said' other than vocally, for example by handsigning (see Wilkins

1989:173), or in printed words. *Ile-* 'tell' is often also used to translate 'say', but always in 'say something **to someone**' contexts:

(15) *Kele, the   tyenge   newe-ke   anteme ile-ke,*
       OK   1SG:A 1SG:DAT spouse-DAT   now   tell-PC
       "Are-tyek-aye   kwenhe ..."
       see-PURP-EMPH   ASSERT
       'So, I said to my husband, "You must have a look ..."'

WANT is expressed by a nominal, *ahentye* 'throat; desire, want(ing)', usually accompanied by the verbal elements *ne-* 'be/sit' or inchoative *-irre-*, as in (1), (5) and (10), but sometimes on its own as in the following:

(16) *Ayenge nhenhe ikwere   alakenhe irre-tyeke*
       1SG:S   this   3SG:DAT thus   happen-PURP
       ahentye-kwenye.
       want-NOMNEG
       'I don't want this to happen.'

Arrernte speakers view the throat as the seat of desire (cf. the link between 'thinking', 'knowing' and another root for 'throat', *ite-*, mentioned above). In its WANT use *ahentye* is a predicative nominal syntactically distinguished by the presence of a dative or purposive complement, as in the above examples. Such a complement cannot occur with *ahentye* when it just means 'throat' (see Harkins 1992b).

11.3 Determiners and Quantifiers

THIS is usually translated by *nhenhe*, as in examples (1), (4), (16), (17) and (41). It is part of a set of demonstratives, the other members of which can probably be defined via *nhenhe* (Wilkins 1989:114–119). When there is no explicit (linguistic) antecedent, *nhenhe* is usually followed by a resumptive pronoun, as in examples (1) and (16). All the demonstratives can indicate location, so *nhenhe* also means 'here' (see section 11.6). By virtue of its opposition to the 'uncertain' demonstratives (see example (2)), *nhenhe* signals certainty that the actual existence of the thing can be asserted, so it might be semantically complex, including concepts such as CAN and KNOW; but more likely *nhenhe* is simply THIS, and the 'uncertain' demonstratives contain an additional 'I don't know' component. For events, THIS is often translated by *alakenhe* 'thus, like this', as in examples (8) and (14); but in (16) we see a contrast between *nhenhe* referring to a particular event, and *alakenhe* (literally 'I don't want **this** to happen **like this**').

ONE and TWO are *nyente* and *therre*, seen in the following example (see also example (21)):

(17) *Ngkweltye nhenhe therre panikene nyente ikwere-iperre.*
piece   this   two   cup   one   3SG:DAT-after
'These two pieces are part of the same (broken) cup.'

As this example shows, *nyente* ONE is also often used to mean THE SAME, in the case of things. For events, *alakenhe* 'thus, like this' is often used as a translation of the related notion THE SAME:

(18) *The   alakenhe   re-nhe   mpware-me.*
1SG:A   thus   3SG-ACC   make/do-NPP
'I can do the same.'

But a better equivalent for THE SAME denoting precise identity may be the particle *(-)anteye* 'same again' (Wilkins 1989:351):

(19) *Jocinta-le   ankerte   twe-ke,   Thomas-le-anteye.*
Jocinta-ERG   lizard   hit-PC   Thomas-ERG-same
'Jocinta killed a (bearded dragon) lizard and Thomas did too.' (i.e. 'did the same')

Anteye is apparently interchangeable with *antime* 'precisely' in some contexts (Wilkins 1989:363–364):

(20) *Ayenge   ahentye-ne-me   the   alakenhe   anteye   /   antime*
1SG:S   want-be-NPP   1SG:A   thus   same   precisely
mpware-tyeke.
make/do-PURP
'I want to do the same.'

It is not clear at present whether *anteye* and *antime* are really synonyms in this context. *Antime* usually co-occurs with *alakenhe*, as in (20), and cannot be substituted for *anteye* in (19). For *anteye* to be used, there must be a reference to some previous event or condition: it conveys 'the same as before', presupposing that what was 'before' is known. In (19) it is known from the previous clause, and in (20) it is signalled by *alakenhe* 'like this'.

There are close conceptual links between 'sameness', 'oneness' (cf. *nyente* in (17)) and 'likeness' (cf. *alakenhe* in (18)), and one might expect some overlaps in use of the equivalents in various languages for THE SAME, ONE and LIKE. What seems to distinguish *anteye* from *nyente* and *alakenhe* is the notion of precise identity, and this may be the core concept involved in THE SAME. *Nyente* ONE, unlike *anteye* THE SAME, does not necessarily refer to any previous conditions; in (17) this is supplied by the context, triggering the reading of *nyente* ONE as 'the same'. *Alakenhe* 'like this', on the other hand, presupposes something that is the object of comparison, but does not ascribe precise identity to the two things or events. In (18) I might be able to do something 'like this' but not necessarily exactly the same, while in (20) either *anteye* or *antime* adds the specification that I want to do exactly the same. Both *anteye* and *antime* are probably derived from the particle *ante* 'only, without exception' (Wilkins 1989:350–351).

The notion of same versus other seems to be highlighted in various ways in Arrernte grammar as well as lexicon, for example in the complex and extensively used switch-reference system, which marks same-subject and different-subject (doing something at the same time, see section 11.6) with the verbal suffixes *-le* and *-rlenge* respectively (Wilkins 1989:454–487). There are several other related particles that might be definable via *anteye*: *(V)-rlke* 'same event, different subject', *kine* 'same event, same subject' (Wilkins 1989:351–352), and *rante-rante* 'same properties' (also derived from *ante*). We are not yet clear as to which of the available contenders (*nyente, alakenhe, anteye, antime, rante-rante*) should be regarded as equivalents of THE SAME. The candidates discussed above all seem to divide along the lines of 'entity' versus 'event' versus 'character', with questionable cross-categorial applicability.[3]

The most common equivalent for OTHER is *arrpenhe*. We have already noted that in a particular grammatical context, that is in the absence of any antecedent, *arrpenhe* may be taken to mean 'someone'. The concept of OTHER does seem to rely upon some prior concept from which the OTHER is to be differentiated, and it is probably this pragmatic fact that gives rise to the effect that when there is no antecedent at all, *arrpenhe* can be interpreted as 'someone' (i.e. someone 'other' than speaker and interlocutor). In all other contexts, *arrpenhe* is interpreted as OTHER with reference to some antecedent.

(21)   *Nwerne knge-ke crowbar therre ware. Crowbar arrpenhe*
         1PL:S take-PC crowbar two   only   crowbar other
         ne-ke arrare-ulkere, kenhe arrpenhe ne-ke ulthentye nthurre.
         be-PC light-kind   but   other   be-PC heavy   very
         'We only took two crowbars with us. One of the crowbars was quite light, but the other one was very heavy.'

Arrpenhe is related to the clitic *-arrpe* 'on one's own, separate, one's self' (Wilkins 1989:357), and *-nhe* is probably originally the accusative case marker, which also shows up at the end of the interrogative forms and the 'certain' demonstratives (Wilkins 1989:114–119).

ALL and MUCH/MANY are translated by *ingkirreke* and *arunthe* respectively:

(22) *"The   are-ke   arne   arunthe   nthurre.   The   ngkwenge*
     1SG:A   see-PC   thing many   very   1SG:A   2SG
     il-eye,"   uterne   angke-ke...   "Mwarre   nthurre   alakenhe,"...
     tell-PERM   sun   say-PC   good   very   thus
     "kele   unte   kaltye   anteme   ane-me   ingkirreke-ke."
     OK   2SG:S   know   now   be-NPP   all-DAT
     "'I saw lots and lots of things. I'll tell you (about them) if you
     like," said the sun (to the moon) ... "It's wonderful," ... "so now
     you know everything."'

There are other terms that indicate groupedness, such as *mape* 'group' (often used as a pluraliser) and *atningke* 'crowd', but these terms indicate that the entities they modify are not only 'many' but also thought of as being in the same place. In uncountable contexts only, *kngerre* 'big' can be used as a synonym for *arunthe* (as in *kwatye kngerre* 'lots of water'). There is no clear dividing line between *urrpetye* 'a few' and *arunthe* MANY, but *urrpetye* can probably be defined in opposition to *arunthe* and *therre* TWO; that is, *urrpetye* is 'not two, not many'.

Ingkirreke ALL does not always imply total exhaustiveness, but it can be made unambiguously exhaustive by adding *nyente* ONE plus negation:

(23)   *Ingkirreke   purte-lhile-tye-lhe-rle,   nyente-kwenye.*
        all   together-CAUS-GO&DO-GENEVT   one-NOMNEG
        'He would gather everyone together, without any exceptions.'

There is a parallel between the use of *ingkirreke* here to mean 'everyone' and the use of *arrpenhe* OTHER for 'someone' (see section 11.1); in both cases *tyerrtye* 'person, people' is the implied antecedent. The intensifier *nthurre* also seems to emphasise the exhaustive sense of *ingkirreke*:

(24)   *Artwe   yanhe   mantere   irlwe-lhe-me,   ingkirre   nthurre!*
        man   that   clothes   remove-REFL-NPP   all   very
        'That man there is taking his clothes off, absolutely all of them!'

This suggests that *ingkirreke* can be exhaustive but is not exclusively so, and that emphasis or intensifiers may be used when the 'without exception' sense needs to be made explicit (cf. Harkins 1991).

11.4   Actions and Events

HAPPEN seems to correspond to *(-)irre-*, as in (16) and the following:

(25) *Itne   apmere   atyinhe   akurne   (-)ile-ke*
      3SG:S   place   1SG:POSS   bad   (-)do/CAUS-PC
      ikwere-iperre   atyenge   akurne   (-)irre-ke.
      3SG:DAT-after   1SG:DAT   bad   (-)happen/INCH-PC
      'They did something bad to my country; because of this, something bad happened to me.'

Irre- can occur as a free form or as an inchoative or intransitivising derivational suffix (Wilkins 1989:261–264), but it seems that in either case its core meaning may be HAPPEN:

(26) *Nthakenhe-irre-ke?*
      how-INCH-PC
      'What happened?'/'How did it happen?'

DO has two likely candidates, *mpware-* 'do, make' and *(-)ile* 'act, cause'. *Mpware-* is usually the best translation in 'someone does something' frames, as seen in examples (1), (18), (32) and (36). Usually, *(-)ile-* (possibly related to *ile-* 'tell') is seen as a suffix deriving causative verbs from nominals, for example: *artwe* 'initiated man', *artwe-ile-* 'to initiate (i.e. cause to become an initiated man)'; *ulkere* 'slippery, smooth', *ulkere-ile-* 'to smooth something'. But *(-)ile-* can also substitute for 'do' in some contexts, as seen in (25).

There is an interesting symmetry between *(-)ile-* and *(-)irre-*. For example, the question 'What is X doing?' would be expressed by (27a) if the expected answer was that X is doing some transitive action (e.g. cooking food). However (27b) would be used if the expected answer was intransitive or stative (e.g. asleep). So, while both (27a) and (27b) can be translated as 'What is X **doing**?', (27a) can mean only this, while (27b) means something more like 'What's **happening** with X?'. (For a discussion of *(-)ile-* and *(-)irre-* see Wilkins 1989:261–264.)

(27) a. *Nthakenhe (-)ile-me   X?*
         how   (-)CAUS-NPP X
         'What is X doing?' (transitive)

      b. *Nthakenhe (-)irre-me   X?*
         how   (-)INCH-NPP X
         'What's up with X?'

Similarly, (28a) and (28b) were both given as renderings of the English *This is a feeling (emotion) which causes your stomach to feel bad*. Sentence (28a) presents the feeling as **doing** something to the stomach, while in (28b) something **happens** to the stomach as a result of feeling something:

(28) a. *Awelhe-ntye nhenhe-le atnerte ngkwinhe*
feeling-NMSR this-ERG stomach 2SG:POSS
akurne-ile-me.
bad-CAUS-NPP
'This feeling makes your stomach (feel) bad.'

b. *Alakenhe awelhe-me atnerte ngkwinhe akurne-irre-rlenge.*
thus feel-NPP stomach 2SG:POSS bad-INCH-DS
'When you feel like this your stomach (feels) bad.'

11.5 Meta-Predicates

NO/NOT is expressed in three main ways: the word *arrangkwe* 'no, not, nothing' seen in the following example, the verb-negating suffix *-tyekenhe* (examples (10) and (35)), and the nominal-negating/privative suffix *-kwenye* (examples (1), (16) and (23)) (Wilkins 1989:235, 355, 375).

(29) *Ayenge ure-ke arrangkwe.*
1SG:S fire-DAT no
'I don't have any matches.'

Arrangkwe typically negates, or rejects, a whole proposition and is used to say 'no' to yes/no questions. The suffix *-tyekenhe* may either negate the whole clausal proposition, or its scope may be just over the content of the verb, but not over (all of) the arguments of the verb. As well as general negation, a verb marked in this way may be used in many situations where 'can't/couldn't' would be the best English translation. In Western Arrernte, where there is no suffix for verb negation, the particle *itye* takes on the full range of functions that, in Mparntwe Arrernte, are shared between *arrangkwe* and *-tyekenhe*. The suffix *-kwenye* only has scope over the nominal it modifies. It seems likely that *-tyekenhe* and *-kwenye* could both be defined in terms of *arrangkwe* (very roughly: N V-tyekenhe = N V-PURP arrangkwe; N-kwenye = N-DAT arrangkwe).

Distinguishing IF and CAN in Arrernte poses a seemingly intractable problem, and one that raises important questions about the relationship between these as primitives. Both are translated easily by a very frequently used word, *peke* 'maybe, perhaps' (Wilkins 1989:361–362). This word expresses possibility or imaginability (but not the 'can' of ability, cf. example (18)):

(30) *Unte   peke   diabetes-kerte, nhenhe-le ngenhe rlkerte*
      2SG:S maybe   diabetes-PROP   this-ERG   2SG:O   sick
      mpware-tyeke.
      make-PURP
      'If you have diabetes, then this will make you sick.'

(31) *Kwart-iperre   arrate-me   yep-arenye   peke,*
      egg-after   appear-NPP   tarvine-ASSOC   maybe
      ntyarlke   peke,   arrpenhe   peke.
      k.o.caterpillar maybe   other   maybe
      'From the eggs might appear tarvine caterpillars, or ntyarlke
      caterpillars, or some other kind (of caterpillars).'

Often, too, no element signalling IF nor CAN seems to appear in the Arrernte sentence, although it occurs in the English:

(32) *Unte   the   mpware-tyeke   ahentye, the   ingwenthe*
      2SG:S 1SG:A   make/do-PURP   want   1SG:A   tomorrow
      mpware-tyenhenge.
      make/do-SBSQNT
      'If you want me to do it, I can do it tomorrow.'

Mparntwe Arrernte also has a hypothetical verbal suffix, *-mere*, which sometimes translates as 'can', 'could' (Wilkins 1989:233–234):

(33) *Dam   itne   mpware-rlenge, kwatye-le   atake-mere.*
      dam   3PL:A   make-DS   water-ERG   destroy-HYPO
      'When they build the dam, then the water could (hypothetically)
      destroy it (and put us all in danger).'

But this suffix is not a satisfactory equivalent for CAN. It is rarely used, and seems to embody a more complex meaning involving I and THINK as well as CAN. Furthermore, it seems relatively easy to propose a definition via *peke*, along these lines: *kwatye-le atake-mere* = *ayenge itirre-me kwatye-le peke atake-tyenhenge* ('water-ERG destroy-HYPO' = 'I think-NPP water-ERG maybe destroy-SBSQNT').

Comparing IF and CAN in their most typical contexts (it CAN/COULD rain tomorrow, IF it rains I won't come), we see that both refer to the 'pure possibility' of an event (e.g. raining). The only difference is that IF points to a further event dependent upon the first (I won't come (because it's raining)). Both of these would be expressed by *peke*:

(34) *Ingwenthe peke   kwatye urnte-me.*
     tomorrow maybe   water   fall-NPP
     'It could rain tomorrow.'

(35) *Kwatye peke   urnte-me   ayenge petye-tyekenhe.*
     water   maybe   fall-NPP   1SG:S   come-VBNEG
     'If it rains I won't come.'

In *if–then* constructions like (32), the ending of the dependent verb is usually *-tyenhenge*, the subsequent marker, which etymologically appears to contain the morphemes *-tyenhe*, the non-past-completive/future tense marker, and *-nge*, the ablative marker, which we propose as the Arrernte equivalent of BECAUSE. Thus, the tense element relates to the fact that the dependent event is after (to the future of) the main event, and the ablative relates, perhaps, to causal connection, although it may simply indicate a direct connection between the events such that one leads naturally from the other. That is, 'something COULD happen (you want me to do it); something else could happen (after this) BECAUSE of this (I do it)'. It may prove possible to match *peke* with IF in the presence of a dependent event and with CAN otherwise, but the question requires further investigation (cf. Harkins 1992a).

LIKE is usually expressed by *-arteke*, the semblative marker (Wilkins 1989:347–348):

(36) *Urreye nhenge-le   mpware-ke   artwe-le-arteke.*
     boy   REMEMB-ERG   make/do-PC   man-ERG-like
     'The boy behaved just like a man (does).'

(37) *Lyete-ulkere   ampe   mape   ne-tyeke   arrenge*
     now-MORE   child   PL(GRP)   be-PURP   grandfather(FF)
     itne-kenhe   ne-tyert-arteke.
     3PL-POSS   be-REMP:HAB-like
     'Nowadays kids should be like their grandfathers used to be.'

Arteke can also indicate 'same', as in example (43), but this may be explained by the conceptual link between 'likeness' and 'sameness' discussed in section 11.3. Notions akin to LIKE are also sometimes expressed using *-ulkere* 'kind' (related uses are seen in examples (21) and (37)). *Alakenhe* 'thus' and *alakenhe-arteke* 'like this' are very commonly used when demonstrating how to do something.

The best equivalent of BECAUSE seems to be the ablative case marker *-nge* (see also example (8)):

(38)   *M-angkwe   unte   are-tyeke   lhe-tyek-aye,*
       mother-2KINPOSS(O) 2SG:S   see-PURP   go-PURP-EMPH
       rlkerte   kngerre-nge   re.
       sick   big-ABL   3SG:S
       'You should go visit your mother because she's very sick.'

This multifunctional suffix can have spatial ('away from') and temporal ('after') reference (Wilkins 1989:185–187), but example (38) is clear evidence of its pure BECAUSE usage: the speaker is certainly not urging the addressee to go 'away from' or 'after' his mother's illness, but 'because' of it.

Arrernte is very rich in ways of expressing reasons for occurrences. In addition to *-nge*, the following are all used to express notions akin to BECAUSE: *-iperre/-ipenhe* 'after' (example (25)), *warte* 'since (as you should know)', the purposive marker *-ke*, the aversive marker *-ketye*, *-arrkngele* 'indirect reason for anger', the causative nominal suffix *-ile-*, and switch-reference (see Wilkins 1989, Ferber & Breen 1984). The main reasons for selecting *-nge* as the basic equivalent of BECAUSE are, first, that it is the best form to use in 'pure' reason contexts like example (38), and second, that the 'because' senses of the other alternatives mentioned above appear to be definable in terms of *-nge*. It is important to note that 'reason' clauses (other than causative constructions) are often presented after rather than before the event they refer to. Thus a sentence like 'I'm crying because he hit me' would often be translated as follows:

(39)   *Re   ayenge   twe-ke.   Ikwere-nge   ayenge   artne-me.*
       3SG:A   1SG:O   hit-PC   3SG:DAT-ABL   1SG:S   cry-NPP
       'He hit me; that's why I'm crying.'

VERY is usually expressed by the intensifier *(a)nthurre*, as in examples (12), (22) and (24). Occasionally *kngerre* 'big' and *arnterre* 'hard, intensively' are also used, but *(a)nthurre* is clearly the main equivalent of VERY.

11.6   Time and Place

In interrogatives, WHERE is translated by *nthenhe*, which may be used with or without the locative suffix *-le* with no apparent difference in meaning:

(40)   *Unte   pmere   nthenhe-le   ne-ke?*
       2SG:S   place   where-LOC   be/sit-PC
       'Which place did you live at?'

Pmere 'place' is a cultural concept of great importance in Arrernte, covering a range of meanings including 'camp, country, place, home, house, shelter, spiritual home'. It is probably semantically complex, denoting something like 'WHERE someone/something belongs or is a part of', and it can take kin possessive suffixes which are usually applied only to people or social entities (see Wilkins 1992b).[4]

Because *nthenhe* seems to be restricted to interrogative use (see also the discussion of 'who' and 'what' in section 11.1), the locative *-le* may be the best equivalent for WHERE. It is used in declaratives, for example:

(41) *Nhenhe-le re   arlkwe-ke-le   inte-ke-rlke.*
      here-LOC 3SG:S/A eat-PC-SS   lie-PC-too
      'This is where it (kangaroo) ate and then slept as well.'

Nhenhe 'here' (also THIS, see section 11.3) is the core of a complex set of spatially deictic demonstratives, all of which (like *nthenhe* 'where') are inherently locative and can thus be used with or without locative *-le* (Wilkins 1989:111–119); *-le* is obligatory in locative uses of all other nominals except place names.

WHEN also has an interrogative form, *ilengare*, which almost certainly comes from *ile-*, a common Arandic base for 'what', plus *-ngare* 'times' (i.e. 'what-times') (Wilkins 1989:131, 341–342). The notion of two events happening at the same time is expressed via the switch-reference construction, with *-le* when the simultaneous events have the same subject, and *-rlenge* when they have different subjects:

(42) *Artwe alye-lhe-me-le   petye-me.*
      man   sing-REFL-NPP-SS   come-NPP
      'A man is coming (while) singing.'

(43) *Re   petye-ke re   lhe-rlenge-arteke.*
      3SG:S come-PC 3SG:S go-DS-SEMBL
      'She came at the same time as he went.'

The switch-reference construction's function of locating an event in time can also indicate the order of events, as in example (41) where *-le* indicates the dependent event (eat) has the same subject as the main event (sleep), while the past completive *-ke* now functions as a relative tense form indicating that eating was completed before the kangaroo slept (i.e. 'This is where, **when** it had eaten, it also slept'; Wilkins 1989:454–487).

But identifying switch-reference with WHEN raises the problem that the switch-reference marker *-le* is etymologically related to the locative suffix (Wilkins 1989:178). Many Arrernte deictics have both spatial and temporal uses, but some are purely spatial and others purely temporal, so clearly the language does distinguish 'time/when' from 'place/where' concepts. An important purely temporal term is *anteme* 'now', seen in examples (15), (22) and (51). The 'associated motion' forms can also mark simultaneity, as well as non-simultaneity, of actions with respect to background motion events that have specific orientations in space (i.e. 'do while moving upwards', 'do while coming back', 'go back and do', etc.) (Wilkins 1991).

While switch-reference seems the device most favoured by speakers for indicating when things happen, *-ngare* may prove to be a better equivalent of TIME. It is used to indicate the number of times a thing happened, and appears in constructions like *nyente-ngare* 'once', *therre-ngare* 'twice', *arrpenhe-ngare* 'another time, again', *mape-ngare* 'a lot of times', *awethe-ngare* 'more times'. More information is needed on its applicability in other contexts (see Goddard's discussion of Yankunytjatjara *ara-*, a probable cognate (Yankunytjatjara, this volume)).

AFTER is probably best matched with *-iperre/-ipenhe* 'after, from', as seen in example (14) above (Wilkins 1989:205–210). This also appears in the *-le-iperre* verb-forms, which indicate 'after V happens, then ...':

(44)   ... nwerne lhe-ke, merne   arlkwe-ke-l-iperre,   dinner-iperre ...
       1PL:S go-PC   food   eat-PC-SS-after   dinner-after
       'We went, after eating some food, after dinner (to hunt for witchetty grubs).'

There is quite a bit of overlap in usage between *-iperre/-ipenhe* and ablative *-nge*. We have already noted that *-nge* can be used to mean 'from' and 'after' as well as BECAUSE; and *-iperre/-ipenhe* AFTER can also be used in 'because' and 'from' senses (see examples (17), (25) and (31)). In narratives, *ikwere-nge* '3SG:DAT-ABL' occurs very frequently meaning 'then, after that', but *ikwere-iperre* '3SG:DAT-after' is also quite common. The distinction between *-iperre/-ipenhe* and *-nge* can be seen by comparing the following example with (38):

(45)   Re   ilwe-ke arrwengkelthe kurn-ipenhe.
       3SG:S die-PC disease   bad-after
       'He died from a bad disease.'

Here *-ipenhe* really means AFTER, but the natural assumption that the disease caused the death is reflected in the gloss 'from'. In (38) the obligation to visit occurs because of, definitely not after, the illness, and *-iperre/-ipenhe* could not be substituted. There are quite a few other ordering terms: *arrwekele* 'before, in front', *ingkerne* 'after, behind' and perhaps *-kemparre* 'first' all have both spatial and temporal reference. *Imerte* 'then, after that', *-urrke* 'before doing anything else', and *urreke* 'later' have temporal reference only (Wilkins 1989:352–353, 366).

ABOVE is one of the senses of *kertne*, which can be used for 'up', 'over' and 'top (part of)'. It is unambiguously ABOVE in a relative location construction in which the ground NP is marked with the ablative *-nge* and *kertne* follows (i.e. *X Y-nge kertne* = 'X is above Y'). UNDER is one of the senses of *kwene*, which can mean 'down, under, below, the bottom of; in, within, the inside'. *Kwene* is an antonym of both *kethe* 'outside' and *kertne* 'top', and suggests surroundedness, an observer above who can't see all sides of the thing that is *kwene*. This could pose problems for identifying *kwene* unambiguously with UNDER.

11.7 Taxonomy and Partonomy

The concept of KINDS of things is expressed in many ways, particularly in relation to kinship and folk-biological classification systems. The notion of 'different kinds' is closely linked with the concept *arrpenhe* OTHER (see also example (31)):

(46) *Thipe   arrpenhe-ante-arrpenhe   nthakentye   unte   are-ke*
     bird   other-ONLY-other   how:many   2SG:A   see-PC
     Darwin zoo-ke   are-tyeke   alhe-me-le?
     Darwin   zoo-DAT   see-PURP   go-NPP-SS
     'How many (different) kinds of bird did you see when you went to the zoo in Darwin?'

Arrpenhe-ante-arrpenhe is formed by reduplication of OTHER and the insertion of *ante* (discussed in Wilkins 1989:350–351); a similar form is *iwenhente-iwenhente* 'what different things, all the different things' (Wilkins 1989:132), but this refers to different individual things rather than different kinds of things.

The other important 'kind' term is *-ulkere*. This form has two distinct uses, both of which are associated with comparison. In its first function, it is used to create comparatives (e.g. *kngerre-ulkere* 'bigger', literally 'big-more'), or to indicate increased temporal range (e.g. *lyete-ulkere* 'nowadays', literally 'now/today-more'). In its second function, *-ulkere* is used to indicate that one thing is of the same general kind as another, or is of the kind being described or indicated. It is common for this clitic to be attached to the demonstrative *nhenge* 'you remember the one', and the resultant form *nhenge-ulkere* is used to signal that the speaker has moved out of discourse into handsigning and is noting that an entity in the story was a thing of the kind indicated in the handsign:

(47) *Unte   warre   kwatye pintye-pintye   nhenge-ulkere*
     2SG:S   REMIND   water   reeds   REMEMB-kind
     mape   itelare-ɸ...
     PL(GRP)   remember-IMP
     'You remember the water reeds of this kind (hand-sign) ...'

(48) *Ayenge   akutne   yanhe   ikwere,   mutekaye   arrpenhe*
     1SG:S   ignorant   that   3SG:DAT   car   other
     ulkere   peke.
     kind   maybe
     'I don't know what it is, but I think it's a kind of car.'

Part–whole relations are also expressed in many different ways in Arrernte. Perhaps the most important of these is a grammatical construction with no specific lexical expression. In this construction a 'whole-NP' and a 'part-NP' can occur, fixed in that order, adjacent to one another with no overt marking of possession and with case marking at the end of the complex NP; or the part and whole can appear, each with independent case marking, as distinct and separated constituents of the same clause (Wilkins 1989:411–413).

The most important lexical indicators of 'parts' are the possessive case marker *-kenhe*, and the proprietive or 'having' marker *-kerte*. These terms have a symmetrical, inverse relationship to one another: the whole 'having' parts (*-kerte*), and the parts 'belonging' to the whole (*-kenhe*):

(49) *Aherre ne-me apethe-kerte, tayele arlpentye-kerte, iltye*
roo   be-NPP   pouch-PROP   tail   long-PROP   hand
therre-kerte, ante ingke therre-kerte.
two-PROP   and   foot   two-PROP
'Kangaroos have a pouch, a long tail, two arms, and two legs.'

(50) *Akaperte apele tyerrtye-kenhe.*
head   FACT   body-POSS
'The head is part of the body.'

(See Goddard's discussion (this volume) of *-tjara* 'having' in Yankunytjatjara.) Two other suffixes can substitute for *-kenhe* in (50): the associative *-arenye* and *(X)-nge-ntyele* 'from (X) onwards', but these suffixes probably encode more complex meanings than *-kenhe* does (Wilkins 1989:187–188, 202–204). Note also that *-iperre* 'after, from' can denote parts (after separation) from a whole, as in example (17).

It is difficult to choose among these possibilities for encoding the notion of PART. The English word *part* is polysemous, and clarification is needed of the specific features of the proposed universal PART. Languages seem to concern themselves with issues of separability, non-separability, inalienability, alienability, individuation, non-discrete continuity and so on when it comes to encoding 'part' notions (see Iris, Litowitz & Evens 1988).[5] Until we know which of these features are involved in the NSM concept PART, no one candidate for Mparntwe Arrernte can be chosen.

11.8 Evaluators and Descriptors

GOOD and BAD are *mwarre* and *(a)kurne*, already seen in examples (11), (12), (13), (22) and (28). *(A)kenge* also means 'bad' (example (10)) and seems to be fully synonymous with *kurne*. These words are nominals and can be used attributively or predicatively, but not adverbially. Therefore a sentence like *X mwarre mpwareke* means 'X did something good', not 'X did (something) well' (see also example (13)).

BIG and SMALL are *(a)kngerre* and *(a)kweke*:

(51) *Kngwelye kweke re   ingkerne mangke-ke; kngerre anteme.*
     dog   small 3SG:S behind   grow-PC   big   now
     'The little dog grew up back there; it was big now.'

As mentioned above, *kngerre* can occasionally substitute for 'much' or 'very'. *Kweke ware* 'only (a) little' is used adjectivally or adverbially as a hedge, or quantificationally to mean 'just a little bit' (Wilkins 1989:362–363).

11.9 Concluding Remarks

It must be borne in mind that this enterprise is premised on a chain of hypotheses that are in the process of being questioned and tested. Unlike most people who propose semantic primitives, Wierzbicka clearly articulated a means by which one could identify the semantic primitives for a particular language. This method was to use the natural language under investigation to continuously create reductive definitional paraphrases that were (semi-)substitutable *salve significatione* (and perhaps *salva veritate*) for the definiendum, and which were constructed according to strict, largely Aristotelian, rules of definition (e.g. avoid obscurity, make sure the correct genus has been identified, make sure the definition applies neither too broadly nor too narrowly, etc.). This would eventually lead to a base set of elements which could not be defined any further without contravening the established principles of definition. This base set is the set of semantic primitives for that language. It is an empirical question whether or not, using this method, all languages would end up with the same number of primitives, and whether these primitives would be semantically equivalent across languages. Thus, it remains to be shown that the base set of elements that would be determined by applying these methods to Mparntwe Arrernte would be the same as the set of elements discussed in this paper, and summarised in the accompanying table (see Appendix).

The hypothesis on which the present volume is founded is that, if we find the set of primitives for one language (English), then the set of primitives in other languages will be coterminous with this first set, since, for Wierzbicka, there is an attendant hypothesis that the primitives correspond to a universal *lingua mentalis*. The authors of this paper have differing views on this hypothesis. It seems possible that semantic primitives could be more like phonological features: while we can identify a useful set that will help us describe all languages, it need not be the case that all languages draw out the same subset (or system) of features. Further, the cognitive status of the primitives also remains an open question for us. At this stage, it is not clear whether such universal primitives, if they do indeed exist, are a result of innate features of brain/mind, or a result of universal semiotic and sociocultural principles and functional pressures which shape natural human language (independently of innate features of mind), or a result of both innate and non-innate factors (perhaps independently or in interaction). In short, even if some lexical universals are identified, this need not be interpreted as evidence that absolutely confirms innateness and/or a psychic unity of humankind.

Finally, the hypothesis that the concepts underlying semantic primitives will correspond to lexical universals is still open to question. The NSM approach has held that syntactic constructions, intonation patterns and simple grammatical morphemes are like lexemes in that they have identifiable and specifiable semantic content. The same would be said about non-concatenative morphological processes, such as tone change in certain West African languages to signal negation, and the various grammatical functions of lenition in Irish (including its being part of the signal for conditionals). However, in the search for lexical universals, there has been a resistance to accepting these other sign structures and meaning-bearing processes as typical, or even possible, loci for the primitives, although they are under consideration for particular languages. The present exercise in cross-linguistic comparison of lexicons could be at odds with the attempt to identify universal semantic primitives, if it excludes the possibility of finding non-lexemic instantiations of semantic primitives. While there is great value in identifying semantic equivalents between languages, in a way that may lead to a useful descriptive system for cross-linguistic comparison of meanings, there is no reason to believe, a priori, that such equivalents are bound to fall within the lexicons of the languages compared. In fact, the method used in this book seems to support the identification of phrasal/clausal equivalents (basic propositional structures that one would want to phrase in NSM), rather than strictly lexical equivalents, although this is what the discussions (including our own) are resolved into. We see a need for further exploration of the utility of the set of elements identified in this paper, for producing monolingual definitions which Arrernte speakers will be able to understand (and verify or modify according to their intuitions).

Thus, the set of elements identified here are, at the very least, our best candidates for English–Arrernte lexical translation equivalents, and for elements that will appear in the basic set of propositional structures that comprise NSM definitions. Perhaps more investigation will reveal that they are truly the reflexes of universal properties of mind. Such a goal, however, seems a long way off, and need not detract from the practical utility of establishing a descriptive metalanguage to facilitate better cross-linguistic semantic comparison.

Notes

1   The majority of the examples are from Wilkins (1989), drawn mostly from natural texts (examples 2, 4, 6, 7, 15, 19, 21–24, 27, 29–31, 33, 36–38, 40–45, 47, 49, 51). Others were sent to us on request by colleagues at the Arandic Dictionary Project, Alice Springs (1, 5, 8, 10, 12–14, 16–18, 25, 28, 32, 46, 48, 50, 52), and some were provided by Arrernte colleagues in discussions with Wilkins in June 1992 (3, 9, 11, 20, 26, 34, 35, 39). We thank Margaret Heffernan, Veronica Dobson and John Henderson for their help, and we thank the Yipirinya

Council for supporting our research into Mparntwe Arrernte and for allowing the publication of this paper. Felix Ameka, Bill Foley, Cliff Goddard, Debbie Hill and Anna Wierzbicka provided useful comments on earlier drafts of this paper. Wilkins' travel in June 1992 was supported by Research Development Funds from the State University of New York at Buffalo. Wilkins thanks the Cognitive Anthropology Research Group at the Max Planck Institute for Psycholinguistics for providing resources and funding which helped in the final development of the paper. Any errors are the responsibility of the authors, who agree to blame each other for them. The following abbreviations are used: Agent (of transitive verb), ABLative, ACCusative, ASSERTive (particle), ASSOCiative, CAUSative, DATive, DS different subject, EMPHatic, ERGative, FACTive (particle), FF father's father, FOCus, GENEVT Generalised event, GO&DO go-and-do (associated motion), GRP group, HAB habilitative, HITHer (associated motion), HYPOthetical verbal suffix, IMPerative, INCHoative, INSTrumental, KIN POSSessive, k.o. kind of, LOCative, mid mid-distant (demonstrative), MORE (particle), Noun, NMSR nominaliser, NOMNEG nominal negator, NP noun phrase, NPP nonpast progressive, Object (of transitive verb), ONLY (particle), PC past completive, PERMissive (particle), PLural, POSSessive, PROPrietive, PURPosive, Question, REFLexive, REMP remote past, REMEMBered (demonstrative), REMINDer (particle), Subject (of intransitive verb), SBSQNT subsequent, SEMBLative, SG singular, SS same subject, THAT (particle), TOPic, UNCERTain (demonstrative), VALADV value adverb derivational suffix, Verb, VBNEG verb negator.

2   Van Valin and Wilkins (1993:523) suggest that *kaltye* has the basic representation 'know (x,y)', while they represent the definition of *itelare-* as 'think (x) about something (x) knows (y)'.

3   Although *antime* usually applies to events, in the following example it seems to apply to an entity:

   Ikwere   antime   alakenhe-irre-ke.
   3SG:DAT   exactly   thus-happen-PC
   'It happened to the same person.'

   More investigation is needed into the structure of this example, but *antime* seems to be modifying the person ('the same person') rather than the event as in (20). In the case of 'The same thing happened to him', *antime* would probably follow *alakenhe*.

4   Strehlow (1944:98) observes with respect to Western Arrernte: "By a peculiar Aranda idiom, 'pmara' (=home, place, conception site) takes 'nguna' [*ngwenhe* 'who?'] and **not** 'iwuna' [*iwenhe* 'what?'] as its interrogative adjective. Thus 'what place' is 'pmara nguna' in Aranda; and 'to what place are you going' is expressed in Aranda as 'pmara ngunauna unta lama?' [*pmere ngwenhe-werne unte lhe-me* 'place who-ALL you go-NPP']." Similarly, Yallop states for Alyawarra (1977:109) that "places count as human for the purposes of interrogative pronoun usage: for example one asks 'at whom?' rather than 'at what (place)'." This suggests that *pmere* is not suitable for the basic primitive notion under discussion; that it may not be exactly correct to define *pmere* via 'where'; and that *pmere* is really a strongly social, rather than physical, notion.

5   "All part–whole schemata are derived originally from physical knowledge of the world. For this

reason, discreteness, formedness, attachment, spatial inclusion, and questions of alienable vs. inalienable possession are all implicated ... Obviously very basic topological issues are implicated; some objects are perceived as cavitied (closed, potential containers, e.g., the body contains the heart) while others are perceived as biplanar or open (e.g., arms have hands) ... Part–whole is, then, not one relation, or even two, but a whole family of relations" (Iris, Litowitz & Evens 1988:284-285).

References

Ferber, Rosie & Gavan Breen. 1984. "Asking Why in Arrernte". *Language in Central Australia* 1.14-15.
Goddard, Cliff. 1982. "Case Systems and Case Marking in Australian Languages: A new interpretation". *Australian Journal of Linguistics* 2.167-196.
Harkins, Jean. 1991. "A Bunch of Ambiguous Quantifiers". Manuscript, Department of Linguistics, Australian National University, Canberra.
Harkins, Jean. 1992a. "Are IFs CANny?". Manuscript, Department of Linguistics, Australian National University, Canberra.
Harkins, Jean. 1992b. "Throat and Desire in Arrernte: Metaphor or polysemy?". Manuscript, Department of Linguistics, Australian National University, Canberra.
Iris, Madelyn, Bonnie Litowitz & Martha Evens. 1988. "Problems of the Part–Whole Relation". *Relational Models of the Lexicon* ed. by Martha Evens, 261-288. Cambridge: Cambridge University Press.
Koch, Harold J. 1984. "The Category of 'Associated Motion' in Kaytej". *Language in Central Australia* 1.23-34.
Strehlow, Theodor G. H. 1944. *Aranda Phonetics and Grammar* (Oceanic Monographs 7). Sydney: Australian National Research Council.
Van Valin, Robert D. Jr & David P. Wilkins. 1993. "Predicting Syntactic Structure from Semantic Representations: *Remember* in English and its equivalents in Mparntwe Arrernte". *Advances in Role and Reference Grammar* ed. by Robert D. Van Valin Jr, 499-534. Amsterdam: John Benjamins.
Wierzbicka, Anna. 1980. *The Case for Surface Case*. Ann Arbor: Karoma.
Wierzbicka, Anna. 1981. "Case Marking and Human Nature". *Australian Journal of Linguistics* 1.43-80.
Wilkins, David P. 1984a. "Nominal Reduplication in Mparntwe Arrernte". *Language in Central Australia* 1.16-22.
Wilkins, David P. 1984b. "How, and How Not To, Say 'And' in Mparntwe Arrernte (Aranda)". *Language in Central Australia* 2.23-30.
Wilkins, David P. 1986. "Particle/Clitics for Criticism and Complaint in Mparntwe Arrernte (Aranda)". *Journal of Pragmatics* 10.575-596.
Wilkins, David P. 1988. "Switch-Reference in Mparntwe Arrernte (Aranda): Form, function, and problems of identity". *Complex Sentence Constructions in Australian Languages* ed. by Peter Austin, 141-176. Amsterdam: John Benjamins.

Wilkins, David P. 1989. *Mparntwe Arrernte: Studies in the structure and semantics of grammar*. PhD Thesis, Department of Linguistics, Australian National University, Canberra.

Wilkins, David P. 1991. "The Semantics, Pragmatics and Diachronic Development of Associated Motion in Mparntwe Arrernte". *Buffalo Papers in Linguistics* 91.207-257.

Wilkins, David P. 1992a. "Interjections as Deictics". *Journal of Pragmatics* 16.119-158.

Wilkins, David P. 1992b. "The Linguistic Manifestations of the Bond Between Kinship, Land, and Totemism in Mparntwe Arrernte (Aranda)". *Center for Cognitive Science Technical Report*, State University at Buffalo (92-13).

Yallop, Colin. 1977. *Alyawarra: An Aboriginal language of Central Australia*. Canberra: Australian Institute of Aboriginal Studies.

Appendix: Summary of Proposed Equivalents

Proposed primitive	Most likely equivalent(s)	Other possible equivalents
I	*ayenge* (S,O); *the* (A)	
YOU	*unte* (S,A); *nge-nhe* (O)	
SOMETHING	*arne* 'thing; tree, stick' (artefact classifier)	*iwenhe* 'what?'
SOMEONE	*tyerrtye* 'person, body' (orig. 'skin') *tyerrtye arrpenhe* 'other person'	*ngwenhe* 'who?' *arrpenhe* 'other'
KNOW	*kaltye* 'be knowledgeable of; wise, learned'	*itelare-* 'know, remember' (orig. 'see with throat')
THINK	*itirre-* (orig. 'throat happen/become')	
FEEL	*awelhe-* (orig. 'hear-REFL-')	
SAY	*angke-*	
WANT	*ahentye* (also 'throat')	
THIS	*nhenhe* (also 'here')	*alakenhe* 'thus, like so' (i.e. with events/states)
ONE	*nyente* (also used for indefinite article; 'alone'; 'do on one's own'; 'one and the same')	
TWO	*therre* (also used as binary coordinate conjunction)	
SAME	?	*nyente* 'one' (nouns) *rante(-rante)* 'same characteristics' *(-)anteye/antime* (verbs) *alakenhe(-antime)* (verbs)
OTHER	*arrpenhe* (orig. 'on one's own/self-ACC')	
ALL	*ingkirreke*	
MUCH/MANY	*arunthe*	*mape* (plural group)

HAPPEN	(-)irre- (inchoative suffix)	
DO	mpware- 'make, do'	
	(-)ile- (causative suffix)	
NO/NOT	arrangkwe (also 'nothing'; 'be without something')	NP-kwenye (privative)
		V-tyekenhe (verb negator)
IF	peke 'might, maybe'; 'if' with a dependent event	V-mere (hypothetical)
CAN/COULD	?	peke 'might, maybe' (basic declarative syntax with assertive intonation)
		V-mere (hypothetical)
LIKE	-arteke (semblative)	alakenhe 'thus, like so' (events/states)
BECAUSE	-nge (ablative; 'from, after'; locative for dynamic events, relative location)	-iperre/-ipenhe 'after' (?switch-reference construction)
VERY	nthurre 'very, really; a true example of'	
WHERE	-le (locative, 'be at'; this form is the same as the ergative and the instrumental form)	nthenhe 'where?'
		(?) pmere 'camp, country, home'
WHEN	?	ilengare 'when?' (orig. 'what-times?')
		-ngare '(number of) times'
		switch-reference construction
AFTER	-iperre/-ipenhe 'happen after, be left over from, because of'	ingkerne 'behind, after'
ABOVE	kertne 'above, over, top (part of), up'	
KIND	?	-ulkere 'kind of; more'
		arrpenhente-arrpenhente ('other-only' reduplicated = different kinds of)
PART	?	part–whole construction
		-kenhe (possessive)
		-kerte (proprietive)
		-arenye (associative)
		kalke 'piece'
		-ngentyele 'from ... onwards'
		-iperre 'after, come out of'
GOOD	mwarre 'good, healthy, well, right'	
BAD	kurne/akenge 'bad, evil, wrong'	
BIG	kngerre 'big, much, a lot, important, loud (of sound)'	
SMALL	akweke 'small, not a lot, soft (of explosion)'	

As this table shows, there are difficulties finding good clear equivalents for the proposed primitives PART, KIND, WHEN, CAN and SAME. Of these, CAN and PART seem to present the greatest problems, and from the point of view of Mparntwe Arrernte they seem to be the most suspect of the proposed semantic primitives/lexical universals.

Longgu

Deborah Hill
Max Planck Institute for Psycholinguistics, Nijmegen

Longgu is an Austronesian language spoken in the north-east coastal region of Guadalcanal, Solomon Islands.[1] The language is a member of the Southeast Solomonic subgroup of Oceanic languages (Pawley 1972; Lichtenberk 1988) and is spoken by around 1 500 speakers. More detail can be found in Hill (1992).

Longgu is a nominative–accusative language which has head-marking characteristics (Nichols 1986). The word order is VOS, although the subject is frequently fronted to indicate a new topic, to re-introduce a topic, to indicate a contrast or to express emphasis. There are three types of simple clause. These are verbal clauses, nominal clauses and semi-verbal clauses.

A verbal clause consists of a predicate whose head is a verb, adjective, numeral or quantifier and, optionally, noun phrases which function as core or peripheral arguments of the clause. As a head-marking language, the subject and object are cross-referenced within the predicate. Example (1) shows a transitive verbal clause consisting of a predicate plus a subject and object argument. Example (2) shows an intransitive verbal clause consisting of the predicate and its subject argument. In (1), the subject is the first-person singular independent pronoun *nau*, which is cross-referenced in the verb phrase by the first-person singular subject pronoun *nu*. The object *mwelageni* 'girl' is cross-referenced by the third-person singular object suffix (*-a*) attached to the verb *pitu* 'wait'. In (2), the subject is *kisugina* 'those blind ones' which is cross-referenced in the verb phrase by the third-person plural subject pronoun *ara*.

(1)   *Nu pitu-a mwela-geni i nau.*
       1SG wait-3SG child-woman ART 1SG
       'I waited for the girl.'

(2)   *M-ara ta'e na kisu-gi-na.*
       CON-3PL ascend/get:in:(canoe) PERF blind-PL-DEIC
       'And those blind ones got in (the canoe).'

The predicate of a nominal clause is a noun phrase or a prepositional phrase:

(3) Tia   ngaia ubu-na   luma-i.
     mother 3SG   inside-3SG   house-SG
     'His/her mother is in the house.'

The predicate of a semi-verbal clause consists of a subject pronoun and a predicate head which is a noun phrase:

(4) E   luma   nau.
     3SG   house   1SG
     'It is my house.'

The open word classes in Longgu are nouns and verbs. Both nouns and verbs can be further subclassified. Nouns may be subclassified into: (a) common nouns; (b) personal nouns; (c) relational nouns; (d) vocatives; and (e) place nouns. The distinction between subclasses of nouns is drawn on the basis of their co-occurrence with other noun phrase constituents, their ability to function as object of a simple prepositional phrase and their ability to function as predicate head of a semi-verbal clause.

Verbs can be subclassified on the basis of their primary valency and of the valency-changing processes they may undergo. On this basis there are four types of verb found in Longgu. These are: (a) verbs that have only a transitive form, consisting of a verb root and an object suffix (e.g. *zaia* 'know it'); (b) verbs that have both a transitive and intransitive form (e.g. *kalea* 'to happen to him/her/it', *kale* 'to happen'); (c) verbs that are intransitive and can be transitivised by means of a transitive suffix and object suffix (e.g. *bere* 'to look', *berengia* 'to see him/her/it'); and (d) verbs that are only intransitive (e.g. *una* 'do/be in the manner, thusly').

12.1 Substantives

The substantives I, YOU, SOMEONE, SOMETHING and PEOPLE all have exponents in Longgu. I and YOU correspond to the independent pronouns *nau* and *oe* respectively. Independent pronouns may function as subject, object or in possessive constructions. In examples (5) and (6) the independent pronouns function as subject or object. As noted in the introduction, subject and object are cross-referenced within the verb phrase.

(5) Nau nu   tali lae va'i-ni-o   i   oe.
     1SG 1SG   want go   COMIT-TRS-2SG   ART 2SG
     'I want to go with you.'

(6)   *Oe   o   tali   lae   va'i-ni-a.*
       2SG 2SG want go   COMIT-TRS-3SG
       'You want to go with him/her.'

(7)   *Nu tali bere-ngi-a   vua   nau-i   i   nau.*
       1SG want see-TRS-3SG grandparent 1SG-SG ART 1SG
       'I want to see my grandfather/grandmother.'

There are two candidates for SOMEONE: *te 'inoni* 'one person' and *te uta'a* 'one person'. Both are compounds consisting of the numeral *te'e/te* 'one' and a head noun. At first glance it seems that *te 'inoni* is the better candidate as it is this phrase that is elicited for the canonical sentence 'I saw someone' (see (8)). However the evidence, presented below suggests that *te uta'a* is the better exponent of SOMEONE. As both the candidates are compound terms, I will first discuss the range of use of the head noun, and then explain the function of *te'e/te* 'one' in the phrase.

(8)   *Nu bere-ngi-a   te   'inoni.*
       1SG see-TRS-3SG one   person
       'I saw someone.'

One argument for choosing *uta'a* rather than *'inoni* is that *'inoni* is restricted in its meaning to humans, whereas *uta'a* can refer to the idea of 'God' as well as humans. Moreover *uta'a* tends to be used to refer to 'unknown someones'. And one can speak of:

(9)   *'inoni ni   komu-gi*
       person LIG village-PL
       'village people'

but not:

(10)   ** uta'a ni   komu-gi*
        person LIG village-PL
        'village someones'

Uta'a 'person' is used when a speaker wants to attract someone's/anyone's attention, but not somebody in particular:

(11)   *Te uta'a ge   la mai   ni   zanga-u.*
        one person OBL go hither PURP help-1SG
        'Someone must come to help me.'

To this point I have discussed *uta'a* and *'inoni* without reference to the numeral *te/te'e* which precedes it. Noun phrases are marked for number by either the singular clitic *-i* or the plural clitic *-gi*. The clitic occurs at the end of the noun phrase and has scope over the entire noun phrase. The singular clitic *-i* is attached to noun phrases where the head denotes a specific, single entity. In example (12), the head nouns *niu* 'coconut' and *alu* 'workplace' are preceded by the numeral *te'e/te* 'one'. However the singular clitic is not attached to the head noun as *te'e/te* does not refer to one specific coconut or workplace, but has the meaning 'any'. By contrast, in (13) the singular clitic is attached to the head noun *niu* 'coconut', which is also preceded by *te* 'one', because it does refer to a single, specific entity:

(12) *Geni   ni   Nangali   oe,   amerua   geni   ni*
     woman LIG Nangali 2SG, 1DU:EX woman LIG
     Bwabwasu-gi   ami   se   puku-a   te   niu
     Bwabwasu-PL 1PL:EX NEG know-3SG one coconut
     ma   te   alu.
     CON one workplace
     'You are a Nangali woman, we two are Bwabwasu women, we don't know **any** coconut (trees) and **any** workplace.' (Implying: 'We don't own any land here and it's difficult for us to collect coconuts and get food here.')

(13) *M-arua   bere-ngi-a   te   niu-i.*
     CON-3DU see-TRS-3SG one coconut-SG
     'And they (both) saw **one** coconut tree.'

Thus *te* can be used to refer to either 'one' or to 'some/any'. The function of *te* in the compound *te uta'a* is therefore not to specify one particular person but to express the meaning 'some/any'. I conclude, therefore, that the exponent of SOMEONE in Longgu is the compound term *te uta'a*.

In addition, an interrogative *te* 'who' is found in Longgu:

(14) *Te   hou   nene?*
     who thither DEIC
     'Who is this?'

The exponent of SOMETHING is also a compound term (*te maa*) consisting of the numeral *te/te'e* 'one' and a head noun (*maa* 'thing'). In some cases (e.g. in (47)) the noun *maa* 'thing' can be translated as the English word *something* but, on the basis of the difference in the range of use of *maa* and *te maa*, I would argue that it is the compound term rather than the noun itself that corresponds to the primitive SOMETHING. As (47) shows, when *maa* 'thing' is modified by an adjective then it can be glossed as 'something' (e.g. something big, something bad) but if there is no modifiying adjective in the noun phrase then it can only be glossed as 'thing'. As (15) shows the canonical sentence elicited *te maa* and not *maa*:

(15) *Nu bere-ngi-a te maa wei i nihou.*
1SG see-TRS-3SG one thing where LOC DEIC
'I saw something over there.'

The function of *te'e/te* 'one, some/any' in the term *te maa* is the same as the function of *te'e/te* discussed in relation to SOMEONE. It refers to a specific, single entity when there is a singular clitic attached to the head noun and is non-specific when there is no clitic attached.

There is also an interrogative noun *tai* 'what':

(16) *Tai hou nene?*
what thither DEIC
'What is this?'

12.2 Mental Predicates

In Longgu the intransitive verb *hanahana* means 'to be thinking' and its transitive counterpart *hana-a* means 'to think of him/her', most commonly in the sense of 'to miss him/her, be worried about him/her'. However this verb is never used in the sense of 'to cross one's mind, to occur to', which is the sense of the English word *think* which is intended to correspond to THINK. For this, the intransitive verb *una* 'thusly' is used. While *una* 'thusly' was elicited in the canonical sentences the central meaning of the word is not 'think, cross one's mind'. Rather *una* reports what has gone through someone's mind just as it introduces direct speech (see discussion of SAY below). It would seem more satisfactory if the semantic primitive (in this case THINK) corresponded to the central meaning of a lexical item. This is not always the case.

(17) *A lahulahu-i nu una.*
ART gecko:lizard-SG 1SG think/in:the:manner
'I thought it was a lizard.' (Literally, 'A lizard I thought.')

(18) *E ani-a na ra'o nu una.*
3SG eat-3SG PERF maybe 1SG think/in:the:manner
'I think she has eaten it.'

Note that in example (18) the post-head modifier *ra'o* 'maybe, perhaps' is present, encapsulating the notion of doubt that is also conveyed by the English verb *think*. The use of *una* to express 'think' in sentences such as (17) and (18) and to introduce direct speech shows a clear link between expressing thought and speech in

Longgu.

SAY is expressed by the transitive verb *ili-a*. Although it is grammatically more complex than the intransitive verb *una* (which is used to introduce direct speech) it is nonetheless semantically closer to SAY. The verb *ili-a* may take either an object NP or a complement. Its range of meaning includes the English speech act verbs *say*, *tell* and *report*. When it expresses the meaning 'say, tell' and takes an object NP rather than a complement, it must also take a dative preposition. The person to whom the thing is said is cross-referenced on the dative preposition; the thing told is cross-referenced on the verb.

(19)   *M-o*   *ili-a*   *wini-u*   *bola-i.*
        CON-2SG say-3SG DAT-1SG jump-NOM
        'And you told me to jump.'

(20)   *Nu ili-a*   *a*   *vali*   *e*   *tihi*   *la*   *mai.*
        1SG say-3SG ART rayfish 3SG first go hither
        'I said that the rayfish came first.'

The primitive KNOW has two exponents, *zai-a* and *puku-a*. These are allolexes. Both are transitive verbs which may take either an object NP or a complement. The verb *zai-a* is found more frequently in narrative texts but *puku-a* seems to be more commonly used by younger speakers. However, at this stage, I can find no semantic difference between the two.

(21)   *Nu puku-a*   *mola*   *i*   *eve*   *e*   *la*   *vu ei.*
        1SG know-3SG just LOC where 3SG go to there
        'I know where he went.'

(22)   *Lahou zai-a*   *e*   *mae ngaia umou-i*
        then know-3SG 3SG die 3SG giant-SG
        burunga-na-i-na.
        spouse-3SG-SG-DEIC
        'His spouse then knows that the giant is dead.'

The allolexy of *zai-a* and *puku-a* is perhaps best shown by an example where both verbs are used. Note that *puku-a* is found in a negative clause while *zai-a* is found in an affirmative clause. This difference is not uncommon, but it does not appear to result from a semantic difference between the two verbs. As far as I can ascertain, the one may always be substitutable for the other.

(23) *Te hou e se puku-o 'ua mole*
who thither 3SG NEG know-2SG CONT all
'inoni ara zai-o na'a.
person 3PL know-2SG PERF
'Who doesn't know you yet, everybody knows you now.'

The exponent of FEEL is the transitive verb *vadangi-a*. Its use is not restricted to the sense of touch, or to physical sensations such as hunger. However a slightly different grammatical construction is used if one wishes to express 'feel an emotion' rather than 'feel a physical sensation'.

The adjectives *meta* 'good' and *ta'a* 'bad' may function as sentential complements of *vadangi-a* 'feel it' or as verbal modifiers. When *meta* 'good' and *ta'a* 'bad' modify the verb, the meaning 'I feel good' or 'I feel bad' is expressed (see section 12.8 for discussion of GOOD and BAD). A verbal modifier is either a verb, adjective or adverb. The verbal modifier always has an adverbial function.

(24) *Nu vadangi meta.*
1SG feel good
'I feel good.'

(25) *Nu vadangi ta'a.*
1SG feel bad
'I feel bad.'

The sentential complements express the meaning 'that it is good', 'that it is bad'. When *ta'a* is the head of the complement clause it can only express that something has been touched, whereas *meta* can express both that something has been touched (e.g. 'the shape of the canoe is good', 'the weave of the basket is even') or that a situation is good.

(26) *Nu vadangi-a e ta'a.*
1SG feel-3SG 3SG bad
'I feel that it is bad.'

(27) *Nu vadangi-a e meta.*
1SG feel-3SG 3SG good
'I feel that it is good.'

When a physical sensation is felt, then it is expressed as the object or complement of the verb:

(28)   *Nu   vadangi-a   nununu-i,   e   kasukasu 'ua.*
       1SG feel-3SG   earthquake-NOM 3SG   shake   CONT
       'I feel the earthquake, it's still shaking.'

There are two words in Longgu which correspond to WANT. These are the transitive verb *ngao-a* and the adverb *tali*. The adverb *tali* appears to be the better exponent. It can only be followed by a verb and thus is used to express wanting actions, events and states of affairs rather than things. When *ngao-a* takes a complement rather than an object noun phrase (as in (31)) then it can also express wanting actions, events and states of affairs, but this is more marked. In addition *ngao-a* expresses the notion of needing as well as wanting something. In eliciting canonical sentences it was always *tali* rather than *ngao-a* that was given (see (29) and (30)).

(29)   *Nu   tali   la   va'i-ni-o.*
       1SG want go   COMIT-TRS-2SG
       'I want to go with you.'

(30)   *Nu   tali   bere-ngi-a   vua   nau-i.*
       1SG want see-TRS-3SG   grandparent 1SG-SG
       'I want to see my grandparent.'

(31)   *Nu   se   ngao-a   zuala-i.*
       1SG NEG want-3SG   stand-NOM
       'I don't want to stand.'

(32)   *Nu   ngao-a   nene.*
       1SG want-3SG   DEIC
       'I want/need this.'

12.3   Determiners and Quantifiers

The proximal deictic *nene* corresponds to THIS. Deictics may refer to both spatial and temporal deixis — thus *nene* expresses 'now' as well as 'here'. In a noun phrase, deictics follow the head noun and specify the referent of that noun:

(33)   boo   nene
       pig   DEIC
       'this pig'

Deictics may also function as the head of a noun phrase and form the subject or predicate of a nominal clause:

(34) *Nene u'unu ni vao-pera-i nina.*
DEIC story LIG weave-basket-NOM DEIC
'This is that story of basket weaving.'

(35) *Bere-ngi-a ga nene.*
look-TRS-3SG ANT DEIC
'Look at this (one).'

The intransitive verb *zada* appears to be the best exponent of THE SAME — although *liva'a-na* 'like this, as though' was given when the canonical sentences were elicited. The fact that the same form can be elicited for two primitives (i.e. THE SAME and LIKE) raises some interesting problems, especially in light of the fact that another word (*zada*) already exists for one of them.

(36) *E zada mola, e se ve'ete.*
3SG same just, 3SG NEG different
'It's just the same, it is no different.'

(37) *Nu tali goni-a ge liva'a-na.*
1SG want do-3SG OBL like-3SG
'I want to do the same/like that.'

As the gloss of (37) shows, I think the canonical sentence accounts for the elicitation of *liva'a-na* rather than *zada* because the English sentence is ambiguous: to do the same thing is to do like that, or in the same way.

Eliciting an exponent for OTHER raised a methodological problem. Using the canonical sentences to disambiguate the primitive from the range of uses of its exponent in English was not always sufficient. The intransitive verb *ve'ete* 'different, other, not the same' is the lexeme which Longgu speakers consider to correspond to the English word *other* (which is, after all, what the canonical sentences are eliciting). It is an antonym of *zada* 'same'.

(38) *Amerua 'inoni ni komu ve'ete-gi*
1DU:EX person LIG village other-PL
amerua se zai-a te maa ina.
1DU:EX NEG know-3SG one thing there
'We two are people of another village, we two don't know anything there.'

The English word *other* has two senses. It can be used in the sense of 'other, different' (as it is in the gloss of example (38)), or it can be used in the sense of 'other, in addition'. The English sentence in (39) is ambiguous between these two readings although it is only the 'other, in addition' sense that is intended by OTHER.

In the following example, the Longgu speaker must choose between *ve'ete* and the general modifier *lou* 'also, in addition, again, other':

(39) *Nu   bere-ngi-o   va'i-ni-a   rua*
       1SG see-TRS-2SG   COMIT-TRS-3SG two
       'inoni-gi   lou.
       person-PL other/in:addition
       'I saw you with two other people/two people in addition to you.'

To use *ve'ete* can only mean 'two people who were of a different kind'. For example, you (a Longgu speaker) and two Europeans, or you (a Longgu speaker) and two people from another part of Solomon Islands.

Thus there is an exponent of OTHER in Longgu (*lou* 'other, in addition') but it is not a straightforward task to elicit it even using canonical sentences. The problem is that the English word *other* covers a wider range of meaning than the primitive. It is clear that even with canonical sentences it is very difficult to separate the meaning of the English word from the semantic primitive which it represents.

There is no problem with TWO, which is expressed in Longgu by *rua*. In the following example the object suffix (*-a* 3SG) does not agree in number with the numeral *rua* 'two' because the verb is followed by a complement clause rather than an object noun phrase. The object suffix agrees with the complement clause as a whole.

(40) *M-e   la   bere-ngi-a   rua   mwela-gi*
       CON-3SG go   see-TRS-3SG   two   child-PL
       ara   bweubweu.
       3PL   play
       'And he saw that two boys were playing.'

The primitive ALL can be expressed by the quantifier *mole*:

(41) *E   ani-a   na   mole uli.*
       3SG   eat-3SG   PERF all   pawpaw
       '(S)he ate all of the pawpaw.'

(42) *mole vata ni   manu-gi*
       all   type LIG bird-PL
       'all types of birds'

As examples (41) and (42) show, *mole* can refer to all of one thing, as in (41), or all of a group of things, as in (42). It can precede nouns with animate or inanimate referents. There is another candidate for ALL — this is *sosoko* which is classed as a general quantifier. *Sosoko* 'all' is not classed with other quantifiers because of its position in relation to the head noun and because it is the only quantifier which occurs in a noun phrase whose head is an independent pronoun (see (43)). In addition, unlike other quantifiers it appears to function as a verbal modifer within the structure of the verb (see (44)).

(43)   *Gira   sosoko   ara   la-u   masu'u.*
        3PL   all   3PL   go-to bush
        'They all went to the bush.'

(44)   *E   wate-sosoko-ra   gale-na   geni-gi.*
        3SG give-all-3PL   child-3SG woman-PL
        'He gave away all his daughters.'

Sosoko is more restricted in its use than *mole* as it is never used to modify nouns which have inanimate objects as their referents. Moreover, although *mole* could never quantify an independent pronoun (e.g. *mole gira 'all of them'), it could be used as a substitute for *sosoko* — compare (44) with (45):

(45)   *E   wate-ra   mole gale-na   geni-gi.*
        3SG give-3PL   all   child-3SG woman-PL
        'He gave away all his daughters.'

12.4   Actions and Events

DO is expressed by the transitive verb *goni-a*. Note that in (47), *maa* 'thing' (see discussion of SOMETHING in section 12.1) is glossed as 'something' in English but that it is modified by an adjective. The singular clitic indicates that the adjective *ta'a* 'bad' is modifying a noun and marks the end of the noun phrase.

(46)   *Nu tali goni-a.*
        1SG want do-3SG
        'I want to do it.'

(47)   *O   goni-a   maa   ta'a-i.*
        2SG do-3SG thing bad-SG
        'You did something bad.' (Literally, 'You did a bad thing.')

HAPPEN TO/IN is expressed by the transitive verb *kale-a* 'happened to someone/something', which has the intransitive form *kale* 'to happen'. As was noted in the introduction, some verbs have both transitive and intransitive forms. The transitive form consists of the verb root and an object suffix. The intransitive form consists of the bare verb. Younger speakers now use the interrogative word *ata* 'what's the matter, what is it' instead of *kale*. It could be argued that there are thus two exponents: one used by older speakers and one used by younger speakers. However it also raises the issue of the correspondence between a primitive and its lexical representation. If the notion of a primitive is something that is basic (and perhaps unchangeable?), then, just as it would be intuitively more satisfactory for the primitive to correspond to the central meaning of its lexical representation (see discussion of THINK, section 12.2), so it would intuitively be more satisfactory if its lexical representation were not so easily supplanted by another lexeme.

(48) *Tai   hou   e   kale.*
      what thither 3SG happen
      'What happened?'

(49) *Tai   hou   e   kale-a   luma-i.*
      what thither 3SG happen-3SG   house-SG
      'What happened to the house?'

(50) *Tai   hou   e   ata.*
      what thither 3SG what:is:it/what's:the:matter
      'What happened?'

(51) *Tai   hou   e   ata   luma-i.*
      what thither 3SG what:is:it   house-SG
      'What happened to the house?'

(52) *Maa   ta'a-i   e   kale-a.*
      thing   bad-SG   3SG happen-3SG
      'Something bad (a bad thing) happened to her/him.'

12.5 Meta-Predicates

There are exponents of both DON'T WANT and NO. In Longgu the intransitive verb *oni* is the exponent of DON'T WANT. There are two exponents of NO which are used in different contexts (the quantifier *bwala* 'no, not' and the negative particle *se*). The quantifier *bwala* 'no, not' also functions as an interjection 'No!'. The negative particle *se* functions as a pre-head verbal particle. Example (53) shows *bwala* used as an interjection and *se* as a pre-head verbal particle. Example (54) shows *bwala* used as a quantifier.

(53) *Bwala! Nu   se   bere-ngi-a.*
      No!   1SG   NEG see-TRS-3SG
      'No! I didn't see it.'

(54)   *bwala u'unu tewa-tewa-i*
        not   story   long-RED-SG
        'not a very long story'

A discussion of IF provides a further example of the replacement of one lexeme with another and raises the same issue as that raised by HAPPEN. The exponent of IF is *zuhu* 'if', but for younger speakers the canonical sentences elicit *liva'a-na* 'like, as though'. Of particular note in the case of *liva'a-na* is the fact that it can also (and more convincingly) be claimed as the lexical representation of another primitive (LIKE). Thus not only is one lexeme being replaced by another, but the lexical representation favoured by younger speakers is the exponent of another primitive.

(55)   *Zuhu ho   uta,   na   ho   se   la   mai.*
        if   IRR   rain   1SG   IRR   NEG   go   hither
        'If it rains, I won't come.'

(56)   *Liva'a-na ho   uta,   na   ho   se   la   mai.*
        like-3SG   IRR   rain   1SG   IRR   NEG   go   hither
        'If it rains, I won't come.'

LIKE is expressed by *liva'a-na*. The form *liva'a-na* 'like, as though' constitutes a word class on its own. It is the only lexeme which functions both as a preposition and as the head of a verbal predicate. No other preposition may form the head of a verbal predicate. *Liva'a-* is a bound morpheme which takes a possessive suffix. As a preposition it functions as a preposition of manner.

(57)   *Ara goni-a   pilu-i   liva'a-na   pilu   ni   boo-i.*
        3PL   do-3SG   fence-SG   like-3SG   fence   LIG   pig
        'They built (literally, do) a fence like a pig fence.'

(58)   *E   se   liva'a-darua   mwela-geni-gi-na.*
        3SG   NEG   like-3DU   child-woman-PL-DEIC
        'It's not like those (two) girls.'

Examples of *liva'a-* in canonical sentences are given in (59) and (60):

(59)   *E   goni-a   liva'a-na   nene.*
        3SG   do-3SG   like-3SG   DEIC
        '(S)he did it like this.'

(60)   *Nene   e   liva'a-na   uli   m-e   se   uli.*
        DEIC   3SG   like-3SG   pawpaw   CON-3SG   NEG   pawpaw
        'This is like pawpaw but it isn't pawpaw.'

COULD (MAYBE) is expressed by *ra'o*. In Longgu, *ra'o* is classed as a post-head modifier. Post-head modifiers function at clause level.

(61) Ho   uta   ra'o   dangi.
      IRR rain maybe tomorrow
      'Maybe it will rain tomorrow.'/'It could rain tomorrow.'

BECAUSE is expressed by the verbal preposition *'ani-a* (which also has an instrumental function and expresses realised purpose). The prepositional object or complement of a verbal preposition is cross-referenced on the preposition. When *'ani-a* expresses BECAUSE it takes a sentential complement:

(62) Nu   se   mauru   'ani-a   ara   ngoengoe ta'ana.
      1SG   NEG   sleep   because-3SG   3PL   noisy   very
      'I couldn't sleep because they were very noisy.'

(63) Nu   angi   'ani-a   e   gumuli-u.
      1SG   cry   because-3SG   3SG   punch-1SG
      'I am crying because (s)he punched me.'

VERY is expressed by the intensifier *ta'ana*:

(64) E   meta   ta'ana.
      3SG   good   very
      'It's very good.'

(65) E   bweina ta'ana.
      3SG   big   very
      'It's very big.'

12.6 Time and Place

There are two exponents of WHEN. The interrogative *angita* is used to ask a question, and *taleasi* 'time' is used to specify a time when something happened:

(66) Angita o   goni-a?
      when   2SG   do-3SG
      'When did you do it?'

(67) Taleasi nu   lae   markete   nu   voli-a   vugi-gi.
      time   1SG   go   market   1SG   buy-3SG   banana-PL
      'When I go to market I buy bananas.'

BEFORE and AFTER can be expressed by the local nouns *na'o* and *buri* respectively. These local nouns also express the spatial notions 'in front' and 'behind'. The terms are derived from terms from the front and back of animals and, spatially, can only refer to featured objects such as a house, canoe or animal. There are other syntactic means of expressing what is expressed by the English words *before* and *after* (e.g. the verb *soko* 'finish' is used to express completive aspect and this can often by best translated by *after*). Thus ambiguity between the spatial and temporal notions need not arise as a speaker has other linguistic means to refer to BEFORE and AFTER. However, the other devices are not lexical representations of the primitives.

(68) *Te'e iola-i   ina   na'o-va-daolu.*
      one canoe-SG there front-NOM-3PAU
      'One canoe there is in front of them (the other canoes).'

(69) *Na'o-va-na   saikaloni bere-bere-a-na*
      front-NOM-3SG cyclone   look-RED-NOM-3SG
      mole vu'a'-i   e   meta.
      all   place-SG 3SG good
      'Before the cyclone everywhere looked good (the look of all the place was good).'

(70) *Ngaia e   zudu buri-na   luma-i.*
      3SG   3SG sit   behind-3SG   house-SG
      '(S)he is sitting behind the house.'

(71) *Oe   ri   ho   zai-a   vaovao tai   hou   o*
      2SG   IMM   IRR   know-3SG   weave   what   thither 2SG
      goni-a   mai   buri-na   zahezahela'i.
      do-3SG   hither   behind-3SG   kind:of:weave
      'Now you know what (kind of) weaving you do after the *zahezahela'i* weaving.'

ABOVE is expressed by the local noun *vavo-*. The local noun *vavo-* 'on, above' forms the head of a possessive construction (with a possessive suffix attached; see description of possessive constructions in section 12.7):

(72) *Parako-bubu   vavo-gaolu.*
      cloud-black   above-1PAU:INC
      'Black clouds are above us.'

WHERE is expressed by the interrogative *eve*, which is always preceded by the locative preposition *i*. It can also be expressed by the noun *vu'a* 'place', as in (74).

(73) I   eve   o   goni-a.
      LOC   where 2SG do-3SG
      'Where did you do it?'

(74) E   kale   ta-na   vu'a   nene, e   se   kale
      3SG happen LOC-3SG place DEIC, 3SG NEG happen
      ta-na   vu'a   ve'ete.
      LOC-3SG place different
      'It happened at this place, it didn't happen at a different place.'

12.7 Partonomy and Taxonomy

There are two means of expressing PART OF in Longgu. One means is by a grammatical construction. The other is by a lexeme, which is itself head of a possessive construction. The lexical representation of PART OF is extremely limited in its range of use and cannot be used to express part–whole relationships.

In Longgu there are two syntactic constructions used to express the relationship between a possessor and a possessee. These are: (a) the inalienable possessive construction; and (b) the alienable possessive construction. Inalienable and alienable possessive constructions are formed by a head noun which refers to the possessee, and a dependent noun or pronoun which refers to the possessor.

Inalienable possessive constructions are formed by directly suffixing a possessive suffix to a head noun (which refers to the possessor). The dependent noun (referring to the possessee) follows the head noun:

(75) E   se   bweina ta'e   tatala-na   mwela-na.
      3SG NEG big   INTENS footprint-3SG child-DEIC
      'That child's footprint isn't really big.'

Alienable possessive constructions are formed by a head noun and a postposed independent pronoun, denoting the possessor. The independent pronoun may be followed by a dependent noun. In (76), there are two possessive constructions: *komu ngaia* 'her village' and *tia ngaia* 'her mother'. The second construction functions as the dependent noun phrase (although within this, the head noun is *tia* 'mother'). The head noun is *komu* 'village'.

(76) *M-arua   lahou   zuala   harehare   na*
      CON-3DU   then   stand   near   PERF
      komu   ngaia$_i$ tia$_i$ ngaia$_j$.
      village   3SG   mother   3SG
      'And they both then stood near her mother's village.'

Longgu's system of possessive constructions means that, in general, the relationship between a whole and its part is expressed through this grammatical construction and is not lexically represented. Longgu speakers do express PART OF lexically, but the range of use of the lexical representation is highly restricted.

For example, *aba-na* can express PART OF. It also means 'side of' but it is possible to find a few examples where it must mean PART OF and cannot be interpreted as 'side of'. The most convincing of these are examples of smaller places which are part of larger places (e.g. Sydney is part of Australia):

(77) *Gizo aba-na   Solomon Islands.*
      Gizo part-3SG Solomon Islands
      'Gizo is part of Solomon Islands.'

However *aba-na* could not be used to express body parts, or relationships within a family. Kinship relations can only be expressed through the grammatical construction:

(78) *rua gale-na   mwane ma   te gale-na   geni*
      two child-3SG man   CON one child-3SG woman
      'his two sons and his daughter'

The existential verb (*to'o*) is used in example (79), but it is the possessive construction itself (*'ai-na ila-i* 'handle of the axe') that expresses the part–whole relationship. Note also that the sentence is interrogative and a declarative form of the sentence would be highly marked.

(79) *E   to'o 'ai-na   ila-i?*
      3SG exist wood-3SG axe-SG
      'Does the axe's handle exist?' ('Does the axe have a handle?')

KIND OF has the exponent *vata*:

(80) *Ami   bere-ngi-a   mola vata ni   i'a-i.*
      1PL:EX see-TRS-3SG just kind LIG fish-SG
      'We just saw (different) kinds of fish.'

12.8 Evaluators and Descriptors

The evaluators (GOOD and BAD) and descriptors (BIG and SMALL) all have exponents in Longgu. These are the adjectives *meta* 'good', *ta'a* 'bad', *bweina* 'big' and *kiki* 'small':

(81)　Maa meta-i　e　kale-u.
　　　thing good-SG 3SG happen-1SG
　　　'A good thing happened to me.'

(82)　Mwane　e　ta'a.
　　　man　　3SG bad
　　　'The man is bad.'

(83)　Nu　bere-ngi-a　　'ai　bweina-i.
　　　1SG see-TRS-3SG tree big-SG
　　　'I saw a big tree.'

(84)　Gale-gu　　e　kiki　'ua.
　　　child-1SG 3SG small CONT
　　　'My child is still small.'

12.9 Conclusion

In general it has not been difficult to find lexical exponents of all of the proposed semantic primitives. Indeed, in most cases (e.g. TWO, ALL, KNOW, WANT) there is a lexical representation which clearly corresponds to the primitive. However, making the link between the existence of an exponent (and, if present cross-linguistically, a lexical universal) and a primitive is clearly not as simple as finding the exponent. In the case of THINK, the evidence suggests that the meaning of the lexical exponent (*una*) is not centred around 'think' but around 'thusly'. This somehow seems unsatisfactory and it raises the question of the expected relationship between a primitive and its exponent.

The ease with which lexical exponents of other primitives (IF, HAPPEN) are being replaced with other lexemes also seems unsatisfactory, even if it can be argued that this merely indicates the existence of two exponents of the same primitive.

The other points that have arisen from looking for these lexical exponents in Longgu have been ones of methodology and, in the case of PART OF, questioning whether the primitive is targeting a range of functions that are not captured by one lexical exponent in the language. The methodological problem was most evident in the case of OTHER. Despite the use of canonical sentences it remained difficult to separate the meaning conveyed by the English lexeme from the primitive.

These problems may not be unsurmountable to deal with but the idea of finding lexical universals which correspond to semantic primitives would be all the more convincing if they could be adequately dealt with.

Note

1   I am grateful to Anna Wierzbicka and Cliff Goddard for their comments on this paper, and to Felix Ameka and David Wilkins for useful discussions on a number of issues raised in this paper and for their comments on the paper. The data comes from fieldwork carried out in 1989 and 1991 (see Hill 1992) and from discussions I had with Florence Besa and Geoffrey Besa in Honiara in 1992. The following abbreviations are used in this paper: 1/2/3 first/second/third-person, ANTerior, ART common article, COMITative, CON coordinating conjunction, CONTinuative aspect, DATive, DEICtic, DUal, EXclusive, IMMediate, INClusive, INTENSifier, IRRealis, LIGature, LOCative, NEGative marker, NOMinaliser, NP noun phrase, OBLigatory particle (mood), PAUcal, PERFect aspect, PLural, PURPose, REDuplication, SG singular, TRS transitive suffix.

References

Hill, Deborah. 1992. *Longgu Grammar*. PhD Thesis, Department of Linguistics, Australian National University, Canberra.
Lichtenberk, Frantisek. 1988. "The Cristobal-Malaitan Subgroup of Southeast Solomonic". *Oceanic Linguistics* 27.24-62.
Nichols, Johanna. 1986. "Head-Marking and Dependent-Marking Grammar". *Language* 62.56-119.
Pawley, Andrew. 1972. "On the Internal Relationship of Eastern Oceanic Languages". *Studies in Oceanic Culture History*, vol 3 (= Pacific Anthropological Records 13) ed. by Roger C. Green & M. Kelly, 103-188. Honolulu: Bernice Panahi Bishop Museum.

Samoan

Ulrike Mosel
Australian National University, Canberra

Samoan is an ergative language whose cases are marked by prepositions.[1] In basic verbal clauses the verb occupies the first position and is followed by its arguments. With a few exceptions, as, for instance, the existential verbs *iai* 'exist' and *leai* 'not exist, be absent', verbs cannot only function as predicates, but also as modifiers in verb and noun phrases. Verbs are subclassified into ergative verbs, which can be combined with ergative arguments, non-ergative verbs, which do not take ergative arguments, and labile verbs which can enter both ergative and non-ergative constructions. There is no distinction between active and passive or antipassive in Samoan. The syntax is neither ergatively nor accusatively organised. For some syntactic processes, such as pronominalisation, S and A function as the pivot, for others S and O, or all three core arguments S, A and O without any restrictions (cf. Mosel & Hovdhaugen 1992, ch. 18).

Samoan differs considerably from English with regard to which information is encoded in the main predicate and which information is given in subordinate predications such as relative and complement clauses. Quantifiers and numerals, for instance, often form the main predication (see examples (39) and (44)), because they give the most important new information. Similarly the Samoan equivalents of LIKE THIS and THE SAME are verbs which often function as predicates (as in examples (37)–(42)). This syntactic difference is closely related to differences in word class assignment. The class of verbs comprises, for instance, property words (see (15), (16), (26), (63)–(76), (78), (79) and (109)), numerals (see (39), (41), (44), (103) and (108)), quantifiers (see (45) and (46)), deictic verbs (see (22), (68) and (69)), the word *pei* 'like' (see (66) and (67)), and the words *muamua* and *mulimuli* which represent BEFORE and AFTER, respectively.

The distinction between nouns and verbs is less rigid in Samoan than in many other languages.[2] We classify all words which form the head of a verb phrase and which can be negated and combined with tense/aspect particles as verbs, whereas all words which form the head of a noun phrase and which are preceded by articles but not by negations are considered as nouns. All words which have been classified as verbs by these distributional criteria can without any morphological alternation function as the head of a nominalised verbal clause, that is, a noun phrase; compare the use of the verb *alu* 'go' in *sâ alu* 'went', *le alu* 'the going'. These verbal noun-phrase heads differ from nouns in that they can be negated, for example *le lê alu* 'the not going'. Another remarkable feature of the Samoan language is that many lexemes can function both as nouns and as verbs and nominalised verbs; for example:[3]

(1)   *le tagata* (noun)   'the person, human being'
       e tagata (verb)   'to be a human being'
       e lê tagata (verb)   'to be not a human being'
       le tagata (nominalisation)   'being a human being'
       le lê tagata (nominalisation) 'not being a human being'

These Samoan data suggest that any classification of lexical universals into categories similar to word classes such as substantives and determiners may be problematic. A further problem is that the proposed canonical contexts cannot always be easily translated into idiomatic Samoan. In some cases all proposed lexical universals of a given canonical context have exponents in Samoan, but they are not combined to render the meaning of the canonical context in question.[4]

13.1 Substantives

13.1.1 *I:* A'u *and YOU:* 'Oe

There are two first-person singular pronouns, the unmarked *a'u* I and the so-called emotional pronoun *ita* 'I, poor me'. Both pronouns have a number of allomorphs (see examples (12) and (26)).

'Oe with its allomorphs is the only second-person singular pronoun, as in (9), (10) and (18).

(2)   *E   fia   alu a'u.*
       GENR[5] want   go   I
       'I want to go.'

(3)   *E   fia   'ai 'oe?*
       GENR   want   eat you
       'Do you want to eat?'

The coordination 'I and YOU' is expressed by the first-person dual inclusive pronoun *tâ'ua* and its allomorphs.

13.1.2 SOMEONE: Ai 'Who?'

The only exponent of SOMEONE is the interrogative proform *ai* 'who' which refers to human beings, spirits (*aitu*) and God (*Atua*):

(4) *'O   ai   na   faia?*
     PRES who   PAST do
     'Who did it?'

The English word *someone* is translated by *se tagata* 'a/any human being' (cf. example (1)), *tasi* ONE or *isi* OTHER.

(5) *'Āfai e   sau   se   tasi ...*
     if   GENR come   a   one
     'If someone comes ...' (Milner 1966:243)

Isi means OTHER when it is used as a determiner, as in (43), but as the nucleus of a non-specific noun phrase it corresponds to English *someone* or *someone else*. Thus a chief calls

(6) *Sau   se   isi!*
     come a   other
     'Someone come!'

when he wants somebody to help him and it does not matter who it is. But since it can also refer to things in the widest sense (cf. (20)), it does not represent SOMEONE.

13.1.3 SOMETHING: Â 'What? Be what?, Be how?'; Mea 'Thing, Place'

The interrogative proform *â* 'what' can function as a noun- and a verb-phrase nucleus, meaning 'what' and 'be what' respectively:

(7) *'O   le   â   le   mea   'ua   tupu?*
     PRES the what the thing PERF   happen
     'What has happened?' (Literally, 'The what (is) the thing (which) has happened?')

(8) *'Ua   â?*
     PERF   what
     'What (is the matter)?'

When it functions as a verb-phrase nucleus, it does not seem to be an exponent of SOMETHING. The word *â* is, however, the same word in both positions, and I would say that it means exactly the same in both positions. The problem is that, as mentioned above, many Samoan lexical items can function both as nouns and verbs; that is, they can form noun phrases in argument function referring to the participants of a state of affairs, but they can also be combined with tense/aspect/mood particles in a verb phrase to form predicates.

Mea is polysemous, meaning 'thing' and 'place'. Usually the context provides sufficient information for the listener to know whether the speaker refers to an object or a place, particularly if *mea* occurs in conventionalised phrases, as in (9) and (10). Taken out of the context, clauses containing *mea* can, however, be ambiguous, as in (11).

(9)   *'O le â le mea e te mana'o*
       PRES the what the thing you:SG GENR want
     (i) ai?
     (LD) ANAPH
     'What do you want?' (Literally, 'What is the thing you want it?')

(10)   *Po 'o fea le mea e te alu i ai?*
       Q PRES where the place you:SG GENR go LD ANAPH
       'Where do you go?' (Literally, 'Where is the place you go to there?')

(11)   *Po 'o fea le mea?*
       Q PRES where the thing/place
       'Where is the place?'/'Where is the thing?'

Similar to (11), example (13) can mean 'Nobody knows that' and 'Nobody knows that place'.

13.1.4 PEOPLE: Tagata *(sp.pl.)* 'The people'; Ni Tagata *(nsp.pl.)* 'Some, Any people'

Tagata (sp.pl.) 'the people' is the plural of *le tagata* (sp.sg.) 'the human being' (as in (57)). Note that the plural is morphologically unmarked, whereas the singular is marked.

13.2 Mental Predicates

13.2.1 THINK: Manatu *(non-erg.v.)* 'Think, Be of the opinion that ...'

(12) Na 'ou manatu 'o se malie.
PAST I think PRES a shark
'I thought it was a shark.'

13.2.2 KNOW: Iloa *(erg.v.)* 'Know, Notice, Recognise'

Iloa means 'to know, notice, recognise something' when it is combined with nominal absolutive arguments or asyndetic complement clauses:[6]

(13) E le'i iloa â e se isi lenâ mea.
GENR not:yet know EMPH ERG any other that thing
'Nobody knows that.' (Literally, 'Any other does not know yet that thing.') (Cain 1979:540)

(14) Ua mafai nei e Ruta ona iloa mea.
PERF can now ERG Ruta that recognise thing[7]
'Ruta (who was blind) can now recognise things.' (Aiavao 1987:15)

(15) 'Ou te iloa 'ua leaga le mea lea.
I GENR know PERF bad the thing that
'I know that that is bad.'

13.2.3 SAY: Fai *(lab.v.)* 'Do, Say'; Ta'u *(erg.v.)* 'Say, Tell, Inform, Call'

The most frequently used and seemingly best candidate for SAY is *fai* which also means DO. *Fai* is used in two kinds of constructions. It introduces direct and indirect speech and combines with noun phrases referring to a speech; for example, *fai le upu* 'say the word', *fai le tatalo* 'say/do the prayer', *fai le tala* 'do a report, tell a story, make a statement'.

(16) Fai mai le tala a Tiva 'ua leaga le fale.
do hither the report of Tiva PERF bad the house
'Tiva told me/said that the house is destroyed.' (Literally, 'The report of Tiva was done hither, the house has become bad.')

(17) *Fai mai Tiva 'ua leaga le fale.*
 say hither Tiva PERF bad the house
 'Tiva told me/said that the house is destroyed.' (Literally, '... has become bad.')

In contrast to *fai* DO, *fai* SAY does not enter ergative constructions (i.e. it is used as a non-ergative verb) and does not occur in the so-called long form *fai=a*. This long form is usually used when an ergative verb is preceded by a preverbal pronoun, but it does not occur with *fai* SAY:

(18) *Na e fai mai ua oti?*
 PAST you:SG say hither PERF die
 'You said he has died?' (Tuitolovaa 1985:59)

Since *fai* DO and *fai* SAY occur in two distinguishable syntactic frames, it seems to be justified to regard them as the two exponents of the lexical universals DO and SAY. A second candidate for SAY which occurs in complementary distribution with *fai* is the ergative verb *ta'u, ta'ua* 'say, tell, inform, call' which, in contrast to *fai*, cannot introduce direct or indirect speech.[8] Being in complementary distribution with *fai*, we can classify it as an allolex.

(19) *Ta'u mai po='o fea le mea*
 tell hither Q=PRES where the place
 'ua togi 'i ai si tamāloa.
 PERF throw LD ANAPH the poor:man
 'Tell me where the poor man was thrown.' (Literally, '... where is the place the poor man was thrown there.') (Moyle 1981:130)

(20) *E le'i ta'ua se isi.*
 GENR not tell any other
 'He did not say anything else.'

Fai would be incorrect in the two preceding sentences. When *ta'u* means 'call someone/something by a particular name', the name is expressed by a noun phrase in the presentative case:

(21) *'O le mea lea 'ua ta'ua 'o le ili.*
 PRES the thing this PERF call PRES the fan
 'This thing is called a fan.'

Fai and *ta'u* do not have the same range of usage as *say* in English. Thus *say* in *He said the same* is not translated by *fai* or *ta'u*, but by a deictic verb:

(22) *Fai mai Seu e   lelei tele le mea lea.*
      say DIR Seu GENR good very the thing this
      'Seu said this is very good.'

      E   fa'apênâ Finau.
      GENR like:this⁹ Finau
      'Finau said the same.'

13.2.4 FEEL: Lagona *(erg.v.) 'Feel'*

Lagona 'feel' is said of physical sensations and emotions:

(23) *'Ua   'ou lagona le   tigâ o lo'u manu'a.*
      PERF I   feel   ART   pain of my   wound
      'I feel pain in my wound.' (Milner 1966:95)

(24) *Ua   lagona e   Ioane lona ita   tele ...*
      PERF feel   ERG Ioane his   being:angry very
      'Ioane felt himself become very angry.' (Tuitolovaa 1985:49)

The canonical context 'I feel bad, I feel good' cannot be directly translated into Samoan, because with *lagona* the kind of feeling must be specified as happy, sad, worried, angry, and so on:

(25) *'Ua   'ou lagona   le   fiafia / fa'anoanoa / popole ...*
      PERF I   feel   ART   happy   sad   worried
      'I feel happy, sad, worried ...'

If you want to say that you feel good in the sense of being healthy and having no problems, you use the verb *manuia* 'fine':

(26) *Olo'o o'u manuia.*
      PROG I   fine
      'I am fine.'

13.2.5 WANT: Fia *(adv.) 'Want to be/do something, Want that something is done'*; Mana'o *(non-erg.v.) 'Want something, Want to do something (and thereby achieve something)'*

Both lexemes seem to be exponents of the semantic primitive WANT. *Fia* is classified as an adverb, because it only occurs in prenuclear adverbial position within the verb phrase:

(27)   *E   fia   'ai   le   teine.*
         GENR want eat the girl
         'The girl wants to eat.'

(28)   *'Ou te   fia   alu i   Apia.*
         I   GENR want go LD Apia
         'I want to go to Apia.'

In contrast to *fia*, *mana'o* is a verb and combines both with noun phrases, the anaphoric pronoun and dependent clauses to express what is wanted:

(29)   *'O   le   mea lea 'ou te   mana'o ai.*
         PRES the thing that I   GENR want   ANAPH
         'That's what I want.' (Literally, 'That is the thing I want it.')

(30)   *Ou te   manao ia   ou foi   mai*
         I   GENR want   SUBJ I return hither
         ma le   mea atoa.
         with the thing whole
         'I want to return here with the whole thing (i.e. all the money).'
         (Literally, 'I want I shall return ...') (Tuitolovaa 1985:45)

Fia and *mana'o* can be combined:

(31)   *'Ou te   mana'o 'ou te   fia   alu.*
         I   GENR want   I   GENR want go
         'I want to go.'

13.3   Determiners and Quantifiers

13.3.1 THIS: Nei *'This, Here, Now' (Mosel & Hovdhaugen 1992:4.3.2.1);* Na *'This (near you)'*; Ia/=a *'This (anaphoric)'*

In noun phrases the demonstratives are combined with articles (e.g. *le*) unless the head noun is inherently specific as, for instance, proper names of places:

(32) 'o   le=nei   mea,   le=nâ   mea
      PRES this:(here) thing, this:(there:near:you) thing
      'this thing (here), this thing (there near you)'

(33) i   Samoa nei
      LD Samoa here
      'in Samoa here'

(34) Sau nei!
      come now
      'Come now!'

The anaphoric demonstrative *ia/=a* is used to refer to something that the speaker assumes to be known from the context or the speech situation. The allomorph *=a* is used in combinations with articles. Note that English does not have a special anaphoric pronoun.

(35) 'o   le mea le=a
      PRES the thing this
      'this thing'

The Samoan translations of the canonical context 'He danced like this' employs deictic verbs which contain the demonstratives:

(36) Sâ   siva fa'a=pê=nei   / fa'a=pê=nâ   /
      PAST dance CAUS=like=this   CAUS=like=this
      fa'a=pe=a
      CAUS=like=this
      'He danced like this.'

Since *nei* and *nâ* locate things with regard to the speaker and the hearer, they do not only represent THIS, but also I and YOU. The notion of 'that', in the sense of 'neither near I nor YOU' is expressed by a number of other demonstrative pronouns. In English the situation is different, because English only distinguishes between *this* 'close to I' and *that* 'not close to I'. There is no explicit link between 'that' and YOU.

13.3.2 THE SAME: Tutusa *(non-erg.v.)* 'Be the same, Identical'

The Samoan exponent of THE SAME seems to be the verb *tutusa* (pl.) 'be the same, identical', which is used when two or more things are compared and are found to be identical.

(37) E   tutusa   le lâ   numela.
      GENR   be:the:same:PL their:3DU   number
      'They have the same size.' (Literally, 'Their number is the same.')

In the suggested canonical contexts, however, we find the deictic verb *fa'apênâ* 'like that (what you said)' and the numeral *tasi* 'one':

(38) E   fia   alu Makerita   i   Niu Sila.
      GENR   want go Makerita   LD   New Zealand
      'Makerita wants to go to New Zealand.'

      E   fa'apênâ   fo'i   a'u.
      GENR   like:that also   I
      'So do I (I want to do the same).' (Literally, 'I am like that (what you said of Makerita) also.')

(39) E   lua   fa'alavelave   na   tutupu
      GENR   two   accidents:SP   PAST   happen:PL
      i   le   taimi   e   tasi.
      at the time   GENR   one
      'The two accidents happened at the same time.' (Literally, 'Two are the accidents which happened at the time which is one.')

Similarly, the English sentence *All the people think the same* can be translated in three different ways into Samoan:

(40) E   tutusa   'uma   manatu   o   tagata.
      GENR   be:the:same   all   think(ing):SP:PL   of   the:people
      'All the people think the same.' (Literally, 'The thoughts of the people are all the same.')

(41) E   tasi   le   manatu   o   tagata   'uma.
      GENR   one   the think(ing)   of   the:people all
      'All the people think the same.' (Literally, 'The thinking of all the people is one; the people have one and the same thought.')

(42) E   fa'apênâ   le   manatu   o   tagata   'uma.
      GENR   like:this   the think(ing)   of   the:people all
      'All the people think the same.' (Literally, 'The thinking is the same as this.')

13.3.3 OTHER: Isi (determiner, n.) 'Other, Someone else, Something else' (Mosel & Hovdhaugen 1992:4.3.4, 6.4.2.3)

The determiner OTHER can be indentified in Samoan without any problems (see also examples (13) and (20)):

(43) 'o   le   isi   mea, 'o   le   isi   tagata
      PRES the other thing PRES the other person
      'the other thing, the other person'

13.3.4 TWO: Lua (num.) 'Two'

Numerals form a subclass of verbs. If the counted items are human beings, the numeral can be combined with the classifier *to'a=*.

(44) E   to'a=lua   ona   afafine, æ   tasi lona   atali'i.
      GENR   HUM=two   his:PL daughter but one his:SG son.
      'He has two daughters and one son.' (Literally, 'His daughters are two, his son is one.')

13.3.5 ALL: 'Uma (non-erg.v.) 'Be all, Be (already) done, Be finished'

ALL is represented by a polysemous verb in Samoan. The core meaning of *'uma* seems to be '(be) all' because *'uma* has this meaning in predicative, attributive and adverbial function, whereas the meaning 'be (already) done, be finished' is only found in predicative function. When *'uma* is used in predicative function, it can take a complement clause as its argument.

(45) 'Ua   'uma le   galuega.
      PERF   all   the work
      'The work is finished (all done).'

(46) 'A   fânau   mai   le   ulugâli'i
      FUT   give:birth hither   the couple
      e   'uma ona   'ai e   le   tama lenei ...
      GENR all   that eat ERG the boy this
      'When the couple had children, they were all eaten up by this boy ...' (Literally, 'The couple will have children, it is all that they are eaten by this boy ...') (Hovdhaugen 1987:34)

The predicative construction *'ua 'uma ona* ... 'it is finished that' (literally, 'it is all done that') is also employed to express the notion of AFTER (see (99), (100) and (102)). In attributive function *'uma* exclusively means 'all' and seems to only modify plural noun phrases.

(47) ... *ma aso uma o lea vaiaso* ...
and the:days all of that week
'... and all days of that week ...' (Aiavao 1987:11)

If *'uma* is used in adverbial function,[10] it seems to mean that the state, process or action entirely involves the core participants:

(48) *E feoti 'uma.*
GENR die:PL all
'They all died.'

(49) *E iloa 'uma pese.*
GENR know all the:songs
'He/she knows all the songs.'

In contrast to its use in attributive function, it does not presuppose an argument referring to a plurality of discrete entities:

(50) *ua tape uma le igoa* ...
PERF wipe:out all the name
'... it (a wave) wiped out completely the name (which was written in the sand).' (Aiavao 1987:11)

'Uma does not take the classifier *to'a=* for quantified human beings (cf. (44)).

13.4 Actions and Events

13.4.1 DO: Fai *(lab.v.)* 'Do, Say'; Faia *(long form, erg.v.)* 'Do' and HAPPEN: Tupu *(non-erg.v.)* 'Grow, Arise, Happen'

The distinction between *fai* (non-erg.) SAY and *fai* (erg.) DO is explained under SAY (section 13.2.3). In contrast to DO, the identification of HAPPEN is without any problems.

(51) 'O   le   â   le mea   'ua   tupu   iate ia?
      PRES the what the thing PERF happen to   him/her
      'What happened to him/her?' (Literally, 'What is the thing (that) happened (to your father)?')

When combined with arguments referring to plants *tupu* means 'to grow', but with arguments like *fa'alavelave* 'trouble', *misa* 'quarrel' and *mala* 'disaster' it means 'to happen'.

13.5 Meta-Predicates

13.5.1 NO: Le, Le'i *(negative particle)* 'Not'; Leai *(non-erg.v.)* 'Not exist, No'; 'Aua *(imperative verb)* 'Don't!'

The distribution of the various Samoan negators is determined by their syntactic functions.

(52) Leai! 'Ou te   le'i faia!
      no   I   GENR   not do
      'No! I did not do it!'

(53) Leai! E   le   'o   a'u na   faia.
      No   GENR not PRES I   PAST do
      'No! It was not me who did it.'

(54) E   leai   se   mea   na   faia.
      GENR not:exist   any thing PAST do
      'He/she/they did not do anything.'/'Nothing was done.' (Literally, 'There is not a thing which was done.')

'Aua 'don't!' is an imperative verb. It expresses negative commands and occurs in direct and indirect speech. In indirect speech it takes tense/aspect/mood particles. The content of the command is expressed by a nominalised verbal clause or a verbal complement clause.

(55) 'Aua le   faia le   mea   lea!
      don't the do   the thing that
      'Don't do that!'

13.5.2 IF: Future Tense[11] 'If (hypothetical), Whenever'; 'Āfai (conj.) 'If (hypothetical), Whenever'; Ana (conj.) 'If (counterfactual)'

The simplest way to express a conditional relationship between two sentences is by juxtaposition. The predicate of the sentence which expresses the condition is marked by the future tense/aspect/mood particle 'â/'a (Mosel & Hovdhaugen 1992:16.2.4).

(56) 'Ā timu taeao ou te lê alu.
FUT rain tomorrow I GENR not go
'If it rains tomorrow, I won't go.' (Literally, 'It will rain tomorrow, I don't go.')

(57) A malaga tagata Lefaga i Apia,
FUT travel the:people Lefaga LD Apia
e malaga i Lolovi i vaa Samoa ...
GENR travel LD Lolovi LD the:boats Samoa
'Whenever the people from Lefaga travelled to Apia, they travelled (first) to Lolovi in Samoan boats (and then by bus).' (Leauga, n.d.:2)

Another possibility is to introduce the conditional clause by 'âfai 'if', which seems to originate from 'â, the future marker, and fai 'do, say'. The remainder of the clause would then be a verbal or nominal complement clause:

(58) 'âfai e timu ...
if GENR rain
'If it rains ...'

(59) 'Āfai 'o se pese silou, ia, 'ua uosi.
whenever PRES a song slow well PERF waltz
'When(ever) it was a slow song, they danced a waltz.'

Counterfactual conditional clauses are introduced by ana (Mosel & Hovdhaugen 1992:16.2.3):

(60) Ana timu ananafi ...
if rain yesterday
'If it had rained yesterday ...'

13.5.3 BECAUSE: 'Auâ *(conj., prep.)* 'Because, Because of'; 'Ona *(conj.)* 'Because'

BECAUSE can be expressed by several words in Samoan. Since *'ona* shows the most unmarked behaviour in terms of text frequency and distribution, we regard it as the exponent of BECAUSE. The semantic difference between *'auâ* and *'ona* is not clear. Sentences describing a negative event which is the reason for what was said before can be introduced by *leaga* 'bad' (Mosel & Hovdhaugen 1992:15.3.6–15.3.8).

(61) 'Ona   'o   le   pisa   e   le'i maua ai
      because PRES the   noise   GENR   not get   ANAPH
      lo'u   moe.
      my   sleep
      'Because of the noise I could not sleep.' (Literally, 'Because of the noise, my sleep wasn't got because of it.')

(62) ... o   le   aso lenei e   mafai   ai   ona
          PRES   the day this GENR   possible ANAPH   that
      momoe   uumi   ona   e   leai   ni   galuega.
      sleep:PL long:PL   because   GENR   not:exist   any:PL   work
      '... on this day they can sleep long, because there is not any work.'
      (Literally, '... this day it is possible that (they) sleep long ...')
      (Larkin 1967:8)

(63) ... auâ   ua   vaivai   lava.
          because PERF exhausted   very
      '(The girl lay down on the beach) because she was very exhausted.'
      (Sio 1984:21)

(64) Ou te   le   taele   leaga   e   lei   sua
      I GENR   not   bathe   bad   GENR   not   contain:water
      le   paipa.
      the   pipe
      'I am not taking a bath, because there is no water in the pipe.'
      (*Faatomuaga o iloiloga*, n.d.:12)

'Auâ and *leaga* in (63) and (64) can be replaced by *'ona*, but *'ona* cannot be replaced by *'auâ* and *leaga* in all contexts. The reason of something can also be expressed by the locative anaphoric pronoun alone (compare (61) and (65)):

(65)   'O   le tele o le pisa e   le'i maua ai
       PRES the big of the noise GENR not get   ANAPH
       lo'u moe.
       my   sleep
       'There was a lot of noise; because of that I could not sleep.'
       (Literally, 'The big(ness) of the noise (I) did not get my sleep
       because of it.')

13.5.4 *LIKE:* Pei *(non-erg.v.) 'Be like, Be as if'*; Fa'apea *(non-erg.v.) 'Be like this/that (anaphoric)'*; Fa'apênei *(non-erg.v.) 'Be like this (here)' (cf.* nei *'this'*); Fa'apênâ *(non-erg. v.) 'Be like that (near you)'*

Pei 'be like, be as if' is a non-ergative verb which takes nominal and verbal complement clauses (Mosel & Hovdhaugen 1992:4.2.1.3.11, 16.6.2). 'A is like B' is expressed by

(66)   E   pei   'o   B A
       GENR be:as:if PRES B A
       'A is like B.' (Literally, 'It is as if A is B.')

where *'o B A* is an equational nominal clause functioning as an argument of the main predicate *e pei*. Therefore, the English translation 'be as if' better mimics the Samoan way of expression.

(67)   'Ua   pei 'o   le   masina oso atu   le   tino
       PERF like PRES the moon   rise thither the body
       o   le   teine lea.
       of the girl   that.
       'The girl's body was like the rising moon.' (Moyle 1981:156)

The deictic verbs *fa'apea, fa'apênei, fa'apênâ* 'like this/that' (Mosel & Hovdhaugen 1992:4.3.2.5) are formed by the causative prefix *fa'a=*, a stem *pe/pê* which seems to be cognate with *pei*, and a demonstrative. They function as predicates and modifiers in verb and noun phrases:

(68)   ... 'ua   fa'apênâ lava   ona fai e   le tama.
           PERF like:this EMPH that do ERG the youth
       '... the youth did it like this.' (Moyle 1981:122)

(69) 'Ua   fiti   atu   fa'apea ...
      PERF jerk thither be:like:this
      'He jerked like this ...' (Moyle 1981:96)

(70) Ioane, e   leai   se   mea   faapena.
      Ioane GENR   not:exist any   thing like:this
      'Ioane, there is not anything like this.' (Tuitolovaa 1985:47)

13.5.5 COULD (MAYBE): Ono *(adv.) 'Can, Might (potentiality)'*; 'Âtonu, 'Ai *(adv.)*
        'Perhaps, Maybe'

In formal Samoan, possibility can be expressed by the preverbal adverb *ono*:

(71) Taotao   ia   mau   ni   mea
      put:weight:on   SUBJ be:fastened   any:PL   thing
      e   ono   lelea   i   se   matagi.
      GENR   can   be:blown:away   LD   a   wind
      'Fasten everything that can be blown away by a wind.' (Literally,
      'Put weight on so that any things which can be blown away ... are
      fastened.') (From a leaflet concerning disasters)

In colloquial Samoan one would use here the negative subjunctive, because what
could happen in this context should not happen:

(72) Fa'a=mau   lelei   ni   mea
      CAUS=fast   good   any:PL   thing
      ne'i   lelea   i   se   matagi.
      NEG:SUBJ   be:blown:away   LD   a   wind
      'Fasten everything well so that it is not blown away by a wind.'

Accordingly the canonical context 'It could break' is also translated by *ne'i*:

(73) Le   ipu!   Ne'i   ta'e!
      the   glass   SUBJ   break
      'The glass! It can break!'[12]

The negative subjunctive is not used to translate the canonical context 'It could
rain tomorrow'. Instead we have the sentence modifiers *'âtonu* and *'ai* 'perhaps,
maybe':

(74)   'Âtonu   e   timu taeao.
       perhaps GENR rain tomorrow
       'Perhaps it will rain tomorrow.'

The difference between *'atonu* and *'ai* is not clear. They can be combined:

(75)   Atonu ai   o   le   ala   lea ...
       maybe perhaps PRES the reason that
       'Maybe this is the reason (why the old man did not talk).' (Maa 1986:9)

13.5.6 VERY: Matuâ *(adv.)* 'Very'; Tele *(non-erg.v.)* 'Many, Much, Very'

Matuâ 'very' precedes the verb it modifies:

(76)   'Ua   matuâ lelei ona fai le galuega.
       PERF very   good   CONJ do   the work
       'The work is very well done.' (Literally, 'It is very good how the work is done.') (Milner 1966:139)

(77)   'O   le   tagata   matuâ   lelei.
       PRES the person   very   good.
       'A very good person.' (Milner 1966:139)

Tele 'very' follows the modified word:

(78)   E   lelei tele le   tama.
       GENR good   very ART boy
       'The boy is very good.'

Matuâ and *tele* can be combined. The semantic difference between the two (if there is any) is not clear. *Tele*, which also means 'much, many', is much more frequent than *matuâ* and could therefore be considered the exponent of the semantic and lexical universal VERY.

(79)   E   laitiiti tele la'u ta'avale.
       GENR small   very my   car
       'My car is very small.'

13.6 Time and Place

13.6.1 WHEN: 'Âfea *'When (in the future)'*; Anafea *'When (in the past)'* and *WHERE:* Fea *'Where'*

The Samoan words representing WHEN and WHERE can be easily identified. What is interesting is their morphological structure. The words *'âfea* 'when (in the future)' and *anafea* 'when (in the past)' are obviously composed of two morphemes, that is, *'â=fea* and *ana=fea*. The second morpheme *fea* is homophonous with *fea* 'where' and *fea* 'which one'. In the latter meaning it occurs in its bare form when it refers to a proper name. Otherwise it is combined with the article, as in *le=fea/lê=fea* 'which one' (Mosel & Hovdhaugen 1992:4.3.3, 10.2.7). The first element of *'â=fea* 'when (in the future)' is also found in some temporal adverbs referring to the future, whereas *ana=* occurs in temporal adverbs referring to the past.

(80) *'â=taeao*   'tomorrow morning'
      ana=taeao 'earlier this morning'

(81) *E   toe   fo'i   mai   'â=fea?*
      GENR again return hither when
      'When will he come back again?'

(82) *'O   ana=fea   na   tupu   ai*[13] *le mea?*
      PRES PAST=when PAST happen ANAPH the thing
      'When did it happen?'

(83) *'O   fea   na   tupu   ai   le mea?*
      PRES where PAST happen ANAPH the thing
      'Where did it happen?'

(84) *O   fea   lou   atunuu?*
      PRES where your:SG country
      'Where is your country?'

(85) *'O   le=fea   e   sili?*
      PRES which:one GENR better
      'Which one is better?' (Milner 1966:134)

Consider the following conversation:

(86) E   sau   'â=fea?
      GENR come   FUT=when
      'When does she come?'

      'O   le   tausaga   fou.
      PRES the year   new
      'Next year.'

(87) 'O   fea   le   masina?
      PRES which the month
      'Which month?'

      'O   Me.
      PRES May.
      'May.'

Fea is a polysemous morpheme which is an exponent of TIME, PLACE and SOMETHING. This reminds us of *mea* 'thing, place'. Interestingly, Samoan does not have an indigenous word for 'time', but only the loanword *taimi*:

(88) Sâ   tupu   i   le taimi e   tasi.
      PAST happen at the time   GENR one
      'It happened at the same time.'

The notion of 'happen at the same time' can also be expressed by a single verb, namely *feagai*:

(89) E   feagai   lava lona sau
      GENR happen:at:the:same:time EMPH his   come
      ma   le   'aumai   o   le   mea   'ai.
      and   the bring   of   the thing eat
      'His arrival coincided with the meal.' (Literally, 'His coming and the bringing of the food coincided.') (Milner 1966:8)

In addition to *'âfea* and *anafea*, Samoans nowadays use questions formed by *'O le â le taimi ...?* 'What time ...?' when asking for a particular time of the day:[14]

(90) O   le   â   le   taimi e   'âmata ai   le   â'oga?
      PRES the what the time   GENR start   ANAPH the school
      'What time does the school start?' (Literally, 'What (is) the time the school starts at it.')

The meaning of 'whenever' is expressed by *'âfai* or the hypothetical use of the future tense, as in (57) and (59).

13.6.2 BEFORE: Muamua *(v.)* '*Come, Go first; Come, Go ahead of someone, (Be) first; (Be) previous, Former*' and **AFTER:** Mulimuli *(v.)* '*Follow; Go, Come last; Be done afterwards*'

The best candidates seem to be the polysemous verbs *mulimuli* and *muamua*, as the following examples suggest. The canonical context 'They live in X now. Before this, they lived in Y' is translated as:

(91) *'Olo'o nonofo nei i Sini, æ nonofo muamua*
PROG live:PL now in Sydney but live:PL first
i Satitoa.
in Satitoa
'They live now in Sydney, but before they lived in Satitoa.'
(Literally, '... they lived first in Satitoa.')

Here the verb *muamua* is used as a modifier of the preceding verb *nonofo*. A similar use of *muamua* is found in the Samoan translation equivalent of 'Tala was born before Felise' or 'Felise was born after Tala':

(92) *Sâ fânau muamua Tala, 'ae mulimuli ai Felise.*
PAST be:born first Tala and follow ANAPH Felise
'Tala was born before Felise.'/'Felise was born after Tala.'[15]

Finally, the phrase *mulimuli ane* 'follow along' can be used adverbially in clause initial position in the sense of 'afterwards':

(93) *Na tagi 'o ia, mulimuli ane 'ua ata.*
PAST cry PRES he afterwards PERF laugh
'He cried, (but) afterwards he laughed.' (Milner 1966:152)

Typical examples for the meanings '(go, be) first, go ahead' and '(be) last, follow' are:

(94) *'o le aso muamua / mulimuli*
PRES the day first last
'the first/last day'

(95)   *Muamua 'oe, 'ae mulimuli a'u.*
       go:first you and follow I
       'Go first, and I'll follow.'

There are, however, many contexts where other constructions than those making use of *muamua* and *mulimuli* must be used in idiomatic Samoan to express BEFORE and AFTER. BEFORE is most frequently expressed by a dependent clause formed by *'a 'o le'i/'ae le'i* 'and/but not yet'.

Before a Certain Event.

(96)   *Fafano lima 'a= 'o le'i 'ai.*
       wash the:hands and/but PROG not eat
       'Wash your hands, before you eat.'

Before a Particular Date.

(97)   *E sau Fa'a'uma 'a 'o le'i o'o i le*
       GENR come Fa'a'uma but PROG not reach LD ART
       Kilisimasi.
       Christmas
       'Fa'a'uma will come before Christmas.' (Literally, 'Fa'a'uma will come, but (we) have not reached Christmas yet.')

Before a Particular Time of the Day.

(98)   *Sau 'a 'o le'i tâina le lima.*
       Come and/but PROG not:yet strike the five
       'Come before five o'clock.'

After a Certain Event. Constructions with *'uma* 'be all' or *ma'ea* 'be finished, be already done':

(99)   *Na 'uma loa le Kilisimasi mâ ô*
       PAST all:(done) just the Christmas 1DU:EXC go:PL
       i Sini.
       LD Sydney
       'We went to Sydney just after Christmas.' (Literally, 'Christmas was just finished, we went to Sydney.')

(100) *Se'i uma   ona fai le lotu   tâtou   ô.*
      OPT all:(done) that do the service 1PL:INC go:PL
      'Let's go after the service.' (Literally, 'Let the meeting be all over, we go.')

(101) *Na   maea   loa   ona tapena   mea   uma*
      PAST finished immediately that get:ready the:things all
      amata   loa   ona savavali.
      started then that walk:PL
      'When they had got ready all things, they walked off.' (Literally, '(They) finished then getting reading all things, then started to walk.') (Asera 1972:6)

(102) *O   ia   mea   uma na   tutupu*
      PRES these things all PAST happen:PL
      ae faatoa uma atu le afa   matautia...
      but just all DIR the hurricane terrible
      'All these things happened just after the terrible hurricane ...'

After a Certain Time Interval. In these constructions an expression denoting the length of the time interval is employed as the predicate:

(103) *E   tasi le tausaga na   galue ai*
      GENR one the year   PAST work ANAPH
      ae   faaipoipo loa...
      and/but marry   immediately
      'After she had worked for one year, she married ...' (Literally, 'The year she worked was one and she married immediately ...') (Falealili 1970:15)

(104) *E   le'i   'umi, 'ae...*
      GENR not:yet long, and/but
      'Shortly afterwards ...' (Literally, 'It hasn't been long yet, and/but ...')

After a Particular Time of the Day. Here the verb *te'a* 'pass' is used:

(105) *Na   sau le tama ina   'ua te'a le lima.*
      PAST come the boy when[16] PERF pass the five
      'The boy came after five o'clock.' (Literally, 'The boy came when the five was passed.')

In Samoan the sequence of events is more often expressed by parataxis than by hypotaxis (see (56) and (99)–(104)). In paratactic constructions we frequently find the adverb *loa* 'immediately, then' and the complex coordinative construction *ona ... (ai) lea* (Mosel & Hovdhaugen 1992:17.3.4) which describe the event in question as a consequence of the event of the preceding clause.

13.6.3 UNDER: Lalo *(loc.n.) 'The space underneath'* and ABOVE: Luga *(loc.n.) 'Top, The space above'*

The spatial primitives UNDER and ABOVE are represented by local nouns in Samoan:

(106) i   lalo   o   le   laulau
       LD   underneath of the table
       'under the table'

(107) i   luga o   le   fale
       LD   top   of the house
       'above/on the house'

13.7 Partonomy and Taxonomy

13.7.1 PART: Vaega *'Section, Division, Part'*

Similar to many other Austronesian languages, Samoan does not have possessive verbs such as English *have* or *belong to*. If you want to express that a certain object has certain parts, you use the existential verb *iai* 'exist' and a genitive construction:

(108) E   iai   le   isu, le   gutu   ma   mata
       GENR   exist the nose, the mouth and the:eyes:SP:PL
       e   lua o   foliga.[17]
       GENR   two of the:face:SP:PL
       'The face has a nose, a mouth and two eyes.' (Literally, 'There is the nose, the mouth and the two eyes of the face.')

If the part is characterised as having a certain property, the property word functions as predicate:

(109) E   'umi le   si'usi'u o   le   solofanua.
       GENR   long the tail   of the horse
       'The tail of the horse is long.'/'The horse has a long tail.'

The genitive preposition indicates that the following NP functions as an attribute of the preceding NP. It is only by virtue of the meaning of both the head noun and the attribute that this genitive construction expresses a part–whole relationship and not some other kind of relationship such as kinship, ownership or a spatial relationship (see, for example, (106) and (107)). Compare:

(110)   E   iai   le fale'oloa   o   Makerita.
        GENR   exist the shop   of   Makerita
        'Makerita has a shop.'

Samoan does, however, have a word for 'part', and this word obviously represents PART, namely *vaega* 'section, division, part'.

(111)   'O   le   gogo   'o   le   vaega   tāua   o   le   malie.
        PRES the fin   PRES the part   important   of   the shark
        'The fin is an important part of the shark'.[18]

(112)   vaega   uma   o   le   lalolagi
        the:parts   all   of   the world
        'all parts of the world' (Aiavao 1987:56)

13.7.2 KIND: Itu'âiga *'Kind, Branch of a lineage'*

(113)   itu'âiga   i'a   'ese'ese
        the:kinds   fish   different
        'different kinds of fish'

(114)   E   tele   ituaiga   taumafa ...
        GENR   many   the:kinds   food
        'There are many kinds of food ...' (Aiavao 1987:56)

13.8 Evaluators and Descriptors

13.8.1 GOOD: Lelei *(non-erg.v.) 'Good' and BAD:* Leaga *(non-erg.v.) 'Bad'*

(115)   'O   le   tama / mea   lelei.
        PRES the boy   thing good
        'The good boy/thing.'

(116) 'O   le   tama / mea leaga
       PRES the boy   thing bad
       'The bad boy/thing.'

13.8.2 BIG: Tele/Telê *(non-erg.v.)* *'Big, Great'*

'Big' is expressed by *tele/telê* (non-erg.v.). In predicative function the variant *telê* seems to be obligatory, whereas in attributive function both variants occur:

(117) E   telê la'u ta'avale.
       GENR big   my   car
       'My car is big.'/'I have a big car.'

(118) 'o   le   ala tele
       PRES ART way big
       'the main road'

(119) 'o   le   leo   tele
       PRES the voice big
       'the loud voice'

BIG in the sense of 'large' is *lâpo'a*. Since *tele* shows a much wider range of usage, we assume that *tele* represents the semantic and lexical universal although there are some problems. *Tele* does not only means 'big', but also 'very' (as in (78)) and 'much, many'. The variant *telê* is found in the meaning of 'very' when it is followed by the emphatic particle *lava* 'indeed', but not in the meaning of 'much, many'. Furthermore, the plural form *tetele* is only found with *tele* 'big', but not with *tele* 'very', and the numeral classifier *to'a*= '(human)' only occurs with *tele* 'many'. We therefore can, I think, distinguish between BIG and VERY, but we must admit that their exponents are very closely related.

13.8.3 SMALL: La'itiiti *(non-erg.v.)* *'Small'*

La'itiiti 'small, little' is the counterpart of *tele/telê* 'big'.

(120) E   la'itiiti la'u ta'avale.
       GENR small   my   car.
       'My car is small.'/'I have a small car.'

Tama'i 'little' only occurs in nominal compounds and denotes small animals, plants and things, particularly tools. While *laitiiti* is used to distinguish objects of the same kind from one another, that is the small ones from those which are not small, *tama'i* subclassifies an object as being of a certain type which besides its small size has certain other characteristics.

(121) Sui   le tama'i ofe   i   le ofe   tele.
       change the small fishing:rod LD the fishing:rod big.
       'He changed the small fishing rod for the big one.' (Aiavao 1987:2)

13.9 Conclusion

The investigation of the proposed 34 semantic and lexical universals showed that 25 were easy to identify. The remaining nine seemed at first sight to be difficult, but when I applied Wierzbicka's method of semantico-syntactic analysis, almost all problems could be solved. The difficult lexical universals were SOMETHING, SAY, DO, WANT, WHERE, WHEN, HAVE (A PART), BIG and VERY. SOMETHING seemed difficult to identify, because the exponent *mea* is polysemous and also means 'place', as in (11), whereas the exponent *â* 'what?' can also be a verb meaning 'what's the matter?', as in (8), and *fea* 'which (one)?' is homophonous with *fea* 'where?', as in (87) and (84). The problem with SAY was again one of polysemy as *fai* means 'say' as well as 'do', as in (16)–(18). Similarly, BIG and VERY are both expressed by *tele*, as in (78)–(79) and (117)–(119). But since *tele* 'big' and *tele* 'very' occur in different morphosyntactic frames, we regard *tele* as polysemous.

It is no problem to identify the Samoan words for WHERE and WHEN. They are *fea* 'where', and *ana-fea* 'when (in the past)' and *â=fea* 'when (in the future)'. What is, however, interesting here and perhaps needs further investigation is that the exponents of WHERE and WHEN contain the morpheme *fea*, which in other contexts also means 'which one' (see (80)–(87)).

The only cases which I could not solve by the analysis of syntactic frames were WANT and HAVE (A PART). The problem with WANT is that there are two candidates, namely *fia* and *mana'o*, which seem both equally suitable as representatives of WANT, and that even more disturbingly, these two can be combined with one another (see (27)–(31)). HAVE (A PART) does not exist in Samoan, but we do have a word for 'part' (see (108)–(112)).

A very interesting aspect of the Samoan language is that the exponents of the semantico-lexical universals do not combine in the same way as the English-based semantic metalanguage would suggest (see examples (22), (25), (26), (38), (39), (41), (42), (73), (88), (89) and (96)–(105)). Thus the exponents of FEEL and GOOD cannot be combined, and 'say the same', 'do the same' and 'want the same' are not expressed by the corresponding Samoan lexemes, but by a deictic verb meaning 'be like this'. Other examples of a single Samoan word corresponding to a phrase in the English-based semantic metalanguage are *tâ'ua* 'I and you', *manuia* 'feel good', *feagai* 'happen at the same time'. In the case of BEFORE and AFTER the main problem is that the contexts in which the exponents *muamua* and *mulimuli* occur are limited. More often than not, BEFORE and AFTER are expressed by very different constructions. With the exception of *tâ'ua* 'I and you', this is not a matter of grammatical rules. We can translate all canonical contexts into grammatical Samoan sentences by using the exponents of the semantic and lexical universals, but many of these translations would not be natural Samoan sentences.

The knowledge of the grammar and the lexicon of a language does not enable us to predict how a native speaker of Samoan (or any other natural language) would put a certain state of affairs into words. In order to say something like a native speaker we must know the conventionalised ways of expression, the idioms and the more or less variable speech patterns.[19]

Notes

1. I would like to thank the Faculties Research Fund for financing four weeks of fieldwork in Satitoa, Western Samoa, which enabled me to check all my data and observe the use of semantic primitives in natural everyday conversation. Special thanks go to Seupule Tiva and his family for their invaluable help and kindness. I am also very grateful to my friend Makerita Va'a who always patiently answered my questions when I visited or phoned her here in Canberra.
2. For further information, see Mosel & Hovhaugen (1992:4.1–2), Mosel (1992a, 1992b).
3. Examples quoted from published texts are given in their original orthography, which often does not indicate glottal stops and vowel length. In the other examples we follow Milner's (1966) orthography and indicate vowel length by ^ and glottal stops by '.
4. Since I am not Samoan, I feel reluctant to create a non-idiomatic technical Samoan metalanguage.
5. The following abbreviations are used: ANAPHoric pronoun, ART specific singular article (if not further specified), CAUSative prefix, CONJunction, DIMinutive, DIRectional, DUal, EMPHatic particle, ERGative preposition, erg.v. ergative verb, EXClusive, FUTure tense particle, GENR general tense/aspect/mood particle, HUM numeral classifier for human beings, INClusive, lab.v. labile verb, LD locative-directional preposition, NEG:SUBJ negative subjunctive particle, non-erg.v. non-ergative verb, NP noun phrase, NSP non-specific, OPTative particle, PAST tense, PERFect, PLural, prep. preposition, PRESentative preposition, PROGressive particle, Q interrogative particle, SG singular, SP specific, SUBJunctive.
6. That is, complement clauses which are juxtaposed to the main clause and which have the same structure as independent clauses.
7. Here *mea* is an incorporated generic noun.
8. I only found *ta'u* in this function in the New Zealand paper *Le Manu Samoa*.
9. *Fa'apênâ* is used here anaphorically in the sense of 'as you said'.
10. That is, as a modifier of a predicative verb-phrase nucleus.
11. The grammatical category future tense expresses that the reported event is or was expected to happen after the moment of the utterance or after a certain point of reference in the past which is

given by the context. All tense categories are relative in Samoan (cf. Mosel & Hovdhaugen 1992:7.3).
12 Said by a woman during dinner when a toddler grabbed a glass.
13 The anaphoric pronoun refers to *anafea*.
14 In Samoan, 'What's the time?' is expressed as

    'Ua   tâ   le   fia?
    PERF strike the how:many?
    'The how many has been struck?'

15 A more idiomatic expression for this state of affairs would be

    E   matua   Tala   iâ   Felise.
    GENR old   Tala   LD Felise
    'Tala is older than Felise.'

16 The conjunction *ina* introduces adverbial clauses. Depending on the tense/aspect/mood marking, these clauses refer to the time, reason or purpose of what is said in the main clause.
17 *Mata* and *foliga* are specific plural.
18 It is the part which is given to high chiefs.
19 Compare Pawley (1991).

References

Aiavao, Tunumafono Apelu. 1987. *Maunu mai loimata o Apa'ula*. Apia: Institute of Pacific Studies and the Western Samoan Extension Centre of the University of the South Pacific and the Iunivesite Aoao o Samoa (National University of Samoa).
Asera, Teuila. 1972. "Galuega i se faatoaga fou". *O le tiuga malie ma isi tala*, 6-11. Apia: School Publications Division, Department of Education, Western Samoa.
Cain, Horst. 1979. *Aitu: Eine Untersuchung zur autochthonen Religion der Samoaner*. Wiesbaden: Franz Steiner.
Faatomuaga o iloiloga. n.d. (Duplicated survey of Samoan grammar with examples for teachers. Probably prepared by the Department of Education, Apia, Western Samoa.)
Falealili, Koke Aiono. 1970. *Olaga i se aiga toatele*. Apia: School Publications Division, Department of Education, Western Samoa.
Hovdhaugen, Even. 1987. *From the Land of Nâfanua*. Oslo: Norwegian University Press.
Larkin, Fanaafi. 1967. *O le tala a Mandy Jane*. Apia: Ofisa e saunia tusi aoga, matagaluega o aoaoga.
Leauga, Fuatia. n.d. *O lau malaga muamua i le motu o Savaii*. Apia: Matagaluega o aoaoga a Samoa i Sisifo.
Maa, Faimasasa. 1986. "O le taui o loimata". *Moana*. Apia: U. S. P. Centre.
Milner, George. 1966. *Samoan Dictionary*. London: Oxford University Press.
Mosel, Ulrike. 1992a. "On Nominalisation in Samoan". *The Language Game: In memory of Don*

Laycock ed. by Thomas Dutton, Malcolm Ross and Darrell Tryon. Canberra: Australian National University Press.

Mosel, Ulrike. 1992b. "Markedness Theory and the Major Word Classes in Samoan". Manuscript, Department of Linguistics, Australian National University, Canberra.

Mosel, Ulrike & Even Hovdhaugen. 1992. *Samoan Reference Grammar*. Oslo: Scandinavian University Press.

Moyle, Richard. 1981. *Fâgogo. Fables from Samoa in Samoan and English*. Auckland: Auckland University Press.

Pawley, Andrew. 1991. "Saying Things in Kalam: Reflections on language and translation". *Man and a Half: Essays in Pacific anthropology and ethnobiology in honour of Ralph Bulmer* ed. by Andrew Pawley, 432-444. Auckland: The Polynesian Society.

Sio, Gaoloaifaana Peseta. 1984. *Tapasâ o folauga i aso afâ. Compass of sailing in the storm*. Apia: U. S. P. Centre.

Tuitolovaa, Agafili Laau. c1985. *Ryhanapoinciana.Tusi tala faa-Samoa*. Apia:Samoa Printing Co.

Semantic Primitives in Japanese

Masayuki Onishi
Australian National University, Canberra

Japanese is a typical SOV language, with all kinds of modifiers such as adjectives, genitive NPs, relative clauses and adverbials preceding their heads.[1] It is an agglutinative language, mainly with suffixing. Cases of NPs are marked by postpositional particles.

Japanese syntax is highly dependent on pragmatics. This introduction will cover those features which are particularly relevant to this paper.

Japanese has three addressee-oriented speech levels in conversational discourse, which are distinguished by the form of the predicate in the main clause. Sentence-final particles attached to the predicate give further shades of meaning concerning the relationship between the speaker and the addressee. Furthermore, the selection of certain lexemes — including pronouns, nouns and verbs — allows the speaker a variety of expressions of respect and deference with regard to the referent (see Ide (1982) and Matsumoto (1988) for a general picture).

In addition, it is said that in Japanese a clear stylistic difference between male and female speakers is observed. Usually the choice of lexemes mentioned above as well as certain discourse devices (cf. Shibamoto 1985) are considered to be the symptoms of such a difference. However, recent literature seems to suggest that at least some of the 'gender-specific' features can be analysed simply in terms of general conversational constraints, which reflect the power relationship of the speakers in Japanese society (cf. McGloin 1991; Ide 1991; Reynolds 1991).

The above issue is crucially important in the discourse of NSM mini-sentences and the choice of Japanese exponents for certain primitives sensitive to pragmatic contexts — notably I and YOU, but also many others. In this paper, I use a somewhat neutralised version of the so-called male familiar style, with plain forms of predicates and no sentence-final particles, as the basic style of mini-sentences. In general, lexemes felicitously used in this style are chosen as the exponents of the primitives.

Perhaps one more feature in Japanese syntax needs a passing remark here. In conversational discourse in Japanese, one class of predicates, which denote the inner state of the speaker, presuppose a first-person subject in a declarative sentence and a second-person subject in an interrogative sentence; and such a subject tends not to be overtly expressed. The candidates for WANT, FEEL and, to some extent, THINK belong to this class of predicates. This phenomenon raises interesting questions about the combinability of 'substantives' and these 'mental predicates'.

Overall, I have tried to stick to the 'radically semantic approach' advocated by Wierzbicka (1991a:18-20). Readers are also referred to the set of exponents in Japanese proposed by Wierzbicka (1991b). Throughout this paper, the language of mini-sentences is based on the Tokyo uptown dialect.

14.1 Substantives

14.1.1 Ore *I* and Omae[2] *YOU*

Japanese has a set of several pronouns for I and YOU, all of which are rather restricted in use. This is so because, firstly, in Japanese a wealth of terms other than pronouns are available for self- and addressee-reference (cf. Suzuki 1976; Ide 1982). And secondly, overt reference to self or addressee is not required syntactically. Usually there are enough clues for the addressee to know whom the speaker is referring to; thus one can easily carry on a conversation without using any of these pronouns. Nevertheless the use of at least one out of each set of pronouns is reported by virtually all the speakers of Japanese (cf. Kokuritsu Kokugo Kenkyuuzyo 1981a:263, 270).

The use of these pronouns is usually characterised by the gender of the speaker and the pragmatic level in which it is used. For example, Ide (1991:73-74) lists the representative first- and second-person pronouns with comments:

	Men's speech	Women's speech
First person		
formal	*watakusi*	*watakusi*
	watasi	*atakusi**
plain	*boku*	*watasi*
	atasi*	
deprecatory	*ore*	∅
Second person		
formal	*anata*	*anata*
plain	*kimi*	*anata*
	anta*	*anta**
deprecatory	*omae*	
	kisama	∅

*marks variants of a social dialect[3]

> Two kinds of differences are noted here. First, a difference in levels of formality can be observed. The level of formality of *watasi* is formal for men, but plain for women and that of *anata* is formal for men, but plain or formal for women. This means that women are required to use more formal forms. ... Second, we notice pronouns of deprecatory level, *ore*, *omae* and *kisama*, in men's speech but none in women's speech. There is no deprecatory word in women's speech.

I basically agree with Ide's first point (except for the fact that *watasi* can be used by women both in formal and plain levels[4]), but not with the second point. To make my points clear, I need to add a few facts which are not stated in the above diagram.

First, gender distinction. The allegedly 'male' second-person pronouns *kimi* and *omae* are used by female speakers in certain circumstances. The use of *kimi* is attested among female students, especially when they address fellow or junior male students in a friendly, but slightly bossy manner.[5] It can also be used by young women to address boys or young males in the same manner. *Omae* is used by elderly women to address their children or grandchildren (regardless of their gender), and by any women (or men) to address an animal endearingly. Even *boku* and *ore* are reported to be used by female students.[6] Similarly, the 'female' first-person pronoun *atasi* is occasionally used by men in casual conversation (cf. Mochizuki (1980) and also note 3). I do not think we can simply categorise all these pronouns under the heading of men's or women's speech.

Secondly, distinctions of formality. It is a well-known fact that *ore* and *omae* are used reciprocally among male friends, as well as by a male talking to an intimate female friend or his wife. Considering that *omae* is also used by a woman addressing her child or pet animal, one might wonder why they are called the 'pronouns of deprecatory level'.

To see how 'gender' and 'formality' are coded in each pronoun, we must clearly distinguish its inherent meaning from contextual factors. In general, whether a particular pronoun sounds rude or polite depends on the context. For example, *anata* may sound quite rude on a formal occasion where the title and *san* or term for social status is appropriate; on the other hand, it definitely sounds polite in a context where the social norm is *kimi* or *omae* (e.g. a man addressing his wife). However, from the fact that *anata* is not used by a male speaker to his friend or junior unless he wants to deliberately show respect or an aloof attitude, we can infer that it implies 'respectful distance' (along the lines of: 'I know you are not a person like me; I couldn't think bad things about you') in addition to the core meaning YOU. The reason *anata* sounds rude in formal context is probably that it is too personal: to address someone who is higher in rank without referring to his title or social status is interpreted as offensive. Similarly, the reason *anata* is used by a female speaker to her friend or junior can be explained by the social expectation that female speech should always be polite. In other words, these pragmatic effects are caused by cultural constraints, not by the meaning of the word.

Anta is commonly used by a female speaker to her close friend of the same sex, and, less commonly, to her husband. It has an intimate overtone which indicates the mutuality of close relationship between the speaker and the addressee (along the lines of: 'I know you are a person like me; I know you think the same').[7]

To illustrate the use of the informal first- and second-person pronouns in Japanese, I quote some passages from a story titled *Tugumi* written by a popular contemporary female writer. In this story, the main character, Tugumi, a young spoilt girl who suffers from a fatal illness, invariably uses *omae* to address her family members (including parents) and close friends, but she switches to a polite womanish style whenever she talks to outsiders. When she and Maria, her cousin and the narrator of the story, encounter a young boy, Kyooiti, on the riverbank for the first time, they merely exchange greetings. In the second encounter, however, Tugumi unconsciously addresses him by *omae*. Their conversation begins when Kyooiti recognises the two girls in the darkness (Yoshimoto 1989:97–100; all the first- and second-person pronouns occurring in the conversation are given in brackets after their English gloss — Ø means it is zero-realised):

"Ah, it's you (*kimi-tati* (NONSG))!"
"Tugumi, isn't that good. Here he is, again," I whispered.
"Yes, I (Ø) know," said Tugumi, and then looking downwards, said in a loud voice, "What's your (*omae*) name, hey?"
He picked up Gengoroo (a dog's name) in one sweep, looked up at us and said, "I (*ore*) am Kyooiti. And you (*kimi-ra* (NONSG informal))[8]?"
"I (*atasi*) am Tugumi. This is Maria. Hey, where do you (*omae*) come from?"
"My (*ore*) house has not been built here, yet ..." ...
We were all filled with happy anticipation that we would become good friends ...
"Hey, you (*omae*), Kyooiti," said Tugumi, her big eyes almost jumping out of their sockets. "I (Ø)'ve been wanting to see you (*omae*) for a long time. Can I (Ø) see you (Ø) again?"
I was startled; he must be even more startled, for he kept silent for a while, and said, "... Yeah, I (*ore*) will be here all summer ..."

After the girls part from Kyooiti, Maria makes remarks on Tugumi's behaviour:

"You (*Tugumi*) were strange. Did you (Ø) realise?"
"What?"
"You (*Tugumi*) were talking to him just like you (Ø) always do."
I knew this from the start, but I had kept silent. Tugumi always goes back to being an ordinary young lady before men, but she had been the usual rough Tugumi, and I was really thrilled to see it.
"Ah!" said Tugumi.
"What's the matter?"
"I (Ø) didn't notice it at all. Oh, I (Ø) was so careless. Stupid me, I (Ø) behaved like *sukeban* (= a group of delinquent girls). Ohh!" ...

Tugumi's verbal behaviour with the use of *omae* is considered vulgar by the social norm-conscious Maria and Tugumi herself, but for the unconscious Tugumi it is a straightforward expression of her emotion. And it is properly understood by Maria and Kyooiti, who are "filled with happy anticipation that they would become good friends".

The above examples show that *kimi* and *omae* imply 'closeness' assumed by the speaker; the degree of 'closeness' implied in *omae* is such that the speaker can say anything he/she thinks/feels/wants to say to the addressee. But if we see the whole matter from the reverse side, this 'closeness' can be interpreted as the mirror image of the cultural constraints of the Japanese society. From this perspective, *omae* can be regarded as bare YOU. As Wierzbicka (1991a:72–78) argues, the norms of Japanese society strongly restrict people from expressing directly what they think/feel in formal social relations; to address someone by bare YOU would violate these norms in most circumstances, especially when it is done by a woman. This explains why *omae* is often labelled 'male', 'deprecatory' or 'vulgar'.

This argument may also apply to *kimi* to some extent. However, if we assume that *kimi* is bare YOU, we cannot satisfactorily define *omae* (it would be against Occam's razor to say that *omae* implies 'closeness' in addition to YOU, once we assume that 'closeness' is the mirror image of social constraints). On the other hand, we will, at least theoretically, be able to define *kimi* via *omae*, by positing a 'respectful distance' component in its semantic structure (to a lesser degree than in that of *anata*) in addition to YOU. This solution also fits our intuition that *kimi* sounds more polite, and sets more distance between the speaker and the addressee, than *omae*.

The choice of the exponent for I is more problematic, because the use of the informal first-person pronouns is much more gender-restricted than that of the informal second-person pronouns.

Watakusi and *watasi* are excluded from consideration due to their obvious implication of 'deference' (along the lines of 'you know I am not a person like you; I think (very) good things about you; I can't think things like that about me').[9]

The other three pronouns — *atasi*, *boku* and *ore* — are comparable with the second-person pronouns *anta*, *kimi* and *omae* respectively. *Atasi* implies 'mutual closeness', and *boku* and *ore* apparently indicate 'closeness' assumed by the speaker, all of which can be analysed along the lines of the argument given above. The fact that at least in certain circumstances *ore* is matched with *omae* is illustrated by the proverb *ore to omae no naka* 'mateship (literally, the relationship between *ore* and *omae*)'. (Note also that Kyooiti spontaneously uses *ore* in response to Tugumi's question with *omae*.) The only problem with regarding *ore* as bare I, I think, is its 'maleness'.

I have no clear explanation why women, even when they address male peers or juniors by *kimi* or *omae*, usually use *watasi* or *atasi* for self-reference, not *boku* or *ore* (note that even Tugumi uses *atasi* for I).[10] At this stage I speculate along the following lines: Because a first-person pronoun is used for the identification of self, it is more indicative of one's social status and gender than a second-person pronoun. In

Japan, female speakers are taught either to identify themselves with polite 'womanish' pronouns, or to avoid referring to themselves, from childhood, in every aspect of social life. Thus, for them, it must be (both socially and psychologically) more difficult to use basic first-person pronouns such as *ore* or *boku*, than to use corresponding second-person pronouns *omae* or *kimi*.

Nevertheless they **are** attested, however sporadically, in female speech.[6] To me it is not at all clear whether the use of *boku* and *ore* in such cases should be regarded as the imitation of 'male speech' on the part of female speakers. It may well be interpreted as the conscious use of more 'basic' pronouns against the socio-cultural constraints.[11]

My tentative solution at this stage is to choose *ore* and *omae* as the closest exponent of I and YOU respectively, though the 'maleness' of *ore* remains an issue of further investigation.

14.1.2 Dare *WHO* (Dare-ka *SOMEONE*), Nani *WHAT* (Nani-ka *SOMETHING*) and Hito *PEOPLE*

Morphologically, *dare-ka* SOMEONE and *nani-ka* SOMETHING consist of the interrogative pronoun *dare* WHO and *nani* WHAT respectively plus the particle *ka*, which denotes indefiniteness. (The same morphological structure is observed in the case of *doko-ka* SOMEWHERE and *itu-ka* SOMETIME; see section 14.6.)

(1) a. *Dare   ga   nani o   si-ta   no   ka?*
        who   NOM   what ACC   do-PAST NOML   INTERROG
        'Who did what?'

    b. *Dare-ka   ga   nani-ka   o   mi-ta.*
        someone NOM   something   ACC   see-PAST
        'Someone saw something.'

Neither *dare-ka* nor *nani-ka* sounds right with a modifier; a common resort is to use the noun *kata/hito/yatu* '(adult) person'[12] or *ko* 'child' in the case of *dare-ka*, or *mono* '(concrete) object' or *koto* 'matter, affair' in the case of *nani-ka*. *Dare-ka* and *nani-ka* can be used in apposition to such an NP to emphasise indefiniteness:

(2) a. *Sore wa   (dare-ka)   hoka no   yatu   ni   oki-ta.*
        it   TOP someone   other   person   L-D   happen-PAST
        'It happened to another (some other) person.'

    b. *Taroo wa   (nani-ka)   warui koto   o   si-ta.*
        Taroo TOP   something   bad   thing   ACC   do-PAST
        'Taroo did a (some) bad thing.'

c. *(Ore wa) onazi mono ga hosii.*
   I TOP the:same thing NOM want
   'I want the same thing.'

Hito, in its indefinite and unspecific reading without a modifier, means 'people/others' (usually it is interpreted as a plural, but a singular reading is possible in certain contexts; *kata* and *yatu* cannot be substituted for *hito* in this reading):

(3) a. ***Hito** wa kami wa nan-de-mo sit-te iru to iu.*
   people TOP [God TOP anything know] COMPL say
   'People say that God knows everything.'

   b. ***Hito** wa minna omae no koto o waruku iu.*
   people TOP all you GEN affairs ACC badly say
   'Everyone says bad things about you.'

14.2 Mental Predicates

14.2.1 Iu SAY, Omou THINK and Sit-te iru KNOW

Iu SAY is easy to identify. See (3a), (3b) and (13b) for exemplification.

There are two candidates for THINK: *omou* and *kangaeru*. *Omou* covers the whole range of thought which may occur in the mind. *Kangaeru*, on the other hand, only refers to a certain idea or opinion which one forms after being engaged in the conscious process of thinking. Thus *kangaeru* seems to be semantically more complex than *omou*:

(4) a. *Ore wa Taroo ga sore o si-ta to*
   I TOP [Taroo NOM it ACC do-PAST] COMPL
   ***omou**.*
   think
   'I think Taroo did it.'

   b. *Ore wa Taroo ga sore o si-ta to*
   I TOP [Taroo NOM it ACC do-PAST] COMPL
   ***kangaeru**.*
   think
   'I am of the opinion that Taroo must have done it.'

Sentence (4b) implies that the speaker formed the judgement after examining all the evidence available; (4a) is more general in meaning, including a casual afterthought without much evidence.

Omou denotes the inner state of the speaker's mind, and thus has only a subjective reading; that is, it has first-person orientation in declarative sentences, and second-person orientation in interrogative sentences. In (4a), *ore wa* is redundant if the speaker wants to indicate a spontaneous reaction of his/her mind. If, however, *omou* takes the auxiliary *iru*, it can objectively describe the mental state of a third-person:

(5) Taroo wa ore ga sore o si-ta to
 Taroo TOP [I NOM it ACC do-PAST] COMPL
 omot-te   iru.
 think-LINK AUX
 'Taroo thinks that I did it.'

Sit-te iru[13] morphologically consists of the verb *siru* with the linking suffix *te*, and the auxiliary *iru*. The *V-te iru* construction indicates either progression of an activity denoted by a 'continuative' verb such as *omou* in (5), or continuation of the effect of a certain activity or action denoted by an 'instantaneous' verb.[14]

The verb *siru* is categorised as an 'instantaneous' verb, with the meaning 'learn, come to know' (Jacobsen 1982:375–376). Thus *sit-te iru* reads as 'be in the state of having come to know', but the resultative reading of this kind is possible only in a specific context, or when it takes a temporal adverb which indicates perfectivity:

(6) *Taroo wa moo sono koto o sit-te*
 Taroo TOP already that affair ACC come:to:know-LINK
 iru.
 AUX
 'Taroo already knew it.'

In other cases, however, *sit-te iru* simply indicates a state. For example, in the following sentence, it takes an object which cannot be learned immediately:

(7) a. *Taroo wa nihongo o **sit-te iru**.*
  Taroo TOP Japanese ACC know
  'Taroo knows Japanese.'

 b. *?? Taroo wa nihongo o sit-ta.*
  Taroo TOP Japanese ACC come:to:know-PAST
  ?? 'Taroo came to know Japanese.'

Sentence (7b) is possible only in a figurative sense. (See also (3a), a sentence of generic type, where the resultative reading is impossible.)

As seen above, *sit-te iru* is polysemous; I regard *sit-te iru* in its stative reading as the exponent of KNOW.[15]

Sit-te iru KNOW can take a complement clause as well:

(8) Ore wa Taroo ga   doko ni   it-ta
     I   TOP [Taroo NOM where L-D go-PAST
     ka   sit-te iru.
     INTERROG]   know
     'I know where Taroo went/has gone.'

14.2.2 Kanziru FEEL and Hosii/-Tai WANT

FEEL has two candidates: the verb *kanziru* (and/or the noun *kanzi*) and the noun *kimoti*. *Kanziru* is used to describe a perception or impression based on a concrete experience; *kimoti*, on the other hand, focuses on the inner feeling or state of mind:

(9) a. Ore wa koo   *kanziru*: ...
        I   TOP like:this feel
        'I feel/have an impression like this: ...'

     b. Ore wa konna   kimoti da: ...
        I   TOP like:this feeling COP
        'As for me, (I have) a feeling like this: ...'

Example (9a) thus describes the quality of the speaker's perception/impression; the stimulus of such perception/impression is implied by the context. Example (9b), on the other hand, is a direct statement about the speaker's inner feeling itself.

'I feel something' can only be translated via *kanziru*. But the translation of 'I feel something good' via the same word sounds very awkward.

(10) a. (Ore wa) nani-ka   (o)   *kanziru*.
        I   TOP something ACC   feel
        'I feel something.'

     b. ?? (Ore wa) (nani-ka) ii   mono o   *kanziru*.
           I   TOP some   good thing ACC feel
        ?? 'I feel something good.'

Sentence (10b), if it takes or implies a dative NP with a human referent (X), means 'I have an impression that X has something good in him/her'.

The closest equivalent to 'I feel good' in Japanese would be:

(11) *(Ore wa)   kimoti   ga   ii.*
      I   TOP   feeling   NOM   good
      'I feel good.'

Sentence (11) is an expression of a self-contained somatic feeling rather than one of an external good feeling triggered by a stimulus. (*Ore wa* sounds redundant.) Thus, when the cause of the feeling is specified it sounds odd:

(12) *Taroo   ga   sore   o   si-ta.*
      Taroo   NOM   it   ACC   do-PAST
      Da-kara   (ore wa)   ?? kimoti   ga   ii.
      because:of:that   I   TOP   feeling   NOM   good
      'Taroo did it. Because of that ?? I feel good.'

Since *kimoti* describes the inner state of the speaker, it is not possible to translate a sentence like 'You/he/she/they feel(s) good' in a straightforward way. We either have to attach an evidential expression, or to embed it in a larger framework:

(13) a. *Taroo   wa   kimoti   ga   yosa-soo da.*
        Taroo   TOP   feeling   NOM   good-it appears
        'It appears that Taroo feels good.'

     b. *Taroo   wa   kimoti   ga   ii   to   it-te   iru.*
        Taroo   TOP   [feeling   NOM   good] COMPL say-LINK AUX
        'Taroo says that he feels good.'

On the other hand, *kanziru*, like *omou* (cf. (5)), can objectively describe the feeling of a third person with the help of the auxiliary *iru*:

(14) *Taroo   wa   nani-ka   (o)   kanzi-te   iru.*
      Taroo   TOP   something   ACC   feel-LINK   AUX
      'Taroo feels something.'

My tentative solution is to choose *kanziru* as the exponent of FEEL, due to its wider syntactic scope than *kimoti*.[16]

WANT has two allolexes: the adjective *hosii* and the desiderative suffix *-tai* (with adjectival endings). *-Tai* is used with a VP complement, the subject of which is coreferential with the matrix subject. If a VP complement has a subject non-coreferential to the matrix one, *hosii* follows the verb and the linking suffix *-te* complex.

(15) a. *(Ore wa)   iki-tai.*
        I   TOP   go-DESI
        'I want to go.'

b. *(Ore wa) omae ni it-te **hosii**.*
   I   TOP you L-D go-LINK want
   'I want you to go.'

Hosii can take an object NP with the nominative case particle *ga* (and marginally with the accusative *o*) — provided that such an NP belongs to the semantic category of *mono*, that is, it is something concrete (cf. section 14.1.2). If the object NP of *hosii* doesn't belong to the *mono* category, but to the *koto* category, a VP complement is necessary:

(16) *(Ore wa) ame ga hut-te **hosii**.*
     I   TOP rain NOM fall-LINK want
     'I want it to rain.'

The NP which has an animate referent usually takes the locative-dative particle *ni* (cf. (15b)).

Hosii and *-tai* belong to the group of adjectives which denote subjective (physical or mental) states. Thus, like in the case of *kimoti*, in (15) and (16) *ore wa* is redundant. The occurrence of a second- or third-person subject in these sentences is restricted, as in (17):

(17) a. * *Omae / * Taroo wa iki-tai.*
        you   Taroo TOP go-DESI
     * 'You/Taroo want(s) to go.'

     b. *Taroo wa iki-ta-gat-te iru.*
        Taroo TOP go-DESI-show:signs-LINK AUX
        'It seems that Taroo wants to go.'

Sentence (17a), as an independent sentence, is possible only when it is uttered in a narrative discourse from the viewpoint of an 'omniscient narrator' (Kuroda 1973:382–389). In such a narrative, the speaker can conceptually identify himself or herself with the second- or third-person subject and describe the mental state of the person from inside.

14.3 Determiners and Quantifiers

14.3.1 Kore *THIS*, Onazi *THE SAME* and Hoka *OTHER*

Kore is one of the three spatial demonstratives: *kore* 'this (near the speaker)', *sore* 'that (near the addressee)' and *are* 'that over there (far from both the speaker and the addressee)'. There is a whole set of proforms which begin with *ko-*, *so-* and *a-* (and indefinite *do-*) (cf. Kuno 1973:282). *Kono* is an allolex of *kore* in attributive function.

(18) a. **Kore** o miro.
        this ACC see:IMP
        'Look at this.'

    b. **Kono** inu o miro.
        this dog ACC see:IMP
        'Look at this dog.'

Kore/kono are used anaphorically only in very restricted circumstances. As pointed out by Kuno (1973:290), "the *ko* series is used semi-anaphorically as if the object being talked about were visible and were at the speaker's side" and not known or accessible to the addressee. (*Sore/sono*, on the other hand, are salient in anaphoric use.) They are not used cataphorically either, except in combination with *yoo* LIKE (cf. section 14.5.2, and (9a) and (9b)).

Onazi THE SAME is an adjective; it can be used either attributively, as in (2c), or predicatively with a copula:

(19)   Kore to sore wa **onazi** da.
        this and that TOP the:same COP
        'This and that are the same.'

Hoka OTHER and *betu* 'different, separate' have a similar range of meaning (the connective particle *no* is attached to either of them in attributive function). While *hoka* simply categorises objects in a group into 'one' and '(any of) the rest', *betu* focuses on the difference of quality between two objects in a group. Thus *betu* cannot be used in the following context:

(20)   Ore wa iku ga **hoka** no / *betu no hito wa ika-nai.
        I TOP go but other   people TOP go-not
        'I will go but other people will not go.'

14.3.2 Hito-/Iti- *ONE*, Huta-/Ni- *TWO*, Minna *ALL* and Takusan *MANY*

Each Japanese numeral up to ten has a pair of allolexes, one of which is combined with original Japanese classifiers, and the other with Chinese-derived ones.

(21)   *hito-ri*   *huta-ri*
       one-CL:person   two-CL:person

       iti-mai   *ni-mai*
       one-CL:thin:object two-CL:thin:object

In the above examples, *-ri* is an original Japanese classifier, while *-mai* is a Chinese-derived one. (See (38a), (40) and (41b) for other examples.)

Minna ALL functions as a verbal modifier. It is a casual form of *mina*.

(22)   *Taroo wa mizu o   minna non-da.*
       Taroo TOP water ACC all   drink-PAST
       'Taroo drank all the water.'

See also (3b).

Zenbu, another candidate for ALL, is either used as a verbal modifier or as a nominal modifier with the connective particle *no*. It can be used only when the speaker sees the object as the assemblage of specifiable parts (etymologically *-bu* in *zenbu* means PART; cf. (38)). Thus it can replace *minna* in (22), but not in (3b). It can best be translated as 'wholly' or 'all the parts'.

Takusan MANY is used as a verbal modifier, or a nominal modifier with the particle *no*:

(23)   a. *Hanako ni wa kodomo ga takusan aru.*
          Hanako L-D TOP children NOM many   exist
          'Hanako has many children.'

       b. *Hanako ni wa takusan (no) kodomo ga   aru.*
          Hanako L-D TOP many   children NOM exist
          'Hanako has many children.'

The adjective *ooi* is another candidate for MANY, but it is used only in predication; its adverbial form *ooku* can be used either in written discourse or in very formal style.

14.4 Actions and Events: *Suru* DO and *Okiru (Okoru)* HAPPEN

Suru DO is easy to identify — see (2b), (4), (25) and (36), among other examples.

HAPPEN has two candidates: *okiru/okoru* (*okiru* is a slightly more colloquial version than *okoru*) and *aru*.

Okiru and *okoru* are 'continuative' verbs (cf. section 14.2.1). Thus, with the auxiliary *iru* they have a progressive reading:

(24) a. *Hanako ni   nani ga   oki-ta / okot-ta   no*
       Hanako L-D   what NOM   happen-PAST   NOML
       ka?
       INTERROG
       'What happened to Hanako?'

   b. *Soko de   nani ga   oki-te / okot-te   iru   no*
      there LOC   what NOM   happen-LINK   AUX   NOML
      ka?
      INTERROG
      'What is happening there?'

As seen in the above sentences, *okiru* and *okoru* can take a patient NP with the locative-dative particle *ni*, or a locative NP with the particle *de*.

Aru means 'exist'. The subject NP of this verb can refer to either an object or event, as far as the speaker sees it statically as a discrete entity; if it refers to an event, *aru* can be translated as 'happen'. *Aru* in this sense can be used to describe a past event which has been completed or a future event which is definitely going to happen, but not an on-going event — because an on-going event can never be seen statically.

Another problem with *aru* is that it describes an event as something spontaneous. It sounds awkward, while *okiru* sounds natural, in a context where the cause of the event is specified:

(25) *Taroo ga   nani-ka   o   si-ta.   Da-kara*
      Taroo NOM   something ACC   do-PAST   because:of:that
      Hanako ni   kore ga   oki-ta / ??at-ta.
      Hanako L-D   this NOM   happen-PAST
      'Taroo did something. Because of that, this happened to Hanako.'

I regard *okoru/okiru* as the exponent of HAPPEN, due to its wider syntactic scope.

14.5 Meta-Predicates

14.5.1 Iya *NO* (-Nai *NOT*), -Ba *IF* and Ka-mo sire-nai *COULD*

NO has two candidates, *iie* and *iya*. *Iie* is a polite form used in formal context, and preferred by women, while *iya* is used more often in informal context or to address friends or juniors, and is preferred by men. I regard *iya* as the exponent.

(26) a. *Omae wa   iku no   ka?*   *Iya, ika-nai.*
        you TOP go NOML INTERROG   no   go-not
        'Are you going?' 'No, I'm not.'

b. *Omae wa ika-nai no ka?* ***Iya, iku.***
you TOP go-not NOML INTERROG no go
'Aren't you going?' 'No, (you are wrong,) I am going.'

NO has a few allolexes, all of which are clause negators used in different syntactic environments: (a) the negative verbal suffix *-nai* (with adjectival endings); (b) the adjective *nai*, used either as the negative form of the existential verb *aru* (cf. section 14.4) or as the negator of nominal/adjectival clauses; (c) the particle *na*, used as the negator of imperative clauses; and (d) the suffix *-n*, used after the polite auxiliary *mas(e)*.

The suffix *-ba* IF is attached to a verb or an adjective to constitute a conditional clause. The conditional form of the copula, *nara*, is the abbreviation of the old form *nare-ba*; the former is often reanalysed as the abbreviation of *nara-ba*, which is also occasionally used.

(27) a. *Omae ga ike-ba ore wa ika-nai.*
you NOM go-COND I TOP go-not
'If you go, I will not go.'

b. *Ore ga omae* **nara(-ba)** *ika-nai.*
I NOM you COP(-COND) go-not
'If I were you, I would not go.'

The copular conditional *nara* can also be attached to an adjectival/verbal clause to constitute a conditional clause; in that case, it has a special predicative force:

(28) *Omae ga iku nara ore wa ika-nai.*
you NOM go COP:COND I TOP go-not
'If it is the case that you go, I will not go.'

The perfect conditional suffix *tara*, often used interchangeably with *-ba*, actually indicates that two events are in an antecedent–subsequent relationship, not a supposition–consequent relationship (cf. Murayama (1985)).[17]

(29) *?? Omae ga it-tara ore wa ika-nai.*
you NOM go-PERF:COND I TOP go-not
?? 'If you go, I will not go.'

Ka-mo sire-nai COULD is morphologically analysable as the interrogative particle *ka*, the concessive particle *mo*, the verb *sireru* 'become known/be knowable' and the negative suffix *nai*. The literal translation of this phrase would thus be 'it is not knowable whether X or not'. But *sireru* as a potential verb requires a nominative NP as a subject, and optionally a locative-dative NP 'to someone'. It never takes a complement clause. *Sire-nai* in *ka-mo sire-nai*, on the other hand, takes a whole nominal/adjectival/verbal clause preceding *ka-mo* in its scope, and predicates a sentential topic. It has no affirmative counterpart.

(30) a. *Asita   wa ame ga   huru **ka-mo sire-nai**.*
       tomorrow TOP rain NOM fall could
       'It could rain tomorrow.'

   b. *Asita   ore wa ika-nai **ka-mo sire-nai**.*
      tomorrow I   TOP go-not   could
      'I may not go tomorrow.'

   c. *Kinoo   Hanako wa soko ni it-ta*
      yesterday Hanako TOP there L-D go-PAST
      ***ka-mo sire-nai**.*
      could
      'Hanako may have gone there yesterday.'

Examples (30b) and (30c) clearly show that *ka-mo sire-nai* is a unitary expression of the speaker's guess or imagination, and the original meaning of *sireru* doesn't fit in any way. Furthermore, in any of (30), *sire-nai* can be omitted in casual conversation.

14.5.2 Yoo LIKE, Kara BECAUSE and Sugoku VERY

Yoo LIKE is a kind of adjectival noun, which obligatorily takes a genitive NP or an adjectival/verbal clause as its modifier. The whole complex with *yoo* as its head in turn functions as an adjective with a copula, or as a verbal modifier with the locative-dative particle *ni*.

(31) a. *bara no   **yoo na**   hana*
       rose GEN   like COP:ATTR flower
       'a flower like a rose'

   b. *Kono hana wa bara no **yoo da** ga bara*
      this flower TOP rose GEN like COP but rose
      de-wa   nai.
      COP-TOP   not
      'This flower is like a rose, but it's not a rose.'

   c. *bara no   **yoo ni** mieru*
      rose GEN   like L-D   be:seen
      'look like a rose'

It has fused forms with demonstrative and indefinite pronouns, which are used much more commonly in conversation: *kono yoo na* becomes *konna*, *dono yoo ni* becomes *doo*, and so on (cf. (9)).

The conjunctive particle *kara* BECAUSE directly follows a nominal/adjectival/verbal clause:

(32) a. *Ame ga hut-ta kara ore wa ika-nakat-ta.*
rain NOM fall-PAST because I TOP go-not-PAST
'Because it rained I didn't go.'

b. *Ame ga hut-ta. Da-kara ore wa ika-nakat-ta.*
rain NOM fall-PAST because:of:that I TOP
go-not-PAST
'It rained. Because of that I didn't go.'

Da-kara can be seen as the abbreviation of *sore-da-kara*, which consists of the anaphoric *sore* 'that' with the copula *da* and *kara*.

No-de, which consists of the nominaliser *no* and the continuative form of the copula *da*, is used in a similar context. It focuses on the speaker's assertion that the event described in the main clause is the logical consequence of the first event. *Kara*, on the other hand, simply connects two events in a causal relationship.

There are several candidates for VERY. Among them, *taihen* and *hizyoo ni* are mostly used in formal style and written discourse. I do not regard these as exponents due to this speech-level constraint.

Totemo is used in a wider context and is preferred by women, probably because it has a sense of reserve which softens the effect of intensification.

Sugoku is commonly used in informal style. On the surface, this intensifier seems to strongly indicate the subjective feeling of the speaker; but I consider this impression the effect of the general cultural rule that people avoid using straightforward emphatic expression in formal settings. Thus I regard *sugoku* as the exponent of VERY.

(33) a. *Hanako wa taihen / hizyoo ni kirei*
Hanako TOP very beautiful
da / desu.
COP COP:POLITE
'Hanako is very beautiful.' (written or formal style)

b. *Hanako wa totemo kirei da.*
Hanako TOP very beautiful COP
'Hanako is very beautiful, I would say.'

c. *Hanako wa   sugoku kirei   da.*
   Hanako TOP very   beautiful COP
   'Hanako is very beautiful.' (informal style)

14.6 Time and Place: *Itu* WHEN (*Itu-ka* SOMETIME, *Toki* TIME), *Doko* WHERE (*Doko-ka* SOMEWHERE, *Tokoro* PLACE), *Ato* AFTER, *Mae* BEFORE,[18] *Sita* UNDER and *Ue* ABOVE

Itu/itu-ka and *doko/doko-ka* constitute parallel pairs of interrogative and indefinite proforms (cf. section 14.1.2). *Toki* and *tokoro* are nouns, with the meaning TIME and PLACE respectively; they can take modifiers, or can be used as the head of a temporal subordinate clause. *Doko/doko-ka/tokoro* need to be followed by the locative particle *de* or the locative-dative particle *ni*.

(34) a. *Omae wa   itu   doko de   sore o   si-ta*
        you TOP when where LOC it   ACC do-PAST
        no   ka?
        NOML INTERROG
        'When and where did you do it?'

    b. *Taroo ga   sore o   si-ta   toki*
       Taroo NOM it   ACC do-PAST   time
       nani-ka   ga   oki-ta.
       something NOM happen-PAST
       'When Taroo did it, something happened.'

    c. *Taroo ga   sore o   si-ta   tokoro de*
       Taroo NOM it   ACC do-PAST   place LOC
       nani-ka   ga   oki-ta.
       something NOM happen-PAST
       'In the place where Taroo did it, something happened.'

In general, AFTER can be translated into Japanese in two ways:

(35) a. *Ore ga   sore o   si-ta   ato*
        I   NOM it   ACC do-PAST   after
        nani-ka   ga   oki-ta.
        something NOM happen-PAST
        'After I did it something happened.'

b. *Ore   ga   sore   o   si-te*
   I   NOM   it   ACC   do-LINK
   kara nani-ka ga   oki-ta.
   from something NOM   happen-PAST
   'I did it and something happened following that.'

Example (35a) simply means that 'something happened at any moment after I did it', while (35b) reads that two events happened in succession. *Kara* 'from' in (35b) is the abbreviation of *sore-kara* 'from that', emphasising the temporal sequence (not the causal relationship) of the two events.[19] Obviously the *te kara* construction in (35b) is semantically complex and is not the exponent we are looking for.

Similarly, BEFORE can be translated in two ways:

(36) a. *Ore ga   sore o   suru mae   ni*
        I   NOM   it   ACC   do   before L-D
        nani-ka   ga   oki-ta.
        something NOM   happen-PAST
        'Before I did it something happened.'

     b. *Ore ga   sore o   si-nai   uti   ni*
        I   NOM   it   ACC   do-not   while L-D
        nani-ka   ga   oki-ta.
        something NOM   happen-PAST
        'I had not done it yet, when something happened.'

The construction in (36a) simply indicates the temporal relationship between two events (*ni* is compulsory in this case). The construction in (36b) indicates that the first event was incomplete when the second event occurred; there is no indication whether the first event eventually occurred or not. Evidently *mae* is the exponent of BEFORE.

The local noun *sita* designates any place below the point referred to by the preceding genitive NP. If no reference point is mentioned, it must be understood deictically. The locative-dative particle *ni*, the locative particle *de*, or the accusative particle *o* is compulsory.[20]

The local noun *ue*, which designates any place on or above the reference point, behaves exactly in the same way as *sita*.

(37) a. *Ore-tati   no   ue   ni   sora   ga   aru.*
        I-NONSG   GEN   above   L-D   sky   NOM   exist
        'There is the sky above us.'

     b. *Ore-tati   no   sita   ni   zimen ga   aru.*
        I-NONSG   GEN   under   L-D   ground NOM   exist
        'There is the ground under us.'

14.7 Partonomy and Taxonomy: *Bubun* PART and *Syurui* KIND

'Have a part' translates into Japanese in two ways:

(38) a. *E   wa   ono no   iti-bu   da.*
       handle TOP axe GEN one-part COP
       'A handle is a part of an axe.'

   b. *Ono ni   wa   e   ga   aru.*
       axe L-D TOP handle NOM exist
       'An axe has a handle.' (Literally, 'To an axe a handle exists.')

Example (38b) sounds much more colloquial than (38a). The construction *NP ni (wa) NP ga aru*, however, is used to indicate 'location' and 'inalienable possession' (cf. (23)) as well:

(39) *Heya ni   hon   ga   aru.*
      room L-D book NOM exist
      'There is a book/are books in the room.'

The part–whole reading of this construction thus depends on the meaning of two NPs in the locative-dative and the nominative slot respectively, and is not inherent in the construction itself.

Iti-bu in (38a) consists of *iti* ONE and *bu* PART, the latter being the abbreviated form of *bubun*, a Chinese-derived word. Observe the following sentence:

(40) *Ono   ni   wa   huta-tu   no   **bubun** ga   aru.*
      axe   L-D TOP two-CL:thing   GEN part   NOM exist
      Hito-tu   wa   e   de,   moo   hito-tu
      one-CL:thing   TOP handle COP:CONT   more one-CL:thing
      wa   ha   da.
      TOP blade COP
      'An axe has two parts. One is a handle and the other is a blade.'
      (Literally, 'To an axe two parts exist ...')

Syurui KIND, a Chinese-derived word, behaves like *bubun*. It has the abbreviated form *syu* when it takes the numeral *iti*, which is assimilated to the following *s* (becoming *is-syu*).

(41) a. *Ki   ni   wa   syurui ga   takusan aru.*
         tree L-D TOP kind   NOM many   exist
         'There are many kinds of trees.' (Literally, 'To trees many kinds exist.')

b. *Matu wa ki no is-syu da.*
   pine TOP tree GEN one-kind COP
   'The pine is a kind of tree.'

Iroiro, normally glossed as 'variety', can be used in the same context as (41a):

(42)   *Ki ni wa iroiro aru.*
       tree L-D TOP variety exist
       (Literally, 'To trees variety exists.')

However, *iroiro* does not necessarily indicate taxonomy. Either example from (43) can follow after (42), while only (43a) is possible after (41a):

(43)   a. *Matu, kaede, sakura ...*
          pine maple cherry
          'Pine, maple, cherry ...'

       b. *Ookii no, tiisai no,*
          big   one small one
          hana ga kirei na no ...
          [flower NOM beautiful COP:ATTR] one
          'Big ones, small ones, those which have beautiful flowers ...'

Similarly, *donna* 'like what' or *konna* 'like this' (cf. 14.5.2) can also be interpreted as 'what kind' or 'this kind'. But, like *iroiro*, these do not necessarily indicate taxonomy. Since only *syurui* encodes a clear taxonomic notion among all the candidates, it is regarded as the exponent of KIND.

14.8 Evaluators and Descriptors: *Ii* GOOD, *Warui* BAD, *Ookii* BIG and *Tiisai* SMALL

(44)   *Taroo wa ii / warui yatu da.*
       Taroo TOP good bad person COP
       'Taroo is a good/bad person.'

(45)   *Ore wa ookii / tiisai inu o mi-ta.*
       I TOP big small dog ACC see-PAST
       'I saw a big/small dog.'

14.9 Conclusion

Let me summarise some of the difficulties, both theoretical and practical, encountered during my investigation.

First of all, I and, to a lesser degree, YOU. As discussed in section 14.1.1, the main obstacles to regarding *ore* and *omae* respectively as the exponents of these two primitives are sociocultural in nature. Since *watasi* (or zero) for I and name or title (or zero) for YOU are the norm in written discourse, *ore* and *omae* may look pejorative in the eyes of sophisticated readers in such a context. One can of course use *watasi* (and *anata*) instead of *ore* (and *omae*) in mini-sentences to avoid such **pragmatic** effects. But I think the fact that the former pair is **semantically** more complex than the latter is indisputable. The problem, however, is a little more serious: in practice it is difficult to formulate the definitions of other first- and second-person pronouns via *ore* and *omae* (and, for that matter, via any pair of pronouns). They have such bizarre effects that they are almost unreadable. I cannot think of any way to get rid of these effects within the NSM framework. Perhaps, as Goddard (1989:306) notes, "semantic representations are limited in their capacity to reflect pragmatic principles", which are maximally at work in the use of these pronouns.

The subjectivity of the mental predicates FEEL and WANT is an intricate issue. It requires a full-fledged discussion far beyond the scope of this paper. Wierzbicka (1991c) suggests the possibility of regarding 'I want', rather than WANT, as a primitive. I think this could solve some of the problems concerning the first/second-person orientation of *hosii/-tai*. On the other hand, the restriction of syntactic scope of *kanziru* (or *kimoti*) FEEL clearly requires subtler interpretation.

Apart from these 'substantives' and 'mental predicates', the exponents of PART and KIND, *bubun* and *syurui* respectively, are slightly problematic in that they sound too formal or literary at the speech level which I assume basic.

There are vast areas where the applicability of the NSM approach should still be tested. I hope the exponents proposed in this paper will serve as a stepping stone for such investigation.

Notes

1   Some of the ideas in this paper, in a premature stage, were discussed and commented on in the Workshop on Semantic and Lexical Universals held on 20th–22nd February 1992, at the Australian National University. I would like to express my gratitude to all who attended this workshop. Special thanks to Anna Wierzbicka, Cliff Goddard and Jean Harkins, who gave me many stimulating ideas and helpful suggestions, and to Catherine Travis, who helped me improve both the content and the language of this paper. I am also grateful to Ulrike Mosel, Toshiki Osada, Voravudhi Chirasombutti and Tony Backhouse for their valuable comments and criticism on an earlier version of this paper. The following abbreviations are used throughout this paper: ACCusative case, ATTRibutive form, AUXiliary, CLassifier, COMPLementiser,

CONDitional suffix/form, CONTinuative form, COPula, DESIderative suffix, GENitive case, IMPerative form, INTERROGative particle, L-D locative-dative case, LINKing suffix, LOCative case, NOMinative case, NOML nominaliser, NONSG non-singular suffix, NP noun phrase, PAST suffix, PERFect suffix, POLITE form, TOPic particle, VP verb phrase.

2   See Wierzbicka's illuminating discussion on I and YOU in Japanese (1991a:12–14, 1991b:340–341, and 1991c, among others).

3   I don't know exactly what this means. In my observation, the pronouns marked by the asterisk are quite commonly heard, though not as often as the pronouns without it. According to the Kokuritsu Kokugo Kenkyuuzyo data in Tokyo (1981b:54), the use of *atasi* and *anta* is reported by 30.9% and 14.3% of the female speakers, and by 5.1% and 10.1% of the male speakers, respectively. (The age range of the informants in this data is 15–69. No data is available concerning *atakusi*.)

4   In fact, women can use *watasi* interchangeably with *watakusi* in most contexts. Mochizuki (1980:467–468) shows that in women's speech: (a) "deletion is marked for a higher degree of politeness and formality" than overt expression of any first-person pronoun; and (b) *watakusi* and *watasi* "do not show a striking stratification along the axes of politeness and formality".

5   See Peng's (1973) data, where 5.5% of the 3rd grade female students in junior high schools in Tokyo report that they use *kimi* when they talk to male juniors or peers. 1.7% of the female speakers in Tokyo report using *kimi* according to Kokuritsu Kokugo Kenkyuuzyo (1981b:54).

6   Jugaku (1979:78–84; summarised by Reynolds 1991:140, 144) reports that many female high-school students in Tokyo use *boku* in order to assert that they are equal in status with male peers. According to Toshiki Osada and Kaori Matsuda (personal communication), the use of *ore* is not rare among female high-school students in the outskirts of Tokyo. I noted a few instances where female speakers used *ore*, with the purpose of much stronger assertion than *boku*, either in exasperation or in a jocular way. According to the Kokuritsu Kokugo Kenkyuuzyo data (1981b:54) in Tokyo, 1.5% of the female speakers report using *ore*, while 0% report using *boku*. The former figure may be due to the dialectal variation of those who originally come from outside Tokyo (cf. note 11).

7   McGloin (1991:36), discussing the "sex difference" of sentence-final particles, argues that "the femininity of *wa* and *no* stems from the sense of conversational rapport they create between the speaker and hearer". We can see "the sense of conversational rapport" in the allegedly feminine pronoun *anta* (and *atasi*) as well.

8   The use of *-ra*, in contrast with *-tati*, clearly reflects the increase of the sense of closeness felt by Kyooiti towards the two girls. However, he does not go so far as to use *omae-tati* or *omae-ra*.

9   It might be argued that since *watasi* is used in informal situations by women, it should be regarded as unmarked I, while its apparent 'politeness' when used by male speakers should be interpreted as a pragmatic effect resulting from the existence of two other 'male' or 'deprecatory' pronouns. This hypothesis, however, does not explain why *watasi*, if it is unmarked, is perfectly compatible with women's formal speech where the choice of lexemes/expressions indicating deference or politeness is obligatory (cf. note 4).

10 When a woman (or a man) talks to juniors in her (or his) family, common practice is to use a kinship term such as 'elder sister' or 'mother' (or 'elder brother' or 'father') for self-reference (cf. Suzuki 1976). As Wierzbicka (personal communication) points out, such a speech practice

suppresses to some extent a woman's use of the bare I, in the context where she is most likely to use it. Even in such cases, however, a woman may use *watasi* or *atasi* instead of a kinship term, but hardly ever *ore*, which a man may use.

11   It must also be noted that the uptown Tokyo dialect is the closest variety to standard Japanese, which is being created by a body of intellectuals and is spreading all over Japan through mass media and schooling. The frequent use of honorifics and formal style is one of the characteristics of this dialect, which is regarded as the indication of sophistication. While the use of *ore* and *omae*, even by women, is quite common in many other dialects, they are disfavoured by both male and female intellectuals in Tokyo, mainly for this socio-cultural reason.

12   These three words constitute allomorphy at three levels of politeness with respect to the referent. I choose the informal *yatu* as a basic term, to be consistent with the speech level of *ore* and *omae*.

13   See Wierzbicka's (1991b:339-340) discussion of this primitive. As she argues, morphological complexity should be distinguished from semantic complexity.

14   This categorisation of verbs follows Kindaichi (1950; summarised by Jacobsen 1982).

15   In negation the resultative *sit-te iru* may contrast with the stative one (cf. Kuno 1983:109-116).

16   In an earlier version of this paper, I regarded *kimoti* as the exponent, mainly due to my intuition that it expresses a more 'inner' feeling and thus would be more difficult to define than *kanziru*. At this stage I have no idea how to decompose *kanziru* via *kimoti*, or *kimoti* via *kanziru*; thus I have opted for a practical solution.

17   The conjunctive particle *to*, similarly, does not indicate the supposition of the speaker (cf. Murayama 1985).

18   See Kuno (1973:153-167) for a detailed discussion of the candidates for AFTER and BEFORE.

19   *Kara* in this construction is the ablative case suffix. *Kara* BECAUSE, on the other hand, is a conjunctive particle, which is always preceded by the conclusive form of the predicate (cf. section 14.5.2).

20   For a discussion of the semantic differences among these particles, see Kuno (1973:96-101).

References

Goddard, Cliff. 1989. "The Goals and Limits of Semantic Representation". *Quaderni di Semantica* 10.2.297-308.

Ide, Sachiko. 1982. "Japanese Sociolinguistics: Politeness and women's language". *Lingua* 57.357-385.

Ide, Sachiko. 1991. "How and Why Do Women Speak More Politely in Japanese?" *Aspects of Japanese Women's Language* ed. by Sachiko Ide & Naomi Hanaoka McGloin, 63-79. Tokyo: Kurosio Publishers.

Jacobsen, Wesley M. 1982. "Vendler's Verb Classes and the Aspectual Character of Japanese *TE-IRU*". *Berkeley Linguistics Society, Proceedings* 8.373-383.

Jugaku, A. 1979. *Nihongo to Onna [Japanese and Women]*. Tokyo: Iwanami Syoten.

Kindaichi, Haruhiko. 1950. *Kokugo Doosi no Itibunrui [A Classification of Japanese Verbs]*. Reprinted in 1976 in *Nihongo Doosi no Asupekuto [Aspect of Japanese Verbs]* ed. by Haruhiko

Kindaichi, 5-26. Tokyo: Mugi Syoboo.
Kokuritsu Kokugo Kenkyuuzyo [The National Language Research Institute]. 1981a. *Daitosi no Gengoseikatsu: Bunseki-hen [Sociolinguistic Survey in Tokyo and Osaka: Analysis]*. Tokyo: Sanseidoo.
Kokuritsu Kokugo Kenkyuuzyo. 1981b. *Daitosi no Gengoseikatsu: Siryoo-hen [Sociolinguistic Survey in Tokyo and Osaka: Data]*. Tokyo: Sanseidoo.
Kuno, Susumu. 1973. *The Structure of the Japanese Language*. Cambridge, Mass.: MIT Press.
Kuno, Susumu. 1983. *Sin-Nihonbunpoo-Kenkyuu [New Researches on Japanese Grammar]*. Tokyo: Taisyuukan Syoten.
Kuroda, S.-Y. 1973. "Where Epistemology, Style, and Grammar Meet: A case study from Japanese". *A Festschrift for Morris Halle* ed. by Stephen R. Anderson & Paul Kiparsky, 377-391. New York: Holt, Rinehart and Winston.
Matsumoto, Yoshiko. 1988. "Reexamination of the Universality of Face: Politeness phenomena in Japanese". *Journal of Pragmatics* 12.403-426.
McGloin, Naomi Hanaoka. 1991. "Sex Difference and Sentence-Final Particles". *Aspects of Japanese Women's Language* ed. by Sachiko Ide & Naomi Hanaoka McGloin, 23-41. Tokyo: Kurosio Publishers.
Mochizuki, Michiko. 1980. "Male and Female Variants for 'I' in Japanese: Cooccurrence rules". *Papers in Linguistics* 13.453-474.
Murayama, Yasuo. 1985. "The Condition and the Use of the Conditionals *To, Tara,* and *Ba*". *Papers in Japanese Linguistics* 10.116-148.
Peng, F. C. C. 1973. "La Parole of Japanese Pronouns". *Language Sciences* 25.36-39.
Reynolds, Katsue Akiba. 1991. "Female Speakers of Japanese in Transition". *Aspects of Japanese Women's Language* ed. by Sachiko Ide & Naomi Hanaoka McGloin, 129-146. Tokyo: Kurosio Publishers.
Shibamoto, Janet S. 1985. *Japanese Women's Language*. Orlando, Florida: Academic Press.
Suzuki, Takao. 1976. "Language and Behavior in Japan: The conceptualization of personal relations". *Japanese Culture and Behavior: Selected readings* ed. by Takie S. Lebra & William P. Lebra, 142-157. Rev. ed. Honolulu: University Press of Hawaii.
Wierzbicka, Anna. 1991a. *Cross-Cultural Pragmatics*. Berlin: Mouton de Gruyter.
Wierzbicka, Anna. 1991b. "Japanese Key Words and Core Cultural Values". *Language in Society* 20.333-385.
Wierzbicka, Anna. 1991c. "Lexical Universals and Universals of Grammar". *Meaning and Grammar* ed. by Michel Kefer & Johann van der Auwera, 383-415. Berlin: Mouton de Gruyter.
Yoshimoto, Banana. 1989. *Tugumi*. Tokyo: Tyuuookooronsya.

Kalam Exponents of Lexical and Semantic Primitives

Andrew Pawley
Australian National University, Canberra

Kalam is spoken in several dialects by about 20 000 people living around the junction of the Bismarck and Schrader Ranges in Madang province, Papua New Guinea. It has only one close relative, Kobon, spoken nearby in the Schraders. Kalam and Kobon are distantly related to other languages occupying central and eastern Madang Province.[1] Kalam data cited here are in the Etp Mnm dialect and Ti Mnm dialects, spoken in the Upper Kaironk Valley. Unmarked data are in Etp Mnm.

Kalam clauses are normally verb-final, although locatives may (and often do) follow the verb. To the extent that there is case-marking, it is nominative–accusative. Free-form subject person-markers are distinguished from object person-markers. Subject nominals are unmarked. Direct object nominals often carry object person-marker clitics if they refer to people or higher animals; otherwise they are unmarked. The person and number of the subject is marked by a suffix on the verb. The form of the suffixes does not vary between transitive and intransitive verbs.

Verb stems are a closed class, with just over one hundred members. Verbs are clearly differentiated from other word classes by their distinctive morphology and syntactic behaviour. A small subset of verb stems, termed 'generic verbs', are characterised by their broad meanings and very high frequency — some 15 generic verbs make up nearly 90 percent of all verb tokens in texts, and 35 verb stems account for nearly 99 percent of all verb tokens. The most common verb stems (with very approximate glosses) include *ag-* 'sound', *am-* 'go', *ap-* 'come, appear', *d-* 'constrain, control, hold, get', *g-* 'do, act, make', *jak-* 'attain an elevated or targeted point; stand, attain, arrive, reach', *ay-* (*l-* in Ti Mnm) 'form, put, stabilise, become', *md-* 'exist, stay, live', *nŋ-* (sometimes *n-* or *ng-* in Ti Mnm) 'perceive, be aware, know', *ñ-* 'transfer, give, connect, apply', *ñb-* or *ñŋ-* 'consume', *pk-* (*pak-* in Ti Mnm) 'hit', *tan-* 'rise, grow', *yap-* 'descend' and *tk-* 'separate, cut across, change suddenly'.

Verb stems can appear either uninflected (that is, as bare stems) — for example, *am-* 'go' — or inflected — for example, *am-jp-in* 'I am going' and *am-i* 'having gone'. Inflected verbs can be further subdivided into dependent and independent verbs. Independent verbs are fully specified for tense/mood/aspect and for person and number of the subject — for example, *am-ab-ay* (go-REC-3PL) 'they have just gone' and *am-igp-ay* (go-PAST:HABITUAL-3PL) 'they used to go'. A clause whose final verb is independent is an independent clause.

The suffixes on dependent verbs specify two things: (a) whether the subject of the dependent verb is the same as (SS), or different from (DS), the subject of the next inflected verb; and (b) relative tense — whether the action of the dependent verb is prior to (PRIOR), simultaneous with (SIM), or future or prospective to (FUT) the action of the next inflected verb. A clause whose inflected verb is dependent is a dependent clause. Since the Kalam method of building complex sentences normally requires the identity or non-identity of subject referents to be marked on non-final clauses, it is classed as a switch-reference system.

(1) *Np   nŋ-i,   a-b-ay.*
    2SG:OBJ perceive-SS:PRIOR   go-PERF-3PL
    'Having seen you they went (earlier today).'/'They went after seeing you.' (Same subject, prior action)

(2) *Kun   g-e-y,   si   a-s<a>p.*
    thus do-DS:PRIOR-2SG   weeping   say-PRES:PROG-3SG
    'You having done thus, he is weeping.'/'He is weeping because of what you did.' (Different subject, prior action)

As in most Papuan languages, extended monologues in Kalam typically contain paragraph-like macro-sentences. Each such sentence contains a series of dependent clauses — that is, clauses containing dependent verbs, with marking of relative tense and relative identity of subject — followed by an independent clause, with absolute marking of tense and subject person and number. However, it is also marked by a high incidence of serial-verb constructions.

In serial-verb constructions an inflected verb stem follows one or more bare verb stems. Under certain circumstances non-verb material (modifiers or nominal arguments) may intervene within the string of verb stems. For example, in the following serial-verb construction, a noun phrase follows the first verb stem (verb stems shown in bold face):

(3) *B   ak   **am** mon   **puk**   d   **ap**   ay-a-k.*
    man   that **go** wood **smash** get   **come** put-3SG-PAST
    'The man fetched some firewood.'

I turn now to the question of how Kalam expresses the stock of lexical and semantic primitives proposed by the editors of this volume.

For most of the proposed primitives it is not hard to find one or more Kalam equivalents. There are, however, a few problematic cases. In anticipation of the discussion of these cases I should make a few brief general remarks about my approach to polysemy. Following Cohen (1971) and Posner (1980), Ruhl (1989) suggests that in treatments of meaning two philosophical biases can often be distinguished: those of 'semanticists' (or 'formalists') versus 'conversationalists' (or 'functionalists'). The former seek an explanation of meaning largely or solely in the linguistic system, tending to assume richness and ambiguity in the literal meanings of words. The latter tend to attribute attribute only minimal meanings to words and to explain different interpretations in terms of conditions of language use, pragmatic rules of interpretation. Ruhl argues that, regardless of their philosophical bias, as a practical procedure in their research, semanticists and lexicographers should first seek a **unitary** meaning for a word, resorting to polysemy (or homophony or idiomaticity) only as a last resort. This is not deny that in many cases a polysemous analysis will in the end prove to be supportable.

My own approach is similar to Ruhl's insofar as I seek as far as possible to explain different understandings of a word in terms of context. In many cases, I believe, one can defend an analysis in which a word associated with a number of contextual senses can be assigned a single, relatively broad, inherent meaning. The variant contextual senses can then be associated, not with the word itself, but with its various linguistic or pragmatic contexts.

Although some data has been taken from my own notes in the Etp Mnm dialect, it has proved useful to draw freely on sources in another dialect, Ti Mnm. Ti Mnm stems ultimately from the Asai Valley but is now spoken next to Etp Mnm in the Upper Kaironk Valley. In morphological and lexical forms the Etp Mnm and Ti Mnm dialects are sharply distinct but they are almost identical in their semantic and grammatical categories and structure. The chief source of Ti Mnm examples is *Kalam hunting traditions* (henceforth *KHT*), a series of working papers comprising the draft of a book by Kalam author Ian Saem Majnep, with translations by Ralph Bulmer (Majnep & Bulmer 1990). In examples from *KHT* details of the source follow the free translation: the first number refers to the chapter or to the text of a folk-tale appended to that chapter, the following number to the paragraph from which the example is taken.

Except where morphological analysis of example sentences is relevant I have not analysed Kalam complex words in the examples. Glosses are thus generally word-for-word rather than morpheme-for-morpheme.[2]

15.1 Substantives

15.1.1 I and YOU

I and YOU (singular) are marked both by free pronouns and (in the case of subjects) by verbal suffixes. The free pronouns each show a number of alternants, including a contrast between grammatical object and non-object forms. The basic non-object free forms are *yad* I and *nad* YOU$_{SG}$ (see examples (4), (48), (67), (82), (89), (96), (101) and (112)) contrasting with the object forms *yp* 'me' and *np* 'you$_{SG}$' (see examples (1), (16), (32)–(37), (56) and (69)). The same pairs of alternants are used for possessor, choice depending on whether the possessor is the grammatical object or not.

15.1.2 SOMEONE, SOMETHING and PEOPLE

In question words, there is a straightforward distinction between an unspecified person (SOMEONE) and an unspecified non-human thing (SOMETHING): *an* 'who?' (plural form *an an*) refers to humans and *etp* 'what?' (plural form *etp etp*) refers to things. Iin Ti Mnm 'what?' is *ti*, with plural *ti ti*.

(4) Wad ebi an gak? Yad an gak ma-nŋbin.
netbag here who he.made I who he.made not-I.know
'Who made this netbag?' 'I don't know who made it.'

(5) Tap kun etp?
thing such what?
'What sort of thing is it?'

Outside of question words, however, the situation is not so simple. There is no noun meaning 'person, human being (singular)' and no pronoun that means uniquely 'someone'. There is, however, a complex lexeme for PEOPLE, namely *bin-b*, literally 'woman-man'. (Kalam builds many generic noun concepts in this way, that is, by combining two or more specific nouns each of which names a salient member of the class. The term for 'children' is *ñ-pan*, literally 'boy-girl'; 'parents' is *nonm-nop*, literally 'mother-father'; 'grandparents' is *aps-basd*, literally 'grandmother-grandfather'.)

For referring to a specific but indefinite person or people there is a productive formula which in Etp Mnm dialect has the nucleus Noun$_{Human}$ + Quantifier. Quantifier may be realised by *ebap* 'a (certain or particular one)' (*olap* in Ti Mnm) — for example, *b ebap* 'a man, a certain man' (see also examples (68) and (70)) —, by *ognap* 'some (particular ones)' — for example, *b ognap* 'some people' — or by another quantifier, such as *omŋal* 'two' or *kawsek* 'several together'.

Under some discourse conditions a quantifier such as *ebap* 'one' and *ognap* 'some' can occur alone in a noun phrase, serving as an anaphoric pronoun. However, as an anaphoric pronoun the quantifier can refer to any kind of noun, not just to humans. In this it resembles English *one* and *some*, or for that matter *two*, *three*, *many*, and so on. So in the following sentence, *ebap* is indeterminate as between a human or non-human referent:

(6)　　Ebap mdp　　kotp-mgan.
　　　　one　it.stays　house-inside
　　　　'One (of them) is in the house.'

I believe that both *ebap* and *ognap* can also be used as non-anaphoric nominals. In the cases I have found (all of *ognap*, none of *ebap*) they always refer to people or higher animals ('someone', 'some people') or to time ('sometimes') and not to inanimate objects. The following is an example of non-anaphoric *ognap* 'some people':

(7)　　Mey　ognap　ñbal,　ji　ognap　mdel
　　　　that　some　they.eat　but　some　they.having.lived
　　　　mdel　　　　　　　　kuñk　aposp...
　　　　they.having.lived　saliva　it.comes
　　　　'But some (people) eat it, some later in life develop a craving (to eat this food) ...' (*KHT* 10:11)

See (74) for an example of *ognap* 'sometimes'.

Perhaps the best candidate for (non–question-word) SOMETHING is *tap* 'thing, stuff', followed by *ebap* 'one' or *ognap* 'some'. *Tap* is the generic noun for all entities, human and non-human; see examples (5), (39), (113) and (126). The uses of *ebap* and *ognap* were noted above. To render 'I see something but I don't know what (kind of thing) it is', one can say:

(8)　　Tap　ebap　ngbin　ak,　mey　tap　kun　etp　ak　ma-ngbin.
　　　　thing　one　I.see　that　that　thing　such　what　that　not-I.know
　　　　'I see something but I don't know what (kind of thing) it is.'

Tap is sometimes used as a classifier before inanimate nouns, as in:

(9)　　Tap　bd　　　　ak　dad　　　　awan.
　　　　thing　bushy:plant　that　carrying　you.come
　　　　'Bring that bushy plant (thing).'

In the following example *tap* is perhaps used as a pronoun or classifier-without-accompanying-noun, to refer to a kind of possum. It has the sense of 'a type of thing', 'members of a class':

(10) Nb   ak   mseŋ   yb   alyaŋ   lak   ak,
      thus that open:country true   down.there   it.forms that
      pen   madaw ak   skol-skol   tek   lak   ak;
      so   madaw the small-small   like   it.forms that
      tap   kub yb   ma-lak.
      thing big very not-it.forms
      'However down in the open country it is the smaller kind of *madaw*
      (*Phalanger gymnotis*, a large terrestrial possum) that is present; the
      very large type is not present.' (*KHT* 11:57)

15.2 Mental Predicates

Perhaps the most problematic members of the list of proposed primitives in Kalam are the 'mental predicates'. It will be convenient first to consider KNOW, THINK and FEEL together, then to turn to the others, WANT and SAY.

15.2.1 KNOW, THINK and FEEL

Kalam has a mental predicate with a meaning more general than KNOW, THINK or FEEL. This is the verb stem *nŋ-* (*n-* or *ng-* in Ti Mnm in some phonological contexts) which denotes awareness, conscious perceiving, that is, both sensing and cognising, in which the perceiver is (at least partly) in control, or at least is a wilful actor. In different contexts *nŋ-*, occurring as the lone content verb in a clause, may be glossed as 'know, be conscious, be aware, be awake, think, see, hear, smell, taste, feel, recognise, notice, understand, remember, learn, study'.[3] The following sentences partly illustrate this range of uses of *nŋ-*:

(11) *Wsn   ma-kjap,   nŋsap.*
      sleeping not-he.lies   he.is.aware
      'He's not asleep, he's awake/conscious.'

(12) *Tmuk   agek   nŋbin.*
      thunder it.sounds   I.perceived
      'I heard thunder.'

(13) *Kaj   kuy   nŋbin.*
      pig   odour   I.perceive
      'I smell pig/pork.'

(14) *Kotp-yp enen m-ap   nŋban?*
     house-my why   not-come you.see
     'Why haven't you come to see my house?'

(15) *Kuj   nŋ-i   cp   ñagngayn.*
     magic   learn-SS:PRIOR   victim I.will.kill
     'I will learn/acquire knowledge of magic and kill people.'

(16) *Np   mapn   nŋbin.*
     you   liver I.feel
     'I feel sorry/affection for you.'

(17) *Apan   ma-nŋbin,   mnm-nad   apan.*
     you.have.said   not-I.know   language-your you.have.spoken
     'I didn't understand what you said; you spoke in your own language.'

(18) *"Apin   ak   nŋ-   dpit?"   agak.*
     I.have.said that understand   you.have.finished   he.said
     Agek   agtek   "Met, nŋ   nŋ
     when.he.spoke they.said   well   understand   understand
     dput   ak,   ma-nput   ak"   agak.
     we.finish that not-understand   that   they.said
     'Then he asked them "Have you (two) completely understood what I've said?", and they replied, "Well, we've understood some parts of it but other parts we haven't."' (*KHT* 9, folk-tale 57)

(The verb *d-* which occurs in the last example (in *d-p-it* 'you have finished', *d-p-ut* 'we have finished') can in other contexts also mean 'hold, grasp, constrain, stop'. In constructions like (18), where *d-* is the final element of a serial-verb construction, *d-* functions as a completive marker, whose scope is the whole serial-verb string.)

Nŋ- also occurs, accompanied by nouns or adjuncts or other verb stems, in a number of lexicalised phrases that translate specific English verbs of awareness, for example, *d nŋ-* (literally, 'touch perceive') 'feel (by touching)', *ñb nŋ-* (literally, 'eat perceive') 'taste', *wdn nŋ-* (literally, 'eye perceive') 'see', *tumd nŋ-* (literally, 'ear perceive') 'hear', *wsn nŋ-* (literally, 'sleep perceive') 'dream' and *nŋ md-* (literally, 'perceive stay') 'watch'. The problem, then, is not that Kalam does not have specific translation equivalents of KNOW, THINK and FEEL, but rather that these notions are aspects of a more general concept. Let us turn now to a more detailed consideration of each.

15.2.2 KNOW

The most common senses of the English verb *know* — 'understand, be aware of, realise' and 'be acquainted with, familiar with' — are translated by *ng-* alone (or by its variants *n-* and *ng-*). There is no complex form meaning simply 'know'.

(19) *(Tp)   mdp   ngbin.*
     (place)   he.stays   I.know
     'I know (the place) where he is.'

(20) *Cn   tap   kun   ak   tap   tmey   ak   ngbun.*
     we   thing   such   this   thing   bad   this   we.know
     'We know that this sort of thing is bad.'

(21) *B   nb   ak   kuj   tmel   ak   ngak   ak ...*
     man   such   this   magic   strong   the   he.knew   the
     'This man knew very powerful magic ...' (*KHT* 11:84)

(22) *Nb   gl   gosp   ngl   apal,*
     thus   having.done   it.recently.did   having.realised   they.say
     "awl   madaw   ak   nokom   apl" ...
     here   madaw   the   one   having.come
     'When people realise that this has happened they say=think, "This can only be a *madaw* possum" ...' (*KHT* 11:36)

15.2.3 THINK

Think in either of the senses 'hold an opinion, believe something to be the case' or 'turn over ideas in the mind, focus one's mind on ideas', is usually expressed by the complex lexeme *gos ng-*. *Gos* is a noun 'thought, idea, mind'.

(23) *Gos   ngl   agak   ypd   mdeb*
     thought   having.perceived   he.said   straight   it.was
     agl   knak.
     having.decided   he.slept
     'Only when he thought everything was in order did he sleep.' (Ti Mnm)

Gos can be possessed, as in (24), or qualified, for example, by *kongay* 'many, a lot' or *pat* 'long'.

(24) *Mnm   agebyn   ak,*
      speech I.am.saying   this
      gos   -yad ak nep   nŋl   agebyn.
      thought my   this only having.perceived I.am-saying
      'What I'm talking about now are only my own thoughts/opinions.'
      (*KHT* Intro:79)

However, *nŋ-* by itself may denote rational thought, as in the following extract from a story about traces left by a mysterious creature or thing:

(25) *"Awl   tap   nŋep   ey!" agak.*
      Here   thing perceiving oh!   he.said
      '"Oh! Here is a thinking/knowing thing [i.e. a creature that is sentient or civilised]", he said.' (*KHT* 11, folk-tale 1:47)

The phrase *gos nŋ-* also translates 'ponder, think over, think about (what to do)' and 'wonder about, be curious, interested in'.

We also find *gos gos ay-* (Etp Mnm dialect) or *gos gos l-* (Ti Mnm), literally 'form thoughts', meaning 'be full of, have something firmly in one's mind':

(26) ... *mab ogok   gos   gos   ll   tanl* ...
          tree the:PL   thought thought having.formed   having.climbed
      '... they climb trees full of such ideas ...' (Ti Mnm)

Thinking (in the senses both of (a) contemplating an idea, wondering, deciding and (b) holding an opinion) is also commonly expressed by the verb *ag-* 'make a sound, speak, say' following a complement which expresses either quoted speech or words as thoughts or a pronoun or noun referring to the same. The thinker may be a human or an animal. In such cases I would argue that *ag-* represents thinking as 'internal speech'. In the following extract, we see both *gos nŋ-* and *ag-* (three times) being used to refer to contemplating a course of action:

(27) *"Nb   gobt"   agtek*
      such we.do   they.said=wondered
      gos   ak nŋl   agtek,
      thought the having.perceived they.said=decided
      "kapkap   ñluk   ll   mdut,"   agl ...
      secretly hiding put we.stay   having.said=decided
      'They wondered what to do, then having thought it over they decided to conceal themselves ...' (*KHT* 9, folk-tale 1:17)

In (28) the complement of *ag-* is explicitly thoughts not words:

(28) *Gos   etp   agi   ap   kun   gpan?*
      thought what   having.said=thought   come   such you.did
      'Whatever were you thinking of that you came and did that?'

In the next example, *ag-* refers to holding an opinion, one that the speaker has just realised is wrong:

(29) *Yad   apin   "b-tud   maj   ma-ñbay"*
      I   I.said=thought   men-white   sweet:potato   not-they.eat
      apin.
      I.said=thought
      'I had always thought that white people don't eat sweet potatoes.'

In some contexts, when following a piece of quoted speech that is understood to be internal, *ag-* can be translated either as 'intend', 'want' or 'try' to do or get the thing specified by its complement.

(30) *Kamget   am am,   "ñn   ay   din"   agek.*
      silently go go   hand   put   I.grab he.said
      'He sneaked up and tried to grab hold of her/intending to grab hold of her.' (Literally, '"I'll grab (her)", he said.')

15.2.4 FEEL

I understand the primitive FEEL to refer to the experiencer's awareness of more or less involuntary psychosomatic conditions, ranging from sensations (e.g. 'I feel hot', 'I feel itchy') to emotions or states of mind (e.g. 'I feel sad', 'I feel lonely').

In talking about bodily and mental processes, Kalam make a basic division between voluntary and involuntary experiences. Involuntary processes are normally expressed by a clause with the structure:

(31) Experiencer   Condition   Verb-TENSE-3SG

where (in the simplest case) Experiencer is a noun or pronoun with objective case-marking, Condition is a noun which denotes a bodily or mental condition or sensation and which acts as the grammatical subject of the clause, and Verb is a transitive verb with third-person singular ending. Roughly speaking, where English says 'Experiencer feels condition X', the Kalam say 'Condition X verbs experiencer'. The verb stem in (31) may be any of several, including *ay-* 'form, set, become', *g-* 'act on, happen to, work, make', *ap-* 'come, appear', *yap-* 'fall' and *jak-* 'rise, stand'.

(32) *Yp ss yowp.*
 me urine it.falls
 'I feel the need to urinate.'

(33) *Yp suk owp.*
 me laughter it.comes
 'I feel like laughing.'

(34) *Yp wsn owp.*
 me sleep it.comes
 'I feel sleepy'/'I am sleepy.'

(35) *Yp wokep tek ayp.*
 me vomiting like it.forms
 'I feel like vomiting.'

(36) *Yp tap gp.*
 me sickness it.works
 'I feel sick.'/'I am sick.'

(37) *Yp sb gp.*
 me bowel/guts it.works
 'I feel emotion (anger, upset, sadness, sympathy).' (Literally, 'The bowels/guts are acting on me.')

The formula represented by (37), referring to activity in the bowels, is neutral between different kinds of emotion: anger, sadness, sympathy, pleasure, delight, envy, and so on. To distinguish between positive and negative emotions one uses other formulae. One of these substitutes *sb-wt* 'guts, intestines' for *sb*, adding *tep* 'good' or *tmey* 'bad' before *g-*, and making the experiencer the possessor of *sb-wt* rather than the object of the verb, as in:

(38) *Sbwt yp tmey gp.*
 guts my bad it.works
 'I feel angry.'

Another strategy is to use *tep* or *tmey*, without any body-part term, to denote positive or negative feelings:

(39) ... *gub   mañmod   tap   ogok   agaknŋ*
        cicada lizard   thing   the:PL   while.they.are.calling
    cnop   tep   gup, ...
    we   good   it.works
    '... when the cicada and *mañmod* lizards call we feel pleasure ...'

In constructions of type (31), choice of verb is partly fixed by the subject noun, that is, some bodily condition nouns require certain verbs. To the extent that there is choice, there is a correlation with the way in which the condition manifests itself. If the condition is the need to excrete urine or faeces, the verb is *yap-* 'fall', as in (32). If the condition is a sudden manifestation that threatens to overpower the experiencer, the verb *ap-* 'come, appear' is selected, provided that the condition is named by a simple noun, as in (33) and (34). If however it is named by a derived noun plus the particle *tek* 'like, similar, as if', the verb *ay-* 'form, set' is selected, as in (35). Most bodily conditions, however, select the verb *g-* 'act on, work, make', as in (36)–(39).

None of the verbs in (32)–(39) can be equated directly with a general meaning FEEL. Instead, the verb denotes the specific manner in which the bodily condition appears to or affects the experiencer. It can be argued that the notion 'cause X to FEEL' is implicit in certain 'involuntary bodily process' constructions but I believe only in the sense that FEEL is implied when we say 'I am sick' or 'I am pleased'.

By contrast, when the Kalam report a sensation that is intended ('I took his hand and felt his pulse', 'I tasted the food') or is the immediate outcome of a deliberate action ('I sniffed and smelt the bark'), they typically use a serial-verb construction containing a final verb explicitly marking feeling or awareness. The experiencer is grammatically the subject of this construction:

(40)   Experiencer   Verb 1   Verb 2(=*nŋ*)-Inflection

Here Verb 1 specifes an action which precedes and is prerequisite to the feeling and Verb 2 (marked for tense/aspect, and person and number of the subject) is *nŋ* 'perceive, know, feel'. Thus, 'smell something, take a sniff of something' is *pug nŋ-* (literally, 'sniff perceive'), 'taste something' is *ñb nŋ-* (literally, 'consume perceive') and 'feel (by handling)' is *d nŋ-* (literally, 'touch perceive').

(41)   *Ap   tap   ñb   nŋ-an!*
       come   food   consume perceive-2SG:IMP
       'Come and taste this food!'

Nŋ- is used in a few formulae for feeling emotion, as in (16).

15.2.5 SAY

Kalam has a verb *ag-*, which may be broadly glossed as 'to sound, make a noise'. Used intransitively with either animate or inanimate subject it denotes a sound, made by an object, normally understood as its characteristic sound. Whereas English uses a specific verb to refer to such sounds — for example, a bird calls, a frog croaks, an engine roars or hums, thunder claps, a bell rings, a person speaks — Kalam frequently uses *ag-* to refer to all such characteristic sounds:

(42) *Yakt asap!*
 bird it.sounds
 'A bird is calling!'

(43) *Balus asap!*
 plane it.sounds
 'There's the sound of a plane!'

(44) *Tmuk agak.*
 thunder it.sounded
 'Thunder clapped.'/'There was a clap of thunder.'

The identity of the subject nominal alone normally allows hearers to infer the distinctive nature of the sound it makes, but such inferences stem from knowledge of the world rather than from polysemy of *ag-*.

If they wish to be more specific about kinds of sound-making, however, the Kalam can be. The language has scores of phrasal lexemes which denote specific kinds of sound-making. Typically these consist of *ag-* used transitively, preceded by a nominal specifying the kind of sound made, and usually functioning as direct object (sometimes as a locative); for example, *gu ag-* 'thud' (literally, 'thud sound'), *kmap ag-* 'sing' (literally, 'song sound'), *si ag-* 'cry, weep' (literally, 'crying sound'), *suk ag-* 'laugh' (literally, 'laughter sound'), *sb ag-* 'fart' (literally, 'bowel sound'), *mukbel ag-* 'belch' (literally, 'belching sound'). It is clear that 'speak, talk' is a complex idea in Kalam: it is distinguished from other sounds as *mnm ag-* (literally, 'speech sound'), where *mnm* is the direct object of *ag-*.

Ag- is usually translatable as 'say' when it is (a) used transitively with a human subject and (b) the direct object is a piece of quoted discourse or a nominal standing for a piece of discourse, for example, *etp* 'what?' or *kun* 'thus, such'.

(45) ... "*agl ak pyow met npin*" *ag-l* ...
 arrow the search not I.have.seen having.said
 '"I've looked but can't find find the arrow" he said ...' (*KHT* 11, folk-tale 1)

(46) *Etp   apan?*
      what you.say?
      'What did you say?'

Conditions (a) and (b) above can be regarded as pragmatic as much as grammatical. Speech is the characteristic sound-making activity of humans and quoted speech obviously requires the reading SAY (or 'ask' if the quote is a question). Example (46) could, in some contexts, be understood as 'What sound did you make?'. (See also examples such as (22), (23), (25), (27), (28), (47), (49) and (50), where the words reported are sometimes internal speech representing thinking or wanting.)

When the direct object is a phrase (P) denoting a subject matter, statement or question, an appropriate translation is often 'talk about, describe, discuss'. When a human object (X, the intended audience) is also present the appropriate translation is often 'tell X about P' or 'describe P to X'.

The evidence, then, suggests to me that the Kalam view saying as a context-specific kind of sound-making, specifically one whose product is speech or discourse. It is true that *ag-* can be used of saying things where there is no sound, for example, to say something by letter or book, by internal speech, and perhaps by messages signalled by gestures. But I would argue that these are extensions of the basic notion of spoken discourse.

15.2.6 WANT

There are at least two partial equivalents of WANT. One is a construction consisting of the verb *ag-* 'sound, say, etc.' and a piece of direct speech comprising at least a main verb marked for hortative mood with a first-person subject that is coreferential with the subject of *ag-*. Basically this construction represents internal dialogue — "Let me do (or get) such-and-such", she said (to herself) — which we may translate as 'She wanted to do/get such-and-such', 'She tried to do/get such-and-such' or 'She intended to do/get such-and-such'. (Note that verbs marked for hortative mood can stand as the main verb of an independent sentence.)

(47) *"Tluk   okyoŋ   amnin"   agen,*
      bush   up.there   I.go   I.said=intended
      gutgat   gab   kbi   opin.
      wet.cold it.acted   leaving   I.came
      'I wanted to/tried to go into the bush but it was very cold and I came back.'

The other obvious candidate is the verbal suffix *-ng* which denotes a prospective act, either because it is intended, desired or inevitable. There is no formal contrast between, say, 'X intends to go', 'X wants to go' and 'X is going to go'.

(48) Yad Simbai am-ng   gpin.
      I   Simbai go-SS:PROSP   I-do
      'I intend to go to Simbai.'/'I want to go to Simbai.'

What happens when the subject of the complement clause is different from that of the main clause? To translate *He wants his daughter to marry Yalk* a Kalam will say 'I intend to give my daughter to Yalk' or else

(49) "Pañ-yad   b-nak   Yalk-nup   dnggab,"   agp.
      daughter-my man-your   Yalk-him   he.will.take=marry he.says
      '"It is my daughter your kinsman Yalk will marry," he says=intends.'

To translate *I believe that Wpc wanted to die* a Kalam will say:

(50) Gos-yad   Wpc   "yad kumin"   agek
      thought-my   Wpc   I   let.me.die=I.die   he.said=thought
      ngbin.
      I.think
      'I believe that Wpc wanted to die.'

or the same construction with *kumngayn* 'I am going to die' substituted for *kumin*.

In summary, it is not clear that there is any means, other than pragmatic context, for distinguishing WANT from 'intend'.

15.3 Determiners and Quantifiers

The concepts in question are THIS, THE SAME, OTHER (additional), ONE, TWO, ALL and MANY.

15.3.1 THIS

The most common determiner in Kalam discourse is *ak*, which in its most central uses is translatable variously as 'the, this/these, that/those'. It indicates or singles out without reference to distance from the speaker or addressee. *Ak* has a near synonym *ok*.

(51)   *Ok dngayn akaŋ ok?*
       this I.will.take question this
       'Will I take this one or that one?'

Examples of *ak* or *ok* appear in (8)–(10), (18), (20)–(22), (24), (51)–(53) and other examples. These two singular determiners have the same plural equivalent, *og-ok* 'these, those, the (plural)', as in (26) and (39). The element *og-* is no doubt cognate with the first part of *og-nap* 'some' (see (7) and (73)) and *og-ni* 'here (of a plural referent); these here' (see (71)).

Often *ak* and *ok* are preceded by another determiner-like word. One of its partners is *mey* 'aforementioned entity, this/these/that/those (previously mentioned)'. Another is a word meaning 'such, like this' (*kun* in Etp Mnm dialect, *nb* in Ti Mnm dialect). The sequence *kun ak* (or *kun ok*) or *nb ak* (or *nb ok*) is sometimes best translated 'this', at other times as 'thus, like this' or 'accordingly'.

(52)   *B nb ak kuj tmel ak ngak ak.*
       man such this magic strong the he.knows this
       'This/that man knows very powerful magic.' (*KHT* 11:84)

(53)   *Pen kmn nakdoy tmaŋ apal,*
       so animal *nakdoy tmaŋ* they.say,
       kmn nb ak madaw ak...
       animal such this *madaw* the
       'Although this animal they call *nakdoy tmaŋ* is a *madaw* (ground possum).' (*KHT* 4:59)

The locative demonstrative *ebi* 'here, this here' (*awl* in Ti Mnm) is used to stress the nearness of the thing indicated but is always tied to physical location.

(54)   *B ebi nup tap gp.*
       man here him sickness it.acts
       'This man here is ill.'

15.3.2 THE SAME

Identity or sameness is distinguished (in principle) from mere similarity or likeness. Likeness is expressed by the particle *tek* 'like, similar, as if', which also serves as the yes/no question marker.

(55) *Suk ak agup ak mey yakt pow*
 call the it.sounds the that bird owlet.nightjar
 ak agup tek.
 the sounds like
 'The call is something like an owlet nightjar's call.' (*KHT* 7:11)

(56) *Yp kumeb tek ayp.*
 me dying like it.forms
 'I feel like dying.'/'It's as if I'm dying.'

Identity is expressed in several ways, of which the most common are:

(a) by the complex verb *jm ñi ay-* 'be joined, be the same', where *jm* is a verb adjunct 'joining, joined, connected', *ñ-* is a verb 'fit, connect', inflected to mark prior action by same subject as final verb, and *ay-* is a verb 'form, become in a stable condition':

(57) *Mluk kuyp jm ñi ayp*
 face their joining=same having.fitted it.forms
 pen wak keykey ayp.
 but skin different it.forms.
 'Their face is the same but their skins (i.e. colour, appearance) is different.'

(b) by the noun *nokom* 'one, unified, together, same', either alone or followed by a modifier, as *nokom kun ak* 'one such that' (*nokom nb ak* in Ti Mnm dialect):

(58) *Yakt nokom kun ok omŋay gi*
 bird same=one like:this the two having.done
 ñag dad opun.
 shoot carrying we.came
 'These two birds we shot and brought back are the same kind/one kind.'

Nokom nb ak 'the very same one' can also be used of a singular referent (see also (65)):

(59) *Mey mnek nokom nb ak nep,*
 that next.day one such this exactly
 katp ak g dlakŋ...
 house the make while.they.are.finishing
 'So that on that very same day the men from the settlement built the house ...' (*KHT* 11, folk-tale 86)

A closely related sense of *nokom* is one which emphasises the unmistakeable or unique identity of a thing: 'none other than, (can) only (be), the very same one':

(60) Nb   gl ...   nŋl   apal,
      such having.done   having.seen   they.say
      awl   madaw ak   nokom   apl ...
      here madaw this same=one having.come
      'When people see that this has happened they know it can only be a *madaw* possum ...' (*KHT* 11:36)

(c) by the reciprocal particle *pen* 'correspondingly, the same in return':

(61) Pen   gpan   gpin!
      reciprocally you.did   I.did
      'I did the same as you did!' (in return)

'Same' in the sense of 'same as a previously mentioned thing' is rendered by *mey* 'aforementioned entity; this/these/that/those previously mentioned', often in association with the temporal *nd* 'first, previously':

(62) Paskoy omŋal ak   nd   nŋnk,
      girl   two   the   previously I.saw
      mey   ksen   nŋnk   ak.
      those later   I.saw the
      'I saw the same two girls again.'

(63) Kmn   nb   ak ...   ognap   ksen   koŋay   dek
      kapul   thus the   some   later many   it.catches
      ñŋngabm   apin,   nb ak mnm juj   ak mey sŋak
      you.will.eat I.have.said so the talk basis the that that
      ned   apin   ak.
      previously I.said that
      'Later in the same trap that I have spoken of many such *kapuls* (game mammals) will be caught and you will eat them.' (*KHT* 7:55)

Mey also occurs in the expression *mey kun-ok* 'like that, thus, the same way as that' (*mey nb ok* in Ti Mnm):

(64) Mey   kun-ok   gnmn.
      that thus-the   you.should.do
      'You should do it the same way (as that just demonstrated or referred to).'

To say 'The same thing happened twice' a Kalam will say 'This thing happened twice'. To say 'This is not the same frog but it is a frog of the same kind' a Kalam will say 'This is a different frog but the two frogs are of the one class'.

(65) As   yenm   key key
      frog yenm   different
      kñŋ   nb   ak   nokom   lak.
      class such that   one   they.form
      'The different *yenm* frogs form a large class.' (Ti Mnm)

15.3.3 OTHER

English *other* has the distinct senses of 'different' and 'additional', though *another* can mean 'distinct and additional'. I believe 'other (additional)' is the meaning we are after here, but I will deal with both.

Other in the sense of 'different, not the same' is usually expressed by the adverbs *key* (singular referent) or *key key* (plural), as in (65). The essential meaning of these words is perhaps 'separateness, individuality, distinctiveness'. They are variously translatable as 'self, each, by oneself, on one's own, separately, differently, distinctively' (or the plural equivalents):

(66) Nuk   key   gnggab.
      He   separately   he.will.do
      'He will do it in his own way/by himself/differently.'

(67) Nad   kawkaw   bep   nokom   ma-aginmn.
      You   potato   spinach   one   not-you.should.cook
      Key key   aginmn.
      separately   you.should.cook
      'You shouldn't cook potatoes and spinach together/the same way.
      You should cook them separately/differently.'

(68) Gos   ak   ŋi,
      thought   that   having-thought
      b   ebap   key   mdp   kotp-mgan.
      man   certain:one different   he.stay   house-inside
      'She thought it was a different man who was in the house.'

(See also (73) below.)

Other in the sense of 'additional, more' is usually expressed by *ebap-sek* 'another' (*olap-sek* in Ti Mnm) or *ognap-sek* 'some other':

(69) *Yp ebap-sek ñan!*
me one-with you.give
'Give me another one!'

If the intention is to distinguish a series of different and additional entities, you repeat the name of the entities with the quantifier *ebap* 'one, a certain one' or *ognap* 'some':

(70) *B ebap amb, b ebap amb ...*
man certain:one he.went man certain:one he.went
'One men went, then another man went ...'

To express 'I and these other men here will go to Simbai' a Kalam will use the form *yp* '(together) with':

(71) *Yad yp, b ogni yp, Sbay amngpun.*
I with men these:here with Simbai we.will.go
'I and these other men here will go to Simbai.'

15.3.4 ONE and TWO

The number ONE is *nokom*. TWO is *omŋal*, with variants *omal, omay, mŋal, mal, may* and (in Ti Mnm) *almŋal*.

(72) *Pañ nokom tktk, ñ omŋal tktk.*
daughter one they.had son two they.had
'They had one daughter and two sons.'

(73) *Kmn wgi ak kmn ognap tek aŋ,*
game.mammal bandicoot the game.mammal some like um
kñŋ ak key key ma-lak; kñŋ ak nokom ak.
kind the distinctive not-it.forms kind the one it.forms
'The bandicoot is not like some game mammals that occur in different varieties, there is only one kind.'

(See also example (22).)

The numbers 'three' and 'four' are expressed literally as TWO-ONE and TWO-TWO:

(74) Mey yb okok   kmn   nb ak kun gup,
      that true thereabouts game.mammal such this thus it.does
      olap   omal gl   kngayt ...
      one (time) two having.done they.sleep
      ognap   omŋal nokom   knbal.
      sometimes two   one (= three) they.sleep
      'Three of these game-mammals will sometimes occupy a single spring-lair.' (*KHT* 11:39)

15.3.5 MANY

MANY is *koŋay*. Modifiers can be added to intensify.

(75) Ñ wagn koŋay nep tkp.
      son group many very she.has.borne
      'She has borne many sons.'

15.3.6 ALL

Magisek (*maglsek* in Ti Mnm) and *spsp* both mean 'all, the whole lot, all together, whole'. The former is more common:

(76) Kuyp   magisek nabŋ   gp.
      them   all   shame   it.does
      'They all feel shamed.'

(77) Yalk-nup magisek ñan!
      Yalk-him all   you.give
      'Give it/them all to Yalk.'

(See also (84).)

15.4 Actions and Events

The semantic elements here are DO and HAPPEN (TO).

15.4.1 HAPPEN

The verb *g-* has intransitive senses 'occur, happen' and 'be active, active, function, operate'.

(78) Tap   etp   gp?
      thing what   it.has.happened
      'What's happened?'

(Note that (78) can also mean 'What has it/he/she done?'.)

(79) Mñab   nb   ak   ned   wagn   ak   g   gek,
      country such   this first origin the   happen it.happened
      mñab   Aytol-jl   alym ...
      country Aytol-jl   down.there
      'The place where this originally happened was down there at Aytol-jl ...' (KHT 3:90)

15.4.2 DO

The same verb-form *g-* has a transitive sense 'do, make, create, work or operate something, cause something to happen'.

(80) Tap   tmey   gpay.
      thing bad   they.have.done
      'They have done bad things.'

(81) ... basd   kay   tap   ti   gelgpal   okok ...
          grandfather group thing what they.used.to.do those
      '... the various things my grandfather's people used to do ...'
      (KHT Intro:81)

(See also (36)–(39), (66), (74), (113) and (122).)

15.5 Meta-Predicates

The semantic primitives to be considered here are NO, BECAUSE, LIKE (similar to), CAN (possible), IF (would) and VERY (intensifier).

15.5.1 NO/NOT

There are two main negative markers: *met* (free form) and *ma-*. *Ma-* 'not' (with variant *m-* before a vowel) is the usual negator of predicates. *Met* is used as an interjection 'No!' and as an emphatic negator before predicates, as in (45). The usual position of the predicate negator is preposed or prefixed to the main verb in a clause although under some conditions it can occur preposed to a verb phrase comprising a serial-verb string or verb with a locative complement. Examples appear in (10), (67), (73) and (111). In the following sentence, the scope of *ma-* covers both the next two verbs, which form a periphrastic future:

(82) Yad   ma-   d-ng   gpin!
      I   not   touch-SS:FUT   I.do
      'I'm not going to touch it!'/'I don't want to touch it!'

The future construction 'will not, do not intend to' or 'X says he will not' may be used to convey a person's unwillingness or refusal to do something:

(83) Nuk   m-amngab.
      She   not-she.will.go
      'She doesn't want to go.'/'She won't go.'

15.5.2 IF

IF in the contrary-to-fact sense ('If I were king'/'If I had been king') is marked by the discontinuous verbal suffix *b...p* or *p...p* (see under CAN, section 15.5.5), especially in association with future tense. Otherwise, conditional relation between events is normally indicated or implied by a sequence of clauses, the first of which contains a dependent verb marked for relative tense and subject identity/non-identity in relation to the final verb in the sentence. There is a choice of three relative tense markers, according to whether the action denoted by the dependent verb occurred prior to, simultaneous with or subsequent to the final verb action; for example, 'X having happened, Y happens', 'while X is happening, Y is happening' or 'in order for X to happen, Y is happening'. (See also the introduction, including examples (1) and (2).) Note that the prior action marker (SS:PRIOR) is *-i* in Etp Mnm or *-l* in Ti Mnm if the subject is the same, but if there is a change of subject between the dependent and final clause, the prior action marker (DS:PRIOR) is *-e-* or, in certain contexts, *-o-*.

A conditional reading is possible if: (a) there is a dependent clause whose main verb carries a suffix marking the action as **prior to** or (in some circumstances) **simultaneous with** that of a following independent clause; and (b) the verb, at least in the independent clause, is in a future tense or optative/irrealis ('should, ought') mood.

Let us consider first constructions with a final verb marked for future tense. Placing the outcome of the event in the future favours an 'if' or 'whenever/if and when' reading. However, such constructions are in principle also open to interpretation as a cause–effect sequence ('X happened so Y will happen') or as a straight-out prediction, a statement about what the speaker thinks will happen ('when X happens, Y will happen'), depending on pragmatic circumstances.

In the next four examples a dependent clause marked as DS:PRIOR is followed by an independent clause marked for future tense.

(84) *Tim nd kum-e-ng-ab,*
Tim first die-DS:PRIOR-FUT-3SG
bin-nuk moni magisek dngab.
wife-his money all she.will.get
'If /when Tim dies first (or because Tim will die first) his wife will get all his money.'

(85) *bin d-e-ngaban, poŋd owngayn.*
wife you.take-DS:PRIOR-FUT-2SG bringing I.will.come
'If/when/because you want a wife, I will bring you one.'

(86) *... mey kmn nb-ak ñb-e-ng-ab,*
so game.mammal such.as.this eat-DS:PRIOR-FUT-3SG
kogi tagengab mdl kumngab.
belly it.will.swell having.persisted he.will.die
'... so if/when/because he eats (will have eaten) this game mammal his belly will swell up and after a while he will die.' (*KHT* 10:55)

(87) *Pug-e-y- pug-e-y*
blow-DS:PRIOR-2SG:HORT blow-DS:PRIOR-2SG:HORT
mon malaŋ yob gaŋ.
fire flame big it.does
'If /when/because you keep blowing the flames get bigger.'

A 'because' interpretation would be required in (84)–(87) if the particle *pen* 'accordingly, so' were added to the final clause or to each clause.

(88) *Jl ogok d-e-te-k, ml ogok mdek,*
joints those take-DS:PRIOR-3DU-PAST heap those it.stayed
ml ogok d-e-te-k, yng ogok mdek ...
heap those take-DS:PRIOR-3DU-PAST backbone those it.stayed
'If/whenever they took some joints from the heap on one side, then the heap on the other side would remain. If they managed to pack up the rump, the backbone would still be there ...' (*KHT* 11, folktale 76)

In the following examples the non-final verbs are marked for prior action by the **same** subject as that of the final verb:

(89) Yad   nd   am   jak-i,   moni   dngayn.
      I   first go   reach-SS:PRIOR   money   I.will.get
      'If/when/because I arrive first I will get the money.'

(90) Am-l   mŋal ...   g-l   knggabit,
      go-SS:PRIOR   two   do-SS:PRIOR   they.will.sleep
      ... bin   anwak   logon ...
          female   with.young   together
      'If/when two (of them) go, they will sleep together, a female with
      her offspring ...' (KHT 11:40)

In the foregoing examples the condition is temporally prior to the consequence. When the condition is not clearly prior, for example in 'If there's a lot of noise going on I won't be able to sleep' or 'If he is at home we will see him', the speaker may choose a relative tense marker that indicates simultaneous and not sequential relation with final verb. In other words, he may say 'if-and-while X is happening ...'.

(91) Nuk   kotp   md-a-knŋ   cn   nup   nŋngabun.
      He   house   stay-3SG-DS:SIM   we   him   we.will.see
      'If/while he's at home we'll see him.'

Although constructions of the kind represented by (84)–(91) are the most common pragmatic equivalents of English conditionals in Kalam, there is another candidate: a construction in which each non-final verb is marked by (a) a same- or different-subject suffix also denoting prior action and (b) the optative suffix -n- 'should'. The final verb may be marked either for optative or for future. Compare English *If you should do X/Should you do X, then Y should/will happen.* The best example I have of this is:

(92) Mab   ñŋeb   ak   ned   gon   ak   l-e-n-mn,
      tree   food   the   first trap   the   put-DS:PRIOR-OPT-2SG
      skoyd   ak   ned   ap   d-o-n-mn ...
      ringtail   the   first come   catch-DS:PRIOR-OPT-2SG
      'If you set a trap at a tree where *kapuls* (game mammals) come to
      feed on dead timber, and if you catch a ringtail possum first ...'
      (KHT 7:33)

15.5.3 BECAUSE

As noted earlier, the morphosyntactic apparatus for indicating that a particular situation (A) occurs prior to another (B) is often used, in combination with discourse context, to imply that B occurs because of A. See, for example, (84)–(87), (89) and associated discussion.

There are however other ways of more explicitly indicating the cause or reason for an event or situation. One is to use the post-nominal particle *nen* 'after (a goal), for (the purpose of)':

(93)   *Etp   nen   amjpan?*
       what   for   you.are.going
       'Why are you going?'

(94)   *Mon-nen   amjpin.*
       wood-for   I.am.going
       'I'm going after firewood.'

Another way of expressing this uses *kun ok* or *kun kun (ok)* (Ti Mnm *nb ak*, *nb nb ak*) 'thus, like this, accordingly, for this (reason)':

(95)   *Kun   ok   kbi   ownk.*
       thus the   having.left   I.came
       'That's why (thus that) I left and came back.'

(96)   *Yad   kunkun   skum   ok   ynab*
       I   accordingly   smoke   the   it.burnt
       kunkun   ŋi   opin.
       accordingly   having.seen   I.came
       'I came back because I saw the smoke.' (Literally, 'I thus seeing the smoke burning this I came.')

The noun *juj* 'root, base, basis, cause, reason' if often used in this sense:

(97)   *Sgaw   nb   ak   agep   juj   ak   gup,*
       wallaby   such   this   saying   reason   the   it.does
       bin-b   yb   ak   gpal   gpal   tek   mey   tagup   ak,
       people   true   the   they.do   they.do   like   that   it.walks.about the
       tawep   kd   omŋal   ak-nep ...
       walking.about   hindleg   two   only
       'One reason for this is that the wallaby is very like a human in the ways that it moves upright on its two hind legs ...' (*KHT* 1:46)

The clause initial conjunction *pen* 'reciprocally, consequently, so' and the complex conjunction *ji pen* (same meaning, except more emphatic) may sometimes be glossed 'because':

(98) *Pen gpan (pen) gpin.*
      reciprocally you.have.done reciprocally I.have.done
      'You did it so I did it too.'/'Because you did I did it too.'

15.5.4 LIKE

The most common exponent is *tek* 'like, similar, resembling', which occurs cliticised to noun phrases:

(99) *Skol wagn ak lak   mey madaw yb   ak lak*
     small kind the it.forms that madaw true the it.forms
     tek ak ...
     like the
     'The small kind is like the common *madaw* (ground possum) ...'
     (*KHT* 11:6)

(100) *... koslam ñu-day tek   ak   pyowl*
          difficult needle like that having.searched
      tanl   pakpal.
      having.climbed they-kill
      '... climbing the trees in search of game mammals is like hunting for needles.'

(see also (10), (35), (56) and (73)); *tek* also occurs cliticised to clauses (see (97)).

15.5.5 CAN

The sense of English *can* that is the proposed primitive is 'potential, possibility' as in 'It could rain tomorrow' and perhaps 'I could have done it, but I decided not to'. Kalam has a verbal suffix that marks hypothetical events that are contrary to fact:

(101) *Yad kaj ñb-n-p.*
      I   pig eat-1SG-CTRF
      'I could have eaten pork (if I'd been there, or if I'd been wicked enough to steal it, but I wasn't).'

However, this suffix cannot be used to mark future events that might happen. It is explicitly counterfactual.

The best candidate for potential CAN is probably the future tense plus the particle *akaŋ*, which marks an either/or question or an option or alternative.

(102) *Mñmon toy pk-ng-ab akaŋ.*
rain tomorrow strike-FUT-3SG question
'It could/might rain tomorrow.'

A few words on how Kalam speakers refer to the 'can of ability'. The generic assertion 'He can climb trees' is expressed by the habitual aspect, 'He climbs trees'. 'He could climb trees when young' is expressed as 'He used to climb trees when young'. A statement about a specific action, such as 'He can climb this tree', is expressed in either of two ways depending whether the statement is seen as applying to an imminent or desirable action or one which is merely hypothetical. If the first, the speaker says 'He will climb this tree'. If the second, he or she uses a contrary-to-fact verb: 'He could climb the tree (but he won't)' or 'He could have ... (but he didn't)'.

(103) *B sŋok, ñn ak tmel gak,*
man like.that arm the bad it.did
mab ak ma-tanub.
tree the not-he.climbs
'A man like that, with a crippled arm, doesn't/can't climb trees.' (Ti Mnm)

15.5.6 VERY

Kalam has several expressions with intensifying function: *yb* 'very, really, truly', *naban* 'extremely, indeed', *sketk* 'extraordinary, monstrous, awesome', *tmey* (Ti Mnm *tmel*) 'bad, excessive' and *o-o-oy!* (drawn out, half-shouted) 'so-o-o, oh so' (compare English *The giant was so-o-o big that* ...). The most common intensifier, *yb*, often follows *tmey*.

(104) *Kaj guk ayab, wak-nupey deg naban mdp.*
pig fat he.put skin-his shiny:smooth very it.stayed
'He put pig fat on his skin and made it very smooth and shiny.'

(105) *Kmn nb yñ tmel yb ak lak.*
game.mammal such strong excessive very the it.forms
'This game mammal is remarkably powerful.' (*KHT* 11:43)

The next example shows three intensifiers combined:

(106) ... *apal kti nb alyaŋ ak tap kub yb o-oy!*
they.say they thus down.there the thing big very wow!
Sketek ak lak!
monstrous the it.forms
'... they say it grows really huge! It is monstrous!' (*KHT* 11:59)

Reduplication of an adjective also has intensifying force; for example, *skoy* 'small', *skoy skoy* 'very small', *kasek* 'quick', *kasek kasek* 'very quick'.

15.6 Time and Place

15.6.1 WHERE and WHEN

Interrogative WHERE is usually *akay?* but sometimes *tp akay?* (literally, 'place where?').

(107) *Akay mdaban opan?*
where you.stay you.have.come
'Where have you been?'

(108) *Tp akay gp?*
place where it.happen
'Where did it happen?'

Interrogative WHEN is *won akay?* consisting of *won* 'piece, bit; period or interval of time' and *akay* 'where, which?'.

(109) *Won akay owngpan?*
time which you.will.come
'When will you come?'

One can also ask 'which day?', 'which month?', 'which year?' and so on using a temporal noun and *akay*. WHEN in the sense of '(at) the time when' is marked by *won* plus any of several determiners, for example, *won ak* 'that time, the time', with a plural equivalent *won (won) ogok* '(at) those times', *won ogni* '(in) these times'.

(110) ... *bapi mdek won ak cptmel apobkop* ...
father he.lived time that white.man if.he.had.come
'... if the white man had come to my area in the time of my father ...' (*KHT* Intro:80)

(111) Won   nb   ogok gos-kti   ak koŋay   ma-mdolgup ...
       time such those ideas-their the many   not-it.exists
       'In those days their ambitions were quite limited ...' (*KHT*
       Intro:78)

As in English the word for 'days' is used also with a determiner to mean 'time, period, era'.

15.6.2 AFTER (BEFORE)

Temporal order is marked by contrasting *nd* 'before, first, prior, ahead, older' (Ti Mnm *ned*), *nab* 'middle, intermediate' and *ksen* 'after, later, younger, new'.

(112) Nt-may   nd   amnmit,   yad yp   ksen   nngayn.
       You-two   before you.two.should.go   I   with later I.will.join
       'You two go should first/before (me), I'll join you later/afterwards.'

(113) Ksen tap   kob   ak   g   g   daglpal ...
       later thing burnt.grassland   this do do they.have.burnt
       'Later this grassland was burnt off ...' (*KHT* 1:87)

(See also (60).)

15.6.3 ABOVE and BELOW

Kalam has an extremely complex system of location-marking, adapted to the mountainous terrain. The locative nouns *at* 'above, on, the top' and *moluk* 'below, underneath' are members of a class that includes *mgan* 'inside, interior', *nab* 'middle, midst' and *ms* 'outside, the outside'. These nouns can occur alone in the locative phrase, as in (114) and (115), or in combination with various dependent orientational markers. Of these markers we need only note two here in their Etp Mnm forms: *yaŋ* 'lower, down, below' and *yoŋ* 'higher, up, above'.

(114) Mab   ak   juj   pug   juwak   ak moluk okok
       tree the root   dislocate   it.came.out   the under various.places
       mdeb,   mab   saj   pagak   moluk okok   mdeb.
       it.lives tree branch   it.broke   under various.places   it.lives
       'It also lives under the roots of fallen trees and under fallen branches.' (*KHT* 11:10)

(115) Tebl *at* mdp.
       table on it.stays
       'It's on the table.'

The combination *at-yoŋ* can be translated 'above, up above, on top of':

(116) Balus asap   seb   *at-yoŋ*.
       Plane it.is.sounding clouds top-higher
       'A plane can be heard above the clouds.'

There are more elaborate ways of expressing ABOVE and BELOW, adding additional orientation markers; for example,

(117) Yi *at* sŋ-yoŋ   ma-knb.
       Far top there-above not-it.sleeps
       'It never sleeps really high above the ground.'

15.7 Partonomy and Taxonomy

15.7.1 PART OF

The PART OF relation is expressed in various ways. Inalienable possession — indeed, any kind of possessive relation — is expressed by a head-plus-possessor construction.

(118) Tob-yad yuwt gsap.
       leg-my pain it.is.acting
       'My leg is hurting.'

The post-nominal particle or clitic *sek* 'with (in the sense of possessing, having), associated with, characterised by' is another way to express possession of a part or of an alienable possession.

(119) Kaj yng-sek dngayn.
       pig tail-with I.intend.to.get
       'I want pigs with tails.'

(120) Tu yj-sek   ak mdp.
       axe handle-with the it.exists
       'The axe has a handle.'

The noun *won* denotes 'part' in the sense of a 'piece, bit, small part, some (of)' and also 'period of time, particular time'.

(121) *Mon tb tb tb ... pñ won pk tki,*
tree cut cut cut topmost part hit sever
ap yap amnak.
come fall it.went
'They cut and cut and cut the tree and the topmost part was cut away and fell.'

(122) *Nunay nd skop kik gyak sb won ok,*
sister older group they they.did dung piece the
ñg won ok, ss won ok gyaknŋ...
water bit the, urine bit the they.were.doing
'The older sisters filled (the container) with pieces of dung and some water and some urine ...'

To say 'X is not part of Y', a Kalam might say 'X and Y are not joined, they are separate'.

There is a particle *ket* which, with an animate possessor, has the sense 'belonging to':

(123) *Kaj Wpc-ket.*
pig Wpc-belonging
'It's Wpc's pig.'

With an inanimate possessor it has the sense 'closely or characteristically associated with':

(124) *As ñg-ket ak.*
small:mammal water-belonging that
'It's a water animal/a small animal of the water.'

But I don't think it can be used to express a part–whole relation:

(125) **Jun tob-ket met.*
head foot-belonging not
'The head does not belong to the leg.'

15.7.2 KIND OF

Two words readily translate 'kind, sort': *wagn* and *kñŋ*. Both have a range of senses which may be translated (a) 'base, lower part of something', (b) 'kin-group, especially extended family co-resident in a house or house cluster', and (c) 'family, class, kind, sort, type'.

(126) ... cn alŋud tap kub wagn ak
          we up.here thing big class the
       skol wagn ak lak   ak.
       small class the it.forms he
       'We up here recognise large and small classes.' (*KHT* 11:5)

(127) Kmn   sgaw ak kñŋ almŋal lak,
       game.mammal wallaby the kind two   it.forms
       tap kub wagn ak, skol wagn ak.
       thing big kind the small kind the
       'There are two kinds of wallaby, one somewhat larger than the other.' (*KHT* 1:4)

15.8 Evaluators and Descriptors

15.8.1 GOOD and BAD

GOOD is *tep*; see (39) and note 3. BAD is *tmey*; see (38) and (103).

15.8.2 BIG and SMALL

BIG is *yob* in Etp Mnm, *kub* in Ti Mnm; see (106), (126) and (127). SMALL is *skoy* in Etp Mnm, *skol* in Ti Mnm; see (10), (99), (126) and (127).

15.9 Conclusion

Most concepts on the list of proposed primitives have one or more translation equivalents. However, there are a few problematic cases, namely those in which:

(a) Kalam has two partial equivalents. See discussion of WANT, section 15.2.6.
(b) Kalam has a translation equivalent but this term has a more general meaning which subsumes the putative primitive. See discussion of the 'mental predicates' (especially KNOW, sections 15.2.1 and 15.2.2, FEEL, section 15.2.1 and 15.2.4, and SAY, section 15.2.5) and of IF, section 15.5.2. The question arises in these cases whether the general meaning is properly analysed into a number of

distinct senses, one of which coincides with the primitive, or whether it is better left unanalysed with specific interpretations determined by pragmatic factors.

Notes

1. Z'graggen (1971, 1975) has grouped these other languages together as the Madang-Adelbert subphylum.
2. Symbols used in morpheme-by-morpheme glosses are: CTRF counterfactual, DUal, DS different subject from next verb, FUTure, HABITUAL, HORTative, OBJective or accusative form (of pronoun), OPTative, PAST, PERFect, PLural, PRESent, PRIOR action to next verb, PROGressive, PROSPective, RECent past, SG singular, SIMultaneous with next verb, SS same subject as next verb, - morpheme boundary, < > infix enclosed, : no morpheme boundary, . morpheme boundaries not marked in Kalam word.
3. The verb *n-* or *ng-* 'perceive' is used for 'feel' in reference to an involuntary sensation. The following example is an exception:

Mñab	ak	tkosp ...	cnop	gos	tep	npun	tep	gup.
land	the	it.clear	us	thought	good	we.perceive	good	it.makes

   'When the weather is fine, ... we enjoy [climbing trees], it feels good.' (*KHT* Intro:61)

Although in the next example the translator renders *gos nb ogok ngl* by 'the feelings of the hunters', a more faithful translation would be 'the thoughts that they have':

B	kmn	pak	ñbal ...
man	game	kill	they.eat

gos	nb	ogok	ngl,	nb	gpal	ok.
thought	such	the.PL	having.perceived	such	they.do	this

'Such are the feelings of hunters who regularly go into the forest.' (*KHT* Intro:67)

References

Cohen, L. Jonathan. 1971. "Some Remarks on Grice's Views about the Logical Particles of Natural Language". *Pragmatics of Natural Language* ed. by Y. Bar-Hillel. Reidel: Dordrecht.

Majnep, Ian Saem & Ralph Bulmer. 1990. *Kalam Hunting Traditions* ed. by Andrew Pawley. University of Auckland, Department of Anthropology Working Papers 85-90.

Posner, Roland. 1980. "Semantics and Pragmatics of Sentence Connectives in Natural Language". *The Signifying Animal* ed. by I. Rauch & G. F. Carr. Bloomington: Indiana University Press. (Reprinted in *Pragmatics and Speech Act Theory* ed. by R. S. Kiefer & J. Searle. Reidel: Dordrecht.)

Ruhl, Charles. 1989. *On Monosemy. A study in linguistic semantics*. Albany: State University of

New York Press.

Z'graggen, John. 1971. *Classificatory and Typological Studies in Languages of the Madang District* (= Pacific Linguistics C-19). Canberra: Australian National University.

Z'graggen, John. 1975. "The Madang-Adelbert Range Sub-Phylum". *New Guinea Area Languages and Language Study*, vol 1: *Papuan Languages and the New Guinea Linguistic Scene* (Pacific Linguistics C-38) ed. by S. A. Wurm, 569-612). Canberra: Australian National University.

16.1 Substantives

The basic exponents of I and YOU in French would be either the stressed pronouns *moi* and *toi* or the unstressed subject pronouns *je* and *tu*. While the former 'look better' in a list of semantic primitives, where each has an autonomy of its own, the latter prevail once the primitives are put to use in the Natural Semantic Metalanguage (NSM). French has two sets of allomorphs: *je/me/moi* for the first person, and *tu/te/toi* for the second. Their use is syntactically conditioned: *je* and *tu* are subjects, and *me* and *te* direct or indirect objects; *moi* and *toi* occur after prepositions and wherever stress is required. Except in the imperative, the subject pronouns are always expressed; in the spoken form of the language, they are, for most verbs and in most tenses, the only indicators of person. The use of *je/me/moi* and *tu/te/toi* is illustrated in (1):

(1)   a. *Je   veux y   aller   avec toi.*
           I   want there go   with you
           'I want to go there with you.'

       b. *Tu   m' obliges à te   parler de moi?*
           You me oblige   to you speak of   me
           'Are you forcing me to talk about myself to you?'

There is no speech level differentiation for the first person; for the second person, the standard language requires the use of *vous* as soon as the speaker wishes to create or to preserve a certain distance. *Vous* is used when talking to superiors, for instance, but also, at times, to younger children (especially those who don't belong to the speaker's family). However, the use of *tu* is rapidly spreading, even in contexts and/or situations where the semantically marked *vous* was traditionally the only choice. It is the preferred exponent for the semantic primitive YOU. *Vous* can be defined in terms of *tu*:

(2)   *je dis "vous"* =
           je ne dis pas "tu"
           si je dis "tu", tu pourrais éprouver quelque chose de mauvais
              envers moi

           'I say "vous" =
           I don't say "tu"
           if I say "tu", you could feel something bad towards me'

SOMEONE and SOMETHING are expressed by means of *quelqu'un* and *quelque chose*. Their morphological build-up mirrors that of their English counterparts. As in English, both are now frozen and can safely be considered to be semantically (and

Semantic and Lexical Universals in French

Bert Peeters
University of Tasmania, Hobart

Regional variation in French (especially at the phonological and the lexical levels) is significant.[1] This chapter looks at semantic and lexical universals in standard, that is Parisian, French (hereafter called 'French'). It finishes with a review of earlier work on French (Wierzbicka 1988) written in the language itself. The explications proposed in that first attempt are open to criticism; one particular explication is analysed and improved upon in the light of various findings reached in this paper. For a recent text in French, the reader is referred to Wierzbicka (1993).

From a typological point of view, French is quite similar to English. The two languages are basically SVO, but French adjectives, unlike their English counterparts, generally follow the noun they qualify. A large proportion of those that usually follow can precede a noun, but will then carry a subjective connotation (*une glorieuse victoire* is different from *une victoire glorieuse*). All adjectives agree in gender and number with the noun they qualify (as do articles, demonstratives, indefinite adjectives and a few others). Old French possessed a case system inherited from Latin. In the modern language, the only case-inflected forms left are to be found among the personal and the relative pronouns.

Verbal inflection remains much further developed in French than in English, although in the case of most regular verbs a majority of forms of the present tense, the imperfect and the conditional are phonetically identical. The future and the conditional are true tenses which do not require an auxiliary. The subjunctive mood is commonly used and may have to be used in the metalanguage (cf. section 16.2).

Further relevant details will be provided when the opportunity arises. As, unlike some other authors, I had little trouble in finding convincing counterparts for each semantic primitive (although there are minor problems with FEEL, TIME and KIND OF), I am not in a favourable position to make critical comments on the need to maintain or replace some elements in the list, and will refrain from doing so.

even morphologically) simple. Pronoun or adjective, *quelque* never loses its final vowel in front of another vowel (cf. *quelque aimable jeune fille* 'some kind young girl'), except in *quelqu'un*; *quelque chose*, on the other hand, is masculine whereas its component *chose* is feminine (cf. *quelque chose de petit* 'something small' versus *une petite chose* 'a small thing'). Note that when an adjective or an adjectival phrase follows, a particle-like element (*de*, or *d'* in front of a following vowel) must be inserted: *someone important* in French is *quelqu'un d'important*. Both *quelqu'un* and *quelque chose* are normally incompatible with a preceding determiner. The notions of THIS SOMEONE/THIS SOMETHING are expressed by means of *cette personne* and *cette chose*, and *personne* and *chose* (both feminine, as indicated by the preceding feminine demonstrative) are held to be allolexes of the basic exponents. The interrogative pronouns *qui* 'who' and *quoi/que/qu'est-ce qui/qu'est-ce que* 'what' are allolexes as well.

The use of all allolexes is illustrated in (3). *Quelque chose* in (3a) can refer, as *something* in English, to events ('You did something') or to entities ('This is something good').

(3) a. *Quelqu'un a vu quelque chose.*
Someone has seen something
'Someone saw something.'

b. *Deux personnes ont vu cette chose.*
Two people have seen this thing
'Two people saw this thing.'

c. *Qui a vu quoi?*
Who has seen what
'Who saw what?'

d. *Qu' est-ce? / Qu' est-ce que c'est?*
What is-it What is-it that it-is
'What is it?'

e. *Qu' est-ce qui est arrivé?*
What is-it that is happened
'What happened?'

As is shown in some of the other papers in this volume, the exponents of a particular semantic primitive do not all have to belong to the same part of speech. The last of our substantives, PEOPLE, is a noun in English. Its French counterpart could be the grammatically plural noun phrase *les gens* (cf. Wierzbicka 1993:17), where the definite article *les* is used to refer to a significant number and differs from the definite article in statements such as *Les baleines sont des mammifères* 'Whales are mammals', where all whales are referred to rather than a significant subset. Since the only universal use of PEOPLE seems to be as a subject, *on* — a pronoun normally glossed in English as 'one' (as in *One never knows*), but actually somewhat different from the English "personal 'one'" — may well be a better choice, however. The use of *on* is illustrated in (4):

(4) a. *Si tu fais ceci, on dira du mal de toi.*
 If you do this, people will-say evil-PART of you
 'If you do this, people will say bad things about you.'

 b. *On dit que Dieu sait tout.*
 People say that God knows everything
 'People say that God knows everything.'

16.2 Mental Predicates

When Descartes formulated his famous statement *Cogito ergo sum* (*Je pense donc je suis, I think therefore I am*), he was using an intransitive verb. *Think* in English and *penser* in French can be used either transitively or intransitively, but it is the former use we have in mind as a primitive. Canonical contexts are given in (5):

(5) a. *Je pensais que c' était un écureuil.*
 I thought that it was a squirrel
 'I thought it was a squirrel.'

 b. *Je pense qu' elle l' a mangé.*
 I think that she it has eaten
 'I think she has eaten it.'

For the verb *know*, many European languages have two words (cf. Wierzbicka 1989a and 1989b); French has *savoir* and *connaître*. In English, one can know (be acquainted or familiar with) a person or a thing, or know something (from memory or from study); one can know how to do something, or know something (be aware of it). *Connaître* is used in the first case, *savoir* in the other three. The only universal use is the last one; *savoir* will normally be followed by a clausal complement or by the substantive *quelque chose*. For instance:

(6) *Je sais par où il est allé.*
 I know by where he is gone
 'I know which way he went.'

If any of the other substantives is used with KNOW, it will be as a subject, not an object (the latter would require *connaître*).

SAY and WANT are extremely straightforward (FEEL is not, and is therefore left till last). In French, *dire* may be used where *say* in English would be wrong, for example, in *dire la vérité* 'tell the truth' (cf. Wierzbicka 1989a). The French verb has a broader range of use, even though it has the same meaning as English *say*. For the rest, it is as 'vague' as the English verb, and is not necessarily tied to the vocal medium. Its range of use as a primitive is identical to the one observed in the case of *savoir* (clausal complement or substantive *quelque chose* in direct object position).

(7) Il   a   dit   la   même   chose.
     He has said the same   thing
     'He said the same.'

Vouloir WANT, once again with a similar range of use, if followed by a subordinate clause, requires the latter's verb to be in the subjunctive, unless a simpler (and more universal?) syntax is preferred, whereby *Je veux que tu fasses quelque chose* 'I want you to do something' is rephrased as *Je veux ceci: tu fais quelque chose* 'I want this: you do something'. In some cases, the subjects in the main and in the subordinate clause may be coreferential, in spite of what is taught in grammar textbooks (cf. Ruwet (1991) for a brilliant new approach based on semantics; see also Peeters, forthcoming a).

(8) a. *Je veux voir mon grand-père.*
        I want see my grandfather
        'I want to see my grandfather.'

     b. *Je veux que tu saches ceci.*
        I want that you know this
        'I want you to know this.'

     c. *Je veux que je sois en mesure d' attaquer à l' aube.*
        I want that I am   capable   of attack   at the dawn
        'I want to be able to attack at dawn.'

It is when *vouloir* and *dire* are used together that caution must be exerted. In English, one would hardly use *want to say* with an inanimate subject, for inanimacy and volition are incompatible (except where the subject is personified). In French, both inanimate and animate subjects are possible. In the former case, *vouloir dire* is best translated as 'to mean', whereas in the latter both a literal interpretation ('want to say') and a frozen one are possible, depending on the context. As a combination of primitives, *vouloir dire* can only have its literal meaning.

(9) a. *Cette phrase ne veut rien dire du tout.*
This sentence NEG want nothing say at all
'This sentence doesn't mean anything at all.'

b. *Maman veut dire qu' elle est occupée.*
Mum wants say that she is busy
'Mum means she's busy' (but didn't say so clearly) or 'Mum wants to say she's busy' (but she's got scissors in her mouth and can't speak)

The one mental predicate we are left with is the only one in fact to be slightly problematical. However, the problem is of a nature different from what appears to be the case in most other languages sampled in this volume. It is not the case that there is no verb for FEEL in French: the catch is that the most obvious translation (*sentir*) is inappropriate. It is an obvious choice because it is, with respect to the meaning at stake, the standard dictionary translation of the **English** word *feel* (in much the same way as English *feeling* has French *sentiment* as its standard dictionary translation). It is an inappropriate choice because, in the NSM context in which it is supposed to be used (*sentir quelque chose de bon ou de mauvais*), *sentir* refers to a good or a bad smell rather than to a good or a bad feeling. Wierzbicka (personal communication) suggests that it may be better to leave out the SOMETHING in a Polish NSM (cf. Goddard (this volume) on 'do something good/bad' in Yankunytjatjara); this would make things only worse in French, as in that case the 'smell' reading is the only one possible. *Elle sent bon* means 'She smells nice'. In order to restore (unambiguously) the intended meaning, the verb would have to be made reflexive; but in that case, it takes an adverb rather than an adjective. *Je me sens bon is wrong; one has to say *Je me sens bien* 'I feel good'. A new problem arises immediately: *Je me sens bien* also means (and probably tends to mean) 'I feel well/I'm fine' and its opposite *Je me sens mal* will be understood as 'I feel unwell/sick', not at all as 'I feel bad'.

Other candidates for FEEL include *éprouver* and *ressentir*. Neither can take a subordinate clause, but I doubt we really want to count that particular syntactic frame among the ones that make up our universal grammar. Both refer, in their relevant meanings, to the perception of feelings such as love and sympathy, hate and rancour, sadness and regret, feelings that can be summarised as either good or bad. Both require the presence of *quelque chose de* before the adjectives *bon* and *mauvais* — which I don't see as a drawback *per se*. But how do we choose?

According to Bénac (1975:873), *ressentir* is typically used for feelings which are the indirect consequences of outside causes (as in Pascal's *L'âme ressent les passions du corps* 'The soul feels the passions of the body') or which subsist long after the event which caused them (as in *ressentir la perte d'un parent proche* 'feel the loss of a close relative'). It may be too specific, for it seems to exclude unspecified or confused feelings and to refer to vivid and/or clear experiences only. NSM phrases such as *quelque chose de bon/de mauvais* are intentionally broad and appear to be more natural after the verb *éprouver* (which is normally used with feelings that as such had not yet been experienced by the subject). A weaker argument in favour of *éprouver* is of a morphological nature: although formal complexity does not make a form unsuitable as an exponent of a semantic primitive, it may plead against its retention if a less formally complex exponent is more or less readily available. *Ressentir* remains clearly related to *sentir*, whereas the link between *éprouver* and *prouver* is purely etymological and has long ceased to be perceived by native speakers, especially when the verb takes on its primitive meaning. While narrower in its range of use than *feel*, *éprouver* is sufficiently broad and seems to correspond to the use of FEEL as a semantic primitive. What is needed is a verb that can be followed by the two evaluators GOOD and BAD, and by phrases such as 'like this'. *Eprouver* is perfectly acceptable under those conditions:

(10) a. J' éprouve quelque chose de bon / de mauvais.
 I feel something PART good PART bad
 'I feel something good/bad.'

b. J' éprouve quelque chose comme ceci.
 I feel something like this
 'I feel something like this.'

16.3 Determiners and Quantifiers

Apart from the first one (THIS), all determiners and quantifiers can be treated in sets of two. Although morphologically complex, the only fitting exponent of THIS in French seems to be *ceci*. It is an invariable pronoun and as such cannot be used adnominally. It has deictic and anaphoric uses (the latter being rather common in semantic explications using the set of lexical universals):

(11) a. Il l' a fait comme ceci.
 He it has done like this
 'He did it like this.'

b. Je fais quelque chose; après ceci ...
 I do something after this
 'I do something; after this ...'

The adnominal allolex (from which *ceci* derives) is *ce*; the latter is also used in subject position, with *être* 'to be' as the main verb. A modal verb may intervene:

(12) a. *Ce   sont   tes   parents.*
       This/it   are   your   parents
       'It's/they are your parents.'

   b. *Ce pourrait être tes parents.*
      It could   be   your parents
      'It could be your parents.'

A 'they' reading seems to be impossible in the case of (12b). On the other hand, adnominal *ce* has a number of allomorphs (*ce* masculine singular, *cet* masculine singular before a vowel or so-called mute *h*, *cette* feminine singular, *ces* plural): it agrees in gender and in number with the noun it qualifies. Among the French exponents of the semantic primitives, there are no masculine words for it to agree with (unless pseudo-primitives, that is, elements which are used as such but must be explicated elsewhere in terms of the primitives alone, are included). The adnominal forms, strictly speaking, require a postnominal *ci* to become entirely unambiguous (cf. *cette personne-ci* 'this person (over here)' versus *cette personne-là* 'that person (over there)').

For THE SAME and OTHER, I suggest *le même* and *autre*:

(13) a. *Je veux faire la même chose.*
       I want do   the same thing
       'I want to do the same.'

   b. *Elle pensait que c' était un autre homme.*
      She thought that it was another man
      'She thought it was another man.'

Both primitives occur pre-nominally; the adjective *autre* has another meaning when used post-nominally (e.g. *un autre homme* 'another (a different) man, one who is not like this one here' versus *un homme autre* 'a different man, one who is not like any other man'; the latter use is admittedly literary). For 'another of the same type, another in a series', different words are used in English (*give me another beer*) and in French (*passe-moi encore une bière*; *passe-moi une autre bière* suggests the drinker wants a different brand).

Le même is preferable to *la même chose* as it seems more easily compatible with *personne* (an allolex of *quelqu'un*; see section 16.1). The combination of both elements requires no more than an agreement in gender (*le même* becomes *la même*). The same agreement would of course impose itself when *chose* follows (an allolex of *quelque chose*). Although agreement in the feminine seems to be inevitable (the reader will recall that there are no masculine words among the primitives), a masculine base form seems more natural to start with. Alternatively, a base form such as *la même chose* would require the existence of a headless *la même* as the allomorph or allolex to be used in conjunction with *personne*. This seems to be a less attractive proposal. Notice that the French exponent of this primitive always requires a nominal head to be explicitly present, whereas in English for instance *the same* can occur independently.

ONE and TWO hardly need any comment: their French exponents are *un* and *deux*. *Un* is the only numeral (it is also, at the same time, an indefinite article) which has a separate feminine form, *une*. MANY can be rendered by means of *beaucoup*, which also means 'much'. I presume the English words would be allomorphs; they bear witness to a distinction between count and mass nouns, which is not observed to the same extent in French. *Beaucoup* can be used on its own (in which case it means 'much'); when it is followed by a noun, the latter is to be introduced with a particle *de* (cf. *quelqu'un* and *quelque chose* above). ALL is masculine plural in French, but there is an allomorph for the feminine gender: *tous/toutes*. There are portmanteau words for the notions of ALL PEOPLE and ALL THINGS: *tous les quelqu'uns* = *toutes les personnes* = *tout le monde* 'everyone' (literally, 'whole the world'); *tous les quelque-choses* = *toutes les choses* = *tout*. The grammatical errors are intentional: *quelques-uns* 'a few (people)' and *quelques choses* 'a few things' are not the kind of plurals I had in mind.

(14) a. *Il a deux fils et une fille.*
He has two sons and one daughter
'He has two sons and one daughter.'

b. *Elle a beaucoup de pantalons.*
She has many PART trousers
'She has many trousers.'

c. *Ils sont tous morts.*
They are all dead
'They have all died.'

d. *Il a marié toutes ses filles.*
He has given-away-in-marriage all his daughters
'All his daughters he has given away in marriage.'

16.4 Actions and Events

DO can be rendered by means of *faire*. The latter also corresponds to most uses of the English verb *make*, which is not a semantic primitive. The kind of usage we have in mind for universal *faire* is illustrated in (13a) and also in (15):

(15)   *Tu   as   fait   quelque chose   de   mauvais.*
       You have done something   PART bad
       'You did something bad.'

There is no difficulty in keeping DO and SAY apart; however, in the past historic (known in French as the *passé simple*), *faire* can be used for *dire* after direct discourse and with subject–verb inversion:

(16)   *"Je suis content",   fit- il.*
       I   am   glad   did he
       '"I am glad," he said.'

It goes without saying that *faire* used in this particular manner is not a lexical universal. On the other hand, wherever *do* is used in English semantic explications using primitives, *faire* seems to be an accurate counterpart.

Se passer and *se produire*, followed by *à*, *en* or *dans* (in complementary distribution), would appear to be adequate exponents of HAPPEN (TO/IN), but they can't be used with an indirect object referring to the person to (*à*) whom something happens. On the other hand, *arriver à/en/dans* may sound a little colloquial; nonetheless, I have preferred it to any other candidate for this primitive in Peeters (1989).

It must be pointed out that *arriver* is polysemous, and that, out of context, ambiguity can arise: *Quelque chose d'autre est arrivé* means either that 'Something else arrived' or 'Something else happened'. We are dealing here with a case of polysemy which is not unlike the one of *-pet* in Mangap-Mbula (Bugenhagen, this volume). Etymologically, *arriver* stems from **adripare* 'come to the shore', which is semantically not unrelated to *-pet* 'to come in a seaward direction'. Subcategorisation in Mangap-Mbula and French is similar as well: when pronominalised, the person to whom something happens appears as a dative pronoun *lui* 'to him/her', whereas the place where something happens (or where someone arrives), when pronominalised, appears for obvious reasons as a locative adverbial (*y* 'there'). *Lui* and *y* always precede the verb (cf. Herslund 1988 for further details; see also Peeters 1991).

(17)   a. *Qu'   est-ce qui   est   arrivé?*
           What is-it   that   is   happened
           'What happened?'

       b. *Quelque chose   de   mauvais   (lui)   est   arrivé.*
           Something   PART bad   (to-him/her) is   happened
           'Something bad happened (to him/her).'

       c. *Quelque chose   de   mauvais   y   est   arrivé.*
           Something   PART bad   there is   happened
           'Something bad happened there.'

16.5 Meta-Predicates

There are several allolexes for the primitive NOT/DON'T WANT/NO! in French (as in English). DON'T WANT has as its French exponent *ne pas vouloir/je ne veux pas* (the former being the negated infinitive, the latter the same verb in the first-person singular of the indicative present). NO! can be expressed as *non!* Finally, if we have to negate one of the universal verbs, the allolex to go for is *ne ... pas*. The dots replace the verb, which normally separates the two elements. Before an infinitive, *ne pas* can appear without an intervening verb (cf. *Je ne vous oblige pas à chanter* 'I don't force you to sing' versus *Je vous oblige à ne pas chanter* 'I force you not to sing').

(18) a. *Je   ne   veux pas que ceci arrive.*
         I   NEG   want not that this happens
         'I don't want this to happen.'

   b. *Non! Je n'   ai   pas fait cela.*
         No   I NEG have not done that
         'No! I didn't do it.'

The reason why, in the morpheme-by-morpheme glosses above, the first element is rendered as NEG and the second as 'not' is that the former tends to become a superfluous particle without lexical meaning: in colloquial speech, *ne* is often not present anymore, *pas* being the only negative marker in a negative statement.

It should not go unnoticed that, when used negatively, *penser* may be followed by a subordinate clause whose verb is in the subjunctive. However, the indicative is not impossible; in general, there seems to be a slight difference in meaning which continues to intrigue grammarians and linguists alike (for a recent overview of the literature and a not entirely convincing new attempt at explaining the difference, see Kampers-Manhe (1991); cf. also Peeters (forthcoming b)). Textbooks often teach that either mood can be used. The difference may well be close to disappearing.

COULD (MAYBE) was proposed as a meta-predicate, in replacement of CAN, at the Workshop on Semantic and Lexical Universals in February 1992. The English exponent (I ignore the bracketed allolex, which can be rendered in French as *peut-être*) is ambiguous between the simple past and the conditional, for which there are two different forms in French (*pouvait, pourrait*); it has the present form CAN (French *peut*, systematically used for instance in Peeters (1993)) as an allolex. The difference between them is conditioned by tense and mood. As the contexts show, the verb is supposed to convey possibility only. The same verb is used in English and French to express permission granted by someone else; this is not part of the meaning of the semantic primitive COULD.

(19) a. *Hier,   il   ne   pouvait pas   travailler.*
       Yesterday he NEG   could   not   work
       'Yesterday he couldn't work.'

   b. *Il pourrait pleuvoir demain.*
       It could   rain   tomorrow
       'It could rain tomorrow.'

   c. *On   ne   peut pas   savoir   s'   il viendra?*
       One NEG   can   not   know   whether he will-come
       'Aren't we allowed to know whether he will come?'

BECAUSE, in universal semantic explications, will almost always be followed by THIS, to which it is linked with a particle. The French way of saying *because of this* is either *en raison de ceci* or *à cause de ceci*. The former is rather formal. A third translation, which cannot be related as easily to other parts of the universal lexicon, would be *voilà pourquoi* 'that's why'. The remaining candidate consists of the noun *cause* 'cause' followed by a particle *de* and preceded by the preposition *à*. If a clause follows, the allomorph to be used is *à cause du fait que*, unless the allolex *parce que* is preferred. In the contexts given below, *cela* 'that' has been preferred to *ceci* 'this'. The result sounds better, but is not semantically simple.

(20) a. *Il   y   avait   beaucoup   de   bruit.*
       it   there had   much   PART   noise
       A cause de cela, je   ne   pouvais pas dormir.
       because of that I   NEG   could   not sleep
       'There was a lot of noise. Because of that, I couldn't sleep.'

   b. *Il est parti parce que je le lui   avais demandé.*
       He is left because   I it to-him/her had   asked
       'He left because I asked him to.'

The remaining meta-predicates are straightforward: IF is *si*, LIKE is *comme* and VERY is *très*. In French, *ainsi* is a portmanteau word for *comme ceci*.

(21)   *S'   il pleut, je   ne   viendrai   pas.*
         If it rains   I NEG   will-come   not
         'If it rains, I won't come.'

(22) a. *Il l' a   fait ainsi...*
         He it has done like-this
         'He did it like this ...'

b. *C' est comme une rose, mais ce n' est pas une*
   It is like a rose but it NEG is not a
   rose.
   rose
   'It's like a rose, but it's not a rose.'

(23) a. *C' est très bon / très mauvais.*
     It is very good   very bad
     'It's very good/very bad.'

   b. *C' est très grand / très petit.*
      It is very big   very small
      'It's very big/very small.'

The combination *very much* may raise a problem: **très beaucoup* is not allowed. One could possibly repeat the adjective (*beaucoup beaucoup*) or else opt for an allolex (?) *vraiment*.

16.6 Time and Place

In French, WHEN can be rendered by means of the interrogative *quand*. *Lorsque* is felt to be too formal. I am a little reluctant to accept *temps* as a possible allolex, although *time* in English is a perfectly suitable allolex of *when*. The problem is that things such as *at that time, at time t, before/after time t* sound fine; their counterparts with *temps* do not. The only exception here would be *en même temps* 'at the same time'. **A ce temps* 'at that time' sounds really bad. *A cette époque* is fine, but it places us in a temporal framework which is too vast for the purposes of a universal semantic explication. Without being as bad, *temps* remains questionable where reference is made to a specific point in time conveniently called *t*. Should there be a definite article? *Au temps t* 'at time t', where *au* is a contraction of the preposition *à* and the definite article *le*, is better than *?à temps t*; on the other hand, *avant temps t* 'before time t' and *après temps t* 'after time t', where there is no article, are much better than *??avant le temps t* and *??après le temps t*, which some native speakers will probably find outright unacceptable.

Wierzbicka (personal communication) tells me that she objects to admitting French *moment* as an exponent of TIME, which deprives us of the most natural and idomatic way of expressing reference to time in French (*à ce moment*, or even better *à ce moment-là*). I suspect her objection is based on the assumption that the French and English words are similarly restricted to **points** in time. This is not so: French *moment* closely corresponds to TIME, is more widely used than English *moment*, and suits all the necessary canonical contexts (*à ce moment-là, au moment t, avant/après le moment t, au même moment*), whether we refer to punctual events or not.

The use of *quand* and *moment* is exemplified in (24):

(24) a. *Quand as- tu fait cela?*
When have you done that
'When did you do it?'

b. *Cela nous est arrivé au même moment.*
That to-us is happened at-the same moment
'It happened to us at the same time.'

c. *À ce moment-là, Pierre était à Londres.*
At that moment-there Peter was at London
'At that time, Peter was in London.'

WHERE is another interrogative, and can be expressed as such in French (*où*). *Endroit* 'place' and *(être) quelque part* '(be) somewhere' are allolexes. Exactly like *somewhere* in English, *quelque part* is morphologically complex; the English primitive is related to *elsewhere*, *nowhere* and *anywhere* in the same way as the French primitive is related to *autre part* (literally, 'other part') and *nulle part* (literally, 'none-at-all part'). *Endroit* has been preferred to *lieu*, which strikes this author as rather too specific.

(25) a. *Où as- tu fait cela?*
Where have you done that
'Where did you do it?'

b. *Cela nous est arrivé au même endroit, pas dans*
That to-us is happened at-the same place not in
un endroit différent.
a place different
'It happened to us in the same place, not in a different place.'

The prepositions AFTER and BEFORE have already been introduced, and the reader is now familiar with their French exponents *après* and *avant*. In semantic explications, they will only be followed by demonstrative *ceci* or, as indicated above, by the temporal reference point *t*. We would have to accept allomorphs if we were to allow clauses or verbs in the (past) infinitive. With clauses, one would have *avant que* (with the subordinate verb in the subjunctive) and *après que* (traditionally followed by a verb in the indicative, but increasingly used with the subjunctive, undoubtedly under the influence of its opposite number). With infinitives, *après* would remain as is, but the following verb would have to be a past infinitive; *avant* would require a particle-like element *de*.

(26) a. *Ils habitent à Paris maintenant. Avant cela, ils*
They live at Paris now. Before that they
habitaient à Rome.
lived at Rome
'They live in Paris now. Before that, they used to live in Rome.'

b. *Après cela, elle est devenue très malade.*
After that, she is become very sick
'After that, she got very sick.'

UNDER and ABOVE are straightforward as well, but are morphologically more complex in French than they are in English. UNDER, at first sight, could have been expressed by means of *sous*; however, as we are dealing with a clear case of antonymy, I feel it is safer to opt for two exponents which unambiguously relate to one another. *Sous* is antonymically related to *sur*, but the latter is not equivalent to ABOVE (*sur la table* means 'on the table', not 'above the table'). We will therefore adopt *au-dessous de* and *au-dessus de* instead.

(27) a. *Il y avait de sombres nuages au-dessus de*
It there had PART somber clouds above
l' horizon.
the horizon
'There were dark clouds above the horizon.'

b. *De notre avion, nous regardions au-dessous de*
From our plane we watched under
nous les montagnes.
us the mountains
'From our plane, we were watching the mountains below us.'

16.7 Partonomy and Taxonomy

PART OF, recently renamed HAS (PARTS), and KIND OF, recently renamed DIFFERENT KINDS, help express relations of partonomy and taxonomy. French has a straightforward exponent for the first one, *partie de* or *avoir (des parties)*:

(28) a. *Beaucoup de livres ont des parties appelées*
Much/many PART books have parts-PART called
chapitres.
chapters
'Many books have parts called chapters.'

b. *Ce   cheval   a   la   queue longue.*
   That horse   has the   tail long
   'That horse has a long tail.'

c. *Le visage a un nez, une bouche et deux yeux.*
   The face has a nose a mouth and two eyes

   'The face has a nose, a mouth and two eyes.'

The translation of KIND OF/DIFFERENT KINDS is a more complex matter. I believe more research is needed; for now, I would say that *espèce de/différentes espèces* is better than *sorte de/différentes sortes* or *genre de/différents genres*. With natural species, neither *genre de* nor *sorte de* seem appropriate. Both sound extremely unidiomatic; at the most, une *sorte de fleur* could make one think of a clumsy drawing of any type of flower rather than a particular subtype or species. With books, *genre* seems to be quite all right, but *espèce* is surely not impossible.

(29) *Quand nous sommes allés au zoo, nous avons vu*
     When we   are   gone to-the zoo we   have seen
     différentes espèces d' animaux.
     different   kinds   of animals
     'When we went to the zoo, we saw different kinds of animals.'

An additional problem relates to the position of the adjective *différent*. When *espèces* is not further qualified (as in DIFFERENT KINDS OF SOMETHING), the adjective seems to be awkward in a pre-nominal position. We would therefore have:

(30) *Ces arbres sont de la même espèce, pas de deux*
     These trees are of the same kind   not of two
     espèces différentes.
     kinds   different
     'These trees are the same kind, not two different kinds.'

16.8 Descriptors and Evaluators

No comments whatsoever are necessary with respect to the way in which GOOD and BAD are to be expressed in French. However, as in the case of *différentes espèces/espèces différentes*, there may be a problem of word order. Where *bon* 'good' and *mauvais* 'bad' relate to moral qualities and qualify a noun (i.e. in the absence of a copula), they must follow the noun they qualify:

(31) a. *Tu   as   fait   quelque chose de   bon / de   mauvais.*
    You have done something   PART good PART bad
    'You did something good/bad.'

   b. *C' est un homme bon / mauvais.*
    It is a man   good bad
    'He is a good/bad man.'

Where other than moral qualities are referred to (but this seems to be a usage which is not universal; note the different English translation), the order is to be reversed.

(32) *J' ai   trouvé la bonne solution.*
    I have found the good solution
    'I found the correct solution.'

BIG is *grand* and SMALL is *petit*. Both usually appear in front of the noun they qualify:

(33) a. *J' ai   vu un grand arbre.*
       I have seen a big   tree
       'I saw a big tree.'

   b. *J' ai   vu un petit chien.*
       I have seen a small dog
       'I saw a small dog.'

It may be useful to note that *big* in English seems to have a broader meaning than *grand* in French. There are cases where *gros* would be a better translation (e.g. *un gros ventre* 'a big belly'). The meaning 'gros' is not a universal meaning of the primitive BIG. *Gros* relates to volume only, whereas *grand* is three-dimensional.

16.9 Conclusion

Until quite recently, the translatability of the semantic primitives had been more or less taken for granted: ever since the publication of Wierzbicka (1972), itself a translation from a Polish original, Wierzbicka herself had continuously written in English, Polish and Russian, using the set of universals, throughout its consecutive developmental stages, in an English, a Polish and a Russian version, in order to explicate the meanings of words in these three languages, and in a host of others. The situation changed somewhat with the publication of Wierzbicka (1986a), where two 'methodological principles' were proposed. I quote in extenso:

There are two methodological principles which I should like to propose. (1) If the meanings encoded in one language A ... are to be made intelligible to people from a different cultural and linguistic background B ..., then those meanings have to be expressed in semantic formulae constructed in simple and generally understandable words from language B. (2) If the semantic formulae constructed in simple and generally understandable words from language B ... are to constitute plausible hypotheses about the native speakers' meanings encoded in language A ..., *then those formulae must be readily translatable into language A.*

(Wierzbicka 1986a:35-36; emphasis added)

Eventually, the two principles were integrated in a broader framework (cf. Wierzbicka 1987). The second one came to be called the 'principle of indigenisation', and was introduced before the first, the 'principle of translatability'. I must add that I am rather puzzled by the way in which Wierzbicka chose her labels: translatability is at the heart of her principle of indigenisation much more than it is at the heart of her principle of translatability.

In early 1988, the French journal *Langages* published Wierzbicka's first paper entirely written in French. Wierzbicka (1988) is about love, anger, joy and boredom as they are linguistically expressed in French and in Ifaluk (a language spoken in the Pacific). The paper had been prepared for publication in Polish, but was eventually translated by Elzbieta Jamrozik, who was responsible for the running text, and by Wierzbicka herself, who assumed the more delicate task of rephrasing the semantic explications. Quite unexpectedly, Wierzbicka failed to translate the explications in a satisfactory way. The formula in (34) was proposed for the French word *colère* (which expresses a kind of anger; the English translation is as literal as possible). I suggest it be rephrased as in (35).

(34)   *X ressent de la colère* =
    (a)   *X pense: Y a fait quelque chose de mal*
    (b)   *je ne veux pas que Y fasse de telles choses*
    (c)   *X ressent un mauvais sentiment envers Y à cause de cela*
    (d)   *X veut faire quelque chose de mauvais à Y à cause de cela*

'X feels *colère* =
    (a)   X thinks: Y has done something bad
    (b)   I do not want Y to do such things
    (c)   X feels a bad feeling towards Y because of that
    (d)   X wants to do something bad to Y because of that'

(35)　　*X est en colère* =
　　　　X pense ceci:
　　　　　　Y a fait quelque chose de mauvais
　　　　　　je ne veux pas ceci: Y fait des choses comme cela
　　　　　　X éprouve quelque chose de mauvais envers Y à cause de cela
　　　　　　X veut faire quelque chose de mauvais à Y à cause de cela

The new formula is simpler in its syntax and takes into account the suggestions made in this paper. Especially disturbing was the use of the phrase *ressentir un sentiment* (as clumsy as *feel a feeling* in English) and the adverb *mal* (which has the same meaning as the adjective *mauvais*). The noun *sentiment* could have been avoided altogether; *ressentir*, on the other hand, is better than *sentir*, but not as good as *éprouver* (see section 16.2). It is surprising that Wierzbicka did not think of the latter, used up to seven times in the body of the translated text. Ironically, elsewhere (Wierzbicka 1986b:590) *éprouver* is explicitly used as an equivalent of *feel*. As a matter of fact, apart from a few marginal problems — nothing in comparison with the ones that arise in some of the other languages examined in this volume — French has clear exponents for all the primitives.

Note

[1]　The author wishes to thank the Australian Research Council for its financial support. Interlinear glossing symbols used are: NEGative, PARTitive.

References

Bénac, Henri. 1975. *Dictionnaire des synonymes conforme au dictionnaire de l'Académie française*. Paris: Hachette.
Herslund, Michael. 1988. *Le datif en français*. Louvain/Paris: Peeters.
Kampers-Manhe, Brigitte. 1991. *L'opposition subjonctif/indicatif dans les relatives*. Amsterdam: Rodopi.
Peeters, Bert. 1989. *Commencement, Continuation, Cessation: A conceptual analysis of a set of English and French verbs from an axiological point of view*. PhD Thesis, Department of Linguistics, Australian National University, Canberra.
Peeters, Bert. 1991. Review of Herslund (1988). *Canadian Journal of Linguistics* 36.94-101.
Peeters, Bert. 1993. "*Commencer* et *se mettre à*: Une description axiologico-conceptuelle". *Langue française* 98.24-47.
Peeters, Bert. Forthcoming a. Review of Ruwet (1991). *Canadian Journal of Linguistics*.
Peeters, Bert. Forthcoming b. Review of Kampers-Manhe (1991). *Word*.
Ruwet, Nicolas. 1991. *Syntax and Human Experience*. Chicago: University of Chicago Press.

Wierzbicka, Anna. 1972. *Semantic Primitives*. Frankfurt: Athenäum.
Wierzbicka, Anna. 1986a. "Semantics and the Interpretation of Cultures: The meaning of 'alternate generations' devices in Australian languages". *Man* 21.34-49.
Wierzbicka, Anna. 1986b. "Human Emotions: Universal or culture-specific?" *American Anthropologist* 88.584-594.
Wierzbicka, Anna. 1987. "Kinship Semantics: Lexical universals as a key to psychological reality". *Anthropological Linguistics* 29.131-156.
Wierzbicka, Anna. 1988. "L'amour, la colère, la joie, l'ennui: La sémantique des émotions dans une perspective transculturelle". *Langages* 89.97-107.
Wierzbicka, Anna. 1989a. "Semantic Primitives and Lexical Universals". *Quaderni di Semantica* 10.103-121.
Wierzbicka, Anna. 1989b. "Semantic Primitives: The expanding set". *Quaderni di Semantica* 10.309-332.
Wierzbicka, Anna. 1993. "La quête des primitifs sémantiques: 1965–1992". *Langue française* 98.9-23.

Part 3: Review

Semantic Primitives Across Languages: A Critical Review

Anna Wierzbicka
Australian National University, Canberra

Hunting for semantic and lexical universals is not like pearl-fishing. Primitives do not present themselves glittering and unmistakable. Identifying them is an empirical endeavour but one that calls for much interpretative effort.

Although the overwhelming conclusion emerging from this survey of languages is that there is indeed a universal "alphabet of human thoughts" (Leibniz 1903 [MS]:435), this by no means implies that no problems have arisen in testing our hypothetical set of conceptual and lexical universals. This closing chapter is devoted mainly to a survey of those problems.

In particular, as the research reported here illustrates, polysemy (in a broad sense, covering also homonymy) is a major problem. If, for example, it is discovered that in a language the same word can be glossed as both SAY and WANT, and that there is no word just for SAY or for WANT, it does not follow from this that this language has no word which means SAY: the question is whether or not the word which can mean either SAY or WANT can be shown to be polysemous. Of course, polysemy must never be postulated lightly. The first assumption should always be that a word or morpheme has only one meaning; but it would be foolish to hold on to this assumption dogmatically in the face of contrary evidence.[1] (For fuller discussion of this problem, cf. Wierzbicka, in press.)

One type of evidence which we regard as particularly telling is syntactic evidence. If 'the same word' can mean either SAY or WANT but each of these senses has a distinct syntactic frame (as, for example, in Mangap-Mbula; see Bugenhagen's paper, p. 104), then we can regard this word as polysemous, and both meanings as having their own lexical exponent.

By positing polysemy wherever syntactic (or other) evidence justifies it, we do not deny the existence of various conceptual affinities between the multiple meanings of the same word or morpheme. Patterns of polysemy recurring in many languages cannot be accidental and must point to affinities of various kinds between the meanings sharing the same exponent. But meanings may be related in many different ways, not necessarily in a compositional way; the rationale for recurring patterns of polysemy is one of the main focal points of this chapter.

Conceptual primitives are mutually independent in the sense that they don't share any identifiable parts. Nonetheless, YOU is obviously related, in a way, to I, I is related to THIS, SOMEONE is related to SOMETHING, WHERE is related to WHEN, WHEN is related to AFTER, IF is related to CAN (MAYBE), and so on. The nature of these different links, and their various reflections in the form of the exponents, provide a fascinating subject for further investigation. But the first task at hand is the cross-linguistic identification and verification of the primitives.

Another problem which has often made itself felt in the research reported here is that of 'allolexy': just as one word (or morpheme) may have two or more different meanings, one meaning may have two or more lexical exponents; and this applies also at the level of semantic primitives. This fact, too, can make cross-linguistic identification of semantic primitives less straightforward than one might wish.

In his classic work *Lexical semantics*, Apresjan postulated that in an ideal metalanguage for the representation of meanings "basic [i.e. elementary] meanings and their names must stand in one-to-one correspondence to one another":

> An ideal lexicon of the semantic language (which has not been produced by anyone yet) must satisfy the following condition: each word of this lexicon must stand for exactly one (basic when possible) meaning; each basic meaning must be expressed by exactly one word of the semantic language, no matter what meaning definition it is used in ...
> (Apresjan 1992 [1974]:49)

One can of course sympathise with this view, but if our semantic metalanguage is to be carved out of natural language, neither of these two postulates (no polysemy, no synonymy/allolexy) can be met in a straightforward manner: natural language simply does not work that way.

Because of polysemy, in Samoan formulae the same element *fai* may represent (depending on the grammatical frame) either the universal element SAY or the universal element DO. Because of allolexy, in English formulae two different elements *I* and *me* may represent the same universal element I (EGO), as in the sentences 'I did something bad' and 'Something bad happened to me'. Since in both cases (the Samoan and the English) meanings can be uniquely identified (and clearly differentiated) in terms of lexical material **and** grammatical frames, in a sense Apresjan's postulates are met, but they are not met in a straightforward manner.

Once again, hunting for semantic and lexical universals is not exactly like pearl-fishing. But it is no less exciting and no less rewarding.

17.1 Substantives

17.1.1 I and YOU

All the languages explored in this volume have words for YOU and I. Among the problems related to these two concepts, three deserve special consideration: the meaning of different case forms, polysemy, and the relationship between semantics and pragmatics.

The question of the meaning of different case forms is raised explicitly by Harkins and Wilkins in their paper on Arrernte, where they say that, for example, the two forms of the word for I, *ayenge* '1SG:S/O' and *the* '1SG:A', "by virtue of their cases ... contain additional specifiable information besides just I" (p. 286). But the authors do not say what this 'specifiable' information is. For example, how does the meaning of *the* I in *the mpware-* 'I do' differ from that of *ayenge* I in *ayenge kaltye* 'I know'? Since the choice of one of these two exponents of I is determined by the choice of the predicate, there is no reason, in our view, why they should not be regarded as allolexes encoding exactly the same semantic element, I.

By saying this, I do not reject the view which I have expressed elsewhere (cf. Wierzbicka 1980b, 1983) that, roughly speaking, cases have meaning, or rather that different syntactic constructions involving different cases differ in meaning. Cases 'have meaning' in the context of complex syntactic constructions which can be explicated in terms of the primitives. But at the level of semantic explications, there are no constructions which could be further explicated. Any attempt to explicate some part of a fully explicated sentence — such as, for example, 'Before this time, I did something bad' — must inevitably lead to a *regressus ad infinitum* (because the new explication itself would contain some parts which one would be tempted to explicate, and so on, *ad infinitum*). Whether in a given language the word for I in the equivalent of the sentence above is in the nominative or in the ergative case cannot make any difference to its meaning. To put it differently, if 'I$_{NOM}$ did' differed in some way in 'meaning' from 'I$_{ERG}$ did', this difference could not be captured in a metalanguage in which both I and DO are regarded as primitives. (All analysis must come to an end, and in semantics this end is reached when one comes to the level of primitives.) This is why the word 'meaning' above has been put in inverted commas: if by 'meaning' we mean 'specifiable meaning', then there is no difference in meaning between 'I$_{ERG}$ did' (as in Arrernte) and 'I$_{NOM}$ did' (as, for example, in Polish), or between 'someone$_{NOM}$ knows' (as in Arrernte) and 'someone$_{ERG}$ knows' (as in Samoan), nor can there be any difference in meaning between 'I$_{NOM}$ know' and 'I$_{ERG}$ do', other than the difference associated with the primitives KNOW and DO. (For further discussion of this problem see Goddard's paper on Yankunytjatjara, pp. 235–236.)

Turning now to the question of polysemy, I will reiterate here the claim made in my earlier publications (cf. Wierzbicka 1989a:109, 1991b:392) that the English word *you* has two distinct meanings, *you*$_{SG}$ (*thou*) and *you*$_{PL}$; and that this polysemy can be established (inter alia) on the basis of the contrast between the forms *yourself* and *yourselves*. For example, in the sentences

(a)   You should try to know yourself.
(b)   You should try to know yourselves.

the choice between the direct object *yourself* and *yourselves* depends on the meaning of the subject, 'you$_{SG}$' or 'you$_{PL}$' (cf. also Goddard, in press). It is interesting to note, however, that in the set of languages discussed in the present volume every single one has distinct, non-polysemous words for the primitives I and YOU. In particular, there is no language in which YOU and I share the same exponent.

I would add that if English did not have a lexical exponent for the primitive YOU$_{SG}$, its expressive power (as compared with that of other languages) would be seriously deficient, and that anyone who would want to claim that the English word *you* is vague rather than polysemous would have to face this consequence.

For example, according to this analysis one would not be able to express in English a simple message such as 'You (i.e. thou) did something bad' — a message which as far as we know can be expressed in any other human language and which is particularly important from a moral, social, legal and religious point of view.

The distinction between polysemy and vagueness is extremely important in semantics, but it is meaningful only if it is drawn with reference to some set of primitives. For example, it makes sense to say that the French word *fille* is polysemous between 'girl' and 'daughter' but vague between 'little girl' and 'big girl' because the shared core of 'little girl' and 'big girl' can be expressed in one definition (built out of primitives), whereas the shared core of 'girl' and 'daughter' can't (cf. Wierzbicka, in press). But there can be no tenable definitions without some set of indefinables (that is, primitives), and so without some set of primitives to rely on, the very distinction between vagueness and polysemy becomes vacuous.

Returning to *you*$_{SG}$ and *you*$_{PL}$ in English, we will note that the alleged vague meaning 'you$_{SG/PL}$' cannot be expressed in the set of primitives explored in the present volume; and that since no-one has ever proposed a definition of the supposedly vague YOU in terms of any other set of primitives, the idea that there **is** such a vague YOU in the English lexicon must be regarded as fanciful.

To say that the English word *you* is vague between *you*$_{SG}$ and *you*$_{PL}$ is like saying that the French word *vous* ('you$_{PL}$' or 'thou:POLITE') is not polysemous but vague. The claim is untenable, because it is impossible to state the common core of *vous*$_{SG}$ and *vous*$_{PL}$ in any verifiable system of primitives. Of course one could claim that this common core is simply 'second person', but this term is neither self-explanatory nor substitutable in context for the words whose meaning it is supposed to express, so it doesn't really explain anything.

Perhaps the most interesting problem arising in connection with the two primitives under discussion concerns the question of the pragmatic markedness of their exponents in a number of languages (e.g. in Thai, Japanese and Acehnese). The chapters by Diller, Onishi, and Durie, Daud and Hasan all provide evidence for the hypothesis that words for I and YOU which are pragmatically marked can nonetheless be semantically simple; and that languages with rich sets of words referring to the speaker and the addressee do in fact have words which strictly speaking mean no more than the English words *you*$_{SG}$ and *I*.

At the same time, it must be recognised that the use of unadorned 'basic level' words for YOU and I in the Thai or Japanese version of the Natural Semantic Metalanguage (NSM) may lead to explications which would strike native speakers as inappropriate and even shocking, and it may thus restrict the practical usefulness of such explications. Difficulties of this kind, however, can be solved by adopting different levels of explications for different purposes, and by using the art of compromise whenever it may be desirable. For example, if one accepts Onishi's arguments in favour of *omae* and *ore* as the Japanese exponents of the pure YOU and I, one could still use 'higher level' words such as *anata* and *atasi* in more approximate explications whenever strict semantic accuracy is not essential.

As Diller points out in his paper (p. 169), normal human discourse is always situated, and NSM explications, which aim at representing meaning apart from any cultural context, are artificial and constitute, so to speak, a genre of speech very different from all other genres. In normal (that is, situated) use, elements which are semantically 'neutral' or 'unmarked' (such as, for example, *omae* and *ore* in Japanese) are never pragmatically 'neutral' or 'unmarked'. The Japanese version of the NSM can be seen as a language different from Japanese, though one which can be comprehended via Japanese. Explications formulated in this metalanguage can only be properly understood if the Japanese NSM is divested of all the normal sociolinguistic conventions. As Chomsky's opponents have often emphasised, a natural language cannot be divested of sociolinguistic conventions, and for natural languages, there is no such thing as an 'ideal speaker/hearer'; but the NSM is not a natural language: rather, it is a semi-artificial language, though one interpretable directly via the natural language from which it has been derived.

17.1.2 SOMEONE, SOMETHING and PEOPLE

As far as we can see, all the languages in the sample have separate words for SOMEONE and SOMETHING. In many languages the same word is used both as an interrogative (WHO or WHAT) and as an indefinite (SOMEONE or SOMETHING); but in one way or another, a lexical distinction between SOMEONE/WHO and SOMETHING/WHAT is drawn in every single case.

In Kayardild, the exponents of SOMEONE and SOMETHING are phrasal (*ngaaka dangkaa* and *ngaaka thungalda*), and since they appear to share a word with an indeterminate meaning (*ngaaka*) it might seem that in this language the distinction between SOMEONE and SOMETHING is not obligatorily drawn. In fact, however, since it is unusual for *ngaaka* to appear alone, and since a person would normally be referred to as *ngaaka dangkaa*, not as *ngaaka*, Evans regards the two phrases *ngaaka dangkaa* and *ngaaka thungalda* as separate lexical items (p. 206).

As one could expect, both SOMEONE and SOMETHING are occasionally involved in polysemies, but not with one another: we have not come across a language where SOMEONE and SOMETHING share the same lexical exponent, as we have not come across a language when YOU and I do. This is understandable, since patterns of polysemy of this kind could lead to unresolvable ambiguities on a very large scale.

Perhaps the most interesting and intricate web of polysemies in which the exponents of SOMEONE and SOMETHING are involved is presented by Kalam. Intriguingly, Pawley says at first that "there is ... no pronoun that means uniquely 'someone'" (p. 390), and gives examples such as the following (his example (6)):

> *Ebap   mdp   kotp-mgan.*
> one   it.stays   house-inside
> 'One (of them) is in the house.'

in which, he says, "*ebap* is indeterminate as between a human or non-human referent" (pp. 390–391).

But in fact Pawley's further comments make it clear that *ebap* has two meanings and two syntactic functions: it can be either a quantifier or a nominal; and it is only its quantifier meaning which is indeterminate between "human and non-human" (or between SOMEONE and SOMETHING). But although *ebap* in the sense 'one' can refer to both persons and things, *ebap* used as a nominal is never vague between SOMEONE and SOMETHING: it can only mean SOMEONE. Accordingly, the sentence above is ambiguous and should be given a second gloss, with *ebap* interpreted as a nominal: 'Someone is in the house' (a gloss which Pawley himself used in an earlier version of his paper).

As Pawley's other example sentences show, the Kalam word for SOMETHING is *tap* (for example 'this thing' is rendered in Kalam as *tap ak*, where *ak* is the word for THIS). But in the absence of any modifier, SOMETHING is realised as *tap ebap*. Since in other contexts, *ebap* means 'one', one may be tempted to analyse the expression *tap ebap* as meaning 'one thing'; but in fact (as Pawley's example (8) shows) *tap ebap* can also be used as a single lexical item meaning SOMETHING.

Despite this potentially confusing web of polysemies, it is therefore quite clear that Kalam does have distinct lexical exponents of SOMEONE (namely *ebap*, used as a syntactic head), and for SOMETHING (*tap*, with the allolex *tap ebap*).

Another interesting example of polysemy involving SOMETHING and another primitive, comes from Samoan. Mosel says in this connection that the primitive SOMETHING is difficult to locate in Samoan "because the exponent *mea* is polysemous and also means 'place' ... whereas the exponent *â* 'what?' can also be a verb meaning 'what's the matter?'" (p. 357); but since these polysemies are clearly associated with different grammatical contexts, they do not present any problems. An ambiguity involving SOMETHING and 'place' may sometimes occur, but the concept WHERE has also another, distinct, exponent (*fea*), and, as Mosel acknowledges herself, "usually the context provides sufficient information for the listener to know whether the speaker refers to an object or a place" (p. 334).

As for SOMEONE, Harkins and Wilkins (p. 288) suggest that this concept may be seen as problematic in Arrernte, where the word for WHO is used only in an interrogative sense. The authors make it clear that there is no difficulty in translating canonical sentences with SOMEONE into Arrernte; but they point out that the word which can translate SOMEONE (*arrpenhe*) can also mean OTHER. Since, however, the two meanings — SOMEONE and OTHER — occur in different grammatical contexts, there can be no objection to treating the word *arrpenhe* as polysemous and to regarding *arrpenhe*₁ as an exponent of SOMEONE, and *arrpenhe*₂ as an exponent of OTHER. The concepts SOMEONE and OTHER are categorially very different, since OTHER requires a semantic 'head' (another what?), whereas SOMEONE is self-sufficient as a referring expression, so there is no reason why these two meanings should not share an exponent. There is a sufficient link between them to explain this particular pattern of polysemy, which is attested in a number of languages: since it is unusual to refer to oneself as SOMEONE, a semantic shift from SOMEONE to 'someone else' (someone other than I) would be perfectly understandable, as would a shift from 'someone else' to SOMEONE.

One test which is particularly helpful in documenting the OTHER/SOMEONE polysemy is provided by a sentence such as *I can see someone, I think it is the same person (as before)*. The fact that in Arrernte there is no problem with using *arrpenhe* in the first clause (Harkins, personal communication) shows that in this context this word cannot mean OTHER or 'another'; here, it can only mean SOMEONE. (For further discussion, see Goddard's paper on Yankunytjatjara (pp. 231–232), where the same polysemy obtains.)

A non-Australian language included in our sample which exhibits the SOMEONE/OTHER polysemy is Samoan (which has also a different word for WHO). As Mosel shows (p. 333), the grammatical contexts in which the two meanings occur are different:

Isi means OTHER when it is used as a determiner ... but as the nucleus of a non-specific noun phrase it corresponds to English *someone* or *someone else*. Thus a chief calls

Sau se isi!
come a other
'Someone come!'

when he wants somebody to help him and it does not matter who it is.

Examples of this kind suggest that in this kind of grammatical context *se isi* means SOMEONE, not 'someone else', and that the second gloss ('someone else') is offered by Mosel only in order to maintain a translational link between the two different uses of *isi*. Just because *se isi* is formally complex (*se* can serve as indefinite article, and *isi* can mean OTHER) does not mean the expression *se isi* is semantically segmentable; on the contrary, it appears to express a single, irreducible meaning. Apparently the reason that Mosel hesitates to recognise *se isi* as an exponent of the primitive SOMEONE is that the same phrase can also refer to things ("since it can also refer to things in the widest sense ... it does not represent SOMEONE" (p. 333)). But we see no difficulty in recognising *se isi* as an exponent of SOMEONE, because when this phrase refers to things it is segmentable (semantically as well as formally) and means 'something else' (cf. Mosel's gloss in her example (20)). Thus:

isi	OTHER (else)
se-isi (nonsegmentable, one word)	SOMEONE (not SOMETHING)
se isi (segmentable, two words)	another thing, something else (not 'someone else')

We are claiming, then, that *se isi* is not vague, covering both SOMEONE and SOMETHING, but polysemous, meaning either SOMEONE or 'something else' (but never 'someone else' or SOMETHING). From a purely formal point of view it is of course tempting to segment *se isi* into *se* (a morpheme homonymous with the indefinite article) and *isi* OTHER, but since semantically *se isi* implies 'otherness' only when referring to things rather than persons, the temptation to segment this phrase in all its uses should in our view be resisted, and polysemy should be recognised.

One of the most fascinating results of the research reported in the present volume is the widespread presence of distinct lexical items for PEOPLE (a concept which has only recently come to be thought of as primitive). In fact, English itself provides a good example of the asymmetry between PEOPLE (plural) and its non-existent singular equivalent (with the word *person* not being as strictly restricted to humans as the word *people* is). In other European languages, too, there is often a separate word for PEOPLE, unrelated to any word for an individual human being (e.g. *Leute* in German, *ljudi* in Russian and *les gens* in French; cf. *Mensch, čelovek, l'homme* 'one human being').

The presence in the languages of the world of a special word for PEOPLE (e.g. *people* in English, *bin-b* (literally, 'woman-man') in Kalam, *tagata* in Samoan, *renmen* in Mandarin) supports the hypothesis that the human conceptual apparatus makes special provisions for a social category of PEOPLE, in addition to the ontological category of SOMEONE (which includes beings other than human, e.g. spirits) and to the psychological categories associated with an individual (such as THINK, WANT and FEEL).

In many languages (especially those which have no obligatory category of number), the word for PEOPLE can also be extended to one human being, but it is often quite clear that without additional marking this word implies plurality. For example, Mosel points out that in Samoan the singular (*le tagata* 'human being') is formally marked, whereas the plural (*tagata* PEOPLE) is formally unmarked (p. 334); Onishi notes that in Japanese the word *hito* without a modifier is usually interpreted as a plural (PEOPLE), although a singular reading is possible in certain contexts (p. 367); and Goddard makes a similar observation about the Yankunytjatjara word *anangu* (p. 233).

Peeters suggests that in French the primitive PEOPLE is realised primarily by the so-called generic pronoun *on*, normally glossed in English as *one* but significantly different from *one* in use (p. 426). This is a very interesting suggestion; but there is no reason to assume that if *on* is an exponent of PEOPLE, then the more obvious candidate, the plural noun *les gens* (PEOPLE), is not another exponent of the same meaning, since the two words — *on* and *les gens* — can be regarded as alloxes of the same primitive.

Do all languages distinguish overtly between PEOPLE (a collectivity of human beings as a social category) and SOMEONE (an individual being, not necessarily human)? Our tentative conclusion from the research to date is that they do, but the formal links between the exponents of these two concepts are sometimes confusing.

For example, in Mangap-Mbula (p. 89) the word *tomtom* by itself can mean either SOMEONE (one, not necessarily human) or PEOPLE (more than one or generic, obviously human), depending on the grammatical frame. If this word is preceded by the overt pluraliser *zin* then it can only mean PEOPLE, and if it is combined with the determiner *ta* then it can only mean SOMEONE. The impression that *tomtom* has one core meaning which is further specified by the addition of *zin* or *ta* is an illusion, because there is no constant meaning which could be attributed to this word in both these contexts: in one context the referent must be human, in the other it may or may not be human, for example, it can refer to God (and if we assumed that the constant meaning is SOMEONE then we could not account for the fact that in combination with *zin* 'plural' this someone must be human).

In addition, it is important to note that Mangap-Mbula also has another word, *wal*, which can only mean PEOPLE (but which cannot be used in a generic sense), and that it has an interrogative pronoun *asiŋ* WHO which is an unambiguous exponent of the concept SOMEONE (not PEOPLE).

Similarly, in Kayardild (p. 207) *dangkaa* without a determiner appears to mean primarily PEOPLE (humans), whereas the phrase *ngaaka dangkaa*, treated by Evans as a single lexical item, means SOMEONE/WHO, and so presumably is not restricted to humans. (In addition, the concept PEOPLE can be expressed unambiguously by the form *dangkawalada*, with an overt pluraliser).

In Ewe, the word for PEOPLE is in my view *gbetɔ́* (referring exclusively to humans; cf. Ameka's examples (10) and (12)), whereas the word for SOMEONE is *ame* (which is not restricted to humans and can, for example, refer to God). Ameka mentions that the range of use of *gbetɔ́* does not correspond exactly to that of the English word *people* (p. 62), but this may be due to non-semantic factors. Crucially, *gbetɔ́* can be used in sentences such as "People will talk of you".[2] Furthermore, as Ameka notes, *gbetɔ́* has a formally more complex variant *gbetɔ́wó* (cf. Ameka's example (11)), and one can expect that the combined ranges of *gbetɔ́* and *gbetɔ́wó* come closer to the range of *people* than does the range of *gbetɔ́* alone.

Thus on the evidence available so far the 'new' primitive PEOPLE appears to fare quite well.

The discovery that the concept of PEOPLE is, in all probability, a semantic universal is both unexpected and exciting.

First of all, it offers a solution to the old and apparently insoluble problem of how the notion of 'human being' can be defined. Is a human being a 'featherless biped' as the cynics maintained in Ancient Greece? Or is it a 'rational animal', as medieval philosophers used to claim? Or is it perhaps, as the French writer Vercors (1956) once maintained 'a being endowed with a religious sense'?

All these and other definitions are clearly deficient, and it is a relief to be able to go to Pascal's (1954 [1658]:579) view that the notion is basic and indefinable, and that all attempts to define it must fail. But this view can be legitimately accepted only if we have satisfied ourselves that the notion in question is universal; if it were not, it **would** require a definition for the benefit of those cultures which didn't have it.

Our evidence suggests, however, that Pascal's view requires a correction. It is not the notion of an individual human being, *l'homme*, which appears to be universal and indefinable, but the notion of PEOPLE, a social, rather than biological, category. Given the universal presence of the concepts PEOPLE, SOMEONE and ONE, the notion of an individual human being does not need to be regarded as primitive. But it is impossible to define both 'human being' and 'people'; and our data suggest that it is the latter, not the former concept, which is indeed universal.

If we think of universal semantic primitives as innate concepts, the idea that a social category of PEOPLE may be innate is unexpected, and it certainly gives food for thought. If we are 'rational animals' (with the notions of THINK and KNOW being part of our genetic endowment), we are also 'social animals', so much so that the idea of PEOPLE as a social category is also a part of this endowment. In fact, of course, according to the innate and universal folk model (cf. Brunner 1990), we are not 'animals' at all: we are PEOPLE, every single one of whom is also SOMEONE and I — all irreducible and apparently universal human concepts.

17.2 Mental Predicates

Mental predicates raise a number of interesting problems involving, in particular, polysemy, allolexy, morphological complexity and differences in the range of use.

17.2.1 KNOW

All the languages surveyed have a word which means KNOW and which can be used to introduce complement clauses (e.g. 'I know which way he went' or 'I know: he went this way'). In some languages, for example in Yankunytjatjara, the exponent of KNOW is an adjective rather than a verb, but at the level of semantic primitives differences in part of speech status do not lead to any differences in meaning, so this is not a problem. Sometimes the word for KNOW is polysemous and sometimes it is morphologically complex, but no difficulties in translating canonical sentences with KNOW have been reported.

For example, in Acehnese KNOW has two exponents, one bound, *tu-*, and one free, *tupeue*. Since the segment *peue* is formally identical with the morphene *peue* meaning WHAT, the form *tupeue* may seem to be morphologically complex and semantically decomposable. As Durie, Daud and Hasan show (p. 176), however, *tupeue* has in fact two different readings, 'know what' and KNOW, and while it is truly analysable and decomposable on the first reading, on the second reading it is both morphologically and semantically simple, and is a perfect exponent of the universal primitive KNOW.

A particularly interesting case involving polysemy of the exponent of KNOW has been reported by Pawley (pp. 392–394). In Kalam, the bare stem *ŋ-* combined with a complement clause means KNOW, whereas the same stem combined with other lexical and grammatical material can mean other things. In particular, if the object stands for a concrete entity and the aspect is punctual, the same stem can mean 'see'.

The fact that the same stem *ŋ-* combined with other words may be used to build more complex meanings involving 'knowing' is perfectly understandable, and there can be no objection to regarding expressions such as *wdn ŋ-* 'eye know' ('see'), *tumd ŋ-* 'ear know' ('hear') or *wsn ŋ-* 'sleep know' ('dream') as both formally and semantically complex, and as including the primitive KNOW.[3]

The question which does need some discussion is the relationship between the primitives KNOW and THINK in Kalam. Since the putative exponent of THINK appears to be morphologically complex and includes the segment *ŋ-* (*gos ŋ-*) it might be argued that *ŋ-* does not in fact mean KNOW but stands for some concept 'more general' than either KNOW or THINK, for which there is no single word in English.

From a semantic point of view, however, nothing prevents us from interpreting *ŋ-* as an exponent of the universal concept KNOW, and the compound *gos ŋ-* as an exponent of the universal concept THINK.[4] It is true that under this analysis not all 'recurring partials' are assigned a constant meaning, but we must distinguish 'recurring partials' linked by an unanalysable family resemblance from compositional relationships. For example, in English, semantically complex words such as *professor*, *doctor*, *tutor*, *actor*, *chancellor*, *debtor*, *mentor* and *suitor* may seem to be morphologically (as well as semantically) complex, but in fact they cannot be segmented into parts with identifiable constant meanings.

This is not to deny that on some level of consciousness Kalam speakers may sense some link between the concepts *ŋ-* and *gos ŋ-* (as English speakers sense some link between *someone* and *something*). But this is a matter of 'resonance' (cf. chapter 2), not of meaning, since the link between *ŋ-* and *gos ŋ-* cannot be shown in Kalam by means of a paraphrase, just as the link between *someone* and *something* in English cannot be shown by means of a paraphrase. The fact that one can say in Kalam, as one can in English, 'I think that such-and-such but I don't know' using *gos ŋg-* for THINK and *ŋg-* for KNOW (Pawley, personal communication) supports the view that Kalam does have the means to express THINK and KNOW as two distinct concepts, despite the formal links between their exponents.

Pawley argues that, in Kalam, KNOW and THINK (and, for that matter, FEEL) "are aspects of a more general concept" (p. 393), but he does not say what this "more general concept" is. He insists that the meaning of *ŋg-* is unitary (in the name of the general methodological principle that "semanticists and lexicographers should first seek a **unitary** meaning for a word", (p. 389)), but again, he doesn't say what this supposedly unitary meaning is.

For our part, we fully agree with the general principle that semanticists and lexicographers should first seek a unitary meaning for a word (Occam's razor), but we require that the unitary meaning one posits be able to be stated and tested in context. Since the supposedly unitary meaning of *ŋg-* cannot be stated (and, consequently, cannot be tested), we regard the claim that there is such a meaning as unfounded and irrelevant to compositional semantics.

From the point of view of compositional semantics the apparent formal complexity of lexemes such as *someone*, *something* or *gos ŋg-* is irrelevant and lexemes of this kind have to be regarded as semantically simple. Similarly, the fact that the Kalam word *ŋg-* KNOW is formally simple whereas the Japanese word *sit-te iru* KNOW (discussed by Onishi, p. 368) is formally complex is irrelevant from the point of view of their meaning (that is, their compositional semantics).

One could still claim, if one wished, that *ŋg-* has an indefinable quality that *sit-te iru* does not have, or vice versa, but as far as we can see nothing much would follow from such a statement. On the other hand, the observation that *ŋg-* **can** be regarded as the Kalam exponent of KNOW, and *gos ŋg-* as the Kalam exponent of THINK, allows us to construct a Kalam version of the NSM, and thus to build bridges between the unique semantic universes associated with different languages and cultures.

17.2.2 THINK

The discussion above has, of necessity, involved the primitive THINK as much as the primitive KNOW, and hopefully has cleared any doubts about the lexicalisation of THINK in Kalam: the apparent compound *gos ŋg-* can do all the work in the Kalam version of the metalanguage that *think* is doing in the English version, *khít* in its Thai version, and so on. This does not mean, of course, that the whole range of use of *gos ŋg-*, *think* and *khít* is exactly the same, but only that they can translate one another in a wide range of canonical sentences.

Occasionally, the availability of a word for THINK is obscured by polysemy. For example, in Longgu (p. 315), the primitive THINK is realised by means of a word (*una*) which can also mean LIKE THIS. The link between the two meanings is clear, as is the link between SAY and LIKE THIS evidenced in some languages, since both THINK and SAY are used to introduce quotational and quasi-quotational complements:

(a)   I thought [about this like this]: she is nice.
(b)   I said [something like this]: she is nice.

(It is particularly interesting to note in this connection the common Yankunytjatjara collocation *alatji kulini* 'think like this', mentioned in Goddard's paper (p. 237).) Obviously, the link in question is not compositional; the two meanings (THINK and LIKE THIS, or SAY and LIKE THIS) are likely to co-occur, but they have no common part, and cannot be reduced to one another in any way.

As in the case of KNOW, THINK is often involved in polysemous relationships with words of perception. For example, in Yankunytjatjara the word which means THINK can also mean 'listen' or 'hear'. Since, however, the syntactic frames in which these two meanings are realised are different, there is no difficulty in establishing polysemy here. Goddard's discussion of this point (p. 237) demonstrates very clearly the incorrectness of Bain's claim, made with respect to the neighbouring dialect Pitjantjatjara, that there is no way to differentiate the concepts of thinking and listening in Pitjantjatjara (Bain 1992:86; for further discussion, see Wierzbicka, in press).

Finally, it should be pointed out that with THINK, as with many other conceptual primitives, there are huge cultural differences between different societies, which may obscure the identity of the underlying conceptual systems. For example, an innocent-looking canonical sentence such as 'I think such-and-such, but I don't know' may in fact be much more congenial to some cultures than to others. In particular, in Anglo culture there is a great emphasis on expressing opinions and on distinguishing opinions from facts. Even in Europe, there are cultures (for example, Polish culture) where the phrase 'I think' is much less common than it is in English because people tend to express their opinions in the same way as they state facts (e.g. by saying 'This is good' and 'That is bad', as they say 'This is white' and 'That is black', rather than 'I think this is good' and 'I think that is bad'; cf. Wierzbicka 1991a:41).

Similarly, Nicholas Evans (personal communication) reports that in Kayardild his informants find it more natural to say 'I don't know' than 'I think ... but I don't know'; in other contexts, too, 'thinking' is rarely mentioned explicitly, so much so that, as Evans reports, he doubted for a long time that the language had a lexical exponent for THINK at all. Nonetheless, Evans has now established (p. 212) that a word for THINK (in the relevant sense) is there (*marralmarutha*, literally 'ear-put') and can be used when needed (for example, in a sentence meaning 'I think that they won't come'). There is no difference in this respect, then, between Kayardild and English as far as conceptual resources are concerned (the basic conceptual and linguistic tools are there); but there are very considerable differences in the exploitation of these resources in the two cultures.

17.2.3 WANT

A word (or morpheme) for WANT is clearly present in all the languages considered in this volume. A number of interesting problems arise in connection with this concept.

First, there is the question of allolexy. For example, in Japanese (pp. 370–371), there are two exponents of WANT, in complementary distribution: the adjective *hosii* and the suffix *-tai*. Similarly, in Samoan (pp. 337–338) there is a verb (*mana'o*) and an adverb (*fia*). Of the two cases, Samoan is more intriguing, because the two exponents of WANT can co-occur. The semantic consequences of this co-occurrence, if any, remain to be investigated.

Second, the range of construction types in which the exponents of WANT can occur may differ from language to language. In particular, many languages do not have a construction corresponding to the English *X wants Y to do Z* construction. The absence of such a construction in a given language is sometimes seen as evidence for the absence of an exact semantic equivalent of the English *want*. In fact, however, what is missing is a certain construction type (with its own semantics), not a lexical equivalent of WANT. (For further discussion of the semantics of different WANT constructions see Wierzbicka 1988:27–45; see also Harkins, forthcoming.)

Third, in some languages (for example, in Acehnese) there are several WANT words, with different functions; and this abundance of WANT words may make the identification of a 'pure' WANT difficult. Thus Durie, Daud and Hasan say at one point that "there is no uncontroversial lexical candidate in Acehnese for WANT itself" (p. 177). On our reading of their paper, however, it shows that in addition to various WANT words specialised in specific grammatical and semantic contexts, Acehnese does have a perfectly general, semantically 'pure' exponent of WANT, namely, the verb *meuh'eut*, which can be used both for wanting actions and wanting events (that is, for wanting to do something and wanting something to happen), and which can refer to someone else's action as well as to one's own (that is, to wanting someone else to do something as well as to wanting to do something oneself). It seems to us, therefore, that the verb in question is a perfect exponent of the universal primitive WANT; and, as we understand it, this is also the conclusion towards which Durie and his co-authors incline.

Fourth, WANT is often involved in polysemy, sharing exponents with various other meanings, in particular with concepts relating to internal body parts or to saying. For example, in Arrernte the word for WANT (*ahentye*) is homonymous with the word for 'throat' (p. 291); and in Mangap-Mbula, *lele-* is homonymous with the word for 'insides' (p. 93). In both cases, differences in syntactic frames allow us to establish polysemy without difficulty. Interestingly, Mangap-Mbula also has another exponent for WANT, the polysemous verb *-so*, which can also stand for SAY and for IF. As shown by Bugenhagen (p. 104), however, the syntactic frames associated with each of these meanings are different. In particular, Bugenhagen shows that so_1 SAY — in contrast to so_2 WANT — may have complements introduced by the complementiser *ta kembei*, imposes no restrictions on the identity or the expression of the subjects (in the main clause and in the complement clause), and can take prepositional objects.

In Ewe, the exponent of WANT (*dí*) has several different meanings linked with different syntactic patterns. One interesting contrast discussed by Ameka (p. 67) has to do with the 'stative' character of the WANT sense and the 'eventive' character of the active 'look for' sense of the verb *dí*, and with the concomitant differences in their temporal interpretation. (For example, the same sentence *Me-dí ésia* can mean either 'I want this' or 'I looked for this', but not 'I wanted this' nor 'I look for this'.)

Another interesting (and common) polysemous pattern illustrated in Ameka's paper on Ewe links WANT with the 'prospective aspect' ('to be about to happen/do'). The 'prospective' sense, too, is clearly distinguished from the WANT sense on syntactic grounds (p. 68).

Polysemy involving WANT and SAY is also evident in Kalam. According to Pawley (p. 400), to ascribe 'wanting' to a third person, one has to do it in the form of an 'internal dialogue', along the following lines: '"Let me do such-and-such," she said (to herself)'. But this analysis begs the question, because it assumes that the verb *ag-* (translatable into English as either *say* or *want*) in fact always means SAY. Since, however, the two different readings of *ag-* (SAY and WANT) are linked with different grammatical constructions, it is more justified, in our view, to posit polysemy here, and to say that in the context of the so-called hortative construction (as described by Pawley), *ag-* means WANT.

Furthermore, we can see no evidence that sentences with *ag-* in the hortative construction, which Pawley glosses in English using the verb *say* rather than *want* (as in the sentence given above), do not mean the same as the corresponding English sentences with *want* (e.g. *She wanted to do such-and-such*). In particular, it seems clear that in sentences about animals WANT cannot be reduced to SAY; so that if, for example, Kalam speakers say of a cat 'He wants to catch that bird', using the stem *ag-* in the hortative construction, they do not mean 'The cat says (to himself), "Let me catch that bird"' (even if this is what the construction itself appears to suggest, on the assumption that *ag-* has a unitary meaning).

Should it be suggested at this point that perhaps Kalam speakers personify animals and so can attribute inner speech to them, I would point out that at this stage this is a totally unsupported conjecture.

But there are other, even more compelling, arguments against the claim that *ag-* always means SAY in Kalam. Judging by Pawley's examples and comments, the stem *ag-* used in the hortative construction can **never** mean simply SAY: it always implies an 'internal dialogue' ('say to oneself = intend'). But elsewhere *ag-* does not imply 'internal speech', it refers simply to speech. It seems, therefore, that on Pawley's account *ag-* is polysemous too: outside the hortative construction it means SAY (whether by sounds, or by other external signs, or internally), whereas in the context of the hortative construction it has to refer to internal speech, and, furthermore, to imply 'intention'. Isn't this really tantamount to saying that in the context of the hortative construction *ag-* means WANT rather than SAY?

Finally, let us consider Pawley's example (50):

> *Gos-yad   Wpc   "yad   kumin"   agek*
> thought-my Wpc I   let.me.die=I.die   he.said=thought
> *nŋbin.*
> I.think
> 'I believe that Wpc wanted to die.'

If *ag-* (in combination with *kumin*) does not mean WANT, where does the meaning given in the gloss come from? Surely a sentence meaning 'I will die, he says' could not be glossed as 'He wants to die', because normally 'I will die' cannot be interpreted as implying 'I want to die'.

From a semantic point of view, therefore, it seems to us misleading to call the use of *ag-* in the hortative construction 'an internal dialogue' (although from an etymological point of view the use of this label may be illuminating).

Polysemy is also involved in the 'story of WANT' in Kayardild, as presented by Evans. According to Evans (pp. 209–210), in Kayardild there is a 'potential inflection', which has three different senses, usually translated into English with *should*, *want* and *can*. Some sentences containing a verb with this inflection are ambiguous. But, crucially, there are grammatical contexts where the potential inflection can only mean WANT and there are others where it can only mean CAN (cf. Evans' examples (19) and (20)). These differences in grammatical contexts associated with the different 'primitive' meanings of the potential inflection establish that this inflection is not simply vague but polysemous, and that one of its meanings is WANT.

As for Kayardild's expressive power with respect to 'wanting', it is important to note that although in natural discourse many sentences (especially sentences referring to the future) may be ambiguous (between a WANT reading and a CAN reading), if needed these ambiguities can be resolved by the use of additional linguistic resources. For example, as pointed out by Harkins (forthcoming), a sentence which on its own can mean either (a) 'He can die in his own country' or (b) 'He wants to die in his own country' can be disambiguated by either adding the particle *marrbi* MAYBE (sense (a)) or by marking the word 'country' with the verbal purposive suffix *-janlija*.

Thus although (as Evans says) in Kayarldild "there is no translation that just means WANT" (p. 210), Kayardild does have a lexical exponent of WANT (namely, the so-called potential inflection). This exponent is a bound morpheme, not a free form, and it is polysemous; but it is certainly not vague between WANT and something else (CAN and 'should'); and its WANT meaning is not any different from that of the lexical exponents of WANT in the other languages under investigation. (For further discussion of the semantic field of WANT in Kayardild, see Harkins, forthcoming.)

Polysemy appears to occur also in the Misumalpan language Ulwa, where, as Hale says, the same word, *walnaka*, "corresponds both to WANT and 'seek'" (p. 269). ("In general, the polysemous *walnaka* ... is used in circumstances in which universal WANT is expected" (p. 270).) As for the other Misumalpan languages considered, Hale says that they use the English borrowing *want*, which perfectly fits the proposed universal. He goes on to say, however, that "the indigenous ways of referring to 'wanting' were not exactly the universal WANT, so far as I can tell. One expression was more like 'seeking', now generally abandoned as a term for WANT in Miskitu; the other referred more to longing or deprivation" (p. 283).

But Hale's suggestion that the older form of Miskitu did not have an exact exponent for WANT appears to be only a conjecture; on the other hand in their current (and therefore more verifiable) form both Ulwa and Miskitu (as described by Hale) clearly do have precise exponents of WANT (although one of them is polysemous, and the other is a loan word). For this reason we feel justified in concluding that Hale's data confirm, rather than cast doubt on, our hypothesis regarding the universal WANT.

The WANT/'love' polysemy noted in Goddard's paper on Yankunytjatjara (p. 238) brings to mind the Spanish verb *querer* (WANT and 'love'), whose two senses are also associated with different syntactic frames; and also the Italian expression *ti voglio bene*, literally, 'I want you good', that is, 'I love you'.

It is important to stress, however, that while all the languages studied in the present volume (and, we hypothesise, all languages in general) have a lexical exponent of the meaning WANT, there are very considerable differences between cultures in the extent of their WANT talk, as there are in the extent of their THINK talk. In particular, in some cultures people are reluctant to speak about other people's 'wants' (in contrast to their own); and differences of this kind may be reflected in grammar. But, once again, the range of use of WANT words and morphemes in different languages must not be confused with their semantics: a difference in the range of use does not have to be accompanied by any specifiable difference in meaning.

17.2.4 FEEL

The primitive FEEL, even more than WANT, raises a whole range of very interesting problems.

To begin with, there are languages which at first appear not to have an exponent for FEEL at all — because it is hiding behind the facade of a body-part word. The idea that a word usually translated as 'stomach' or 'belly' can actually mean FEEL, that is, have two distinct meanings, 'stomach' and FEEL, and that the use of the 'stomach' word in the sense of FEEL is not a case of metaphorical extension but of plain polysemy, was originally put forward by Cliff Goddard at the Semantic and Lexical Universals Workshop in 1992. When applied to other languages (in Australia and elsewhere) this idea has proved to be extremely fruitful, and has brought to light a widespread pattern of polysemy, involving body-part words and the concept FEEL. The Yankunytjatjara word *tjuni*, discussed in Goddard's paper (pp. 239–241), and the Kayardild word *bardaka* ('stomach'/FEEL), described in Evans' paper (p. 212; see also Evans' recent dictionary of this language (1992)), provide particularly striking examples of this pattern.

Furthermore, there are languages like Mangap-Mbula (pp. 91–92) which do have a separate word for FEEL but which rely also on body-part words (such as 'liver', 'stomach' or 'body'). The exact relationship between the different exponents of FEEL in such languages remains to be investigated. For example, for Mangap-Mbula it could be suggested that the words *lele-* 'insides' and *ni* 'body' may — in another meaning — be allolexes of the verb *-yamaana* FEEL. If the semantic range of these three words was the same there would be no problem with such an analysis (even if *lele-* tended to be used primarily in connection with emotions and *ni* with bodily feelings). But if *lele-* is exclusively restricted to emotions and *ni* to sensations (as appears to be the case) then it could be argued that the meanings of these words are more complex than that of *-yamaana* FEEL (and different from one another). Be that as it may, it is certainly remarkable that in our sample of **fourteen** different languages not a single one has turned up which does not provide some means for treating emotions and sensations in a unitary way, as simply 'feelings' (such as the Mangap-Mbula verb *-yamaana*).

It is true that, for example, in Misumalpan languages (p. 269) there appears to be a contrast between sentences such as 'I feel good in my body' (physical) and 'I feel good' (predominantly emotional or psychological), but contrasts of this kind suggest an unspecified FEEL rather than a strictly emotional (or psychological) one (with the bare FEEL being used predominantly, but not exclusively, for non-physical feelings).

A different problem arises in Kalam (and other Papuan languages, cf. Foley (1986:119)), where the stem *g-*, glossed by Pawley as 'do/act/work/happen', appears to serve as a lexical exponent of three distinct primitives: DO, HAPPEN and FEEL. It is clear, however, that here — as in other similar cases where different primitives share the same lexical exponent — each primitive is associated with a distinct grammatical construction, and that in the context of the 'experiencer construction' described by Pawley (p. 396) it can only mean FEEL (Pawley, personal communication):

    Yp yuwt gp.
    me pain it.acts/works/does
    'I feel pain.'

Pawley favours an analysis according to which in a sentence such as this the verb *g-* means 'do/act/work/happen', as it does elsewhere, and the idea of feeling is conveyed by the whole construction, not by the verb as such. But from our point of view, this is equivalent to saying that in this particular construction the verb *g-* means FEEL.

In our view, this interpretation (assigning the meaning FEEL to the verb *g-* in the experiencer construction) is confirmed by sentences such as the following ones (Pawley, personal communication):

    Yp tep gp.
    me good it.acts/works/does
    'I feel good.'

Yp tmey gp.
me bad it.acts/works/does
'I feel bad.'

If the sentences above mean what Pawley says they mean (that is, 'I feel good' and 'I feel bad'), then to our way of thinking it is proper to conclude that the verb *g-* used in these sentences means FEEL, rather than 'work' (or 'act', or DO). The fact that in a different grammatical construction the verb *g-* means DO is not, in our view, a sufficient reason for saying that it means DO (or 'work', or 'act') in the experiencer construction as well. Pawley's use of glosses such as 'Good works on me', 'Bad works on me' or 'Pain works on me' is clearly motivated by a desire to assign to the word *g-* a unitary meaning and to avoid postulating unnecessary polysemy. We understand and appreciate such an attitude, but in our view in this case the positing of polysemy is justified. Even if one could defend with some degree of plausibility glosses such as 'Pain works on me' or 'Hunger does me' (with respect to sentences referring to physical sensations such as pain or hunger), we believe that glosses such as 'Good/bad works on me' (applied to sentences which clearly mean 'I feel good' or 'I feel bad') are too far-fetched; and that it is necessary to acknowledge that in this particular construction *g-* means not 'work' or DO but FEEL.[5]

The controversy hinges largely on the interpretation of the notion 'literal meaning'. In Pawley's analysis, a sentence such as *Yp tep gp* ('me good *gp*') means, literally, 'Goodness does/works/acts on me', and if it is normally understood as 'I feel good', this happens by virtue of some sort of pragmatic implicature. But what kind of pragmatic implicature can explain the transition from the alleged 'literal' meaning 'Goodness works on me' or 'Goodness does me' to the communicatively real meaning 'I feel good'? In the absence of such an independently justified implicature, to say that *Yp tep gp* means ('literally') 'Goodness works on me' and only implies 'I feel good' is a bit like saying that the English sentence *I understand* means, literally, 'I stand under', and only implies, by some unspecified pragmatic implicature, something like 'I comprehend'.

In addition, the controversy hinges on the question of how to distribute the meaning of a sentence among its components (cf. Zawadowski 1975:134). Pawley is quite prepared to agree that *Yp tep gp* really means 'I feel good', and he uses such glosses himself, although he insists on distinguishing this communicative meaning from the 'literal' meaning. He is not prepared, however, to link the element *gp* as such with the meaning FEEL, because in his view, *gp* must always mean ('literally') the same: 'do/act/work on'.

We agree that it is not the element *gp* which 'as such' means FEEL, but only the element *gp* in the context of the experiencer construction. But from our point of view it is significant that in a sentence such as *Yp tep gp* the element *yp* means 'me' (as it does in other contexts), the element *tep* means 'good' (as it does in other contexts), and consequently that it is the element *gp* which — in the context of this particular construction — can be regarded as the bearer of the meaning FEEL (although in other constructions it is associated with other meanings.

Another interesting problem arises, in connection with FEEL, in Samoan (p. 337), where the primary exponent of this concept, the verb *lagona*, has a range of use which is much more restricted than that of, for example, the English word *feel* (in the relevant sense). In particular, as Mosel points out, "the canonical context 'I feel bad, I feel good' cannot be directly translated into Samoan, because with *lagona* the kind of feeling must be specified as happy, sad, worried, angry, and so on" (p. 337).

In fact, however, it appears that what is involved is not the 'semantic syntax' of FEEL (in the sense of combinability of semantic elements) but the phraseology and idiomatic usage. For example, if to say 'I feel good' in Samoan one normally uses the verb *manuia* 'feel good' rather than a combination of *lagona* FEEL and *lelei* GOOD, this appears to be a matter of usage, not of any semantic obstacles. Significantly, although Mosel says that "the exponents of FEEL and GOOD cannot be combined" (p. 357) she goes on to say that "with the exception of *tâ'ua* 'I and you', [these translation problems are] not a matter of grammatical rules. We can translate all canonical contexts into grammatical Samoan sentences by using the exponents of the semantic and lexical universals, but many of these translations would not be natural Samoan sentences" (p. 358).

But sentences formulated in the English version of the NSM will not always sound like natural English sentences either. If in Samoan there is an idiomatic way of saying something like 'I feel good' by using means other than the basic exponents of FEEL and of GOOD, then it is understandable that a combination of these basic exponents may sound unnatural. Facts of this kind, therefore, do not demonstrate any differences in the semantic syntax of FEEL (that is, in its combinability with other meanings).

I should add that although our proposed canonical sentences with FEEL included 'I feel good' and 'I feel bad' (which sound quite idiomatic in English), it may have been more justified from a semantic point of view to phrase these canonical sentences differently, namely as 'I feel something good' and 'I feel something bad'; and the latter versions do not sound too good in English either.

Similarly in Polish and Russian, counterparts of the sentences 'I feel good' and 'I feel bad' sound quite good:

(Ja)	*czuję*	*się*	*dobrze/źle.*
Ja	čuvstvuju	sebja	xorošo/ploxo.
I	feel	REFL	well/badly

'I feel good/bad.'

whereas the counterparts of the sentences 'I feel something good' and 'I feel something bad' sound highly unnatural, indeed strange:

(Ja)	*czuję*	*coś*	*dobrego/złego.*
Ja	čuvstvuju	čto-to	xorošee/ploxoe.
I	feel	something	good/bad

'I feel something good/bad.'

And yet it seems that these unnatural, unidiomatic sentences in English, Polish or Russian capture the shared semantic component of 'positive feelings' better than the natural, idiomatic sentences such as 'I feel good/bad' do. For example, the English sentences *I am relieved* and *I feel relieved* imply that 'I feel something good' (unidiomatic as this sounds) rather than 'I feel good'. Similarly, the English sentences *I am disappointed* and *I feel disappointed* imply that 'I feel something bad' rather than 'I feel bad'. The sentences 'I feel good' and 'I feel bad' imply an over-all well-being or ill-being, and so they may be less appropriate for modelling the meaning of sentences referring to feelings than 'I feel something good' and 'I feel something bad', with their implication of only partial well- or ill-being.

Returning to Samoan, the sentences combining FEEL with GOOD and BAD in this language may be not much stranger than the sentences *I feel something good* and *I feel something bad* in English (or their counterparts in Polish or Russian); and yet the Samoan informant may quite understandably reject them as being outside the range of 'normal' Samoan speech. For the present purposes, the most important fact is that Samoan clearly does have a lexical exponent of the universal FEEL (the verb *lagona*). At the same time, we wish to acknowledge that the 'combinatory potential' of FEEL raises problems which will need to be addressed in future research.

Finally, FEEL raises some interesting problems in French, where, as Peeters puts it, "the catch is that the most obvious translation (*sentir*) is inappropriate" (p. 428). The reason why *sentir* is (in Peeters' judgment) inappropriate is that it is polysemous and that in some of our canonical contexts (such as 'I feel something good', *Je sens quelque chose de bon*) it would normally be understood in another, non-primitive meaning ('smell'). Peeters' solution is to propose the verb *éprouver* as the primary French exponent of FEEL. But in my view, this solution, too, raises some difficulties (since *éprouver* may in fact be closer in meaning to the English *experience* than to FEEL). Another possibility discussed in Peeters' paper is the verb *ressentir*, morphologically more complex than *sentir* but semantically, I think, equivalent to it.

The general point illustrated by the French data is that an elegant, idiomatic rendering of a canonical sentence may introduce subtle (but undesirable) differences in meaning, whereas a semantically fully equivalent rendering may sometimes sound inappropriate due to interference from the idiomatic meaning of another phrase, apparently composed exclusively of primitive elements.

17.2.5 SAY

The primitive SAY is usually easy to locate in a language and does not present too many problems, but it does tend to be involved in certain recurring patterns of polysemy, some of them involving other primitives (notably DO, WANT and IF).

To begin with, many languages do not make lexical distinctions of the SAY/'speak' type. This does not mean, however, that these languages do not have an exponent for the primitive SAY as such, since the two meanings occur in different syntactic frames (roughly speaking, with a sentential complement the meaning is SAY, whereas without a complement it is 'speak' or something like 'speak'; cf. Harkins and Wilkins on Arrernte (p. 290), Goddard on Yankunytjatjara (pp. 238–239), Diller on Thai (p. 154), or Chappell on Mandarin (p. 118)).

Another pattern of polysemy involves SAYING and 'making sounds' of different kinds. The existence of this pattern in a given language may create the impression that this language does not have an exponent of the primitive SAY. Pawley raises this point with regard to Kalam (p. 339), where *ag-* can mean either SAY or 'utter sounds of a recognisable kind' (e.g. *kmap ag-* 'sing' (literally, 'song sound'), *si ag-* 'cry/weep' (literally, 'crying sound'), *sb ag-* 'fart' (literally, 'bowel sound'), *mukbel ag-* 'belch' (literally, 'belching sound') and *gu ag-* 'thud' (literally, 'thud sound').

Pawley suggests on the basis of such facts that "the Kalam view saying as a context-specific kind of sound-making, specifically one whose product is speech or discourse" (p. 400). In our view, however, this conclusion is not justified, because *ag-* can also be used in Kalam to refer to silent (i.e. soundless) SAYING of various things. In particular, *ag-* can be used in Kalam in sentences such as 'The book says ...', 'The letter says ...' and 'The fool said in his heart: there is no God' (Pawley, personal communication). To our way of thinking, if one can use the same verb *ag-* to say that a frog croaks and that a letter says something, then this verb must be polysemous; for while the frog makes sounds, the letter does not, and while the letter says something (that is, conveys a message), the frog does not.

Furthermore, it can be conjectured that *ag-* could also be used in Kalam to refer to the use of gestural sign systems. It is worth noting that in the Australian Aboriginal language Warlpiri, where the word for SAY is also used to refer to various non-linguistic sounds, the same word can be used to refer to signed messages (David Nash, personal communication); and Harkins and Wilkins report the same for Arrernte (p. 290). It seems reasonable to conjecture (as Pawley does, p. 400) that the same is true of Kalam. Obviously, it would be good to obtain further information on Kalam in this respect, but even without further information, what Pawley tells us about Kalam is in our view sufficient to establish that *ag-* has two distinct meanings. The fact that there is a well-established pattern of polysemy SAY/'make a sound' lends support to the hypothesis that *ag-*$_1$ means simply SAY in Kalam (without any reference to sounds), despite the fact that there is also a homonymous word *ag-*$_2$, which stands for 'sound-making', not for SAYING.

Significantly, the two meanings in question can be differentiated by means of syntactic frames: the SAY *ag-* can take a complement clause whereas the 'sound' *ag-* cannot. In fact, grammatical differences of this kind are commonly associated with the SAY/'sound' polysemy. Thus Goddard (pp. 238–239) reports that in Yankunytjatjara, the SAY sense of the verb *wangkanyi* selects an ergative case subject, whereas the same verb in its 'sound' sense (as in the sentence 'A fly is buzzing') selects a subject in the nominative case.

We would venture to suggest that the key to the SAYING/'sound making' polysemy may well lie in words such as the Kalam *mnm ag-* 'speak' (literally, 'speech sound'), which serves as a kind of 'semantic bridge' (cf. Mel'čuk 1984:4) between saying without sounds and sounds without saying:

ag-	'say'
mnm ag-	'make sounds like one does when one says things to people (i.e. speak)'
mukbel ag-	'make sounds like one does when one has eaten a lot (i.e. belch)'

Although *ag-* SAY and *ag-* 'make sounds' share no semantic components, they both share components with the compound *mnm ag-* 'speak', and so they are linked by a semantic bridge.

Turning to polysemies involving SAY and some other primitive, a very simple example is provided by the Samoan verb *fai*, which can mean either SAY or DO. Since, as pointed out by Mosel (p. 336), the two meanings are associated with different syntactic frames (as *fai* SAY does not enter ergative constructions), it is clearly justifiable to posit polysemy here. The fact that *fai* SAY does not occur in the so-called long form *fai=a* provides additional evidence for the distinctness of the two lexemes (*fai*$_1$ SAY and *fai*$_2$ DO).

It is not difficult to understand how the meanings SAY and DO are related and how they could come to share the same exponent, even though they are both semantically simple and therefore cannot have any common parts. Surely, the clue to this pattern of polysemy lies in the quotative complement: a sentence of the 'X said: Y' type can be seen as describing what X did as much as what X said. Thus, there is a natural link between SAY and DO, but this link is not compositional. (The SAY/DO polysemy is also very common in Papuan languages (cf. Foley 1986:119).)

The common pattern of polysemy involving SAY and WANT has already been discussed in section 17.2.3 (pp. 458–460) on WANT and has been illustrated with data from Kalam and Mangap-Mbula. Again, while there is no compositional relationship between SAY and WANT there is a kind of link between them, in so far as a person's wants may be hidden from outsiders and become fully accessible to them only if he or she says what these wants are. Of course, this inaccessibility applies also to the other mental predicates (knowing, thinking and feeling), but perhaps wanting has a privileged position in this regard: in social life, it is not essential for people to say what they know, think or feel, but saying what one wants occupies a very important place in human interaction (although some cultures, for example Japanese culture, impose limits on the expression of wants). The fact that in some languages one cannot say 'He wants' in the way one says 'I want', and that one has to say instead something which looks more like 'He says: I want' or 'He says: I will', is understandable in the light of the inaccessibility of other people's wants as well as their potential importance and interest. At the same time, it is perfectly understandable how an expression meaning 'He says: I want' could come to mean 'He wants', and how polysemies involving SAY and WANT could develop.[6]

As noted earlier in section 17.2.3 (pp. 458–460) on WANT, languages which use the same exponent for SAY and WANT may tempt the analyst to try to reduce these two concepts to one, and to say that 'He wants to go' means the same as 'He says: I will go' (or at least that the speakers of some languages cannot distinguish wanting from saying). But as Bugenhagen's and Pawley's papers in fact illustrate, the use of the same lexical exponents for SAY and WANT does not prevent clear differentiation of the two concepts, because they are linked with different constructions.

The polysemous pattern involving SAY and IF (illustrated in the present volume in Bugenhagen's paper on Mangap-Mbula, p. 96) has a parallel in the occasional use of the verb *say* for IF in English (e.g. 'Say it's a good day tomorrow — let's go fishing' or 'But say it happens again — what then?'). The codification of shifts such as *suppose* to *if* in English-based creoles and pidgins provides another instructive analogy. The basis for shifts of this kind can be represented as follows:

> if this happened, then ...
> if I (you) say that this happened, then ...
> if I (you) suppose that this happened, then ...

Shifts of this kind illuminate the raison d'être of the SAY/IF patterns of polysemy. At the same time, as pointed out by Bugenhagen with respect to Mangap-Mbula, "there would never be true constructional ambiguity between SAY and IF because of various syntactic differences" (p. 97).

17.3 Determiners and Quantifiers

17.3.1 THIS

All languages in our sample have a clear and unproblematic exponent for THIS. The other demonstrative pronouns often do not match semantically across language boundaries (for example, of the three Japanese demonstrative pronouns *kono*, *sono* and *ano*, neither *sono* nor *ano* corresponds exactly to English *that*, but *this* can be matched semantically with *kono*).

It might of course be claimed that if *this*, *kono* and other basic demonstrative pronouns enter into different contrastive sets, then their meanings must therefore be different; but in fact nobody has ever been able to identify any semantic difference between the basic demonstrative pronouns of different languages. (Generally speaking, the a priori assumption of non-equivalence of all the individual elements in two non-equivalent sets has never been empirically verified.)

Exponents of THIS, like those of many other primitives, are often involved in polysemy and allolexy.

To begin with polysemy, the word which means THIS frequently also has the meaning 'here' (for example, in Kayardild, Arrernte and Mangap-Mbula), and sometimes also the meaning 'now'. Since 'here' can be analysed as 'in this place', and 'now' as 'at this time', the three meanings in question clearly have a common core, and this core corresponds to the meaning of the demonstrative pronoun itself. In all the languages examined, the frames within which these meanings are realised are different, so the polysemy can be established without any difficulty. (For example, Evans notes that "the complex agreement rules of Kayardild can assign different cases to spatial adverbs than to demonstratives" (p. 213).)

But while there are many languages where the exponent of THIS has been extended to other meanings (above all, to 'here'), there are also many languages in which the single meaning of THIS is served by more than one exponent. Good examples of such allolexy are provided by Japanese, French and Yankunytjatjara (among many other languages). For example, in Japanese (p. 372) the form *kore* is used as a nominal (e.g. in 'Look at this!') whereas the form *kono* is used in an adnominal position (e.g. in 'this thing' or 'this person'). Similarly, in French (p. 429) the form *ceci* is used as a nominal, whereas in the adnominal position *ce* is used (with its allomorphs *cette* (feminine singular) and *ces* (plural)); and in Yankunytjatjara (p. 242) *nyanga* is used adnominally, while *nyangatja* is used as a referring word (as in 'This is bad').

One apparent difference in the use of the THIS primitive in different languages concerns its ability to function as a nominal referring to clauses. For example, in Thai (p. 161) or in Mangap-Mbula (p. 94) one would not normally say the equivalent of 'because of this' but rather 'because of this thing'. It is not clear at this stage, however, whether differences of this kind relate to idiomatic usage, or whether they have some deeper significance.

In all the languages under investigation, the word for THIS can be used both to point to extra-linguistic situations and to refer to some elements within the discourse. Mosel points out that Samoan, unlike English, has a special anaphoric pronoun, but she acknowledges that the basic demonstrative *nei* can also be used anaphorically (p. 339).

Mosel also raises the question of the status of THIS as a semantic primitive. She observes that "since *nei* and *nâ* [another demonstrative] locate things with regard to the speaker and the hearer, they do not only represent THIS, but also I and YOU" (p. 339).

But first, in their monumental Samoan grammar Mosel and Hovdhaugen (1992:131) gloss *nei* as 'this here (near the speaker or another focal point)', thus acknowledging that *nei* can refer to any 'focal point', not necessarily to the speaker; in other words, that it is just like the English word *this*, or any other word for THIS in any other language.

Second, the traditional definition of the basic demonstrative pronoun as 'near the speaker' cannot be right, because in all the languages examined (including Samoan), the word for THIS can also be used to refer to internal parts of the speaker's body, and a sentence such as *It is this tooth that hurts* (said to a dentist) cannot be interpreted as meaning 'It is the tooth near me which hurts' (cf. Wierzbicka 1980a:37). It is hardly necessary to add that 'this day' does not mean 'the day near the speaker', nor does 'this song' mean 'the song near the speaker'.

This is not to deny that there is an intuitive link between the concepts THIS and I, but this link is not compositional (as the examples above show, one cannot define THIS in terms of I).

17.3.2 THE SAME and OTHER

The notion of THE SAME has clear exponents in all the languages examined, but its range of occurrence is often narrower than it is in English. For example, in Samoan (and in a number of other languages) THE SAME (realised as a verb) can only be used as a predicate (p. 339). One can use it, therefore, to say that two people do, think, say or want the same, but not that 'the same person' came.

As pointed out by Harkins and Wilkins, "there are close conceptual links between 'sameness', 'oneness' ... and 'likeness' ... and one might expect some overlaps in use of the equivalents in various languages for THE SAME, ONE, and LIKE" (p. 292). The papers included in the present volume show that such overlaps do indeed occur, and that in some languages (for example, Arrernte, Kalam and Samoan) one says, for example, 'These two pieces are parts of one cup' rather than 'the same cup'; or 'I can do like this' rather than 'I can do the same'. It is important to note, however, that in all the languages considered there are nevertheless separate exponents for all of the three concepts in question. For example:

	Arrernte	Kalam	Samoan
THE SAME	*anteye*	*jm ñ-*	*tutusa*
ONE	*nyente*	*nokom*	*tasi*
LIKE	*-arteke*	*tek*	*pei*

Glosses such as 'one, unified, together, same', offered by Pawley (p. 403) for the Kalam word *nokom*, can be misleading, because they can be seen as implying that the speakers of the language in question make no distinction between the concepts THE SAME and ONE. In fact, however, lexical evidence shows that, for example, the speakers of Kalam do make this distinction (*nokom* ONE versus *jm ñ-* THE SAME). The fact that they may use the word for ONE more broadly than English speakers do, and the word for THE SAME less commonly, has to do with usage, not with semantics in the strict sense.

Differences of this kind (which concern usage, not meaning) should be distinguished from cases where two primitives — for example, THE SAME and ONE — share the same lexical exponent (with two independently identifiable senses). As we will see (section 17.3.3, p. 472), an example of the latter situation occurs in Acehnese, where the two meanings of the form *sa* can be distinguished on the basis of different allomorphy.

In Kayardild, the word *warngiida* is cited by Evans (p. 213) as a possible translation equivalent of both ONE and THE SAME, with the latter sense being illustrated with the sentence glossed as 'They two are from the one womb, from the same womb'. It seems likely, however, that this sentence constitutes an example of the use of the primitive ONE in a context where *the same* would normally be used in English; and we agree with Evans that it is better to consider another word (*niida*), illustrated with a sentence glossed 'You two are the same colour', as the primary (and perhaps only) exponent of the sense THE SAME.

As for OTHER, a very recent addition to the set of primitives, it may seem to be decomposable into THE SAME and negation ('not the same'), and so be entirely superfluous as a primitive. There are, however, contexts where OTHER cannot be replaced with 'not the same'. In particular, a substitution of this kind does not work in canonical phrases such as 'You and two other people' or 'I and two other people'. This shows that OTHER cannot be defined away.

In many languages (e.g. in Acehnese and Mandarin), the word for OTHER covers also the meaning 'different' ('not the same, not like this, not of the same kind'). In all the languages examined, however, there is a clear exponent of the primitive concept OTHER, which can be used in canonical contexts such as 'I and two other people' or 'You and many other people' (though not necessarily in contexts such as 'Pass me another beer', which, as Peeters (p. 430) points out, is an idiomatic English usage).

Hill says that "eliciting an exponent for OTHER raised a methodological problem. Using the canonical sentences to disambiguate the primitive from the range of uses of its exponent in English was not always sufficient" (p. 319). What she means is that in some contexts the English word *other* would be translated as *ve'ete* (which she glosses as 'different, other, not the same') and in others as *lou* (which she glosses as 'other, in addition'). Using the primitives, however, *ve'ete* could be glossed as 'not the same' (or 'not of the same kind'), and *lou* as OTHER. (For example, it is only *lou* which can be used in the canonical phrase 'You and two other people'). On this interpretation, which is compatible with all of Hill's examples and comments, there is no problem with OTHER in Longgu.

As mentioned earlier, in some languages the word for OTHER is formally related to, or even homonymous with, the word for SOMEONE. For example in Samoan, *isi* means OTHER (p. 341), but *se isi* (where *se* is homonymous with the indefinite article) means SOMEONE (p. 333). In Arrernte the word *arrpenhe* by itself (with no antecedent) means 'person', but when it is used as a modifier (*tyerrtye arrpenhe* 'another person') or with an antecedent it means OTHER (p. 288); and the same applies to the Yankunytjatjara word *kutjupa* (pp. 231–232).

17.3.3 ONE and TWO

ONE and TWO are entirely straightforward. In Acehnese, the word for ONE (*sa*) is homonymous with the word for THE SAME, but, as Durie, Daud and Hasan (p. 181) point out, the former, in contrast to the latter, is involved in *sa/si* allomorphy, and so can be regarded as a different word.

In many languages, the word for ONE is polysemous (as it is of course in English). For example, in Mangap-Mbula the element *ta* functions not only as the numeral ONE, but also as an indefinite article, as a relative clause marker, and as a formative in some demonstratives and conjunctions (p. 106, note 11).

In Japanese, ONE and TWO have two different allolexes, one of which combines with original Japanese classifiers, and the other, with classifiers of Chinese origin (p. 372). The primitive TWO also has two allolexes in Mandarin (p. 125).

17.3.4 ALL

Very clearly, all the languages in our sample have a word (or words) for the concept ALL. This fact is particularly significant in view of the recurring claims that in some 'primitive' cultures people not only do not make generalisations, but don't even have linguistic resources necessary for making them; and that they do not distinguish the concepts ALL and MANY (cf. e.g. Hallpike 1979; for discussion, see Wierzbicka, in press). Since claims of this kind are usually illustrated with the languages of Australia, Papua New Guinea and the Pacific, it is worth noting that all the Australian and Austronesian languages discussed in the present volume, as well as the Papuan language Kalam, have clear exponents of the concept ALL, and that these exponents can be used for making 'absolute generalisations' (as in the Lònggu example 'all types of birds' (p. 320) or in the Kayardild example 'all kinds of yam' (p. 214)).

This is not to say that the range of use of the semantic equivalents of ALL is necessarily the same in all the languages examined. While the papers included in the present volume did not aim at examining the range of ALL, there are reasons to think that this range may vary in different languages. In particular, Green (1992) states that in the Australian language Marrithiyel the exponent of ALL can only combine with semantic undergoers, and Foley (personal communication) has made a similar observation about the Papuan language Yimas. No reputable linguistic description, however, has reported the absence of any word for ALL. The papers included in the present volume provide clear evidence for the lexicalisation of this concept in all the languages examined.

One point raised in the discussions of ALL (for example, in the paper by Harkins and Wilkins, p. 294) concerns its implication of total exhaustiveness: do words for ALL always imply 'all, without exception', or can they be interpreted as 'nearly all'? In our view, the evidence presented in the present volume suggests that all languages do have a word for ALL in the sense of 'total exhaustiveness'; but that the attitudes to precision and accuracy may differ from culture to culture. If in some cultures people tend to say ALL in situations when it would be more accurate to say 'nearly all' this does not mean that the word glossed as ALL does not mean ALL, but rather that they are not aiming at complete accuracy, and that they readily permit themselves the use of a rhetorical overstatement.

17.3.5 MUCH/MANY

In a number of papers included in this volume, the authors report the presence of a clear exponent for the concept MUCH/MANY (which we treat here as a unitary concept). Some languages, for example Thai, have separate exponents for MUCH and MANY (like English), whereas others (for example Mandarin) do not make this distinction (note, however, that the expression *a lot* does not make this distinction either); but all the languages which have been investigated from this point of view do have at least one word for the meaning (or meanings) in question. Unfortunately, in this case (unlike that of the other primitives) we do not have information on all the languages included in the volume, because at the time when the present research proposal was formulated, MUCH/MANY was not included in our hypothetical set of primitives, and so not all the contributors were asked to look for it.[7]

Nor have we asked the contributors to look for the exponents of what is traditionally regarded as the 'opposite' of MUCH/MANY, namely 'little/few'. As will be discussed in section 17.8.1 (pp. 494–496) on BIG, SMALL and VERY, the relationship between the so-called semantic opposites MUCH/MANY and 'little/few', as well as BIG and SMALL, requires further investigation, as does also the relationship between the concepts MUCH, BIG and VERY.

17.4 Actions and Events (DO and HAPPEN)

With one exception (to be discussed below), DO and HAPPEN are easy to identify across the languages under investigation, although they do raise various interesting problems.

To begin with, there are interesting patterns of polysemy, some of them involving some other primitives. In particular, as mentioned earlier, in Kalam DO and HAPPEN share a single lexical exponent, which furthermore functions also an an exponent of the primitive FEEL.

The DO/HAPPEN polysemy has come to light in a number of languages not included in the present volume. But Kalam (and, apparently, a number of other Papuan languages, cf. Foley (1991:334)) goes even further than that, using the same lexical exponent for DO, HAPPEN and FEEL (pp. 396, 407–408). Both the DO/HAPPEN and the DO/HAPPEN/FEEL polysemies are clearly associated with different grammatical frames. (The same applies to the DO/SAY polysemy in Samoan, discussed earlier in connection with SAY.)

In Ewe (p. 71), DO and HAPPEN have their distinct exponents (wɔ and dzɔ respectively), but the primary exponent of DO (wɔ) can also be used in a special construction (with the experiencer as its direct object) as an exponent of HAPPEN. Ameka comments that "this kind of criss-crossing is ... undesirable and calls for further investigation" (p. 72), but we do not see such 'criss-crossing' as a problem, since the two senses (DO and HAPPEN) are kept perfectly distinct by different syntactic frames.

Among polysemies which involve DO or HAPPEN and some more complex meanings, a recurring one is the DO/'make' polysemy, present, for example, in Misumalpan languages (p. 272); and the HAPPEN/'appear' or HAPPEN/'arrive' polysemies, present, for examples, in Mangap-Mbula (p. 95), Ewe (p. 71) and French (p. 432).

From the point of view of form, it is interesting to note that while both DO and HAPPEN are commonly expressed by verbs (as in English), they can also be expressed in other ways. In particular, in Arrernte (p. 295) and Yankunytjatjara (p. 243), and a number of other Australian languages, HAPPEN is expressed by means of a suffix (the so-called inchoative suffix); in Kayardild (p. 216), it is expressed by means of a noun (rather like *event* in English); and in Thai (p. 159), by means of a discontinuous lexical item (serial-verb expression) *kòe:t ... khû'n* ('occur ... arise').

As far as the syntactic possibilities of the primitives under discussion are concerned, Durie, Daud and Hasan have raised some questions with respect to the combination of HAPPEN with a second argument ('something happened to ...') in Acehnese (pp. 185–187). Their discussion suggests that Acehnese differs in this regard from, say, English, in grammatical structure rather than in the range of semantic possibilities. For example, one can easily say 'Something good happened to me' in Acehnese using a construction which allows a noun phrase referring to the experiencer/patient to be topicalised before the verb. Durie, Daud and Hasan make the generalisation that in a case like this the noun phrase in question is understood as "the 'location' ... of the event" (p. 186); but, as they acknowledge, in a sentence like 'Something good happened to me' the term 'location' cannot be interpreted literally (WHERE). As they suggest, therefore, this construction can provide an adequate way of rendering in Acehnese sentences such as 'Something happened to someone'.

A different kind of problem arises in Mandarin, where, as Chappell (pp. 127–129) reports, the majority of verbs of happening, including the most basic one, *fasheng*, have adversative overtones, and where a sentence such as 'This kind of thing often happens to her' implies a misfortune. At first sight, this appears to suggest that Mandarin does not have a suitably neutral exponent of the hypothetical universal HAPPEN. Chappell, however, has provided a key to the solution to this difficulty, by pointing out that when the verb *fasheng* HAPPEN is used with non-human patients (e.g. 'Something happened here' or 'Huge changes have taken place') it can have a perfectly neutral interpretation. This suggests that any 'adversative' overtones of this verb in sentences with human subjects are pragmatic rather than strictly semantic.

For the purposes of the metalanguage, then, the verb *fasheng* appears to be quite an adequate exponent of the primitive HAPPEN, even though one would normally not use it in a sentence such as 'Something good happened to me' (resorting instead to the expression *zou-yun*, glossed by Chappell as 'good luck').

Turning now to the only really problematic case mentioned in the present volume, in Kayardild the primitive DO appears to be realised primarily by means of the interrogative verb *ngaakawatha* 'do what', as in *nyingka ngaakawath*? 'What are you doing?' (p. 215). Outside interrogative contexts, DO can be rendered by the verb formative *-yalatha*, which Evans himself has glossed in his grammar of Kayardild as 'do'; for example, *birdiyalatha* 'do evil things, act immorally' (literally, 'bad-do') and *mirrayalatha* 'do well'. Other examples are *thista-yala-tha* 'look after, care for' (literally, 'sister-DO' (from *thista* 'sister, nurse'), that is, 'do (things) like a nurse'), *marndurra-yala-tha* 'act (do) as if one were dead' (literally, 'dead-DO'), and *malawarri-yala-tha* 'shallow-DO' ("used by a man who jumped out of a boat, on the mistaken assumption that the water around was shallow" (Evans 1985:230)). Examples of this kind suggest that the formative in question is at least semi-productive.

Thus, Kayardild clearly does have at least one lexical exponent for the concept DO (*-yalatha*). But the range of this exponent's occurrence appears to be fairly restricted, and in a number of contexts where *do* would be used in English, in Kayardild more complex words would have to be used (that is, words whose meaning combines DO with something else). For example, there is a verb in Kayardild which means 'do the same' ('copy, imitate'), and this word would normally be used to render the sense 'do the same'. Evans remarks that "DO can usually be translated, but not in a consistent way", and that this "would make the manipulation of DO in Kayardild definitions extremely difficult" (p. 216).

From our point of view, however, the statement that DO **can** be translated into Kayardild is welcome and significant; and the observation that it cannot be translated into Kayardild in a consistent way is not necessarily a problem (since we recognise, and indeed expect, allolexy). As for the impression that manipulation of DO in Kayardild definitions would at times be very difficult, we hope that continuing research on Kayardild will bring solutions to these difficulties.

In particular, one wonders whether the interrogative verb 'do what' cannot in some situations be pressed into service to double as 'do something', the way the interrogative pronouns WHO and WHAT can be pressed into service in Australian languages to double as SOMEONE and SOMETHING (cf. Goddard's discussion of a comparable phenomenon in Yankunytjatjara (p. 245) and Evans' own comments on Kayardild (pp. 206–207)):

(a) He saw something/what — a kangaroo. (i.e. he saw a kangaroo)
(b) He saw someone/who — that fella Witjiki. (i.e. he saw that fella Witjiki)

(c) He did what — lost it. (i.e. he lost it)
(d) He did what — hit her. (i.e. he hit her)
(e) She did what — the same thing again. (i.e. she did the same again)

As Goddard (p. 245) points out, the interrogative verb 'do what' can also be used in Yankunytjatjara as an indefinite verb 'do something' (without the implications of suspense or excitement that a similar construction has in English). It would not be surprising if it turned out that the same applies to the Kayardild verb 'do what'.

17.5 Meta-Predicates

17.5.1 NO (DON'T WANT)

Negation is probably the least controversial of all the lexical universals which have been posited in the present volume. Nobody has ever reported coming across a language without negation, and exponents of negation — unlike those of the other conceptual primitives posited here — are routinely reported in all descriptive grammars.

It is true that negation was absent from the first tentative lists of universal semantic primitives proposed by the present writer (cf. e.g. Wierzbicka 1972, 1980a) — a fact which has puzzled or even dismayed some readers. Instead, however, those early lists included the element DON'T WANT (DISWANT) or I DON'T WANT (I DISWANT); and although now it seems wiser to regard interjections or particles analogous to the English word *no* (the opposite of *yes*) as the primary exponent of the primitive in question, we would still argue that negation is closely related to 'rejection' and to 'not wanting'; and that the phrase 'I don't want', which cannot always be decomposed into negation and 'wanting', is but an allolex of negation.

The English phrase *I don't want* is ambiguous. Sometimes, it functions as a negated version of *I want* (for example, in *I don't particularly want to do it*). But it doesn't always function that way. For example, in a case when we resist outside pressure to do something by saying *I don't want to do it!*, we are not denying that we want to do something, but rather we are rejecting a proposed action, that is, we are saying that we 'diswant' to do something. It is certainly remarkable that many languages — including several investigated in the present volume (e.g. Acehnese, Longgu, Samoan, Kayardild) — do have a special exponent for this sense of the phrase 'I don't want'. Equally remarkable is the fact that many languages (e.g. Samoan) have a special 'negative imperative' ('don't').

If we assume that 'I don't want' (on one reading) is an allolex of negation, then two problems require some explanation: first, what exactly is it that we 'don't want' when we use a negative sentence (e.g. 'It is not black'); and second, how is 'not wanting' related to 'wanting'?

The answer to the first question (suggested to me in part by Cliff Goddard, personal communication) can be represented, schematically, along the following lines:

It is not black. =
No, it is not black. =
when I want to think: "I can think: 'it is black'", I think "no"

What this means is that to reject a thought, one must first, so to speak, try to accept it.

As for the relation between 'I don't want this' (rejection, 'negative volition') and 'I want this' ('positive volition'), an affinity is certainly there (and in many languages the exponents of the two are morphologically related), but since it cannot be represented by means of a paraphrase, it has to be regarded as non-compositional ('I don't want this!' ≠ 'It is not the case that I want this').

In any case, whatever the relationship between negation and 'rejection' or 'diswanting' and wanting, it is clear that all the languages investigated in the present volume do have lexical exponents of negation. Typically, there is a great deal of allolexy in this area, with interjections and particles (comparable to *no*) being supplemented in the linguistic system by verbs, verbal affixes and various other morphological devices. The topic requires further investigation, but apart from the question of the relationship between negation and volition, it is not particularly controversial.

17.5.2 LIKE

All the languages investigated in this volume have one or more words which can translate (without any discernible difference in meaning) the English word *like* (as in *like this*).

Several languages (e.g. Yankunytjatjara, Samoan, Arrernte) have portmanteau exponents for semantic molecules including LIKE, such as 'like this', 'do like this' and 'say like this' (cf. the English words *thus* and *such*, both corresponding to 'like this'). It is not clear at this stage whether the meanings in question can always be expressed in those languages (be it unidiomatically, but intelligibly) with combinations of the exponents of the simple atom-like elements LIKE, THIS, SAY or DO as well as by means of those molecules.

In several languages (as in English), there is allolexy, and the different exponents of LIKE can often be compared to the English allolexes *like*, *as*, *how* or *way*.

In some languages, there is evidence of polysemy. One pattern of polysemy illustrated in this volume links LIKE with counterfactual expressions such as 'as if' or 'one would/could think such-and-such' ('A is like B' = 'looking at A, one would/could think that it was B'). Discussing the presence of this pattern of polysemy in Kayardild, Evans (p. 227, note 20) raises the question of a possible paraphrase relation between 'X is like Y' and 'one would think it was Y'. (Cf. also Mosel's remarks concerning the Samoan verb *pei* 'be like', that "the English translation 'be as if' better mimics the Samoan way of expression" (p. 346); and Hill's observation

(p. 323) that while Longgu has a perfectly unambiguous exponent of IF, namely *zuhu*, younger speakers tend to replace it with the word *liva'a-na*, which is the prime exponent of LIKE.)

But despite the intuitive links between LIKE and conditional and 'counterfactual' expressions such as IF, 'as if' or 'one would think', LIKE cannot be reduced to any combination of other simple meanings. In particular, the combination of LIKE and THIS (e.g. 'I want to sing like this') cannot be reduced in any way to 'one would think' or 'as if'. Furthermore, a sentence such as 'I want to be like you' can hardly be paraphrased without some allolex of LIKE. (Even the implausible paraphrase 'I want to be such that one would/could think that I was you' includes the word *such*, which is a portmanteau exponent of LIKE THIS.)

Assuming, then, that LIKE is semantically irreducible, it is gratifying to be able to state that there are no problems with finding clear exponents of this concept in the languages investigated in the present volume. In view of recent theories concerning the role of 'prototypes' in human categorisation, it is important to emphasise that all these languages have means for distinguishing LIKE from KIND (so that in any of them one can say, for example, 'This fish is like that fish, but it is not the same kind'). (Cf. also the Kalam sentence quoted by Pawley (p. 413): 'The small kind is like the common *madaw* ...'.)

In some languages, for example in Yankunytjatjara and Arrernte, there are formal links between the exponents of LIKE and THE SAME. For example, in Yankunytjatjara *puṟunypa* means LIKE and *palupuṟunypaṯu* (literally, 'LIKE THIS-emphatic', since *palu* means THIS) means THE SAME (p. 242). Harkins and Wilkins seek to explain such facts in Arrernte by pointing to "the conceptual link between 'likeness' and 'sameness'" (p. 298). But the affinity between the two concepts is not compositional. The fact that one can say, for example, 'This fish is like that other fish, but it is not the same fish' (and as far as we have been able to ascertain, one can say this in all the languages under investigation) shows that there is an irreducible difference between these two concepts.

17.5.3 BECAUSE

BECAUSE is one of those concepts whose fundamental role in human thinking has often been taken for granted (especially by philosophers) but whose universality has sometimes been questioned on linguistic grounds (cf. Evans 1986). It is important to emphasise, therefore, that all the papers included in the present volume corroborate the view that BECAUSE is indeed a universal human concept.

In some languages causation can be expressed, as in English, by means of unambiguous intersentential connectives analogous to the English word *because* (e.g. *yīnwei* in Mandarin (p. 133), *tana* in Mangap-Mbula (p. 99), *parce que* in French (p. 434), *'ona* in Samoan (p. 345), *'ani-a* in Longgu (p. 324)).

In some other languages the basic exponent of BECAUSE is a noun, like *cause* or *reason* in English (e.g. *kareuna* in Acehnese (p. 189), *juj* in Kalam (p. 412)) but this noun can be used perfectly well to render the meaning BECAUSE in sentences such as 'I'm crying because ...' (cf. 'The cause of my crying is ...' or 'The reason why I'm crying is ...'). There are no grounds for saying, then, that a noun such as *kareuna* or *juj* means anything different from the English conjunction *because*.

The only group of languages in the present sample which at first sight may appear to be problematic as far as the expression of causal relations is concerned are the Australian languages (Arrernte (pp. 298–299), Yankunytjatjara (p. 247) and Kayardild (p. 220)). In all these languages, the concept BECAUSE is expressed by a grammatical morpheme which can also be used to express temporal sequence (AFTER) or the origin of motion ('from'). As the authors of the relevant papers show, however, in all of these languages the sense BECAUSE can be clearly distinguished from the other ones. In particular, the BECAUSE sense cannot be seen as a contextual interpretation of a more basic temporal sense, because in crucial examples adduced in these papers (in support of a separate BECAUSE sense) an interpretation in terms of AFTER does not make sense.

For example, in the Arrernte sentence glossed by Harkins and Wilkins (p. 299) as 'You should go visit your mother because she's very sick' the only possible interpretation of the polysemous ablative suffix -*nge* ((a) 'away from', (b) AFTER, and (c) BECAUSE) is BECAUSE. (As Harkins and Wilkins point out, "the speaker is certainly not urging the addressee to go 'away from' or 'after' his mother's illness, but 'because' of it".)

A particularly clear test for establishing polysemy of elements which can mean either AFTER or BECAUSE has been proposed by Goddard (1991), who has shown that in Yankunytjatjara the ablative suffix (normally used for temporal succession) can also be used to refer to concurrent cause, and who has thus established the independence of the temporal and causal senses of this suffix. The fact that the same test when applied to Kayardild gives the same results has led Evans to revise his earlier view on the "unimportance of CAUSE in Kayardild" (Evans 1986) and to conclude that the so-called consequential suffix "is polysemous between 'temporal consequence' and 'causal consequence' meanings" (p. 221). (For further discussion, see Goddard (1991).)

17.5.4 IF

Like BECAUSE, IF is one of those concepts which play a particularly important role in the controversies concerning the fundamentals of human thought (cf. Wierzbicka, in press). Like BECAUSE, IF has been claimed to be an indispensable element of human thought; and yet its universality has been questioned. The papers included in the present volume support the view that IF is indeed universally present; and they also point to recurring patterns of polysemy as the main source of the widespread confusion regarding the universality of this concept. (Another source lies in the fact that in many languages, for example in Samoan and Kayardild, the conditional relation is commonly expressed by simple juxtaposition of clauses, with a suitable intonation pattern.)

One pattern of polysemy involving IF has been discussed in the section on SAY. As shown in Bugenhagen's paper on Mangap-Mbula (p. 104), the IF/SAY polysemy of the element *so* in this language is clearly associated with different grammatical properties (e.g. *so* SAY, in contrast to *so* IF, can take prepositional complements, or sentential complements introduced by the complementiser *ta kembei*; and the sentential complement *so* IF never has an overt noun phrase subject).

Another recurring pattern of polysemy involves IF and MAYBE (or CAN). As shown by Goddard (pp. 248–249), in Yankunytjatjara the free particle *tjinguṟu* means MAYBE (as does also the verbal inflection *-ku*), but the same word may also introduce a conditional clause. For example, in sentences such as

Tjinguṟu-la wiyampa iluma.
'If we'd been without (a radio) we would've died.'

the word *tjinguṟu* cannot be interpreted as MAYBE; for the sentence to make sense, it must be interpreted as IF.

As Harkins and Wilkins show in their paper (pp. 296–298), a similar situation appears to obtain in Arrernte, where the word *peke* can be used in a simple sentence to mean MAYBE, but in a complex sentence (with the verb of the main clause marked by a special 'subsequent' suffix, unless this clause contains negation) can only mean IF. Schematically:

(a) 'It could (*peke*) rain tomorrow.'
(b) 'If (*peke*) it rains tomorrow, I will come-SEQU.'

In Kayardild, the concept IF is realised by means of a polysemous suffix glossed by Evans as 'potential'. As Evans points out, "some tense/mood sequences (notably the past–future) only allow the conditional interpretation [of this suffix], others (e.g. precondition–actual) also allow a 'when' interpretation" (p. 217). The fact that there are grammatical environments where the potential suffix can only mean IF establishes, in our view, the polysemy of this suffix, and proves that IF is one of its distinct meanings.

The fact that many other Australian languages (not included in the present volume), exhibit demonstrable IF/WHEN polysemy, supports the analysis of Kayardild summarised here.

As McConvell (1991:15) notes, "lack of a formal distinction between *if* and *when* in Aboriginal languages, in contrast to English, is supposedly linked to absence of hypothetical conditional statements in Aboriginal discourse". Rejecting such claims McConvell argues that Aboriginal languages do have lexical and grammatical resources to mark hypotheticality, and he points out that even if the words for IF and

WHEN are identical, they may appear in different frames. For example, "in the Ngarinman language the concept of *if* is distinguished from *when* by the use of the doubt suffix *nga* following the subordinate clause marker *nyamu* and the pronoun clitic complex" (1991:16).

This brings us to what for a long time looked like the only exception to the universality thesis, namely to the Kalam data. In the earlier versions of Pawley's paper on Kalam, the section on IF started with the following two sentences: "There is no distinct conditional marker. Conditional relation between clauses is inferable from a combination of grammatical and pragmatic conditions."

In an exciting recent development, however, Pawley (p. 411) has been able to identify what does look like a distinct conditional marker: not a single morpheme but a combination of two elements, a 'prior' suffix (whose form depends on the identity or non-identity of the subjects in the dependent and independent clause) and the so-called optative suffix *-n-*. Pawley glosses this optative suffix as 'should', and likens the construction in question to English sentences such as *If you should do X/Should you do X, then Y should/will happen.*

From our point of view the crucial fact is that while in a simple clause the suffix *-n-* means 'should', in a complex sentence containing a different-subject prior suffix *-e-* (or, presumably, an same-subject prior suffix *-i*), this suffix means IF, as seen in Pawley's example (92):

> *Mab ñŋeb ak ned gon ak l-e-n-mn,*
> tree food the first trap the put-DS:PRIOR-OPT-2SG
> *skoyd ak ned ap d-o-n-mn ...*
> ringtail the first come catch-DS:PRIOR-OPT-2SG
> 'If you set a trap at a tree where *kapuls* (game mammals) come to feed on dead timber, and if you catch a ringtail possum first ...'

Furthermore, Pawley (p. 409) reports that Kalam does have a distinct marker for the counterfactual IF, in the form of a discontinuous morpheme *b...p* (or *p...p*). For example, counterfactual clauses such as 'If I were God ...' can be rendered in Kalam in a completely unambiguous way (Pawley, personal communication).

Since a counterfactual proposition is more complex in its meaning than an ordinary conditional one, and is built upon it, a language can hardly have a concept of a counterfactual IF without having a concept of IF in the first place. (For further discussion of the expression of IF in Kalam, see section 17.6.1, p. 484.)

17.5.5 CAN and MAYBE

Experience suggests that to explicate meanings across a wide range of semantic domains we need an indefinable concept corresponding to at least some uses of the English word *can* (and so identified provisionally as CAN). The numerous attempts to define away CAN (or 'can't') undertaken by different writers (including the present writer) have in our view failed, and that is why we have included CAN in the list of primitives to be tested cross-linguistically in the present volume. But while we have reasons to believe that some primitive having to do, roughly speaking, with the realm of possibility is needed, we are still not quite certain that we know exactly what we are looking for. The fact that, by and large, the hypothetical primitive CAN has proved itself in the research reported in the present volume, is in itself quite amazing, given that in this area perhaps more than in any other we felt that we were groping in the dark.

Traditional distinctions such as 'the can of ability' versus 'the can of possibility' or 'the deontic can' versus 'the epistemic can', cannot be taken for granted. As is often the case with similar clarifications, the notions of 'possibility' and 'ability' may in fact prove more complex than the notion of CAN itself, vague and obscure as it might seem.

Since examples are usually much more illuminating than labels it will be useful to list here a few sentences illustrating the hypothetical semantic primitive CAN:

> This rope could break.
> It might rain tomorrow.
> Maybe it will rain tomorrow.
> He can't sleep (in this noise).
> Fasten everything that can be blown away by the wind.
> One can't say things like that.

The data reported in the present volume suggest that there is no problem with rendering sentences such as those listed above in the languages under investigation: they all have some words or morphemes which can be used as equivalents of the English words *could*, *can*, *might* and *maybe*. Sometimes, these words or morphemes may be involved in polysemies (for example, we have already discussed the CAN/IF polysemies in Yankunytjatjara and Arrernte); but these polysemies can always be resolved on the basis of different grammatical frames with which the different senses are associated. Perhaps the least clear case reported in the present volume is that of Kayardild (pp. 217–219), where the so-called potential suffix has a number of different senses which are difficult to sort out. But whatever results future research on Kayardild may bring in this area,[8] it is significant that, as Evans reports (p. 218), Kayardild also uses a loanword from English, *marrbi* (from *might be*), and this is in fact the most common way of expressing the meaning in question. As Hale points out with respect to the word for WANT in Misumalpan languages (p. 283), it seems inconceivable that a word like *might be* or *maybe* could be borrowed from another language unless the concept was already there. What seems to happen in a case like this is that an indigenous polysemous marker of a basic meaning is either partially or totally replaced with a borrowed monosemous one.

A particularly interesting case of polysemy involving the notion of possibility has recently been reported by Pawley (p. 413), according to whom the primary exponent of this notion in Kalam is a discontinuous morpheme superficially analysable as a combination of a future marker and the word for 'or'. For example, to say something like 'It may rain tomorrow' one says something that looks more like 'It will rain tomorrow or ...'. But although the elements glossed by Pawley as 'future' and 'or' have their own functions (different from the function of expressing possibility), the combination of these two elements has a unique meaning (roughly, 'it's possible').

Undoubtedly, the expression of 'possibility' or CAN in different languages requires further investigation, and so the role of CAN in the Natural Semantic Metalanguage requires further thought; but the papers included in the present volume support the view that CAN is a universal human concept, lexicalised in one way or another in all languages.

17.5.6 VERY

For discussion of VERY, see section 17.8.1, pp. 494–496.

17.6 Time and Place

17.6.1 TIME (WHEN)

It has often been pointed out that not all cultures give anywhere near as much attention to the concept of 'time' as modern Western culture does. LePan (1989:90) says that even in England, "incredibly, the question 'what time is it?' does not appear in our written language until 1597"; and he remarks that "a lack of chronological awareness — and a lack of a sense of 'whenness' generally — is one of the most immediately striking aspects of medieval historical writing" (1989:113).

According to LePan, the lack of a sense of 'whenness' is equally characteristic of mediaeval European mentality as it is of 'primitive thought' elsewhere in the world. Given this background, it is particularly interesting to note that all the languages in our sample do have a word for WHEN.

It is true that Samoan appears to have no general 'epistemological classifier' for time and seems to distinguish lexically between 'when in the future' (*'âfea*) and 'when in the past' (*anafea*). But since the words *'âfea* and *anafea* "are obviously composed of two morphemes, that is, *'â=fea* and *ana=fea*" (p. 349), it seems reasonable to suggest that the second morpheme in each pair, *fea*, represents the general concept WHEN — a suggestion confirmed by the fact that the element *â-* is also found in adverbs referring to the future, and the element *ana-* in adverbs referring to the past.

Admittedly, the morpheme *-fea* has also two other meanings, WHERE and 'which', but as Mosel points out (p. 349), these can occur in different frames, and can be easily separated from the temporal sense on distributional grounds (*fea* 'which' occurs in combination with the article *le* — *lefea* — except when it refers to proper names; *fea* WHERE always occurs in a base form, whereas *fea* WHEN occurs only in combination with *'â-* 'in the future' or *ana-* 'in the past').

Furthermore, Samoan has a word which situates an event in time with respect to another event (schematically, 'X happened when Y happened'). The word in question is *ina* WHEN (Mosel, personal communication), and arguably it can be regarded as an allolex of *-fea* WHEN.

Not surprisingly, the formal links between the exponents of WHERE, WHEN and 'which', characteristic of Samoan, have their parallels in other languages. Among the languages studied in the present volume, a case in point is Kalam (p. 415), where the word *akay* combined with a noun means 'which', whereas the same form *akay* on its own means WHERE, and where the word for WHEN is *won akay* (*won* being glossed by Pawley as 'piece, bit; period or interval of time'). It is clear, however, that both in Kalam and in Samoan the three concepts in question (WHERE, WHEN and 'which') are quite distinct (and are differentiated on formal as well as semantic grounds).

It is interesting to note in this connection that although in the past Pawley has raised some difficulties in connection with IF (suggesting that in Kalam it may be impossible to distinguish IF from WHEN), he has never had any problems in identifying the Kalam exponent of WHEN (namely *won akay*). But if WHEN can be unambiguously located in Kalam, this means that Kalam does draw a distinction between WHEN and IF. The fact that in the latest version of his paper Pawley was able to identify an exponent of IF is exciting but it is not altogether surprising: since Kalam clearly has an unambiguous exponent of WHEN (in the expression *won akay*), it was to be expected that the blurring of WHEN and IF in this language was more apparent than real and that sooner or later an exponent of IF would show up too.

The presence of a word for WHEN in all the languages examined suggests that even if it is true that some cultures may have a greater awareness of, and interest in, 'whenness' than others, the concept of WHEN is indeed one of the universal human concepts.

LePan argues that mediaeval people, like 'primitive man' in general, were "often unclear on the distinction between time and space" (1989:112). The fact that all the languages in our sample do distinguish lexically between WHEN and WHERE suggests that **some** distinction between time and space is universally drawn. (The Samoan morpheme *fea* is only an apparent counterexample to this statement, since as we have seen *fea* WHERE is always formally distinguished from *-fea* WHEN; and in addition there is also the relative WHEN marker, *ina*.)

17.6.2 WHERE

As mentioned in the section on WHEN, it has often been claimed that the distinction between time and space is not always sharply drawn. There is plenty of evidence supporting the view that there are some conceptual links between time and space (for example, as the papers included in the present volume show, the words for BEFORE and AFTER are often related to, or even homonymous with, the words for 'front' and 'back'). We have also seen that in Samoan the same segment, *fea*, stands for both WHEN and WHERE, although the two senses occur in different environments.

Nonetheless, in all the languages investigated time and space (WHEN and WHERE) are distinguished, and each of these concepts has its own distinct exponent.

In some languages, as in English, there is an allolexic relation between a locative adverbial (WHERE, 'somewhere') and a locative noun ('place'). In others, there does not seem to be a noun corresponding to 'place', but there is always an 'epistemological classifier' corresponding to WHERE. We assume that in a language which does not have a noun corresponding to *place* (for example, in Yankunytjatjara) it is still possible to convey, for example, the idea that 'something happened in the same place (as something else)'; but the matter requires further investigation.

17.6.3 AFTER and BEFORE

It has often been pointed out that the idea of 'temporal succession' plays a much greater role in modern Western culture than it does in other cultures; and a 'linear' conception of time has often been contrasted with a 'cyclical' one. For example, LePan (1989:89) writes that "primitive man's intuition of time was dominated by his sense of rhythm rather than by the idea of continual succession" (cf. also Hall 1983).

We regard it as an important finding of the present volume, therefore, that all the languages under investigation do have words for temporal succession (AFTER and BEFORE), and that in all of them one can form sentences such as 'B was born (died) after A' and 'A was born (died) before B'. Mosel (p. 359, note 15) notes that in Samoan it is more natural to say 'A is older than B' than 'A was born before B' (or 'B was born after A'), but of course this would not necessarily apply to a family where some children died in infancy (A may have died before B was born, and may have never reached the age reached subsequently by B). Similarly, it makes sense to say of twins that twin A was born before twin B (or twin B after twin A), but one wouldn't say (unless in jest) that twin A is older than twin B.

One or two of the contributors to the present volume have suggested that in the language described by them a word meaning 'first' rather than BEFORE would be used in situations described above; upon further questioning, however, it emerged that in such cases the word traditionally glossed as 'first' would also be used in the case of three or more children, as in 'A was born before B, and B was born before (*first) C'. In this case, one can say that B was born before C, but not that B was born first. It is clear that while in the case of a first-born child it may be difficult to distinguish these two meanings (BEFORE and 'first'), in the case of a second or a third child the word traditionally glossed in a given linguistic tradition as 'first' must in fact mean BEFORE.

But if a word clearly means BEFORE, why is it that the tradition of glossing it in English as 'first' arose in the first place? Apparently, the reason lies in different formal properties of the BEFORE word. In English, *before* is usually used as a preposition or as a conjunction ('before that' or 'before that happened'), and its adverbial use is restricted to the temporal reference point (e.g. 'I've never done that before', that is, before now, but not 'He was born before', that is, before someone else). But, for example, in Samoan (p. 351), the BEFORE word (*muamua*) glossed traditionally as 'come first, go first, be first' is in fact a verb and has a range of uses different from that of the English word *before*. For example, it can be used in sentences such as 'Go first, and I will follow'; compare English *Go before me*, but not *Go before. But since, as pointed out earlier, the Samoan word in question (*muamua*) can also be used in sentences such as 'B was born before C' (where it cannot mean anything other than BEFORE), it is reasonable to conclude that it does in fact mean BEFORE.

Similarly, in Kayardild (p. 222) the concept BEFORE is expressed by means of a verb, *yuulutha*, literally, 'go ahead', which Evans glosses as 'first, happening first' (e.g. 'X died first, before'). Assuming that this verb can also be used in canonical sentences such as 'A was born before B', there is no difficulty in regarding it as the exponent of the primitive BEFORE.

What applies to BEFORE, also applies to AFTER. For example, in Samoan (p. 351) the word for AFTER (*mulimuli*) is also a verb (like *follow* is in English), and the range of constructions in which it can appear is of course different from that of the English word *after* (which is either a preposition or a conjunction); but since there is no problem with using this word in canonical sentences such as 'B was born after A', it is perfectly justified to conclude that this word does in fact mean AFTER.

BEFORE and AFTER are considered as somewhat problematic by Durie, Daud and Hasan (p. 192), who write with respect to Acehnese:

'X comes after Y' is ... rendered as, for example, 'At a particular time, Y is finished or complete but X is not'. In such constructions the actual temporal sequence is strictly speaking an inference, and because of this, as far as temporal sequence is concerned, the meanings AFTER and BEFORE find no lexical realisation in Acehnese in such constructions. If such aspectual notions as 'complete' and 'incomplete' are to be decomposed in terms of AFTER and BEFORE ... then we would have a serious problem for NSM methodology ...

But notions such as 'finish', 'complete' or 'incomplete' do not apply to punctual events. The crucial question is how — if at all — a temporal sequence of punctual events can be expressed in Acehnese, that is, how — if at all — one can say, for example, 'A was born before B', 'A died before B', 'B was born after A' or 'B died after A'.

As one would expect, thoughts of this kind are neither unthinkable nor unsayable in Acehnese, and the words necessary to formulate them **are** available (Durie, personal communication). The words in question are *awai* BEFORE and *dudoe* AFTER. According to Durie, Daud and Hasan (p. 192), these words are usually glossed in English as 'earlier' and 'later', rather than BEFORE and AFTER, but this seems to be motivated by syntactic rather than semantic considerations.

Like other primitives, BEFORE and AFTER can be involved in polysemies. One recurrent polysemy links BEFORE with 'front' and AFTER with 'back' (as in Longgu). Clearly, in a sentence such as 'Before the cyclone everywhere looked good' (quoted by Hill, p. 325) the word which can mean either 'in front' or BEFORE means in fact BEFORE.

The pattern of polysemy linking the concepts AFTER and BEFORE with spatial and body-part terms such as 'back, behind' or 'front, in front of' is also evidenced in Ewe. Ameka makes in this connection the following remark: "From a localist viewpoint, the body parts ... are more basic and more concrete than the primitive notions they have developed into" (p. 84); and he asks what is semantically more basic and conceptually prior, the spatial (bodily) sense or the temporal sense.

An objection along these lines may also occur to some readers of the present volume, but Ameka answers it himself when he continues (p. 84):

One can defend the primitive status of these terms [for BEFORE and AFTER] by saying that although there is a semantic and conceptual link between their historical sources and the primitive notions, one cannot define these primitive terms through the body-part terms, so from a decompositional point of view these [temporal] terms are primitive.

Just so.

Several contributors to the present volume emphasise that English sentences with the words *before* or *after* would be translated into their respective languages in a variety of ways, and that these different ways are not always semantically equivalent to the English sentences. In particular, it has been claimed that in some languages (e.g. in Acehnese or Samoan) aspectual notions such as 'completed' and 'incompleted' play a greater role than purely temporal notions BEFORE and AFTER, and would often be used to translate sentences with the words *before* and *after* (cf. Durie, Daud and Hasan's remarks quoted above).

We do not dispute this. It is all the more important to emphasise, however, that **all** languages which have been investigated from this point of view have words which denote pure temporal sequence (BEFORE and AFTER) and which can be used to express the temporal order of punctual events, as in 'A was born before B' or 'B died after A'. This finding is all the more striking in that from a logical point of view it might seem that either BEFORE or AFTER would be sufficient, and that a language could get by with only one of these concepts. In fact, however, it appears that all languages have lexical resources for expressing both of them. This suggests that from the point of view of human conceptualisation of reality, 'Y happened after X' means something different from, and cannot be reduced to, 'X happened before Y'.

17.6.4 UNDER and ABOVE

In most languages, there are no problems with finding semantic exponents of the concepts UNDER and ABOVE. In two languages (Arrernte and Yankunytjatjara), however, problems do arise as far as UNDER is concerned, and in Ewe there appear to be some problems with ABOVE. On the other hand, ABOVE is easy to identify in Arrernte and perhaps in Yankunytjatjara as well, whereas UNDER is easy to identify in Ewe. Since we have posited (so far) only one relational locative primitive, we could now hypothesise that the same basic conceptual primitive is realised in some languages as UNDER and in others as ABOVE; and this possibility should undoubtedly be explored in future research. But it is also possible that with time the difficulties which emerged with respect to the two Australian languages and Ewe will be resolved.

Let me summarise briefly the nature of these difficulties. In Arrernte, Harkins and Wilkins (p. 301) report that the word for UNDER (*kwene*) can also mean 'inside'; and they make a case for a unitary interpretation in terms of 'surroundness' and 'invisibility' (an observer placed above an object cannot see all its sides, just as an object which is inside something else cannot be seen). Since, however, *kwere* is perceived as an antonym of both *kethe* 'outside' and *kertne* 'top' it is possible that upon further investigation it may turn out to be polysemous, with the two senses UNDER and 'inside' being related (in the way suggested by Harkins and Wilkins) rather than identical. A similar situation applies in Yankunytjatjara (Goddard, personal communication).

As for Ewe, it is not entirely clear to us why Ameka regards it as problematic, in view of the fact that he does provide a satisfactory translation of the canonical sentence 'There are black clouds above us'. Ameka (p. 80–81) notes that the word used for ABOVE in the Ewe translation, namely *tame*, can also mean 'peak, top of', but surely, this cannot be the meaning of *tame* in this particular sentence. Rather, it would seem that *tame* is polysemous, and that one of its two meanings is ABOVE. But more data would be needed to clarify this point. Be that as it may, we have to conclude that the status of UNDER (or UNDER/ABOVE) as a hypothetical universal requires further investigation.

17.7 Partonomy and Taxonomy

17.7.1 PART

The concept of PART is perhaps the most difficult one in the entire set of the three dozen or so primitives investigated in the present volume. The first observation is that while many languages examined, for example Japanese, do have a word corresponding, semantically, to the English word *part*, many others (e.g. Acehnese, Kayardild and Yankunytjatjara) appear to not have such a word.

Should PART, then, be crossed off the list of universal semantic primitives? Or in any case, should it be crossed out from the lexicon of the Natural Semantic Metalanguage?

We could of course do that — nothing would be simpler. But then we would have to face the consequences, and one consequence of such a move would be to have to accept the conclusion that certain thoughts which can be easily expressed in English cannot be expressed in many languages at all — not that it would be very difficult to express such thoughts in those languages, but that it would be absolutely impossible to do so. Furthermore, we would have to admit that these apparently inexpressible thoughts are not philosophical, scientific or technical in character, but very simple and accessible to anyone in the English-speaking world. Two examples:

(a) This thing has two identical parts. (said, for example, of scissors)
(b) This thing has two parts, one to hold and one to cut with. (said, for example, of an axe)

Is it true that there are languages in which thoughts of this kind could not be expressed at all?

The research reported in the present volume does not support such a conclusion. Rather, it suggests that while a special word for PART (and only for PART) may be lacking there is always some lexical material which — in combination with some grammatical machinery — allows the speakers to express the idea of HAVING PARTS. For example, if one wants to say the equivalent of the English sentence *This thing has two parts* in a language which doesn't have a special word for PART (and only for PART), one may be able to say the equivalent of one of the following sentences:

(a) This thing has two things.
(b) This thing has two whats.
(c) This thing, there are two things (to it).

Admittedly, in sentences about human beings, HAVING PARTS may be expressed in the same way as 'possession'. But inanimate things do not 'own' other things, and so in sentences with inanimate subjects the ambiguity between HAVING PARTS and 'possessing things' does not arise. (A sentence such as 'Person X has two Ys' could refer to two personal possessions, but 'This thing has two Ys' could not.)

The idea of PART implies the existence of other parts (an object cannot have just one part). For this reason, HAVING PARTS is more basic than 'being a part of'. If X is a part of Y, this presupposes that Y has parts. We conjecture that in any language the idea of HAVING PARTS can be expressed in an unambiguous way. But it is quite conceivable that the idea of 'being a part of' can only be expressed in an unambiguous way in the context of a prior statement that something has parts (e.g. 'A knife has two things: a blade is a thing of the knife, a handle is a thing of the knife').

Durie, Daud and Hasan argue that since in Acehnese one would use the same construction to say 'The knife has a blade' and 'The knife has a sheath', this construction cannot be regarded as an exponent of the part–whole relation. They also point out that "any PART OF meaning that can be found in an expression like 'John's leg' is presumably to be located in the meaning of *leg*, rather than in the adnominal construction itself" (p. 194).

We don't dispute these contentions; and we accept the point that while in English there is a special word associated with the PART meaning (*part*), in Acehnese there is no such special word. On the other hand, we hypothesise that in Acehnese, too, one can express the thought that something has two parts, and that one could do so using a combination of the 'possessive/existential' construction described by Durie, Daud and Hasan with the word for 'thing', or SOMETHING, along the lines of 'This thing has two things' (or 'This thing, there are two things').

One way to interpret such facts is to say that in some languages the word for 'thing' when used in a particular construction means PART. Another way is to say that it is the construction itself which — in conjunction with the word 'thing' or WHAT — encodes the part–whole relation.

As for sentences such as 'The knife has a sheath', we would point out that in this case the nature of the relationship between the two referents (the knife and the sheath) is specified in the lexical meaning of the word *sheath*. The same applies to a sentence such as 'This fridge has three lumps of meat (in it)', which according to Evans (personal communication) would be rendered in Kayardild by means of the same construction as 'This bike has three wheels'. The lexical meaning of the word *fridge* implies a container–contents relationship, and so it opens a possibility of a semantic interpretation other than HAVING PARTS. But the word *thing* has no implications of the kind that *fridge* or *sheath* do. For this reason, as proposed by Goddard (pp. 255–256), the crucial test for the primitive PART (or, more precisely, HAVING PARTS) must come from sentences where both arguments are lexically bare, so to speak, and are realised by the word for 'thing' (or WHAT, or SOMETHING), such as the following ones:

(a) This thing has many things.
(b) This thing has two identical things.

We expect that in all languages sentences of this kind would normally be interpreted as referring to parts. This, of course, requires further testing.

In summary, we hypothesise that the idea of HAVING PARTS can be unambiguously expressed in any language even if there is no special word for PART (different from the word for 'thing'). We are less confident about the possibility of unambiguously expressing the converse idea of 'being a part of', but we suspect that this idea, too, can be expressed, though the way of expressing it may be more complex than that of expressing the idea of HAVING PARTS.

Having argued that the notion of PART or HAVING PARTS can probably be expressed in all languages, it is important to note considerable differences in the cultural salience of this concept in different societies, and in the culturally acceptable discourse on parts.

The fact that, for example, Acehnese speakers are uncomfortable with sentences such as 'What is this a part of?' is hardly surprising. (In fact, if I were asked to translate this sentence literally into Polish, I would also feel uncomfortable with the Polish equivalent.) Similarly, it is not surprising that a sentence such as 'A bicycle has many parts' may seem bizarre to those from a technologically simple traditional society; and not only because bicycles may not be a daily occurrence in that society, but also because in a culture with a fairly stable range of common 'cultural kinds', recognisable parts of recognisable artifacts have their own names, and are unlikely to be spoken of abstractly as simply 'parts'. I suspect that growth of technological inventions facilitates an expansion of talk about parts — a point which can be illustrated with the remarkable career that the expression *spare parts* has made in recent times in the English-speaking world. It is only in a technological society where mass production of complex machines and devices, with many different parts, plays an important role that a need may develop for a trade in 'spare parts'; in traditional societies there is hardly any need for any talk about 'spare parts', and, presumably, there is much less room for any talk about 'parts' at all. Thus, here as elsewhere, the availability of cognitive and lexical resources must be distinguished from their utilisation.

As a final illustration of this point (with reference to PART) let us consider the situation in Mandarin. Chappell writes in the concluding section of her paper (pp. 143–144):

... it was shown that some primitives may be syntacticised in Mandarin rather than lexified. This was the situation for meronymy, for example, where inherent part–whole relations and simple possession are expressed by means of two different syntactic constructions rather than at word level. No lexemes for 'part' or 'belong' could be identified that were able to express the same unrestricted range of meaning.

At the same time, however, in the section on PART (p. 139) Chappell does identify a word which, as far as we can see (on her evidence), means no more and no less than PART. The word in question is *yī-bùfēn*. Chappell provides the following example (her example (98)):

Shùzhī   shì   shù   de   yī-bùfēn
branch   be   tree   DE   one-part
'Branches are parts of trees.'

Nonetheless, Chappell suggests that *yī-bùfēn* should be excluded from consideration as the Mandarin exponent of the (putative) universal concept PART because it cannot be applied to people. For example, one would normally say in Mandarin that someone is a member (*yī-yuán*) rather than a part (*yī-bùfēn*) of a certain family.

But this is probably true of most languages. Certainly in Polish one would normally say that a person was a *członek* ('member') rather than a *część* ('part') of a family, a group or an organisation. In fact, even in English a sentence such as *She is a part of the Jones family* sounds a bit strange and requires a special context or a special communicative intention to justify it.

But even if we establish that in some languages (for example, in English) the word for KIND can be more readily applied to people than in others (for example, in Mandarin), this does not mean that there is an identifiable semantic difference between the words in question (for example between the English word *part* and the Mandarin word *yī-bùfēn*). Once again, it is a matter of the utilisation of lexical resources rather than of their availability.

17.7.2 KIND

A number of chapters in the present volume make the point that one does not need a word for KIND to say 'X is a kind of Y' (e.g. 'Oak is a kind of tree') and that in this or that language one would simply say, instead, that 'X is a Y' (e.g. 'Oak is a tree'). But one does need a word for KIND to say that, for example, there are three kinds of bat, or that this fish is a fish of the same kind as that fish (though it is not the same fish).

Most of the languages examined in the present volume (Kalam, Samoan, Longgu, Mangap-Mbula, Yankunytjatjara, Thai, Japanese, Arrernte, Kayardild, French, Ewe and Mandarin) present no problems in this regard.

In Kayardild (pp. 223–224), the situation is somewhat less clear than in most of the other languages considered, but this is due to an abundance of possible exponents of KIND rather than to their shortage. However, the word *wuranda* is clearly the exponent of KIND in the collocations *niida wurand* 'same kind' and *jangkaa wurand* 'another kind'. Furthermore, Evans reports that in some contexts the word *minyi* (usually translated as 'colour') can serve as an equivalent of KIND. He also mentions that to speak of 'kinds of' (in the plural), one uses a reduplication of a derived ('proprietive') form of the word *minyi*: *minyiwuru minyiwuru*, literally 'kind-having kind-having'.

In Misumalpan languages the concept KIND is expressed by means of a borrowing from English (*sat*, from *sort*), which, Hale says (p. 281), is fully integrated into the Miskitu and Panamahka lexicons. In addition, it appears that original Misumalpan terms meaning 'person', 'thing' or 'animal' can also be used in some contexts as exponents of the notion KIND. Exactly how these terms are used, or what the relationship between them and the English borrowing *sat* is, is not quite clear, but in any case the concept KIND is clearly present in these languages as well.

The only case regarded as somewhat problematic is that of Acehnese, but in our view the data discussed in Durie, Daud and Hasan's paper (pp. 197–199) show that in this language, too, KIND does have an exponent, even though this exponent is homonymous with the word for WHAT (*peue*). Even though the Acehnese sentence which means 'There are many kinds (*peue*) of bat' is the same, word-for-word, as one which would translate as 'There are many whats (*peue*) of bat', it seems quite clear that in this context *peue* cannot possibly mean WHAT but must mean KIND. Similarly, if to say that A and B are the same kind of bird (fish, animal, tree) one uses again the same word *peue*, which in other contexts can mean WHAT, it seems clear that in this particular context *peue* means KIND, not WHAT.

Since *peue* KIND has a different range of grammatical frames from *peue* WHAT, there is no difficulty in recognising polysemy here. Durie, Daud and Hasan say that "*lè peue* 'many kinds' may in fact mean 'many somethings', where 'something' is understood to have an adnominal modifying function" (p. 199). But since to give the expression 'many whats' some sense we have to interpret it as either 'many kinds (e.g. of fish)' or 'many things' (i.e. many items), and since the authors make it clear that of these two interpretations only the first one is valid, *peue* can only mean KIND here (in *lè peue*).

What is potentially confusing in the Acehnese data is that a sentence like 'What kind of fish is it?' would be translated into Acehnese as 'What fish (is it)?' (*peue eungkôt*). Arguably, in this context *peue* does not mean KIND, but WHAT, with the notion of KIND being implicit rather than explicit. But in other contexts, such as *lè peue* ('many kinds'), *peue* expresses KIND, not WHAT.

The indispensability of a word for KIND (whether polysemous or not) can be illustrated with the following scenario. You have caught a fish, you have thrown it back into the water, and then you have caught a fish again. Your companion says "It is the same fish", but you want to reply "It is not the same fish, but it is the same kind of fish". To convey this thought in a particular language one needs a word for KIND (because one cannot build this meaning out of any other meanings). The question is whether one can convey this thought in any language, or whether there are some languages which make it impossible for their speakers to express it (because they don't have a word for KIND).

The data surveyed in the present volume suggest that — as one would have expected — one can indeed convey this thought in any language, because all the languages examined here do have a word for KIND. This word may be homonymous with the word for WHAT (as in Acehnese), with the word for 'colour' (as in Kayardild) or with the word for 'name' (as in Yankunytjatjara), but a sentence such as 'It is not the same fish, but it is the same what of fish' can only make sense if the word glossed here as 'what' is in fact polysemous and can also mean KIND.

In addition to the KIND/WHAT polysemy it is also worth noting that in a number of languages the exponents of KIND have formal links with those of OTHER. As Harkins and Wilkins say discussing Arrernte data, "the notion of 'different kinds' is closely linked with the concept ... OTHER" (p. 302); and indeed in Arrernte the word *arrpenhe-ante-arrpenhe* 'different kinds' (literally, 'other-only-other') is formed by reduplication of OTHER and the insertion of a particle (*ante*).

But although the concepts KIND and OTHER are indeed closely linked (an oak can only be called a kind of tree because there are other kinds of tree), this link is not compositional: one cannot define KIND in terms of OTHER (or the other way around). The formal connection between one of the exponents of KIND and OTHER in Arrernte (and in a number of other Australian Aboriginal languages) highlights the fact that formal links (including polysemy, that is, formal identity) may reflect semantic affinities of a non-compositional nature.

What applies to the relationship between KIND and OTHER applies even more to that between KIND and LIKE. Human categorisation is based on the concept of KIND, and the fact that all languages appear to have a word for KIND, different from the word for LIKE, points to the importance of taxonomies in the human conceptualisation of reality. Taxonomies do not have to be based on resemblance, and the fact that all languages appear to distinguish lexically between the concepts KIND and LIKE highlights the mutual independence of these concepts. At the same time, taxonomies are indeed often associated with resemblance (for example, while dogs do not necessarily resemble one another, cats, horses, elephants or mice do); and in many languages the distinction between KIND and LIKE may at times be blurred. Even in English, the word *kind* can be used not only as a categoriser, as in 'An oak is a kind of tree', but also as a hedge, as in 'Her eyes are kind of blue' (although there is a formal difference between *a kind of* and *kind of*). But it is important to recognise that all languages which have been studied from this point of view do have a distinct exponent for the categorising KIND (distinct from the exponents of resemblance).

17.8 Evaluators and Descriptors

17.8.1 BIG and SMALL (and VERY)

BIG, SMALL and VERY have turned out to be surprisingly unproblematic: in every single language under consideration, the exponents of all these three concepts can be identified without any difficulty. In some languages (for example in Polish, not represented in this volume), BIG shares an exponent (or one of its exponents) with the primitive MUCH/MANY,[9] in others (for example in Arrernte) with the primitive VERY, and in others (for example in Samoan or Thai), VERY shares an exponent with MUCH, but the grammatical contexts are always different.

The polysemies involving BIG, MUCH and VERY are clearly not accidental, as the three meanings in question are intuitively related; but their relationships are not compositional. In particular, attempts to define VERY as 'in a big (large) degree', MUCH as a 'big (large) quantity' and MANY as a 'big/large number' fail, because they leave us with undefined terms such as 'degree', 'quantity' and 'number'.

In some languages, the primitive VERY has two exponents which are, by and large, in complementary distribution. For example, in English in combination with adjectives and adverbs it is realised as *very*, whereas in combination with verbs it is realised as *very much* (e.g. *I love you very much*). Similarly, French *très* corresponds to the English word *very*, and *beaucoup* to the phrase *very much*. In Samoan VERY is realised as either *matuâ* or *tele*; *matuâ* precedes the verb it modifies, whereas *tele* follows the modified word (p. 348). On the other hand, we do not consider words such as *real*, *proper*, *true* or *dinkum*, which modify nouns, as alternative exponents of the same primitive VERY (cf. Evans' discussion of this point, p. 221). Words of this kind, which can usually combine with adjectives and/or verbs as well as with nouns, do not mean exactly the same as VERY. (For example, *She is very intelligent* does not mean the same as *She is really intelligent*, and in fact *really* can combine with a much wider range of adjectives than *very*; compare *It is really black* with *?It is very black*.)

It should be noted, however, that in some languages the word for VERY can occur in contexts where the English word *very* seems to be excluded for semantic reasons. For example, in Mangap-Mbula (p. 95) the word *kat*, which is the primary exponent of VERY, can also be used in combination with the word *raraate* THE SAME ('exactly the same', *very the same*).[10] It is possible, however, that on further investigation words such as *kat* will prove to be polysemous.

It is interesting to speculate why the three meanings BIG, MUCH/MANY and VERY tend to share some of their exponents, if they are not compositionally related. Evidently, there are some inherent links between size, quantity and intensity. For example, if there is MUCH (more idiomatically, a lot of) sand in a heap of sand then this heap will be BIG (and if there is LITTLE sand, the heap will be SMALL); or if there is MUCH (a lot of) sugar in the tea this tea will be VERY sweet. It is also very striking how easily exponents of MUCH/MANY and of VERY can be paraphrased in terms of exponents of BIG ('much' = 'big quantity', and so on). It is therefore very tempting to try to reduce the three concepts in question to one, and to define, for example, MUCH and VERY in terms of BIG; but so far all attempts to do so have failed, and the fact that in all the languages investigated all three concepts can be very easily identified supports the hypothesis that they are indeed linguistic and conceptual universals.

One might ask why both BIG and SMALL are being posited as universal primitives, whereas 'few' or 'a little' are not posited next to MUCH/MANY, given that the relationship between BIG and SMALL on the one hand and MUCH/MANY and 'little/few' on the other seems to be very similar, and since both pairs have often been called 'antonyms' (just as the pairs 'bigger/smaller' and 'more/less' have both been called 'converses').

We acknowledge that the two cases may indeed be parallel, and that if SMALL cannot be defined in terms of BIG ('small' ≠ 'not big'), neither can 'few/little' be satisfactorily defined in terms of MUCH/MANY ('few' ≠ 'not many', 'little' ≠ 'not much'). The lack of equivalence between SMALL and 'not big' or between 'little' and 'not much' is particularly noticeable when one considers the fact that neither 'not big' nor 'not much/not many' can combine with VERY in the way SMALL or 'few/little' can: 'very small' versus *'very not big', 'very few' versus *'very not many'. For example, if one wanted to say that 'Very little water was left' one could not convey this idea using 'not much'. Unfortunately, we have not asked the contributors to the present volume to look for exponents of the concepts 'little/few' in the languages under investigation.

On the other hand, while it is possible that 'few/little' may turn out to be a universal semantic primitive, alongside MUCH/MANY, BIG and SMALL, it seems clear that VERY does not have a common antonymic counterpart indicating a 'small degree' (although many languages do seem to have a word meaning 'not very').

17.8.2 GOOD and BAD

Words for GOOD and BAD are apparently quite easy to find in all the languages investigated. In Ewe (p. 81), the adjective meaning GOOD (*nyuí/nyoé*) is derived from the verb *nyó* 'be good', but the difference between these two words appears to be purely syntactic, not semantic. GOOD and BAD as semantic primitives can function predicatively in all languages (e.g. 'do/say something good/bad', 'be good/bad'), and whether a language uses for this purpose an adjective combined with a copula ('X is good') or a verb equivalent to 'be good', is irrelevant from a semantic point of view. This is not to deny that part of speech membership is, generally speaking, semantically relevant (as I have argued in Wierzbicka 1988), but only to note that it loses its relevance at the level of semantic primitives.[11]

The range of use of the words for GOOD and BAD is not always the same as that of the English words *good* and *bad*, but these differences appear to be idiosyncratic and do not suggest any differences in meaning. For example, Durie, Daud and Hasan report that the Acehnese word *göt* GOOD can also be used for 'beautiful, scenic, handsome' (p. 199). Nonetheless, one can contrast 'goodness' and 'beauty' in Acehnese, saying, for example, of a woman 'She is good but she is not beautiful' or 'She is beautiful but she is not good' (Durie, personal communication).

Idiosyncratic extensions of this kind (as well as idiosyncratic restrictions) are quite common in the area of GOOD and BAD. For example, in French, one speaks of 'bad weather' (*mauvais temps*), but not of 'good weather' (**bon temps*). Similarly, in Russian the words *xorošij* GOOD and *durnoj* BAD can in certain contexts refer to beauty and ugliness. Idiosyncratic uses of this kind are interesting to note and to compare across languages, but they do not present any real problems as far as the identification of the primitives GOOD and BAD is concerned.

BAD is a little more problematic than GOOD in so far as it is not always clear how BAD is related to 'not good'. For example, in Thai (p. 165), the word for GOOD is *di:*, and the word for BAD appears to be *mây di:*, literally 'not good'. But is the expression *mây di:* an exact semantic equivalent of BAD? Or is it somewhat 'weaker' in its negative evaluation than BAD?

In some languages which have both a morphologically simple word for BAD and a word or expression corresponding to 'not good', the BAD word appears to be 'stronger' than the 'not good' one. For example Durie, Daud and Hasan (p. 199) say that in Acehnese the word for BAD is *brôk*, but in an earlier version of their paper they noted that it is more common to use *hana göt* 'not good' for BAD, and they commented that this is perhaps because *brôk* has a "rather stronger negative sense than English *bad*". But if so, then does the Thai word *mây di:* 'not good' correspond in meaning to the Acehnese *hana göt* 'not good' or to the Acehnese *brôk* BAD? And which of the Acehnese words, *brôk* or *hana göt*, is the real semantic equivalent of the English word *bad*?

Since in nearly all the languages under investigation the identification of both GOOD and BAD is extremely straightforward, we tentatively conclude that either the Thai expression *mây di:*, literally 'not good', means BAD, or that one of the other words listed by Diller (p. 165) as quasi-equivalents of BAD is in fact a semantic equivalent of BAD, even though for cultural reasons Thai speakers use 'not good' more readily than BAD.

In Acehnese, too, if *brôk* BAD appears to have "a rather stronger negative sense" than the English *bad*, the reasons for this may be cultural rather than semantic: in many situations in which speakers of English use the word *bad* it may be more culturally appropriate for speakers of Acehnese to say 'not good'. (Durie, Daud and Hasan's unqualified identification of *brôk* as BAD in the final version of their paper suggests that they themselves have reached this conclusion.)

Similarly, although Chappell says that in Mandarin *bù hǎo* 'not good' may be a better exponent of BAD than *huài* (BAD) since *huài* "is more semantically specialised at its end of the scale to mean 'immoral', 'nasty' or 'evil' than *hǎo* is on the 'saintly' end of the scale" (p. 142), we tentatively conclude that the reasons for the asymmetry in use may be cultural rather than purely semantic.

We are suggesting, then, that in languages which have a word for BAD unrelated to the word for GOOD, the expression meaning 'not good' may function as a culturally appropriate euphemism for BAD, whereas in languages where the only word for BAD combines negation with the word for GOOD, the combination 'not good' may in fact mean BAD.

All the facts discussed in the present volume are compatible with such a hypothesis, but the evidence is not conclusive and further research in this area is undoubtedly needed.

17.9 Conclusion

As the foregoing survey shows, the studies included in the present volume on the whole support the hypothesised set of thirty-seven universal semantic primitives. Perhaps the most controversial case has proved to be that of PART, which requires a good deal of further research. Remarkably, in a number of languages various primitives have been supported against the initial scepticism of the researchers themselves. Again and again, an initial report along the lines of "There is no word or morpheme for the primitive X in my language" was followed after months of further investigation (and sometimes after additional field-trips) with a "Eureka!" report. The primitives repeatedly vindicated in this way include, in particular, SOMEONE, THE SAME, ALL, WANT, THINK, FEEL, BECAUSE, IF, CAN, AFTER and KIND.

Identifying a set of primitives in fourteen or so different languages is not the same thing as constructing fourteen full-blown versions of the Natural Semantic Metalanguage. To achieve the latter goal, much more work remains to be done; in particular, the combinability of the primitives in different languages needs to be further investigated.

The use of canonical sentences (built entirely, or largely, out of the primitive concepts), which has been introduced in the present volume, has proved fruitful beyond all our expectations; and we would suggest that this method can be adopted as a primary tool in the construction and validation of a whole series of Natural Semantic Metalanguages. But the foundation for such an enterprise has been laid; and the aim of tentatively identifying a set of universal semantic primitives and of validating them through cross-linguistic correspondences has, in our estimation, been achieved.

Notes

1 It is worth recalling in this connection Zawadowski's comment: "The most prominent feature of prestructural semantics (and its present day epigenes) is its exuberant polysemism: the opinion that every sign has many meanings" (1975:128). It is essential to reject what Zawadowski called "parasitic polysemism" (1975:117–118). But it is equally essential to recognise what Zawadowski called "real polysemy".

2 The fact that, according to Ameka, this word cannot be used to translate the sentence "People say that God knows everything" is puzzling and requires an explanation.

3 Glosses such as 'eye know' or 'ear know' are of course mine, not Pawley's, as Pawley glosses the segment *nŋ-* as 'perceive'.

4 Pawley suggests that *nŋ-* by itself may denote 'rational thought' (p. 395), but the example he offers in support of this suggestion, example (25), lends itself to an interpretation in terms of KNOW as much as in terms of THINK.

5 We note that the three meanings which we assign to single stem *g-* correspond to the three senses assigned by Foley to the single stem *ti-* in another Papuan language, Yimas. Foley glosses these three senses as 'do, feel, become' (1991:334).

6 In earlier work (cf. Wierzbicka 1972 and 1989b), I in fact suggested that 'I want' may be semantically simpler than WANT. I have now rejected this idea mainly because all the attempts to analyse sentences such as third-person sentences ('He wants ...') in terms of first-person ones ('I want ...') have failed. But it is undoubtedly the case that many languages have special exponents (e.g. particles) for 'I want', and that in many cultures it is much easier, and much more common, to talk about one's own wants than about those of other people.

7 It should also be said that the semantic relationship between the two words *much* and *many* requires further investigation. Is it justified to treat the two as exponents of the same primitive, conditioned by the environment in which they occur? Generally speaking, the two words do appear to be in complementary distribution (e.g. *How many/*much boys?*, *How much/*many*

butter?), but is this always the case? Even assuming that many apparent exceptions such as *How many coffees?* versus *How much coffee?* can be accounted for in terms of ellipsis (*How many portions of coffee?*), the matter certainly deserves further exploration.

8   Unfortunately, it is possible that future research on Kayardild may not reveal very much, given the fact that the language is dying out and the number of reliable informants is dwindling.

9   Compare also in English *little* (adjective) *boy* and *little* (adverb) *butter*, though not *big boy* and *big butter or *small boy* and *small butter.

10 One can of course say *the very same*, but this is clearly different from the combination of the meanings of VERY and THE SAME; and in most languages other than English and Mangap-Mbula the word for VERY does not combine with the word for THE SAME.

11 For example, the Latin sentence *Rosa rubet*, roughly 'The rose is red', does not mean exactly the same as the English sentence offered here as its gloss because the verb *rubet* has its own semantics, more processual than that of the adjective *red* (cf. Bally 1920), and differences of this kind can be identified in a semantic paraphrase. But if conceptual primitives such as GOOD, WANT or KNOW are realised in different languages by means of different parts of speech (an adjective or a verb) then any residual quasi-semantic differences between them have to be interpreted as a matter of 'resonance' rather than meaning (since they cannot be identified in a semantic paraphrase).

References

Apresjan, Jurij D. 1992. *Lexical Semantics: User's guide to contemporary Russian vocabulary*. Ann Arbor: Karoma. (English translation of: Jurij D. Apresjan. 1974. *Leksičeskaja Semantika — Sinonimečeskie sredstva jazyka*. Moscow: Nauka.)

Bain, Margaret. 1992. *The Aboriginal-White Encounter in Australia: Towards better communication* (SIL-AAB Occasional Papers 2). Darwin: Summer Institute of Linguistics, Australian Aborigines Branch.

Bally, Charles. 1920. "Impressionnisme et grammaire". *Mélanges d'histoire littéraire et de philologie offert à M. Bernard Bouvier*, 261-279. Geneva: Sonor.

Brunner, Jerome S. 1990. *Acts of Meaning*. Cambridge, Mass.: Harvard University Press.

Evans, Nicholas. 1985. *Kayardild: The language of the Bentinck Islanders of North West Queensland*. PhD Thesis, Department of Linguistics, Australian National University, Canberra.

Evans, Nicholas. 1986. "The Unimportance of CAUSE in Kayardild". *Language in Aboriginal Australia* 2:9-17.

Evans, Nicholas. 1992. *Kayardild Dictionary and Thesaurus*. Melbourne: Department of Linguistics and Language Studies, University of Melbourne.

Foley, William A. 1986. *The Papuan Languages of New Guinea*. Cambridge: Cambridge University Press.

Foley, William A. 1991. *The Yimas Language of New Guinea*. Stanford: Stanford University Press.

Goddard, Cliff. 1991. "Testing the Translatability of Semantic Primitives into an Australian Aboriginal Language". *Anthropological Linguistics* 33.1.31-56.

Goddard, Cliff. In press. "Who Are 'We'? The natural semantics of pronouns". *Language Sciences*.

Green, Ian. 1992. "ALL in Marrithiyel". Manuscript, Department of Linguistics, Australian National University.

Hall, Edward T. 1983. *The Dance of Life: The other dimension of time.* New York: Anchor Books.

Hallpike, Christopher R. 1979. *The Foundations of Primitive Thought.* Oxford: Clarendon Press.

Harkins, Jean. Forthcoming. *Desire in Language and Thought: A study in crosscultural semantics.* PhD Thesis, Department of Linguistics, Australian National University, Canberra.

Leibniz, Gottfried Wilhelm. 1903 [MS]. "Sur la caractéristique" (*Philosophie*, VII, C, 160-161). *Opuscules et fragments inédits de Leibniz* ed. by Louis Couterat, 435. Paris: Presses Universitaires de France. (Reprinted 1961, Hildesheim: Georg Olms.)

LePan, Don. 1989. *The Cognitive Revolution in Western Culture,* vol 1: *The birth of expectation.* London: Macmillan.

McConvell, Patrick. 1991. "Cultural Domain Separation: Two-way street or blind alley? Stephen Harris and the neo-Whorfians on Aboriginal Education". *Australian Aboriginal Studies* 1:13-24.

Mel'čuk, Igor. 1984. "Un nouveau type de dictionnaire: Le dictionnaire explicatif et combinatoire du français contemporain". *Dictionnaire explicatif et combinatoire du français contemporain: Recherches lexico-sémantique I* ed. by Igor Mel'čuk et al., 3-16. Montreal: Les Presses de l'Université de Montréal.

Mosel, Ulrike & Even Hovdhaugen. 1992. *Samoan Reference Grammar.* Oslo: Scandinavian University Press.

Pascal, Blaise. 1954 [1658]. "De l'esprit géométrique et de l'art de persuader". *Œuvres complétes de Pascal* ed. by Jacques Chevalier, 575-604. Paris: Gallimard.

Vercors [Jean Bruller]. 1956. *Les animaux dénaturés, suivi de La marche à l'étoile.* Paris: A. Michel.

Wierzbicka, Anna. 1972. *Semantic Primitives.* Frankfurt: Athenäum.

Wierzbicka, Anna. 1980a. *Lingua Mentalis: The semantics of natural language.* Sydney: Academic.

Wierzbicka, Anna. 1980b. *The Case for Surface Case.* Ann Arbor: Karoma.

Wierzbicka, Anna. 1983. "The Semantics of Case Marking". *Studies in Language* 7.2.247-275.

Wierzbicka, Anna. 1988. *The Semantics of Grammar.* Amsterdam: John Benjamins.

Wierzbicka, Anna. 1989a. "Semantic Primitives and Lexical Universals". *Quaderni di Semantica* 10.1.103-121.

Wierzbicka, Anna. 1989b. "Semantic Primitives — The Expanding Set". *Quaderni di Semantica* 10.2.309-332.

Wierzbicka, Anna. 1991a. *Cross-Cultural Pragmatics: The semantics of human interaction.* Berlin: Mouton de Gruyter.

Wierzbicka, Anna. 1991b. "Lexical Universals and Universals of Grammar". *Meaning and Grammar: Cross-linguistic perspectives* ed. by Michel Kefer & Johan van der Auwera, 383-415. Berlin: Mouton de Gruyter.

Wierzbicka, Anna. In press. "Semantic Universals and 'Primitive Thought': The question of the 'psychic unity of [hu]mankind'". *Journal of Linguistic Anthropology.*

Zawadowski, Leo. 1975. *Inductive Semantics and Syntax: Foundations of empirical linguistics.* The Hague: Mouton.

Notes on Contributors

Felix K. Ameka is a lecturer in African linguistics at Leiden University. He studied at the University of Ghana, Legon, where he obtained a BA (Hons), and at the Australian National University, Canberra, where he obtained his MA and PhD. His main research interests include linguistic typology, semantics, pragmatics, contact linguistics, cross-cultural communication, anthropological linguistics and (West) African linguistics. He has published a number of articles in these areas with special reference to Ewe, his mother tongue. He was the Guest Editor for the special issue on interjections of the *Journal of Pragmatics* (vol 18(2/3), 1992). He is the Assistant Editor of the *Journal of African Languages and Linguistics*.

Robert D. Bugenhagen is a member of the Summer Institute of Linguistics who has been working with the Mangap-Mbula people of Papua New Guinea since 1982, facilitating vernacular literacy, doing linguistic analysis and translating the Bible. He received his PhD in Linguistics from the Australian National University in 1992.

Hilary Chappell completed her PhD on Chinese Linguistics at the Australian National University in 1983; this included one year's fieldwork at Bei Da (Peking University). From 1984 to 1986, she continued her research on Mandarin at the University of Cologne with the Language Universals and Typology project as an Alexander von Humboldt Fellow. Since 1987, she has taught in the Linguistics Department at La Trobe University, Melbourne, where she is now a Senior Lecturer. Her current research work is a four-year project investigating the extent of grammatical and morphological variation in Sinitic languages.

Bukhari Daud and **Mawardi Hasan** are both graduates in English from Universitas Syiah Kuala in Banda Aceh, Indonesia. Both are currently pursuing Masters programs in the USA: Bukhari Daud at the State University of New York at Buffalo, and Marwardi Hasan at Oregon State University, Corvallis.

Anthony Diller is presently Director of the National Thai Studies Centre, located in the Faculty of Asian Studies, Australian National University, Canberra. His research interests focus on Thai syntax, semantics and sociolinguistics and on comparative–historical studies of the larger language family of which Central Thai is a member.

Mark Durie studied linguistics at the Australian National University from 1976–1983. Then he spent a year in the Netherlands researching the Dutch manuscript tradition on Acehnese, and two years in the USA on a Harkness Fellowship. Since 1987 he has been a member of the Linguistics program at the University of Melbourne, where he is now a Senior Research Fellow.

Nicholas Evans teaches in the Department of Linguistics at the University of Melbourne, which he joined in 1988; from 1985 to 1987 he taught at the School of Australian Linguistics in Batchelor, Northern Territory. His main areas of research are grammatical and semantic typology, polysemy, the interaction of pragmatic and grammatical systems, and Australian Aboriginal languages. He obtained his doctoral thesis from the Australian National University in 1986 with a description of the Australian language Kayardild, currently being revised for the Mouton Grammar Library; he has also carried out extensive research on several languages of Western Arnhem Land, and is preparing a comprehensive pan-dialectal grammar of Mayali. He has published articles on many aspects of Australian languages, including multiple case-marking, semantic change, phonology, noun incorporation, quantification and ellipsis.

Cliff Goddard is presently a lecturer in linguistics at the University of New England, Armidale. He has worked extensively on the Western Desert Language of Central Australia, having published a dictionary and a semantically oriented grammar of the Yankunytjatjara dialect. He has authored articles on NSM semantic theory and on descriptive and theoretical topics in cross-cultural semantics and pragmatics, in journals such as *Anthropological Linguistics, Man, Journal of Pragmatics, Quaderni di Semantica* and *Australian Journal of Linguistics*. He is currently researching semantic topics in Malay (Bahasa Melayu).

Kenneth Hale received his BA in Anthropology from the University of Arizona in 1955; from Indiana University he received an MA in Linguistics in 1958, and a PhD in Linguistics in 1959. He is presently Ferrari P. Ward Professor of Modern Languages and Linguistics at the Massachusetts Institute of Technology. His current research interests include languages occupying different positions in the typology of the languages of the world, including languages from North America and Aboriginal Australia; research on the Lexicon, involving the Central Australian language Warlpiri, the Misumalpan languages of Eastern Nicaragua, and English; and research on the educational potential of theoretical linguistics as a medium for the teaching of the methods and attitudes of scientific inquiry.

Jean Harkins is completing her doctoral thesis, a semantic–typological study of desiderative constructions across languages and cultures, at the Australian National University, Canberra. She has worked as a teacher and linguist in Central Australia and has published several papers on cross-cultural semantics and pragmatics. Her book on Australian Aboriginal English is to be published by the University of Queensland Press in 1994.

Mawardi Hasan: see Bukhari Daud.

Deborah Hill trained in linguistics at the Australian National University, Canberra, and carried out fieldwork on Longgu (Solomon Islands) for her PhD thesis (*Longgu grammar*). She is currently working with the Cognitive Anthropology Research Group at the Max Planck Institute for Psycholinguistics, Nijmegen, The Netherlands, and is continuing fieldwork on Longgu (with special emphasis on collecting data on spatial terminology). Her interests are primarily in the areas of semantics and Oceanic linguistics.

Ulrike Mosel (Dr. phil., Dr. habil., University of Munich) studied Semitic languages and later specialised in Austronesian languages, linguistic typology, grammatical description and sociolinguistics. Her books include *Tolai and Tok Pisin* (1980), *Tolai syntax* (1984) and *Samoan reference grammar* (1992, together with Even Hovdhaugen). She is a senior lecturer in the Department of Linguistics at the Australian National University, and is currently working on the expression of time in Samoan.

Masayuki Onishi was born and brought up in Japan. He obtained a BA in modern British literature at the University of Tokyo, and then spent several years in India, teaching Japanese and studying Bengali language, literature and music, as well as carrying out fieldwork on the folk culture of Bengal in both India and Bangladesh. He is experienced in teaching language in the Silent Way. At present he is at the Department of Linguistics, Australian National University, Canberra, writing his PhD thesis on the grammar of Motuna, a non-Austronesian language spoken in southern Bougainville, Papua New Guinea.

Andrew Pawley is Professor and Head of the Department of Linguistics at the Research School of Pacific Studies at the Australian National University. He received his PhD from the University of Auckland, New Zealand, and is a Fellow of the Royal Society of New Zealand and the Australian Academy of the Humanities. He is particularly interested in languages of the Pacific, including both Austronesian and Papuan, as well as in Australian English and the language of cricket. Professor Pawley has published widely in descriptive and comparative linguistics and lexicography. He is particularly well known for his accounts of aspects of Kalam, a Papuan language of the Madang Province of Papua New Guinea. He was recently elected President of the Australian Linguistics Society.

Before becoming a lecturer in French at the University of Tasmania, Hobart, **Bert Peeters** (born in Belgium in 1960) spent two years at the Australian National

University, where he obtained his PhD in 1989. Over the last dozen years or so, he has published numerous books, papers and reviews, and he is currently working on a new framework for semantic research in French called conceptual axiology.

Anna Wierzbicka was educated at Warsaw University where she obtained her MA in 1958. She received her PhD (in 1964) and her 'Habilitation' (in 1968) from the Polish Academy of Sciences. In 1973 she joined the staff of the Department of Linguistics at the Australian National University in Canberra, where she now holds a personal chair. In addition to several books in Polish (on semantics, stylistics, syntax and general linguistics) she has published in English: *Semantic primitives* (Athenäum, 1972); *Lingua mentalis* (Academic Press, 1980); *The case for surface case* (Karoma, 1980); *Lexicography and conceptual analysis* (Karoma, 1985); *English speech act verbs* (Academic Press, 1987); *The semantics of grammar* (John Benjamins, 1988); *Cross-cultural pragmatics* (Mouton de Gruyter, 1991); and *Semantics, culture and cognition* (Oxford University Press, 1992).

David Wilkins is an assistant professor in the Department of Linguistics at the State University of New York at Buffalo, and is also a member of the Center for Cognitive Science at Buffalo. He received his PhD from the Australian National University, Canberra, in 1990; his dissertation was entitled *Mparntwe Arrernte: Studies in the structure and semantics of grammar*. Wilkins' major research interests are ethno-semantics, lexical semantics, ethno-pragmatics, semantic change, aphasiology and Australian Aboriginal languages. He has done extensive fieldwork on Mparntwe Arrernte (Alice Springs Aranda, Central Australia), and has published several papers on morphological, syntactic, semantic and pragmatic aspects of this language.

Index

ablative 35, 247
ABOVE 22, 46, 79-80, 101, 138, 163, 166, 193, 222, 253, 279-80, 301, 325, 354, 416-7, 437, 488
Acehnese 171-201, 448-9, 455, 458, 471, 472, 474, 476, 479, 486-7, 488, 496-7
action *see* DO
actions and events 42-3, 71-2, 95-6, 127-9, 159-60, 182-7, 215-6, 243-6, 272-3, 294-6, 321-2, 342-3, 373-4, 407-8, 431-2, 473-6
adversative 127-9, 159-60, 474-5
AFTER 22, 46, 78-9, 83, 84, 101, 137-8, 163, 166, 191-2, 221-2, 252-3, 278, 301, 325, 331, 351-4, 358, 378-9, 416, 436-7, 479, 485, 498
agency 42
agent 236
ALL 22, 41, 70-1, 93-4, 125-6, 157-8, 182, 214-5, 241, 272, 293-4, 320-1, 328, 341-2, 373, 407, 431, 472-3, 498
allolexy 12, 13, 23, 33-4, 83-4, 446, 447
allomorphy 33-34
alphabet of human thoughts 1, 3, 20, 445
Arabic 174, 190
Aranda *see* Arrernte
Arrernte 21, 61, 71, 232, 235, 285-310, 447, 451, 458, 466, 469, 470, 471, 474, 477, 479, 480, 482, 487, 488, 489-91, 492-3, 493-4
aversive 299
BAD 22, 45, 47, 82, 83, 103-4, 142-3, 165, 199, 224, 240, 245, 258, 282, 303, 317, 327-8, 355-6, 381, 419, 429, 438-9, 464-5, 496-7
BECAUSE 22, 35, 36, 44-5, 74, 83, 84, 98-100, 133-4, 161-2, 166, 189-90, 219-21, 247, 276, 298-9, 301, 324, 345-6, 377, 411-3, 434, 478-9, 498
BECOME 21
BEFORE 22, 46, 79, 101, 137-8, 166, 191-2, 221-2, 278-9, 325, 331, 351-4, 358, 379, 416, 436-7, 485-7
BELOW *see* UNDER
BIG 22, 47-8, 82-3, 143, 165, 166, 224, 258, 303-4, 327-8, 356, 357, 381, 419, 439, 473, 494-6
body-part words 84, 105, 240, 461-2, 487
CAN (COULD, MAYBE) 22, 36, 44, 73, 97, 132, 161, 188-9, 217-9, 225, 248, 274-5, 291, 296-8, 324, 347-8, 375-6, 413-4, 433-4, 446, 460, 480, 481-3, 498
canonical sentences 23, 59, 83, 328, 358, 471, 498
case allolexy 235-6, 286-7, 447
categorisation 46, 478; *see also* KIND OF
causality 23
causation *see* BECAUSE
causative *see* BECAUSE
cause *see* BECAUSE

classifier *see* KIND OF, PART OF
classifiers 121, 124, 125, 155-6, 157, 158, 166-7, 172
cognition 21
colours 44
combinatorial properties 13, 32, 225
complementation 39
componential analysis 8
conditional 375; *see also* IF
COULD *see* CAN
counterfactual 97, 344, 413; *see also* IF
cultural factors 35, 457
cultural kinds 46
cultural psychology 2
cultural scripts 38
decomposition 8
definitions 448
deixis 40
desiderative 209-10
determiners and quantifiers 39-42, 68-71, 93-5, 121-7, 155-9, 181-2, 212-15, 241-3, 270-2, 291-4, 318-21, 338-42, 371-3, 401-7, 429-31, 468-73
DO 22, 32, 34, 42-3, 44, 71, 72, 84, 90, 95, 127, 159, 166, 182-5, 215-6, 225, 230, 235, 236, 244-6, 259, 272, 295-6, 321, 335-6, 342-3, 357, 373-4, 408, 431-2, 446, 447, 462-3, 467, 473-6, 477
DON'T WANT 21; *see also* NO
dual 40
Dutch 76
emotions 39, 44; *see also* FEEL
English 21, 31-32, 33, 34, 35, 38, 40-1, 42, 45, 46, 47, 131, 164, 211, 221, 230, 233, 234, 251, 424, 427, 430, 435, 439, 446, 447-8, 452, 457, 464-5, 472, 473, 474, 477, 478, 485, 492, 494
epistemological classifiers 173-4, 175, 177, 181, 182, 190, 191, 198
evaluators and descriptors 47-8, 81-3, 103-4, 142-3, 165, 199, 224, 258, 281-2, 303-4, 327-8, 355-7, 381, 419, 438-9, 494-7
event *see* HAPPEN
events 43
Ewe 21, 57-86, 453, 459, 474, 489, 488, 492, 496
exhaustive analysis 8
experiencer constructions 39
FEEL 21, 22, 23, 32, 35, 36, 39, 65-7, 83, 91-2, 105, 116, 118-20, 143, 153, 166, 176-7, 212, 239-41, 269, 290, 317-8, 337, 357, 362, 369-70, 382, 392-3, 396-8, 419, 423, 428-9, 452, 456, 461-5, 473, 498
formal complexity 33, 456
French 32, 38, 40, 117, 251, 423-442, 452, 453, 465, 469, 474, 478, 492, 494-5, 496
fuzzy-set theory 8
generativism 15-17
genitive 355
German 116, 117, 122, 175, 205, 452
GOOD 22, 36, 45, 47, 81-2, 83, 103-4, 142-3, 165, 166, 199, 224, 240, 244, 245, 258, 281, 303, 317, 327-8, 355-6, 357, 381, 419, 429, 438-9, 464-5, 496-7
grammatical frames *see* synactic frames
HAPPEN (TO/IN) 22, 42-3, 44, 71-2, 84, 90, 95-6, 127-9, 159-60, 166, 185-7, 216, 230, 233, 236, 243-4, 272-3, 294-6, 321-2, 323, 328, 342-3, 373-4, 407-8, 432, 462-3, 473-6
HAVE PARTS *see* PART OF
hedge 44
homonymy 32, 445; *see also* polysemy
hypotheticality 480; *see also* IF
I 21, 22, 33, 35, 36, 37-8, 41, 59, 83, 88, 110, 150-1, 167-9, 172-3, 206, 230, 266-7, 286-7, 312-3, 332, 339, 362-6, 382, 389-90, 424, 446, 447-9, 454, 470

identity 41; *see also* THE SAME
IF 22, 36, 43-4, 45, 72, 96-7, 104-5, 130-2, 160-1, 166, 188, 217, 225, 248-9, 259, 273-4, 277, 296-8, 323, 328, 344, 375, 409-11, 419, 434, 446, 468, 478, 479-81, 482, 484, 498
ignorative 190, 206, 231
illocutionary forces 39
imagination 43-4; *see also* IF
IMAGINE 21, 44
implication 44; *see also* BECAUSE
inchoative 243, 295
indefinables 448
independence 36
intensification *see* VERY
intensionality 7
inter-translatability 12
interjections 39
interrogative 37, 111
Irish 305
irrealis *see* COULD, IF, WHEN
Italian 461
Japanese 21, 34, 37, 40, 61, 361-385, 448-9, 452-3, 456, 458, 468, 469, 472, 488, 492
Javanese 35
Kalam 387-421, 450, 452, 455-6, 459-60, 462-3, 466-8, 470, 472, 473, 478, 479, 481, 483, 484, 492
Kayardild 13, 61, 98, 203-28, 449-51, 453, 457, 460, 461, 469, 471, 472, 474, 475-6, 477, 479, 480, 482, 486, 488, 490, 492, 493
KIND OF 22, 46, 80, 101-2, 141-2, 164, 166, 197-9, 223-4, 257-8, 259, 281, 302, 326-7, 355, 380-81, 382, 418-9, 423, 438, 478, 492-4, 498
kinship 44
KNOW 21, 22, 23, 31-2, 36, 39, 42, 47, 64, 90-1, 117, 150, 154, 166, 175-6, 208, 235, 236-7, 268, 283, 289-90, 291, 316-7, 328, 335, 368-9, 392-4, 419, 426-7, 447, 454-6
Latin 33, 34
lexicography 10
LIKE 13, 22, 40, 41, 44, 46, 73-4, 98, 121-2, 132-3, 144, 161, 166, 189, 219, 242, 246, 247, 270, 276, 292-3, 298, 319, 323, 331, 356-7, 372, 376-7, 413, 434-5, 456-7, 470, 477-8, 494
Longgu 81, 311-29, 456, 471, 472, 476, 478, 487, 492
Malay 35, 176
Mandarin 13, 21, 109-47, 452, 466, 471, 472, 473, 474-5, 478, 491-2, 492, 497
Mangap-Mbula 32, 39, 87-108, 432, 445, 453, 458-9, 462, 467-8, 469, 472, 474, 478, 480, 492, 495
MANY 22, 70, 124, 126-7, 143, 157-8, 166, 214, 241, 293-4, 356, 373, 407, 431, 473, 494
markerese 11
Marrithiyel 472
Matagalpa-Cacaopera 263-4
Mayali 207
MAYBE *see* CAN
Meaning-Text Model 19-20
mental predicates 39, 62-8, 90-3, 115-21, 153-5, 174-81, 208-12, 236-41, 268-70, 289-91, 315-8, 335-8, 367-71, 392-401, 426-9, 454-468
mental processes 36
meronymy *see* PART OF
meta-predicates 43-5, 72-5, 96-100, 129-35, 160-2, 187-90, 217-21, 246-9, 273-7, 296-9, 322-4, 343-8, 374-8, 408-15, 433-5, 476-83
Miskitu *see* Misumalpan
Misumalpan 14, 263-83, 460-1, 462, 482, 492
Moscow School 18-20
Mparntwe Arrernte *see* Arrernte
MUCH *see* MANY

Natural Semantic Metalanguage (NSM) 10, 12, 20-4, 34, 36, 498
natural kinds 46
negation 41, 43, 47, 477; *see also* NO
negative imperative 43
negative *see* NO
Ngarinman 481
NO (NOT, DON'T WANT) 22, 43, 44, 72, 96, 129-30, 144, 160, 166, 187-8, 217, 246, 275-6, 296, 322-3, 343, 374-5, 408-9, 433, 476-7
non-compositional 36-7
non-decomposability 17
NOT *see* NO
NOT WANT *see* NO
NSM *see* Natural Semantic Metalanguage
Nyawaygi 15
ONE 22, 40, 69-70, 122, 124-5, 197, 213, 214, 241, 271-2, 291-3, 294, 333, 372-3, 380, 406-7, 431, 454, 470-1, 472
OTHER 22, 32, 41, 70, 93, 123-4, 158-9, 166, 181-2, 213-4, 230, 231, 241-2, 271, 288, 293, 294, 302, 319-20, 328, 333, 341, 372, 405-6, 430, 451, 470-1, 493-4
Panamahka *see* Misumalpan
paraphrase 36-7
PART OF (HAVE PARTS) 13, 21, 22, 40, 45, 46-7, 80-1, 102-3, 138-41, 164-5, 166, 193-7, 222-3, 225, 235, 254-7, 259, 280-1, 283, 302-3, 326-7, 328, 354-5, 357, 373, 380, 382, 417-8, 437-8, 488-92, 497
partonomy and taxonomy 46-7, 80-1, 101-3, 138-42, 164-5, 193-9, 222-4, 254-8, 280-1, 302-3, 326-7, 354-5, 380-1, 417-9, 437-8, 488-94
parts of speech 12, 23
part–whole 88, 143-4, 280-1, 302-3, 355; *see also* PART OF
patient 43, 236

PEOPLE 22, 38, 41, 61-2, 113-5, 143, 152, 174, 207-8, 230-5, 250, 267-8, 288-9, 334, 366-7, 390-2, 425-6, 431, 452-4
perception words 39, 205, 457
PERSON *see* SOMEONE
phenomenologists 36
Pitjantjatjara 255, 229, 237, 457
PLACE *see* WHERE
place 45
Polish 21, 447, 457, 464-5, 491, 492, 494
polysemy 13, 23, 31-32, 35, 389, 445, 447-8, 463, 474
portmanteau morphemes 13
possession 138-41, 303
possessive 326-7, 417
possibility 44; *see also* CAN
potential 209-10, 217-8, 225, 248, 460, 480, 482
potentiality *see* IF
pragmatics 35, 167-9, 361, 382, 448-9
primitive thought 1-2
primitives
    conceptual 282
    lexical 20-24, 31-54
    semantic 1, 8-13, 16-20, 20-24, 305, 497-8
pronouns 37-8
proprietive 303
prototypes 44, 478
psychic unity 1-2
purposive 35, 209, 299; *see also* BECAUSE
quantification 21
range of use 23, 34-5, 470, 472
rejection 43, 477; *see also* NO
resonance 35-6, 455
respect 38
Russian 21, 47, 221, 452, 464-5, 496
Samoan 331-360, 446, 447, 450-2, 458, 464-5, 467, 469-70, 471, 473, 476, 477, 478, 480, 483-4, 485, 486,

487, 492, 494, 495
Sanskrit 176, 189
SAY 21, 22, 32, 39, 42, 44, 64-5, 83-4, 92-3, 97, 104-5, 118, 154-5, 176, 212, 235, 236, 238-9, 268-9, 290-1, 315-6, 335-7, 342,357, 367, 399-400, 419, 427, 432, 446, 456-7, 459-60, 465-8, 473, 477, 480
semantic
  bridge 467
  complexity 33
  metalanguage 10, 18-20, 446; *see also* Natural Semantic Metalanguage
  primitives *see* primitives, semantic
  universals *see* universals, semantic
semantics 7-24
  denotation-based 7
  formal 7, 10
  generative 16
  interpretative 16
  reference-based 7
  truth-conditional 7
sensations 39; *see also* FEEL
similarity 41, 46; *see also* LIKE
Slavic 15
SMALL 22, 47-8, 82-3, 83, 143, 165, 166, 224, 258, 303-4, 327-8, 356-7, 381, 419, 439, 473, 494-6
SOMEONE (WHO, PERSON) 21, 22, 23, 32, 33, 36, 37, 40, 41-2, 44, 59-61, 88-9, 111-2, 151-2, 166, 173, 206-7, 230-5, 241, 255, 267, 287-9, 313-4, 333, 366-7, 390-2, 424-5, 446, 449-52, 453-4, 471, 475-6, 498
SOMETHING (WHAT, THING) 21, 22, 33, 37, 40, 41, 42, 44, 59-60, 89-90, 95, 105, 112-3, 136, 144, 151-2, 173, 206-7, 230-5, 241, 244, 255, 256, 267, 287-8, 314-5, 321, 333-4, 350, 357, 366-7, 390-2, 424-5, 428, 431, 446, 449-52, 475-6, 490, 493
space 21

Spanish 461
speech act verbs 39, 44
speech-level 35, 167-9, 361, 382, 448-9
structuralism 15-16
subsequent marker 298
substantives 37-8, 59-62, 88-90, 110-5, 150-2, 172-4, 205-8, 230-6, 266-8, 286-9, 312-5, 332-4, 362-7,389-92, 424-6, 447-454
Sumu 263-4
symbolic logic 10
syntactic frames 32, 36, 445, 446, 474
syntax 11-12, 39
taxonomy 46, 257; *see also* KIND OF
tense 34
Thai 35, 37, 149-70, 448-9, 456, 466, 469, 473, 474, 492, 494, 496-7
THE SAME 22, 33, 41, 68-9, 70, 83, 93-5, 122-3, 124, 156-7, 164, 166, 181, 197, 213, 242-3, 270-1, 292-3, 298, 319, 331, 339-40, 372, 402-5, 430-1, 470-1, 472, 478, 495, 498
THINK 21, 22, 32, 36, 39, 42, 47, 62-3, 83, 92, 97, 104-5, 115-7, 153-4, 174-5, 210-2, 225, 235, 236, 237, 240, 268, 290, 315-6, 322, 328, 335, 362, 367-8, 392-6, 426, 452, 454, 455-6, 456-8, 498
THIS 21, 22, 33, 34, 39-40, 44, 68, 93-4, 121-2, 133, 155-6, 166, 181, 213, 242, 246, 270, 291, 300, 318-9, 338-9, 371-2, 401-2, 425, 429-30, 434, 446, 468-70, 477
TIME *see* WHEN
time 21, 42-3, 45
time and place 45-6, 75-80, 100-1, 135-8, 162-3, 190-3, 221-2, 249-53, 277-80, 299-301, 324-6, 349-54, 378-9, 415-7, 435-7, 483-8
translative 209
Twahka 264
TWO 22, 40, 70, 93, 124-5, 143, 156,

166, 182, 214, 241, 271-2, 291-2, 294, 320, 328, 341, 372-3, 406-7, 431, 472
Ulwa *see* Misumalpan
UNDER (BELOW) 22, 46, 79, 83, 84, 101, 138, 163, 166, 193, 222, 253, 279-80, 301, 354, 416-7, 437, 488
universal concepts 15
universalists 1
universals
   formal 14
   lexical 1, 14, 225, 305, 497-8
   semantic 1, 7-24, 225
   substantive 14
vagueness 32, 448
VERY 13, 22, 45, 74-5, 100, 134-5, 162, 190, 221, 249, 276-7, 299, 324, 348, 356, 357, 377-8, 414-5, 434-5, 473, 494-6
volition 177-8, 184-5, 205, 477; *see also* WANT
WANT 13, 21, 22, 23, 32, 35, 36, 39, 42, 47, 67-8, 93, 104-5, 120-1, 153, 166, 177-81, 187, 209-10, 225, 235, 236, 237-8, 259, 269-70, 283, 291, 318, 328, 337-8, 357, 362, 370-1, 382, 400-1, 419, 427-8, 452, 458-61, 467-8, 482, 498
Warlpiri 193, 223, 254, 466
Western Arrernte 296
Western Desert Language *see* Yankunytjatjara
WHAT *see* SOMETHING
WHEN (TIME) 22, 40, 45, 72, 75-6, 77, 100-1, 135-6, 144, 162-3, 190-1, 221, 249-52, 277, 300-1, 324, 349-51, 357, 366-7, 378, 415-6, 423, 435-6, 481, 483
WHERE (PLACE) 21, 22, 33, 40, 45, 76-8, 101, 136-7, 144, 163, 191, 221, 249-52, 279-80, 299-300, 325-6, 349-51, 357, 366-7, 378, 415-6, 436, 446, 450-1, 474, 483-5

WHO *see* SOMEONE
WORLD 21
Yankunytjatjara 21, 32, 35, 220, 229-62, 287, 301, 303, 428, 447, 451, 453, 454, 457, 461, 466-7, 469, 471, 474, 475-6, 477, 479, 480, 482, 485, 488, 492, 493
Yimas 472
YOU 21, 22, 32, 36, 37-8, 41, 43, 59, 83, 88, 110, 150-1, 167-9, 172-3, 206, 230, 266-7, 286-7, 312-3, 332, 339, 362-6, 382, 389-90, 424, 446, 447-449
zero anaphora 167

In the STUDIES IN LANGUAGE COMPANION SERIES (SLCS) the following volumes have been published and will be published during 1994:

1. ABRAHAM, Werner (ed.): *Valence, Semantic Case, and Grammatical Relations. Workshop studies prepared for the 12th Conference of Linguistics, Vienna, August 29th to September 3rd, 1977.* Amsterdam, 1978.
2. ANWAR, Mohamed Sami: *BE and Equational Sentences in Egyptian Colloquial Arabic.* Amsterdam, 1979.
3. MALKIEL, Yakov: *From Particular to General Linguistics. Selected Essays 1965-1978.* With an introd. by the author + indices. Amsterdam, 1983.
4. LLOYD, Albert L.: *Anatomy of the Verb: The Gothic Verb as a Model for a Unified Theory of Aspect, Actional Types, and Verbal Velocity.* Amsterdam, 1979.
5. HAIMAN, John: *Hua: A Papuan Language of the Eastern Highlands of New Guinea.* Amsterdam, 1980.
6. VAGO, Robert (ed.): *Issues in Vowel Harmony. Proceedings of the CUNY Linguistics Conference on Vowel Harmony (May 14, 1977).* Amsterdam, 1980.
7. PARRET, H., J. VERSCHUEREN, M. SBISÀ (eds): *Possibilities and Limitations of Pragmatics. Proceedings of the Conference on Pragmatics, Urbino, July 8-14, 1979.* Amsterdam, 1981.
8. BARTH, E.M. & J.L. MARTENS (eds): *Argumentation: Approaches to Theory Formation. Containing the Contributions to the Groningen Conference on the Theory of Argumentation, Groningen, October 1978.* Amsterdam, 1982.
9. LANG, Ewald: *The Semantics of Coordination.* Amsterdam, 1984. (English transl. by John Pheby from the German orig. edition *"Semantik der koordinativen Verknüpfung"*, Berlin, 1977.)
10. DRESSLER, Wolfgang U., Willi MAYERTHALER, Oswald PANAGL & Wolfgang U. WURZEL: *Leitmotifs in Natural Morphology.* Amsterdam, 1987.
11. PANHUIS, Dirk G.J.: *The Communicative Perspective in the Sentence: A Study of Latin Word Order.* Amsterdam, 1982.
12. PINKSTER, Harm (ed.): *Latin Linguistics and Linguistic Theory. Proceedings of the 1st Intern. Coll. on Latin Linguistics, Amsterdam, April 1981.* Amsterdam, 1983.
13. REESINK, G.: *Structures and their Functions in Usan.* Amsterdam, 1987.
14. BENSON, Morton, Evelyn BENSON & Robert ILSON: *Lexicographic Description of English.* Amsterdam, 1986.
15. JUSTICE, David: *The Semantics of Form in Arabic, in the mirror of European languages.* Amsterdam, 1987.
16. CONTE, M.E., J.S. PETÖFI, and E. SÖZER (eds): *Text and Discourse Connectedness.* Amsterdam/Philadelphia, 1989.
17. CALBOLI, Gualtiero (ed.): *Subordination and other Topics in Latin. Proceedings of the Third Colloquium on Latin Linguistics, Bologna, 1-5 April 1985.* Amsterdam/Philadelphia, 1989.
18. WIERZBICKA, Anna: *The Semantics of Grammar.* Amsterdam/Philadelphia, 1988.
19. BLUST, Robert A.: *Austronesian Root Theory. An Essay on the Limits of Morphology.* Amsterdam/Philadelphia, 1988.
20. VERHAAR, John W.M. (ed.): *Melanesian Pidgin and Tok Pisin. Proceedings of the First International Conference on Pidgins and Creoles on Melanesia.* Amsterdam/Philadelphia, 1990.
21. COLEMAN, Robert (ed.): *New Studies in Latin Linguistics. Proceedings of the 4th International Colloquium on Latin Linguistics, Cambridge, April 1987.* Amsterdam/Philadelphia, 1991.

22. McGREGOR, William: *A Functional Grammar of Gooniyandi*. Amsterdam/Philadelphia, 1990.
23. COMRIE, Bernard and Maria POLINSKY (eds): *Causatives and Transitivity*. Amsterdam/Philadelphia, 1993.
24. BHAT, D.N.S. *The Adjectival Category. Criteria for differentiation and identification*. Amsterdam/Philadelphia, 1994.
25. GODDARD, Cliff and Anna WIERZBICKA (eds): *Semantics and Lexical Universals. Theory and empirical findings*. Amsterdam/Philadelphia, 1994.
26. LIMA, Susan D., Roberta L. CORRIGAN and Gregory K. IVERSON (eds): *The Reality of Linguistic Rules*. Amsterdam/Philadelphia, 1994.
27. ABRAHAM, Werner, T. GIVÓN and Sandra A. THOMPSON (eds): *Discourse Grammar and Typology*. Amsterdam/Philadelphia, n.y.p.